WOMEN IN AMERICAN SOCIETY

Women in American Society

An Introduction to Women's Studies

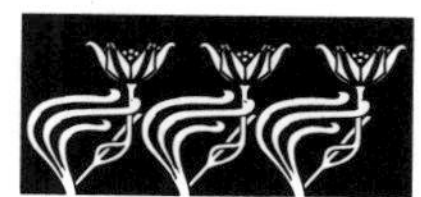

THIRD EDITION

Virginia Sapiro
University of Wisconsin–Madison

MAYFIELD PUBLISHING COMPANY
Mountain View, California
London • Toronto

To my family:
William and the memory of Florence,
Graham,
and Adam Ross Wilson, who can now read this whole book

Library of Congress Cataloging-in-Publication Data
Sapiro, Virginia.
Women in American society : an introduction to women's studies / Virginia Sapiro —3rd ed.
p. cm.
Includes bibliographical references and index.
ISBN 1-55934-225-0
1. Women—United States. 2. Women's studies—United States.
I. Title.
HQ1421.S27 1994
305.42'0973—dc20 93-27335
CIP

MANUFACTURED IN THE UNITED STATES OF AMERICA
10 9 8 7 6 5 4 3 2 1

MAYFIELD PUBLISHING COMPANY
1280 Villa Street
Mountain View, California 94041

Sponsoring editor, Franklin C. Graham; production editor, Sondra Glider; manuscript editor, Margaret Moore; text designer, Joan Greenfield; cover designer, Donna Davis; manufacturing manager, Martha Branch. Cover image: *Bramble,* 1980, by Louisa Chase, oil on canvas, 72 x 96 inches. Copyright © 1980 Louisa Chase. Courtesy Brooke Alexander, New York. The text was set in 10/12 Galliard by ExecuStaff and printed on 50# Butte des Morts by Banta Company. Illustration credits appear on a continuation of the copyright page, p. 549.

This book is printed on recycled paper.

Contents

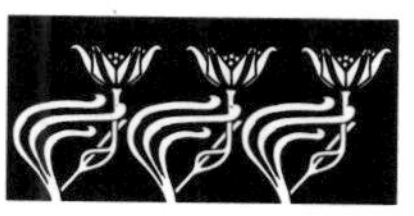

List of Tables

Preface

WOMEN IN AMERICAN SOCIETY is a woman-centered introduction to the study of gender in the United States. It emphasizes knowledge gained from research in the various social sciences. Designed to be used as the main text in courses such as Introduction to Women's Studies and Women in the United States, it assumes no prior college-level background in either women's studies or the social sciences. This book grows out of many years' experience teaching an introductory women's studies course as well as other courses, plus the comments of many students, teachers, and scholars on earlier editions.

Because this book is intended as an *introduction* to women's studies, I have traded depth for breadth. Nevertheless I make no attempt to cover all the possible approaches and issues. Writing this book required making many choices and solving many problems. My choices reflect my training, research experience, and disciplinary background. Let me emphasize some choices I have made and their significance for those who read this book.

Scope and Coverage

Women in American Society focuses primarily on the United States. At the same time, it often views this one nation from a *comparative* perspective, placing the United States in the contexts of both national and international diversity. Writing a good cross-cultural text takes more comparative knowledge and training than I have. It is better to weave together several high-quality single-country studies than to use one study that offers snippets of different cultures without underlying care in applying comparative theory and method.

This book is based in the social sciences. It relies especially on research and approaches used in economics, education, history, law, mass communication, political science, psychology, social work, and sociology. It emphasizes the languages and methodologies of the social sciences in a way that makes them accessible to students with no social science background. It treats social science methodology critically, but it is also shaped by social science methods. My choice to limit the book primarily to social science does not suggest that this mode of theory and research is "better" than the humanities or that the humanities has little to contribute to the questions raised here. But these are different approaches, each worthy of careful and coherent interpretation. In recent years, women's studies has come to mirror the values of the surrounding academy. While the "outside" (mainstream) world undervalues the humanities and "soft" fields in favor of the sciences, women's studies has increasingly tended to undervalue social science approaches. This book shows the kinds of problems the social sciences have dealt with especially intelligently.

The focus on the social sciences is further defined by emphasizing the grounding of gender in social institutions and institutionalized relationships. I discuss cultural values and psychological character and processes within the context of social structure and specific social institutions. The social institutions approach also leads to an emphasis on the legal and policy aspects of sex/gender systems.

This book surveys a wide range of topics and themes necessary to an understanding of women's status, roles, and experiences today, and includes most topics usually treated in women's studies courses regardless of their cultural or methodological focus. The text emphasizes the importance of both theory and empirical research. Although I focus primarily on contemporary society, I show the reader how an understanding of historical developments places the current situation in context and enlightens us about the nature and processes of social change, both worldwide and in the United States. Many women's studies instructors have found their students lacking in the historical background needed to discuss contemporary issues. This book assumes that it is not possible to understand the social phenomena of today without understanding something of their historical dynamics.

Women in American Society reflects the state of the field of women's studies, but it is also a unique contribution to that field. The newness of the field means that conventional wisdom, accepted methodologies, and established models do not exist to the same degree as they do in other fields. Even so, women's studies has built up a core of shared views and commonly cited works. This book, however, does not take even these for granted; many of the observations and works cited in women's studies are already out of date. In some cases this means that "old friends" in the literature do not get the treatment to which they have grown accustomed. In other cases I discuss works that are not widely known inside the women's studies community.

An Interdisciplinary Approach

The interdisciplinary approach used in this book interweaves the approaches, methods, and findings of different social science disciplines and subfields to examine common themes and problems. This is not easy to accomplish; the range of difference in assumptions, focus, language, method, and interpretation is enormous. Different fields use the same terminology to discuss different ideas, and different terminology to discuss the same ideas.

It is especially difficult to achieve integration in a *rigorous* way; interdisciplinary research is not just a pastiche of bits from various disciplines selected because they seem attractive or confirm one's original beliefs. Good interdisciplinary teaching requires careful discussion of epistemology (the study of the nature of knowledge) and research methods. In order to build "the findings" of diverse enquiries into knowledge, we must understand how researchers arrived at their findings.

The rewards of an interdisciplinary approach are great, however. Some disciplines are often accused of focusing on individuals to the neglect of social structure; others receive the opposite criticism. Some approaches consider human thought and behavior without explicitly recognizing the power of public law and policy; others investigate law and policy without examining their relationships to human thought and behavior. An interdisciplinary approach promotes a more realistic understanding of human life.

Diversity: An Integrated Approach

My treatment of the diversity of women is also unusual in the integrated rather than segregated approach followed here. There is no special chapter on the unique situation of black women, older women, lesbians, or any other subgroup of women that usually receives such segregated treatment. The segregated approach tends to suggest to readers that unless otherwise specified, the text is "about" specific groups of women, such as those who are white and middle class. The segregated approach often does less to encourage decentered and multiperspectival views than it appears at first. It tends to emphasize a relatively few more popular "different" perspectives while ignoring others. In the United States context, for example, feminist work now usually emphasizes marginality based on race, age, sexuality, and class. It is not usually as cognizant of marginality based on region, urban-rural dimensions, or religion. If multiple perspectives are fostered primarily by using special chapters, the recognition of a few specific groups overruns the larger theoretical issues involved in the constitution of multiple versus singular perspectives.

The integrated approach involves two specific aspects. First, I assume that women's situations and experiences vary systematically because of differences in culture and their position in the social structure. Even if gender shapes social life in substantial ways, these effects mediate and are mediated by other structural and cultural differences. Understanding the significance of these differences must be a part of each theme this book undertakes. Where I do not name a specific group of women, the reader should not assume that I am referring to any specific group. I have tried not to make generalizations about women that violate or ignore the experience of particular groups of women. If social divisions—for example, by race or age—make a difference in the gendered aspects of women's lives, the discussion of difference is integrated into that discussion of that aspect of gender.

The second aspect of my integrated approach is that in the opening theoretical section of the book I focus on difference and unity among women, emphasizing both the fact that gender cannot be fully understood without understanding other social divisions and some of the different approaches scholars have used to encompass difference among women without losing sight of gender.

Research Guided by Feminist Theory

This text is designed to be a rigorous academic work and is based on careful analysis of research guided by feminist theory. Most of the studies I draw on employ social science methods, including survey, clinical, and experimental techniques, participant observation, and institutional, documentary, and content analysis.

Many students begin with at least some fear of or antagonism toward science-oriented writing, especially if it includes quantitative data analysis. Some women's studies scholars reinforce this anxiety by using the excellent literature in feminist theory on methodology and epistemology to attack quantitative analysis or some strategies such as experimental or survey research as incompatible with women's studies. *Women in American Society* is based in the assumption that systematically gathered and theoretically grounded empirical research can be done in a feminist mode and in a manner that serves humane purposes. Methods of research must fit the task. Some questions are best answered by one method and some by another, and the questions we will consider are the ones social scientists happen to ask.

The text is largely devoted to discussion of the research literature and its theoretical and practical significance. I include numerous references and bibliographic comments both to document the observations I make and to provide readers with the resources they will need to learn more. Studies, bibliography, and statistics are not all there is to learning this material, of course, and at each turn it is crucial to reflect on it to decide how it fits and doesn't fit with the reader's own observations, and why. To assist this process I provide study questions before each unit asking readers to "reflect before you read."

Feminist theory and women's studies are diverse. Sometimes I present alternative theories and viewpoints without reaching a definitive conclusion about which is "best." I have attempted to avoid the mind-numbing claim that knowledge and theories are all relative, while giving the student room to make theoretical and epistemological choices.

REVISIONS. Each revision of this work is enriched not only by the growth of general knowledge in the research and literature of women's studies scholars but also by the changes and events in the world at large. Past users of this work will find that this third edition incorporates many important additions reflecting recent events and issues that are only now emerging into our consciousness or which have become revitalized in often unanticipated ways.

Important changes and events that have influenced the content of this edition include the widely debated issue of women in combat that became intensified by the Gulf War, the upheavals in the political and social map of eastern Europe and elsewhere that inevitably affect the status of women in those societies, and recent U.S. Supreme Court decisions and hearings, such as the U.S. Senate Anita Hill–Clarence Thomas hearings, that focused on sexual harassment in the workplace. The 1992 presidential election has also served to spotlight the debates on women's access to political decision making, political appointments, and election to public office. These topics, as well as increased attention to sexually transmitted diseases, access to new reproductive technologies, the feminization of poverty, and the ordination of women in religious denominations, represent some of the new and expanded coverage in the third edition.

Organization: What Lies Ahead

Those familiar with women's studies may find that the book's topical organization is unique, although the text is divided into subsections to facilitate restructuring it for reading assignments. I based this structure on careful consideration of theory and pedagogy and the demands of working in a specifically interdisciplinary fashion. For example, rather than segregating the discussion of *violence* against women I have integrated it with the text in subsections of relevant chapters, such as those on health, the law, and relations between women and men, in order to show how pervasive violence is in women's lives. At the same time, many women's studies works highlight violence with such lengthy and distinct treatment that victimization seems to be the most central aspect of women's lives.

I begin and end the book with theory, but I end (rather than begin) with a full-fledged discussion of feminism, feminist (and antifeminist) movements, and feminist theory per se. An introduction to women's studies must help the reader understand what feminist analysis is and how it differs from other kinds of study. Nevertheless, my experience in introductory women's studies courses taught me that discussing feminism as a social movement before describing and analyzing the situation of women is putting the cart before the horse. Therefore, questions of feminism are inseparably woven throughout the pages of this book, but explicit treatment of the topic is reserved for the finale.

The book is divided into four parts, corresponding to four of the most important themes in the field of women's studies.

Part One, "Developing Frameworks for the Study of Gender and Society," introduces the field of women's studies, especially its underlying themes theories. Chapter 1, "Women's Studies: An Introduction," presents many of the basic facts about women's and men's lives *as* women and men. It shows, for example, that women and men have different home lives, health problems, education, and occupations; that they commit different kinds of crimes and have different kinds of crimes committed against them; and that they take different roles in influencing both their own and other people's lives. In other words, Chapter 1 shows that gender still makes a considerable difference in the quality and characteristics of our lives. But facts do not speak for themselves; they need people to interpret them, and people interpret facts through particular constructions of theory. Because theory is the framework that makes an otherwise shapeless set of facts and pieces of information coherent and useful, theory construction and evaluation are among the most important tasks of students in any field. Chapters 2 and 3 discuss a variety of theories offered to explain the development and significance of sex/gender systems, or the pattern of relationships between women and men in society. As we shall see, a wide variety of theories could be, and have been, used to explain sex/gender systems.

The difference between the theories presented in Chapters 2 and 3 lies in what they attempt to explain. The first type (outlined in Chapter 2, "How Did Society Get This Way?") includes theories that focus primarily on large-scale social, political, and economic forces to explain how sex/gender systems came to be what they are—that is, why women's and men's places in society are what they are. The theories presented in Chapter 3 ("How Did Individuals Get This Way?") focus on individuals and explain how people fit themselves into societies, institutions, and groups. Sometimes people argue about which level of explanation—societal or individual, macro or micro—is better. This question does not make much sense in the abstract. These two types of theories explain different things, equally important and equally partial on their own. Chapter 4, "Commonality and Difference Among Women," emphasizes the importance of understanding difference among women if we are to comprehend the meaning of gender in society.

Part Two, "Gender-Defining Institutions," presents the second major theme of the book—that there are many different kinds of power and control. One of the most important is normative power, or the power to define the values and standards against which we measure ourselves and others. There are a number of social institutions with the primary purpose of setting, teaching, and enforcing values, standards, or norms. We will look at education (Chapter 5), health care (Chapter 6), religion (Chapter 7), communications media (Chapter 8), and government and politics (Chapter 9) to see how they define and enforce norms of good and bad, normal and abnormal, healthy and sick, skilled and unskilled, important and unimportant, valuable and not valuable. You might notice there is not a single chapter in this section devoted to the family. In fact, there is hardly a page of this book that does not discuss some aspect of the family. Instead of looking at the family as simply one more institution, we will look at different aspects of the family throughout this book. The family is most consistently and thoroughly discussed in Part Three.

The chapters in Part Two show, first, how interrelated these institutions and their underlying values are and, second, how they both shape and depend on gender norms. We will look at these systems as parts of a larger sex/gender system and consider how their values control women's lives and how women have influenced these values and used them to exert control over their own lives. We will also explore the development of the current norms and the potential for change within the institution.

Part Three, "Choice and Control in Personal Life, the Family, and Work," examines some of the types of problems, decisions, and experiences most women face in their adult lives. We will look especially at how much choice women have in life decisions and how women make these choices. Chapter 10, "Gender, Communication, and Self-Expression," suggests that there are many gender-related limitations on people—and especially women—even in what they say and how they act with other people. Chapter 11, "Consenting Adults? Personal and Sexual Relationships," looks at another kind of social interaction and relationship: intimacy. We will focus on different kinds of intimacy, including sexual and nonsexual, heterosexual and homosexual, heterosocial and homosocial relationships, and look at one of the most widespread structures of heterosexual relationship: marriage. We will also examine some of the problems in distinguishing between sexual and nonsexual relationships and between sexuality and violence.

Chapter 12, "Reproduction, Parenthood, and Child Care" focuses on the decisions women make about whether to have children, under what circumstances women have children, and what women do about children when they have them. We will also examine the effects these experiences have on women.

Chapter 13, "Work, Employment, and the Economics of Gender," discusses many different types of work: paid and unpaid (housework); professional, white collar, blue collar, and agricultural; traditionally female and traditionally male. We will look at the ways in which women attempt to exert influence over their work lives and economic situations. We will also look at some sources of income other than paid labor and at questions of women's poverty, wealth, and economic resources and strategies.

Part Four, "Feminism and the Global Context," explains women's movements of the past and present and makes some educated guesses about what the future holds.

ACKNOWLEDGMENTS

Many people have helped me write this book. At the top of my list are my students; the many scholars in the field with whom I have talked and whose work I have read over the years; and those who have used the book and made comments and suggestions.

The students in my various women's studies classes at the University of Wisconsin—Madison have been important in the writing of this book. They are my audience in writing: I see their faces while writing much as I do when I lecture. When I lecture, I do not see an abstract "student," but many different individuals in what some theorists call their "concrete situations." My students are women and men who come from many backgrounds and have many different interests. They range from adolescence to old age. Many, of course, are full-time students, but some are working people from the community taking a single course because they are interested or because it relates to their work. Some come in as radical feminists; some are as skeptical and anxious as a student in this kind of course can be. Some are new to academic study; some are relatively advanced scholars in other fields who are investigating women's studies for the first time. This book has been written for all these people. I assume that my readers are even more diverse than the students I have already met. I once again acknowledge the impact of my colleagues in Women's Studies at the University of Wisconsin—Madison. I continue to learn from them.

I also wish to thank the following reviewers of the book for their suggestions: Helen Bannan, Florida Atlantic University; Lisel Blash, Kansas State University; Jane Smith Boyd, San Jose State University; Sandra Coyner, Kansas State University; Mary Margaret Fonow, Ohio State University; Irene C. Goldman, Ball State University; Angela E. Hubler, Kansas State University; Audry T. McCluskey, Indiana University; Faye Plascak-Craig, Marian College; Kim Romenesko, University of Wisconsin, Milwaukee; and Judith Wishnia, State University of New York, Stony Brook.

My greatest debts are to Graham Wilson and Adam Wilson—the former because, as always, he was wonderful in all the ways one could want, and the latter because his impending arrival kept me writing the first edition of this text. The little boy who was a newborn when the first manuscript was delivered to the publisher now plays a different role. Audre Lorde (1984) said it best:

> I am thankful that one of my children is male, since that helps to keep me honest. Every line I write shrieks there are no easy solutions.

WOMEN IN AMERICAN SOCIETY

PART ONE

Developing Frameworks for the Study of Gender and Society

WHAT IS THE situation of women in society, and how did it get that way? Over the centuries, many theorists and scholars have attempted to answer this question. In the process of seeking the answers, they have developed alternative theories or frameworks that we can use to organize our analysis and interpretation of the role of gender in society. In the past few decades, scholars interested in the study of women and gender have organized a field of inquiry known as "women's studies." This book is an introduction to part of that field of women's studies, and this part of the book introduces many of the frameworks used by students of women's studies.

We begin with a look at the nature of women's studies as an academic field of study, then turn to an overview of the "facts of life" for women in the United States today. Chapter 1 emphasizes mostly basic facts with very little embellishment. As you read them, think about the significance of these facts and figures, what they might mean, and how we might explain them.

Chapters 2 through 4 then explore some of the theories and approaches used by women's studies scholars, especially in the social sciences, to understand women and gender in society. Chapter 2 focuses on theories used to explain how *societies* develop particular patterns of relationship between the sexes over time, through history. These theories ask how we might explain the development of particular sex/gender systems, or social structures of gender. Chapter 3 focuses on a different level of explanation, looking at theories used to explain how *individuals* develop gender-related patterns of behavior through their own experiences in the context of the larger society. These theories ask how we as individuals come to be the kind of women and men we are. Finally, Chapter 4 offers ways of understanding women that take full account of the fact that women do not constitute a homogeneous group but, rather, have differed crucially in their history and life experiences on the basis of race, class, and religion, among many other characteristics. These approaches ask how it is we can talk about "women" if "women" are so different from each other. In order to understand women's situation in society, it is necessary to understand all of these types of theories.

Reflect Before You Read

1. Some people say that men and women are very unequal in society today. Others say that, although there used to be inequality between the sexes, society has changed so that men and women now have equal opportunities to live the lives they choose. What position do you take? Why?
2. Women constitute a very small proportion of the people who have top positions in education, government, and business. Why? Does this matter?
3. Construct a list of the five most important problems facing people like you today. Who did you define as "people like you"? Why? What other choices might you have made in defining "people like you"? How many of the problems you selected truly affect women and men in the same way? What role can or does feminism play in the solutions to these problems?
4. Construct a list of the five most important problems facing women today. Now think about the relationship of these problems to different kinds of women. Do women of different classes face these problems in the same way? Women of different races? Ages? Religions? Sexual orientation? How did your own personal situation and experiences affect the way you defined the problems of "women"?

1

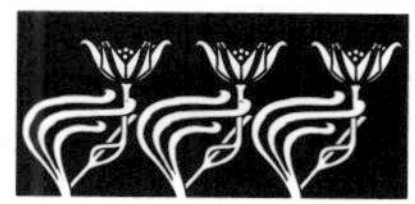

Women's Studies: An Introduction

Representing Women

IMAGINE A philosophy textbook beginning with the question "What is Man?" What would you expect the book to be about? Most likely you would expect an exploration of how man differs from other animal species, or from angels, gods, and other celestial beings.

Now imagine a philosophy textbook beginning with the question "What is Woman?" What would this book be about? You probably would not anticipate a discussion of women and animals or gods, but rather an analysis of the similarities and differences between women and men.

Why would most people's expectations of these two books be so different? One answer is that *man* is often considered a generic term, but *woman* is not; in other words, *man* can be used to refer either to one sex or to human beings as a species. But isn't this confusing? How do we know when *man* means males and females and when it means only males? Perhaps we can judge by the context. Unfortunately the immediate context often does little to solve the ambiguity. To avoid such ambiguity in this book, from now on *man* and *men* will be used only to refer to males.

This remedy for confusion and ambiguity is simple enough, but the important issue remains. How did it happen that one word came to refer to both the whole of humanity and one specific half of it? Why does *man* represent both males and females, whereas *woman* refers very narrowly to females? This question recurs as a theme throughout this book.

The answer suggested by many feminist theorists in recent centuries is that the use of the word *man* to represent human society reflects our tendency to view men as the central actors or characters in human society and to consider what we view as male characteristics, manliness, or masculinity as the defining characteristics of human beings.

The word used to describe this situation is *androcentrism*, which means "centered on men." This word was used as long ago as 1911 by sociologist and feminist theorist Charlotte Perkins Gilman in *The Man-Made World: Our Androcentric Culture*. *Androcentric* has parallels in three words that are more widely used and understood: *egocentric*, *ethnocentric*, and *anthropocentric*. *Egocentric* refers to the tendency of individuals to see themselves as the center of the world, as though everything revolves around them. *Ethnocentric* refers to people's tendency to view their own culture as normal and to think of other cultures only as deviations from their own—better—way of life. *Anthropocentric* refers to our tendency to view the human species as the most significant entity in the universe. *Androcentric*, then, refers to the tendency to think of men as the norm against which women are compared and to the view that men are the main actors in—the center of—the social world.

An analogy using the ideas of characters and actors will illustrate the point. Consider one of the most famous plays in Western literature, William Shakespeare's *Hamlet*. Why is this play called *Hamlet*? The Danish prince is not the only person in the play; he is not even the only character who seems to have an interesting history, faces a tragedy, or dies. The title reflects the fact that the play is essentially about Hamlet and his role in the story. The events that occur in the play—even when Hamlet is absent—are significant in the eyes of the audience primarily for the ways they affect or are affected by the young prince. Although the perspectives of the other characters are significant, it is really Hamlet's perspective and problems that move the play and us.

Nearly four centuries after Shakespeare wrote *Hamlet*, another English playwright, Tom Stoppard, took the same material and twisted it inside out. His play, *Rosencrantz and Guildenstern Are Dead*, presents the same set of events and the same characters, but from the point of view of two of the most minor characters in the original play. In Stoppard's version Rosencrantz and Guildenstern, who cannot even remember themselves which one of them is which, become the central actors. The events, the characters, and the play itself suddenly become vastly different and make a very different point from the original.

Just as all the other characters in *Hamlet* revolve around, support, and gain their significance from the central character, women are socially defined as revolving around, supporting, and gaining their significance from men. In *Hamlet* we care that the prince is on a ship to England; it is less important to us that Rosencrantz, Guildenstern, and the ship's captain are there as well. Likewise, the centrality of men in society leads observers of society and history to write, as did one eminent political scientist, "The analysis which this book contains is based on what might be called the storybook truth about American history: that America was settled by men who fled from the feudal and clerical oppressions of the Old World" (Hartz 1955, 3). Some people would not notice anything odd about this sentence. Others would notice a problem: Surely American history would not have lasted this long had women not settled in America too. Acknowledging that women were also "on the ship" makes a great difference to understanding American history.

A well-known study by a group of psychologists shows that this "man–woman–human" question is not a mere matter of playing with words (Broverman et al. 1970). These psychologists asked a number of mental-health clinicians to define the characteristics of a "healthy man," a "healthy woman," and a "healthy adult." The results showed that the clinicians defined the healthy adult and the healthy man in much the same way: rational, independent, ambitious, active, and so forth. Their healthy woman, however, had very different characteristics: She was emotional, dependent, and submissive. Thus not only in our language but also in the eyes of those who define our standards of health, the man is the real adult. To act like a healthy woman, one cannot act like a healthy adult. This situation has not changed as much as we might hope (O'Malley and Richardson 1985).

Another example from a very different area of life offers another perspective on our definitions of women and men. One of the most important recent constitutional questions affecting women concerned the issue of jury service. At one time women were not allowed to serve on juries; during most of this century different states had different rules, but most of them tended to exclude women. Only in 1975 (*Taylor* v. *Louisiana*) did the Supreme Court decide that women could not be systematically excluded from juries because of their sex. In a 1946 case (*Ballard* v. *U.S.*), Justice William O. Douglas considered the question of whether women and men were simply exchangeable puzzle pieces. Many people argued that they were, but exchangeable in the sense that it did not matter that only men were on juries; a jury composed only of men was "as truly representative as if women were included." Douglas countered by offering the following problem for consideration:[1]

> [It] is not enough to say that women when sitting as jurors neither act nor tend to act as a class. Men likewise do not act as a class. But, if the shoe were on the other foot, who would claim that a jury was truly representative of the community if all men were intentionally and systematically excluded from the [jury]? The truth is that the two sexes are not fungible; a community made up exclusively of one is different from a community composed of both; the subtle interplay of influence one on the other is among the imponderables. To insulate the courtroom from either may not in a given case make an iota of difference. Yet a flavor, a distinct quality is lost if either sex is excluded.

Douglas's point is clear. There are two alternative arguments on which to base a claim that men can fully represent women. The first is that women and men are in this context fully interchangeable persons, in which case it would make no difference whether juries (or, for that matter, Congress or almost any other organization) were composed entirely of men or entirely of women. Few people seem to worry that Congress is composed of mostly males, but would the same be true if Congress were suddenly to become composed mostly of females? The other argument is that men can adequately represent women, but women cannot adequately represent men because women are narrower creatures, more parochial, less competent, or, like children, dependent on the better judgment of men. Is this an acceptable argument?

Notice what has happened in the discussion thus far. We began by talking about the meaning of words and by asking what real-life things the words *man* and *woman* represent. It became clear that words, meanings, and definitions have a great deal to do with real-life issues of power and choice, and we have gradually turned to this problem of representation: Who can represent whom in society? Can women's interests and needs be satisfied if men are invested with the power to act and make decisions for them? If men can act for women, why can't women act for men? If men and women are not precisely the same, as Douglas argued, what are the differences? What is the significance of these differences for the way we arrange important social, economic, and governmental institutions? These are some of the questions we will probe throughout the book.

In the course of participating in a decision of the Supreme Court, Justice Douglas had to face a series of important problems. Do men or women act as a "class"? That is, is there a set of orientations or types of behavior that are common to one sex and not to the other? How, if at all, would community or organizations composed only of men, only of women, or of both differ? As Douglas suggested, differences could emerge because women and men act differently from each other or because people's behavior varies depending on whether they are in a single-sex or mixed-sex group. But above all Douglas apparently felt we did not have enough knowledge to be able to argue that one sex or the other can be excluded from the important activities of society.

Two decades later, and despite the vast increase in the education of women and men in the 20th century, many students, scholars, and others began to realize how little knowledge we had about women and men as women and men, and especially, how little we knew about women's history and current situation. There are at least three reasons for this ignorance:

1. Many aspects of women's lives are ignored or dismissed as unimportant compared with most aspects of men's lives. Basic philosophy courses usually pay considerable attention to what philosophers said about men and very little to what they said about women. In history we learn more about the changes in men's activities, strategies, and equipment in battle than about changes in childbirth practices. If an event in history caused great suffering to men, we (justly) take great interest in how and why it happened because we hope to avoid similar suffering in the future. If an event caused great suffering only or primarily to women (for example, the European witch burnings, which led to the deaths of at least thousands of women), it does not seem quite as important to study.
2. We continue to view men as "generic," as representative of us all. Sometimes we are almost fooled into thinking we have studied women when we have really studied only men and simply assumed that all of us have been covered. In psychology a large proportion of "general" research involves males

only but is discussed as though it applies to everyone (Holmes and Jorgensen 1971). In sociology scores of people who claim to study social status and how it is determined in fact gather and look at evidence about men only.

3. The view we often get from books and courses is a narrow perspective on women, usually focusing on their roles, behavior, and significance as wives, mothers, lovers, or supporting muses. These roles are important, but they are not the only aspects of women that are important. This perspective provides only a limited and distorted view of women.

In most of the social sciences, women have been discussed as though they were merely a component of "the family," which is composed of an employed husband, a wife who is a homemaker, and some number of dependent children who live at home. The woman who lives in such a family is probably most people's image of the "typical woman." It is a shock to find how rare this "typical woman" really is. If we eliminate women who are currently unmarried, women who are employed outside the home, and women who have no children or whose children are grown up and have left home, we are left with only 14% of women in the United States. If we limit our view even further to women who are homemakers and live with their husbands and at least one preschool child, only 7% remain. How very different is the reality from the image! (Statistics calculated from U.S. Bureau of the Census, data for 1980.)

How can there be such disparity between image and reality, especially as we are talking about basic facts of women's existence? One answer is that women are seen as people want to see them: as comfortable, nurturing, always-available mothers. Another answer (which does not contradict the first) is that women are seen through stereotypes. This allows us to deal with women without really having to pay close attention to them or to any contradictory evidence in the facts of their lives.

French feminist Hélène Cixous (1976) makes a similar point in a different way. She reminds us of the Greek myth of the Medusa, the snake-haired woman who would supposedly turn anyone who looked directly at her to stone. She could be viewed only indirectly, through a reflection. Cixous argues that the myth is more dangerous than the woman herself. When the Medusa—or any woman—is seen only indirectly, through the distorted reflections of cultural fears and stereotypes, we are harmed. The accepted "facts" (like the appearance of the "typical woman") are often wrong. Women's studies is a field that looks directly at women: at their roles in society, at their impact on society, and at the impact of social institutions and processes on them.

Women's Studies as a Field of Study

The field of study called *women's studies* has developed since the reemergence of the women's movement in the late 1960s. At first women's studies consisted mainly of handfuls of students and instructors who met in often informal, unofficial study sessions. In the early years the participants spent much of their time trying to figure out what questions they needed to ask and searching for any information they could find on women's history and roles in society. Those participants, mostly young women, seemed radical to everyone else and, frankly, slightly obsessive and weird.

Women's studies has grown and changed considerably in the last quarter century. Most universities now have some women's studies courses, and many have programs or departments devoted to the field. Thousands of instructors and students are involved, and they are a much more heterogeneous group than the early participants. Although many women's studies students are motivated by their feminist activism, increasing numbers of students take these courses not because they are involved in feminism or the women's movement (at least not at first), but simply because they wish to learn. There are as many reasons for taking a women's studies course as there are for taking a course in any other field.

Defining the Field

What, then, is this field called *women's studies*? The answer might seem obvious at first. In economics we study economics, in political science we study politics, in women's studies we study women. In fact the definition is not as simple as that. Academic fields are defined not simply by what they study but also by how they study it. For example, the novel *1984* could be assigned reading in either a literature course or a political science course. But the reasons for reading the book, the questions asked about it, and the lessons learned from it would be somewhat different in the two fields. So students of women's studies approach their topic in different ways from other students of women, and you must understand the differences to understand this book.

Women's studies scholars look at the meanings that events, ideas, and social institutions have for women as well as for men. They investigate experiences that only (or almost only) women have with the same care and attention that others use in examining experiences that only (or almost only) men have. They notice that even when men and women do the same sorts of things, those things are often interpreted or valued differently. When men tell each other stories about another man, it is called the "old boys' network." When women do the same, it is called "gossip" or a "hen session."

It probably would not surprise anyone that women's studies focuses heavily on such aspects of life as the family, women's employment, abortion and contraception, and family and child-oriented issues, because these are often thought of as *women's* issues. But women's studies probes beyond this conventional wisdom and questions widely accepted views of male and female in society. We ask why these are considered especially "female" issues, when they affect men in substantial ways also. But further, the topics included within women's studies cannot be limited to these things because we would then miss an important point. Women's and men's roles in most social institutions are different. Many social problems and policies have very different—and often unnoticed—relevance to the two sexes, whose day-to-day lives are different in many respects. Women's studies seeks to understand how and why being female or male shapes their lives and experiences so much. This chapter outlines some of these basic "facts of life," and the remainder of this book will explore the whys and wherefores.

Women's studies focuses on understanding women. But it is impossible to learn about the female half of society without also learning something about the male half. In some cases we will *compare* the thoughts, behavior, and roles of men and women. At other times we will look at the *interactions* between men and women, including how they think about and act toward each other and how they influence each other. By examining the lives of both sexes we will gain a much wider and more profound understanding of our society as a whole. Gender, the sociocultural construction of male and female, is an important part of the social structure. Indeed, we cannot understand the structure and operation of our society without understanding gender.

Perhaps the overriding difference between women's studies and other studies of women is the special kind of skepticism women's studies scholars bring to their studies. A good student in any field should be questioning, skeptical, and wary of easy answers. But in women's studies, skepticism plays a particularly important role because of the nature of the subject and its relationship to our day-to-day lives and even to our very senses of self (male and female). Women's studies students are deeply skeptical of conventional wisdom about women for the reasons already mentioned. Too often it proves false or distorted when we consider systematic evidence. For example, have labor-saving devices in the home diminished the amount of effort women put into their housework over the course of the past century? The answer is no, as we shall see later. What other people use as assumptions about women, women's studies scholars pose as questions.

Thus women's studies is not just a simple matter of filling in gaps in information. It is a matter of reevaluating what we think we know. We consider some very basic questions: What is important enough to know? To whom is it important and in what ways? Women's studies involves constant critical evaluation of our own and other people's understanding of and reactions to women. Both women and men find that women's studies entails much learning and questioning about themselves.

Feminism shapes the practice of women's studies. Although many students who take women's studies courses do not think of themselves as feminists, women's studies is both a result and a part of the feminist movement. In the 1960s and early 1970s, women's movement activists realized they needed to know more about the social forces that shaped their lives. When they thought about what they previously had learned about women, they realized they had been taught very little. Thinking, studying, and learning became an important part of feminist political and social action. Although there are many different types of feminism (discussed in the final chapter), they share a central core of ideas and attitudes revolving around the desire to see women take control of and responsibility for their own lives and become participants and leaders in society.

Women's Studies and Other Disciplines

Women's studies is not unique in the fact that it links academics and current political and social issues. Many traditional social science disciplines (sociology and political science, for example) were also children of the social and political movements of their founding days. None of the social sciences is immune to pressing world problems. After World War II many people began to study public opinion and the psychology of politics because they wanted to know how people came to tolerate (if not participate in) fascism and the Holocaust in order to try to avoid a repeat performance. In the 1960s many social scientists turned their attention to questions of poverty, urban life, and race relations because these were the problems that seemed to need solving. In the 1980s awareness of AIDS spurred social as well as medical research. Contrary to the "ivory tower" cliché, scholarship is indeed part of the real world, and this relationship has been valued in some—although not all—areas of the social sciences.

Only the rare student in women's studies courses never becomes angry, frustrated, anxious, or elated. The topics that are discussed, such as relations between parents and children or sexuality and violence between men and women, touch all of us very deeply. Scholars in some fields of study argue that feelings and personal experiences should play no role in our academic efforts to discover truth. Women's studies scholars, even in the sciences and social sciences, tend to argue that our personal understandings and experiences play important roles in learning. But at the same time, if the personal nature of the subjects and themes of women's studies makes it difficult to think analytically or to comprehend and use unfamiliar or uncomfortable information, the ability to learn is substantially limited. This means that in women's studies we must maintain some skepticism about ours and others' immediate reactions while at the same time valuing them.

Women's studies is *interdisciplinary;* that is, it draws on and weaves together theories, research, and insights from numerous fields throughout the humanities and social and biological sciences. This interdisciplinary nature grows in part out of necessity. Suppose I, as a political scientist, deliver a lecture on why few women achieve high political office. Among the questions people usually ask me are the following: "But don't women's hormones make them less aggressive and less competitive than men?" "Didn't this system grow out of a historical division of labor that goes all the way back to hunters and gatherers, with women staying close to home and men going out to hunt and fight?" "Isn't the division of labor, with women in the home and men out in society leading and working, functional and efficient? Doesn't this system exist because it works well and not because women are any less valued?" "Doesn't it all come down to capitalism?" To answer these questions I need to know something about biology, psychology, history, anthropology, sociology, and political economy.

Just having some information from a lot of fields is not enough for understanding human social life. Imagine a massive bag filled with the bits and pieces necessary to construct a Rolls Royce. The pieces are useful only if you know how to put them together, which in turn requires understanding the underlying principles of engineering and design. The bits of information obtained from a variety of different academic fields can be like the car pieces: a useless and confusing jumble of unlinked or incorrectly linked parts.

Academic disciplines are at least as differentiated by their assumptions, theories, and methods as by the bits of information they provide. Thus, to use interdisciplinary approaches for understanding women's situation, we must learn about the methods and approaches of different kinds of research and develop the skills to integrate them coherently. For this reason we will pay attention not only to the *findings* of research on women (the bits of information such research has produced) but also to the *process* by which people have arrived at these findings and the *uses* to which they have been put.

A women's studies approach to understanding women's lives in the United States (or anywhere else) requires rethinking the questions people have asked before, criticizing conventional wisdom and the assumptions that are built from earlier scholarship, and crossing the boundaries of academic fields as they have been defined. Because of the pervasiveness of androcentrism, stereotype, and sheer ignorance about gender issues and women in most academic fields, we have to start with very basic questions. Let us, then, turn to our main subject—women and gender in the United States—to sketch a basic portrait of their situation. We will spend the remainder of this book filling out the picture.

Women in the United States Today

What are the basic facts about women's lives in the United States today? How can we describe the situation of women? How different are women's and men's lives? The goal of the remainder of this chapter is to provide a foundation of some basic information about women's lives and to begin thinking about how to interpret this information. For now we place special emphasis on outlining similarities and differences between women and men. (Later we will redefine this focus.) We will also highlight basic and especially statistical information. Soon it will become clear that these "facts" alone do not tell us all we need to know. We will delve more deeply into each of the areas discussed here in later chapters.

A Demographic and Social Portrait[2]

LIFE, DEATH, AND HEALTH. The world is not evenly divided between men and women; there are 95 men for every 100 women in the United States. More males than females are born (about 105 males for every 100 females), but males die earlier. The average age of American women is 34 years; for men the average is 32. Among people aged 65 and older, there are only 67 men for every 100 women. The ratio of males to females varies among different social groups. Among African Americans there are 90 men for every 100 women; among whites, 95 men for every 100 women; and among Hispanics,[3] 105 men for every 100 women. Throughout this century women have had longer life expectancies than men. A white male born in the United States in 1980 could expect to live 70 years compared to 77 for a white female; an African American male born that year could expect to live to 64 compared with 73 for an African American female.

This apparent male fragility is attributable to a number of causes. More males are born with genetically based diseases such as hemophilia and are more likely to die from infant diseases, heart disease, most forms of cancer, cirrhosis of the liver, AIDS, accidents, homicide, and suicide. Women, on the other hand, are more likely than men to die of cerebrovascular disease, diabetes, arteriosclerosis, breast cancer, genital cancer (except among people over 65), pregnancy and

What do you know about these two children by knowing their sex? Are they different kinds of people? Will they lead different kinds of lives?

abortion, and old age. Men are more likely than women to be heavy drinkers, but only slightly more likely to smoke cigarettes. As the dangers of cigarette smoking have become more publicized, fewer people now smoke than in earlier years. About 31% of men and 25% of women smoke. (Health is discussed in Chapter 6.)

Although men seem more fragile than women by these standards, women visit doctors and hospitals more than men do. In 1989 the average woman visited a doctor six times and a dentist two times; the average man visited a doctor five times and a dentist two times. Part of the explanation for this difference is that women seek more preventive care and, especially, they go to doctors regularly when they are pregnant. The female population is also older, which means that women have more of the problems afflicting the aged. Women also spend more time in hospitals: per year, 907 days of care for every 1,000 women compared to 757 days for every 1,000 men. If we break these figures down by age, we find that women have more total days of hospital care than men only during their childbearing years.

In 1989 there were 67 births for every 1,000 American women. Not surprisingly, birthrates are the highest among women in their late twenties (117 per 1,000 women), but birth is not rare among women in their early thirties

(76 births per 1,000 women), late thirties (30 births per 1,000 women), or late adolescence (58 births per 1,000 women).

Women who are pregnant against their wishes have had the legal option to terminate their pregnancies through abortion since 1973. Taking into account all pregnancies, abortion rates are highest among adolescents, women over 40, and unmarried women.

Pregnancy and childbirth are much safer than they once were, but not as safe in the United States as in some countries. In 1989 there were about 6 maternal deaths for every 1,000 live births, tremendous improvement from 1970, when there were 14 maternal deaths for a comparable number of live births. Among the other nations that have lower maternal death rates than the United States are Luxembourg, Iceland, Ireland, Denmark, Belgium, Norway, Switzerland, Sweden, and Spain (Snyder 1992, 396). The pregnancy and childbirth experiences of black and white women are shockingly different; in 1989, 6 white and 18 black women died because of pregnancy or childbirth for every 1,000 live births. This is probably partly due to the fact that African American, Native American, and Hispanic women are much less likely than white women to receive prenatal health care early in their pregnancies. (Reproduction is discussed in Chapters 6 and 12.)

FAMILIES AND OTHER LIVING ARRANGEMENTS. Children are more likely to live with their mothers than with their fathers. In 1990 about 73% of children in the United States lived with both parents, while 22% lived only with their mother, 3% lived only with their father, and 3% lived with neither parent. Race and ethnicity make a considerable difference in children's living situations. Whereas about 79% of white children live with both parents, the same is true of 67% of Hispanic children and 38% of black children. While 16% of white children live only with their mothers, 27% of Hispanic children and 51% of black children do. Of these the majority of the Hispanic and white children live with mothers who are divorced or widowed; the majority of the black children live with mothers who were never married.

During early adulthood, women are more likely than men to live with a spouse or other relative and slightly less likely to live alone. This changes dramatically later in life. Among people 65 and older, 42% of women and only 16% of men live alone; 40% of women live with a husband and 74% of men live with a wife at that time. Many more women live alone than we sometimes think. Although black women are less likely than white women to be married, they are slightly less likely to be living alone during their old age because older black women are much more likely than older white women to be living with other relatives.

Women generally marry younger than men do. In 1988 the median age at the time of first marriage was 24 for women and 26 for men. The median age at first divorce was 31.9 for women and 34.4 for men. These figures represent a significant change over recent years; age at first marriage has increased by 2 years since the beginning of the 1980s and 3 years since 1970.

Men are more likely to be married than women are. In 1990, among people aged 18 and over, 64% of all men and 60% of all women were married. Adult women and men are somewhat less likely to be married and more likely either to be divorced or never to have married than was true 20 years ago. Gender differences are much larger among the elderly. About 77% of all men over 65 were married, and only 14% are widowed. At the same time, 41 percent of women over 65 are married, while 49% are widowed. Men are also slightly more likely to remarry after a divorce than women are, in part because they tend to seek younger women. In 1990, 7% of all men and 9% of all women 18 and older were divorced. (Marriage is discussed in Chapter 11.)

Being married and having children mean very different things to women and men. Surveys show that women are much more likely than men to place the blame for unachieved aspirations in education, employment, and other activities on their family obligations (Campbell, Converse, and Rodgers 1976). Men's family ties do not seem to interfere with other aspects of their lives as much as women's do. Women spend considerably more time directly serving other members of the family, shopping for them, cooking and cleaning for them, and ministering to their emotional and physical needs. This is true regardless of whether they are employed outside the home (Robinson 1980).

Men's jobs are more likely to create work for their wives than women's jobs are to add burdens to their husbands. More male-dominated jobs seem to require the spouse to make a direct contribution, including the jobs of corporate executives, the noncelibate clergy, politicians, and farmers. More male-dominated jobs require travel and relatively lengthy stays away from home, thus adding to the spouse's domestic labor. Researchers disagree about the distribution of power between husbands and wives, but it seems clear that husbands and wives have different degrees of power over the outcome of different types of decisions (Lips 1981). With regard to household consumption patterns, for example, men's opinions weigh more heavily in car buying, and women's weigh more heavily in the purchase of children's clothing or food.

EDUCATION, WORK, AND WEALTH. Women now achieve nearly the same overall level of education as men. The median level of education for Hispanic and black women and men is about 12 years compared with almost 13 for both white women and men. In addition, women constitute a majority of people engaged in adult education. In 1990 women earned 53% of the bachelor's degrees and 53% of the master's degrees awarded. On the other hand, they earned only 36% of the doctoral degrees (Ph.D.s), 42% of the advanced law degrees (LL.D.s and J.D.s), 34% of the medical degrees (M.D.s), and 31% of the dentistry degrees (D.D.S. and D.M.D.). If we also consider the fields in which people earn their degrees, we find considerable segregation, as Table 1-1 shows. Although women earn a higher proportion of master's degrees than bachelor's degrees in only four fields (by marginal amounts), in all fields but art and nursing, women have a smaller share of the doctorates than of any lower degree except liberal studies, generally by a fairly substantial amount. The proportions of women haven't changed much in the past decade in most fields. (Education is discussed in Chapter 5.)

TABLE 1-1
Proportion of Degrees Awarded to Women, 1990

Field	*Bachelor's*	*Master's*	*Doctor's*
Agricultural and natural resources	31	33	19
Anthropology	64	58	52
Business and management	46	34	24
Communications	63	67	48
Computer and information sciences	30	28	14
Economics	31	25	20
Education	78	76	58
Engineering	15	14	9
English	68	67	56
Ethnic studies	63	58	*
Fine arts	67	60	55
Foreign languages	73	69	59
Health sciences	86	78	55
History	38	38	33
Home economics	92	86	72
Liberal studies	58	65	58
Library and archival science	81	78	71
Life sciences	51	51	38
Mathematics	47	40	19
Music	50	51	36
Philosophy	32	29	22
Physical sciences	31	26	19
Political science	41	33	26
Psychology	72	68	58
Social work	86	81	70
Sociology	68	59	48
Theology	24	36	12

*Too few cases.

Source: U.S. Department of Education (1992, 246–52).

Turning to work, we already have seen that women do more unpaid work in the home regardless of their employment status. More women than men also report doing volunteer work. This means that among married people, employed women work much longer hours than employed men, especially if there are children present, and that women have less time for sleep, leisure, or recreation than men do. People generally think of "work" as something one is paid to do, however, which means that a higher proportion of men's labor is generally counted as work. (Work is discussed in Chapter 13.)

In 1990, 76% of all men were in the labor force compared with 58% of all women.[4] About 58% of black women and white women were in the labor force

Donna E. Shalala, the first woman to head a Big Ten university (Wisconsin—Madison), later became Secretary of the U.S. Department of Health and Human Services.

compared to 53% of Hispanic women. Labor force participation differs more among men by race: 77% of white men, 70% of black men, and 81% of Hispanic men are in the labor force. Of those who are employed, women are more likely to be working full-time. Women constituted about 44.7% of the labor force in 1987. Table 1-2 compares the education and labor force participation of women in the United States and other industrialized countries. As that table shows, women's education and labor force participation in this country are relatively high.

Women's marital status and, especially, whether or not they have children, affects their employment rates. About 58% of married women with husbands present are in the labor force compared with 66% of single women. This constitutes a considerable change from past years—for example, in 1970 when 41% of married women were in the labor force, and in 1960, when 31% were. Table 1-3

TABLE 1-2
Education and Labor Force Participation of Women:
Cross-National Comparisons

Country	*Women's Share: Bachelor's*	*Women's Share: Grad Degrees*	*Labor Force Participation*	
			Women	*Men*
Australia	50	32	57	85
Canada	54	44	66	87
Finland	56	27	73	81
France	49	41	57	78
Germany (West)	38	26	52	80
Italy	48	33	43	78
Japan	26	12	58	87
Netherlands	35	*	41	74
Norway	65	32	74	89
Spain	53	26	36	82
Sweden	53	22	81	86
United Kingdom	45	35	65	88
United States	52	46	68	87

Note: Education figures are for 1990; labor force participation figures are for 1987.

*Figure not available.

Source: Office for Economic Cooperation and Development (1988); U.S. Department of Education (1992, 418).

shows that although women with young children are less likely to be in the labor force than those with older children, it is no longer true that most mothers stay "at home" while their children are young. A majority of mothers of young children are in the labor market. This was not true before the 1980s. As we shall see later, work organizations and public policy are only beginning to adjust to these changes.

TABLE 1-3
Labor Force Participation of Married Mothers, 1990,
by Race and Age of Children

Age of Children	*All Women*	*White*	*African American*
1 year or less	54	53	64
2 years	61	60	75
3–5 years	64	63	80
6–13 years	73	73	78

Source: U.S. Bureau of the Census (1992, 388).

Employment remains relatively highly sex segregated; most people work in jobs in which a clear majority of workers are people of their own sex. Women are more heavily concentrated in fewer jobs than men. About 35% of employed women are in clerical jobs. Adding sales clerks to these accounts for 39% of employed women. Private household-service workers, waitresses, and other food-service workers bring the figure to 49%. The addition of teachers and registered nurses accounts for a majority of the female work force—almost 55%. This is a large proportion of people in a very small number of job categories.

Table 1-4 shows which are the most- and least-segregated jobs in the United States in 1991. In the first column are jobs in which more than 90% of the workers are women. In the third column are the jobs in which 10% or less of the workers are women. The middle column shows the jobs that are the most integrated: those in which 47–55% of the workers are women. The numbers show the exact proportion of women in each job. Notice that the "female" jobs are mostly clerical or personal-service jobs, and the "male" jobs are mostly blue-collar jobs. Women are also underrepresented in labor unions; they constituted 35% of union members in 1987 (U.S. Department of Labor 1989, 225).

TABLE 1-4

Most- and Least-Segregated Occupations, 1991

Most Segregated: Female	*Least Segregated*	*Most Segregated: Male*
Dental hygienists (>99)	Secondary school teachers (55)	Electricians (10)
Secretaries (99)	Administrators: education and related fields (55)	Clergy (9)
Prekindergarten and kindergarten teachers (99)	Bartenders (54)	Architects (8)
Dental assistants (98)	Designers (53)	Engineers (8)
Receptionists (97)	Advertising and related sales (53)	Airplane pilots (3)
Private household childcare workers (97)	Accountants and auditors (52)	Truck drivers (2)
Private household cleaners and servants (96)	Real estate sales (52)	Telephone installers (2)
Childcare workers (96)	Editors and reporters (51)	Supervisors, police, and detectives (2)
Practical nurses (95)	Painters, sculptors, and craft artists (51)	Vehicle and mobile equipment mechanics (1)
Registered nurses (95)	Dispatchers (51)	Construction trades (2)
Typists (95)	Technical writers (50)	Firefighters (1)
Welfare service aides (95)	Weighers and measurers (50)	Carpenters (1)
Dietitians (94)	Mail clerks (49)	Auto mechanics (<1)
Health records technologists (94)	Postal clerks (48)	
Teacher aides (93)	Cooks (47)	

Note: Figures show the proportion of women in each occupation.

Source: U.S. Department of Labor (1989, 181–88).

Jobs are segregated not only by field but also by level. Women are concentrated in jobs at lower levels with less pay, even in "female" areas. In the public schools, for example, 1990 figures show women constituted 93% of the teacher aides, 99% of kindergarten and prekindergarten teachers, 85% of elementary school teachers, and 54% of secondary school teachers at roughly the same time women were 39% of faculty at 2-year colleges, 31% of faculty at 4-year colleges, and 20% of faculty at doctoral-level universities (Fox 1989, 228; U.S. Department of Labor 1989, 181–88). The problem is equally apparent in the ranks of federal employees. Table 1-5 shows that, as in many other types of employment, "the higher, the fewer" is the rule that holds in governmental employment. Whereas about 75% of the workers in the lowest-paid federal jobs are women, less than 10% of those in the highest-paid jobs are women.

The result of differences in training and employment is that women earn much less than men do. In 1990 women earned 72 cents for every dollar men earned—a considerable improvement over even the recent past.[5] Using 25- to 34-year-olds as an example, Table 1-6 shows that at every level of education, from those who have fewer than 8 years of education to those who have gone beyond 4 years of college, women earn less than men do. And these pay differences emerge regardless of race, for a number of reasons. "Women's" jobs tend to pay less than "men's" jobs, and women are still paid less for doing the same job as men.

If we consider that besides commanding lower salaries women are also more likely than men to be caring for children on their own and more likely to be over 65, it should not be surprising to find that more women live under the poverty line. In fact, in recent years women's share of poverty has been increasing, a pattern known as the "feminization of poverty."

The high rate of poverty among women creates vast additional poverty among children because women are primarily responsible for children. This point is best illustrated by the evidence that families maintained only by women are much more likely to live under the poverty line than families maintained by either men or a

TABLE 1-5
Proportion of Women in Different Pay Grades of
White-Collar Federal Employment

		Percent Female	
Grade Level	*Maximum Pay*	*1970*	*1989*
GS 1–6	$23,628	72	75
GS 7–10	$35,369	33	54
GS 11–12	$46,571	10	33
GS 13–15	$76,982	3	17
GS 16–18	$78,200	1	9

Note: 1989 pay levels are shown.
Source: U.S. Bureau of the Census (1992, 330).

TABLE 1-6
Median Annual Income for Year-Round Full-Time Workers
Aged 25 and Over, 1990

Years of Education	*Men*	*Women*	*Women's Salary as Percentage of Men's*
≤ 8 years	$17,394	$12,251	70.4
4 years high school	26,653	18,319	68.7
4 years college	39,238	28,017	71.4
5+ years college	49,304	33,750	68.5

Source: U.S. Department of Education (1992, 391).

married couple. Although this is generally true regardless of race, the rates of poverty are most shocking among the families of nonwhite women. In 1990 about 30% of whites living in female-headed families were below the poverty line as were 51% of African Americans and 53% of Hispanics. (Wealth and poverty are discussed in Chapter 13.)

CRIME AND VIOLENCE. Women and men have different experiences in the social life of the nation; they also have different experiences in its "antisocial life." In 1986 only about 17% of the people arrested for crimes in the United States were women, and in 1990 women constituted about 9% of the U.S. jail population and 4% of state inmates.

Women and men commit different types of crimes. Table 1-7 shows the "most male" and "most female" crimes—that is, those in which men are at least 90% of the perpetrators and those in which women are at least 75% of the perpetrators. Men predominate among the crimes of violence and the most serious property crimes. Men are more likely to kill themselves or other people than women are; indeed, men are more likely to die from accidental or intentional violence than women are, as Table 1-8 shows. Those figures also demonstrate the devastating problems of violence suffered by African Americans, especially African American men. Men are more likely to be the victims of crimes against people except for rape and offenses against family members. According to the Federal Bureau of Investigation (FBI), there were almost 97 reported rapes per 100,000 females aged 12 and older in the United States in 1990. There has been a dramatic increase in reported rapes; in 1980 the figure was 86 per 100,000 females and in 1970 it was 46. Moreover, rape and wife battery are two of the most underreported crimes in the country; the FBI estimates that at best only a quarter of all rapes are actually reported to the police. Some researchers note that as many as one half of all marriages involve some physical abuse of the wife. According to the FBI, 30% of the 4,399 female murder victims in 1990 were killed by their boyfriends or husbands.[6] (Criminal justice is discussed in Chapter 9; violence against women is also discussed in Chapters 6 and 11.)

TABLE 1-7
Proportions of Women and Men Committing Specific Crimes, 1987

Most "Female" Crimes	*Most "Male" Crimes*
Prostitution and commercialized vice (65)	Forcible rape (99)
Juvenile runaways (57)	Weapons crimes (92)
Fraud (44)	Sex offenses (92)
Embezzlement (38)	Robbery (91)
Forgery, counterfeiting (34)	Drunkenness (91)
Curfew, loitering (25)	Motor vehicle theft (90)

Note: Numbers in the "Female" column show the proportion of women within category; numbers in the "Male" column show the proportion of men within category.
Source: U.S. Bureau of the Census (1989, 173).

TABLE 1-8
Death from Violence, by Race and Sex, 1989

	White		*Black*	
Cause of Death	*Men*	*Women*	*Men*	*Women*
Motor vehicle accident	27.0	12.1	28.3	9.3
Other accidents	24.5	12.7	37.0	15.0
Suicide	21.4	5.2	12.2	2.2
Homicide	8.2	2.8	61.1	12.9

Note: Figures show the number of deaths per 100,000 population.
Source: U.S. Bureau of the Census (1992, 89).

Women are only a minority of crime prevention and control personnel. They are 10% of the police officers and detectives. In 1987 they were 8% of the officers of the FBI and 6% of the Secret Service. In 1986 they were 11% of nonsupervisory police and detectives (McGuinnes and Donahue 1988). In 1991 they were only 2% of police and detective supervisors and a very small percentage of prison corrections officials and administrators. In 1988 they were twenty percent of the nation's lawyers and judges (U.S. Department of Labor 1989).

AUTHORITY AND LEADERSHIP. We already have seen that in occupations and education, we can describe the situation of women as "the higher, the fewer," even when in female-dominated fields. Women similarly constitute only a small proportion of leaders in industry and labor. Although by the end of the 1980s women owned about 30% of the business firms in the United States, their business accounted for only 17% of sales and receipts. They owned a majority of the business in two industries: apparel and textile manufacturers (55% of firms) and personal services (52%). In no industry did women-owned firms earn a majority of the sales and receipts. Women are only beginning to break into leadership in labor unions. The first woman was appointed to the executive council of the AFL-CIO in 1980. This pattern also held in other domains such as in the mass media and other cultural institutions.

The same pattern emerges in politics. Women make up half the population but hold only a small minority of all political offices. Following the 1992 elections about 11% of the members of the House of Representatives and 6% of the U.S. senators were women, a great increase over the past. They also held 20% of all state legislative offices. There were 3 female governors and 11 female lieutenant governors. In 1992 women held 145 of the mayoral positions in the approximately 900 cities with populations over 30,000. One of the nine Supreme Court judges was a woman; a second was added in 1993. Within the Native American commu-nities of the United States, the degree of power women traditionally held in tribal governance was quite varied, although it tended to decline during the nineteenth century (Bonvillain 1989). In recent years, women's prominence in tribal leadership has been rising. In 1987, for example, Wilma Mankiller was elected the first female chief of the Cherokees.

Table 1-9, which lists in descending order the female proportion of the members of the chief national legislative body (in cases of bicameral legislatures, generally the lower house) in a number of countries, shows that women have a worldwide problem in achieving positions of political authority. In no country except, perhaps Norway, have women achieved parity. In Norway government policy calls for all public bodies to be gender balanced so that neither men nor women have less than 40% of the positions. Women are also underrepresented in international organizations. In the United Nations, for example, women hold 8% of the senior positions, and they are only 29% of the U.N. employees overall (Kirshenbaum 1992). (Government and politics are discussed in Chapter 9.)

Women now also serve in the military in greater numbers than ever before; about 11% of U.S. military personnel are women,[7] and about 35,000 women served in the Gulf War in 1991.[8]

A Psychological and Social-Psychological Portrait

Thus far we have considered demographic differences between women and men; most people also seem to think they can identify at least some psychological differences between the sexes. Women are said to be nurturant, emotional, soft, weak, peaceful, and jealous; and men are said to be aggressive, competitive, strong, and particularly good at mathematics and abstract reasoning. As we have already seen, a person's emotional health is often judged by how well the individual conforms to psychological characteristics attributed to his or her sex. This section looks at both conventional wisdom and research on the relationship between gender and psychological characteristics and at the meanings of *femininity* and *masculinity.*

TABLE 1-9
Women as a Proportion of National Legislators

Country	*Percent Female*	*Year*	*Country*	*Percent Female*	*Year*
Finland	39	1991	Australia	11	1987
Sweden	38	1988	Ghana	11	1987
Norway*	36	1989	Mexico	11	1987
Denmark	33	1990	United States	11	1992
Netherlands	27	1989	Belgium	9	1987
Iceland*	24	1991	Ireland*	9	1989
Germany	21	1990	Israel*	9	1987
Austria	21	1990	Portugal	8	1991
Switzerland	18	1991	India*	7	1986
Canada*	14	1990	United Kingdom*	7	1991
Italy	13	1987	France	5	1990
Luxembourg	13	1991	Sri Lanka*	5	1987
New Zealand	13	1987	Greece	5	1989
Spain	13	1989	Zaire	4	1987
Costa Rica	12	1987	South Korea	3	1987

*Indicates nations that have had a female head of government.

Source: "Women in Government Around the World" (April 1987, 97–101); Snyder (1992, 399); Ries and Stone (1993, 440).

MASCULINITY, FEMININITY, AND STEREOTYPES. The packages of psychological characteristics people tend to associate with one sex or the other are summarized by a pair of commonly used but often unexamined concepts: masculinity and femininity. What do these words mean? *Masculine,* the *Concise Oxford Dictionary* tells us, means, "of men; manly, vigorous; (of women) having qualities appropriate to a man." *Webster's Ninth New Collegiate Dictionary* defines *feminine* as ". . . appropriate or peculiar to women." Notice that these definitions turn not on whether men and women actually possess masculine or feminine qualities, but on whether we think of these qualities as appropriate for one sex or the other. It is possible to say that a woman is "not feminine" or that she is "masculine" and possesses "masculine characteristics." It is also possible to say that a man is "not masculine" or that he is "effeminate" and possesses "feminine characteristics." When we use these phrases, we are saying that there are certain characteristics we think women and men *should* have because we think they are more appropriate for one sex than the other.

Notice that people do not just describe *people* as masculine or feminine; they also describe many personality characteristics as masculine or feminine, regardless of the sex of the person who has the characteristics. Regarding personality traits as having a gender of their own is confusing, as the following example shows.

Suppose that we are interested in sex differences in nurturing behavior and that we think of nurturance as feminine, regardless of the sex of the person we are describing. Research on this characteristic provides conflicting evidence, but it offers little reason to believe that women and men as groups differ very much in the degree to which they have nurturing personalities, although women's roles in society involve them in more situations in which they can act out their nurturant propensities. What do we conclude? Do we say that women and men are roughly equivalent in their potential to nurture, although we regard this behavior as more appropriate for women? If so, we would then have to consider strategies for making sure men don't live up to their potentials so that they won't act inappropriately. Are we arguing, as some psychologists do, that nurturant men are "cross-sex typed" (behave in a way appropriate to the other sex)? This too suggests that something is wrong with nurturant men. The problem is that the definitions of *masculine* and *feminine* are usually based on stereotypes.

Some people try to avoid the problem associated with the labels *masculine* and *feminine* by using the terms *androgyny* or *androgynous*. Some of these people believe an androgynous person is one whose personality is constituted of both "masculine" and "feminine" characteristics. Some go further and say that an androgynous person combines the best of both sexes, meaning the "good" characteristics stereotypically associated with males and females. (No one seems to have devised a term for a person who combines the worst characteristics of both sexes.) Others define *androgyny* more in terms of flexibility, or the ability to call on a range of characteristics conventionally labeled masculine or feminine, depending on circumstances.

Over the years many different researchers have investigated masculinity, femininity, and androgyny, often by asking people how well each of a long list of personality characteristics describes them. A list of the traits often used in this research appears in Table 1-10. The researchers then tally the score to categorize the subjects as masculine, feminine, or androgynous. One of the most important things these studies show is how many people do not conform to traditional images of gender typing. Regardless of the method used, one common finding emerges: Most people do not describe themselves in anything like uniformly "gender appropriate" terms (Cook 1985). These findings cast even more doubt on the usefulness of the concepts *masculine* and *feminine*.

Many researchers have tried to discover what difference it makes if people seem to be particularly masculine, feminine, or androgynous. Some, for example, have found that "androgynous" people are more flexible in their ability to deal with different situations, but others (e.g., Jones, Chernovetz, and Hansson 1978) have found that "masculinity" is associated with greater levels of flexibility. Leanne K. Lamke (1982) and others have found that "masculinity" is associated with higher levels of self-esteem among both adolescent females and males and that "androgynous" adolescents have higher self-esteem than "feminine" adolescents. The literature on androgyny is too large and varied to detail here, but many people have suggested that androgyny is a healthy alternative to rigid sex typing because of the flexibility it implies. But that doesn't change this fact: If we think of androgyny as the combination of "masculine" and "feminine" traits, we are still implying that there are ideal male and female personality types. We are still talking about how well individuals conform to stereotypes. Psychological research

TABLE 1-10

Gender Stereotypic Personality Traits

The following terms describe different personality traits, most of which are widely viewed as "masculine" or "feminine." They also have been incorporated into tests used by psychologists to determine whether individual women and men are "masculine," "feminine," or "androgynous." Which of these terms are "masculine"? Which are "feminine"? Why?

affectionate	forceful	sensitive to others' needs
aggressive	gentle	shy
ambitious	gullible	soft-spoken
analytical	independent	strong personality
athletic	individualistic	sympathetic
cheerful	leadership ability	tender
childlike	loves children	theatrical
compassionate	loyal	understanding
competitive	makes decisions easily	warm
conceited	reliable	willing to take a stand
conscientious	risk taker	yielding
defends own beliefs	self-reliant	
dominant	self-sufficient	
flatterable		

Note: These items are derived from the Bem Sex-Role Inventory (BSRI). See Bem (1974).

certainly gives us no reason to believe that people who conform to these stereotypes are healthier, happier, or better adjusted (Cook 1985).

Stereotypes are beliefs or expectations people have about members of particular social groups. When we say that a person views women through stereotypes, we are saying that person holds certain beliefs about the nature of women as a group (for example, that they are nurturant, passive, or emotional) and applies those beliefs to any given woman, regardless of her actual characteristics. To determine what is and is not a stereotype, it is necessary to review research on the psychological and personality characteristics of women and men.

PERSONALITY AND COGNITIVE SKILLS. Consistent and conclusive evidence of psychological sex differences of any type is very rare. In article after article in professional psychology journals, we find the words "No sex differences were found." The existence of differences between men and women has been exaggerated, partly because people pay more attention to the relatively few studies that find differences than to the vast number that do not.

Reviews of the literature on psychological differences almost uniformly lead to the same conclusion: Psychologists have not found significant sex differences in most personality characteristics or cognitive skills (e.g., Maccoby and Jacklin 1974; Hyde 1991; Lips 1993). Let us look briefly at cognitive skills, then turn to other personality traits. In both cases we will rely for our conclusions primarily on published reviews of many research studies focusing on the actual behavior of women and men rather than on individual studies or on people's stereotypes of how women and men act and think.[9]

Turning first to *cognitive abilities,* despite the stereotypes, research—especially the most recent studies—offers virtually no overall evidence of gender differences in verbal abilities (Hyde and Linn 1988). Males and females seem to develop slightly more strength in different kinds of perceptual skills relating to sight, hearing, and touch (Hyde 1991; Lips 1993). Males tend to outperform females on certain kinds of visual–spatial tasks. Small but consistent differences appear in tests of mental rotation (imagining a figure from a different angle) and rod-and-frame tests (being able to make a tilted rod vertical despite a confusing context). Despite common claims, no consistent gender differences emerge in embedded-figure tests, that is, identifying a figure that forms a part of a more complex figure (Linn and Peterson 1985).

Certainly considerable attention has been paid over the years to gender differences in mathematical skills. One group of researchers (Hyde, Fennema, and Lamon 1990) meta-analyzed 100 different articles published between 1962 and 1988, representing research on 3 million people. Their results would surprise many people. Overall they found females and males virtually indistinguishable in mathematical ability. No gender differences appeared during elementary or middle school in understanding mathematical concepts or problem solving, although girls showed slight superiority in computation. In high school and college, on the other hand, males performed better than females in mathematical problem solving. The conventionally expected male edge in mathematics performance is more likely to appear in specialized and selective settings (such as among college entrance exam takers) than in more general populations (such as students in high school classrooms). Finally, gender differences have declined over the years.

There is also little evidence to support the idea that the specific *personality traits* of women and men are basically different. There seems to be general agreement, though, that from an early age males exhibit more aggressiveness (especially physical rather than verbal aggressiveness) than females do. Certainly males seem to engage in more acts of antisocial aggression than females do (Hyde 1984). Research also suggests that females and males use somewhat different means to get their way and to influence people, as we shall discuss further in Chapter 10.

Research regarding most other personality characteristics, including those that are most stereotypically masculine and feminine, shows scanty and often conflicting evidence of sex differences when females and males are given similar opportunities to display these characteristics. A review of 127 different studies of activity levels found little difference in how active girls and boys are (Eaton and Enns 1986). Likewise, a review of the research on conformity and influenceability shows only some tendency for females to be more influenceable than males, and only under some circumstances—such as when men rather than women are the psychologists doing the research (Eagly and Carli 1981). Although women are thought to be nurturant, research finds men more likely to engage in helping behavior in most of the forms of behavior psychologists usually investigate (Eagly and Crowley 1986). Females report themselves to be more empathetic than males report themselves to be, but research involving observation of behavior rather than self-perception has not revealed much in the way of gender differences (Eisenberg and Lennon 1983).

Following the publication of Carol Gilligan's (1982) book, *In a Different Voice,* many researchers focused on possible differences between women and men in the way they understand and solve moral dilemmas. Many feminist writers have concluded along with Gilligan that women and men think differently about social and moral dilemmas. Women's thinking and feelings, they argue, are more shaped by social connectedness and a stance of caring and relating to others, whereas men's are more shaped by more abstract and individualistic notions of rights and justice. As we shall see in Chapter 3, there is little consistent evidence for gender differences in thinking about rights and justice, although women's thinking may be more embedded in social relations than men's.

SUMMARY Of PSYCHOLOGICAL DIFFERENCES. We have only touched on research discussing differences between women and men. Throughout this book we will see other examples. But by and large research on the psychology of gender suggests that the most fruitful approach to understanding the gender basis of human characteristics and behavior is not to focus on global, abstract skills and characteristics removed from their social context, as we have been doing thus far, but rather to discuss these skills and characteristics in the context of social institutions and organization. When people ask whether women are happier, more anxious, more dependent, or more nurturant than men, the best answer is probably, "Under what circumstances? With regard to what situations?"

Human beings are very complex and tend to respond in different ways to different situations. Although there may be people so thoroughly dominated by particular characteristics that they always act in the same manner, these people are a minority constituted of saints, devils, or people so out of touch with their surroundings and circumstances that they need protection from themselves. Personality characteristics depend very much on the context of behavior, and people's particular skills and motivations depend on their experiences. For this reason we will discuss psychological gender differences and the psychology of gender throughout the remainder of this book, but always in the context of specific social settings.

What Does It All Mean?

This chapter has been presented as though understanding gender in society is a simple matter of looking at the facts. Having looked at a wide range of facts it is now time to consider one more: Even grasping the "basic information" about women's situation in society and what role gender plays in it is not as simple a matter as it first appears. The remainder of this chapter focuses on two problems that need addressing before we move on: (1) research and analysis methods and (2) interpretation of the social significance of the information.

When Is a Difference Really a Difference?

Until now we have focused primarily on gender differences, including differences in the life situations of women and men, differences in the treatment they receive, and differences in their personal characteristics and skills. We have not yet discussed when a difference is really a difference. What do we mean when we talk about gender differences? What makes a gender difference worth talking about? A number of problems make it difficult to answer these questions.

The first problem we encounter in analyzing gender differences is the very language we use to express differences. Unfortunately the language used to describe gender differences is often imprecise, exaggerated, or otherwise misleading, thus leaving us room to read our own expectations into the situation. Suppose a test of mathematical skills was administered to 42 men and 42 women, and the distribution of scores on this particular test was as follows:

Grade	*A*	*B*	*C*	*D*	*F*	*Average*
	(4.0)	(3.0)	(2.0)	(1.0)	(0.0)	
Number of women	5	15	16	4	2	2.4
Number of men	6	17	15	3	1	2.6

How could we put these results into words? Women demonstrate a lower level of mathematical skills than men? The average woman has a lower level of mathematical skills than the average man? Women are twice as likely to fail a particular test of mathematical skills than men? A majority of the people who got A's on a test of mathematical skill were men? Reading these words without thinking carefully or looking at the evidence might lead one to conclude that women are pretty poor indeed at mathematics. One might decide that a man would be a much better bet than a woman if you needed help with a mathematical problem. Look again at the actual numbers. Do the "sex differences" in these scores really mean that you should look for a man to help you with your math problem? Wouldn't you rather have the advice of one of the five women who got A's than of the four men who got D's and F's?

Words like *average, most, more,* or *a majority* are summary terms for numbers, and it is impossible to understand their significance without knowing more about the numbers. Unfortunately too many people think they can understand problems of difference without any attention to precision. This much is clear: Saying that the average male and the average female possess certain skills or personality traits almost never means that all members of one sex are better at the skill than all members of the other sex or that all members of one sex display the trait and the others do not. In fact, research usually shows much more variation *among* men and *among* women than there is *between* men and women.

A second difficulty with interpreting sex differences stems from the problems of constructing and analyzing appropriate measures of characteristics and skills. Let us pursue the example of mathematical skills. Before we can compare the abilities of the sexes, we need to devise a specific test or set of tests that we think provides a valid measure of mathematical skills, a test that actually measures what we want it to measure and only that.

Many of the widely circulated reports of sex differences are faulty because the tests used in the research did not measure only what the researchers claimed to be testing. There are many different ways of measuring any given skill or personality characteristic, and differences in measures can make considerable difference in the results. Unfortunately many students find questions about research methods and statistics boring or intimidating and therefore do not pay attention to these important methodological problems.

A third difficulty in identifying gender differences even if one is attempting to be precise is the impact of bias on observation. Researchers can be as prejudiced as anyone else, so two different researchers may observe the same situation or event and see different things happening depending on their own expectations and stereotypes (Lyons and Serbin 1986).[10]

A final problem in trying to identify gender differences is that we sometimes unintentionally make it more difficult to see the role gender plays in our lives because we have deemphasized other aspects of human experience. We already have seen, for example, that the family experiences of women of different races are different in some respects. In order to understand the role of gender in women's lives, therefore, it is also necessary to look at the role of race. Although being a woman or a man shapes people's lives regardless of race, it shapes their lives somewhat differently depending on race. (The relationship between gender and other forms of social differentiation is discussed further in Chapter 4.)

When and Why Are Gender Differences Interesting?

It probably doesn't seem strange to devote so much space in a women's studies book to gender differences. But why and under what circumstances are gender differences of interest to us? What types of gender differences are worth attention? The main reason to pay attention to certain types of differences is that we think they have some social relevance: They might make women's and men's lives and experiences different in some significant way. We pay little attention to the well-documented fact that men and not women may have visible hair in their ears. We pay considerably more attention to the more contentious assertions about gender differences in the ability to nurture or fight.

Again consider the case of skills. If we find that men and women differ in their visual–spatial skills, we presumably have found out something about the special abilities and limitations of each sex that might determine how they function in day-to-day life and what activities might better suit women or men. But deriving the social significance of basic gender differences is not as simple as it might seem. If we find that on average girls do better on one spatial–visual skill test and boys do better on another, should we give boys and girls training only in the skill on which they do better? Should we base our occupation counseling on these results, sending girls and boys into different occupations? This might be an appropriate conclusion if *only* boys showed *any* talent on one skill and *only* girls showed *any* talent on the other, and if these differences resulted entirely from innate sex differences, and if girls or boys could reach the full extent of their abilities with only a little training. However, none of these things is true.

Even if we found that there were indeed many more men than women with the particular skill needed for a certain job, we cannot rule out women from that job on the grounds that they are not as likely to be qualified. Some women probably will be as qualified as, and possibly even more qualified than, any man. This understanding of gender differences now forms part of the basis of American law on employment. After the passage of the 1964 Civil Rights Act, which (among other things) banned discrimination in employment on the basis of sex, the Equal Employment Opportunity Commission (EEOC) ruled that employers may not refuse jobs to women because of "assumptions of the comparative employment characteristics of women in general" or because of "stereotyped characterizations of the sexes."

> Such stereotypes include, for example, that men are less capable of assembling intricate equipment and that women are less capable of aggressive salesmanship. The principle of nondiscrimination requires that individuals be considered on the basis of individual capacities and not on the basis of any characteristics generally attributed to the group (Goldstein 1988, 500).

Thus people must be considered on the basis of their individual merit, not on the basis of stereotypes about the social groups of which they are a part, even if the stereotype is true of a majority of the members of the group.

It is not even as simple as some people think to determine which human characteristics best enable a person to perform specific tasks or roles in society. For example, most people assume that a relatively high degree of competitiveness and aggression is required to be active in politics. They therefore assume that it is reasonable to compare women's and men's levels of competitiveness and aggression to help explain differences in male and female political participation. But is the initial assumption true, that is, *do* people need an extraordinarily high level of competitiveness and aggression to be active in politics? There is no clear indication that they do. True, a person who wishes to be elected to a political office must compete in an electoral contest, but this does not necessarily mean that person is especially competitive or particularly cares for competition. To argue otherwise would be like suggesting that to be a doctor a person has to like taking tests, because one has to take a lot of tests to become a doctor. Thus social significance of sex differences is rarely as obvious as it seems, and it requires careful thought and analysis.

Above all, when looking at gender differences, it is important to bear in mind what is interesting about them and what questions we are asking. We cannot simply continue to use men as a representation of the norm and ask how women differ from them. Exploring gender differences is a matter of asking how women and men are similar to and different from each other.

Finally, remember that in women's studies differences between women and men is not the only area of interest. We can also be interested in women's history and situation for its own sake. If we are interested in the variety of forms women in the arts have used to express their understanding of womanhood, for example, we probably would focus on women and not on men at all. Understanding pregnancy and childbirth is not a matter of looking at gender *difference,* but rather gendered *existence.* Many other examples will appear throughout this book.

Difference and Inequality

It is clearer than ever that differences exist between the activities and situations of women and men. There is, as sociologists would say, a system of differentiation of women and men in the United States. But can we also say that the two sexes are so differentiated as to give them unequal value or power? That is, are they not only differentiated but also stratified? Do women and men have not only different roles and activities but different statuses as well?

People can engage in different types of behavior without appearing unequal. For example, if I always have ice cream for dessert and you always have apple pie, or if I play piano as a hobby and you play basketball, there is no reason to believe that we are revealing a pattern of inequality. It is also possible for different people to engage in the same activities or have the same resources and be regarded unequally. If a black family and a white family with equal incomes try to buy the same house in the same neighborhood, they—and their money—may not be valued equally. Difference does not necessarily indicate inequality, just as certain kinds of sameness may not reflect equality. We want to know not just about sameness and difference but also about the values we use to measure the worth of people, activities, and resources.

We can evaluate the degree of equality between women and men by asking several questions:

1. To what degree do women and men possess similar levels of valued resources?
2. To what degree do women and men have similar ranges of life options?
3. To what degree are women and men and their major activities valued similarly?
4. To what degree do women's and men's psychological states—their mental health and degree of happiness or contentment—seem to indicate that their situations are good?

If we consider control over or possession of valued resources, we find strong indications of lower status for women. Women, as we have seen, are financially poorer than men. They hold far fewer positions of authority in society, which means considerably less control over the disposition of valuable resources, including time, labor, and deference as well as tangible goods. By this measure, we live in a very unequal society indeed.

We can also evaluate equality in terms of the degree of personal independence and choice in life options that people have. How much control over our own lives do we have? If women and men have before them an equivalent range of options from which to choose and have equal freedom to make their own choices with equivalent amounts and types of risk, we could say that they have equal status even if they choose different options.

Do women and men have the same degree of control over their lives? We already have some indication that they do not. Men have control over more valuable resources, which in turn expands the number of options they have. Men are in more positions of authority, which gives them control over both others and themselves. Public officials, for example, make major decisions about the distribution of resources and about what people may and may not do in a community or nation, and that community or nation includes the public officials themselves. The very concept of democracy is based on the principle of self-government. As we have seen, men are vastly predominant among those who do the "self-governing." In personal life and day-to-day decision making, women also seem to have—or at least to make—a much smaller range of choices. But we must go considerably beyond the mere presentation of figures to understand the relative degree of choice women and men have. We will attend to this task throughout the remainder of this book.

We can also consider equality by looking at the relative worth attached to people and their activities. According to one of our most tangible measures of worth, money, women and their activities are valued much less than men and their activities. "Women's" jobs have lower salaries than "men's" jobs, and women tend to be paid less even when they do equivalent jobs. Indeed, many of women's activities are not paid at all.

Money is not the only measure of worth, of course. People still value having a male child (an heir to carry on the family name) more than having a female child. *Who's Who* lists only a few women. Many women speak of their major day-to-day activity as being "just a housewife," thus devaluing their own work. To say that a woman writes or thinks "like a man" is supposed to be a compliment, but it indicates that the way women write or speak is viewed as less good. Many historians of women note that even when women have done remarkable and valued things, they tend to be forgotten. We will see many other such examples later in this book.

Psychological states are also important to consider when we talk about equality. When confronted with the degree to which men's and women's experiences and resources differ, many people argue that there really isn't a problem because many women are happy and content with their segregated lives. Although a majority of people still think women are happiest when devoting themselves to motherhood and homemaking, some surveys show that women in the homemaking role are unhappier than employed women. Women in traditional roles seem to have more psychological problems (including "middle-aged depression") than other women. (The relationship between gender roles and mental health is discussed further in Chapter 6.)

Simone de Beauvoir (1952) suggested an even more profound criticism of the "happiness and contentment" principle for evaluating the relative status of women and men. People can learn—or be taught—to be happy in all sorts of situations, including slavery and extreme poverty; the human population is amazingly varied. If we use only happiness and contentment as the criterion for judging whether a group has a problem, we could make wrongs right merely by convincing people to be happy with their lot. Some people are happiest when they save a life; others are happiest when they kill. Are all forms of human happiness morally equivalent? Is happiness the criterion we wish to use to evaluate human activity? Some suggest it is, others say it is not. The measure that de Beauvoir uses, for example, is not contentment and happiness, but liberty.

We can conclude, even from the small amount of information we have examined thus far, that men's and women's lives and activities are not just different; they are unequal. Before we can probe more deeply into the ways this system of inequality works and how it can be changed, we must first find out how it came about. We turn to that question next.

NOTES

1. The full text of this Supreme Court case and most others cited in this book can be found in Goldstein (1988) and Kay (1988).
2. Unless otherwise stated, all figures presented in this chapter refer to and are taken from the U.S. Bureau of the Census 1992.
3. "Hispanic" is a term used by the Census Bureau to refer to Spanish-surnamed people, which means it includes people from many diverse national backgrounds. This is important to remember when trying to understand what these summary statistics mean.
4. *Labor-force participation* refers to people who are employed or are seeking employment. *Employment* refers only to people who hold paid jobs.
5. Sylvia Nasar, "Women's Progress Stalled? Just Not So, *New York Times,* October 18, 1992.
6. Don Terry, "Stabbing Death at Door of Justice Sends Alert on Domestic Violence, *New York Times,* March 17, 1992.
7. Eric Schmitt, "Ban on Women in Combat Divides Four Service Chiefs," *New York Times,* June 19, 1991.
8 Eric Schmitt, "Survey Finds Majority of Army Women Favor Ending Ban on Combat Roles," *New York Times,* September 11, 1992.
9. Many of these reviews are in the form of meta-analyses, in which researchers use statistical techniques to summarize the findings of many different specific studies. Meta-analysis helps the reviewer to determine whether, taken together, these different and often disparate studies allow one to conclude that a difference exists and, if so, how large a difference it is. For a brief introduction to meta-analysis in gender research see Hyde (1991, 76–78). See also Hyde and Linn (1986).
10. Many other important issues are involved in understanding the process of research and learning. For a more complete introduction to social science methodology and feminist research, see Eichler (1980; 1988).

2

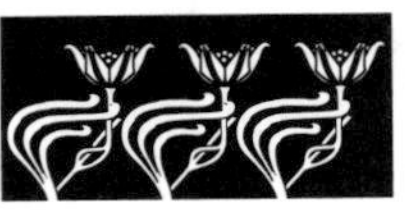

How Did Society Get This Way?

AMERICAN SOCIETY is marked by both sex differentiation and sex stratification. How did this situation come about? How did these inequities develop historically? How do we explain how societies and cultures become structured with one or another general pattern of gender relations? A number of different theories have been suggested over the centuries. Each theory is based on somewhat different kinds of evidence, looks at slightly different aspects of women's lives, and suggests different implications for the possibility of social change.

This chapter examines five kinds of theories about sex differentiation and stratification: (1) static theories, usually based on theology or biology, that see the structure of gender relations as unchanging and inevitable; (2) progress theories, emphasizing modernization and learning from one generation to the next that result in inevitable change for the better; (3) economic or materialist theories, which focus on economic needs and structures as determinants of other aspects of society and change; (4) functionalist evolutionary theories, which emphasize the development of efficient and harmonious social structure, especially in its divisions of labor; and (5) sex war theories, which identify conflicts of interest and power struggles between women and men as the key dynamic in understanding the structure of gender relations.

Each of these approaches represents an attempt to understand the history of gender in society by providing a framework through which to look at and analyze the structure of societies, cultures, and social institutions. Theory helps us make sense of the specific facts of women's experiences and social change. Four important themes or questions can be used to compare these alternative theories:

1. What assumptions do they make? What evidence do they employ?
2. How adequate is the theory for explaining women's situation? Does it help you make sense of the situation?

3. What is the historical context of each theory? Why was each theory developed when it was?
4. What are the political implications of each of these theories? How can each be used, and how have they been used, to justify different strategies for maintaining or changing the status of women and men? What are the differences between feminist theories and explanations and those offered by nonfeminists or opponents of feminism?

The last question is an especially important one. Each of these frameworks suggests political points of view about that history and situation and strategies for the future. Sometimes the same general theory has been adapted by some people to show why gender inequality is a good thing (or at least natural or normal) and by others to show why it must be overcome.

The rest of this chapter outlines each of these approaches, discusses their historical origins, shows how they have been applied to understanding the structure of gender relations in society, and briefly evaluates their utility and drawbacks.

The "Eternal Feminine": Static Theories of God and Nature

There is something about the idea of the eternal or universal that human beings seem to find attractive. People sometimes describe things that are quite evidently variable as eternal and universal. This has often been the case with sex differences.

Although theories of gender inequality that call on biology or theology do not necessarily justify inequity or pose static views of women and men, those that do so have been among the most influential and historically persistent. These frameworks are based on ideas of naturally created eternal truths or principles of human existence that create difference and inequality between women and men. Although these static theories are less widely held than they once were, they are still accepted by many people.

Biological Nature

The Greek philosopher Aristotle (384–322 B.C.) was the first influential theorist to use biological knowledge to explain sociopolitical differences between women and men. Using the biological knowledge of his day, Aristotle argued that the main difference between the sexes was that women are more passive. Because of their passivity and weakness, he argued, women may be regarded as a deformity, although a natural one.

Aristotle—and many later theorists—found evidence of women's passivity in two aspects of procreation. First they argue that men are more active in courtship and sexual behavior and draw from this the conclusion that women are *in general* less active and more passive than men. (Some even suggest that the fact that men are more likely to rape than women shows that women are more passive and, therefore, socially subordinate.) Second, Aristotle also believed that the male is the active principle in procreation itself in that the male sperm creates a baby out of the female material in a woman's body, much as a candlemaker forms a candlestick out of the impassive brass. Later sociobiologists derived their conception of female passivity from different misinformation, for example, that sperm fight their way upstream like so many (female) salmon and then compete with each other in a mad rush to conquer the demure, stationary egg.[1] The concept of natural passivity, however derived, has generally been one of the cornerstone arguments for explaining and justifying the inequality of males and females.

These perceptions of biological passivity are often interpreted as proof that females are naturally inferior, dependent, and submissive. One of the most striking aspects of the history of debate over the nature of women is that although both the methods and the findings of biological science have changed drastically from Aristotle's time to ours, the dominant conclusions derived from biological science remained largely the same for most of that time. Many students of the history of science use this history of scientific interpretation as an example of how science is often shaped by culture, values, and the perspectives of the scientists (Bleier 1984).

Theorists have searched for many biological explanations for what they regard as women's weakness, especially of mind. People once thought that women's menstrual cycles indicated that they were unduly influenced by the moon, which causes craziness or *lunacy*, a word derived from the Latin word for moon. Later people argued that menstruation sapped the strength of women, leaving them weak. Many people now accept the "raging hormones" explanation of women's supposed instability and mental weakness. Women's wombs have also been defined as the cause of their weakness. For a long time people believed that the womb emitted vapors that caused instability. Others believed that the womb traveled around the body, sometimes causing women to faint. The word *hysteria* is derived from the Latin word for womb. The conclusion is obvious: If women are lunatic and hysterical, they are certainly not fit to take care of themselves, let alone others. (But why are women entrusted with the care of children?) These and other views of menstruation will be discussed more fully in Chapter 6.

Biological arguments about the inevitability of inequality have also been grounded in women's reproductive capacities, suggesting that because of pregnancy and childbirth, women need a protector to watch over and act for them. This idea of women's natural need for protection has been used by governments to justify not only what is known as "protective labor legislation" (which we shall examine more closely in Chapter 6) but also many restrictions on women's activities. In 1873, for example, a Supreme Court justice used the following argument to explain why a woman should not be allowed to practice law, even if she was qualified to do so (*Myra Bradwell* v. *State of Illinois*): "Civil law, *as well as nature herself*, has always recognized a wide difference in the respective spheres and destinies of man and woman. Man is, or should be, woman's protector and defender" (emphasis added).

These static theories offer an unchanging view of the structure of relations between the sexes based on "eternal" and "universal" characteristics of women that do not allow either equality or similarity between men and women. They are useless in any real attempt to understand either the well-documented historical changes in relations between the sexes or possible future variation and change. Without arguing that biology has changed dramatically during recorded history or varies from culture to culture, these theories cannot possibly account for the fact that the structure of relations between the sexes has been variable.

Biological theory need not be, and often is not, static in its understanding of women. It can also underscore the malleability or flexibility of human life. But here we have begun with the tradition of biological thinking that has predominated in intellectual history.

Women's God-Given Nature

Many theological interpretations of women's nature have also provided static explanations for sexual inequality. Within the Judeo-Christian tradition, the stories of creation and the expulsion from the Garden of Eden have served as the basis for ethical systems arguing for a God-given moral necessity of women's submission to men. God the Father created women second, we are told, to be a helpmeet to her husband. The Italian theologian St. Thomas Aquinas (1225–1274) argued that God had a very specific type of helper in mind. "It was necessary for women to be made, as the Scripture says, as a helper to man; not indeed as a helpmate in other works, as some say, since man can be more efficiently helped by another man in other works; but as a helper in the work of generation" (1945, 880). Aquinas accepted Aristotle's idea that women were a deformity, but one that could be turned to good. He argued that women should be submissive to men because men had greater quantities of the active principle of reason. Women were created for the purpose of having babies so that men could carry on with God's work. In the order of life on earth, men are answerable to God, and women are answerable to men.

Another biblical event has also been used to prove the need for female submission: Eve's disobedience to God when she eats fruit from the forbidden tree of knowledge. Genesis 3:16 states: "Unto the woman (God) said, I will greatly multiply thy sorrow and thy conception; in sorrow thou shall bring forth children; and thy desire shall be to thy husband, and he shall rule over thee." There have been some differences of interpretation of these words within Christianity and Judaism, but the most common interpretations include these arguments:

1. Eve's actions reveal women's moral weakness.
2. Adam's own weakness in accepting the fruit shows that women are dangerous temptresses who must be controlled if men are to be morally strong.
3. God ordained that there must be a division of labor by which women bear children (in sorrow and pain) and men produce the means of existence (by the sweat of their brow).
4. Men shall rule over women.

Note that this theological view appears to admit of more possibility for variation in human life than the crudest of the biological theories. It is *possible* for human beings not to follow some aspects of the divine order, just as it is possible for humans to violate most other divine laws. But, of course, the consequences of choosing to act against God's will are dire. (In Chapter 7 we will look more closely at the role of religion in structuring women's lives.)

The traditions of biological and theological thinking described here suggest that attempts to change the relative conditions of men and women are dangerous because that requires violating the laws of God or nature. As we shall see later, these are not the only explanations that have been offered by scientists and theologians. Calling on God or nature to understand the structure and history of relations between the sexes by no means necessitates taking either a static view or one that justifies inequality. Unfortunately, however, these have been the dominant views not just of the ancients but also of many contemporary leaders. As late as 1972, for example, U.S. Senator Sam Ervin opposed passage of the Equal Rights Amendment on the grounds that "when He created them, God made physiological and functional differences between men and women" (Sayers 1982, 70).

The Inevitable Progress of Enlightenment and Modernization

The 18th century witnessed the formulation of a new view based on Enlightenment philosophy that continues to be the most widely accepted basis for understanding social relations in the West, especially the United States. It emphasizes that gradual progress of human society will result if—and only if—we can be free to learn from our collective mistakes and develop science and technology to improve our lives. This new approach to thinking about society, which formed part of the basis for both the American and French Revolutions, framed the liberal assault on the old feudal order of power relations in society and government. It was quickly adopted by a number of early feminists as a means of understanding and criticizing inequalities between the sexes.

Foundations of Liberalism

The liberal argument introduced by philosophers like John Locke (1672–1704) and Jean-Jacques Rousseau (1712–1778) opposed certain aspects of the patriarchal structure of political and economic power. *Patriarchy* means "rule of" (*arch*) "fathers" (*patri*). Most of the early critics of patriarchy did not, however, focus on the family as such. Rather, they attacked rule by monarchs and the privileges of the aristocratic class of men over other men in society. The logic of the patriarchal order was right, privilege, and power by birth. There were a number of different patriarchal views of society, but a good example is philosopher Jean Bodin's (1530–1596) observation that

> a family is like a state: there can be but one ruler, one master, one lord. A father . . . is the true image of God, our sovereign Lord, the Father of all

> things. . . . A father is obliged by nature to support his children while they are still weak and helpless, and to bring them up in honorable and virtuous ways. On the other hand, a child is obliged . . . to love, revere, serve, and support his father; to execute his commands in loyal obedience; to shield his infirmities; and never to spare his own life or property in order to save the life of him to whom he owes his own (Jones 1963, 561).

The monarch and relations within the realm were analogous to the father and relationships within the family. Some writers went even further. Robert Filmer (1588–1653) argued in his *Patriarcha* that royal authority is not only analogous to but also derived from the power God gave to fathers over the family. Kings, he claimed, derived their power through inheritance of the power the Father gave to the first father: Adam.

The liberal attack on patriarchalism is exemplified in the famous lines from the Declaration of Independence: "We hold these truths to be self-evident: that all men are created equal, that they are endowed by their Creator with certain inalienable rights, that among these are life, liberty, and the pursuit of happiness."

What was so new and revolutionary about this view? First and foremost it rejected the idea that only monarchs or certain classes of people were "endowed by their Creator" with rights and power. It argued that each individual (white) man (for at first this was not applied to women or to men who were not white) had an equal birthright of basic or natural rights. These rights were "inalienable"; that is, in place of the patriarchal notion that all rights stem from or are granted by the king, Enlightenment theorists argued that individuals have certain autonomous rights that could not be taken away from them. The idea of the autonomy and independence of individuals was critical; men should not owe obedience to other men merely because of some condition of birth.

Liberalism and Women

It did not take long for some people to extend these principles to cover the situation of women. The first person to undertake this task in a comprehensive way was Mary Wollstonecraft (1759–1797). In 1792 Wollstonecraft published her important treatise, *A Vindication of the Rights of Woman*, which argued that autocratic and patriarchal power relations between the sexes were as unjust and indefensible as those between monarch and subject. Much of the best-known and most influential feminist ideas on women's status, particularly on the United States and Western Europe, has been based solidly in this liberal tradition.

The liberal approach to explaining women's status revolved around the importance of reason in human development and the conditions of individual liberty that nurture reason. Like men, it argues, women should be considered free and equal at birth, with a virtually limitless potential for improvement. But this potential can be developed only if society places no artificial constraints on their lives so that they can be free to use their reason to discover what is good for them.

How do liberals explain the difference in status and roles of women and men? Wollstonecraft argued that the oppression of women, like the subjection of slaves to masters or people to an autocratic king, was the result of the artificial constraints of law and social institutions that stem from people's irrational prejudices (Sapiro 1992). If women appear very different from and inferior to men, it is because they have been made that way by social forces instituted by human beings who did not know any better. Such a system of inequity harms women because their rights are taken from them and they are denied the opportunity to develop reason and thus improve themselves. But men are also harmed because, like kings and slave masters, they have been corrupted by holding excessive power over others. Indeed society as a whole is harmed because inequities and the lack of freedom within it makes the entire society unjust and impedes progress of the whole and its parts. Another important early liberal text on this problem was written by John Stuart Mill (1806–1873) in his *Subjection of Women* (1869; reprinted in Rossi, 1970). Mill claimed that the right of men over women was the last bastion of the bygone and unenlightened days when "might was right."

In liberal theory the key to social change is the enlightenment of individuals by reason that requires stripping away old blinding prejudices. Liberal feminists identified education as the primary instrument for progress. But progress also involves tearing down the barriers that keep women from the freedom to

Patriarchy begins at home.

develop themselves as individuals, including laws that barred women from doing certain kinds of jobs, voting, or, if they were married, holding their own property. This emphasis on enlightenment and progress is embedded in contemporary *modernization* theories used by many students of historical change. These theories argue that the growth of markets, technology, and science necessarily lead to other aspects of "progress" such as growing egalitarianism, including equality between the sexes.

The liberal view of social change is an optimistic one. It suggests that the ills of the past are irrelevant to today's world because people in the past simply did not know as much as we do now; past problems were caused by human stupidity and prejudice. Progress appears natural and almost inevitable, depending simply on increased education and technology and decreased interference with our individual lives by the government. Although widely accepted today, this perspective has some problems. As a theory of history it is very weak; indeed, some would argue that it offers no theory of historical changes at all. Human history has not been a matter of slow and steady progress from less enlightened to more enlightened ages. The history of women and women's status offers many examples of this.

Historians and anthropologists alike note that political and economic development, both in the United States and elsewhere, has often been marked by increased inequality in women's and men's status, at least at the early stages of change. In the United States, women became increasingly restricted at the beginning of the nineteenth century. A similar phenomenon is noted immediately following World War II, when the idea of women's "proper" role at home was reestablished with renewed vigor. Students of African society and history have found that in many places the sexes became more unequal and the power of women was decreased by the impact of "enlightened" Western law and custom (e.g., Hafkin and Bay 1976).

Liberal theory gives us little idea of what conditions cause changes in the roles and status of women. It gives no hints of what creates movements for change other than a vague notion that some enlightened (or unenlightened) people become active and push for change. It suggests no reasons why cultures differ in how they arrange relations between the sexes, except for a vague notion that people in different cultures somehow have different ideas about what is right and proper. It suggests that all we have to do to achieve changes in the status of women is change people's minds, or "resocialize" them. As we shall see, the matter is not as simple as that.

Finally, although the optimism of liberalism has spurred many people to action, it can also breed a kind of complacency. If we expect human beings to progress merely because we become "smarter" about ourselves as we gain experience in the world, we have little reason to do anything about the status of women other than go about the business of improving ourselves as individuals. It is interesting to see how often just this argument has been launched against feminism over the past century. It seems that each generation feels that the battles for equality have been won and that the only thing holding women back is women's own lack of initiative. Unfortunately good works by single individuals have rarely enabled any subordinate social group to achieve changes toward equality and liberty.[2]

Economic and Historical Materialist Theories

By the middle of the 19th century another major approach to understanding social relations and social change gained influence. This approach emphasizes the impact of economic structures and relations on the other aspects of society and culture. The most famous of the early theorists associated with this view were Karl Marx (1818–1883) and Friedrich Engels (1820–1895), whose writings became the source for the most influential materialist theory of social relations.

Marxist Foundations

The differences between the Marxist, or historical-materialist, analysis of society and the liberal, or Enlightenment, analysis can be approached through Marx and Engels's assertion in *The German Ideology* (1845–1846) that "the first premise of all human history is, of course, the existence of living human individuals" (Marx and Engels, 1947, 7). This sentence may not appear remarkable at first, but the conclusions Marx and Engels drew from it make all the difference in the analytical world. They suggested that people may well argue that human beings "can be distinguished from animals by consciousness, by religion or anything else you like" (7), but the first fact of human life is their physical existence and sustenance. "Life involves before everything else eating and drinking, a habitation, clothing and many other things" (16). The key to seeing the impact of these ideas is to understand that "before everything else" refers not just to the historical fact that human beings learned to feed and clothe themselves before they learned to read and write, but also to the idea that the physical maintenance of life is primary in our social existence and substantially shapes consciousness and culture.

Marxists argue that consciousness, thought, language, religion, law, and other such manifestations of the human mind flow from and are shaped by material needs and the social and institutional arrangements of economic production through which people satisfy these needs. Language and the ideas it expresses are developed to help fulfill these needs and experiences of day-to-day life. Dominant thought systems (religion, theory, and so forth) reflect the interests of those in power and justify the economic, social, and political arrangements by which that power is maintained.

According to Marxist theories, the history of the world is "the history of class struggle." Divisions of labor within the economy do not simply mean that different people do different jobs. Within the divisions of labor that have developed under feudalism and later under capitalism, those in control of the means of production also control the products and the labor of those who make them.

Labor power, and therefore laborers themselves, is exploited by capitalists in the following sense. It is in the capitalists' interest to get as much production out of workers for as little money as possible just as it is in the workers' interest to get as much money for as little work as possible. The struggle between employer and worker is far from even, however, because the capitalists control the material means of living and production and the ideology of society.

Marxists argue that this struggle will end only when the workers retrieve control over their own labor, life situations, and consciousness, if the capitalist system is replaced by one in which no single individual or class can own the means of production. Only by substantially rearranging economic institutions can political and social values and structures be truly altered.

How was this theory applied to understanding the condition of women? The earliest exposition of a Marxist analysis can be found in Friedrich Engels's *Origins of the Family, Private Property, and the State* (1884) and somewhat later in August Bebel's *Women and Socialism* ([1910] 1970). Marx and Engels suggest that in subsistence economies, in which all individuals participate in the production process and provide for themselves with no significant amount of surplus, men and women are fairly equal because they have equal control over their labor and over the products of their labor. Women's subservience began with the development of private property. As agricultural production became more efficient, people created a surplus beyond what they needed for immediate consumption that could be exchanged for other products. Because men were the producers of goods with exchange value, they owned and controlled the production of surplus products. According to Marxist analysis, this is the key to power in exchange economies. The division of labor between men and women in the family paralleled the division in the larger society into capitalist and proletariat classes.

With the invention of private property, men sought to ensure they could pass their property on to their own children (for reasons not entirely explained). Because of the nature of reproduction, this concern about inheritance gave men the motivation to control women in monogamous (at least for the woman) marriages. Property and family law were therefore designed by men to keep women under their control. For Marxists the condition of women, like other social inequities and oppression, has its source in the class system—the structure of property ownership and production—found in capitalist societies. Thus for orthodox Marxists the liberation of women can occur only when working-class women participate with men in overthrowing the capitalist economic structure that causes their oppression. Change will not simply happen because people become wiser and more modern from one generation to the next, and a separate women's movement apart from the more general class struggle cannot accomplish real change either because of the source of women's oppression in the economy.

Contemporary Economic and Materialist Theories

Although much historical and anthropological research contradicts the details presented by Engels, several aspects of economic and materialist explanations of women's situation remain widely influential. First, the divisions of labor and power between men and women, and the different value placed on men's and women's work seems to depend at least partly on the structure of the economy as a whole. Research on many countries around the world including the United States shows that industrialization and the shift to a fully capitalist economy is often marked by an increasing gap between the power and value of men and women. As production moves out of the home, the divisions of labor between women and men leave men with the greater share of economic and other forms of power.

Many experts fear that this widening gap due to the creation of a new capitalist economy is occurring again, this time in eastern Europe and the former Soviet Union as those countries are restructuring their economies. In many of those countries women are suffering greater unemployment and social services that assisted mothers are disappearing or threatened. A common belief among men in the former Soviet Union is that one of the benefits of the new system is that women will stay home as homemakers and can now be kept out of the labor force. At the same time some feminist theorists, especially those working in the formerly communist countries, argue that it is not capitalism per se that is causing the restructuring of gender relations, because the working of the communist systems had also reinforced a culture of male dominance even if those systems diminished many of the actual signs of gender inequality. Indeed, the reintroduction of increasingly severe gender inequality is *preceding* the establishment of new capitalist systems. But the upheavals in the economy, and the increasing emphasis on markets and market efficiency, seem to be having even more negative effects on women's work lives than on men's (Rosenberg 1991).

These approaches to women's situation also emphasize that the structure of power within different major social institutions is interdependent. Although Marxist theory and its variants are not the only theories that make this point, it is central to them. The relationships—and similarity—between divisions of labor inside and outside the family are so obvious we may sometimes forget how remarkable they are. Women's roles outside the family and the degree of social power they have are dependent on divisions of labor within the family. The jobs viewed as most appropriate for women to hold are those that seem most to resemble the tasks that women are supposed to undertake in the family. Even people who claim to desire equality for women in the marketplace tend to feel that women can seek employment only if their children are already taken care of. We do not ask the same of men. It is important to remember that these theories pay close attention to the fact that *divisions* of labor usually mean more than different people doing different types of work. Divisions of labor often also entail division of power and control.

Consider the division of labor in marriage. In the traditional arrangement (reinforced by law), men are supposed to seek employment to support the family, while women are supposed to do most of the labor required for family upkeep. Some might argue this is simply a functional and efficient arrangement, not to mention (as some people would) a particularly nice one for women because they get to care for the people they love while men are out working in competitive, alienating jobs. A closer look suggests this is no mere system of cooperation between equals, as the man's designation as "head of the household" suggests. Participating in the labor market and bringing home wages give men in traditional marriages added power and prestige over their wives.

Economic analyses of the structure of gender relations also emphasize that cultural definitions of women's and men's roles are grounded in the concrete, material aspects of life and that they therefore are subject to great historical change. American history offers some clear examples. Historians note that the idea that pregnancy is a glowing, happy time developed in the United States only after the facts of reproductive life had improved considerably. In the colonial era, for example, when one out of five reproductively active women died as a result of childbirth and many babies did not survive past one year, what women were taught about pregnancy and motherhood had a lot more to do with resignation to possible death than with the joys of motherhood.

People are sometimes startled to realize how recent are our supposedly traditional ideologies of womanhood. In the early 19th century as "productive labor" (and with it, men) moved increasingly out of the home, women began to be viewed as delicate, frail, asexual, and as the keepers of the home fires to which men could return after a harrowing day in the world. This new ideological framework for understanding women, now known as the "cult of true womanhood" (Welter 1966), could not make sense in an economy in which women and men must toil together to survive. Moreover, it should not be surprising that this ideology was applied only to specific classes of women. Southern slaveholders did not apply the cult of true womanhood to the black women they owned, and late 19th century Boston Brahmins did not worry about the femininity and delicacy of their Irish maids.

More recent examples underscore the point that ideology often flows from institutional and social arrangements rather than the reverse. During World War II, the figure of "Rosie the Riveter" had been used to convince women that armaments manufacturing was important and appropriately feminine work for women. After the war, how could women be convinced to give the jobs back to men? Freudian psychoanalysis became popular in the 1950s as one way to justify why an increasingly educated population of women—and one that had experienced employment during World War II—should feel happy staying at home having babies. Ideas about women's roles began to change again later, as the structure of the economy changed and masses of new auxiliary jobs (such as clerical work) opened up, education expanded dramatically, and more workers were needed in the "helping professions" such as nursing and social work.

Thus, many feminist theorists find Marxist and other materialists' analyses of consciousness and ideology especially useful. Materialists argue that our social relationships and ideas about ourselves reflect and justify the social arrangements and institutions that exist, and especially the power relations within them. In short, ideologies support the power of the powerful. Dominant ideas of what is natural for women and what women "want" change over time, but they support existing arrangements and shape our perceptions of people and events. Psychological research shows that these ideological constructions of men and women affect not just how men perceive and treat women but also how women perceive and treat themselves, both as a group and as individuals.

If people's views of social arrangements are shaped by those arrangements themselves, how can change occur? At some times in history some portion of a subordinate group (in this case women) become conscious of their situation; that is, something happens to make them understand their situation is determined by their membership in a particular subordinated social group and they begin to see through the cultural justifications of their subordination. Change, then, might occur as these women become active in a social movement to mobilize other women to the same recognition and to political action based on this new group consciousness.

Consider the masses of women in recent decades who never thought they would have to earn their own living but found that they had to seek employment to support themselves and their families because of widowhood, divorce, or economic recession. Many women probably blamed themselves for their inabilities to earn enough money, explaining their situation by saying, "I don't have sufficient skills," "I didn't get enough training," or "I dropped out of school to support my husband and to have children." Group consciousness could lead such women to see that the fault is not theirs alone but is common to women because education and training are not considered to be as important for women as for men and because women are encouraged to get married and have babies at a young age and drop out of school if necessary. Women without a group consciousness simply regret their "fault" and do whatever they can as individuals to better themselves. When the system is rigged against them, such solutions are doomed to failure. Women with a group consciousness work to change the situation of women as a group.

Structural-Functionalist and Evolutionary Theories

The 19th century saw the development of a second influential set of explanations for the development of societal sex differentiation and stratification: evolutionary theories. These grew out of the work of Charles Darwin (1809–1882) and Herbert Spencer (1820–1903) and sought to understand and link together the biological and social history of human life. These were among the first of the *structural-functionalist* theories of the structure gender arrangements in society; that is, they explored the development of particular institutionalized gender relations to see how they function as means by which human beings ensure their own survival as individuals, as societies, and as a species. Social arrangements that contribute to survival are functional; those that do not are dysfunctional. Although the earliest examples of this approach focused specifically on biological adaptation and evolution, later versions were more sociological in their emphasis. Most of the theorists who have used evolutionary perspectives to explain the situation of women have concluded that both differentiation and stratification are inevitable, or at least desirable, if human life is to progress. This type of functionalist and evolutionary theory is often called social Darwinism, although Darwin himself did not subscribe to it.

Foundations of Structural-Functionalist Thought

Herbert Spencer believed that human society evolves through physiological adaptation to its surroundings in order to ensure its own survival. Through the mechanism of the "survival of the fittest" those best adapted to the needs of human life will survive and reproduce their characteristics while others will not survive. As human beings discover the social arrangements that are most functional (that contribute most to their ability to survive), these arrangements will become the order of society, and people will also develop and emphasize the characteristics best fitted to this order. Nature is naturally progressive; evolution is the path to survival. Spencer believed that the hallmark of progress in human life is the division of labor into specialized functions. Students of evolution noted that higher species were more specialized than lower species and argued that divisions of labor within human life were necessary for human survival and progress.

For Spencer and many others, the most important division of human labor is that between men and women because it directly shapes the efficiency with which human life is reproduced and maintained. According to the early versions of evolutionary theory, as human life progresses, women become increasingly relieved of the burden of breadwinning and increasingly fitted to the exclusive tasks of childbearing and taking care of the home. The higher the level of society, the more differentiated women and men are. Some noted that there was less differentiation between the sexes in the "lower orders" of society, by which they meant the working class, immigrants, and the poor. This only went to show, they said, that the more evolved human society is, the more different men and women are. Of course to accept this argument we also have to accept the idea that people in different classes or societies are on different rungs of the evolutionary ladder: They are biologically different. Many people did just that, and social Darwinism became an important justification of racism, class exploitation, and imperialism.

Spencer argued that the sexes are not merely different but also necessarily unequal. Women have become increasingly well fitted to domestic duties but have had no need to become fit for anything else. Only men have evolved the characteristics necessary for other aspects of social, economic, and political life. Since it appears that men continue to evolve while women do not, men must dominate women and reinforce their inequalities if society is to continue to progress.

A century ago many people used functionalist and evolutionary theory to argue that women should not be allowed to vote. Many proponents of this view of evolution have claimed that it is a mistake to make laws and policies designed to increase equality between women and men because these are doomed to fail; nature has not developed women and men for equality. Although many evolutionary theorists have claimed to trust evolution to move society in the direction of progress, they also seem to feel that only men know what that direction is.

Early Feminist Critiques

Evolutionary theory was also adopted by some observers of the division of labor between the sexes who came to very different conclusions about the nature of inequality between women and men. Antoinette Brown Blackwell (1825–1921), an American feminist who began her career as a theologian, was very influenced by but also critical of the writing of Darwin and Spencer. Her book, *The Sexes*

Spencer's biological arguments do not appear to have applied to pioneer women.

Throughout Nature, written in 1875, is a fascinating early discussion of bias in scientific research (for extensive excerpts from the text, see Rossi, 1988). She believed in evolution as the basis of human development and accepted the conclusions that the division of labor between the sexes was caused by evolution and that men's and women's personalities and abilities had evolved to be very different. But she objected to the conservative conclusions about the natural dominance of women by men the social Darwinists had drawn from evolution.

Blackwell thought that the sexes had developed different characteristics. But instead of arguing that the sexes were therefore naturally unequal she claimed they were complementary; men and women constituted two balanced halves of the whole of humanity. Therefore, she said, sex differentiation cannot give men grounds to restrict women or declare them unfit to do anything but take care of children and the home. Male dominance of women and the exclusion of women from public life is dysfunctional—contrary to the proper functioning of society. Both women and men must be free to contribute their special skills and attributes to society at all levels. Men could contribute the force and rationality necessary to society, women could contribute the gentleness and spirituality. Using the principles of evolution, therefore, Blackwell reached exactly the opposite conclusion from Spencer's, as she wrote, "No theory of unfitness . . . can have the right to suppress any excellence which Nature has seen fit to evolve. Men and women, in search of the same ends, must co-operate in as many . . . pursuits as the present development of the race enables them both to recognize and appreciate" (quoted in Rossi 1988, 377).

A similar argument was made by many proponents of women's suffrage, such as the great social worker Jane Addams (1860–1935), who thought that if women took a full role in politics, the addition of their propensity for nurturance and their skills as housekeepers would upgrade the quality of politics and political decisions (see, e.g., the selection in Rossi 1988).

The sociologist Charlotte Perkins Gilman (1868–1935) offered a different feminist interpretation of functionalist and evolutionary theory. She also thought that divisions of labor between the sexes had developed through the struggle of human beings to survive. At one time, when human life required both grueling labor for production and nearly constant attempts to reproduce simply to replace the current population, a relatively strict division of labor was functional—it made sense. But many aspects of modernization meant that divisions of labor as they had existed in the past were no longer functional. In industrialized societies, work depended decreasingly on physical force and increasingly on intellectual and technical skills. Women did not need to become pregnant as often as they once did to ensure survival of the race. In her view, human beings had become "oversexed," by which she meant that they were exaggerating and overemphasizing differences between the sexes in a way that was becoming dangerous to the preservation and improvement of the human race.

Gilman thought that men would only hold themselves back if they continued to try to restrict women. Human society was wasting half its brain power and turning the female half of society into useless parasites living off the work of others. Better, Gilman said, to advance useful divisions of labor based on skill, training, and efficiency and to do away with harmful ones such as those based on sex. She thought that rather than having all women do cooking, cleaning, and child care in their individual homes whether they were good at these things or not, such tasks should be done cooperatively by trained specialists outside the home whenever possible. Society had become dysfunctionally *androcentric*—that is, focused on and dominated by men.[3]

Evolution and Sexual Differentiation: Current Views

Debates over the role of evolution in the development of sexual differentiation and stratification continue today. One influential theme among anthropologists and sociologists is the idea that in primitive times social arrangements between the sexes developed into a functional division of labor between men the hunters and women the gatherers and nurturers and that our social arrangements since that time have continued to diverge from that original division. Encumbered by pregnancies and children, women could not travel far and in any case did not have the strength to engage in the hunt. Although women contributed considerably more than men to daily subsistence—some estimates suggest that at least 80 percent of the food consumed was the result of women's labor—men gained dominance and control in society as their hunting bands were transformed into warring bands and, ultimately, into governments. Sociobiologists such as E. O. Wilson (1975) claim that male dominance and divisions of labor have been reinforced by genetic differences through the evolution process. Sociobiologists disagree about how much equality is possible in the future, but almost all are deeply skeptical about the possibility of full equality.

Criticisms of sociobiological theories based on evolution stand on a number of points (e.g., Hrdy 1981; Sayers 1982; Sperling 1991).

1. Recent research questions some of the assumptions often made about hunting and gathering societies. Female gatherers apparently traveled long distances to accomplish their tasks. Moreover, the division of labor was not always as rigid as many theories suggest; in some hunter-gatherer societies, men participated in what we now think of as domestic tasks.
2. Sociobiologists tend to select examples to suit their arguments, examples ranging from the most primitive times to modern, postindustrial societies, without any careful systematic historical analysis.
3. Sociobiologists often seem to confuse human evolution (changes in the physiological structure of the species) with human history (changes in culture, social structure, and human events). Some sociobiologists seem to accept the Lamarckian position that suggests that characteristics acquired during a person's life are passed on to that person's children through biological mechanisms.[4] Although social structures and culture have changed during recorded history and even during living memory, there is little, if any, evidence that relevant physiological and genetic characteristics have changed in significant ways during that time.

4. Even if sexual divisions of labor and dominance were once functional, we must still ask Charlotte Perkins Gilman's question: Are these divisions still functional, or should they be erased for better adaptation to our needs at this point in history?

Current biological research offers little support for the thesis that men and women have evolved into creatures that are well suited for the divisions of labor and dominance we see in society. Although all known societies are marked by some division of labor between the sexes, the exact content of that division varies from one culture to another and from one historical period to another. Recent American history shows a tremendous shift in one aspect of division of labor: Female civilian labor force participation rose from about 18% in 1900 to 34% in 1950 to 58% in 1990 (Ries and Stone 1992, 308). On almost any personality or psychological test devised, men and women as groups reveal the same range of traits or characteristics. Biological science has failed to establish direct links between physiological characteristics and social roles and arrangements. If these divisions are natural, it is difficult to understand why people have had to work so hard to enforce and maintain them.

Structural Functionalism in 20th-Century Social Theory

Structural-functionalist approaches gained new life in the 1940s and 1950s with the influence of the sociologist Talcott Parsons and his colleagues in their development of social systems theory.[5] Structural-functionalist systems theory, which became one of the dominant approaches to social science, describes society as an integrated system of individuals interacting in their various social roles that depend on their status or positions in society. These social roles, in turn, are embedded in social institutions that coordinate performance of the various functions of society. Culture is the set of underlying values and symbols that help lend coherent meaning to the whole and its parts. To the degree that personality is socialized or taught to the young rather than innate, personality can be seen as the internalized or learned aspects of culture that help individuals become motivated and able to carry out their part in this scheme. Thus we end up with a picture of society as a system of coordinated, interlocking parts that contribute to the functioning of the whole.

Among the most important functions of society is reproduction and the nurturing and socialization of the young; therefore the family and family roles take on major significance in structural-functionalist social analysis. Within this tradition of research the division of labor of males and females in and out of the family becomes an important determinant of the ability of societies to maintain themselves effectively.

Talcott Parsons outlined the basic argument in his 1942 essay on "Age and Sex in the Social Structure of the United States," in which he discussed how from an early age boys and girls are socialized into "feminine" and "masculine" personalities and work roles so that they may become appropriately differentiated into their different adult roles to keep society working smoothly. Parsons writes, for example, that "it is of fundamental significance to the sex role structure of the adult age levels that the normal man has a 'job,' which is fundamental to his social status in general" (Parsons 1954, 94). In contrast, "The woman's fundamental status is that of her husband's wife, the mother of his children, and traditionally the person responsible for a complex of activities in connection with the management of the household, care of children, etc." (Parsons 1954, 95).

Parsons pointed out that while it is true that women might hold jobs, men might be unemployed, adults might not marry, or they might not even develop heterosexual orientations at all, these results are all dysfunctional. That is, they would disrupt the ability of society or its parts to work well. Thus structural-functionalist approaches in the social sciences have tended to define gender divisions of labor and status as part of the support system of society, necessary for its functioning.

Sex War: The Struggle for Dominance

When one nation or class or people dominates another, we can usually reasonably assume that this situation was brought about and is maintained through competition and force. At first glance men and women seem to pose the major exception to this rule. The very idea of a battle or struggle for dominance between the sexes is greeted either by laughter (perhaps nervous) or anger and anxiety by most people. Could women and men have such opposing interests in society? After all, if men and women were at war, they certainly wouldn't choose to live with each other, would they?

The idea of a primeval struggle through which men have asserted their dominance over women is more deeply embedded in many cultures than we might at first think (Sanday 1981a). Recall the story of the Medusa, discussed earlier, in which man must struggle to overcome woman or women's evil. A similar theme occurs in numerous myths and stories, such as the Greek myth of the Sirens, in which dangerous women drive sailors to self-destruction; the story of Eve, in which Eve seduces Adam from grace; and the Mozart opera, *The Magic Flute*, in which the deceptive Queen of the Night is overcome by male rationality.[6] Many cultures have myths of an originally powerful goddess—the Mother Goddess—who was overthrown by men or a male god, who thereby put the world in proper order. Marx and Engels and numerous later theorists argued that there must have been a struggle for men to win control over women and property.

In fact many theorists have suggested that the current power relations between the sexes are the result of a war between the sexes that women so far have lost. Some theorists see a struggle that is derived from conflicts of interest in the roles and personalities of women and men, and some point directly to sexuality as the battleground. Susan Faludi's (1991) book, *Backlash,* offers the influential argument that the 1980s witnessed the renewal of conflict in the rise of an "undeclared war against American women" in reaction to the gains that women were beginning to make. She points to evidence in the mass media, the economic system, fashion, politics, and intellectual life. It is important to note that the view that relations between women and men are determined in part by power struggles between them has been held in different forms by both feminists and antifeminists. We shall look briefly at both versions.

Freud and the War Between the Sexes

Sigmund Freud (1856–1939), the founder of modern psychoanalysis, was one of the first writers to try to understand the roots of antagonism between the sexes. Although Freud and, indeed, psychoanalysis are most discussed in relation to understanding *individual* development (as we will see in Chapter 3), they also provide a framework for examining social change and *historical* development. Freud's thoughts on history, culture, and society, including his story of the battle between the sexes, may be found in its most complete form in *Civilization and Its Discontents* ([1930] 1961). His essay on "Femininity" ([1933] 1965) focuses most clearly on the development of femininity and masculinity.

According to Freud, the trauma of a girl's life is the discovery that she is not male, that she has no penis. (Some feminist theorists accept the outline of this argument but interpret the discovery symbolically. To them the penis, or phallus, is simply the symbol of male power, which women lack.) This causes her to grow hostile to her mother, who made her deficient like the mother herself, and to attach herself first to her father and later to potential fathers. She also develops the need to acquire the missing penis, at least symbolically, by giving birth, particularly to a boy. She is thus set on the track toward heterosexuality; her choice of a love object is conditioned by her struggle for restitution of the penis.

But even getting married and having a son does not end a woman's struggle. She may place on her son all the ambitions she as a woman cannot or is not allowed to fulfill, which causes a struggle for autonomy between them. She also will try to achieve her ambitions through her husband. Although to remain attractive to him she must seem passive and submissive, in fact her insecurity leads her to strengthen her hold on him in marriage by turning her husband into her child and in acting as a mother to him.

Finally, according to Freud, the battle between men and women is carried to a broader field. Women's energies are focused on the home and family; men's energies are devoted to the larger society. As men increasingly turn their energies outward and away from the family and home, a struggle develops between men and women. Women resent men's lack of attention to them and battle against it, and they come to resent civilization itself, which stole men's attentions from them. Men are destined to win this battle, however, because, after all, they have what women want.

Some psychoanalytic scholars suggest that Freud may have been on the right track but that womb envy rather than penis envy is the main issue in dominance struggles between women and men. Men, they argue, resent the fact that only women can produce life from within their bodies and have spent most of their history trying both to control this powerful force and to make up for their own deficiencies (e.g., Horney 1967). It is important to remember that the role of fathers in procreation is not readily apparent; women's power in reproduction is considerably more obvious.

Societal Stress and Cultural Strain

Researchers in other scholarly traditions have also pondered the origins of dominance struggles between women and men. Anthropologist Peggy Reeves Sanday (1981a) explored evidence from over 150 tribal societies from around the world to understand the sources and dynamics of male dominance, which she defined as "the exclusion of women from political and economic decision making" plus male aggression against women, defined as "the expectation that males should be tough, brave, and aggressive; the presence of men's houses or specific places where only men may congregate; frequent quarreling, fighting, or wife beating; the institutionalization or regular occurrence of rape; and raiding other groups for wives" (Sanday 1981a, 164).

Sanday found that the degree of male dominance seemed to depend on other environmental and historical conditions, especially relatively recent migration, an undependable, fluctuating food supply, chronic hunger or protein deficiency, and chronic or endemic war. Her research led her to conclude that "the aggressive subjugation of women must be understood as part of a people's response to stress" (Sanday 1981a, 184). Sanday argues that men and women tend to respond differently to stress; men tend to respond with aggression although not always with domination, and not always with the subjugation of *women.* Under what stress circumstances do men blame or turn against women?

She argues that there is a complex interaction within any society among the cultural meanings attached to male and female, the specific stresses it is undergoing, and the range of culturally possible solutions to its problems. Sanday points to circumstances in which life and death become threatening in such a way as to make male aggression and control of female fertility appear a key to security. Women, she argues, will not engage as a group in pitched battle against men, which makes it relatively easy for men to subjugate them. There are many historical examples in the past century of large-scale social struggles of men to control women, for example, in the context of the upheavals of the creation of new nations, such as those that occurred in many Islamic nations (Jayawardena 1986; Kandiyoti 1991; Sapiro 1993).

Writers from a wide spectrum of viewpoints suggest that even if we don't know how male dominance began, it is maintained through struggle and violence. As early as the end of the 18th century, Mary Wollstonecraft argued that the division of power and labor between the sexes created a constant war between them. Although the balance of power is on men's side, human nature leads women to pursue their own interests by using whatever power they might have over men. If men force women to be mere sex objects or objects of beauty, women will use their sexuality and beauty against men. If women are not allowed to be forceful and direct, they will be cunning, manipulative, and sly.

The only way to end this battle, Wollstonecraft argued, was to grant both men and women the human dignity that comes through independence and equality.

Sex War: Current Versions

Modern feminists have further developed the theme of sex war, finding different types of evidence to show the signs of struggle and antagonism. Although not all feminists are women, and not all antifeminists are men, the history of feminist movements is in part a struggle to gain rights and increased powers for women from governments, employers, and other male-dominated organizations. Women gained their new rights slowly, through considerable effort, and sometimes bloodshed.

Many feminists point not just to legal battles but also to what Kate Millett (1970) called the *sexual politics* of everyday life. Social psychologists and linguists have documented numerous ways in which men take control from women even in normal conversation (Colwill 1982). Feminists point out that the battle is often violent and that rape and wife battery can be seen as means of physical control of women. Many contemporary feminists also agree with the liberal democratic theorist John Stuart Mill, who argued that men do everything in their power to make women "willing slaves" (for the text, see Rossi 1970). Other feminists point specifically to sexual control, the signs of which one can see in double standards of sexual morality and in the "privileges" women receive when they are associated with men, especially through marriage.[7] Whether the sex war is fought on the battleground of sexual politics or sexual control, many argue that men have numerous privileges they derive merely from being men and will not give up without a struggle.

Feminists are not the only observers of gender systems who see the condition of women as the result of a sex war. The conservative sociobiological theory of the "selfish gene" suggests that men seek to dominate women to be sure they reproduce themselves by passing on their genes to a new generation. Along similar lines, many sociobiologists argue that men have an instinct to control women sexually (and even have a natural tendency to rape) because they are driven to impregnate as many women as possible. Nor is the battle ended if pregnancy occurs. The man, having accomplished what he wanted, has little interest in the child he helped create, but the woman, who has made a significant investment in the child through her pregnancy, focuses her attention on the child.

Some sociobiologists see relations between the sexes as a continual battle in which each sex seeks to outwit and control the other; they argue that these relations are essentially mutually exploitative. Others argue that men dominate women simply because they are biologically capable of doing so; men are stronger and more aggressive. The conclusion these sociobiologists reach is that a battle between men and women is inevitable, and it is also inevitable that women must lose. These theories are currently very influential.

One of the most interesting antifeminist approaches to the sex war theory is found in Helen Andelin's best seller, *Fascinating Womanhood* (1974). Andelin bases her book on her antifeminist, fundamentalist Christian beliefs. The book is intended to help women improve their marriages and their relationships with their husbands. Women, Andelin argues, must be childlike and submissive to their husbands. The reason she offers is not that women are inferior or naturally submissive, but that men have such weak egos and such difficult, insensitive, and crude personalities that women must learn to manipulate them through coquettishness and apparent passivity. Andelin says that men and women have very different and basically antagonistic characters. Women are gentle, sensitive, religious, and nurturant, and men are insensitive, aggressive, and temperamental. Much of her advice to women is of the kind generations of mothers have passed on to their daughters: Never appear threatening. Never nag if your man is being bad (as he is wont to be, because men are like that). Never show that you are your man's equal, and certainly never take an obvious lead in sex or appear smarter or more skilled at anything than he is. Andelin also takes matters a step further. If a woman's husband beats or physically abuses her, Andelin says, the woman should pout, stamp her foot, shake her curls, perhaps pound weakly on his chest and say, "How can such a big strong man hurt such a poor little girl?"

Several important points can be made from the sex war theories of male dominance:

1. These theories are not the sole property of feminists. The view that dominance grows out of sexual antagonism goes back in antifeminist thought at least to the time of Charles Darwin.
2. Different theories regarding the sex war have different implications for the future. Generally antifeminist sex war theories suggest that both antagonism and male dominance are inevitable. Most feminist theories argue that equality is possible and, therefore, more harmonious relations between the sexes are also possible.
3. Acceptance of sex war theories does not necessarily mean that one believes this war is a conscious conspiracy of nasty people. Sociobiological approaches generally assume that sex war is fostered by unconscious biological instincts and capabilities. Feminist theorists usually suggest that war is a natural outcome of inequity and therefore can be ended if inequity is defeated. As long as inequity exists, at least some members of the group with less power will fight for increased control over themselves, and at least some members of the group with power will try to justify their strength and will not willingly relinquish it.

Toward Understanding Social Change and Women's History

The five types of theories discussed here attempt to explain how societies develop particular structures of power and relations between women and men. They suggest the somewhat different historical routes societies may have followed, and they also suggest different possible futures. Although most of these theories have both positive and negative points, none is perfect, and all must be evaluated carefully in light of the evidence. With the exception of the static theories, none is necessarily and exclusively feminist or antifeminist. People with a variety of political viewpoints have found something appealing in most of the theories outlined here. The difference lies in how the theories are formulated and applied and in how evidence is brought to bear on them.

NOTES

1. Recent scientific research shows this widely held view of conception is mistaken. Sperm are not entirely self-propelling but are carried along by the actions of the woman's body and the fluids within it.
2. For further discussion of liberal theory, see Jaggar (1983) and Eisenstein (1981).
3. For Gilman's theories see especially her *Women and Economics* ([1898] 1970), *The Home* ([1903] 1972), and *The Man-Made World: Our Androcentric Culture* ([1911] 1970).
4. The most famous example of the Lamarckian principle is the suggestion that if the tail of a rat is cut off during its lifetime, its offspring will be tailless.
5. For the primary exposition of Parson's work, especially as it concerns gender, see Parsons (1951; 1954) and Parsons and Bales (1955).
6. For Mozart fans (of which the author is one) it is important to remember that both Pamina and Tamino (the heroine and the hero) are allowed to enter a condition of enlightenment.
7. By *privileges*, feminists mean the higher status and social respect women have when they are married or are at least associated with a man, and such benefits as the relatively greater degree of safety women have in traveling or even walking around their own communities when accompanied by a male "protector." (See, e.g., Rich 1980).

3

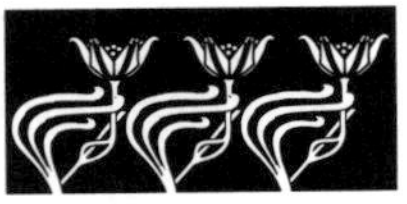

How Did Individuals Get This Way?

A THEORY THAT explains how the social structure and culture of relations between women and men developed over historical time does not necessarily explain why, in a given society, individual women and men behave as they do. Marxist theories of social differences, for example, suggest that the relative status of women and men depends on historical changes in the structure of the economy. But how do individual people come to "fit into" this system? How do we acquire the beliefs, ideology, personality characteristics, or patterns of behavior that are appropriate to a given social or cultural system?

Consider the example of trying to understand the gender basis of work. Theories discussed in Chapter 2 might help explain why and how the gender structure of work and occupations shifted in the United States from the 18th to the end of the 20th century. But they do not provide any direct help with understanding what forces shape the specific career paths of Jane and Bob, both born in the United States in 1985. What makes Jane become part of the statistics that show women are more likely to become secretaries than men? To answer this question, we must turn to different kinds of theory and evidence.

This chapter discusses five approaches scholars use to help explain how individuals come to adopt particular variations of gender norms. The first calls on biology for explanation. In this case we look to genetic structures, the brain, or the hormonal system to understand why males become "masculine" and females become "feminine." The second theory is psychoanalytic theory, especially that proposed by Sigmund Freud, who understood the development of gender and sexuality as a conflictive process involving psychological adaptation to the demands placed on the psyche by both biology and the environment. According to psychoanalysts, much of the work of becoming male or female is accomplished by reining in and giving culturally acceptable shape to our unconscious drives.

The third theory, cognitive development, also defines gender as involving an interaction between biology and environment. Cognitive-developmentalists believe people progress through different stages of cognitive organization or structures of thinking. Thus, for cognitive-developmentalists, the question we should focus on is how gender comes to shape and become part of the structure of thinking. Fourth, we turn to social learning theory, which emphasizes the impact of the social and physical environment on individuals. In this perspective, people learn about gender through their experience in the world, especially the models it presents them, and they are influenced or conditioned to become male or female in specific ways because of the rewards and punishments they receive from others.

After pausing to consider some attempts to synthesize the different learning and development theories, we will conclude with a final important approach to understanding how individuals become "gendered": discrimination theory. This approach suggests that the whole story of living a gendered life is not told when we have taken account of how individuals learn or internalize gender norms. The discrimination model reminds us of the possibility that individuals can be forced into gendered behavior against their will.

The Biological Basis of Female and Male

To what degree does nature bestow on each of us limits or capabilities that depend on whether we happen to be male or female? How much are our individual lives shaped by our sex? These are two of the most controversial questions among those who study women.[1]

The Genetic Basis of Sex

Fertilized human egg cells, and thus human beings, normally contain 23 pairs of chromosomes. Sex is determined by a specific one of these pairs. The ovum, or egg, contributed by the mother to the sex-determining pair, contains only X chromosomes. Every human being therefore possesses an X chromosome, which contains genetic information affecting a wide range of physiological functions. The father, through the sperm, randomly contributes either another X or a Y chromosome to the egg. If it is an X chromosome, the baby will have an XX pair and be a girl. If it is a Y chromosome, the baby will have an XY pair and be a boy. This is the only sex difference in genetic structure. What is the effect of having an XX or XY sex-determining pair of chromosomes?[2]

At first there is no apparent sex difference among fetuses. At about the sixth week of fetal development, the genetic information on the sex-linked chromosomes begins to send out signals that turn one set of glands into either ovaries or testes which will, in turn, produce powerful chemicals called *hormones* that aid further development. The same hormones are produced in both males and females, but the amounts produced tell the body whether to develop a male or female structure. Other than stimulating different hormone production, what specifically genetically based sex differences are there? Males are prone to many more recessive genetically transmitted diseases and disorders such as hemophilia and colorblindness. There is no conclusive evidence that the Y chromosome carries any other information that causes behavioral, cognitive, or personality differences between women and men. For this reason, scientists focus more attention on the hormonal basis of sex differences.

The Role of Hormones

For ethical reasons, much of the research on the hormonal basis of sex differences uses animals other than human beings. Our discussion will be restricted to conclusions based on observations of human beings, not because research on other species is irrelevant to understanding human physiology, but because this field is complicated enough to introductory readers without the added problem of discussing findings not validated through research on human beings.

Hormones are crucially important in determining our physical existence as male or female. The hormones that play the most important role in sex differentiation are *testosterone*, produced in much greater quantities in males than females, and *estrogen* and *progesterone*, produced in much greater quantities in females than males. When these hormones begin to be released, they stimulate the body to develop a male or female structure. If the glands produce enough testosterone,

Women's athletic ability has increased dramatically as they receive better athletic training.

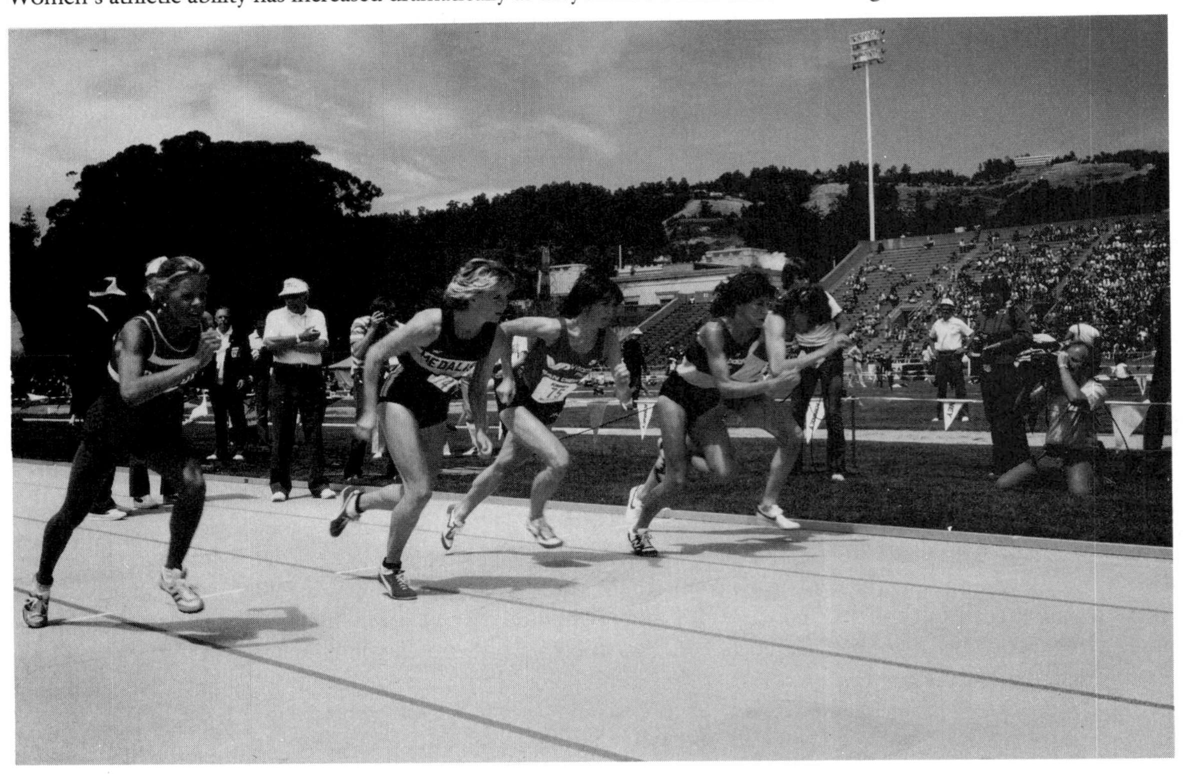

the fetus will become male; if they do not, the normal path of development is to become female. Male and female bodies are analogues of each other—shaped from the same basic form. One part of the body becomes either a clitoris or a penis; the breasts will grow and eventually develop functioning mammary glands or remain small and functionless.

Females develop more quickly than males do. Some research suggests that testosterone is responsible for slowing down the process of physiological development, thus causing males to grow more slowly, develop coordination at a later stage, and reach puberty at an older age. How these differences affect the process of learning and eventual adult roles and behavior is unclear.

Male bodies develop stronger muscular structure and more red blood cells on average than female bodies do, although female bodies are more agile in certain ways. Sex differences in strength have been vastly exaggerated by the different types of training and experiences males and females receive. Because of changes in training, the gender gap in some skills and sports has diminished considerably.

Although men and women may never compete with each other directly in sports that depend on strength, the larger social significance of strength differentials depends on the social construction of human tasks. Technological advances, for example, have decreased the importance of strength in many types of jobs. Protective labor legislation used to keep women out of jobs that required carrying loads "too heavy for women," but many of these limits were lower than the weights of the small children, grocery packages, and laundry baskets that women commonly carry.

Sex hormones also have effects during adulthood. Although the evidence on effects on human beings is still uncertain, research has offered some clues. Research links raised rates of testosterone in males with increased aggression and raised rates of testosterone in women, at least under certain circumstances, with increased sex drive.

Hormonal changes stimulate and accompany puberty in males and females and menopause in women. The balance of hormones in women shifts throughout the menstrual cycle. Many scientists have hypothesized that this shift causes mood and behavioral changes, some of which may have a great impact on women's capabilities and social activities. Many nonscientists, of course, suspect the same thing because of conventional wisdom. How many times have we heard people worry about menstruating pilots crashing airplanes or menstruating presidents blowing up the world?

As usual, early consensus has dissolved in the face of contradictory evidence and interpretation. Many of the symptoms conventionally associated with menstruation in one society do not commonly appear in others (Paige and Paige 1981). Although researchers agree that women tend to experience mood changes in association with their menstrual cycles, the symptoms and timing vary considerably. Changes that appear to be associated with the menstrual cycle may not actually be caused by the hormonal changes themselves. In her research comparing women using birth control pills (which affect hormone levels) and those not using them, Karen Paige found that negative psychological symptoms were related to how heavy the menstrual flow was. She also found that the degree of acceptance of traditional menstrual taboos and gender ideology was related to menstrual distress. Further, as most women have found at one time or another, stress—which often causes mood changes—can affect a woman's normal cycle. And finally, many critics have pointed out that most of the research that finds a correlation between menstrual cycles and mood changes is not designed to rule out the possibility that negative reactions to menstruation might be caused by a socially constructed negative attitude toward menstruation and menstruating women. (There is more discussion of menstruation in Chapter 6.)

These criticisms point to a problem that plagues the study of women and social science in general: Correlation does not necessarily indicate causation. In other words, just because two events happen at the same time, we cannot be sure, without further investigation, that one causes the other. Hormonal changes can affect moods, but moods can also induce hormonal changes. Hormonal changes bring on menstruation, and mood changes may be associated with the menstrual cycle, but something else—for example, a feeling that menstruation is embarrassing or that one's lover can't abide sexual relations with a menstruating woman—may actually cause the mood changes.

Recent research has added a new twist to the study of hormonal fluctuations and cycles: Men have them too (Doering et al. 1974). Men appear to have cycles in a variety of physiological and psychological respects. Whether these are related to fluctuations in sex hormones is still open to question. We do not yet know whether we should ground male pilots at "that time of the month." In any case, with regard to the basic question of what kind of sex differentiation is caused by hormones, we see some important ones, including the basic functioning of our reproductive system. But it does not seem that hormones create as sweeping a set of basic personality differences between women and men as many people have thought.

The Structure of the Brain

Much research has focused on sex differences in the brain. In the 19th century one popular notion was that female brains were smaller than male brains and that therefore women's capacities were more limited than men's. These observations led theorist and politician John Stuart Mill to remark that by the same logic we should conclude that elephants are much smarter than people because of the relative sizes of elephant and human brains.

Current research focuses more on the organization of the brain and the functions of its component parts. One of the most interesting and controversial arguments concerns brain lateralization (that is, which hemisphere, or side—if any—is dominant in what functions) and its effects, especially on verbal and spatial abilities. Many brain researchers believe that which side of the brain is specialized for specific functions and how concentrated functions are in one specific side of the brain affect how those functions are performed. Many researchers have argued that male and female brains are differently lateralized. Some have claimed that women (and some men) are less lateralized than men;

that is, women's processing is less concentrated in one or the other half of the brain. Others argue that sex differences in lateralization occur only early in life, but that these differences have long-term effects in the development of cognitive skills such as verbal or spatial ability. Yet others believe that young females are more lateralized than males, but at later ages males are more lateralized than females.

What difference would sex differences in lateralization make? When conventional wisdom and some research suggested there were broad differences between females and males in spatial, verbal, and mathematical ability, scientists thought that brain lateralization could explain these differences. Now that more systematic research shows no evidence of general differences in verbal ability (Hyde and Linn 1988) or mathematical ability (Hyde, Fennema, and Lamon 1990), and more limited differences in spatial ability than people formerly thought (Linn and Peterson 1985), there is less cognitive difference to explain in the first place. Moreover, research scientists still do not agree whether brain lateralization studies distinguish between *innate* and *developed* brain capacity. Training and environmental factors not only enhance or limit capacity but also affect what part of the brain does what. It is possible that even some of the differences observed in young children are the result of the different types of games and activities undertaken with male and female children, just as some of the differences between left- and right-handed people could be caused by the common attempt to force left-handed children to become right handed. It is possible, therefore, that gender differences in training could help shape gender differences not only in acquired skills (that is, how much of their potential they actually fulfill) but also in apparent biological potential.

Although the search for differences and effects of brain structure remains an interesting and active field, for now it has no clear results to offer those interested in understanding sex differences. There is no consistent and widely accepted evidence for sex differences in brain lateralization, and no fully accepted connection drawn between lateralization and any other cognitive, personality, or behavioral difference between women and men.

From Sex to Gender

Biological research alone has not yet been able to point clearly to a reason for the degree of gender differentiation and stratification in our society, and it certainly has not accounted for the varying levels of differentiation and stratification across societies, although there are still many avenues open for further investigation. Scientists generally agree that human life and activity are products of an intriguing relationship between biology and society, nature and invention. In order to begin the task of thinking about the differences and relationship between the impact of biology and society on the development of women and men *as* women and men, women's studies scholars have long emphasized the distinction between two related terms: sex and gender. To state the point simply (although it will not remain simple as we proceed), *sex* is a physiological phenomenon, *gender* is a sociocultural one.

Our search for the roots of distinctions between female and male in genetics, the hormonal system, and brain structure was an exercise in exploring sex differences. At the simplest level, we know that sex determines whether we can menstruate, bear children, and lactate and helps determine how much upper-body strength we have. Gender involves these phenomena and much more. Sex doesn't tell us whether it is socially acceptable to wear a dress or to train as a nurse or a doctor. Even if biology determines the contribution women and men make to the physical reproduction of human beings, there is no clear evidence that it offers any clear guidelines on any other psychological or behavioral aspect relating to having children or being a parent. It sometimes seems that the more sophisticated biological research becomes, the less compelling is the evidence that nature provides us with very much guidance about how to be female and male.

Gender is best understood as our sociocultural interpretation of the significance of sex. Gender roles are organized patterns of behavior we follow that are based on our interpretation of the significance of sex. They structure our choices and guide our behavior in ways that are viewed as gender appropriate. Thus gender roles lead people in many cultures to believe that men should be doctors and women nurses, or that menstruating women shouldn't walk in agriculturally productive fields, or that if a child is sick the mother rather than the father should be called home from work.

The insistence of many scholars that we make a clear conceptual distinction between sex and gender does not mean that in the real world it is easy to tell what is a function of sex and what is a function of gender. In fact it is difficult to make this determination for a number of reasons. First, our views tend to be colored by our own ideological preferences. Antifeminists, for instance, are often eager to label differences as biologically based and to view them as the major cause of the inequities we observe in society. On the other hand, some feminists are loathe to see any influence of biology at all—unless it "favors women"—and are even suspicious of anyone who studies biology. Believing in sex differences that do not exist can have real effects on human beings: Such beliefs become the basis of sex discrimination. Rejecting the possibility of sex differences where they may actually exist doesn't make these differences any less real. In neither case is the cause of learning advanced.

Another reason it is difficult to distinguish between sex and gender is that one of the most powerful functions of gender is to tell us what our culture regards as natural. In some cultures, for example, there is a belief that if a man has sexual intercourse with a menstruating woman, he will become impotent. And sure enough, many men who accept this belief do become at least temporarily impotent when they find that the woman with whom they wanted to have sexual relations has "the curse." Cultures also vary in how they view childbirth, and research shows that the physical experience of childbirth differs from culture to culture depending on that view. If a society believes that women have no natural ability to be great artists and thus doesn't waste valuable resources training them, showing their work, or writing about it, it will be easy to "prove" that women aren't capable of being great artists.

It is also difficult to disentangle sex and gender because of the difficulty of determining causation: Which causes a person to act in a certain way—biology or society? In order to be absolutely sure whether an individual's personality is caused by nature or nurture, we would have to be capable of examining an individual totally removed from the context of society and any prior social training. Indeed, many scientists argue that biological and social factors have important interactive effects; to believe that important and complex aspects of human existence must be caused by biology *or* society displays a primitive understanding of human nature and society. (See, e.g., Bleier 1984.)

Most fascinating of all is the study of how human cultures and social life construct such complicated and nuanced systems of gender distinctions and gender-based rules of human behavior and interaction of which we all become willing or unwilling parts. Even people who reject traditional ideas of how women and men in their class and culture are supposed to act are usually very aware of those ideas and of their power. Everyone knows that women's and men's lives are just not the same; the more one studies the ways gender structures human life the more impressive its power becomes.

Thus far we have referred to the "structure of relations between the sexes" and to "systems of differentiation and stratification." These concepts are encompassed by the term *sex/gender system* (Rubin 1974), which refers to the system or structure of roles, power, and activities predominant within a society that are based on the biological distinctions between males and females and further elaborated and interpreted through culturally defined gender norms. The remainder of this book will use this term to look at the role different social institutions and processes play in taking the basic biological "facts" of male and female sex differentiation and turning them into one of the basic organizing principles of human culture and society.

Psychoanalytic Theory: The Creation of Masculinity and Femininity

As we have seen, biological research has not been very successful in explaining how individuals in society come to be (or not be) part of the prevailing sex/gender system. Let us now turn to approaches arguing that although becoming a "masculine" male or a "feminine" female is in many respects a matter of biology (they differ in what role they assign to biology), the human mind as it encounters its environment after birth is the predominant determinant of masculinity and femininity. In trying to understand how individuals come to be the kind of people they are, these theorists emphasize the degree of change that occurs in individuals' lives over time, especially the different phases or stages that occur during the course of individuals' development.

We begin with one of the most influential psychological theorists of the 20th century, Sigmund Freud. In Chapter 2 we looked at the role of conflict between women and men in Freud's psychoanalytic theory. Now we review his theories of psychosexual development.

Sex Similarity

According to Freud, the structure of the psyche and human personalities are not sex differentiated at birth. The development of females and males is very similar for the first few years, when any observed "sexual differences are not . . . of great consequence: they can be outweighed by individual variations" ([1933] 1965, 118). The bulk of the psyche—male and female—is composed of human instincts or drives. Freud called this part of the psyche the *id* ("it" in Latin). These drives and instincts are defined as psychic energy. Like other types of energy, they have no particular form or object other than self-gratification and can be channeled to have any of several forms, objects, or effects. This is why a single feeling (for example, hatred of another person) can take on either a destructive form ("I'll kill him") or a constructive form ("I'll show him—I'll get this done faster and better than it's ever been done before").

Because Freud believed that females and males are born essentially undifferentiated, he also believed they are essentially bisexual (or, more accurately, pansexual). If the human drive for pleasure is unshaped or unchanneled, as is the case in infants, it cannot care how that pleasure is achieved. A human infant will try sucking on almost anything, it is happy to have almost any part of its anatomy stroked, and it feels no shock if a person of one sex or the other strokes it. The *libido*, or pleasure-seeking drive, knows nothing of sex or gender, even if it is the source of sexuality and eroticism. For a human being to become heterosexual, which to Freud is central to appropriate sexual maturity and gender roles, this part of the human psyche has to be repressed and rechanneled.

How do these relatively undifferentiated masses of gurgles, cries, and burps acquire masculinity and femininity and develop particular psychosexual orientations? In Freudian theory, the process is posed as a series of stages through which people must pass to achieve maturity. Progress through these stages is not easy; it might best be described as a hazardous struggle both within individuals and between individuals and the social world around them. It can go wrong at any stage because of events in the child's environment or relationships between the child and others.

The early stages of psychosexual development are similar for boys and girls. The first stage, the oral phase, is marked by the importance of the mouth in receiving pleasure. Sucking and feeding is the primary business of infants' lives. This changes when children face the first demand that they become self-conscious and exert control over themselves during the anal phase, triggered by the experience of toilet training. This is a very complex transition. The infant finds that he or she can please another person, but only under certain circumstances. The child can give a gift of properly deposited feces, but this act requires a certain amount of self-denial. Because of the role of self-denial (the first of many instances of self-denial to be learned), this stage is achieved only with resistance. The assault on the id by the *ego* (the "I," or potentially conscious or self-conscious self) has begun. The third phase, the phallic phase, is the time during which the child begins to learn about genital pleasure. Now the trouble begins.

Development of Difference

The Freudian picture described thus far pictures girls and boys as relatively undifferentiated and unrestrained pleasure seekers. The pleasure drives have yet to be regulated; in other words, both the ego and the *superego* (literally, "over I") have yet to be developed. The superego is often described as the conscience, the (relatively small) part of our consciousness that flows from the world around us. It contains the moral rules and personal sense of right and wrong learned from parents and others who transmit cultural norms. The superego pushes the ego into battle against the dark unruly drives of the id. It is the ego and superego that have to learn what masculinity, femininity, and sexuality are about; the id can never learn and remains in conflict with the ego and the superego. Freud thought that this task is more difficult for females than for males because it takes females two extra steps to achieve the final goal of maturity.

Both boys and girls originally derive their pleasure from the mother. This poses a special problem for girls. In finding his mother his primary erotic object (source of pleasure), a boy is on the way to "mature masculinity." He will have to give up his mother as a consciously sexual object, but to become heterosexual he merely has to turn to other women. This involves a struggle, but it is not as difficult as the task girls face to become "mature" heterosexual women. They must shift their focus of eroticism from women to men.

What could wrench girls' affections from women so completely that the original pleasurable feelings associated with physical relations with women are replaced with horror or profound anxiety in most women? For Freud, the answer lies in the female version of the castration complex. "After all, the anatomical distinction between the sexes must express itself in psychical consequences. It was, however, a surprise to learn from analyses that girls hold their mother responsible for their lack of a penis and do not forgive her for being thus put at a disadvantage" (Freud [1933] 1965, 124).

Like many people Freud could not imagine that a woman's body could be regarded as complete. His standard and, he seemed to assume, everyone else's, for a "complete" human body is the male anatomy. According to Freud, one sight of a male's "superior equipment" ([1933] 1965, 126) and a girl is overcome with mortification for her own body, envy of the male's, and a need to place blame for her mutilation. She becomes hostile to her mother who, she finds, is deformed like herself and is responsible for creating her without the essential organ. By generalizing her view of herself and her mother, women become "debased in value for girls just as they are for boys" ([1933] 1965, 127). The girl is now on the road to maturity. She rejects women and turns to her father who, after all, possesses a penis. She also begins to suppress her former feelings for her clitoris, or deficient penis, to pave the way for vaginal eroticism, which prepares her for heterosexuality and motherhood. This transfer of erotic feeling from one organ to another is the other major developmental step that girls, and not boys, must take.

When she discovers her castration, the girl begins a very difficult journey. According to Freud she may take any of three roads:

1. She might develop "sexual inhibitions or neurosis," especially frigidity. This happens if the girl is so traumatized by her discoveries that she suppresses not only her "infantile" sexuality but also all sexuality.
2. She might develop a "masculinity complex." In this case, she rebels against femininity and retains her more "infantile" form of sexuality, which means, among other things, homosexuality.
3. She may "renounce" infantile sexuality, which includes both women as love objects and her own clitoris as the focus of erotic pleasure to achieve "normal femininity."

Some feminists have pointed out that the idea of vaginal orgasms—difficult to achieve because of the relative lack of nerve endings in the vagina compared to the clitoris—is particularly convenient to a male-centered definition of sexuality and dangerous for women's senses of self-esteem. What about penis envy? This becomes transformed into a desire for a child, and, if at all possible, a child with a penis.

What differences between males and females develop as a result of this process? Freud believed that women become oriented toward home, husband, and child, and men turn their interests outward. Men also develop a stronger superego, or conscience, than women do. To explain this, Freud turned to the castration complex and the child's feelings toward the mother and the father. Boys continue to be sexually oriented toward their mothers and toward women in general. What force imposes itself against the id to keep boys from becoming incestuous? Boys compete with their father for the mother's attention, but they also fear the power of their father and, especially, the punishment of castration. (This psychic relationship with the father is called the Oedipus complex.) This fear keeps males in line and strengthens their abilities to integrate societal rules into their psyches.

Women do not have to fear castration because it has already happened, and thus they have less reason to develop this social orientation. Rather than learning to be governed by societal rules, they become passively oriented toward men's will to achieve their goal of having a child. Notice that unlike other theorists who put women in "their place," Freud argued that women are not passive by nature. In the course of their psychosocial development they "give preference to passive aims" (Freud [1933] 1965, 115). Thus for Freud, although it is normal for women to become passive, he did not believe it is especially easy for women to do this.

Women's development has other effects that distinguish women from men, according to Freud. Women's repression of their "masculinity" (especially their aggressiveness) makes them masochistic. Drives like aggressiveness do not disappear when they are repressed but remain alive in the id. The woman who achieves "normal femininity," therefore, turns her aggressive energy inward. Women also remain dominated by the envy sparked by their discovery of their castration. They therefore have less sense of social justice than men because social justice is incompatible with envy. They become more rigid than men and age more quickly, primarily because of the more arduous path they have taken. Freud thought that women appear tired out, spent, and aged by the time they reach 30 years of age in comparison with men, who at this age are just reaching their peaks.

Evaluating the Psychoanalytic Perspective

The psychoanalytic perspective on the development of males and females offers a rich body of theories and observations. In its variety of interpretations and applications, it has been both celebrated and rejected from every point of view, from the radically antifeminist to the radically feminist. What are the sources of these reactions?

Many criticisms revolve around the research methods Freud and many of his followers used to reach conclusions. Numerous observers point out that the subjects of Freud's study were his patients and his colleagues' patients. To accept Freud's arguments, we must accept generalizations made on the basis of observing only women who went to psychoanalysts' offices at the beginning of this century. These researchers made no effort to compare these findings with observations of other women.

The nature of both the clinical method (in-depth discussion with and observation and interpretation of one person by another) and psychoanalytic theory itself creates a problem for confirmation of the theory. Psychoanalytic method involves seeking the subjective meanings of people's perceptions and actions. As we have seen in the earlier example of how hatred can lead to either destructive *or* constructive activity, different acts can have the same meaning or motivation, and different people can engage in the same activity for very different reasons.

The psychoanalytic method is vulnerable to the charge that one can see whatever one *wants* to see. Consider penis envy. From the Freudian viewpoint, if a girl asks her mother why she can't have a penis like her brother, she is displaying penis envy. If she suggests that it must be neat to be able to urinate standing up (or tries it), or if she playacts at having a penis, she is also expressing penis envy. But what if, as many girls do, she expresses the feeling that having a penis must be strange or uncomfortable or that it might get in the way when one is riding a bicycle? The psychoanalyst might argue that this too is a sign of penis envy, expressed through her hostility to the male body. Many psychoanalysts go even further and regard almost any attempt by a woman to enter a traditionally masculine domain as a sign of penis envy. In fact, attempts to confirm Freud's conclusions by using other methods, such as experimental evidence and even projective techniques, have found little confirmation for important cornerstones of Freud's theory such as the universal existence of penis envy.

Another important issue in Freudian theory subject to intense debate is the relative roles of biology and society in shaping individuals. Many of his greatest critics, including many feminist scholars, claim that Freud totally neglected the role of society and culture in his examination of female and male development. This is not true. First, much of the struggle in developing the ego is fueled by the superego, formed by the individual's interaction with the social world. Because psychoanalytic theory regards the human psyche as shaped not exclusively by nature or society but by the struggles between the two, it can encompass the effects of tangible reality, biology, social relationships, myths and symbols, the rational, and the irrational. Many feminist theorists have found great potential in this aspect of psychoanalytic theory.

Freud argued that human suffering and unhappiness, both male and female, comes from three sources: "the superior power of nature, the feebleness of our own bodies and the inadequacy of the regulations which adjust the mutual relationships of human beings in the family, the state and society" ([1930] 1961, 33). A large part of the human struggle, therefore, is to civilize humanity and remove the sources of suffering as much as possible. This observation has opened the way for feminist theorists such as Juliet Mitchell (1974) and Nancy Chodorow (1978) to suggest that Freudian theory can be used to explain the particular nature of suffering under patriarchal conditions and to point out how the restructuring of social institutions can have profound and positive effects on psychosexual development.

Nancy Chodorow has influentially argued that arranging our social institutions so that women do most of the child raising has gender-specific effects on the psychosocial development of children that results in reproducing gender differentiation and inequality. She believes that women think more in terms of connectedness among people because of the continuities between themselves and their mothers. Males are more dominated by the task of separation because of the early need to distinguish themselves from their mothers in order to develop a masculine identity. The "problem" for males is that because men tend not to take a full share in nurturing children, they cannot gain the same sense of connection and continuity as girls, who are nurtured by their same-sex parent. Thus,

> Because women are themselves mothered by women, they grow up with the relational capacities and needs, and psychological definition of self-in-relationship, which commits them to mothering. Men, because they are mothered by women, do not. Women mother daughters who, when they become women, mother (Chodorow 1978, 209).

Chodorow concludes that the institution of the family needs to be changed so that men develop the emotional structure that can equip them to expand their relational capacities and needs and that will equip women to develop greater autonomy.

Freud's discussion of the human drive toward "civilization" points to another key issue in the significance of psychoanalytic theory: its perspective on sexuality. Many feminists consider Freud a patriarchal, oppressive "Victorian" (a word many people use to mean prudish). In fact, his views are not so easily categorized. Civilization, he argued, is necessary to help us divert our self-destructive tendencies. It can help in the struggle between the id and the superego to channel our destructive energies into creative social projects. But "at the same time we have been careful not to fall in with the prejudice that civilization is synonymous with perfecting, that it is the road to perfection preordained for men [sic]" (Freud

[1930] 1961, 43). Civilization, Freud believed, is no friend of liberty, and civilization has rarely been based on justice.

Freud was dismayed at the degree of sexual repression he saw in society. "The requirement . . . that there shall be a single kind of sexual life for everyone, disregards the dissimilarities, whether innate or acquired, in the sexual constitution of human beings; it cuts off a fair number of them from sexual enjoyment, and so becomes the source of serious injustice" (51). As we have seen, Freud thought that homosexuality was an infantile form of sexuality, but he did not think it dangerous or wrong and didn't favor social or legal penalties for the homosexual. The man who pointed to the nature of the unconscious and the id, and who declared that human beings are naturally bisexual, not to mention incestuous, found little favor with the public or most of the medical establishment—and certainly the moral establishment—of his day.

Certainly Freud and a great many of his influential followers were patriarchal and, in some cases, misogynistic. The great majority of Freudian psychoanalysts seem to accept the notion that the penis is superior equipment and that women who achieve normal femininity are uncreative, jealous, unjust, and masochistic creatures. Psychoanalysis has been used to try to make women interpret their problems in light of penis envy and the need for a child. Psychoanalysis is one of the many modes of thought that view women's own perceptions as unreliable. In one of Freud's most famous cases, a woman traced her problems to a childhood experience of being raped by her father. Freud reinterpreted the woman's story as a fiction that revealed an extreme case of normal childhood penis envy and father love. His "evidence" that the child only wished to have sex with her father was the father's claim that he had not raped his daughter.

Freudian orthodoxy has been extremely harmful to women in many respects. Many feminists, however, have begun to return to psychoanalysis and the theories of Freud and others such as Karen Horney (1885–1952), a contemporary of Freud's. Some argue that men both fear women and, in a sense, "envy" the womb (Horney 1967).[3] This, they argue, accounts for the male need to dominate women, in contrast to the Freudian idea that penis envy leads women to seek domination by men. Some argue that the general outline of Freudian theory is correct, although the substantive conclusions often reached have been shaped by androcentric ideology. They suggest that Freud's writing on women should not be taken as a theory of what *must* happen but as a description of what *does* happen in a patriarchal or androcentric society. One could argue that Freud's conclusions about "normal femininity" serve as an excellent guide to the pernicious nature of "normal femininity" as an ideal women should seek to attain.

Psychoanalytic theory is also one of the few theories that explicitly consider the importance of sexuality in social and cultural life and that suggest the important relationship between social construction of sexuality and social construction of gender. If one accepts Freud's argument that children's psyches are not naturally differentiated, but are pressed to diverge because of the pursuit of what Freud calls "normal" sexuality, the theory begs us to reconsider our views of what is normal. Some feminists conclude that Freud's view of penis envy is also correct, but only within the context of a culture that perceives the phallus as a symbol of power, dominance, and liberty. If our cultural conceptions of sex and gender were not "phallocentric," if the phallus were not a symbol of power, there would be little reason to be jealous of those who possess a penis. This interpretation has bolstered the argument that no change in society can occur until our social construction of sexuality is changed and the penis is regarded as merely an anatomical organ. In any case, psychoanalytic theory offers an excellent example of a theory that can have different and conflicting implications depending on how it is interpreted and used.

Cognitive-Developmental Theories

Psychoanalytic theory is only one approach to understanding the differentiation of individual males and females that uses the concept of stages of development. Cognitive-developmentalists do also, but in a way that is very different from that of psychoanalysts.

Unlike psychoanalysts, cognitive-developmentalists focus on the conscious part of the mind, especially the skills, structures, and styles of thought and reasoning. They are interested in the development of the frameworks people use to understand, analyze, and cope with questions of self-identity, social and physical relationships, and principles such as morality. Many (although not all) developmentalists have a more rigid notion than psychoanalysts of the succession or hierarchy of stages through which an individual passes. Most claim that once an individual has passed from one stage to the next, she or he will not return to a previous stage. Psychoanalysts make no such claims; in fact, the ideas of regression to previous stages and of constant tensions between earlier and later impulses figure very importantly in their views. The difference exists largely because psychoanalysts and cognitive-developmentalists focus on different aspects of the mind. For the developmentalist focusing on the stages of learning specific problem-solving skills, a person would no more return to an earlier mode than he or she would forget how to ride a bicycle.

Becoming Boys and Girls

Most developmentalists see growth as a product of the interaction of the human organism with the environment. During the earliest stage of life, infants develop both basic physical capabilities, such as seeing and hearing, and the ability to manipulate physical objects purposefully. At this time, for example, a baby learns the wonderful game of repeatedly throwing things on the floor during feeding time. During the next stage, babies become capable of some awareness of objects that are not physically present; they begin to show signs of imagination and memory. Until this stage an object that is taken away from a baby ceases to exist for the child. In the next stage it is not so easy to take candy from a baby.

More sophisticated cognitive abilities such as the ability to classify objects and understand the relationship among them develop in the third stage. Children learn that not all fruits are apples, that apples and oranges are both fruits, and that although both apples and ice cream cones are edible, they are not both fruits. Finally they reach an even more sophisticated stage when they learn to solve more complex problems that require the ability to manipulate symbols and abstract ideas. But they cannot do this until they have passed through the prior stages.

Cognitive-developmentalists investigate many different aspects of human thought in this same way, including how children develop gender identification and learn to be girls and boys. Lawrence Kohlberg, one of the most important cognitive-developmental theorists, wrote, "[Basic] sexual attitudes are not patterned directly by either biological instincts or arbitrary cultural norms, but by the child's cognitive organization of his social world along sex role dimensions." Developing gender is a process of making sense of the world. "It is not the child's biological instincts, but rather his cognitive organization of social role concepts around universal physical dimensions, which accounts for the existence of universals in sex role attitudes" (Kohlberg 1966, 82).

According to Kohlberg, the process of gender development begins early in life when little girls figure out that they are girls and little boys figure out they are boys; that is, they engage in cognitive self-categorization. They acquire gender identity. It normally takes up to 3 years for this to happen. Children next learn that everyone has gender; everyone is a boy or a girl. Only after this do children begin to learn that gender does not change (if you are a girl, you are going to be a girl forever) and that gender has meaning. At this stage children begin to recognize that girls and boys do different things, like different things, and have different amounts of power. They begin to learn about masculinity and femininity.

Learning about gender is one thing, learning to follow gender norms is another. How does this happen and why? Learning has both a cognitive (thinking and analysis) dimension and an affective (feelings and emotions) dimension. Children learn about themselves but they also learn to value themselves and, through generalization, people like themselves. As children learn about their gender, they begin to value it. Boys want to do "boy" things, and girls want to do "girl" things. Once children develop a framework for understanding the world, ambiguities are painful until they acquire considerably more sophisticated analytical abilities. Young children thus not only become careful to uphold gender standards but also are often more rigid in their adherence to gender standards than are older children.

Research by Rebecca S. Bigler and Lynn S. Liben (1992) is a good example of cognitive-developmental research on the development of gender. They were interested in the findings that young children seem especially rigid in their gender stereotyping. They hypothesized that this happens because most young children have not yet reached a cognitive level at which they can understand that one object can fall into more than one category; rigid stereotyping is, after all, partly a matter of making simple and inflexible gender categorizations. This rigid stereotyping can be self-reinforcing, because children tend to remember gender-stereotypes information better than information that contradicts stereotypes. They cited evidence that children with more advanced classification skills hold less rigid stereotypes.

Bigler and Liben did a study involving a sample of white middle-class 5- to 10-year-olds. They investigated the children's level of occupation-related gender stereotyping and its relationship to their classification and verbal skills. Their findings support cognitive-developmental theory. Regardless of age or sex, the more advanced the children's multiple classification skills the more gender egalitarian (the less rigidly stereotyped) they were. Among the younger children in the sample, if the experimenters taught the children skills in multiple classification using social examples (sorting people into categories), the children became more egalitarian. Among the older children, if the experimenters taught skills in multiple classification using examples of sorting either people or physical objects into categories, the children became more egalitarian. (This is probably because the older children are more cognitively advanced and can generalize from a skill learned with respect to people or things while the less sophisticated, younger children have to learn about people to generalize to people.) Bigler and Liben also found that the children who became more flexible in gender stereotyping

Young children still learn to grow into stereotypic roles.

Even young children understand how their society defines masculinity and femininity.

because of classification training with social examples also gained more memory for counterstereotypic stories.

Psychologist Lawrence Kohlberg (1966) believed that boys and girls have different motivations for learning gender. As boys become acquainted with male social power and prestige, their desire to act like males increases. Boys identify with their fathers and want to act like them. They begin to want only to be with other boys and to avoid anything that seems girlish. But if boys want to be boys because of male power and prestige, what motivates girls to become girls? Kohlberg thought that girls also know males have more power and prestige and, like boys, girls define the male body as the "basic" body and the female's as the negative of the masculine rather than as a positive entity. But nevertheless, he argues, girls also want to identify with and act like their same-sex parent. Why? Part of the answer, Kohlberg said, is that instead of power and prestige, girls value the "feminine" attributes of niceness and nurturance. These observations presumably help explain another: Many studies show that girls are generally not as rigid in their gender stereotypes as boys are (e.g., Jessell and Beymer 1992), and they are not as adamant about doing only "girl" things (witness the "tomboy") or about playing only with other girls. Within Kohlberg's view, the issue of power and privilege would make boys more eager to conform to gender norms.

More important, however, is the developmentalist's argument that people are very egocentric with a strong motive to value themselves and people like themselves. The higher prestige of males might reinforce their egocentric reasons for conformity, but children of both sexes tend to think their own sex is better. Kohlberg also believed that children tend to view physical and social regularities in moral terms, citing Piaget's observation of a "tendency for the young child to view any deviation from the social order as bad or wrong, even if such a deviation would not be considered bad by adults. The child does not distinguish between conventional social expectations and moral laws and duties." Thus, he argues, "The physical constancies underlying the child's concepts of gender identity tend to be identified with divine or moral law, and the need to adapt to the physical realities of one's identity are viewed as moral obligations" (Kohlberg 1966, 122). This brings us back to the question of cognitive-developmental paths and the relationship of gender identity to the ability to tolerate ambiguity and multiple classification.

Gender and Moral Development

Beside these attempts to understand how children come to develop basic gender identity, cognitive-developmental theory has also opened up another train of research focusing on gender differences in the cognitive frameworks people use for analyzing moral questions. Kohlberg's research revolved around asking people to solve moral dilemmas, such as the one about a man whose dying wife could be saved by a drug manufactured by a local pharmacist who was charging much more than the cost of production. The man could not afford the drug. Should he steal it? Kohlberg's work did not focus on the final answer his subjects gave (i.e., to steal or not to steal). Rather, he was interested in the cognitive framework or reasoning they used to arrive at their answer. Did the answers refer to the need to obey rules? Avoid punishment? Gain others' approval? Maintain order in society? Follow one's conscience? Kohlberg and his colleagues argued that just as cognitive-developmentalists believe other kinds of problem solving follow certain stages of development, so does moral thinking. Thus, they outlined a series of six stages of development, ranging from one displayed by most little children—choosing action only to get rewards and avoid punishment—to one they argued very few adults ever reach as a *consistent* base of action: using an abstract principle internalized in conscience such as the Golden Rule or Kantian categorical imperative.

There is little controversy over the earliest stages posed by Kohlberg. The issue for gender development occurs at the middle and higher stages. Some of the early studies indicated that while most adults fall into the "middle" range known as "conventional" morality, women tended to score lower than men. The women's answers were more likely to be framed in terms of the dynamics of social relationships within the stories, and the men's more in terms of rules of fairness. According to the original scale, this seemed to indicate women were less morally developed.

Psychologist Carol Gilligan launched an influential critique published in *In a Different Voice* (1982), in which she argued that the original moralism scale was biased toward more "male" ways of thinking. She suggested that men's moral reasoning is based more on principles of individualism, rights, and justice, whereas women's is based more on caring, obligation, and responsibility to others. She attacked the notion, implicit in the conventional moral development literature, that the "justice" mode of approaching morality in fact demonstrates higher development than the "caring" mode. Her views are similar to Nancy Chodorow's (1978) interpretation of connectedness and separation in women's and men's lives. Along similar lines, Sara Ruddick (1982) argued that women use a form of thinking that she calls maternal thinking, which is shaped by the caring work that women do in society. None of these authors claims that these gender differences in thinking stem directly from biological differences; instead, they maintain that our ways of thinking are shaped by social practices or experiences, which tend to be gender differentiated. These arguments about women's and men's moral thinking have been very influential for many reasons. They are among the few claims about psychological gender differences that appear to place women in as good or even better light than men.

Although many researchers continue to explore Gilligan's idea that the structure of female and male roles leads young women's development to be specially shaped by personal relationships of caring (Gilligan, Ward, and Taylor 1988; Gilligan, Lyons, and Hanmer 1990), these arguments have also been the target of considerable criticism (e.g., Kerber et al. 1986). Some writers are uncomfortable with the degree to which they resemble and justify traditional stereotypes. Systematic comparative research has in fact not uncovered consistent gender differences in moral reasoning; rather, it suggests that women's and men's *reputation* for differences outstrips their *actual* differences in this regard (e.g., Brabeck 1983; Walker 1984; Lifton 1985; Ford and Lowery 1986). No research provides evidence that most men think differently from most women. Most research suggests that women and men do not differ in their use of "justice" or "rights" frameworks in understanding moral and social dilemmas, although women may also use a "caring" framework more than men do. Although women's nurturance is supposed to make them more peace oriented than men, analysis of public reactions to the Gulf War of 1991 shows that while American women were less supportive of military engagement in the Gulf before the war began, and they had more negative emotional reactions to it once it did occur, women supported and assessed the war in much the same way as men after it was over (Conover and Sapiro 1993). No doubt debates about gender and modes of thinking will continue.

Evaluating Cognitive-Developmental Theory

Cognitive-developmental theory offers a handle on the growth of gender identity, its associated meanings, and the importance it plays in individuals' lives. The developmental approach regards the individual as struggling to adapt to or cope with the social and physical world (sometimes labeled *competence strivings*) and to develop and preserve a positive and stable self-image. This struggle leads children to develop gender identity, gender stereotypes, and a motive to become gender typed early in their lives. Many researchers find utility in the idea of gender as a framework through which people understand themselves and their social environment.

Other aspects of cognitive-developmental theory have been subject to greater attack. The idea of a relatively rigid and universal "stage and sequence" process of development is probably the most controversial aspect. It raises many important questions. Even if researchers find a general pattern of stage and sequence in development in some groups of people, is that pattern necessarily the same across cultures and classes? At minimum, might it be that the development of some cognitive skills follows a similar path cross-culturally but the development of others doesn't? Certainly the debates over moral development illustrate some of the problems in generalization.

Childhood Socialization and Social Learning

The most widely used approach to understanding how gender differentiation at the individual level occurs is based on the process of social learning or socialization. Social-learning theory focuses the effects of individuals' experiences. Gender socialization occurs as children learn to imitate the models or examples they see in society, and as people reward them for behaving in gender-appropriate ways and punish them for acting otherwise. The social learning approach to socialization leads researchers to investigate the ways in which agents of socialization such as parents, peers, schools, and the mass media encourage different types of behavior in males and females.

Development of Difference

It is easy to observe the important people in children's lives designing their world to produce gender-appropriate behavior. From the moment of birth, girls and boys are treated differently, even by their parents. Parents interact with their male and female babies differently in how they respond to their crying, how much they handle and talk to them, and what tone of voice they use toward them. Parents treat baby girls as though they are more fragile than baby boys, and they treat baby boys as though they are more independent than baby girls. Of course parents aren't the only ones who do this; most other people do too.

Could parents be treating baby girls and boys differently simply because they are different? Mothers and fathers certainly think that baby girls and baby boys act differently (Rubin, Provenzano, and Luria 1974). But research also shows that if a person is told that a baby is a girl or boy, regardless of what the sex of the child really is, that person is likely to describe the child in "gender-appropriate" terms; that is, they perceive the baby as boyish or girlish regardless of its real sex. Parents give female and male children different kinds of clothes, games, and books. As the children grow and are given more responsibility within the home, parents begin to teach them "gender-appropriate" tasks.

Often this training for gender is neither conscious nor direct. Parents and other agents of socialization may give the child explicit gender messages: "Go and help your mother in the kitchen so that when you grow up you'll be a good mommy too." "You don't want that toy—that's for girls!" "Don't sit like that—it's not ladylike!" "No, you may not phone Sam. A girl should wait for the boy to phone." More often, the teaching is not explicit or even conscious. Gender-typed toys simply appear. A study of mothers reading stories to their children found evidence that they unconsciously taught their children to think of the male as the norm. In 95% of the cases in which the sex of the character was indeterminant, the mothers referred to the character as a male (DeLoache, Cassidy, and Carpenter 1987). Parents and other teachers set a constant example. If Mommy and Daddy are equally capable of driving, but Mommy never drives if Daddy is in the car, children learn who is "supposed" to drive the car.

These parental actions make a difference. Research shows that fathers' and mothers' own level of gender stereotyping, their preference for traditional family roles, and their encouragement of their children to play with gender-typed toys is associated with how well 2- and 3-year-olds recognized the gender of people in pictures they were shown and how much gender stereotyping the children's own thinking showed (Weinraub et al. 1984; Fagot and Leinbach 1989; Fagot, Leinbach, and O'Boyle 1992). Parents of children who learn gender labeling earlier seem to care about gender typing more than do parents of other children (Fagot and Leinbach 1989). Modeling alone without systematic reinforcement may have only limited effect; research on children of gay and lesbian parents, for example, shows that these children do not differ from others in toy or television program preferences, in their relationships with peers, or in their own sexual preference (Patterson 1992).

Parents are not the only teachers of gender norms. As later chapters will show, schools, the mass media, religious institutions, and many others have changed in recent decades, but they still send out important messages about what constitutes appropriate behavior for females and males. Given that research suggests that television still presents very gender-typed messages (Ferrante, Haynes, and Kingsley 1988), it is not surprising that the more television children watch the more gender stereotypic are their attitudes toward jobs (Signorielli and Lears 1992). A child's peers also get involved in the process of socialization; peer pressure is a very effective weapon in making sure children and adolescents toe the line on gender-appropriate behavior.

This process of socialization does not stop at the end of childhood. University and occupational training continues the task of gender-role teaching, as do family members and peers. Perhaps even more than during childhood people expect different things from adult women and men, and they reward people who act as expected and punish those who do not. Women who pursue nontraditional careers or activities often find that the only way they can succeed without tremendous opposition or disapproval is to make sure they also play their more "feminine" roles very carefully.

The Complexity of Learning

The social-learning model of socialization has proven useful in providing insights about how gender differentiation and stratification are maintained from one generation to the next. It is not, however, without its problems.

Girls and boys and women and men are not given only one message about how they are supposed to think, feel, and act. The social environment is complex and varied, offering many different values and patterns from which to choose. As parents know only too well, even carefully structuring a child's life so as to enforce certain values doesn't always work. Moreover, the world itself changes during the course of an individual's lifetime. The fact that no one in the 1930s or 1940s was encouraged to be an astronaut didn't mean that no one was available in the late 1950s to fly in space rockets. In fact we can argue that one of the norms children learn today is not only to expect change but also to participate in it. Young people expect that they will be different from their parents' generation in many ways, and they learn to be able to be different. In fact the multiplicity of messages means the outcome of gender socialization is less predictable than we may sometimes think. People sometimes excuse their behaviors by saying, "Well, I was socialized in this way," as though socialization precludes active, independent thought. It does not.

Perhaps the best caution against using socialization theory as an excuse to maintain the status quo is to review the findings regarding gender differences presented in Chapter 1. If social learning had produced unidimensionally "feminine" girls and "masculine" boys, we should be seeing many more differences between males and females in abilities, attitudes, personality characteristics, and behavior. Doubtless that the pressure to conform to gender stereotypes is quite strong, but there is still considerable room for variation. We must be careful to avoid painting a portrait of oversocialized, passive, conforming people (Weitzman 1979).

More on Learning Theories

Although cognitive-developmental and social-learning theories offer alternative ways of thinking about how gender differences occur, researchers are increasingly weaving together some of the insights from both to arrive at a more complete picture of how gender develops. Here we look at two themes. First is a set of reflections on the timing of learning, especially the amount of gender learning that takes place in adulthood. Then we turn to the concept of gender schemas and "doing gender," two related ways of understanding how gender helps to structure our behavior and thinking.

Adult Life and Learning

The developmental and social-learning approaches to understanding individual gender roles emphasize the processes by which people develop values, attitudes, abilities, and patterns of behavior as they grow up. These theories suggest that by the time people reach adulthood, they are prepared to perform their adult roles. Socialization theorists use the concept of ***anticipatory socialization*** to label the process by which children acquire the attitudes and behavior patterns that become appropriate only when they grow up. A good example of this activity is the child's game "playing house."

Many sociologists have pointed out that anticipatory socialization is not all it is cracked up to be. Sociologists Jessie Bernard (1972) and Helena Lopata (1971), for example, point out that adjustment to adult roles, including the roles of wife and husband, mother and father, is much more difficult than most romantic young people expect. Books, television, homemaking classes in school, playing house, and even the experience of growing up in a family leave women and men only vaguely prepared for the lives that lie ahead. The amount of attention paid to socialization and learning during childhood and adolescence sometimes obscures the fact that females and males become increasingly differentiated after adolescence and that people continue to learn their gender roles as they go through adulthood. This is particularly important because many young people now believe that their adult lives will be very different from those of the current older generation.

Many researchers argue that although some of the groundwork for gender differentiation is laid during childhood, only when people actually live in the adult world do they begin to conform to gender stereotypes. They do this because of the demands placed on them by the specific situations they encounter. As the situations in which people find themselves channel their behavior and options, they establish patterns of appropriate gender-role behavior.

In 1980 Joanna Bunker Rohrbaugh reported on a pair of studies that suggest the effects of situational factors on adult women. The first, done by Alice Rossi (1965), found that among women in their twenties, those who chose marriage and child rearing as full-time occupations seemed happier, had a higher sense of self-esteem, and were less anxious than women who chose careers. Young career women worried about whether they had made the right choices and whether they were good enough to do well in their jobs. Rossi suspected that at some point the homemakers would begin to feel less satisfied and complete, especially as their children went off to school and needed them less. The career women, she believed, would eventually find more satisfaction in their jobs and would feel more challenged and competent to handle the challenges.

The second study, done by Judith Birnbaum (1975), confirmed Rossi's suspicions. Birnbaum compared full-time homemakers who had been top students in college 15 years before with both married and single professional women. Compared to all the professional women, the homemakers had a low sense of self-esteem and personal competence, felt lonely and unattractive, and missed a sense of challenge and creative involvement. They were also much more likely than the married professional women to think that marriage was restricting, demanding, and burdensome.

One study of young adults shows very clearly how the pressure of adult life continues to shape the enactment of gender roles. Even though large numbers of young women (and men) now think that they will follow less traditional, more egalitarian paths than earlier generations did, the pressure of day-to-day adult life still tends to shape their career decisions to reflect the older patterns in which the man's career takes precedence (Foster, Wallston, and Berger 1980; Machung 1989).

Many women find that their adult family lives, their jobs, and their household commitments shape them in ways they did not expect. They may take a few years off to have children and find they never quite get back on track. Because the job market is still segregated, men and women spend their work lives in very different kinds of jobs. Thus the socialization effects of employment can continue to create increased differentiation by gender. The obligations of child and household care—especially on top of a job—continue to push women away from doing things they might otherwise do.

Adulthood can also be a time in which people who have learned traditional gender and sexual orientations can experience a process of resocialization toward very new and different roles and identities. The feminist movement has been an important agent of socialization to new gender orientations (Sapiro 1989). In their introduction to a collection of life stories of women in the arts and sciences, for example, Sara Ruddick and Pamela Daniels described the experience of a group of women "educated in the 1950s, at the height of the feminine mystique." This is a group of women who "encountered the women's movement late, usually in [their] thirties" (Ruddick and Daniels 1977, xxviii). As a result of contact with the women's movement, all of us have had to relearn our pasts. We have had to reevaluate our purposes in working and re-view our commitments to our work and to those we love. Raised consciousness, whatever its ultimate value, has brought vulnerability and has invited risk. It has insisted on change. Our stories are the evidence that significant changes can and do occur in adult lives—after we are supposed to be "grown up" and "settled down" (Ruddick and Daniels 1977, xxix).

Synthesizing Learning Theories: Gender-Schema Theory and Doing Gender

Some scholars are now attempting to combine the insights of cognitive-developmental and social-learning theories by developing what they call gender-schema theory. Sandra Bem, a leading theorist in this field, defines *schema* as a "network of associations that organizes and guides an individual's perception" (1983, 603); a gender schema, therefore, is a network of associations with the concepts of male and female (or masculinity and femininity) that organizes and guides an individual's perception. Bem notes that these gender-related networks encompass

> not only those features directly related to female and male persons—such as anatomy, reproductive function, division of labor, and personality attributes—but also features more remotely or metaphorically related to sex, such as the angularity or roundedness of an abstract shape and the periodicity of the moon (1983, 603).

As social-learning theorists would argue, the content of the gender schema (the ideas found within it) is learned in large part from interaction with the social environment and the gender-linked practices of the social world. The gender schema is then used by the individual to process information by structuring and organizing perception and by helping the individual to evaluate incoming information (including information about the self) with regard to gender norms. The emphasis on cognitive frameworks and the active role of the mind in learning and processing information reflects cognitive-developmental theory.

The most important insight of gender-schema theory is that people follow gender schemas to different degrees and in different ways. Some people, for example, organize many of their thoughts, perceptions, and evaluations around concepts of male and female, masculine and feminine. These people, whom we might describe as highly gender typed, rely heavily on gender stereotypes and symbols to understand the social world. They see a wide variety of human characteristics, behavior, roles, and jobs as decidedly masculine or feminine and evaluate themselves and others according to how well they conform to gender norms and stereotypes.

Other people follow gender schemas less closely or not at all. This does not necessarily mean that they lack what the highly gender-typed person might regard as appropriate masculine and feminine characteristics. Gender may not be the central means by which they organize their perceptions of themselves and the social world. Whereas the highly gender-typed person might immediately understand words such as *pink*, *nurturant*, *blushing*, *librarian*, and *curved* as "feminine," these words might not have any immediate gender connotation to the person with no gender schema.

Research shows that by 3 years old children have already begun to learn the figurative or metaphorical meanings of gender. As one set of researchers concluded in a study in which very young children distributed toys in conventionally gender-appropriate ways, including giving bear toys to boys and cat toys to girls, children learn an underlying framework for understanding the nature of masculine and feminine that does not depend on the specific models having appeared in their environment.

> Few men keep bears, and cats do not belong only to women. Rather, it appears that children, like the rest of us, make inferences on the basis of what they see or know about the nature of things. Children, even at these early ages, may have begun to connect certain qualities with males and other qualities with females (Fagot, Leinbach, and Boyle 1992, 229).

Even in childhood these frameworks or schemas shape perception; highly gender-typed children cannot remember details of stories that are inconsistent with traditional gender stereotypes as well as other children can. Marianne Carlsson and Pia Jaderquist (1983) found that not only did first-graders remember gender-typed information better; they also tended to reconstruct the gender-inappropriate stories in memory to conform more closely to gender stereotypes. This tendency was even stronger when children were questioned about the stories 7 days later.

These studies support the notion of gender schemas discussed earlier. This is consistent with Claudia Cohen's (1981) research on person perception and memory. After showing her subjects a short movie that identified the main character's occupation and included some details that conformed to their stereotypes and some that did not, she asked the subjects in her experiment to tell her what they remembered about the movie. She found that her subjects "were selectively more accurate in remembering those characteristics that fit their prototype than those features that were inconsistent with the target person's occupation" (1981, 447). Dana Christensen and Robert Rosenthal (1982) found that men's expectations bias their perceptions of other people more than women's do.

Other evidence also shows that gender schemas have important social implications. A study of adults showed that when they were asked to remember a conversation, those who described themselves in highly gender-schematic ways were more likely to make mistakes remembering which person of the other sex (as compared with their own sex) said what. Those whose self-description did not conform to traditional male or female stereotypes were equally likely to make mistakes about people of their own or the other sex. The title of the research report said it all: "If you are gender schematic, all members of the opposite sex look alike" (Frable and Bem 1985).[4]

It is important to remember, however, that gender schemas are not just used to organize perception of and thinking about *other* people; people also use them to integrate *self*-understanding (Markus, Crane, Bernstein, and Siladi 1982). People differ not just in how they describe themselves, but in the degree to which gender serves as one of the major frameworks for thinking about and evaluating themselves.

Discussions of gender schemas focus our attention on the way we think about gender. But it is clear that gender is more than ideas and symbols. It involves action and interaction, behavior that displays and even asserts femininity, masculinity, or the rejection of these concepts. Recognition of the importance of action, interaction, and display has led Candace West and Don H. Zimmerman (1987) to write about "doing gender." They argue that "a person's gender is not simply an aspect of what one is, but, more fundamentally, it is something that one *does*, and does recurrently, in interaction with others" (140). Gender, they contend, is not just a matter of roles that have been learned and are repeated automatically; reproducing gender in everyday behavior takes continual work. Because gender is an important basis for social organization, doing gender, even while we are engaged in other activities, helps define our place and keep social relations orderly.

Women may be especially aware of doing gender while they are deciding how to dress for specific situations each day. How "feminine" should one appear at a job interview? At work? It depends on the job and special circumstances. The same woman may highlight her gender much more forcefully when dressing to go to a party than when she goes to work. Sometimes deciding how much to do gender takes very careful thought.

Gender-schema theory can be used to understand the meanings (and variability of meanings) of gender, while Zimmerman and West's notion of doing gender reminds us of the effort and activity it takes to learn and display (or refuse to display) our gender. The insights of cognitive-developmental theory can contribute to understanding the relationship between identity and gender meanings. This theory emphasizes that individuals actively participate in their own socialization and in their everyday maintenance or breaking of gender expectations. Social-learning theory, on the other hand, focuses our attention on the social order and the means by which social interaction imposes rules and meaning.

Discrimination: Being Forced to Be Different

Up to this point we have emphasized the ways in which individuals develop gendered character, cognitive frameworks, and styles of action and interaction through learning or internalizing cultural norms. Here we explore another explanation: Men and women do not just *learn* to be different or *choose* to be different but are *forced* to be different. In the learning perspective we might argue that because of their experiences in life, women learn to prefer and be better at some jobs, while men learn to prefer and be better at other jobs. Thus, women and men enter different jobs because, for whatever reason, they choose to do so. According to the discrimination view, women are forced out of certain roles and activities because their passage has been barred through discrimination. This point is important: If we argue that most differences between the lives women and men lead develop because they have learned to choose different paths, we arrive at one set of solutions to the problem of gender differentiation and stratification; if we find that, regardless of what people have learned, they take different roles because they are forced to do so through discrimination, the solutions will be different.

The verb *discriminate* is derived from the Latin *discernere*, meaning "to distinguish between." Not all forms of discrimination are necessarily bad. In art and music, for example, we talk about the discriminating eye or ear. We discriminate between children and adults in meting out punishment. The type of discrimination with which we are concerned here, however, is not so commendable. Our use of the word refers to the act of singling out a person for special treatment not on the basis of individual merit, but on the basis of prejudices about the group to which that person belongs. When a woman is barred from a job or receives relatively low pay not because of her lack of abilities but because she happens to be a woman, we say that she has been discriminated against on the basis of sex.

Supreme Court Justice Ruth Bader Ginsburg and Senator Diane Feinstein have spent their careers fighting to end discrimination.

At one time many graduate and professional schools explicitly required higher entrance qualifications for women than for men. Many employers announced their jobs as designed for men or women but not both. Now it is illegal to discriminate in jobs or education on the basis of sex. But still, many employers and schools or departments would prefer to rule out women in some areas on the grounds that few women are likely to be qualified. These people might claim that they are not discriminating; they are only looking for qualified people. But as long as these employers automatically rule out women and do not consider them on the basis of individual merit they are discriminating, and according to the 1964 Civil Rights Act they are engaging in an illegal activity.

A person does not have to be conscious of what he or she is doing to discriminate. Unconscious discrimination is more difficult to identify. None of us sees people objectively all the time; as the discussion of gender schemas suggested, our expectations of people affect how we see them. In other words, people apply the beliefs and attitudes they hold with regard to a *group* of people to individual members of that group. These group-based beliefs or attitudes are called *stereotypes.* They become the basis for discrimination when employers, for example, perceive a woman as not likely to be capable of strong leadership because she happens to be a woman or a man as not likely to be capable of caring for children because he happens to be a man.

Numerous studies have investigated the possibility that people see women and men and their qualifications differently even when they are objectively the same. One of the most widely used research designs follows a model first used by Philip Goldberg in 1968: The subjects are asked to evaluate an essay, speech, job application, piece of artwork, or musical composition. All subjects are given the same work to evaluate, but some are told that a man created the work and some are told that a woman did.

Many of these experiments (although not Goldberg's) found evidence of prejudice against women. A meta-analysis of 123 such studies concludes that we do not have the evidence to say simply that women are evaluated more negatively than men because of the great differences in the results of these studies. That study concluded, "Gender-biased evaluations indeed occur, but the complexity of the conditions under which such evaluations occur and the flexibility of social perceivers' thinking must be taken into consideration" (Swim, Borgida, Maruyama, and Myers 1989, 424).

These experiments suggest that people are more likely to be prejudiced in their evaluations if the situation or activity is stereotypically masculine. Also, the more information people are given about an individual the less they rely on stereotypes (Swim, Borgida, Maruyama, and Myers 1989). Discrimination is particularly likely to emerge in evaluations involved in hiring decisions (Glick, Zion, and Nelson 1988). In addition, some research finds men more likely to be prejudiced against women than women are (e.g., Sapiro 1982b).

These types of research suggest first that people who discriminate may not know they are doing so and second that it may be very difficult to identify cases in which discrimination has occurred. Considerable evidence shows that there is sex discrimination in job and education counseling, letters of recommendation, and evaluations of individuals that affects hiring, salary, and promotion. How much discrimination is there? As long as discrimination can occur unconsciously and most of the important decisions about us are made confidentially, we cannot know.

Individual Development and Social Change

We have looked at six different approaches people use to explain the existence of differences between women and men at the individual level. Each is based on a different type of research and evidence, employs different assumptions, and comes to different conclusions.

Which of these theories is "correct"? The answer is that no single theory completely explains the process of gender-role development and differentiation. Each has drawbacks, and each focuses our attention on a slightly different aspect of the problem. These different approaches are by no means mutually exclusive; one can argue, for example, that psychoanalytic theories explain some aspects of gender development, cognitive-developmental theories others, and discrimination theories still others. These different theories can provide complementary insights that fill in the whole picture. The task for the student of gender development is to learn to evaluate and use these theories skillfully and appropriately.

These theories of individual differences also need to be integrated with the theories of social differentiation and stratification reviewed in Chapter 2. We began this chapter by observing that theories used to explain how a given sex/gender system evolves and is maintained in a given society do not necessarily tell us how individuals in a given society come to fit or not fit into that system. By the same token, theories that explain how individual gender development occurs do not tell us how the society as a whole comes to be structured in a particular way. The theories offered in this chapter may help us understand why so many young women today will become secretaries rather than business executives. They do not tell us why in this century secretaries are usually women, although in the 19th century they were usually men, or why, since secretarial positions have come to be primarily female jobs, they have fewer promotion prospects than lower-level business jobs held predominantly by men. Societal theories can help explain how and why the institution of marriage came to be based on patriarchal norms (and why those norms seem to be threatened now) and how the institution of marriage is linked to other social, political, and economic structures of society. Individual theories suggest some of the reasons why most women continue to participate in those arrangements and why some do not.

Women's studies scholars are interested, therefore, in the insights offered by both the societal theories outlined in Chapter 2 and the individual theories outlined in this chapter because they investigate both the historical development of sex/gender systems and the development of individuals within given societies. For this reason each of the following chapters of this book includes discussion of both levels of analysis.

NOTES

1. This discussion of biology is very basic and nontechnical. A good basic text on female biology is Sloane (1993). Two important works on women's health also contain relevant information: *The Black Women's Health Book* (White 1990) and *Our Bodies, Ourselves* (Boston Women's Health Book Collective 1992).
2. In fact, human beings are not neatly divided into two sexes, female (XX) and male (XY). About 1 in 2,500 females is born with only one X chromosome, a condition known as Turner's syndrome. As a result they are relatively short and their ovaries don't function. About 1 in 700 males is born with two X chromosomes and one Y, and the same proportion has two Y chromosomes and one X. "Normal" people can have a variety of combinations of X and Y chromosomes. Research has not identified clear personality or behavioral effects of these differing genetic structures.
3. Horney's book is a compilation of papers that Horney wrote between 1922 and 1936.
4. For purposes of this discussion I am contrasting those who, on the BSRI scale used, were either gender typed or cross gender typed with those who were androgynous or aschematic.

4

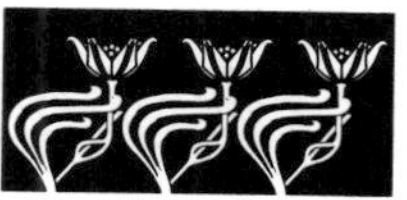

Commonality and Difference Among Women

THE MAJOR PREMISE of women's studies—and of this book—is that we can use the concept of gender to organize important aspects of our knowledge of the social world. The idea of a sex/gender system leads us to suppose that whatever else also shapes social life, societies are structured in such a way as to "make something of" the sex into which people were born. We investigate the ways in which societies accommodate, build on, institutionalize, and give significance to biological sex. Thus the study of gender and sex/gender systems tends to focus our attention on differences between male and female in terms of their character, thinking, or behavior, or the ways they are perceived, interpreted, and treated.

The obvious implication of what has been said thus far is that we can make meaningful generalizations about women (and also about men) as a group. In the first chapter we saw evidence of aggregate and average gender differences, for example, in criminal behavior and employment. The subsequent two chapters made claims about aspects of history and day-to-day social existence that affect women as women and men as men in specific, gendered ways.

This chapter considers the significance of an obvious but crucial fact of life for our study of gender: Almost anyone past the age of 6 could hypothetically divide most of the people on earth into two groups, one labeled *women* and one labeled *men*. But differences *among* the people labeled one way or the other are so numerous that it seems difficult to make any simple but meaningful generalizations about either collectivity. Even if we narrow our sights down to one nation or one community, a realistic look at gender and gender difference shows that it is crisscrossed and complicated by the simultaneous existence of other important structural bases of social life, such as race and ethnicity, class, age, and religion, to name just a few. Are the differences between the lives of rich women and poor women or those of Unitarians and fundamentalist Muslims or those of lesbians and heterosexual women so great that they render our concepts of *gender* and *women* useless? Or are these differences so trivial that we can talk about the "average" woman without wondering whether she is African American, Hmong, a Chicana, or Swedish American, whether she is just reaching puberty or has already passed menopause?

These and related questions discussed in this chapter have both *analytical* and *political* significance. The *analytical* question was just posed: Can we understand women, or the significance of gender in women's or men's lives, if we do not also understand and take account of the other crucial bases of social life? The argument that will be made here is that sex/gender systems both depend on and shape other aspects of social structure and identity such as race, ethnicity, and class. The *political* significance of difference among women is related to the claims made by feminist and antifeminist political groups alike. Both feminists and antifeminists claim that they can speak on behalf of women and their interests. But this assumes that some underlying commonality of interest can be represented. Now we are back to the analytical question: What difference for our understanding of gender does difference among women make?

Even though our primary focus is the nature of sex/gender systems, there are four reasons for analyzing these social divisions: (1) to recognize the variety of lives that women lead, (2) to evaluate the different ways that sex/gender systems affect people, (3) to untangle the effects of different stratification systems on people, and (4) to understand the impact of the multiple contexts of people's lives. The remainder of this chapter will look at how studying social divisions other than gender helps us to understand gender, sex/gender systems, and women's lives.

Recognizing Difference

The obvious truth is that women live many different kinds of lives, and to understand women we must understand these differences. But this is not easy, and women's studies scholars have found they have had to work hard to eliminate the blinders that make these differences and their significance difficult to see.

Consider the claim that feminist scholars make about scholars (and other people) whose perceptions of women are shaped by androcentric perspectives. We claim that group-based stereotypes distort the ability to understand women, in part by making it difficult to comprehend the variation in women's character, abilities, and experiences. Indeed, psychological research shows that people who think of themselves in terms of gender stereotypes have trouble telling people of the other sex apart (Frable and Bem 1985).

Many critics point out that feminist scholars have also "homogenized" or overgeneralized about women. Just as most traditional scholarship was blind to the experiences and perspectives of women because women had very little influence in creating that scholarship, much of women's studies scholarship has been blind to the experiences of women other than middle-class, white women—that is, blind to the perspectives of the women who have least influenced that scholarship. Many scholars have detected pervasive biases in women's studies research based not on gender but, for example, on race and class (e.g., Spelman 1988).

It may seem ironic that scholars who put so much effort into thinking about equality are themselves subject to charges of parallel kinds of bias. Adrienne Rich's (1979) essay on racism points to the irony of how many white feminists revealed their racism just at the point when they are trying to be antiracist. Consider how this occurs. Feminists historically emphasize sisterhood and the commonalities of women's lives. Many white feminists have been so eager to emphasize their common womanhood and equality with African American women that they have ignored or denied race-based differences in their histories, experiences, and perspectives that make real differences in their lives. But this overgeneralization of commonality is usually framed in a very ethnocentric way; that is, the "observer" assumes that her own perceptions, feelings, experiences, and aspirations are shared by others, thus devaluing those of others. Whites in a white-dominated society do not usually experience themselves as having "race" or "color." In such a society it is likely that when a white person says she is "color blind," it means she sees everyone as "white like me."[1] Remember the men who think it is a compliment to tell a woman she "thinks like a man."

Neither historical nor psychological research reveals any mechanism that means that someone who is consciously antisexist will necessarily be antiracist or vice versa. History offers many examples of racist and class-biased feminist movements, sexist and racist labor organizations, and sexist movements for racial or ethnic equality. Some white women's suffrage leaders made very racist statements in defense of the vote for native-born white women, claiming that these women could then help "outvote" the immigrant and "colored" vote (Kraditor 1965). Indeed, although the KKK has not supported equality between white Protestant women and men (and they have never been allied with feminist organizations), earlier in this century it did claim belief "in the purity of womanhood and in the fullest measure of freedom compatible with the highest type of womanhood including the suffrage" (Blee 1991, 49).

Many movements of national or ethnic liberation placed restrictions on women and their roles in the service of the apparent interests of the group as a whole (Jayawardena 1986; Enloe 1989; Sapiro 1993). Movements based on race, class, or ethnic solidarity face many pressures to appear and, indeed, to perceive themselves as completely unified and undivided. They have tended to see women's movements as secondary to "the cause" or as divisive and detrimental to the general good of that group or of society. Workers' organizations historically have argued that separate women's organizations are divisive to organization of the working class and that women's problems will be solved anyway when the problems of labor and capital are relieved. Some writers, like E. Frances White (1990), worry that the particular way in which black nationalism and African American social identity are being developed collapses the ability to see differences within the community and acts to the detriment of understanding women's problems. Many African American leaders have argued that separate black women's organizations are divisive to the organization of blacks and that black women's problems will be solved anyway when blacks as a group become free and equal to whites. The same argument has been made within the Chicano movement (Mirandé and Enríquez 1979). Leaders of primarily white and middle-class groups use similar arguments when they claim that the most important social ills are human problems and that distinct organizations of women are divisive and misguided.

Many leaders of various movements argue that the "woman problem" may be a problem for *other* social groups—but not theirs. Middle-class representatives argue that working-class families suffer the most patriarchal norms, and working-class activists claim that the middle class foists the ideal of feminine fragility on women. Black activists have pointed to the long history of black female employment and the image of the strong black mother to show that feminism is a white problem. Chicano activists claim that behind the stereotype of machismo is veneration for the Chicana, who holds social life and the family together as the Anglo mother no longer does. Christians attempt to prove that theirs is the liberated group by pointing to the New Testament declaration that there is "neither male nor female," and Jews point out that because Judaism is a home-based religion women's leadership in the home gives them a unique power and authority. Meanwhile, in none of these groups do women have the range of opportunities men have, and in none of them are women who are trying to support themselves and their families paid as much as men are. These varying groups seem to be able to agree about one thing: Women who try to organize women on behalf of their own quality of life are out of line.

Thus, analyzing and comparing women in different social groups can reveal important differences but also commonalities in women's lives that might otherwise be ignored. Just as conventional history has left women out of the picture, focusing only on men and men's experiences, it has often happened that women who are not part of dominant social groups are simply left out. For example, women's historians have revealed the tremendous number of women involved in volunteer and public service groups in the late 19th century, but for a long time it seemed as though this was a white, middle-class phenomenon simply because historians had paid less attention to the participation by African American and working-class white women. In any case, it is not possible to understand women's lives without considering these differences. For this reason, a tremendous growth in research in many disciplines has focused on specific groups of women and an increasing amount offers comparisons among different groups of women.

The Differential Impact of Sex/Gender Systems

Studying difference among women gives us a more accurate picture of the experiences of women. In the preceding two chapters, however, we probed a more theoretical or analytical question than this. Rather than just describing what different women's lives look like, we are trying to understand what role gender plays in shaping women's lives. Looking at difference among women underscores a crucial point: Arguing that there is a sex/gender system that structures women's experiences does not imply all women are affected by this system in the same way any more than arguing that there is a political or economic system in a country means it affects all social groups the same way.

The structure of a sex/gender system is composed of the underlying rules and norms that determine how male and female, masculinity and femininity are defined; what expectations are made of men and women on the basis of their gender; and how they, their behavior, work, and ideas are treated. Let us imagine a very simple androcentric sex/gender system. In such a system all women might be expected to be passive and submissive to men's will, "feminine" in the manner suggested by early 1960s situation comedies and family shows, and required to do just as they are told, reproduce, and take care of the children and home. Any other woman must be punished and will never be allowed to fit into the "good" side of the system. For example, if a woman is too sexually active, she will never be able to attract a husband, or at least not one who can offer the rewards of the system.

Even under this very simple sex/gender system in which all women are judged by the same narrow standards, not all women will have the same experiences, and they will not be affected in the same way in their day-to-day lives. The most obvious point is that women who *will not* or *cannot* fulfill the expectations for femininity will be affected very differently from those who will or can. The simple but important fact is that if women are rewarded for being dependent on and deferential toward men, both women who conform to that norm and women who do not are caught in that same system; they are treated differently and their experiences are different *because* of it. The prostitute and the traditional wife, the lesbian and the married heterosexual woman are judged by the same values. In fact, one of the social mechanisms that control the lives of traditionally married women is that they may fear being treated like a lesbian or a prostitute if they violate the behavioral norms expected of them.

Thus, at minimum, the stereotypic images of women are double-sided: one image for women who fulfill the cultural ideal of proper womanhood and one for those who don't—one for the good girls and one for the bad girls. Feminist observers of Western society have long argued that there is a central double image of woman drawn from Christian imagery. On the one side is Mary, the asexual, self-sacrificing, moral mother, devoted to caring for her family, and on the other is Eve, the sexual, morally weak temptress responsible for the Fall of Man. There are many cultural variations on this theme, but the central point is that the more moral mother is the preferred ideal while the sexual object deserves what she gets. Although only one of these images is the *ideal* for women, both are culturally regarded as desirable to men, but for obviously different purposes. Thus, there is pressure on women to conform to both the ideal and its flip side.

Very few—if any—sex/gender systems are as simple as that just described. The norms of most human communities are complex, nuanced, and partial. Even those governed self-consciously by leaders attempting to enforce very narrow and specified gender norms for women, as in the more conservative Islamic countries, are more complicated than they appear to outsiders at first (MacLeod 1991).

Closer inspection of recognizable and dominant sets of cultural norms defining male and female usually reveals contingencies based on situation, place, and other definers of social membership and status. Let us return briefly to the concept of "doing gender," discussed in Chapter 3. Any woman who attempts to fulfill cultural requirements of "femininity" knows that dress and demeanor are important aspects of doing gender properly. But she also knows that she cannot appropriately "do gender" in exactly the same way in different settings. To display appropriately feminine dress and demeanor in different situations or settings in the course of a day will require her to change her clothes and behavior. She is expected to be feminine, but the definition of "feminine" is contingent on situation and setting.

The norms and rules of sex/gender systems also include contingencies based on women's social identity and status. In the 19th century and early 20th century United States, the new "cult of true womanhood," idealizing femininity in terms of passivity, delicacy, and moral superiority, could apply fully only to white women—and native-born, Protestant, middle- and upper-class white women at that. Dominant views of ideal femininity were in fact unattainable for *most* women not just because it was only in wealthy families that women could scorn hard labor and display the requisite frailty, but also because women who were not white and northern European in origin were defined by those who were as naturally incapable of achieving the ideal. Indeed, in the 19th century the working class and poor, even when they were white, northern European, and Protestant, were widely believed to be naturally inferior and incapable of attaining full ideal femininity.

More progressive whites rejected these ideas of natural inferiority. Middle- and upper-class reformers throughout the United States (for example, missionaries in the South and western areas) often tried to help nonwhite and immigrant women learn how to achieve the ideal. Two little-known examples are found in some schools for young Native American women (Trennert 1988) and in the efforts of German Jewish women to integrate newer Eastern European Jewish immigrant women into appropriate roles and character (Sinkoff 1988). Of course, although these reform efforts were well intentioned, they often were based on the idea that only one form of femininity—their own—was morally and socially acceptable. Thus, while hoping to free another group of women, those involved in reform movements at the same time often helped perpetrate restricted views of femininity.

The fact that most 19th-century women could not live the life that some relatively wealthy white women led does not mean they were unaffected by the cult of domesticity. The feminine image fostered by this view became an unreachable goal to which women often aspired despite their circumstances. For those, such as black women, whose aspirations were futile because of racism, the image must have had especially devastating effects (hooks 1981, 48; see also Perkins 1983). Their attempts to fulfill the requirements of the predominant definition of femininity after emancipation were met by the racial hatred of whites. As hooks observes, "A black woman dressed tidy and clean, carrying herself in a dignified manner, was usually the object of mudslinging by white men who ridiculed and mocked her self-improvement efforts" (55). Aspiring women from most subordinate social groups were also chastised for reaching "above their station" or "putting on airs."

In complex societies marked by stratification and gender divisions of labor, the sex/gender system is composed of a plurality of gender-based stereotypes and expectations that depend on other aspects of social position and identity. As we have seen, there may be a central, widely unattainable ideal that can be met only by the highest-status women, but the dominant society also develops stereotypes and expectations aimed specifically at women in different social positions. White American society, for example, imagined Native American women either as the silent, oppressed, laboring squaw or as the romantic and noble princess, captured by the popular stories of Pocahontas (Clinton 1985; Tsosie 1988). African American women came to be characterized either as promiscuous, earthy women who could be used as beasts of burden or as Mammy, a loyal member of a white household with a special knowledge of nature and children (Clinton 1985). The late 20th century added another African American female figure: the welfare cheat, placing burdens on the system through having uncontrollable numbers of children for whom she cannot care or provide.

Esther Ngan-Ling Chow (1987) offers further examples from the stereotyped views of Asian American women, defined in a variety of closely related roles: Suzie Wong, geisha, picture bride, and sexpot. In each case, the definition of the Asian American woman depends on both race and sex. Stereotypes of the Jewish American princess (JAP) are based on both gender and ethnicity. Neither gender nor race or ethnicity is alone sufficient to understand most women's situation. In each case, scholars have noted, the special character of the stereotypes is not just an accident; it serves the ideological needs of both an androcentric structure of power relations and the racial/ethnic structure of power by not just *describing* but also *justifying* these power relations.

The cast of subculturally differentiated female characters could be extended indefinitely if we turn to depictions based on other ethnic/racial groups or on class, sexuality, geographic region, or other aspects of sociocultural diversity. Lillian Faderman (1991) and Donna Penn (1991), among others, have written about the historical development of stereotypes of lesbian women during the 20th century, including the pervasive view that lesbians can be categorized as either "butch," in which case they are hypermasculine predators of other women, or "femme," the feminized victim who might be rescued if the right man came along. The construction of female (and male) gender is also partly determined by region, as in the case of the Southern belle (Clinton 1985; Silber 1989), the Boston "bluestocking," the "gentle tamer" of the West, the "madonna of the Plains," or the "tall women" and "mountain belles" of Appalachia (Mathews 1987). We shall look at many of these characters later in this chapter and book.

When we analyze sex/gender systems, we are not talking about just the cultural stereotypes in people's minds but also the structure of social institutions and their roles in creating and maintaining divisions of labor and differences of value based on gender. This will become clearer in later chapters as we investigate the role of many major social institutions in the sex/gender system. As the overview in Chapter 1 showed, despite the many changes in the past few decades, women and men still have different kinds of education and jobs, and they play somewhat different roles and receive different treatment from other social institutions as well. But now we must add to the picture that those gender divisions are also contingent on the other aspects of social stratification and identity we have been discussing.

Evelyn Nakano Glenn's research on service work offers an excellent example of the institutionalization of specific racial/ethnic norms of womanhood (Glenn 1992). She reminds us that woman's central role has been defined as both physical and social reproduction, or the "creation and recreation of people as cultural and social, as well as physical beings" (Glenn 1992, 4). This means having responsibility for care of (but not financial provision for) the household and the people within it. But Glenn points out an important contradiction in the expectations placed on women that arose from the 19th century cult of womanhood.

Domestic labor is, in many respects, dirty, difficult, labor-intensive work, especially in a society without electricity. The image of the "domestic angel," therefore, is largely inconsistent with the domestic labor required to keep homes in the preferred domestic order. Not surprisingly, therefore, in the era of industrial development, when labor was both plentiful and cheap, families of any means employed servants to do much of the domestic labor. First, the work was intensive enough that most women probably welcomed help; only the most upper-class women tended to shift the entire burden of domestic labor to servants. Second, shifting the work to servants could reduce the contradiction within the gender role of the "lady" of the house.

An apparent contradiction remains. This domestic labor was placed in the hands of women because it was gender-specified labor. But isn't there as much contradiction between the image of the domestic angel and the dirty, laborious work for the women hired to do the labor as for the "lady" of the house? In the eyes of the employing class there was not, because their gender norms did not depend just on a woman's *gender* but on her *class* and *race/ethnicity* as well. For some women, serving the domestic labor needs of strangers was entirely consistent with dominant-culture definitions of appropriate womanhood. As Evelyn Nakano Glenn points out, the classification of women who performed these tasks changed historically and differed from geographic region to geographic region. In the northeastern United States at the turn of the century, recent European immigrants, especially Irish women, were thought to be specially fitted to do domestic labor. White women in the South turned to African Americans, in the Southwest Mexican women filled the service roles, as did Japanese women on the West Coast and in Hawaii.

These groups of women engaged in paid domestic service because they needed the money, and they lived in those geographic areas in large numbers. But in each region these women came to be culturally reinterpreted as a servant class *by nature*, marked out and determined by their gender and race/ethnicity. Glenn argues that in each case the women, marked by their race/ethnicity, were understood to have inherent traits suiting them for service, and they were not perceived as mothers and wives in their own right but as servants. Thus, Glenn

Society's definitions of appropriate roles for women depend on their race/ethnicity and class.

shows, in each region young women were institutionally tracked into fulfilling their "natural" destiny. She found examples of how Mexican girls in the Southwest and Japanese girls in Hawaii were blocked from school programs other than those that would lead to domestic service. Even in the jobs programs run by the federal Works Project Administration (WPA) in the New Deal response to the Great Depression of the 1930s, Chicanas and African American and Asian women were funneled in to domestic service jobs and out of others.

The View from Different Groups of Women

Let us now add one further layer to this discussion of the differential impact of sex/gender systems on different women. As we have argued, a single sex/gender system, like an economic system or a political system, contains a complex of norms and rules that place different expectations on people depending on their situation and group membership. But in a complex society, the large sex/gender system contains a number of subsystems whose norms and rules are shaped by the larger national community, but also by the more specific communities defined, for example, by geography, race/ethnicity, religion, or class. From this perspective, we might say that the entire system is like a game with very complicated rules, but in which there are also a number of sub-games with rules of their own that may conflict with the rules of the larger game. The players may thus be subject to different sets of rules at the same time, some of which fit together coherently, and some of which do not.

The section you just read takes the perspective of the "larger game" in the United States—that is, the norms and rules of the dominant national sex/gender system. Within this system women who are not native-born, white, middle class or upper class and, in many areas, Protestant or of Northern European extraction have historically been seen as incapable of fulfilling the ideal of femininity as presented in the "cult of womanhood," but were offered another version of stereotypic femininity that assumed they were specially fitted to do "female" but "dirty" work or other families' domestic labor. But at the same time, the "second class" women—immigrants, racial minorities, those from working-class communities or from the urban slums or farming communities—developed their own understandings of gender because of the circumstances in which they lived and the cultures they carried with them from one era of history to the next.

This means that women's actions can be—and are—interpreted simultaneously through the multiple perspectives contained within the system. Thus, when African American, Hispanic, and Asian American women went into domestic service in large numbers, from the "large game" perspective they were fulfilling the roles of second-class femininity; they were acting in gender and race-appropriate ways. From their own points of view, many were being good mothers; they were struggling to help their families garner enough resources so that their daughters would not have to go into domestic service to support themselves (Glenn 1992, 19).

For another example, consider the story of Pocahontas. To Euro-American society the story of Pocahontas is a romantic tale of a beautiful Indian princess who falls in love with an Englishman, who generously marries her and takes her off to England, where she is the talk of the town. This story can be seen as symbolizing to the Euro-American the unique "marriage" of the civilized European with the wildness of nature on the new continent, with all living happily ever after as the Indian and wilderness are "tamed." Native Americans are more likely to hear the rest of the story and, presumably, to take a different message from it. Pocahontas was offered to John Smith as part of a policy of alliance, much as European aristocrats and royalty intermarried to solidify international agreements. When she went to London, although she was displayed in society, neither her husband nor the society in which she was now isolated ever accepted her, and while longing to return home, she died before her 25th birthday.

Each of these subcultures, defined by race/ethnicity, class, and geography (among other characteristics), display distinctive ways of understanding gender and different norms about how women and men should "do gender" to some degree. For communities defined by race/ethnicity, religion, or geography, distinctive rituals and practices, cultural figures, myths and stories, and graphic representations offer a way of understanding the specific subcultural constructions of male and female. The Navajo Changing Woman, for example, responsible for the growth of crops and the birth of new life, presents a model of the woman warrior and defender of her home that is a cultural ideal for Navajo women (Tsosie 1988). Young Jewish girls dress up at Purim as "Queen Esther," a savior of her people, as often as they might, like many other American children, appear as fairy princesses and witches at Halloween. Many Appalachian authors incorporate the locally well-known image of the "tall women," so named because of the saying that "a tall woman casts a long shadow." This image of "strong women, who can manage the household and children as well as milk the cows and cultivate the fields," served as a positive cultural image of femininity for Appalachian women for whom the image of the Southern belle must have seemed foreign (Mathews 1987, 39).

The closer we look at women's lives, the more clear it becomes that there is immense variation in the ways gender is shaped and represented in a complex sex/gender system. Nevertheless, these representations are not completely independent. They are linked through the common social institutions which tie them all together into the larger society including, for example, the government, the mass media, and the school and health-care systems. Thus, women (and men) "do gender" within sex/gender systems that often demand different and sometimes conflicting behavior of them at the same time in order to act in a "gender-appropriate" way.

Untangling Oppressions

The subordination of women on the basis of their gender is one of the facts of life that women's studies seeks to understand. How prevalent is it? How does it work? How does it change? Chapters 2 and 3 looked at alternative theories that can be used to offer answers to these questions. But once we have accepted the idea that understanding sex/gender systems also requires understanding the structures of power based on other social markers, we are led to an obvious question: What are the relative effects of gender and, for example, race or class on social power structures?

The literature on gender and social difference suggests four different general approaches people have used to understand the simultaneous dynamics of gender and other structures of social inequality: the parallel model, the distinct components model, the complex model, and the hierarchical model.[2] Let us look briefly at each.

The Parallel Model

The parallel model is perhaps the most widely used way of thinking about oppression and inequality. This view does not attempt to *integrate* an understanding of gender with other forms of social inequality, although the parallel view allows us to try to *compare* them. The parallel view sees gender, age, class, and race (for example) as different principles of social structure and power that have their own distinct effects. In social science research, scholars tend to study gender *or* race *or* class *or* age, but not to pay serious attention to all of these.

Day-to-day thinking in the broader culture also shows evidence of parallel thinking. The phrase "women and blacks" is often used in a way that suggests these groups are not overlapping.[3] For example, discussions of post–Civil War movements to broaden the franchise often discuss the debates over whether reformers should fight to secure the vote for women as well as blacks or just for blacks. In the end, we are told, blacks were given the legal right to vote. In fact, of course, "blacks" were not given the legal right to vote; it was black men whose legal rights had technically changed. If we can only account for race or gender at a given time, it does little to understand anyone if we assume that in a race- and gender-conscious society everyone's race *and* gender must play some role in shaping their experiences.

The parallel model often underlies the tendency for groups focusing on different forms of oppression to engage in comparative oppression measuring. There is little point in debating whose oppression hurts more; such debates tend to lead people almost to express pride in their oppression. The "whose oppression is bigger" debate defeats the whole purpose of comparing women's lives, because it tends to lead the participants to reject or downplay the claims of other women. Moreover, attempts to rank oppression is for many women an exercise in self-fragmentation. Individual women have many different social identities. How does a woman decide which bit of her is the source of her oppression? Cheryl Clarke, a black radical feminist, arrives at perhaps the only sane response to women's self-fragmentation when she writes, "So, all of us would do well to stop fighting each other for our space at the bottom, because there ain't no more room. We have spent so much time hating ourselves. Time to love ourselves" (1981, 137).

The Distinct Components Model

The distinct components model offers a widely used way of thinking about how different bases of social structure work together. The distinct components model, very much like what Elizabeth V. Spelman (1988) and Evelyn Nakano Glenn (1992) call an "additive perspective," attempts to weigh different aspects of people's social identification in their overall experience. According to this view we should attempt to parse out an individual's experience into its various components of gender, race/ethnicity, class, and age to understand the whole. Spelman correctly claims that most feminist research and theory on racism falls into this category. Glenn points out that the widespread view of research on women is that white women are oppressed by gender, while women of color are "doubly" subordinated. In this perspective, "White women have only gender and women of color have gender plus race" (Glenn 1992, 33). A distinct components or additive model of oppression could also argue that all African Americans are oppressed by racism and some are further oppressed by sexism, or that all poor people are oppressed by class oppression and some are further oppressed by ageism. In each of these cases we imagine piles of distinct burdens that are added onto an individual.

Most social science research on gender using statistical techniques for analyzing data such as those gathered from surveys, experiments, and censuses takes a distinct components approach. Consider research on wealth and income. An economist who has access to data that include information on people's income, job, education, family status, race, gender, age, and other characteristics can use a number of statistical techniques to determine what the relative "weight" of these different factors is in determining someone's income. Within any given class or job, for example, research shows that on average people's salaries are lower if they are female rather than male. Both black and white women earn less than both black and white men, even if we control for their levels of education. Within each sex, blacks earn less than whites, although the gap is much wider among men than among women. The conclusion researchers draw from this work is that apart from education, training, and skill, both gender and race/ethnicity have *independent* effects on where people stand on the economic ladder. The effects of gender are slightly different for blacks and whites, and the effects of race/ethnicity are slightly different for women and men.

The distinct components or additive model has seemed very useful for trying to understand gender in relation to other aspects of social status. But it has also been widely criticized by scholars because while it may prove useful in some cases, such as the income problem just described, it is very flawed in dealing with questions of social identity, which is crucial in trying to untangle the sources and effects of prejudice, discrimination, group-based violence, and other aspects of oppression.

Let us say I fit the following description: I am female, Chinese American, Roman Catholic, born and raised in San Francisco, I went to UCLA, and I am currently living and working in Washington, D.C. A distinct components model suggests not only that could I name these different aspects of my identity but also that they are identifiably distinct and independent components of my experience and sense of self and that it would be possible to sort out the specific impact of each aspect of my identity independently.

Can I actually look at myself physically or psychologically and point out distinct parts of me that are, for example, Chinese American, female, and urban? Is there an essential "Chinese Americanness" that would not change at all if I were male instead of female, or rural born and raised instead of urban, or Unitarian instead of Catholic? Is there an essential "femaleness" that would not be different if I were Spanish American rather than Chinese American and Jewish rather than Catholic? As Spelman writes,

> Selves are not made up of separable units of identity strung together to constitute a whole person. It is not as if there is a goddess somewhere who made lots of little identical "woman" units and then, in order to spruce up the world a bit for herself, decided to put some of those units in black bodies, some in white bodies, some in the bodies of kitchen maids in seventeenth-century France, some in the bodies of English, Israeli, and Indian prime ministers (1988, 158).

Consistent with Spelman's point, there is no psychological theory of identity development or structure that suggests that an adequate theory can be based on the idea of distinct components of group identification.

This discussion should also raise another question in your mind: If we should try to understand gender by understanding it in relation to other aspects of social identity, which ones and how many should we consider at any given time? For many writers on this subject, race is central to this discussion. Others add class or sexual orientation or age. We can also argue that religion, language, region or locale, urbanicity, and any of a wide range of other factors are central in shaping human experience and—the relevant point for our purposes here—shape the meaning of gender and the way sex/gender systems are structured and affect people. For this reason many scholars are turning to what we can call (for lack of a better term) a complex model of gender and difference in order to understand the dynamics of oppression.

The Complex Model

This view is based on the following observations. First, in the real world of human subjective experience, it is impossible for many purposes to make generalizations about women's experiences *as women*; that is, to imagine an abstract woman whose "womanness" is raceless, classless, ageless, and is based in no particular geographic place. This is largely because of a point repeated throughout the discussion thus far: Gender is a function not simply of biology but of culture and society. Gender is constructed through the arrangements of particular sex/gender systems which are themselves complex. Thus, the definition of men's and women's gender is socially constructed in a way that makes it contingent on many aspects of a person's situation.

The second important point in a complex view of gender and difference is that the other markers of social identity that are most important to take into account in understanding gender also depend on the situation. It is not reasonable to expect that every time we discuss the significance of gender we have to place it explicitly in the context of race/ethnicity, religion, class, sexual orientation, language, region, urbanicity, health status, and any of the range of other aspects of social existence that may be important in defining identity and experience. But the complex model does demand at least two things. First, any time we discuss the structure or impact of sex/gender systems or the meaning of gender, or we attempt to explore the experiences of "women," it is necessary to be very conscious of what women we are talking about and what are the limitations of the range of women encompassed by our descriptions. Second, it is important to understand that part of exploring the role of gender in people's lives is identifying the circumstances under which the role of gender is especially contingent on other specific aspects of social existence. The different types of social identification listed previously are not equally and similarly relevant to gendered experience under all circumstances.

Hierarchical Models

Some people have argued that not only are the meanings of different social statuses and identities interrelated and contingent, they are also hierarchically related. This model assumes that certain kinds of oppression are, in a sense, master oppressions and that some kinds of oppression are derivative of others. The classic example of this is the traditional Marxist view of class divisions and class oppression. The basic social division is based on property relations and the division of labor and control between the workers and the owners; all other forms of oppression flow from that. Early Marxist theorists who expressed concern with women's condition argued that there is no distinct or particular social problem that afflicted women that did not flow from class relations, and therefore to solve the class problem would lead to a solution for women (Bebel [1910] 1970). Traditional Marxist theorists also tried to explain race oppression as derived from the different class positions of the different races. As noted earlier, in the past century's history of social movements it has become commonplace for movements to declare one or another form of social division as primary and therefore prior to gender divisions.

In recent decades some theorists have again posed the idea of a hierarchy of oppressions to understand gender.[4] Two well-known attempts to do this in the early stages of the contemporary women's movement are found in Kate Millett's (1970) *Sexual Politics* and Shulamith Firestone's (1970) *Dialectic of Sex.* Firestone took the family as the fundamental unit of society and therefore saw the basic form of oppression as patriarchy, or the domination of women by men because of the domination of the father. For Firestone, racism was the domination of one race by another in a manner that follows the logic of the primary form of oppression. Kate Millett likewise made an influential (among some white women) argument that sexism is more fundamental than racism. These arguments have been widely criticized as being based in ignorance about the conditions of race and racism.

Some feminist theorists have recently argued that race should be understood as the primary social condition. Evelyn Brook Higgenbotham, for example, describes race as a meta-language with a "powerful, all-encompassing effect on the construction and representation of other social and power relations, namely, gender, class, and sexuality" (Higgenbotham 1992, 252). She argues that race "subsumes" other sets of social relations. This formulation, like the traditional Marxist approach and Firestone's and Millett's arguments, is based in a world view that is derived from a particular location in social and historical space, oversimplifying social relations, and ignoring the dependence of social meaning on situation. Gender relations are not equally linked with race relations in all circumstances. Both race relations and gender relations (and, for that matter, class relations) have different importance and meaning in different historical, national, and cultural settings. Different societies don't even categorize races and classes in the same way. It is certainly true that race can and often does serve as a meta-language for social relations, just as gender sometimes does. But neither race nor gender is the essential "master" language of oppression in all times, cultures, and circumstances.

To summarize, theorists have used different perspectives to try to understand the social bases of oppression. This book is based on the complex model, assuming that it is necessary to integrate understanding gender with other types of social relations and that these relationships are variable. Social phenomena that may seem at first to be entirely based on gender relations are in fact also based on other social divisions; those that may seem to be based on race or class are often also based on gender. Let us look at two examples: sexual violence and slavery.

Exemplifying Complexity: Gender, Race, Sexuality, and Violence

Rape would seem at first to offer a clear example of a form of oppression or violence based solely on gender. Slavery would seem at first to offer a clear example of a form of oppression or violence based solely on race. But in fact, for a complete understanding of rape it is necessary to look beyond gender, and for a complete understanding of slavery it is necessary to look beyond race.

Gender is a crucial determinant of the degree to which women are regarded and treated as sex and rape objects, but their race, ethnicity, class, and whether they are recent immigrants are also important. The lower a woman's status is by almost any measure, the more likely she is to be a target of sexual violence. Some examples of how this works follow.

Bell hooks (1981) offers a powerful analysis of the intertwined effects of race and gender on sexual oppression. Rape was an integral part of the female slave experience beginning with the sea voyage, during which the slavers did what they could to break the Africans' spirits and make them passive and compliant. For the women this process included rape. Neither race nor gender alone accounts for the experience of slavery because, "While racism was clearly the evil that had decreed black people would be enslaved, it was sexism that determined that the lot of the black female would be harsher, more brutal than that of the black male slave" (hooks 1981, 43; see also Jennings 1990). Women were subjected to slavery because of their race, but they were also used as sexual objects and as breeders because of their sex. The same was true for the Indians held as slaves in the Southwest (Mirandé and Enríquez 1979). There are many other situations in which rape is clearly dependent not just on gender, but on the race, ethnic, or class relations between perpetrator and victim. Susan Brownmiller's (1975) argument that rape has often been used as a tactic of war and imperialism depends on recognizing that rape does not occur just because of gender and sexual relations. The massive and systematic use of rape in Serbia against Muslim women in 1992–93 during the civil war that followed the breakup of Yugoslavia offers only a recent example in a long history.

Gender played other roles in differentiating the slave experience. Bell hooks points out that an important aspect of slavery was the requirement that women do labor regarded in America as men's work. Male slaves were less often subjected to the complementary treatment of being required to do women's work (1981, 20; Mann 1989, 780).

Race and gender also combined to affect the experience of slaveowners in 19th-century America. White men could own slaves because of their race and gender. Their sex gave them the right to own property (married women could not own property), and their race gave them the right to own human beings (very few nonwhites owned slaves [Schwendinger 1990]). In one sense this gender difference among whites is little more than a technical nicety; white women had great power over their husband's slaves. Moreover, because during the Civil War about three-quarters of white Southern men were in the military, wives had to take over the management of plantations, including the slaves. Drew Gilpin Faust's historical analysis shows that many of these women were especially uncomfortable with this role and were caught in a web of conflicting social norms. They lived in a society based on violence, in which white people could hold black people in bondage and enforce their power with violence against them; on the other hand, gender norms defined women as nurturant and nonviolent (Faust 1992).

Gender distinguished among white slaveholders in one important respect: White women knew about their husband's, brothers', and sons' sexual treatment of their slaves. They knew that the children of some of the enslaved women were progeny of their "loved ones" through rape. This knowledge motivated some white women like the Grimké sisters to become abolitionists, but many others simply stored their resentment or even blamed the victimized black women. Hooks suggests another dimension to this complex picture of gender and race by speculating, "Surely it must have occurred to white women that were enslaved black women not available to bear the brunt of such intense anti-woman male aggression, they themselves might have been the victims" (1981, 38).

As Chapter 11 will discuss in more detail, blaming the victim plays an important role in all forms of sexual- and gender-based violence. But just as enslaved women were often held responsible for their own victimization, women of low-status groups, especially those perceived as alien, are often regarded as excessively sexual (and even animal-like) and thus become special targets for sexual violence and exploitation. Hooks explains that defining black women as initiators of the sexual relationships with men that were in fact rapes, whites reinforced a stereotype of black women as "sexual savages" who, in effect, could not be raped (1981, 52). The same principle applied to Hispanic and Indian women (Mirandé and Enríquez 1979). Likewise, in the late 19th and early 20th centuries native-born whites often claimed that immigrant women—Irish, Italian, Jewish, or whatever—were especially promiscuous and likely to ruin the morals of innocent American men. Young immigrant women, especially those helping to support their families, were constantly subjected to sexual harassment and exploitation and then labeled promiscuous.

These examples demonstrate that the forms of gender-based oppression and exploitation people experience depend in part on their other social characteristics and that racial/ethnic- or class-based forms of oppression and exploitation depend in part on gender (see also Hurtado 1989; Mann 1989). In fact, we can argue that the exploitation of gender relations is often a means of enforcing other types of oppression. Some examples from the legal control of sexuality and marriage follow.

The state's control over marriage and sexual relations gives it leverage to pursue many different goals. (This will be further discussed in Chapter 11.) Among these is the preservation of particular racial or ethnic hierarchies. In order to preserve a particular racial/ethnic social order, societies must ensure that different races or ethnic groups cannot intermarry or develop the mutual loyalty and commitment owed to intimates and family members. Thus nations with an apartheid history, such as the United States and South Africa, declared miscegenation, or racial intermarriage, illegal in that era.

Laws against interracial sexual relations or marriage may seem to fall equally on the shoulders of women and men, and on those of different races or ethnic groups, but in fact they do not. Higher-status men, however defined, tend to have sexual rights over lower-status women, or at least they are not punished as severely as their partners in interracial sexual contact. In the American past, sexual relations between white women and nonwhite men were punished more severely than relations between white men and nonwhite women. The first American antimiscegenation law, passed in 1664 in Maryland, declared that a white woman who had sexual relations with an enslaved black male must herself become a slave. No such law applied to white men who had sexual relations with enslaved black women.

We also can see these dynamics not just through law but in the way societies have often treated mixed -race, -ethnicity, or even -class couples and their babies. If a low-status female becomes pregnant by a high-status male, it has little effect on their relative status. Patriarchal ideology keeps the male in control; if the woman makes too many claims he can abandon and reject her with relatively little social cost, partly because he can accuse her of promiscuity. A situation involving a low-status male and a high-status female is very different. For example, a baby of mixed-race parentage born to a white woman has been regarded as a "pollution" of the white race. Because women are regarded as the property of male protectors in a patriarchal society, a nonwhite male who has sexual relations with a white woman is ultimately seen as taking something from white men. The effects of this dual system of racial and sexual oppression lasted long after the end of slavery. The rape of a white woman by a nonwhite man has usually been treated by white society as the most serious type of heterosexual rape, whereas rape of a nonwhite woman by a white man has not often been regarded as rape at all. False charges of rape of white women were often used as excuses for lynching African American men.

Almost a generation ago, women's studies researchers began to emphasize the need to take gender into account to understand important social issues. In recent years they have been demanding yet more sophistication and argue that gender analysis is not complete without integrating it with an understanding of other structural bases of social life. Maxine Baca Zinn offers a good example in her writing on the family and poverty (1989). She shows that efforts to understand and solve the problems of poverty are doomed to failure if we look only at culture or race and class structures or gender structures. Society and social relations are constructed of all of these.

Some Sketches of Unity and Diversity

This chapter has focused on general questions of comparison, commonality, and difference across different social groups. Let us now briefly look at some problems raised in considering the relationship between gender and a few specific categories of social relations, including age, class, race/ethnicity and geographic community. Among those topics that will receive more detailed attention later are religion (Chapter 7), sexual orientation (see Chapter 11), marital status (see Chapter 11), maternal status (see Chapter 12), and employment status (see Chapter 13). Once again, the point at this stage of the discussion is not to *describe* different groups of women, but to underscore some of the analytical issues that will help us explore the commonalities and differences in women's lives later.

Age

When we discuss the problems and roles of "women," it is important to remember that we are talking about experiences that have special relevance for women of some ages, while we may be neglecting those especially important for women of other ages. More specifically, like the society around us, women's studies has tended to devote more attention to the young than the old and to engage unconsciously in age-specific generalizations. For example, in arguing that an important aspect of the way women are treated in society is that they are viewed by men as sex objects, we must also be aware of the severe age basis of cultural definitions of sexuality and beauty. There is not as booming a market for middle-aged or older models as there is for adolescents and women in their twenties.

Until recently, when social scientists turned to older women, the topics that seemed to come to mind were middle-aged depression and menopause, widowhood and the "empty nest" and poverty. These are important topics, but they are not the only aspects of older women's lives.

Older women's lives offer important illustrations of the workings of gender ideology because they do not fulfil dominant cultural definitions of femininity.[5] Older women are not treated as sex objects because American culture defines attractive females as young. Most have no dependent children. Their lives, much less likely than younger women's, revolve around men because of gender differences in life expectancy. Although the aged suffer from dependencies due to health and financial circumstances, in one sense older women are among the most self-reliant of people; they are the Americans most likely to live on their own. Regardless of how women spend their younger adult years, there comes a time in most women's lives when they do not conform to some of the stereotypes of womanhood and femininity because these are built around age-specific norms.

Because older women do not easily fit into traditional definitions of womanhood, they are often viewed as though they are not real women but a kind of third sex (somewhere between male and female) or, worse, sexless. Many women react to menopause not just with the common anxiety most of us feel when confronted with the realization of our aging and mortality, but also with depression over a loss of femininity. What does it mean that women are defined in such a way that any woman who lives out a normal lifespan will come to a point when she no longer seems to be a real "woman"? A parallel problem affects men, although not to the same degree. For example, the term *old man* is used as an epithet to indicate that a man is weak and not in command—in other words, not masculine enough. Degrading treatment of older people is based primarily on age but also on gender norms.

Old age can release women from some of the problems they faced when younger. In some cultures women gain respect and power only with age. Although the structure of American families has changed as people have become more geographically mobile, the matriarch of a family is still often regarded as the center of the extended kinship network and the person who defines and holds the family together. Women often feel they gain some gender-based and sexual freedom as they grow older. Many find their sense of sexual enjoyment increases when they no longer need worry about getting pregnant. The period of life often defined as the "empty nest" is also a time when women no longer have to balance their interests and pursuits against the demands of dependent children. Many women also readily admit, at least to each other, that they feel freer to act, speak, and dress as they wish because they feel less pressure to conform to the stereotypes of femininity.

Old-age interest groups such as the Grey Panthers, long led by Maggie Kuhn, and the women's movement in general have sought changes in the material and cultural conditions of older women. In recent decades the material condition of older Americans has improved to some degree, at least relative to what has happened to younger people and children. There are still many issues that need to be resolved, especially with respect to health and housing. Some problems will become worse as the proportion of retired people in the population increases, thus increasing the financial burden on the young and middle aged. The even more difficult battle is against cultural stereotypes and social relations among people of different ages. It is not polite to refer to someone as an old woman or man because *old* has many negative connotations. When someone says "I am old," it is likely said in a tone of defeat. Instead, we use such euphemisms as *senior citizen*, *golden ager*, *mature*, or perhaps *aging* or *older*. It will take much work to make *old* a proud word.

Class

Assessing the effects of class on women's lives is difficult because most definitions of *class* are gender biased. People's "class background," the class with which they are identified when they are children, is usually defined according to the status of their father's occupation. People's adulthood class definition depends on their gender. For men we usually refer to the status of their occupation. This is also true for single women. Jobs can be categorized in several ways. Most analyses use a variation on the basic framework of blue-collar, white-collar, and professional or managerial occupations. But married women's class is usually defined by their husband's occupation. Even if we wanted to define married women's class by their own occupations, the work that a very large proportion of women do—homemaking—is not defined as having a class ranking of its own. Moreover, because wives usually have lower-status, less-well-paid jobs than their husbands, does it make sense to say that in most families women have lower class standing than their husbands do? Or should we argue, as many have, that women's

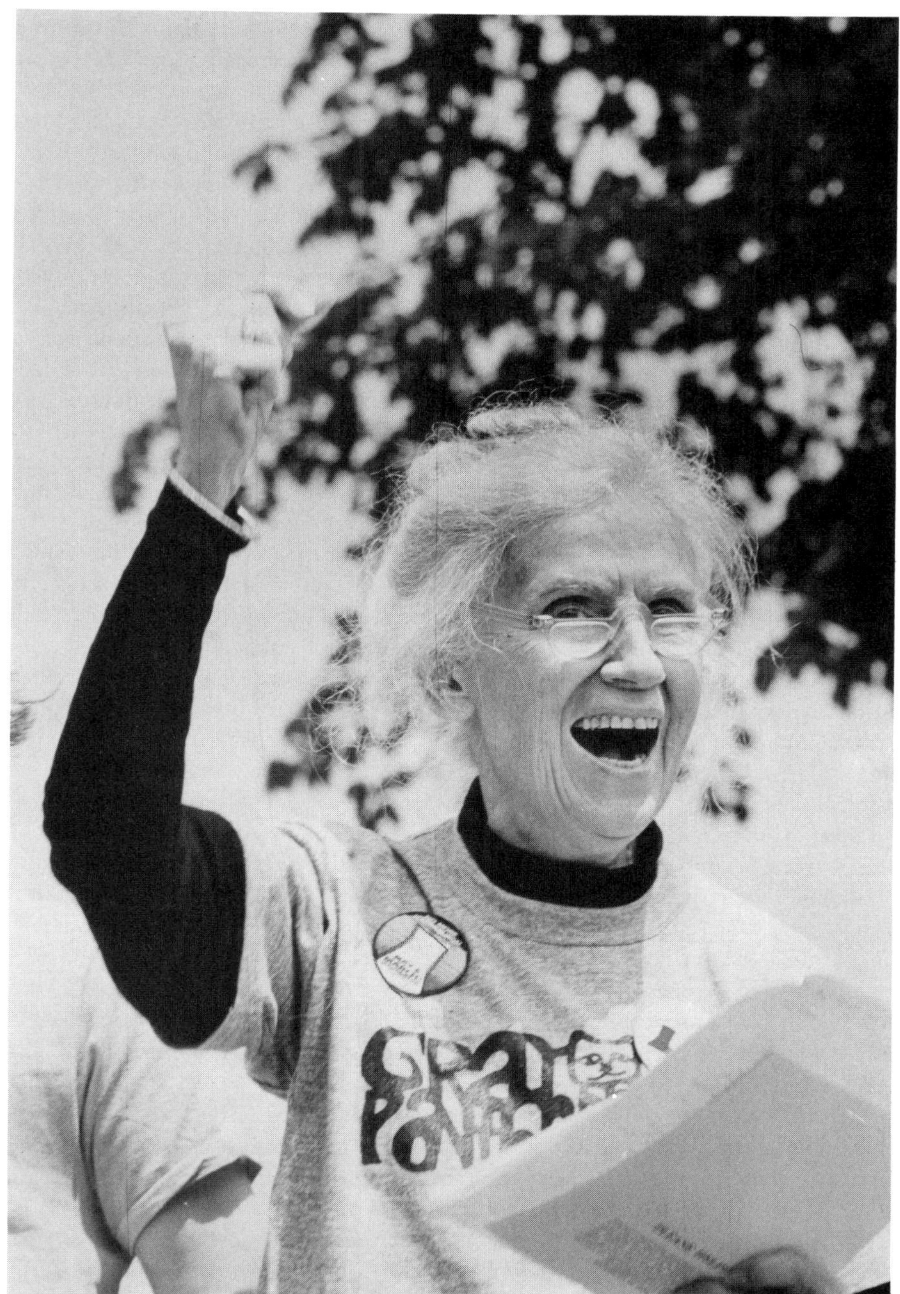

Maggie Kuhn, leader of the Gray Panthers.

class standing is usually derivative of their father's or husband's? Should class be defined according to the structure of one's own labor? What kinds of arguments underpin the idea that we should use different definitions to identify women's and men's class standing?

These definitional problems highlight some important points about the nature of women's social roles and status. As Roslyn K. Feldberg and Evelyn N. Glenn (1979) have argued, whereas men's status and economic worth are defined largely by their work, women's status and economic worth are defined by their marital status and, if they are married, by their husband's work. Women's employment is defined as secondary to their family roles, which is the reason a married woman's class status is often judged by her husband's work even if she is employed. Women's domestic work is not defined as real work, or at least not the kind that shapes her place in socioeconomic and class relations.

If we think of class in terms of wealth and control over economic resources, we find again that women's class status is determined somewhat differently from men's. It is much more vulnerable to change and depends more on family relationships. Regardless of the wealth of the family in which women were raised, women are much more vulnerable to a descent into poverty than men are. Chapter 13 will go into more detail on this point and the related issue of the feminization of poverty. Women's responsibility for children and their experiences after divorce have more effect on their economic well-being than on men's.

The usual class definitions of occupations are not adequate to inform us about the nature of women's work, and they obscure some of the most important aspects of the structure of women's work and its function in the economic system and economic relations. Traditional categorizations of class distinguish among farm, blue-collar, white-collar, business/managerial, and professional work, but they mask the gender-based divisions of labor within these categories. Because women's roles do not fit neatly into class designations developed with men's work in mind, many feminist scholars add a category that crosses all the others and refers to women's work: pink-collar or auxiliary service work. Unpaid housewives, blue-collar service workers, pink-collar clerical workers, and professionals in traditional women's occupations such as nursing and social work are included within these terms. These efforts to construct new definitions have provoked controversy (Abbott and Sapsford 1988). Examining the concept of class as it applies to women reveals how important gender is in governing social and economic relations.

Despite the difficulty of developing an adequate definition of class, many people have fruitfully used different definitions to probe commonalities and differences in the gender-based experiences of women. Once again, generalizations about women that are not class-conscious are often also class biased. When we say that "women" are increasingly entering the labor market we are not referring to the poorest women; they have always had to work for pay to survive, even if much of their work has been illegal (such as prostitution) or black market labor. Women breaking into traditionally male middle-class jobs have received more attention than those in traditionally male working-class jobs, and less progress has been made in the latter than in the former.

Research by Theodore Caplow and Bruce A. Chadwick (1979) offers an interesting picture of class-based changes in women's roles during the 20th century. In 1929 and 1937, sociologists Robert Lynd and Helen Lynd published two influential books based on studies of life in "Middletown," a fictional name for Muncie, Indiana. Caplow and Chadwick's research examined some of the differences between white working- and middle-class women in Middletown in 1978 against the backdrop of the Lynds' findings in the 1920s. They found that many changes had occurred in half a century, one of the most notable being the convergence in the lives of working- and middle-class women.

In the 1920s working-class women did much more domestic labor than middle-class women did. Middle-class women did very little washing and ironing, and they did less sewing, mending, and baking than working-class women did. In 1924, 95% of the working-class women but only 10% of the middle-class women had no paid help in the home; 33% of the middle-class women and none of the working-class women had full-time paid help.

The picture was very different 50 years later, largely because of the increase in the amount of domestic labor done by middle-class women. By 1978 working- and middle-class women did essentially equivalent amounts of housework, including each of the tasks mentioned earlier. In the 1970s women, especially middle-class women, did more laundry than they did earlier in the century, and they were more likely to bake bread than they had been earlier. In 1978, 91% of working-class women and 83% of middle-class women had no paid domestic help; 1% of both middle-class and working-class women had full-time help. Caplow and Chadwick also found there was no longer any difference in the educational aspirations middle- and working-class women had for their children. Surprisingly, perhaps, especially for those who romanticize the traditional family, both mothers and fathers reported spending more time with their children in 1978 than they did in the 1920s.

Scholars have painted many different pictures of working-class women's lives. In some cases, working-class women appear as oppressed members of the most patriarchal kinds of families (Rubin 1976), and in others they are brave, tough people with magnificent coping reactions (Seifer 1976). Most people who discuss class and gender emphasize the differences among women of different classes. Some of these are profound. But just as the effects of class are sometimes ignored, they can also be exaggerated.

Race and Ethnicity

It might seem that race is easier to analyze than class because it should be easier to define. Any appearance of simplicity, however, is a pernicious illusion. As Michael Banton (1983) shows in his history of racial definition, different societies at different times vary considerably in how they define race. Race is not a biological classification, even though it is built around biological characteristics such as parentage or skin pigmentation. It is a social category defined by cultural norms.

A few brief examples illustrate how elusive the concept of race is. Some cultures define Jews as a race, others do not. At one time most Hispanic leaders in the United States objected to being categorized as a race distinguished from "white," but by the late 1970s many Hispanic leaders wished to be regarded as a distinct race. Even so, this demand is made only by some people of Latin American ancestry. A very large proportion of American blacks are descended from the union of white slave masters of European ancestry with black slaves of African ancestry. The children of a black-white union have generally been regarded as black even if their gene pools come from white parentage as much as black. Today there is a movement in some multiracial families to allow their children to define themselves as "biracial" rather than forcing them to identify with only one of their parents. As in other cases in which one race is regarded as inferior to another, it takes only a small fraction of the blood of the lower-status race for an individual to be treated as a part of that race. Thus the relevance of race to an individual's life is ultimately determined not by biology but by how societies deal with a clue that biology gives them.

Ethnicity is an even more subjective cultural concept, especially in a society in which there is a relatively high degree of intermarriage. Ethnicity is largely, although not entirely, defined by the nationality of one's forebears, often buttressed by differences in religion or language.

The history of African American women is especially revealing of the nature of sex/gender systems in America because of the way in which they have been caught in a cross fire of demands based on the interplay of gender and racial politics. Their lives and experiences defy dominant stereotypes of femininity. They have worked at hard physical labor, and they have been the primary breadwinners in their families in larger proportions than is true for most other groups of American women. These aspects of black women's lives have often served as the basis for accusations that black women "emasculate" black men (Collins 1989b). Bonnie Dill reminds us that

> it is a cruel irony that the black woman's role as a worker has been used to represent dominance over and emasculation of black men. This predisposition ignores both historical and socioeconomic realities. Black workers were brought to this country for two economic reasons: to work and to produce workers. Although they were valued for their reproductive function, as were white women settlers, it was only of equal importance to their labor (1979, 550).

Black women have been exploited by white society for their ability to depart from feminine roles and slapped down by the same society for attempting to conform to the dominant norms of femininity.

As the realities of black women's experiences are finally being examined more extensively, they are also serving as the basis for a new symbolism and mythology. Just as African Americans have become the American symbol of poverty and oppression, in feminist and black writing the African American woman has become the symbol of strength against odds, the wonder woman. Although pride in the history and strength of black women has taken too long to arrive, turning black women into romantic symbols has its dangers. Bell hooks is wary of these romantic interpretations of black women's history, claiming that "they ignore the reality that to be strong in the face of oppression is not the same as overcoming oppression, that endurance is not to be confused with transformation" (1981, 6). The romanticizing of any women's lives, however, and especially their oppression, can lead to complacency.

White women sometimes use black women as symbols for their own purposes. Hooks points out an irony in this treatment:

> When the women's movement was at its peak and white women were rejecting the role of breeder, burden bearer, and sex object, black women were celebrated for their unique devotion to the task of mothering; for their "innate" ability to bear tremendous burdens; and for their ever-increasing availability as sex objects (1981, 6).

Hooks also points out that although white feminists have rarely devoted much effort to learning about or from black women's lives, they have long used the analogy of black oppression and struggle to underscore the oppression of women, sometimes to excess. "A white woman who has suffered physical abuse and assault from a husband or lover, who also suffers poverty, need not compare her lot to that of a suffering black person to emphasize that she is in pain" (hooks 1981, 142).

Women's experiences in America cannot be understood without reference to both race and sex. This includes understanding the role of race in white women's lives. Women who are not white have had to be more conscious of their race because in a white-dominant society those who are not white are defined more by their race. Indeed, even in scholarly books it is rare to refer to an African American, a Hispanic American, an Asian American, or a Native American unless one means to say something about race. Whites are allowed to forget their race. But that doesn't mean that race is unimportant in their lives.

Geography and Culture

Any student of American history knows that one of the most important sources of division has been geography. American history is marked by economic and political struggles for power between, for example, different regions of the country and between urban and rural interests. There are obvious differences between living in rural Nebraska and living in New York City (although, no doubt, there are many unfounded stereotypes as well). Despite great geographic mobility and the pervasiveness of the mass media, the regions of the country continue to differ considerably in economic structure, culture, and demography.

One of the interesting aspects of American women's history is the regional variation. Some of the differences are obvious. The story of women under slavery is a story of the South, the story of 19th-century immigrant women working in sweatshops is a story primarily of the Northeast. Parts of the country found it in their interest to encourage women to be property holders, while others didn't. The territory of Oregon, for example, offered single women settlers (but not single men) a large parcel of free farmland because it was thought that would encourage both men and women to settle and develop the territory. The Midwest was relatively quick to develop coeducational higher education, first at private colleges such as Oberlin in Ohio and Lawrence in Wisconsin, and then at the public land-grant colleges that are now state universities.

Observers sometimes exaggerate regional variation and sometimes minimize it. Life in the Old South (including gender norms) was undoubtedly different from that in other parts of the country. But the stereotype of the white Southern belle is an overdrawn portrait that historians have labored to correct. Most white Southern women were not ladies of the manor; they were farm women. For most Southern white men the ideal wife was not in fact a delicate lady, but a woman who could help run farm and family (Hagler 1980). Regardless of region the ideal of the lady was a luxury only the wealthy could afford. In her history of Southern women, Anne Firor Scott (1970) focuses on the much-neglected story of women who became involved in politics and struggles for change. Gerda Lerner's (1971) biography of the Grimké sisters, who devoted themselves to abolition and women's rights, shows the determination of these women to fight against a system their own family helped perpetrate. Nina Silber's fascinating history of the immediate post–Civil War era shows that Northern and Southern antagonisms were played out in highly gendered terms, in which Northerners redefined their images of the sexuality and gender of Southern men and women to "define their regional distinctiveness and, in the aftermath of the war, to establish their regional and political superiority" (Silber 1989, 634). White Southerners' masculinity and femininity came to be seen as corrupt and dishonorable.

Most women's studies scholars now accept the charge that the field has been dominated by the experiences of middle-class white women. Less well recognized is a charge articulated by Southern scholars such as Jacquelyn Dowd Hall: Women's studies is "New Englandized," or based largely on the experiences and perspectives of women from the Northeast. Hall points out that the interpretive framework used most often for American women's history

> turned on the industrial revolution, which, beginning in the 1830s, severed work from life, the public from the private sphere, and transformed the household from a unit of production to a woman-dominated haven from a heartless world. Women lost their productive roles but gained access to education and a conviction of moral superiority. Above all they acquired the sense of grievance and group identity that would inspire them to form voluntary associations, oppose slavery, and launch a movement for women's rights (1989, 904).

This story is not exclusively of the Northeast, but it is certainly not an adequate rendition of conditions in the South of that period.

Comparing women in urban and rural settings offers another example of the way in which attention to commonalities and differences among women helps create a more complete picture of the meaning of gender in America. Certainly the growth of cities and development of suburbs changed the structure and effects of gender roles (Hayden 1981). Experts in policy and planning are coming to realize that the structure and design of communities has a special impact on women because of their gender roles and that women's needs must be given more attention in, for example, urban planning ("Women and the American City" 1980).

Although cities are often the base of progressive attitudes and social change, we should not exaggerate the differences. We already have seen that the 19th-century cult of domesticity, which counterposed the rough and tumble world of male commerce with the serene woman's domain of the home, or the Victorian-era image of the frail, swooning lady, had little relevance to—indeed, could provoke economic disaster in—the farmlands. Some of the almost entirely agricultural midwestern states were among the first to grant women the right to vote.

One other type of cultural and geographic division among women should be considered. Although this book is about the United States, it is important to know whether the evidence provided by the American experience is similar to that found in other countries and what aspects of the American experience are unique to this society. The question of how much change has occurred and how much change can occur is a relative one. How do the types and degrees of change that have occurred in the United States compare with those that have occurred elsewhere? It is impossible to make more than a few brief comments here, but these will indicate directions for further inquiry.

This chapter has consistently emphasized two crucial points in considering diversity among women and the relationship between gender and other social divisions. First, we should not take the experience of some women and generalize to all women. Second, people tend to generalize from their own experiences without realizing it. This is certainly the case with national differences. Throughout this book there will be comparisons with situations in other nations in order to help us understand the particular case we are looking at—the United States—more clearly.

If we read through the literature on women of the various social sciences, the tendency to overgeneralize is noticeable. Sociologists studying specific American communities speak of "the" relationship between class or race and gender without noting that what they see is conditioned by the specific history and structure of the country they are studying. Psychologists probably are most likely of all to make no reference to the national setting of their research, assuming that if we do "good" research we can claim our work is representative of "people" in general. History, social structures, the particular design of the state, and the place of that state in the global order make a difference in human meaning and social relations.

Conclusion: Learning from Difference

Doing good social science research on women involves two seemingly contradictory tasks. The first is to be able to make some nontrivial statements about what we know about women, their lives and experiences. The reason to look specifically at women is to claim there is something that makes them a collectivity, distinct from men, which implies some commonality. But the second task is not to seek false commonality and, especially, not to comprehend women in such a way that makes some women represent all women in our minds. Recall the problem of representation that opened this book; the argument of feminists has long been that men have been taken to represent humanity as a whole. The problem here is to make sure that in the study of women in the United States, white, middle-class women (and perhaps those who are urban, Northern, and Christian) are not taken to represent American women as a whole.

People have a tendency to generalize from their own experience, so it is no surprise that scholarship dominated by one or another social group tends to generalize from its own standpoint. Psychologists also find that where we find social divisions, no matter how trivial, people tend to see exaggerated differences between the two and to see their own group as more complex and differentiated than the other group. The first cognitive habit would tend to make us minimize differences from our own experience, the second would make us maximize differences between "us" and "them" and trivial differences among "them." We can see all of these effects in research on women and gender.

Writing on commonality and difference among women sometimes exaggerates commonality, sometimes difference. Certainly the exact experiences of different groups of women are quite different in detail, but as we have seen there can be important parallels, or we can see where differences emerge because of a common rule that is being applied to them. Even now, as writers engage in what they see as sensitivity to difference, they can still overgeneralize. It is simply not adequate to generalize about gender relations in "white, middle-class" America as though religion and ethnicity make no difference, for example. We cannot generalize about the gender relations among Native Americans; the different nations have different structures, cultures, and histories (Bonvillain 1989). "Hispanic" and "Asian American" mask large differences in national heritage. Nor can we confound the historical inheritance and situation faced by "African Americans" whose families arrived recently from the West Indies and those whose families came from the slaveholding South or those raised in Southern rural versus Northern urban communities.

In recent years, women's studies writers have tended to emphasize differences among women, especially on the basis of race and sexuality. Many feminist theorists are now arguing that the dominance of "difference talk" threatens the very ability to say anything analytically or politically about women and gender (Gordon 1991). We can say this: To capture human existence, even only the female part of it, in all of its truly human variety and detail is to be able to say nothing about groups and be able to do nothing for or on behalf of a group.

To capture human existence, or only the female part of it, only in its specific commonality, is to misunderstand the nature of the group.

NOTES

1. This phrase is a play on the title of an influential book and movie, *Black Like Me* (Griffin 1961), in which a white man disguised himself as black and learned how profound a difference race makes.
2. I have made up these different names to distinguish among general tendencies that emerge from reading in this area; none of these are self-conscious "schools" of thought.
3. For this reason, one of the first major books on black women's studies was named *All the Women Are White, All the Blacks Are Men, But Some of Us Are Brave* (Hull, Scott, and Smith 1982).
4. Spelman embeds what I am calling a hierarchical model in her discussion of the additive model. The additive model does not logically imply a hierarchy of oppressions, thus I discuss them separately.
5. Older women are defined here as at least 60 years old.

PART TWO

Gender-Defining Institutions

IN THIS SECTION we take a closer look at some social institutions and organizations whose primary function is defining cultural norms, the values through which we understand ourselves, other people, and the world in which we live. We focus on educational and health-care institutions, organized religion, the mass and cultural media of communication, and government.

Each chapter examines the ways in which these institutions define, create, maintain, and change gender norms and sex/gender systems. The chapter on education, for example, shows how gender norms are taught in educational institutions, while the chapter on health care shows how definitions of health and health-care practices shape and are shaped by definitions of gender. We explore how these institutions shape women's lives and the influence women have had on these institutions. In looking at women's influence we, of course, focus on women's leadership positions within these institutions as, for example, clergy, doctors, teachers, and government officials, but also look at the kinds of influence women have had as community and family members. In this way we will see that although women's power has been limited by androcentric sex/gender systems, women also have had much more scope for shaping their own and others' lives than is often realized.

Although it is an underlying theme throughout this section, the most important norm-defining institution, the family, does not have its own chapter here. Instead, because of the importance of understanding families as social institutions when studying gender, and especially, women, each chapter devotes considerable attention to the family. Part Three will focus directly and intensively on women and the family.

Reflect Before You Read

1. Think about the education you have had up to this point, including, if applicable, your religious training. What did you learn about women? About

men? Did your education give you any hints or guidelines about what it should mean to you that you were born male or female? If you had been born of the other sex, how might your education have been different?

2. Enjoy yourself this week. Watch television, go to the movies or a play, read a novel or a poem, listen to music on the radio, watch MTV, or watch a sporting event. What do you see women and men doing? What are their characteristics? What do these entertainments teach you about women and men, femininity and masculinity?
3. The vast majority of members of state legislatures, the U.S. House of Representatives, and the U.S. Senate are men. Why is this? What would it take for more women to get elected? Imagine for a moment that most members of these institutions were women. What difference would it make? Why do so many people think that politics is "men's business"?

5

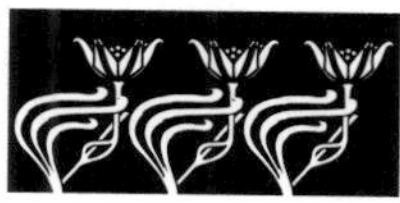

Education: Learning to Be Male and Female

EDUCATION HAS BEEN a central focus of women seeking to improve their condition and raise their status for well over two centuries. Some of the reasons should be obvious. Education imparts skills that create options for individuals in economic, social, and political life. It is an instrument for attaining high-status positions. Education earns respect. The educational system is also one of the most important definers of gender norms and one of the most important institutional components of a sex/gender system. No wonder so many women have fought for education when it was denied to them. We look first at the historical evolution of women's education, then at the relationship between gender and the contemporary American educational system.

Historical Perspectives on Women's Education

We begin with three premises:

1. To think of education only as what happens in school buildings on weekdays from early autumn to late spring is to ignore much of what has constituted education, especially women's education, during most of history.
2. Observers and theorists of education have long recognized that the substance and process of education impart far more than the three R's or even what we generally think of as school subjects. It also helps shape people's values and ways of living in society.
3. For most of modern history, education has been designed to help children find their "place" in society. Their "place," and thus their education, has been defined partly by their gender.

Early Efforts

Until the 19th century, relatively few people had formal education of any sort. Most people learned what they needed to know by trial and error or from someone more experienced. Trades and other work were learned by apprenticeship or from parents or other relatives. Mothers and fathers passed their skills and knowledge on to their daughters and sons. Women taught women what they "needed" to know, and men taught men what they "needed" to know. For those who attained literacy the only textbook was frequently the Bible, for that was the only book people "needed" to read.

Formal education was largely restricted to the wealthy and well connected, generally the men of the upper class. Formal education was considered irrelevant for most free citizens, and dangerous and even illegal for the enslaved. With few exceptions, education for upper-class women was confined to a bit of literature, a bit of music, and perhaps a bit of foreign language, all taught at home. The purpose of this education was to train the woman for her station. She should be pretty, witty, and, above all, a good complement to her husband.

The first American battle over women's education revolved not around schooling per se but around whether women should write and speak and what they should write and say, especially with respect to religion. In colonial America, women were active as religious teachers, but they faced severe restrictions. In 1637, for example, "A synod of elders resolved that women might meet 'to pray and edify one another,' but when one woman 'in a prophetical way' resolved questions of doctrine and expounded Scripture, then the meeting was 'disorderly'" (Koehler 1982, 41). Women could preach, but only to each other, and they could teach only thoughts derived from their husband's or minister's thoughts. Those who went too far posed a danger to social order and even to their own sanity. In 1645 Governor John Winthrop of Massachusetts wrote that Anne Hopkins, the wife of Connecticut's governor, had gone insane because she spent too much time writing and reading. Her sanity might have been saved had she "attended her household affairs, and such things as belong to a woman" (Koehler 1982, 37).

Perhaps the most famous battle over women's education during the colonial period was waged between Anne Hutchinson and the religious authorities of the Massachusetts Bay Colony. Although the strict Massachusetts colony dealt harshly with all cases of suspected heresy, part of the reason offered by the authorities for excommunicating and banishing Hutchinson was that her teaching activities stepped beyond the bounds of women's proper role.

As Chapter 2 showed, Enlightenment theorists emphasized the development of rationality and knowledge as the keys to a better and more democratic future. To create a new kind of society based on reason, individual merit, independence, competition, and achievement required creating individuals who would fit into that society. But should women and men—could they—be educated in the same way? The theoretical debates began in Europe.

Some theorists of education such as Jean-Jacques Rousseau (1712–1778) thought that men should be educated in reason and independence to enable them to carry on the major work of society. But Rousseau and others thought that extending this education to women would be counterproductive because women's tasks were to get married, be submissive and ornamental to their husbands, raise their children, and do or supervise the necessary domestic work. Other theorists, like Mary Wollstonecraft in England and the Marquis de Condorcet (1743–1794) in France, argued that the values of a liberal society must also extend, at least in some degree, to women. They agreed that most women would be primarily wives and mothers, but they couldn't imagine how women could be proper companions to these "new men" or be fit mothers to their children if they themselves had not learned reason and independence of mind.

This debate also raged in the new American republic. What kinds of men and women are needed in this new country? How should they be trained? Liberal European ideas on education had great influence in America, and, as in Europe, some included and some excluded women. Many experts argued that it was "necessary that our ladies should be qualified to a certain degree by a peculiar and suitable education, to concur in instructing their sons in the principles of liberty and government" as educator Benjamin Rush (1745–1813) did in his address to the Young Ladies Academy, established in Philadelphia in 1786 as the first American school for girls (Kerber 1982, 91). Women should be good "republican mothers" able to educate the sons of liberty, hardly a radical view in our eyes, but in the 1780s it was a significant move forward.

That women should be educated for motherhood was not a new view, but the conception of what type of education would accomplish this was changing. An intellectual leader like Rush probably knew that the verb *educate* is derived from a word meaning "to rear." Most of all he and others realized that all mothers are teachers and are involved in education regardless of their own schooling.

Some were more radical. Judith Sargent Murray (1751–1820), writing as "Constantia," was one of many women arguing that as long as women's education was aimed at producing wives and mothers, it would create dependent people rather than the independent people required by a republic. She was also one of the first American feminists declaring that females and males do not *naturally* have different characteristics but, rather, are *shaped* to be different. In one of her most famous passages she asked her readers,

> Will it be said that the judgement of a male of two years old is more sage than that of a female's of the same age? I believe the reverse is generally observed to be true. But from that period on what partiality! how is the one exalted and the other depressed, by the contrary modes of education which are adopted! the one is taught to aspire, the other is early confined and limited! (Rossi 1988, 19.)

Others were even more direct. In her 1793 graduation speech at the Young Ladies Academy, Pamela Mason made a charge that was remarkably similar to Wollstonecraft's of the previous year: "Our high and mighty Lords . . . have denied us the means of knowledge, and then reproached us for the want of it" (Kerber 1982, 87).

Despite these arguments, women gained little formal education in those early days. They continued to teach each other and to learn informally at home and in church. That many women learned despite the lack of formal opportunities is evidenced by the number of women writers. Even during colonial days some women joined their husbands in publishing newspapers and took over when their husbands died. Many women also submitted their writings to newspapers, often under assumed names (a practice also employed by men). We still read the poems of women such as Anne Bradstreet (1612–1672) and Phyllis Wheatly (1753?–1784), one of the first black American poets. Mercy Otis Warren (1728–1814) was the first historian of the American Revolution, and the letters of her friend Abigail Adams, wife of President John Adams, remain examples of the prolific writings of many early American women. Finally, women continued to learn trades and skills such as millinery, midwifery, and, as we can see from the number of widows who took over their deceased husbands' businesses, business and accounting.

Expanding Access

More formal educational opportunities for women opened up in the 1830s and 1840s. As free public schools were founded, especially in the Northeast, girls joined boys in elementary school. Public education at higher levels was available almost exclusively to boys until after the Civil War. Although the first American colleges opened their doors in the 17th century (Harvard in 1636, William and Mary in 1693), all barred women. In 1821, however, Emma Willard (1787–1870) opened the Troy Female Seminary, offering a curriculum similar to men's colleges. Willard instigated the expansion of women's educational opportunities, but in directions now considered conservative. She wished her students to be good American mothers or teachers. Her school, which still exists as the Emma Willard School, fared better than one of the first schools for black girls opened in 1833 by Prudence Crandall in Connecticut. Crandall was jailed on false charges, and her school was burned down.

The 1830s saw the beginnings of coeducational colleges. Oberlin College (Ohio) opened its doors to men and women, whites and blacks in 1832, followed in 1847 by Lawrence College (Wisconsin). Wheaton College was founded as the first women's college in 1834, followed by Mount Holyoke in 1837. The New England Female Medical College was started in 1848, followed closely by the Philadelphia Women's Medical College in 1851.

Only a tiny proportion of women went to these schools, but they had a major influence on American life. Among the earliest female college graduates we find many leaders of the post–Civil War feminist movement, as well as the first formally trained female doctors, clergy, and other professionals.

These formal schools were not the only places women taught and learned. Women continued to read and write in an effort to educate themselves and others. They organized their own study groups or seminars on many topics. In the mid-19th century, women not only met together to learn but also began to develop self-conscious feminist theories of women's education. Margaret Fuller (1810–1850), a member of the American Transcendentalist group (along with Emerson, Thoreau, and Bronson Alcott) and editor of their journal, *The Dial*, held "Conversations," or seminars, at which only women were allowed. She believed, as many feminists do today, that there must be at least some separate time and space in which women can learn among themselves, unimpeded by the hierarchical relations between the sexes.

While Fuller discussed philosophy, the classics, and other topics in the rarefied atmosphere of Boston, thousands of women across the country traded information and knowledge among themselves at quilting bees and other such gatherings. And women by no means restricted themselves to such safe, though revolutionary, activities. Despite the fact that it was illegal to teach black slaves to read, many women did so; after the Civil War women organized missionary societies that sent women throughout the South to teach newly freed blacks. Others, organized by Catharine Beecher (Harriet Beecher Stowe's sister) in the late 1840s, went west to teach on the frontiers.

By 1873, 60% of all American secondary schools had mixed-sex classes. The number of coeducational colleges increased to 22 by 1867 and 97 by 1872 (Leach 1980, 72). Although opportunities for formal education increased during this period, women's education lagged behind men's in two respects. Women still received less education than men and even if they went beyond the elementary level, their education continued to be oriented mostly toward producing good wives and mothers. Few educators thought education for females and males should be the same.

Increasing Leadership Roles

Women also gained some ground as teachers, administrators, and other shapers of education. Throughout the middle decades of the 19th century, the proportion of teachers who were women increased; in the first part of the century the vast majority were men, but by the late 1880s the majority (up to 90% in some cities) were women (Sklar 1982, 146). Some estimates suggest that by the mid 19th century, up to one-fifth of all New England women served as teachers at some point in their lives (Jones 1980, 48). Was this growth a sign of progressive enlightenment on the part of school administrators? Kathryn Kish Sklar (1982) argues that it was more a matter of practical finances. Three arguments justified paying women considerably less than men as teachers:

1. Women did not have to support families as men do.
2. Women deserved less pay because they would quit their jobs when they married.
3. Women's low salaries were merely determined by the free market; women would accept lower salaries, and so they got them.

Hiring women was a practical way of allowing mass education to grow cheaply. For women, the expansion of teaching jobs, even if they were poorly paid, meant the opening of a sector of jobs appropriate for a decent lady.

Women made less progress in entering administrative and policy-making roles, although these expanded somewhat as well. Their efforts to open their own

Mary McLeod Bethune, educator and political activist, turned a small school into what is now Bethune-Cookman College.

schools increased over time. Most of what became the "Seven Sisters" colleges (Mt. Holyoke, 1837; Vassar, 1861; Wellesley, 1870; Smith, 1871; Radcliffe, 1879; Bryn Mawr, 1880; and Barnard, 1889) were opened by women late in the last three decades of the 19th century. In 1904 Mary McLeod Bethune (1875–1955), a daughter of slaves, opened a small school for blacks in Daytona Beach, Florida. She herself had been educated by missionary teachers. She began her school using charred splinters of wood as pencils and elderberry juice as ink; she eventually turned the school into what is now Bethune-Cookman College (Bethune [1941] 1982).

Even in women's schools, however, women remained constrained by restrictive views of women's place. Emily James Putnam (1865–1944), dean of Barnard College in New York, was threatened with the loss of her job when she married. Although she survived that round, when she became pregnant she was forced to leave: Employment and marriage didn't mix well, and employment and motherhood was even worse. Until World War II most school boards demanded that women resign when they married; some wouldn't let them wait until the end of the school year. These laws finally disappeared in the mid 1950s. Such laws, if they applied only to women, would now be illegal under the 1964 Civil Rights Act.

Women's roles in shaping education also grew in other ways. In 1837 property-owning (white) widows in Kentucky with children in school were allowed to vote in school board elections. As time passed, more states and localities extended the school board vote to women because education came to be viewed as an appropriate arena for women's action. The right to vote in school board elections was followed by the right to run for school board offices (first in Illinois in 1872). By the end of the 19th century a number of women served on school boards, some even as school superintendents, across the country.

As the number of educated women rose at the end of the 19th century, they became increasingly active in trying to shape education. The number of women's clubs and organizations directed at improving education mushroomed. The 1870s saw the rise of "moral education" or "moral science" societies, groups of women who discussed among themselves topics such as sexuality, marriage, and birth control (Leach 1980). Suffrage groups and others interested in women's roles in society held lectures, seminars, and other such meetings to educate women for citizenship.

The rise of social science and the view that the knowledge gained from the social science research could help make a better society created another avenue for women's involvement in education. Women not only were active in the American Social Science Association (ASSA) but also formed their own social science associations and clubs beginning in the 1870s. As early as 1874 a leader in the ASSA argued, "The work of social science is literally women's work, and it is getting done by them more and more; but there is room for all sexes and ages in the field of social science" (Leach 1980, 316). These women's groups, which later took leading roles in the politics of the Progressive era, lobbied for educational reforms.

Many women also began to take on radical issues, as demonstrated by Dr. Alice Stockham's 1878 address to the Illinois Social Science Association. She argued that it should be obligatory "that every child should get special instruction in procreation and reproduction. Let us see to it that no girl should go to the altar of marriage without being instructed in the physiological function of maternity" (Leach 1980, 321). Margaret Sanger (1883–1960) brought education about reproductive issues to working-class women in the immigrant ghettos. Feminists were just as concerned as others about the quality of women's lives as wives and mothers, but their approach was then, as it is now, quite different from that of nonfeminists.

By the end of the 19th century a new group of women had to be considered in the design of education: immigrants and the children of immigrants. School administrators, other government officials, and a variety of women's groups, including the newly formed groups of social workers, reached a consensus: Education should help immigrant women be good American wives and mothers. Immigrant women needed to know English so that they could run their households properly and teach their children. They needed courses in household arts or home economics so that they could make proper American homes and learn to budget properly to ward off the discontent of poverty. They needed to be Americanized enough to be able to control their children and ward off juvenile delinquency. And they needed to be taught trades (appropriate for females) so that they could avoid being drawn into the "white slave trade," or prostitution, until they got married.

Special efforts devoted to the education of immigrant women had only mixed success. Much more effort was devoted to educating immigrant men. Even in public schools, overcrowding meant school officials were more willing to let girls drop out to create places for boys. The norm in the majority of immigrant families was that girls should leave school early to help support their families and put their brothers through school. Maxine Seller (1982) suggests that many of the most popular and successful programs were run by ethnic and cultural groups and churches, such as the Polish Women's Alliance of America, the Union of Czech Women, the National Council of Jewish Women; by trade unions, such as the Ladies Waist Makers Union or the International Ladies Garment Workers Union (ILGWU); or by socialist groups.

The turn of the century witnessed another development in women's education. Home economics and domestic science courses were introduced into secondary school and college curricula to teach women how to be modern housewives. The modern housewife, experts claimed, needed more than her mother's recipes to be successful; she needed firm knowledge of nutrition, psychology, sociology, and even biology and organic chemistry to run her household scientifically. If a mother was going to be nurturant and helpful to her children, she needed some advanced mathematics and even physics to help them with their homework. However, if a woman wanted a career, it should be one that fit in with her "inevitable" family commitments and could be dropped for a few years when her children needed her most. Motherhood was still woman's primary mission, but in modern times it was a subject to be studied scientifically. (For further discussion of this topic, see Chapter 12.)

Achieving Higher Education

Education for women continued to grow in the 20th century despite resistance and occasional slowdowns. Resisters worked hard to keep women back, sometimes calling on the assistance of supposedly "scientific" theories, such as

Edward Clarke's, who argued in the 1880s that if women became too educated the energy that should go to their wombs would be diverted to their brains, leaving them too feeble to produce good children. By the middle of the 20th century, the question of whether women should be educated up to the secondary level had been resolved, and the battle focused more on facilitating women's access to university education, advanced degrees, and training programs in traditionally male fields such as business and industry.

Women and men have now reached parity in the number of B.A. and M.A. degrees they earn (see Table 5-1). It is clear from these figures that progress has not been slow and steady. The proportion of women earning B.A.s increased until World War II, fell, and then increased again. Some of the drop, especially in the 1950s, can be accounted for by the fact that colleges were filled by male veterans of World War II assisted by the G.I. Bill. The year 1930 marked a high point for women earning M.A.s that was not surpassed until the 1970s. Likewise, women's share of Ph.D.s rose until 1920, then dropped until an impressive upward shift during the 1970s. The decline in the proportion of higher degrees gained by women occurred not because the absolute number of women fell but because the number of men seeking these degrees rose so steeply in a time of massive discrimination against women. Progress in the traditionally male fields of medicine, dentistry, and law began in the 1970s and has been impressive since then. The decade from 1980 to 1990 witnessed substantial change. (For further discussion of women's education today see Chapter 1.)

TABLE 5-1
Proportion of All Degrees Awarded to Women, 1890–1990

Year	*B.A.*	*M.A.*	*Ph.D.*	*Medicine (M.D.)*	*Dentistry (D.D.S.)*	*Law (L.L.D. & J.D.)*
1890	17	19	1			
1900	19	19	6			
1910	23	26	10			
1920	34	30	15			
1930	40	40	15			
1940	41	38	13			
1950	24	29	10	10	1	
1960	35	35	11	6	1	2
1970	42	40	13	8	1	5
1980	47	49	28	23	13	30
1990	53	53	36	34	31	42

Source: U.S. Bureau of the Census (1982). U.S. Department of Education (1992, 171).

The first clear legal or policy statement from the U.S. government supporting equal education and forbidding gender discrimination was written in Title IX of the Education Amendments Act of 1972 which reads, "No person in the United States shall, on the basis of sex, be excluded from participation in, be denied the benefits of, or be subjected to discrimination under any education program or activity receiving federal financial assistance." This act covers all public schools and many private ones. Do we now see gender equity in education?

Twenty years later, in 1992, the American Association of University Women published a major report (hereafter the AAUW report). The AAUW report points out that following a major study by the U.S. Department of Education in 1983 that urged the need for educational reform, at least 35 other reports by different task forces and commissions discussed the problems of education today. The AAUW noted that few women were among the leaders of these study groups and that few of the studies took gender or the problems of girls seriously. In response, the AAUW did its own study. Their conclusions are clear from the very title of the report: *How Schools Shortchange Girls.*

How Much Education?

Two questions need to be asked about the quantity of women's education: (1) Do women and men get the same amount of education? (2) Do women get the amount of education they need? These are not merely different wordings of the same question. Even if levels of education are similar for men and women, we cannot necessarily assume that women are getting the amount of education they need. To earn the same amount of money as men, for example, women need more education than men. The law requires that all children, male and female, go to school from age 5 or 6 to 16. Thus, let us look at gender comparisons in amount of preschool education and education after 16.

Education before first grade has become increasingly popular since World War II. Kindergartens and nursery schools are seen as important settings for the transition to "real school." The popularity of these programs was bolstered by the increased value placed on education in general; the growth in the number of employed mothers; and the growth of programs such as "Project Head Start" in the 1960s, which were seen as means of helping children from impoverished families "catch up." In 1967 government figures showed that about 32% of all children age 3 to 5, and a slightly higher proportion of white children, were enrolled in pre-primary education programs; in 1989 about 55% of all children were enrolled in such programs. Experts assume that roughly the same number of boys and girls are enrolled (AAUW 1992, 18).

The AAUW report shows that boys outnumber girls in special-education programs for the mentally retarded, speech impaired, emotionally disturbed, and learning disabled by a very wide margin; about two-thirds of students in special-education programs are boys. It has long been believed that more boys suffer from these problems than girls, thus explaining enrollment differences. Research now indicates that gender differences in actual incidence of these difficulties may be much smaller, which means that teachers and others may be diagnosing and treating boys and girls with similar problems differently. It may be that boys are more often incorrectly placed in these classes because they are more likely to "act out," while girls who are in need of help are not as readily identified because they are not noticed (AAUW 1992, 19–20).

The law does not require students to finish high school. Are there differences in dropout rates and characteristics? Girls are more likely to finish high school than boys, especially among African Americans. On the other hand, among those who do drop out, men are more likely to return for a GED. It is commonly believed that the main reason girls leave school is because of pregnancy; although this is true for many, 50–60% of female dropouts cite other reasons. Many more girls than boys cite other "family-related problems"; more boys than girls mention work as a reason for leaving (AAUW 1992, 48).

As Table 5-1 shows, the proportion of males and females going beyond high school has also evened out, at least to the M.A. level. Colleges and universities are not the only types of postsecondary education available; adults may also enroll in technical, vocational, business, and other kinds of training programs. Women are a majority of those enrolled in adult-education programs.

Women also get their adult education from different sources than do men. They are more likely to take courses from local schools and 2-year colleges, private tutors and instructors, or private community organizations. The courses men take are more likely to be provided by their own employers (U.S. Department of Education 1992, 345).

Women are also continuing their long tradition of educating themselves outside the school. Women's church groups, professional and labor organizations, and political and social clubs continue to hold lectures, meetings, courses, and training institutes for women to learn a wide range of subjects and skills. One of the most important functions of the new women's movement has been education. It has spawned innumerable lectures, seminars, and small informal discussion groups, as well as books, articles, newspapers, magazines, and publishing houses.

Thus far we have compared the amount of education received by boys and girls by looking at how many are sitting in what kinds of classrooms. But even when they are in the same classrooms, there is evidence that girls and boys receive different amounts of education. The AAUW report found differences as early as preschool, where teaching often focuses on competencies girls already have; thus girls may be more ignored than boys. The skills that boys may have more developed at that time and in which girls need the most encouragement—large-motor skills—are regarded as "free play"; thus education may not be as well balanced for the needs of girls as for those of boys (AAUW 1992, 18–20).

Teachers tend to react differently to girls and boys and have different amounts of contact with them. Numerous studies show that boys get more negative treatment or criticism from teachers, although there is contradictory evidence as well (Bank, Biddle, and Good 1980). Criticism in the classroom, however, is not necessarily harmful to education. One study (Dweck et al. 1978) found that boys get more criticism from teachers, but it is a very different kind from that which girls receive. In that study, boys were more likely to be criticized for not trying hard enough to do well, which seems to assume they could do better if they wanted. Girls were more likely to be criticized for their academic performance itself, which may be a less encouraging evaluation. Another study finds that girls, particularly black girls, get less feedback than boys do (Irvine 1986).

One study of second-graders shows that teachers made more contacts with girls during reading classes and with boys during mathematics classes (Leinhardt, Seewald, and Engel 1979). Another study suggests that girls and boys have to act differently to get the same amount of attention from their teachers (Serbin et al. 1973). In that study, girls who were physically close to their teachers received more attention than boys who were physically close; boys who were aggressive received more attention than girls who were aggressive. Perhaps that is why boys initiate more interactions with teachers than girls do (Irvine 1986). These findings support the assertion that schools provide a hidden curriculum of gender-role training. The AAUW Report cites other research showing that boys get more feedback and attention in general.

What Did You Learn in School Today?

We already have argued that schools and school curricula are designed in part to teach fundamental cultural values, including gender norms. Until the current era there was widespread consensus about the gender norms girls and boys should learn. To what degree do schools continue to teach gendered lessons? Do they still help track girls and boys into different kinds of lives, or do they prepare girls and boys to make their own choices?

Educators talk about two different types of curricula: the overt curriculum, or the lessons teachers are consciously and explicitly trying to teach, and the hidden curriculum, or things that may be taught consciously or unconsciously but are not part of the apparent lesson plan. Critics of American education argue that the hidden curriculum still strongly supports traditional gender roles and, more specifically, discourages girls who might otherwise stretch themselves beyond traditional gender boundaries in intellectual skills and interests.

Consider the content of textbooks. This book's Introduction briefly discussed the content of school curricula and showed women's very small place in what we learn in school. Even in the 19th century some educational reformers realized it was necessary to give girls examples of women who had achieved notability in a variety of fields in order to expand their ambitions and horizons (Leach 1980). In the 1970s a group of women published a study of 2,760 children's stories to demonstrate the lessons girls and boys learn about women's potential (Women on Words and Images 1972). They found females notably absent from the world presented to children. There were five boy-centered stories for every two girl-centered stories, three adult male characters for every adult female character, and six biographies of males for every biography of a female. Although males were considerably more present than females, the word *mother* appeared more often than the word *father*, and the word *wife* appeared three times as often as the word *husband*. Similar findings have emerged from studies of textbooks at the primary and secondary levels (Weitzman 1979). It does not look as though there has been much change since that time (AAUW 1992, 62).

Bias in school books is by no means limited to the primary and secondary levels. Reviews of college- and graduate-level textbooks show the same pattern. A review of medical textbooks, including those used in obstetrics and gynecology classes, shows that women are often presented in thoroughly negative terms and used gratuitously as sex objects in illustrations and examples (Scully and Bart 1973). Little changed in later years (Elder, Humphreys, and Laskowski 1988). Perhaps even more shocking if we are concerned with possibilities for change in education is Sadker and Sadker's (1980) content analysis of the most widely used education textbooks, which found the same pattern of bias. Despite all research on gender and sexism in education done in recent decades, only one book the Sadkers looked at devoted even .5 percent of its space (1 page out of 200, for example) to issues of sexism. Another book discussed guidelines for nonsexist language but did not itself follow the guidelines. A review of introductory sociology textbooks published between 1982 and 1988 also found little material on women (Hall 1988).

Does this bias in textbooks make a difference? Many psychologists emphasize the importance of role models in developing children's senses of identity and in giving them examples to follow. These books not only support traditional and relatively restrictive roles for women but also present an unrealistic view of contemporary social life. In the schoolbook world women are mostly wives and mothers; in the real world many are wives and mothers, but they are many other things as well. Two pieces of research show how textbooks affect what children learn and think. In one study, Ashby and Whittmaier (1978) read to fourth-grade girls either a story presenting women only in their traditional family roles or a story showing women in nontraditional activities. The girls were then asked to rate a series of jobs and characteristics according to how appropriate they were for women. The girls who had heard the stories with the nontraditional themes rated traditionally male jobs and characteristics as appropriate for females more frequently than did the other girls.

In another study (Schneider and Hacker 1973), researchers gave college students titles for chapters in a forthcoming general sociology textbook and asked them to select appropriate photographs for each chapter. Some of the students were given the chapter titles "Social Man," "Industrial Man," and "Political Man." The others were given chapter titles "Society," "Industrial Life," and "Political Behavior." The latter chose pictures with a greater number of women in them. Apparently the first set of titles supported images of a predominantly male world in the minds of the students.

The gendered messages children receive are not simple; they are self-contradictory. On the one hand, they are told that in a democracy all children are given an equal chance. They are all told that math, science, and technology are important in the modern world. But schools blunt these messages by offering conflicting ones to girls. Girls are still often subtly told that their most important role is that of wife and mother (even if she also studied physics) and that a girl should not "sacrifice her femininity" to pursue education or a career.

Children learn very young that some subjects are "masculine" and some are "feminine." We have already discussed some of the problems surrounding mathematics. One study (reported in Tobias and Weissbrod 1980) found that adolescent girls refrain from studying mathematics because they think boys don't like girls who study mathematics. Julia Sherman (1980) found that the degree to which high school girls considered mathematics a male domain affected their performance in the subject, and among 11th-grade girls it affected how much confidence they had in their abilities to learn math. Thus a girl who thinks that mathematics is a masculine subject will not have much confidence in her ability to learn mathematics or will feel it is better to avoid the subject for social reasons. Neither of these attitudes will help her performance.

The gender messages in education are not restrictive only to girls. Labeling different subjects masculine or feminine restricts girls and boys. In the United States (although not in all countries), girls tend to be better than boys at reading in the younger grades. Carol Dwyer (1974) studied the problem and found that boys who did poorly in reading were more likely to consider reading to be a "feminine" occupation. Both boys and girls do well on school problems that are directly related to what they view as appropriate gender norms and poorly on those at odds with these norms (Christoplos and Borden 1978). It is, of course, quite possible for young people to assert themselves against these norms, but, as Michelle Stanworth has written, "It takes considerably more determination (and support) for [boys and girls] to choose a subject or career which is not considered appropriate to their gender" (1983, 17). Unfortunately we have little evidence that many teachers, even at the university level, are willing to help young people assert themselves in this way partly because they are unaware there is a problem.

Gender and Evaluation

Young people's interest and confidence in their abilities seem to be linked to how gender appropriate they find a particular subject or activity. Gender expectations help people to explain their successes and failures. Experimental research shows that people tend to express male success and female failure in terms of possession or lack of skills and to explain male failure and female success in terms of other factors, often things out of their control. (For a review of this research, see Deaux 1976.) In one study, for example, people were told about males or females who did well or poorly in school. They were then asked to make up stories to explain these successes and failures. The same pattern found in other studies emerged: In the stories the subjects composed, males did well because they were smart and poorly because they were unlucky. Females did well because the test was easy, because they tried harder, or even because they cheated; they did poorly because they were not smart. This pattern holds particularly for gender-inappropriate tasks.

These findings hold for African American as well as white students. When black girls specifically do as well as white boys in school, teachers seem to attribute the "equality" to the black girls' hard work and the white boys' lack of trying. Black girls have lower academic self-evaluations than black boys in some areas in which the girls' actual performance was as good as or even better than the boys' (AAUW 1992, 71).

Perhaps the most disturbing aspect of this body of research is that males and females apply these different perceptions to their own experiences. Girls learn not to expect much from their own abilities, which leads many to underrate themselves. By the same token, males show a tendency to overrate their own work. Three studies provide examples. A study of third-grade and junior high school students in math showed that girls self-evaluated their abilities and expected grades lower in mathematics than boys did, and attributed their failures more to lack of ability and their successes less to high ability than did boys. Girls who did badly were more likely than boys to want to hide their papers from others. Among the junior high students (but not the fourth-graders), girls who had not expected to do well on a test continued to be pessimistic about their future math prospects even just after they received good test results. Girls were less likely than boys to think that trying hard could guarantee doing well (Stipek and Gralinski 1991). These kinds of results have been found relatively consistently for other subjects and students of other ages. For example, research on an undergraduate economics course showed that while male and female students who did well explained the outcome in much the same way, among less successful students more men attributed their failure to their lack of effort while more women than men blamed a lack of ability (Halperin and Abrams 1978).

In her investigation of British adolescents' self-evaluations, Michelle Stanworth (1983) also found evidence of girls' lack of confidence and boys' overconfidence. When students and teachers ranked students according to how well they were doing academically, 19 of the 24 students ranked themselves differently from the way the teacher ranked them. All the girls who differed from the teacher's evaluation underestimated their own ranking. All but one of the boys who differed from the teacher overestimated their own ranking. In most of these cases, the girls incorrectly ranked themselves lower than a boy, and the boys incorrectly ranked themselves higher than a girl.

Parents also assess their children's school work and abilities on the basis of gender. A study of seventh-grade mathematics students found that among students of average ability fathers (but not mothers) held lower achievement standards for daughters than for sons. Parents (especially mothers) attributed their daughters' math successes more to effort than they did for sons, and attributed their sons' successes more to talent than they did for daughters (Yee and Eccles 1988).

Gender norms have direct effects on school performance. One study shows what wide effects these attitudes have throughout American culture. A study of groups of adolescent Hopi and black girls who were highly skilled at playing dodgeball found that the girls reduced their level of competitiveness—actually held back their own performances—when playing with boys, especially when playing with boys who were relatively unskilled. Further investigation showed that the girls were unaware of what they were doing (Weisfeld, Weisfeld, and Callaghan 1982). Similar behavior in boys, playing girls, would be regarded as chivalrous, but because the girls' behavior is unacknowledged, the implication is different. It simply offers further, although mistaken, evidence to all involved that boys are better than girls.

Of course much evaluation of students is based on tests. Do tests offer an "objective" and unbiased means to ensure that we can evaluate girls and boys fairly? Both gender bias and race bias in testing has been the subject of debate for a long time. The AAUW report shows some evidence of continued gender bias in testing. For example, in the 1970s test companies began efforts to balance gendered references in tests, for example, by embedding math problems in stories about measuring lengths of fabric as well as football fields. In the 1980s, however, many standardized tests, including the crucial SAT exams found extreme bias in the number of references to males and females. Their review shows that test structures can greatly influence the relative performances of girls and boys (AAUW 1992, 55–57).

This research on the impact of test structures reminds us that treating all students exactly the same does not necessarily create fairness and equitable education, because people's needs may differ. The AAUW report shows that different teaching methods are sometimes differentially effective for girls and boys, but where this is the case the method that is better for boys is more often used. Specialists interested in teaching computer science have found that males and females may often use different routes to solve the same problems; thus, if computer instruction is done only one way, some students—usually the girls—will be disadvantaged (Kramer and Lehman 1990; Turkel and Papert 1990).

Segregation and Schooling

One of the oldest debates over women and education concerns the benefits and drawbacks of mixed- versus single-sex education. In some education traditions and subjects, gender segregation was long enforced. Many fields of study were available only to one sex. Girls were barred from subjects thought too indelicate for them. For example, women had particular trouble training as artists because they were not allowed into classes with (nude) life models. Medical training also posed problems because of the parts of the body that must be discussed and viewed. The very idea of women working on cadavers was considered indecent.

Many reformers of the 19th century advocated mixed schools. As William Leach (1980, 78) notes, "At the heart of the coeducational rationale lay the conviction that everything 'one-sided' and dangerous happens in a segregated sexual world where everything is hidden." In her *Vindication of the Rights of Woman* ([1792] 1975), Mary Wollstonecraft argued strongly for mixed-sex schools for these reasons. She was adamant about the "immodesty" and impropriety of behavior in single-sex boarding schools; no doubt one of the things she feared was exploration of homosexuality among the young. But also, she wondered how men and women could be good companions for each other if they had never had a chance to get to know each other as ordinary human beings. In 1870 Elizabeth Cady Stanton wrote, "In opening all high schools and colleges to girls we are giving young men and women better opportunities of studying each others' tastes, sentiments, capacities, characters in the normal condition" (Leach 1980, 80).

By the 20th century most public schools were mixed, and as the century continued, so was an increasing proportion of colleges and universities, including most of the long-segregated "Seven Sisters" and "Ivy League" schools of the Northeast. The number of women's colleges declined from 228 in 1969 to 94 in 1989.[1] Considerable sex segregation remained, however. Physical education classes were (and are) rarely mixed, even in sports that could easily be played by mixed groups. Many schools segregated the sexes into special "gender-appropriate" classes: Girls learned cooking and sewing, and boys learned metal or wood working or mechanical drawing. In sex-education classes, boys and girls are often segregated, giving boys, for example, no opportunity to learn about menstruation, which can heighten girls' embarrassment about the subject because they know how ignorant boys are (AAUW 1992, 77).

By the time students seem to have more options, in secondary school and especially in college, males and females still "choose" different subjects, resulting in further segregation. Any male or female interested in a "gender-inappropriate" field knows how daunting it can be just to enter the classroom. Consider a survey of eighth-graders in 1988 that asked students to identify the subjects they looked forward to, those in which they were afraid to ask questions, and those they thought would be useful for their future. As Table 5-2 shows, there were gender differences in how the students reacted to some subjects; girls looked forward to English more than boys did, and boys looked forward to social studies and science more than girls did. At the same time, it is important not to exaggerate the gender differences. In fact, segregation increases as we move up the levels from secondary school through college and graduate programs (see Table 1-1, p. 15). Although gender segregation has decreased in some academic fields, widespread segregation remains, especially at the highest levels.

The amount of gender segregation depends on the social context. As Table 5-3 shows, the amount of gender imbalance in professional degrees awarded varies by race and ethnicity. Dentistry is a much more male-dominated field among whites than among students of other ethnic groups. Only among African Americans do roughly equal proportions of women and men receive medical degrees.

Is segregation in education always bad? When segregation limits opportunities to learn, there is a problem. Can we afford to lose potential participants in any field? Why is it good for men to be unable to make themselves dinner or sew buttons on their shirts or to be ignorant of how women's bodies work? Why should women not know the basics about how to build shelves, or not learn skills that might open up interesting job possibilities? It is not conducive to learning to be the odd woman (or man) out in a classroom filled with people of the other sex. One of the things people learn in school is how to understand, work with, respect, and get along with others. There is much justification in Elizabeth Cady

TABLE 5-2
Eighth-Graders' Attitudes Toward School, Selected Subjects, 1988

		Male	*Female*
Mathematics:	Look forward to	59	55
	Afraid to ask questions	19	23
	Useful in my future	89	87
English:	Look forward to	52	62
	Afraid to ask questions	16	15
	Useful in my future	81	88
Social studies:	Look forward to	62	55
	Afraid to ask questions	14	16
	Useful in my future	61	57
Science:	Look forward to	65	58
	Afraid to ask questions	14	16
	Useful in my future	72	65

Note: Numbers show proportion of students agreeing with each statement.
Source: U.S. Department of Education (1992, 134).

Stanton's and Mary Wollstonecraft's belief that it is detrimental for women and men to grow up regarding each other as mysterious and foreign creatures.

But segregation may have benefits in certain circumstances. Advocates of women's colleges point out that when women at these schools take physics or chemistry classes, they cannot be discouraged by being in the minority; there is no peer pressure from male classmates not to be smart. When women at women's

TABLE 5-3
Proportion of First Professional Degrees Awarded to Women, by Race and Ethnicity, 1990

Field (% White)	*White, Non-Hispanic*	*Black, Non-Hispanic*	*Hispanic*	*Asian/ Pacific Islander*	*American Indian*	*All Women*
Dentistry (74)	27	50	40	43	*	31
Medicine (80)	32	52	35	36	42	34
Pharmacy (70)	58	66	63	63	*	60
Veterinary medicine (94)	58	54	61	70	67	58
Law (88)	41	56	44	49	51	42
Theology (84)	25	32	16	9	27	25

Note: "% White" indicates the total proportion of degree recipients who are white. All other figures indicate the proportion of degree recipients who are women.

*Fewer than 10 degree recipients in this category.

Source: U.S. Department of Education (1992, 283).

colleges take women's studies courses, men are not there to make fun of them. Women at these schools are not distracted by heterosexual courtship rituals in the classroom and have no reason to hide their assertiveness or brains. A study by Elizabeth Tidball (1980) shows that twice as many of the women who appear in *Who's Who of American Women* went to women's colleges as to coeducational colleges.

Many educators in former women's colleges that have since become mixed or merged with men's colleges regret the change. In many cases, men have become dominant in the traditionally male fields. In some cases, such as that of Harvard and Radcliffe, the schools have not merely been merged; the women's college has, for all intents and purposes, been swallowed up by the men's school.

Some feminists look back at intellectual forebears such as Margaret Fuller, who felt that women needed to meet among themselves to learn from each other, and Virginia Woolf, who talked about woman needing a "room of her own." Although most of these feminists do not suggest that all education should be segregated, they do argue that under certain circumstances it should be. One example is segregating classes in traditionally male fields to help women become self-confident. Another area in which segregation might be useful is courses on topics directly relating to questions of gender and sexuality. Men often regard women's discussion of these topics as hostile and become antagonistic and defensive when women talk honestly about their perceptions and questions. Many women worry about hurting men's feelings if they discuss some important issues, such as violence against women, in front of men. Further, feminists point out that women have long been expected to learn about themselves through the opinions of male "experts." As we shall see in Chapter 10, the gender composition of a group affects who talks and how they talk: Men tend to dominate discussions even if they are a minority. If women are to learn to think and talk independently and honestly, especially about gender and sexuality and the areas of life they affect, there may be some times during which they must withdraw to work among themselves. Some male feminists make the same point, arguing that before men can deal honestly with women about questions of sexuality and parenthood, for example, men must be able to talk honestly among themselves.

Women as Educators

We are told education is a woman's field. But is it? What proportion of the people responsible for shaping and dispensing education are women? Table 5-4 shows the proportion of women who are educators or are preparing to be educators. Despite women's involvement in education, men clearly predominate at the highest levels. The higher the degree, the lower is women's share. The higher the teaching position, the lower is women's share. In every type of college or university, the higher the rank, the fewer the women. Men clearly hold the majority of positions of education governance.

What holds women back in the field of education? We will look more closely at women and employment in Chapter 13, but for now we can say that many of

TABLE 5-4
Women as a Proportion of Educators

	Education Degrees: Proportion Granted to Women, 1990		
	B.A.	*M.A.*	*Ph.D./Ed.D.*
Pre-elementary	98%	98	*
Elementary	93	91	77
Secondary	62	67	63
Education administration	*	59	51
All education fields	78	76	58
Elementary and Secondary Educators, 1990			
Teacher aides	93%		
Prekindergarten and kindergarten	99		
Elementary teachers	85		
Secondary teachers	52		
Full-Time Faculty, Higher Educators, 1986			
Institutional Type			
Two-year colleges	39%		
Four-year colleges	31		
Universities	20		
Rank, all institutions			
Lecturer	50%		
Instructor	53		
Assistant professor	38		
Associate professor	25		
Professor	12		
Education Governance, 1990			
School principals	28%		
School superintendents	5		
School board members	34		
Chief state school officer	18		
College chief executive officer	10		

Source: U.S. Department of Education (1992); U.S. Department of Labor (1992); AAUW (1992).

*Fewer than 100 degrees total.

the same problems exist in education as in other jobs. Although certain parts of the field of education are considered particularly appropriate for women, the more the job departs from traditional stereotypes of women's nature and interests, the more obstacles women face. Many people argue that women are naturally suited to be educators, but few seem to believe that women's natures fit them to control the education process or to work at the higher educational levels. They see women as nurturers fit for kindergartens, not scholars fit for universities. In the 19th century, women were not encouraged to teach in secondary schools because it was felt they could not discipline older children as well as men could; they were not encouraged to be administrators because management was believed to be a man's job (Strober and Tyack 1980). Some of these attitudes linger.

Are women held back because they possess lower academic qualifications than men? Government figures show that in 1986 about 60% of male classroom teachers and about 46% of female classroom teachers had degrees beyond the B.A., a fact that is reflected in the greater numbers of men at the secondary level. While this could suggest one reason why males are more likely than females to be promoted into school administration, it does not account for the size of the difference in male and female administrators. Differences in experience and length of service do not account for the great discrepancy either. In 1986 the median number of years served by male public school teachers was 17; the median number of years served by females was 14 (U.S. Bureau of the Census 1989). Even in the mid 1970s a review of research on women as leaders in public education pointed out that about equal numbers of male and female teachers had the credentials needed to become administrators; however, women put in an average of 15 years and men put in an average of only 5 years in the classroom before they became elementary school principals (Estler 1975). An analysis of one case study of a parent–teacher organization suggests that there is a similar pattern of discrimination in favor of males in PTAs as well (Sapiro 1979). In that study, men who became presidents of the PTA had less experience in the organization than women did.

Similar patterns emerge at the college and university levels. The amount a professor publishes is a better predictor of men's rank and salary than of women's; women's publications apparently do not guarantee women's promotion the same way that men's do (Unger 1979, 439). Even student evaluations of teachers are gender biased, although males' evaluations show more evidence of bias than females' do (Martin 1984; Basow and Silberg 1987; Kierstead, D'Agostino, and Dill 1988; but see also Wheeless and Potorti 1989). Women are evaluated less highly on traditionally male characteristics.

Organizations of women in science try to draw attention to the barriers that face them in pursuing their goals. In 1991, for example, only 5 of the 60 new scientists inducted into the National Academy of Sciences were women, a proportion that has been roughly constant over the preceding two decades. One of the new members, Dr. Jane Richardson of the Duke University Medical School, explained part of the problem: "It's an old boys' club, elected by its own members. They're really trying hard, but still, you vote for somebody you know,

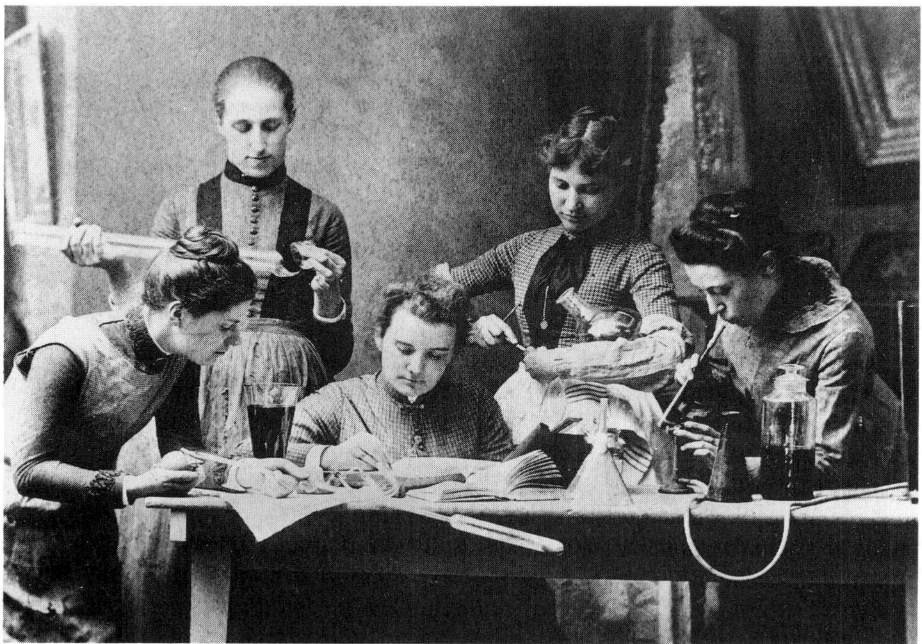

While these Smith College students studied chemistry in 1889, some theorists argued that too much education was bad for women's health.

and men just tend to know each other better than they do women."[2] Others point out that at the higher levels fields such as science are structured around the lives of people who have been left free to devote all of their attention to their work because someone else takes care of them and, if they have them, their children. Linda Wilson, a chemist and the president of Radcliffe College, claims that women won't make greater entries into science until the culture of science changes so that it does not require excluding every other human activity. She considers the following dilemma for women: "Her critical scientific years, in which she is establishing her reputation, and her peak reproductive years coincide. This is a dirty trick." She and other education leaders ask whether science and other research areas must be structured as they are.[3]

What difference would it make if more women entered the higher ranks of education? It would make considerable difference to women who wish to pursue careers in education. Whether it would make a difference in the type of education people receive is a more complex question. It is not clear that women would run their schools or school districts very differently from men. At least the presence of more women at higher levels would provide more heterogeneous models for students to follow. In colleges and universities, women certainly have led the efforts to bring women into the curriculum, remove bias from evaluation procedures, and end sexual harassment on campus.

What difference does the gender of a teacher make in the classroom? Some research suggests that students benefit from contact with teachers of their own sex. One study found that children perform better on intelligence tests with an examiner of their own sex (Pedersen, Schinedling, and Johnson 1968). Another concluded that students in science classes are more likely to consider science as a career for themselves if their teacher is of their own sex (Stake and Granger 1978). There can be few female college and university professors who have not had small hordes of female students beating paths to their doors because they are women. (On the other hand, too many female college professors find an unusual number of both male and female students wanting to hand in papers late because they thought "a woman might be nicer than a man.")

Unfortunately it is clear that female teachers participate in the hidden curriculum we have been discussing. This should not be surprising. They grow up in the same sexist society, sit in the same classrooms, and read the same biased textbooks that men do. Many women become teachers because it is an occupation that is regarded as particularly appropriate for women. It will take considerably more than simply putting more women into positions of responsibility to eliminate the sexist bias of schools. Educators are becoming increasingly aware of the problem, however, and are beginning to seek solutions to it.

Education and the Future

It should be clear by now that certain problems need to be addressed for education to serve women and men better. Let us review some of them.

The Question of Choice

Do girls and boys and women and men have the fullest possible opportunity to get the education they choose? Research suggests they do not. Subtle and not so subtle messages still track students according to gender and limit girls' attainment especially. One of the most striking conclusions of the AAUW report is that girls learn in school to devalue themselves.

Some questions affecting choice in education are particularly difficult to tackle. Much of the sexism of people's attitudes and behavior is not conscious; teachers, for example, are often not aware that they treat female and male students differently. When female and male students make their choices in education, they are not always aware of the pressures that have led them to their decisions. Much of the evaluation that goes on in schools and universities—test results, letters of recommendation, promotions, and committee meetings—is confidential, which means it occurs in a secret way that often does not allow the subjects to know how they were evaluated.

Some of the clearest examples of unconscious or subtle sex discrimination in education are seen in the process by which colleges and universities handle promotions among faculty. When considering individuals for tenure or promotion, these institutions usually look for a complex combination of scholarship (generally, publication of original research), teaching (both how much and how well), and service to the institution (participation on committees and other decision-making bodies in the institution). Measuring these qualities and determining how well the individual will do in the future is immensely difficult.

How do we know when a teacher is really good? A teacher may be relatively unpopular with students but prove in the long run to have given them a fine education. Another may be very popular but may be dispensing educational cotton candy: fun and even interesting at the time but insubstantial over the long run. Some people may produce a great deal of research that is forgotten before the ink is dry on the paper; others may write very little, but what they write may continue to teach people for years. Or they may do research in areas that are unpopular with or considered unimportant by their colleagues—areas like women's studies. Because these judgments are in large part necessarily subjective, considerable room is left for conscious or unconscious discrimination. Moreover, these judgments are supposed to be collective and confidential; that is, *individuals'* decisions and the rationales for them are not supposed to be revealed. It should be no surprise that in recent years there have been court battles over the process and substance of decision making in educational institutions.

Unfortunately the appearance of choice is too often an illusion. How can the degree of choice be increased? Two common answers, "We must change people's minds or resocialize them to be less sexist," and "We should make laws against discrimination," are inadequate. The first is too vague, and the second is too narrow, primarily because for the most part it already has been done and hasn't worked out as well as we hoped.

Education for What?

Until recently, women's schooling was designed almost exclusively to prepare them to be good mothers and wives. Women are still tracked into areas that are supposed to be compatible with the roles of wife and mother. Schools also play a role in tracking women into lower-status jobs than men.

Schools and school boards are often unwilling to handle the problem of gender stereotyping directly within school curricula. Most have made few real strides in correcting gender biases in teaching methods and school curricula. In the early 1990s a backlash developed in many areas of the country that claimed schools had gone too far in teaching "alternative lifestyles" and in mixing up people's gender roles and belittling women's traditional roles.

It is ironic that many school officials who want their female students to grow up to be responsible wives and mothers balk at the idea that schools should teach students about sexuality and reproduction. As a result many American children still think babies come from cabbages, storks, and supernatural acts or from parts of the body not connected to the reproductive system, whereas children in countries such as Sweden, where sex education is introduced in the first grade, understand the basic facts of life at an early age (Parsons 1983). By the time American schools get around to teaching sex education—late in high school if at all—up to one-half of the students have already begun having sex, and many have accidentally found out where babies come from (Zellman and Goodchilds 1983). The spread of AIDS has increased the need for sex education among adolescents. Most probably do not realize that about a third of women with AIDS were infected through heterosexual contact (AAUW 1992, 78).

Research shows repeatedly that education does not "pay off" for women in the same way it does for men. Men get better jobs, more pay, and higher social status for the same amount of education. It is no wonder that many women become discouraged and curtail their studies even when they are fully qualified to continue them. Helen F. Durio and Cheryl A. Kildow (1980) found that of the 273 women and 1,953 men enrolled in an engineering program at the University of Texas during the mid and late 1970s the women who left the program (unlike the men who left) did not leave because of academic failure and in fact tended to be better qualified academically than the men.

Education for and about Women

Some progress has been made in including women in the world about which students learn. The most progress has been made in relatively ghettoized women's studies courses and programs in colleges and universities and, to a lesser extent, in high schools. For the most part, "women" are still a special topic, and women have to work hard to make their own space in existing schools. Many advocates of traditional education have criticized women's studies as being harmfully ideological and nonacademic, claiming it refuses to acknowledge the value in studying "dead white males."[4] Female students have to work particularly hard to learn about themselves and to do what Adrienne Rich (1979) calls "claiming an education."

It is daunting to consider the vast web of institutions involved in education when we consider how to find the keys to change. Of one thing we can be sure: The battle must be fought on several fronts. Students themselves can take an active part in creating their own education by being watchful and demanding changes in their educational institutions when they see evidence of bias or closed opportunities. Most colleges and universities have women's groups or caucuses, and many high schools do as well. Parents also have a role to play, either as individuals or through groups such as the PTA.

Teachers and school administrators can also work to achieve change. There are women's groups within most professional societies and unions, and there are professional journals devoted in whole or in part to discussing the problem of sexism in schools. These professional and labor organizations, as well as feminist groups such as the National Organization for Women, increasingly have special reports, programs, and training sessions designed to help teachers and administrators fight sexism in schools.

One point that must not be forgotten is that most educational institutions in the United States are run by the government; they are paid for and regulated by a complex web of local, county, and state school boards and superintendents of schools; local, county, and state legislators; and Congress and the U.S. Department of Education. Politics thus play a major role in education.

A case in point is the battle over implementation of Title IX of the 1972 Education Amendments, which bars discrimination in educational programs. One of the areas of university education in which discriminatory treatment is most obvious is sports, particularly in schools with big money-making male sports. The NCAA originally fought intense legal battles to try to make sure Title IX would not cover college athletics, even trying to claim that would be unconstitutional (Carpenter and Acosta 1991). A 1990 survey of Division I members of the National College Athletic Association (NCAA) showed that women were 50% of the full-time undergraduates but only 31% of the athletes. Women received 30% of the athletic scholarship money, 23% of the operating expenditures, and 17% of the recruiting expenditures.[5] In 1992 the Big Ten Conference unanimously passed a new rule requiring member universities to increase the proportion of female athletes. They have vowed to provide 40% of their athletic funding to women by 1997. The Big Ten is the only conference to make such a policy.[6]

Title IX is still in place, and lawsuits may be launched against schools either by the Office of Civil Rights in the U.S. Department of Education or by private individuals. In addition to Title IX, numerous other laws and policies aim to equalize educational opportunities for women and men, although most observers argue that they are either not sufficient or not enforced rigorously enough. Programs such as those under the 1974 Women's Educational Equity Act (WEEA) have been developed to provide funds for new programs or research projects designed to promote women's education. Sex discrimination in employment, including employment in education, remains illegal under Title VII of the 1964 Civil Rights Act, and sex discrimination in pay is illegal under the Equal Pay Act of 1960. Experts, however, cite two particular problems in using legal means to redress sexism: (1) The laws are vague (Vladeck 1981), and (2) the courts generally approach each case on the basis of its individual merit, thus making it difficult to focus the battle on the real issue, which is discrimination against a group of people (Abel 1981).

Women have formed interest groups to combat sexism in education. Joyce Gelb and Marian Palley (1987) report that at least 60 different women's groups have been involved in Title IX battles. Some, such as the Women's Educational Action League (WEAL), the National Organization for Women (NOW), and the National Women's Political Caucus (NWPC), are clearly associated with the feminist movement. Others, such as the League of Women Voters, the American Association of University Women (AAUW), and the Girl Scouts, are more traditional women's organizations. The National Council for Research on Women (NCRW), a federation of research centers on women, pursues issues of interest to research in this area. There are now electronic mail bulletin boards and networks, such as WMST-L, devoted to international discussion on women's studies concerns. Issues concerning education have often united women from diverse backgrounds and political perspectives, however, and these groups have joined to form the National Coalition for Women and Girls in Education.

Many people feel strongly that education must continue to change; the dilemma is how to create change and where to start. There probably cannot be major changes in the status and roles of women in society in general until education changes, but it is doubtful that education can undergo major changes until other social institutions change as well.

NOTES

1. Edward B. Fiske, "Lessons," *New York Times*, June 14, 1989, p. 24.
2. Natalie Angier, "Academy's Choices Don't Reflect the Number of Women in Science," *New York Times*, May 10, 1992.
3. Shirley M. Tilghman, "Science vs. Women—A Radical Solution," *New York Times*, January 26, 1993.
4. For a partial list of dead white males discussed in this book, look up the following names in the index: Aristotle, Jean Bodin, Charles Darwin, Sigmund Freud, John Stuart Mill, Talcott Parsons, Jean-Jacques Rousseau, and Benjamin Rush.
5. Douglas Lederman, "Men Outnumber Women and Get Most of Money in Big-Time Sports Programs," *Chronicle of Higher Education*, April 8, 1992.
6. Debra E. Blum, "Athletic Conferences Struggle with Issue of Sex Equity," *Chronicle of Higher Education*, January 13, 1993.

6

Normal Gender: Health, Fitness, and Beauty

A PREGNANT WOMAN chats with a friend during their lunch break. "Are you hoping for a boy or a girl?" her friend asks. "Oh, I don't care what sex it is—as long as it's a healthy, normal baby I'll be happy!" A student wakes up the first day of final exams and refuses the breakfast offered by her roommate. "I feel really ill," she explains, and both of them believe it but make no move to get her to a doctor because they know there is nothing physically wrong with her. A 95-year-old woman dies in her sleep, and her children comfort themselves by expressing happiness that she was "healthy and in good shape up to the end." A man walks down the street in high heels, skin-tight leather trousers, and heavy eye makeup. "That's really sick!" someone comments. In 1982 John Hinckley, who shot President Ronald Reagan, was judged not guilty of a crime "by reason of insanity," causing people to argue that the high crime rate in the United States is evidence of a "sick society." In 1973 the American Psychological Association, changing its collective mind, declared that homosexuality is not a sickness.

Words connoting health and sickness, normality and abnormality are among the most common and important we use to describe and evaluate people as individuals and groups, but they also are among the most confusing and difficult to define. What constitutes health or normality is culturally and historically variable. What doesn't change is the *evaluative* connotations of these concepts: Health is good and its absence bad. The absence of health (or the presence of sickness) should be corrected if at all possible.

David Mechanic, an influential medical sociologist, argues, "The concept of disease usually refers to some deviation from normal functioning which has undesirable consequences because it produces personal discomfort or adversely affects the individual's future health status" (1978, 25). Notice the importance of the concept of *normal* in this definition. Mechanic points out that we (including both health professionals and lay people) compare the way we feel or act to some standard of normality to determine whether we are healthy or not.

How do we establish standards of health or normality? Mechanic argues that they depend on the state of health institutions and health science as well as the "social and cultural context within which human problems are defined" (1978, 26). Even the simplest health problems show how definitions of health shift and leave leeway for subjective interpretation. The average temperature of the human body is 98.6 degrees Fahrenheit. If my temperature is 99 degrees, is this a problem? Possibly not; some people's normal temperature is higher or lower than average. So at what point has my temperature deviated enough from the norm to say that I am not healthy? Defining health is even more difficult with respect to addressing more complex physiological problems, not to mention those involving human psychology, mental health, and social behavior.

Observers generally agree that cultural and social values play large roles in defining health and that this aspect of health science and care can be very dangerous. But if health is understood in terms of normality, and normality is culturally defined, isn't there a problem? Here is a plaguing question: If healthy people are those who fall within "normal" ranges, if they are "like most people," isn't it easy to define as "unhealthy" people who are different or unique or violate social custom? Who or what can guard against this tendency?

Not surprisingly, definitions of health are related to definitions of normal gender roles, femininity, and masculinity. In the book's Introduction we briefly discussed a study (Broverman et al. 1970) that found that many health professionals define health for males and females differently. Thus, in the process of teaching us how to be healthy, health professionals also teach us how to conform to gender norms. While restoring us to health when we show signs of abnormality, they may also be restoring us to "normal" masculinity and femininity.

Like the family and schools, health institutions impart values and knowledge, define what constitutes personal and social problems, and then seek to prevent or correct these problems. This chapter examines the relationship between gender and standards of health and health care. We show the ways in which institutions and people charged with managing our health also manage gender. *Health* is used very broadly here and includes physical, mental, and social health. A wide range of interrelated institutions fall into our view, including those most obviously concerned with health, such as hospitals and clinics, and other less obvious institutions, such as families, schools, social welfare agencies, and even the criminal justice system.

Like most other fields of human science, medicine is an imperfect science. Even when the state of knowledge about a given medical problem is limited, doctors still try to help, relying if necessary on educated guesses. The fact that some portion of the practice of medicine is subjective (although educated) guesswork leaves considerable room for the influence of ideology, including gender ideology. Procedures that represent the best guesses and the values of a given era may appear wrongheaded and even disgraceful at a later period.

Let us look at how these problems are manifest in the health care of women.[1]

How are sex, gender, and women's gender roles related to definitions of health and illness? How have health practitioners viewed and treated women? We begin with medical views of women's anatomy and reproductive systems. We then turn to the relationship between women's health and their roles in the family and at work. Finally we look at the relationship between women's health and conceptions of female beauty and fitness.

Anatomy and Health

A doctor addressing a medical society in 1870 noted that it seemed "as if the Almighty, in creating the female sex, had taken the uterus and built up a woman around it" (quoted in Ehrenreich and English 1979, 108). Although the Bible claims that God began with a rib rather than the uterus, writers and practitioners of health care have tended to view women largely in terms of their reproductive organs and capacities. Women's reproductive organs have not merely been seen as different from men's; they have been regarded as the defining characteristics of women and their potential for health. In fact they generally have been treated as special health hazards women would be better off not having.

In the late 19th century, women's ovaries came to be regarded as sources of danger to mental health. Because of their link to women's periodicity, ovaries were assumed to control women's personalities, causing their apparent emotional instability. This "psychology of the ovary," as Ehrenreich and English (1979) call it, had disastrous effects on women when doctors set their minds to figuring out how to care for women. Many doctors claimed that ovariotomy, or surgical

An early chastity belt.

removal of the ovaries, cured women of a variety of "problems." An estimated 150,000 women underwent the operation in 1906 alone. There were many specific reasons for these operations such as helping women who ate too much, masturbated, had "erotic tendencies," had attempted suicide, or suffered from persecution manias (and no wonder!). In some cases, husbands brought their wives to the doctor for this surgery hoping to cure them of unruly behavior (Ehrenreich and English 1979, 111–12).

Women's potential for sexuality has often been seen as dangerous and unhealthy. Although Victorians believed that women only tolerated rather than enjoyed sex, many also thought women were insatiable,"raging volcanos of desire." To control women's sexuality and its "dangerous" effects, men have used various means, including chastity belts and segregation, the latter especially by religious law and authority.

In the mid 19th century American doctors found a new cure for such problems as "nymphomania," masturbation, and other sorts of unruly feminine behavior: clitoridectomy, or surgical removal of the clitoris. Once again, some husbands at a loss to control unmanageable wives presented them to doctors for "female circumcision," as it is often mistakenly called. This gruesome practice has disappeared among Western doctors, although it remains part of some cultures' female initiation rites, particularly in parts of Africa. Feminists and such organizations as the World Health Organization have mounted a worldwide campaign to eliminate this dangerous practice (see Hoskin 1980).

The womb has long been regarded as the cause of both physical and emotional problems, or "hysteria." Many experts thought the uterus traveled around the body, causing grave danger (Shorter 1982). As recently as the 19th century most of women's diseases were attributed to the presence of a womb (Ehrenreich and English 1979).

Hysterectomy—the removal of the womb—has become one of the most important life-saving procedures in the history of women's health. The medical profession might have been as wrong in pursuing this procedure as it was in the cases of the clitoridectomy and the ovariotomy, but it was not; hysterectomies regularly save the lives of women with uterine cancer. However, numerous observers argue that there is considerable abuse of hysterectomy because of androcentric views of women and their health. According to these critics, hysterectomies are among the most overdone surgical operations in the medical repertoire. In the calculation of risks, costs, and benefits, doctors seem especially inclined to perform hysterectomies on older women because "they don't need their wombs anymore." In this case, age stereotypes combine with gender stereotypes to create problems for women.

Like cancer of the uterus, breast cancer has always plagued women. In the 1880s radical mastectomy—the removal of the breast plus underlying muscles and lymph nodes—was introduced to treat breast cancer patients. Although this procedure greatly reduced recurrence of cancer, in recent years observers have concluded that the radical mastectomy, like the hysterectomy, is overdone; too much surgery is done too often. Again this surgical technique seems particularly likely to be overused on older women partly because of the cultural view that older women don't need their breasts.

Thus the organs of women's bodies that are most different from men's—those that compose the reproductive system—have long been identified as sources of peculiar mental and physical health problems. Part of the willingness to excise women's reproductive organs seems based on the perception that they are extraneous in any case, especially in women past the age at which they are likely to bear children or appear sexually attractive to men. There seems to have been no analogous tendency to remove men's unique reproductive organs (except, at some times in history, as a cure or punishment for rapists)—but men's reproductive organs are regarded as normal and necessary to the healthy male.

Most observers who call attention to this situation do not suggest that doctors intend to hurt women; to the contrary, they argue that an underlying androcentric view of women's bodies, combined with imperfect knowledge, causes the harm in the course of attempting to help. This suggests two solutions, neither of which is sufficient by itself: (1) continued research to improve our understanding of both male and female bodies and (2) continued efforts to destroy androcentric conceptions of human health. But even with these efforts, controversies over appropriate care for women arise. In the early 1990s, for example, the American Cancer Society (ACS) stepped up its campaign to convince women to do self-examinations of their breasts and to get regular mammograms in order to reduce the unnecessary death and disfigurement due to cancer. During its campaign the ACS emphasized the statement that women face a 1 in 9 chance of getting breast cancer. Critics argued that the ACS had greatly exaggerated the odds to scare women into preventive medicine. The ACS figure tells us the cumulative probability that any woman will develop breast cancer sometime between birth and the time she is 100 years old. The odds that any given woman has not-yet-detected cancer at any given time are dramatically lower. Who is right: The ACS, which points out that 70% of women are not getting mammograms and could die unnecessarily, or the critics who say the campaign scares women about their bodies unnecessarily?[2]

Reproduction and Health

Like the organs themselves, the normal functions of women's reproductive organs have been seen as health problems. Let us look briefly at two examples: menstruation and pregnancy and childbirth.

MENSTRUATION. Menstruation has often been regarded as almost a community or public health problem. Most cultures have some menstrual taboos: beliefs that menstrual blood can make crops fail, wine go sour, infants die, and men become impotent. In many cultures, men view sexual relations with a menstruating woman as disgusting and many women find the idea embarrassing. Some religions, including Orthodox Judaism, ban sexual relations during menstrual periods and require women to undergo cleansing rituals after their periods are over.

There is little doubt that menstrual periods were once considerably more unpleasant for most women than they are now. Modern ideas of hygiene, such as the importance of regular bathing, are quite recent. As recently as the middle of the 20th century many people still believed that bathing or showering was dangerous for menstruating women. Fresh menstrual blood is no more unhealthful than blood from any other part of the body; but left to sit in warm dark places it is certainly both unappealing and a good breeding ground for germs.

Despite the present availability of sanitary pads, tampons (invented in 1933), and sponges, the old menstrual ideology persists. Consider advertisements for "feminine hygiene products" (Toth 1980) implying that even a menstruating woman can be normal and feminine—if she is careful to cover all signs of her condition. Recent developments in the "feminine hygiene" industry have even created some real health dangers. The search for bigger tampons led to the distribution of tampons that increase the risks of toxic shock syndrome, a potentially fatal illness. Rather than wearing bigger tampons longer women should change them more frequently.

We briefly discussed the controversy over physical and psychological menstrual distress in Chapter 3. Many women suffer from problems associated with menstruation and menstrual cycles. For some women these difficulties are caused by the physical functioning of their reproductive or hormonal systems. Some women experience physical and emotional difficulties at puberty and menopause. Excessive amounts of bleeding and the lack of bleeding in women of reproductive age can be symptoms of other health problems. Uncomfortable amounts of weight gain or cramps are not just products of the mind. But what is the relationship among menstruation, menstrual cycles, and women's normal health and well-being?

Beginning especially with the work of Katarina Dalton (1964), many researchers, doctors, journalists, and the public seized on the idea of premenstrual syndrome (PMS) to explain women's apparent mood swings and erratic behavior. Medical researchers disagree about the definition, existence, or causes of PMS. They do not agree which psychological and physical correlates of menstruation are more generally caused by the *physiological* aspects of the menstrual cycle and which are caused by people's menstrual beliefs or expectations or the way menstruating women are treated. Indeed, there is little agreement over what are the psychological and behavioral correlates of menstrual cycles and how many women might be affected. Some research shows that even when women believe they are being affected by PMS their own behavior and performance doesn't necessarily show it (Richardson 1989). Certainly women's interpretations of their own menstrual cycles and menstrual symptoms are based on their bodily sensations. But experimental research shows that women who were told they were premenstrual on the basis of a (make-believe) "scientific test" detected more menstrual symptoms in themselves than women who were told on the basis of the same test that they were not premenstrual (Klebanov and Jemmett 1992).

Research by Jeanne Brooks-Gunn and Diane Ruble (1982) offers important evidence that at least some menstrual difficulty is social in origin. As early as the fifth-grade girls have clear ideas about what symptoms accompany menstruation.

Interestingly, girls who had begun to menstruate reported experiencing less severe menstrual distress than those who hadn't yet begun expected to have. The level of distress young girls expected was related to the level they felt when they actually reached menarche. And girls who had learned more about menstruation "from male sources rated menstruation as more debilitating and negative than those who learned less from male sources" (1576). Females who live in close proximity (for example, in a dormitory room) often find that their menstrual cycles begin to become more similar over time (McClintock 1971). Biology alone is not responsible for whether a woman who is menstruating feels good. Even this basic physiological event is partly shaped by culture and society (Buckley and Gottlieb 1988; Delaney, Lupton, and Toth 1988; Lander 1988).

Nevertheless, both the institutions of health care and mass media have fostered the idea that there is a clearly defined and common set of disturbing and dysfunctional correlates of menstruation. The 1987 edition of the *Diagnostic and Statistical Manual of Mental Disorders* (*DSM*-III) (APA 1987) for the first time included a disorder called "late luteal phase dysphoric disorder" (LLPDD), derived from research on PMS. For menstruating women, a mental-health practitioner should look for the following symptoms (among others) in the week before and the first days after the onset of menses to determine whether a woman is suffering from this mental disorder: marked instability of moods; persistent and marked anger, irritability, anxiety, tension, or depression; decreased interest in usual activities; becoming tired easily or lacking in energy; subjective sense of difficulty in concentrating; marked change in appetite; insomnia; or physical symptoms such as breast tenderness, headaches, pain, or weight gain.[3]

Many experts in this area of research have objected to the definition of this disorder on the grounds that evidence is at best too contested to warrant such a designation (Caplan, McCurdy-Myers, and Gans 1992; Parlee 1992). Many prefer Jeanne Brooks-Gunn's notion that we should talk about premenstrual symptoms rather than any kind of stable "syndrome" (Brooks-Gunn 1986). If the evidence is not good enough, why does the psychiatric establishment treat this "syndrome" as if it is uncontested? Feminist scholars like Mary Brown Parlee point out that the creation of particular diagnostic categories is in large part a cultural activity related to the structure and needs of particular institutions. Thus the creation of a formal medical term such as PMS or LLPDD must be understood not just in relation to specific scientific tests and results but also in relation to the history of the cultural construction of the meaning of menstruation and menstruating women. Parlee also argues that once these designations become formally recognized diagnostic categories different health professionals are in a position to compete over who is supposed to handle these cases. Parlee thinks it is "quite comprehensible as a claim [mental health professionals] make to advance their case as they compete with gynaecologists for a 'new' (medically insured) patient population—women who 'have' PMS/LLPDD" (Parlee 1992, 107). Meanwhile, while health researchers and practitioners debate these issues, the mass media continue to portray women as crazed by their menstrual cycles (Chrisler and Levy 1990).

There is also great controversy over the effects of menopause. Although the majority of women experience some symptoms such as hot flashes, estimates are that 5–15% of women seek medical attention for menopause-related symptoms. In recent years, doctors have increasingly used hormone-replacement therapies to help. While this seems to offer relief, there are also negative side effects, including some that are dangerous. Until recently there had been little research on this subject because doctors did not regard women's menopause-related complaints as serious. But as women began to demand more attention to their health needs, and the possibility of more widespread use of hormone replacement therapy became more widely known, a major 10-year study was initiated in the early 1990s that should offer some needed answers.[4]

PREGNANCY AND CHILDBIRTH. For much of women's history childbirth was tremendously dangerous to women's health, first, because of the general state of women's physical health and second, because of the treatment of women during pregnancy and childbirth. Historical changes in nutrition, for example, affect reproduction. The widespread problem of rickets posed a special difficulty for pregnant women because rickets causes deformities of the pelvis that make labor and delivery difficult and dangerous (Shorter 1982). Other types of malnutrition also affect women's muscular structure or energy level. Because of women's low status in the family, women used to eat considerably less (and often less nourishing) food than their husbands, which placed them at increased risk of malnutrition.

For women of the wealthier classes, clothing caused problems during the middle and end of the 19th century. Corsets could exert 28 pounds of pressure (in extreme cases, considerably more) on internal organs. Over time this constant pressure would deform their body structure. Women's clothing was very heavy; street clothing averaged 37 pounds in the winter, 19 of which were suspended from the waist (Ehrenreich and English 1979, 98).

The process of childbirth has changed dramatically over the past two centuries. Let us look at these changes in relation to women's health.[5] The now common practice of having doctors deliver babies in hospitals, with the mother on her back and her feet in stirrups, is very recent. Most babies were born at home until World War II; the proportion of hospital births rose from 37% in 1935 to 79% in 1945 and 99% by the end of the 1970s (Shorter 1982, 157). Midwives delivered about half the children born in the United States at the turn of the century; after 1910 the majority of women were assisted by male doctors. The use of the lithotomy position for birthing (back down, feet up; named after the operation used to remove gallstones) accompanied the anesthetized deliveries that became prevalent after the middle of the 19th century. Before that women gave birth lying on their sides, squatting, standing, or sitting.

At one time delivery of babies was thought to be beneath the dignity of doctors. In the late 17th and 18th centuries, however, doctors began to compete with midwives, especially in cities where people had the money to pay. (Doctors were apparently happy to leave births to midwives in rural areas and among the poor and immigrants, at least until the early 20th century.) The doctors charged that midwives were incompetent. Most research shows something quite different; midwives were at least as competent as doctors, and trained urban midwives were even more competent than the other midwives and, therefore, probably than the average doctor. Note that "medical incompetence" refers not just to whether practitioners help solve health problems but also to whether they create health problems. We shall see that in trying to do the former practitioners sometimes inadvertently do the latter.

The innovations doctors brought to childbirth included new technology and surgical skills. The forceps were invented by barber-surgeon Peter Chamberlin in the early 17th century and remained a family secret for many years. Eventually other doctors began to use them. Forceps are appropriately used only in problem deliveries and only under certain circumstances. Their use can be painful and, if they are misused, dangerous to mother or child. Unfortunately forceps were too often used incompetently, and after the 1920s doctors began to use forceps with increasing frequency. Forceps deliveries have declined partly because so many doctors have turned instead to birth by surgery (caesarean section), a much safer procedure.

Two forms of surgery have become common in connection with childbirth. The first, episiotomy, is designed to enlarge the opening to the vagina by cutting the tissue at its base. If an episiotomy is not done in some cases, this tissue may be torn (perhaps dangerously) by the emerging infant's head. Episiotomies have become routine; they are performed in 70–80% of births in North America.[6] They are much more common in hospital births than in home births (Rothman 1982). In any case, some research suggests that episiotomy actually causes some of the problems it is designed to prevent (Rothman 1982, 58), and a more recent Canadian study shows that episiotomy generally offers no benefits.[7]

The other surgical procedure that has been used increasingly frequently is the caesarean section, or surgical delivery of the baby through the abdomen. Caesareans were used in emergencies (usually unsuccessfully) as early as the 16th century. They became considerably safer at the end of the 19th century, although they were rarely used in the United States until very recently. The rate of caesareans increased dramatically from an average of 6% of births in 1970 to 25% in 1987.[8] Caesareans are more frequent in private than in public hospitals, suggesting that finances play an important role in decision making along with health considerations. Some observers suggest that the high rate of caesarean sections is caused partly by hospital staff choosing the delivery time according to their own convenience. Further, because caesarean births are now extremely safe, doctors may prefer this strategy to riskier procedures (including a lengthy and difficult labor), partly because of the widespread incidence of malpractice suits (Taffel, Placek, and Less 1987).

At one time women who had one caesarean section had to use the same method for all subsequent births. In 1970, for example, only 2% of postcaesarean births were vaginal births. Now, partly because of changes in technique, more women are being urged to try vaginal births for postcaesarean deliveries. By 1988 about 13% of postcaesarean births were done vaginally; about 6 out of every 10 women who tried were successful. Many of the (40%) women who are evaluated as medically eligible do not try.[9]

Debates also rage over other aspects of current birthing practices. Medical personnel often prefer the lithotomy position for birth because it makes it easier for doctors to monitor the fetus and deliver the baby, but it also makes it harder for women to give birth by increasing the risk of tearing, working against gravity, thus rendering it more difficult for women to push because their feet are elevated. When women are ordered to stay immobile in bed rather than walking around, labor lengthens. To compensate for these problems, some doctors do episiotomies, use more drugs to decrease the added pain, and induce births or perform caesarean sections to shorten labor.

The invention of anesthesia in 1847 made it possible to relieve the pain of childbirth and increased the feasibility of the surgical procedures discussed above. Far from being restricted to cases of extraordinary pain or emergency, however, the use of a wide variety of tranquilizers and anesthetics has become routine. Many women have been grateful for the pain relief, of course, but there are costs when anesthetics are used. While they are in effect, a woman's ability to use her voluntary muscles is diminished or lost, making it difficult for her to participate actively in childbirth and making surgery more likely. Women may find themselves too drugged even to hold their newborn infants. And if the mother is drugged, so is the fetus. Unfortunately, women are given very little information about what drugs they are receiving and why. One study of women who had "normal vaginal deliveries" found that the average woman is exposed to 11 different drugs during pregnancy and 7 different drug administrations during childbirth (McManus et al. 1982).

What conclusions can we draw about women and health from this brief survey of the relationship between health professionals and birth? The history of childbirth in the West, especially the United States, is marked by the growing influence of the "medical model" of pregnancy and childbirth. As Barbara Rothman describes it,

> [Within] the medical model the body is seen as a machine, and the male body is taken as the norm. Pregnancy and birth are at best complications, stresses on the system. At worst, they are disease-like states. In either case, in that model, they need treatment, medical management (1982, 24).

Pregnant women are transformed into "patients" and are treated, and expected to act, as though they are sick people. Many medical definitions of what is normal during pregnancy are based on norms for nonpregnant women (a more "normal" state), which means doctors end up attempting to cure women of "abnormalities" that are actually normal in pregnant women (Rothman 1982, 141–57). Sometimes it seems as though the doctor and not the woman births the baby.

Women have learned to accept the medical model, including the notion that something in their body is likely to go wrong. They have also learned to think of pain as the most salient feature of childbirth. The medical model has turned pregnancy and childbirth into one set of precautions after another. Some of these precautions are overused or of dubious utility for most pregnant women.

Most doctors and women still prefer hospital births "just in case," that is, because medical technology, drugs, and specialists are available in hospitals. But in the hospital, "just in case" procedures may be routine. Further, as Judith Leavitt (1983) points out, when birthing women began to use hospitals rather than delivering at home, they lost control over the process—a point we will discuss more later in this chapter.

Pregnancy and childbirth have become safer for women and babies in recent history, largely because of advances in medicine. On the other hand, infant and maternal mortality rates are higher in the United States than they are in much of Western Europe, which tends to use less interventionist and lower technology approaches. There are two issues here. One is whether, after a certain point, the value added by extra technology and intervention really gains us more life and health. In some cases, as we have seen, the medical and technological models of dealing with pregnancy and childbirth result in losses as well as gains. Current birthing practices often make the experience less healthful and satisfactory than it might be, partly because normal women are treated as though they are unhealthy. Many women and health-care practitioners are beginning to seek more healthful alternatives.

The other crucial issue has to do with the availability of affordable and appropriate health care for pregnant women. The United States has had one of the most restricted public-health systems in the industrial world, and the per capita cost of health care is much more expensive than elsewhere. While prenatal care is crucial for insuring the life and health of mothers and babies during and after childbirth, a large proportion of pregnant women in the United States get little or no health care. Over a quarter of women of reproductive age have no health insurance, and the insurance of another 9% does not cover maternity care (Muller 1990, 189). A study of a West Virginia community in the mid 1980s that had a free prenatal health-care program for a 2-year period showed significant improvement in fetal death rates during the period the program was in operation (Foster, Guzick, and Pulliam 1992). In the early 1990s, with the election of the Clinton administration, the federal government finally began to engage in serious thinking about developing a health-care system that would make health care available to more pregnant women. (For more discussion of reproduction and family issues see Chapter 12.)

Families, Family Roles, and Health

In 1963 Betty Friedan published *The Feminine Mystique*, a book that became very influential in the rise of the new women's movement. Friedan took a second look at the presumably happy, hopeful world of post–World War II suburbia, and she found a problem among homemakers that was widespread but had no name. In her book she offered some doctors' views of the problem:

> [One] found, surprisingly, that his patients suffering from "housewife's fatigue," slept more than an adult needed to sleep—as much as ten hours a

> day—and that the actual energy they spent on housework did not tax their capacity. The real problem must be something else, he decided—perhaps boredom. Some doctors told their women patients they must get out of the house for a day, treat themselves to a movie in town. Others prescribed tranquilizers. Many suburban housewives were taking tranquilizers like cough drops. "You wake up in the morning, and you feel as if there's no point in going on another day like this. So you take a tranquilizer because it makes you not care so much that it's pointless."

Many people began to wonder: Is it possible that family life was not as healthy for women as people had thought?

Over the years scholarly research added evidence that family life as it is commonly constructed creates special health problems for women. Influential research in the early 1970s showed gender differences in the relationship between marital status and mental health that continue to hold up (Gove 1972; Gove, Style, and Hughes 1990). Married women have higher rates of mental disorder than married men, but single, divorced, and widowed women have lower rates of mental disorder than similarly situated men. What could be the cause of these differences? Many observers point to the burdens and stresses that individuals assume or relinquish when they marry or when their marriages break up. Jessie Bernard (1972) argues that when men and women marry, they do not really enter into the same situation; they enter what she calls "his" and "hers" marriages.

Marriage is a different experience for men and women, especially when children arrive. Indeed, research suggests that marriage itself has similar positive effects on women and men, as does employment, but that when children arrive the stresses on the marriage and the gender divisions of physical and psychological labor have different effects on them (McLanahan and Adams 1987). Married men continue to have much less responsibility for their own or their family's day-to-day maintenance such as cooking, cleaning, or shopping (Hochschild 1989). While at work they are not held as responsible for the care and supervision of their children as married women are when they are at work. Men who find themselves on their own must manage these things themselves. Given their socialization and lack of experience this can be very difficult indeed. Some studies show that after a divorce fathers often find interacting with their children very stressful because they have not developed child-care skills, even with their own children.

The situation for women is different. Married woman tend to shoulder most of the care-taking responsibilities in the household; the husband is, among other things, another person within the family needing care. Besides doing domestic labor, a "good" wife is supposed to provide emotional support to the husband. The husband's job is generally regarded as more important than the wife's, and his job-related problems take precedence over hers. If a woman is a full-time homemaker, she is supposed to be understanding and helpful when her husband comes home from work regardless of what her day was like. Arlie Hochschild struck a chord in many households when she published her book, *The Second Shift*, on the stressful results of this division of labor (Hochschild 1989). Women with children face tremendous burdens when their marriages break up, but they are also left with one less person to manage.

Of course, there are many problems that men and women are likely to share. And for the approximately 20% of dual-career married couples in which the husband and wife share the domestic responsibilities, or "second shift," both the health problems and benefits are likely to be similar. But for the majority of married couples, the "his" and "hers" marriage model still has some negative health implications for women in particular. Among these are the effects of isolation and loss of autonomy, the stress of juggling the demands of family and work, and the widespread problem of domestic violence.

Women suffer more than men from a loss of autonomy in the early years of marriage (Lopata 1971). Sometimes the reaction is particularly destructive, causing *agoraphobia* (fear of open spaces), making women fearful of venturing outside the home and, sometimes, even of answering the door or telephone or leaving the curtains open. Ironically, agoraphobia, which is most common among young married women, renders them incapable of carrying out many normal homemaking tasks.

Many social scientists have pointed to the construction of gender divisions of labor in the family as potential health hazards for women. Consider the effect on a woman's life of having small children. Because a large minority of women but not men with small children are withdrawn from the labor force for some period of time, they are more likely than men to be socially isolated and spend much more of their day without any adult contact. Research suggests that such isolation is related to both depression and loneliness. An interesting perspective on this problem is provided by research showing that 6 hours is the maximum contact with children that day-care workers can tolerate before their abilities to function are diminished (Seiden 1976). Watching television, an activity many women may use to pass the time and to give themselves "contact" with people other than children, is not without its dangers. One study (Shaver and Freedman 1976) found that the more hours women spent alone with children, the more lonely they felt and that the more television they watched, the more worthless they felt. As one newspaper reporter who had recently returned from maternity leave put it in her article on maternity leave, "Let's face it. Being a full-time mom can beat out any desk job for stress, fatigue, unpredictable predicaments and tense moments. Besides, if working at home were so easy, men would be lining up to do it."[10]

In recent years, increasing attention has been paid to another family health hazard: domestic violence. Estimates are that about 4% of American children aged 3 to 17—2 million children—are abused each year, and some violence between spouses occurs in approximately 16% of couples (Gelles, 1980). Most research agrees that even where both partners engage in violence men tend to be the primary perpetrators (women's violence is more likely to be a response to violence) and women suffer greater injuries. At least 20% of women treated in hospital emergency rooms are injured by domestic violence. The FBI claims that in 1990 about 30% of women murdered in the United States were killed by their boyfriends or husbands.[11]

Wini Breines and Linda Gordon (1983) conclude from their research that there are two apparently contradictory images of the family: the "peaceful haven" and the "cradle of violence." It may be precisely some aspects of the family that make it a peaceful haven that also transform it into a cradle of violence. Breines and Gordon say, "Intimate and family relationships are filled with contradiction, with longing and expectations so ambiguous and ambivalent that they may not be conscious" (493).

Research in many fields suggests that gender ideology and the gender-based structure of families help to create the amount and type of violence we find in families. Certainly stress of various sorts may trigger family violence, but stress alone is not the cause of violence. Millions of people face the stresses of crying babies, poverty and strained resources, time conflicts, intrafamilial disagreement, or other tensions without engaging in violence against partners, parents, or children. Something else must lead individuals to turn their stress into violence against their family members. More specifically, something must explain why so much family violence is directed against *women.*

This transformation of stress into family violence is likely to result under two circumstances. First, individuals under stress may feel unable to pursue alternative coping mechanisms. The isolation of mothers of young children, discussed earlier, offers an example. This study was of a group of women at a clinic for mothers who had abused their children and a control group of mothers who hadn't done so. The main difference between the two groups was that the abusive mothers were under more stress and were more socially isolated. They were pressed for time, often because besides taking care of small children they were employed or in school, and they had smaller social networks, especially fewer adult friends (Salzinger, Kaplan, and Artmeyeff 1983). Research also suggests that women and men generally tend to express distress differently; whereas women exhibit distress through such symptoms as depression and anxiety, thus turning their distress inward, men are more likely to exhibit distress through aggressive behavior or substance use, which can help lead to aggressive behavior (Aneshensel, Rutter, and Lachenbruch 1991). The fact that men are more likely to turn stress outward against others than women may help account for their relatively high use of violence in the family compared with women's.

But why is so much domestic violence directed against women in particular? Why does such a large proportion of the violence that women—and children—suffer occur at the hands of their "loved ones"? The answer must lie largely in whether domestic violence, against women *or* children, is considered a "normal" or justifiable part of family life and intimate relations. To what degree is violence against women treated as less unhealthy than other kinds of violence?

Consider the norms uncovered in a national study of family violence. Using a national sample, Ursula Dibble and Murray Straus (1980) found that 63% of Americans admitted to having pushed, shoved, slapped, or thrown something at their children. Almost 82 percent thought that slapping a 12-year-old child is necessary, normal, or good, and 65% thought that slapping a 12-year-old child is necessary, normal, *and* good. A majority of the U.S. population, in other words, considers some level of violence by parents against their children a normal, presumably healthy part of family life. It is no wonder that defining child abuse is so difficult; where do people draw the line?

Evidence shows that a certain amount of gender-based violence against women is still widely considered normal, acceptable, and justifiable. "Gender-based violence" refers not just to any violence between women and men, but to violence that is understood and justified in part by people's understanding of the gendered character of men and women or their appropriate relative roles and relationships to each other (Sapiro 1993). For example, until the 1970s, nowhere did the law recognize that a man could rape his wife. The fact of a woman's marriage was taken as a legal sign that she had given consent to having sexual relations with him. Thus, instead of regarding it as abnormal or unhealthy for a man to force an unwilling woman to have sex with him if they were married to each other, the law suggests we should regard a woman who at any time does not want to have sex with her husband as abnormal or unhealthy.[12]

The law also used to regard some degree of wife battery as healthy and normal.[13] Many people still think it is necessary for men to hit their wives from time to time. In observations of staged street fights, psychologists found that male passersby would aid a man attacked by another man or a woman, and a woman attacked by a woman, but not a woman being attacked by a man. Why? A man attacking a woman might be her husband, which means that the violence is a "private matter" (cited in Rohrbaugh 1980, 351).

Thus the sex/gender system can make the family an unhealthy breeding ground for violence against women if it is based on patriarchal and androcentric ideas about the appropriate relationship between women and men in their families. Research shows, for example, that the risk of violence between spouses is particularly high when there is a great status difference between husband and wife, especially when the wife's occupation is of higher status than the husband's (Hornung, McCullough, and Sugimoto 1981). It is often very stressful for men to have wives with higher-status occupations because they have learned they are supposed to be superior to their wives.

People learn these ideas about violence as children. A national sample survey study (Ulbrich and Huber 1981) shows that childhood observation of intraspousal violence helps men come to accept violence against women as normal, even when they do not engage in violence against women themselves. Men who had seen their fathers hit their mothers were more likely to think that violence against women can be justified than those who hadn't. In contrast, women who had seen their fathers hit their mothers were less likely to think violence against women can be justified. Both men and women were more likely to find justification for violence against women if they saw their mothers hit their fathers. There is no inevitable cycle of violence, especially given new health, counseling, and relief agencies designed to help both the perpetrators and victims of family violence, but this research shows living with violence against women as a child can help socialize men to accept that violence.[14]

Work and Health

In the late 19th century many psychologists and medical practitioners were disturbed by women's tendency to seek more education and employment. As

Ehrenreich and English argue, "Medical men saw the body as a miniature economic system, with the various parts—like classes or interest groups—competing for a limited supply of resources" (1979, 114). If women used either their brains or their brawn to study or work, they would deplete the energies needed to bear and raise children. Some found evidence in the tendency (which still exists) for female college graduates to be less likely to marry and to have fewer children than females who are not college graduates (Ehrenreich and English 1979, 115). This theory has long since lost its popularity, but the relationship between employment and women's health, especially reproductive health, is an important theme in women's economic history. We will look at some of the issues beginning with the effects of combining employment and family roles, then turning more directly to health and the work place.

What is the relationship between health and women's employment? The evidence is mixed. Some studies find employed women healthier than full-time homemakers while others do not. A survey of married black women found no difference between homemakers and employed women in their levels of depressive symptoms but did find more depression among unemployed women (Brown and Gray 1988). Another survey observed no difference in the psychiatric status of employed women and homemakers but found that homemakers liked their work less, found it less interesting, and felt less adequate in their jobs (Newberry, Weissman, and Myers 1979).

Not surprisingly, health depends on the combination of burdens people shoulder. A national study of mental health found that among married women who were not employed the presence of children was associated with increased depression, whereas among married women who were employed depression was not affected by children per se, but by the level of difficulty they had in arranging child care and whether or not their husbands participated in child care. Employed mothers who had sole responsibility for children and difficulty in arranging child care showed the highest levels of depression. Neither the presence of children nor the availability of child care affected husbands' levels of depression (Ross and Mirowsky 1988).

Women's experience of combining roles also depends on their attitudes toward them. Consider a study of first-time mothers of babies 5 to 9 months old who had left the labor force to care for their children. The study compared women who had been very involved with their work before the birth with those who hadn't. Those who previously had been very involved in their work showed greater irritability, decreased marital intimacy, greater depression, lower self-esteem, and they perceived higher costs of motherhood than did mothers who had not been so involved in work before their babies were born (Pistrang 1984).

Another issue in work and health is occupational health and safety—that is, not just the impact of the simple fact of being employed on women's health, but the impact of the job itself and the work environment. At the turn of the 20th century many groups pressed for legislation that would offer special protections to women workers. This "protective labor legislation" assumed that certain jobs involve tasks or situations that are more dangerous to women than to men or put them at risk in ways that are unacceptable.

Until 1908 the Supreme Court remained antagonistic to the idea of protective labor legislation, not because it was worried about sex discrimination but because, as it said in *Lochner* v. *New York* (1905), any type of protective legislation for workers (regardless of sex) constituted interference with the right to enter freely into a contract. In 1908 the Court changed its mind in the case of *Muller* v. *Oregon*, which concerned a maximum hours law applying only to women. The justification offered by the Court for allowing such legislation contains the classic argument for restricting women's employment:

> That women's physical structure and the performance of maternal functions place her at a disadvantage in the struggle for subsistence is obvious. This is especially true when the burdens of motherhood are upon her. Even when they are not, by abundant testimony of the medical fraternity continuance for a long time on her feet at work, repeating this from day to day, tends to injurious effects upon the body, *and as healthy mothers are essential to vigorous offspring, the physical well-being of woman becomes an object of public interest and care* in order to preserve the strength and vigor of the race (emphasis added).

Whether or not an individual woman was either pregnant or a mother, the Court now said she should be treated as though she were. The law has a special interest in protecting women's health because "her physical structure and a proper discharge of her maternal functions—having in view not merely her own health, but the well-being of the race—justify legislation to protect her from the greed as well as the passion of man." The restrictions "are not imposed solely for her benefit, but also largely for the benefit of all," said the Court.

Most special protective labor legislation for women has disappeared because it conflicts with employment sex discrimination law, especially Title VII of the 1964 Civil Rights Act, which bars discrimination in employment on the basis of race and sex. But employment-related protection of women's reproductive systems continues to spark controversy. The Federal Occupational Safety and Health Administration (OSHA) was established in 1970 to develop and enforce guidelines to protect workers from health and safety hazards at work. Jeanne Mager Stellman (1977) argues that relatively little attention has been paid to women's special occupational health problems, although some are quite widespread and serious. For example, she points out, hospital jobs generally held by women have the greatest risk of skin diseases. Other jobs that place workers at special risk of skin diseases are cleaning, hairdressing, food service, and homemaking—heavily female sectors of the economy.

Many employers have tried to protect women, especially pregnant women, from substances considered hazardous to reproductive health. They usually do this by barring pregnant women or women of childbearing age from doing jobs that would bring them in contact with these substances. Employers fear lawsuits by women who may not have known they were pregnant when exposed to substances dangerous to the fetus' health. Many critics have charged that this kind of policy is discriminatory and results in inequitable treatment of women and men.

Many of these substances are hazardous to *both* sexes, but only women are barred from the affected jobs while men's health is left at risk.[15]

Many of the rules and laws that "protected" women's health at work have come to be viewed as roadblocks selectively placed in the path of women's advancement. Many protective labor practices have been applied less rigorously in traditionally female jobs than in traditionally male jobs. More effort is expended to protect women from hazardous "male" jobs than from hazardous "female" jobs, showing the gender ideology underlying the policies.

Women now have more choices, but as Vibiana Andrade says, such choices also give women the opportunity to pay with their own flesh (1981, 78). Women face a range of health hazards at work that we are only beginning to understand. Among these are stress, which has important psychological and physical effects. Not only are women entering more stressful jobs, but also they are doing so without the same sort of help at home that men receive. Women are also entering fields in which they are likely to encounter discrimination and sexual harassment, which also affects women's health by increasing stress. Although old-style protective labor legislation is not the answer, some means must be found to protect the health of the nation's work force.

Beauty, Fitness, and Health

Recent years have witnessed increasing attention to physical fitness for both men and women. Definitions of health have become more linked to conceptions of beauty and appearance. Consider the trends in advertisements; shampoos, nail polishes, and skin creams are now guaranteed to make our hair and skin not just beautiful but also "healthy looking." Women athletes and dancers are increasingly used as models and promoters in television commercials. These changes stand in stark contrast to the past, when women and girls were discouraged from athletics and other activities that might promote health but were thought to make women unattractive and unfeminine. Standards of feminine beauty have often been remarkably detrimental to women's health. Let us look at some of the connections between health and beauty.

THE PURSUIT OF BEAUTY. Shifting standards of health and attractiveness have affected both sexes, but women have had to endure more than men in the pursuit of beauty. Women with the means and time to do so have become convinced to resculpt, recolor, and otherwise alter their bodies in a wide range of ways, sometimes dangerously, in the pursuit of current standards of beauty. Many of these alterations have been encouraged, or at least aided and abetted, by both the medical profession and the business world including the fashion industry and pharmaceutical companies. Only rarely has the natural shape, color, or smell of the female body been promoted as attractive. Hair coloring, especially coloring to hide the normal signs of aging, is more common among women than men. Women have used countless forms of coloring on their faces. Even in the rare times when their lip color has been regarded as appropriate, lipsticks have been created to look "natural." Besides attention to and possible artificial alteration of

How to achieve the "classic" hourglass figure: with a stiff corset.

a woman's overall dimensions, the size of many individual parts of her body has been the object of special attention, including her eyes, eyelashes, nose, lips, cheeks, breasts, fingernails, abdomen, buttocks, and thighs.

Consider changes in the ideal weight and shape of women's bodies. For white, middle- and upper-class women in the 19th century, the "consumptive look"—that is, the thin and fragile look of tuberculosis—was the beauty ideal. Women tried to make their waists appear even smaller by wearing corsets which, over time, could literally change the shape of the body, cramping and moving vital internal organs in the process. Swooning became a fashionable show of delicacy (and no wonder given the effects of the corsets). Of course this ideal delicacy could be pursued only by relatively few women. Working-class and agricultural white women and women of color of all classes were considered naturally stronger and hardier, fit to be workhorses, not swooning feminine ideals. In the early part of the 20th century, weight standards rose for women (look at the robust chorus girls in early movies), then fell again after the 1960s to an almost emaciated look. Now, with the fitness craze, the size of women's bodies is once again rising. At various times in the past century women's breasts have been bound to make them look small, raised by stiff brassieres to make them look large, exaggerated with padding, and left virtually undressed.

In the 19th century white women were supposed to remain as pale as possible, which required avoiding the sun and fresh air. These women, then, did not only *look* consumptive; their behavior contributed to large rates of tuberculosis among women. In the 20th century standards changed; white women began to bake themselves mercilessly in the sun, go to "tanning spas," or use chemicals to simulate a tan. By the late 1980s medical experts began warning that this pursuit of a tan was leading to an epidemic of skin cancer and premature aging of women's skin. Women were urged to be more careful about protecting their skin from the sun. Black women meanwhile have sometimes been urged to try to bleach their skin.

In the post–World War II era, surgery was increasingly used to alter bodies. Women have had facelifts and "nose jobs" and operations to remove layers of fat ("liposuction") and augment their breasts. Female models often have their back teeth removed to give them hollow cheeks and the appearance of high cheekbones. In the early 1990s the problem of breast implants became headline news. By 1990 at least 150,000 women a year were having breast implants. Although many of these women had medically related reasons for implants, such as previous mastectomies, about 80% were for nonmedical reasons.[16] By the late 1980s reports of implant-caused tragedies began to filter into the news. Implants caused scar tissue buildup and other problems when they leaked or ruptured, and many women began to report they developed autoimmune diseases. In 1991 widely publicized lawsuits rewarded women damages due to the effects of their implants. Although the major manufacturer, Dow Corning Wright, argued that no scientific evidence showed that breast implants caused autoimmune diseases,[17] it did offer to pay the cost for any woman who wished to have her implant removed. In January 1992 the Food and Drug Administration (FDA) imposed a moratorium on the use of breast implants, arguing that their safety had not been proved. The FDA initiated a study to determine their safety.[18]

Feminists raise five criticisms about these "beauty" practices. The first points to the double standard of beauty. Research shows that women's physical attractiveness simply makes more difference for the way they are perceived and treated than it does for men (Jackson 1992). Why should women require so much ornamentation and alteration—and so much more than men—to be considered attractive? Second, these practices require a considerable investment and, many argue, waste of women's time and money. Women have less of either resource at their disposal than men do, but are pressured to spend these precious resources in search of passing and often unattainable beauty ideals.

The third criticism concerns choice and control. Standards of beauty are established and guided in large part by the pharmaceutical, fashion, and cosmetic industries through advertising and by the commercial entertainment media such as television and motion pictures. Although these industries may not be able to manipulate women as though they were lifeless puppets, their powers of direction are considerable. To what degree do women look the way they want to look, and to what degree do they look the way other people want them to look?

The fourth criticism of these fashion and style practices concerns the negative impact on women's health. Many of these "beauty practices" put women's health at risk and some are downright dangerous, as shown by the breast implant controversy. The chemical composition of some women's toiletries is harmful. Women's clothes generally have not been designed with comfort in mind and can be restrictive to women who are or might otherwise be active. Women's shoes are a good case in point. Looking at the historical parade of high spindly heels, pointed cramped toes, and high platforms who would guess that the primary function of feet is transportation? It is no wonder that dress reform has been a major goal of feminist movements since the 1840s.

The final criticism is that the combined effects of these beauty standards lead women to low self-esteem and self-devaluation to an extent that can become extremely dangerous. It is important to remember that the standards of beauty perpetrated through the advertising and entertainment industries are unattainable for most women. The women who serve as models are 9% taller and 16% thinner than the average woman.[19] They also are very young, leaving most women over age 35 "over the hill" as far as public images of beauty are concerned. These beauty standards generally require substantial financial resources. To the degree that they dictate appropriate skin or hair color, body shape, or hair texture they also support racial and ethnic stereotypes and inequality.

WEIGHT AND DIET. It is no wonder that research consistently shows that girls and women are more discontented with their bodies than men are and spend more time dieting and engaging in other efforts to make their bodies conform to ideal standards (Jackson 1992). Standards women use to evaluate their own weight differ by ethnicity (Dawson 1988), although discontentment among women with their body shape reaches across racial and ethnic lines. Research suggests, for example, that African American and white women are similarly discontented with their own body size, although white women are more likely to think that their being "overweight" will actually have negative repercussions in the way men treat them (Thomas and James 1988).

One study of pregnant women and maternity clothes reveals an interesting aspect of women's reactions to weight gain, especially how their self-evaluations are mediated by external forces and social class. A survey of department stores found that the location of the maternity clothes was related to the "class" of the store (Horgan 1983). In more expensive stores, maternity clothes were near the lingerie department. In stores aimed at working-class women, maternity clothes were located near the large-size women's department and uniforms. (Why, in any case, do large women—usually meaning women size 16 and over—need a segregated section of department stores?) In the same study, a survey showed that wealthier pregnant women felt sexier and more attractive than other women, and the less wealthy and working-class pregnant women felt fatter and unattractive.

There is considerable prejudice and discrimination against overweight people (Jackson 1992; Rothblum 1992). In fact, women hold more negative stereotypes of the obese than men do (Jackson 1992, 166). Esther Rothblum (1992) writes that while observers frequently have explained the often-noted connection between poverty and obesity by looking for the conditions of poverty that lead to obesity (such as the types of available food), she believes discrimination against the obese is great enough to argue that part of the cause of poverty may lie in the way people treat obese people. For women who are in fact overweight, then, there is plenty of pressure to internalize self-hatred.

Those concerned with women's health have focused increasingly on related "eating disorders" found principally among women: anorexia nervosa, or self-starvation, and bulimia, or binge eating alternated with self-induced vomiting and fasting. Both are serious illnesses, not just cases of "going too far" in attempts to lose weight. They involve compulsive and dangerous behaviors, often hidden from family and friends until they are well advanced, and they result in emaciation, other physical symptoms, and in some severe cases death. The anorexic continues to regard herself as fat and ugly even after she has lost a dangerous amount of weight.

From 85% to 95% of all anorexics and bulimics are women (Jackson 1992). A large number of college women exhibit symptoms of bulimia or anorexia. Most research suggests that the majority of afflicted women are in their late teens and early twenties and are somewhat overweight, although not necessarily extraordinarily so. They tend to be "good girls" from affluent homes who have well-educated parents and are under pressure to succeed. Anorexia seems to strike at the time when major changes are occurring in a young woman's life—as she prepares to go to college or to get married.

Other research is beginning to suggest that this portrait may be due more to bias in research than to the reality of which women suffer from eating disorders. For example, a study of Chippewa women showed that the majority in the sample were trying to diet and the majority of them were using unhealthy methods (reported in Jackson 1992, 185). There is a widespread problem of eating disorders among women of color, and it seems to be increasing (Jackson 1992).

Many theories have been advanced to explain these illnesses. Most experts agree that eating disorders are linked to gender roles and sexual pressures on young women. They disagree, however, about the precise cause and meaning of these problems. Some argue that anorexia is a flight from femininity. Others consider it an attempt to fulfill norms of femininity and feminine beauty run amok. Still others argue that anorexia is based on feelings of dependency and unworthiness. One study of the life histories of Latina, African American, and white women found in each group that many women who were survivors of sexual abuse also suffered from eating disorders, and many of them made an explicit connection in their minds between the abuse and eating (Thompson 1992). Many described the eating in terms of a numbing hatred of their own body or a means of protecting it. In these cases it may not be obsession with the way the women's bodies look that triggers eating disorders, but rather the act of eating.

EXERCISE. All other things being equal, body weight and tone depend on both diet and exercise. Females have tended to diet and males to exercise to control their weight (Dwyer and Mayer 1968), partly because until recently girls were discouraged from most forms of exercise that would strengthen and tone their bodies. Muscles were considered unflattering in women, and engaging in most sports was thought to be either unfeminine or dangerous. Since menstruating and pregnant women were considered disabled, until the last few years exercise was considered especially bad for them. Attitudes are changing, however, and now even pregnant women are encouraged to exercise.

The issues and debate surrounding Title IX and sports in schools (see Chapter 5) point to the degree to which sports have been institutionalized as a male domain. Philosopher Jane English (1982) argues that our very concept of sports has been androcentric. She writes that "the few athletic activities permitted to women—mostly forms of dance—were not thought to fall under the concept of sport, and are still classified as arts or entertainment instead. Speed, size, and strength seem to be the essence of sports. Women are naturally inferior at 'sports' so conceived" (266). Women's bodies, their "small size, flexibility, and low center of gravity combine to give women the kind of natural hegemony in some sports activities such as the balance beam that men enjoy in football" (265). English suggests that if women rather than men dominated the sports world, "competitions emphasizing flexibility, balance, strength, timing, and small size might dominate Sunday afternoon television and offer salaries in six figures" (266). Even this is beginning to change, as more people are paying attention to women's sports such as college basketball.

As more athletic opportunities are opening to women and girls are receiving better training, the gap between women and men in such abilities as speed and strength has been considerably reduced. Indeed, even though men and women still perform differently in many sports requiring these abilities, women athletes now match or break records set by men a few decades ago—a feat that seemed biologically impossible then.

Which sports are most lucrative and whether top female athletes can compete against top male athletes are questions of only tangential interest to most of us. Our activities are not chosen on the basis of whether we can beat everyone else. Regular exercise is important for physical health, and women who try to control the way they look through dress, cosmetic alterations, diet, or surgery are often unsuccessful unless they also include exercise in their lives as well.

Women and the Practice of Health Care

Thus far we have looked at the way women's health is shaped and defined by different social institutions and practices. Let us now look to the health-care system to reach some general conclusions about women's health care. To what degree do we find evidence of androcentrism or sexism in health-care systems?

Some evidence suggests that health-care professionals view and treat males and females differently, although the differences may not be as great as they once were (Smith 1980). As mentioned earlier, in 1970 Inge Broverman and her colleagues found that mental-health clinicians described a "healthy male" and a "healthy adult" in roughly the same way and used other terms to characterize a "healthy female." Later studies obtained similar results (Aslin 1977; Kravetz and Jones 1981; O'Malley and Richardson 1985).

Other studies also show that judgments of health among patients and clients may be based on gender ideology. In one study, when hypothetical female patients expressed conventionally "male" attitudes, evaluators judged them as more disturbed than when they expressed attitudes or preferences conventionally considered neutral or feminine. The same statements did not affect evaluators' views when they were made by males (Zeldow 1976). In another, counselors listening to tapes of either a man or a woman expressing the same concerns about work rated the woman as more masculine than they rated the man, possibly because these concerns, apparently normal in a man, seem abnormal in a woman (Hayes and Wolleat 1978). Another found that counselors had more complete memory of what male clients had said than they did of what female clients had said (Buczek 1981).

Other aspects of health practitioners' ideology also appear to affect their judgments of patients. One study in which professional counselors were presented with bogus client profiles found that examiners who were politically conservative perceived greater psychological maladjustment in women who leaned left politically than in men with a similar political bias (Abramowitz et al. 1973). Another found that the higher the social class of a male patient, the more favorably the clinical psychologist viewed him, but the higher the social class of a female patient, the less favorably the therapist viewed her. If we assume that patients of higher social class are more articulate (which does not mean smarter), less deferential, and apparently less dependent, we can see how class and gender interact to produce this result. The males of higher social class would be acting in ways therapists find preferable in males, and females of the lower social class would be acting in ways therapists find preferable in females (Settin and Bramel 1981). When psychiatrists were presented with similar case histories, they tended to diagnose patients differently depending on their gender and race. The same symptoms led them to diagnose white women as having histrionic personality disorders and black women as having paranoid personality disorders. Male clinicians were especially likely to perceive women as depressed (Loring and Powell 1988).

Some research suggests that clinicians' attitudes have changed over time so that the problem is less that they see women and men differently per se and more that they define the situations in which they expect to find women and men differently. These clinicians defined mental-health characteristics differently for people in the home and at work. Appropriate characteristics for people in the home were the ones traditionally regarded as feminine while appropriate characteristics for people at work were those traditionally regarded as masculine (Poole and Tapley 1988). Of course the result will continue to be differential evaluation of women and men if they think of women at home and men at work.

Thus far we have considered differences in practitioners' attitudes toward and perceptions of men and women. Research also suggests that male and female patients are treated differently. An interview study of 253 physicians found doctors more likely to consider emotional factors important in diagnosing a woman's problems and more likely to expect a psychosomatic diagnosis of a woman's problem. These differences were especially evident among patients who did not, during the course of the medical interview, mention experiencing any personal problems (Bernstein and Kane 1981).

Both psychotic and neurotic males are kept in mental hospitals longer than are females with similar disorders, and psychotic males are channeled into psychiatric treatment more quickly than females (Tudor, Tudor, and Gove 1977). Thus it seems, "Standards of normality for females are reported to be lower than standards for males, and females are apparently less stigmatized for symptoms of mental incompetence" (Tudor, Tudor, and Gove 1977, 101) demonstrating again that from the medical point of view a normal female is not quite as healthy as a normal male or that an unhealthy female is more normal than an unhealthy male.

More psychotropic drugs such as sedatives and tranquilizers are prescribed for women than for men, and while women are more likely than men to use prescribed psychoactive drugs, men are more likely to use self-prescribed (for example, over-the-counter drugs and alcohol) or illegal drugs (Cooperstock 1971). This pattern exists even in specialized populations. Even if we hold levels of anxiety constant, elderly women are given more major tranquilizers than elderly men are (Milliren 1977), and women in prisons are given more psychotropic drugs than men in prisons are (Shaw 1982). Interviews with physicians reveal a variety of reasons for the prescription differences, including beliefs that women are more vulnerable and need drugs more, that men are reluctant to use drugs, and that women have the kinds of stress that can be alleviated by these drugs. Both women and doctors are likely to understand women's problems in psychological rather than purely physical terms. Some doctors believe that the side effects of psychotropic drugs are less troublesome to women because women don't have to be as alert as men do (Prather and Fidell 1975).

Drug advertisements play an important role in helping doctors to match drugs with patients and symptoms. Content analysis of drug ads shows that they tend to associate psychoactive drugs with women and nonpsychoactive drugs with men. Men in these advertisements have more specific or work-related problems, and women have more diffuse anxieties and tensions and are shown as difficult patients (Prather and Fidell 1975). Some drug advertisements suggest that a woman's reluctance or inability to do housework is a sign of mental illness, recalling Betty Friedan's picture of tranquilizer-popping housewives in the 1950s. (Seidenberg 1971. For more discussion of commercials and advertisements, see Chapter 8.)

Several factors combine to create problems for women in the health-care system. If a culture is sexist or androcentric, health-care practitioners and patients alike assimilate these attitudes and perceptions. Moreover, women may be especially hesitant to question their treatment. Doctors and patients are unequal in status, a female patient and a male doctor are even more so. Although consumer movements in health care have grown recently, "doctor's orders" are still commanding, particularly for women who, because of gender ideology, feel incompetent to question males in what is regarded as a male field.

These problems are exacerbated by the training of health-care professionals and the organizations in which they work. Textbooks and teaching methods used in medical schools reinforce sexist views of women. One doctor, for example, reported that during her first day at medical school the lab instructor told the students to cut off the female cadaver's breasts and discard them, as though there is nothing a doctor can learn from them despite the near-epidemic of breast cancer.[20] Feminist critics have expressed dismay at the ignorance of women in medical research and technology. Health problems of special concern to women have received little serious research attention until recently; this includes menstruation, menopause, and osteoporosis (bone deterioration). Heart disease has been treated much less aggressively in women than in men, and the instruments used in heart surgery are designed for men's bigger bodies.[21]

A considerable amount of medical research, including drug testing, is done on men only because researchers are worried about the effect of "abnormalities" of women's bodies such as menstrual cycles and pregnancy. This means we do not know to what degree and how many drugs may affect women and men differently or how they respond to the normal changes in women's bodies. In the early 1990s it became clear that because most of the AIDS attention and research had focused on men, experts had not caught on to the fact that the AIDS-causing human immunodeficiency virus (HIV) may have different effects on women's and men's bodies, thus leaving many HIV-positive women undetected. It is no wonder that many feminist health professionals are discussing the possible development of a formal medical specialty in women's health. But would such a move ghettoize women's health concerns? This is a topic for serious debate.[22]

Medical definitions of femininity are changing, and increasing health activism among women is pressuring the health-care system to be more responsive to women. In many communities, medical personnel and hospitals have become more favorable toward women taking more control of childbirth. Doctors increasingly expect women to take birth preparation courses such as Lamaze classes. Fitness among women is emphasized as it never was before. Women who do not conform to traditional female roles appear less likely to be suspected of being psychologically unhealthy.

Altering health-care institutions and procedures requires changes in the training health-care practitioners receive. But change appears risky, and neither the public nor health-care professionals are likely to take risks that might threaten health. As much as many of us would like to shape our own health care, few of us are likely to feel confident to question the training and experience of the professional. Patients may feel they have increased their power by using the threat of medical malpractice suits, but this threat both increases the cost of health care dramatically and tends to make doctors even more resistant to using anything but their own medical judgment and high-technology safeguards.

Health care is expensive in the United States. Unlike most other industrialized nations, the U.S. health-care system has long been based on the principle that except under certain circumstances, the person receiving health care should be responsible for paying the bill. The facts that women are poorer than men, care for more children, and live longer make the economics of health care particularly relevant to them. A growing consumer movement and the women's movement have argued that the public must be more active in shaping their health care. We therefore turn to the question of women's influence in health-care systems.

Women's Roles in Shaping Health Care

Women are now, and generally have been, the people who have provided most of the world's health care. However, the study of women in society repeatedly shows that a group constituting a numerical majority is by no means necessarily a group that has the most power and control.

Thus far this chapter has investigated how women's health is defined and treated by various social institutions. We now look more closely at the people who shape health care and values. What have been the roles of women? What contributions have women made to health care? We begin by looking at the people whose primary job it is to provide health care: health professionals and other workers. We then turn to health activists and social movements and organizations that attempt to influence health-care institutions and practices. Next we consider one of the largest groups of health-care providers: mothers. We conclude with the largest group of all: patients and health-care consumers.

Healers, Doctors, and Other Health-Care Professionals

Most health care is not now, and certainly was not in the past, provided by professional physicians. Until this century in the United States, midwives performed most gynecological and obstetrical care. Many women, often these same midwives, also served as healers, employing herbal remedies and other means to manage the people's health. Although many of their remedies were at best useless and at worst harmful (as were the strategies of male doctors of the same era), many were also very helpful. In fact, medicine recently has been returning to some of these "natural" remedies.

Professional medical training is a very recent phenomenon. Until the 17th century, doctors trained in academies concentrated their study primarily on philosophy, theology, and perhaps astrology. Certainly some of the women's herbs were at least as good as the men's stars and prayers. Even in the 19th century much of male doctors' training, especially with regard to gynecology and obstetrics, was theoretical in nature, so doctors were ill prepared when they began their practice on real women (Leavitt 1983). Part of the reason for this questionable training was the constraints placed on men because of gender ideology: A man should not offend the delicacy of a woman who is not his wife by looking at her naked body. Surgery was a relatively low-status occupation performed by men who doubled as barbers; the red and white barber pole, symbolizing a bloody rag, is a reminder of the dual role barbers once played. Most medical knowledge, including that of healers and midwives, was learned on the job from those who were more experienced.

As late as the 1840s about 70% of all male physicians in the United States had no formal medical training. In a sense, this information casts a slightly different light on the fact that the first female to finish formal medical training in the United States didn't do so until 1849. As Mary Roth Walsh has written, Elizabeth Blackwell (sister-in-law of Antoinette Brown Blackwell, discussed in Chapter 2) "was recognized as the first woman medical doctor because she was the first woman who earned a degree from a medical college, a criterion which, if applied to her male colleagues, would have sharply reduced their numbers" (Walsh 1979, 448).

Competition and antagonism between female healers and male doctors (and other male-dominated institutions) developed as early as the 14th century and was well established by the 15th and 16th centuries. This growing antagonism was manifested in part in the witch hunts of the late medieval period when, it is estimated, thousands of people were executed as witches, about 85% of whom were women (Ehrenreich and English 1979, 31). Among the charges leveled against the women were the crimes of healing, using drugs to ease pain, and assisting with contraception and abortion.

Although in early American history women continued to serve as healers and midwives, their activities became increasingly restricted during the 19th and 20th centuries. Medicine came under increasingly strict licensing requirements and eventually required training that at first only men could receive. Women's medical colleges began to open in the 1840s, and other medical schools began to admit women in the 1870s. By 1900 there were about 5,000 trained women doctors, but at about that time the mixed medical colleges that admitted women began to impose quotas restricting the number of women. Those women who did gain admission were often harassed by their male colleagues. The powerful professional organization and interest group, the American Medical Association (AMA), admitted women to full membership only in 1951, 104 years after it was founded. Medical schools explicitly imposed tougher entry standards on women than on men until the 1970s, when such actions became illegal. As soon as women were required only to be as good as men rather than better to get into medical school, the proportion of women in medical schools rose dramatically.

The late 19th and early 20th centuries saw the rise of a number of health-care fields such as nursing, social work, and mental health, some of which became predominantly female. Nursing is a very interesting case study of women health professionals. At first nurses were generally trained on the job, as ward workers in hospitals and clinics, for example. The first training school for nurses was established at Bellevue Hospital in New York City in 1873. Nursing

Nursing was always a "women's occupation," but different from its stereotype. In this photo, a nurse crosses New York rooftops to visit her patient.

education expanded and was gradually professionalized, although it was not regulated and licensed until after World War II. Since then nursing organizations have worked to foster a view of nurses as highly trained health-care professionals rather than the old "Nurse Nancy" view of nurses as cocktail waitresses or maids in white. In the 20th century, especially in the recent era of rapid technological and scientific development in medicine and health care, the number of female technicians and laboratory workers has also grown.

Men continue to hold higher proportions of the high-status roles in health-care organizations. In 1988 only about 20% of the nation's physicians and 9% of the dentists were women. Among the female-dominated health jobs in 1991, women constitute 99% of the dental assistants, 98% of the dental hygienists, 96% of the practical nurses, 95% of the registered nurses, and 94% of the dietitians (U.S. Bureau of the Census 1992). Women doctors have tended to go into fields with high patient interaction and, often, relatively low pay and status, such as general practice, psychiatry, and pediatrics, although these patterns are now changing.

Some evidence shows that patients and clients tend to prefer male health-care practitioners in some fields, although not in others (Chesler 1971; Tanney and Birk 1976; Mandelbaum 1978). Nevertheless, women provide a large proportion of health care in some fields. A 1977 study shows that in community mental-health clinics, psychiatrists, one-tenth of whom were female, provided 15% of the therapy hours; psychologists, one-third of whom were female, provided 8% of the therapy hours; and psychiatric social workers and general clinicians, two-thirds of whom were female, provided the other 77% of the therapy hours (cited in Rohrbaugh 1980). Many women, on the other hand, prefer women as health-care practitioners, particularly, one might suspect, as gynecologists and obstetricians and, as Mary Faith Tanney and Janice M. Birk (1976) show, as therapists for personal and social problems.

Little research has been done to see whether women and men perform differently as health-care practitioners. Alice Aslin (1977), who conducted a survey among male and female therapists and members of the feminist Association for Women in Psychology, found that only males still described "healthy women" and "healthy adults" as different. Another study of clinicians (Sherman, Koufacos, and Kenworthy 1978) found women more informed about issues relating to the psychology of women. One study shows that female doctors are more likely than male doctors to let their patients talk (West 1984). In hospitals staffed by women doctors, there are fewer operative deliveries of babies and lower maternal mortality rates. It is certainly true that women do most of the feminist research in health-care fields. But in some health-care areas the important differences in treatment of women may be most due to generational rather than gender differences in approach, with younger and more recently trained doctors more sensitive to gender issues and women's health.

Health-Care Activists

No discussion of the people involved in shaping health care can be restricted to people actually employed as health-care workers. One of the most striking aspects of the history of women's organizations and feminist movements is the degree to which these groups were active very early in trying to improve the quality and quantity of health care in America. Women were active in the health-care reform movements of the 1820s, 1830s, and later periods. Amelia Bloomer, a feminist and editor of the *Lily*, and proponent of more healthful and functional dress for women, was only one of the many women who organized the dress-reform movement of the 1840s and 1850s. Throughout the 19th century feminists were committed to and involved in ideas of "preventive hygiene," which included not just medical treatment but also what we now call environmental health, fitness, mental health, and social health. It is no coincidence that numerous suffragists and other feminists were active in the temperance movement. Their motivation was, by and large, protection of the health of women and children who suffered at the hands of drunken husbands.

These "health activists" often saw individual health as related to morality, equality, justice, and the "health of society." The women involved in these reform movements understood that health and health needs are based on and shaped by the structure of society and social relations. Jane Addams and others involved in the settlement house movement, which emphasized the needs of immigrants; Margaret Sanger, Emma Goldman, and others in the birth control movement, which focused on working-class women; and Ellen Richards and others who developed the field of home economics (endorsed in 1899 by the AMA) were motivated in part by a concern for the health of individuals and of society as a whole.

As the 19th century came to a close, women pushed to have government directly involved in ensuring the health of society through regulating and improving sanitation facilities, hospitals, parks, and prisons. They found allies in the Progressive Movement, an early 20th-century movement dedicated to these and related social and political reforms. By the end of the century, women, including many feminists, were actively involved in state and city politics and government and the agencies that managed sanitation, health, and health education in schools. Today these same concerns remain prominent in the feminist movement and in women's social and political activity more generally. Many groups are involved in educating women on health issues of concern to them. Since 1971 the Boston Women's Health Book Collective (1992) has published a valuable book written in lay language, now titled *The New Our Bodies, Ourselves.* The National Black Women's Health Project, begun in 1981, focuses especially on the health needs of African American women. The Native American Women's Health Education Resource Center, founded in 1987, offers information on Native American women's health, and the National Latina Health Organization, founded in 1986, focuses on many issues including especially reproductive choice. The National Women's Health Network is an umbrella organization including a membership of over 20,000 individuals and organizations.[23]

Mothers and Daughters as Health-Care Providers

One relatively unchanged aspect of the role of wife and mother is caring for the family's health, both by creating a healthful home and by dispensing most of the immediate health care and making sure that family members who need treatment from professionals receive it. As Eugenia S. Carpenter notes, "Women are the principal brokers or arrangers of health services for their children and spouses" (1980, 1214). This responsibility of women for family health care entails certain problems.

David Spiegel (1982), among others, argues that this responsibility is in many ways a burden. "Because we have been willing to believe that mothers do something special for their children—something that cannot be replaced by anyone other than the mother—mothers have been given an inequitable share of the responsibility for child care and undue blame for the mental illness of their children" (105). This burden becomes greater when a woman is employed for much of the day outside the home without any major change in the division of labor at home. "Both the monetary and nonmonetary costs women incur in fulfilling their family responsibilities for health care of other family members are increasing" (Carpenter 1980, 1215).

Mothers have more responsibility and take more blame than fathers in family health matters because they are given more responsibility in general for family care. But even beyond this, people tend to blame parents for gender-linked problems in their children (Kellerman 1974). For example, a child's problems may be blamed on a "domineering mother" or a "henpecked father," both pejorative judgments of women.

Gender ideology plays an important role in shaping views of mothers' impact on their children's psychological and physical health. During the 20th century courts almost always have awarded children to their mothers in child custody disputes on the assumption that children need a mother's special care. (This imbalance in decisions is beginning to change; for more discussion see Chapter 12.) If the mother was a lesbian, however, children were not usually awarded to her on the grounds that she could not provide a healthful environment for the child, even though research finds no greater likelihood of emotional problems among children in single-lesbian-parent households than in single-heterosexual-parent households (Kirkpatrick, Smith, and Roy 1981; Patterson 1992). In fact, research reveals virtually no differences in gender identification or gender-linked toy preferences among children in these two groups (Hoeffer 1981; Kirkpatrick, Smith, and Roy 1981; Patterson 1992). Courts are beginning to take the view that a parent's homosexuality should not play a role in determining custody arrangements.

The Influence of Women as Health-Care Consumers

It is all too easy to think of health-care consumers as passive patients whose only real source of power in health care is to pick a doctor wisely. Much feminist writing about women and health emphasizes women's role as passive victims of health-care institutions. In fact, new research into the history of health and medicine point out that health-care consumers do not have to be passive recipients and that they never have been devoid of power as a group. They have provided much of their own training and passed on their knowledge, often disparagingly referred to as "old wives' tales."

Women have often taken a strong hand in determining what treatment they received (Smith-Rosenberg 1975; Leavitt 1980; 1983; Leavitt and Walton 1982). Childbirth is a good example. Birth was a cooperative effort among women before the widespread use of physicians and hospitals, including the mother, midwife, and female relations and friends. That control did not disappear suddenly; medical science did not simply appear at the door and force women to accept new models and practices and ship women off to hospitals to have their babies. Women continued to exert considerable control as long as birth occurred in "their" territory: the home. A doctor could be thrown out of the birthing room by a woman if she disapproved of the doctor's methods. Doctors found themselves without patients if they were known to engage in practices women didn't like. Judith Walzer Leavitt cites the advice one doctor gave to others about attempting to shave a woman's pubic area before birthing:

> In about three seconds after the doctor has made the first rake with his safety [razor], he will find himself on his back out in the yard with the imprint of a woman's bare foot emblazoned on his manly chest, the window sash round his neck. . . . Tell him not to try to shave 'em (1983, 294).

Taking control was no easy task for the doctor.

Women have often staunchly searched for and demanded the best treatment they thought they could obtain, including trained doctors in preference to midwives and state-of-the-art procedures and drugs. "Old-fashioned" practitioners who refused to use new procedures often found themselves rejected in favor of those who were more "modern." Eventually women began to seek hospital rather than home care for childbirth. Once they left "their" territory, however, they also lost their control of birth. Increasing numbers of women are now trying to regain that control.

Toward a New Understanding of Women's Health

Standards of normal health cover a wide range of our characteristics and activities and are intimately tied to definitions of gender and gender roles. Incomplete medical knowledge means that in the pursuit of high standards of health, gender ideology is likely to play a role in the development and application of health-care values and procedures. In any case, despite the tangible reality of physical states of body, a significant amount of how we think about health is socially constructed.

The study of women and health is highly charged and controversial. Some writers, such as Mary Daly (1978) and Barbara Ehrenreich and Dierdre English (1979) suggest that women have been passive victims of medical professionals' purposeful attempts to destroy them; others, such as Edward Shorter (1982), suggest that medical science has single-mindedly saved women from their self-destructing bodies. The truth seems to be somewhere else. The practice of medicine and, more broadly, health care has saved women's lives and improved the quality of their lives in very gender-specific ways. It has also hurt women at times and not lived up to its potential for improving the quality of women's lives in other gender-specific ways. Women have been victims, sometimes passive victims. They also have often taken active charge of themselves and their health care and struggled to increase their control, sometimes for better and sometimes for worse.

The health-care system in the United States has changed in recent decades with respect to women's health care. There is considerably more organization on behalf of women. More and more hospitals and Health Maintenance Organizations (HMOs) include designated women's centers or women's programs. The question is whether these centers are providing something fundamentally new or are simply repackaging and marketing something old. Perhaps most important of all, even where these special organizations do not exist, women are beginning to take their health and fitness more seriously.

NOTES

1. For more discussion of the history of women and health in America, see Leavitt (1984).
2. Sandra Blakeslee, "Faulty Math Heightens Fears of Breast Cancer," *New York Times*, March 15, 1992.
3. This is only a partial list. Mental-health practitioners attempting to diagnose LLPDD would look for a combination of symptoms that were consistent over an extended period of time. Do not try to diagnose yourself on the basis of this list!
4. Jane E. Brody, "Can Drugs 'Treat' Menopause?" *New York Times*, May 19, 1992.
5. There is considerable controversy on this subject. Compare, for example, the very different interpretations of the history of women's health and health care offered by Ehrenreich and English (1979), Rothman (1982), and Shorter (1982). For further discussion of the history of childbirth, see especially Leavitt (1986).
6. "Study Faults Surgery on Women Giving Birth," *New York Times*, July 2, 1992.
7. Ibid.
8. Warren E. Leary, "Alternative to Caesarean Grows More Popular," *New York Times*, August 29, 1991.
9. Ibid.
10. Cindy Skrzycki, "Maternity Leave Is No Vacation," *Washington Post*, October 5, 1992.
11. Don Terry, "Stabbing Death at Door of Justice Sends Alert on Domestic Violence," *New York Times,* March 17, 1992.
12. For more discussion of the legal and social issues, see Chapter 11.
13. See further discussion in Chapter 9.
14. For more on the legal issues involved see Chapter 9.
15. For more discussion of occupational safety and health see Chavkin (1984).
16. Lena Williams, "Girl's Self-Image Is Mother of the Woman," *New York Times*, February 6, 1992.
17. Tamar Lewin, "As Silicone Issue Grows, Women Take Agony and Anger to Court," *New York Times*, January 19, 1992.
18. Felicity Barringer, "First Steps Taken in Revived Use of Breast Implants," *New York Times,* May 3, 1992.
19. Lena Williams, "Girl's Self-Image Is Mother of the Woman," *New York Times*, February 6, 1992.
20. Tamar Lewin, "Doctors Consider a Specialty Focusing on Women's Health," *New York Times,* November 7, 1992.
21. Ibid.
22. Ibid.
23. National Black Women's Health Project, 1237 Ralph David Abernathy Blvd., SW, Atlanta, GA 30310. National Latina Health Organization, P.O. Box 7567, Oakland, CA 94601. National Women's Health Network, 1325 G. Street, NW, Washington, DC 20005. Native American Women's Health Education Resource Center, P.O. Box 572, Lake Andes, SD 57358.

7

Women and Religion

In 1780 JUDITH Sargent Murray, an American writer and the daughter of a minister, argued against interpretations of Scripture presenting women as inferior and dangerous. In 1837 the English social observer Harriet Martineau argued that American women's morals were crushed by the repressive teachings of religion. In 1848 the participants at the Seneca Falls convention, a meeting often described as the beginning of the American feminist movement, denounced the treatment of women by organized churches. In the 1880s Elizabeth Cady Stanton, Matilda Joslyn Gage, and many other feminists published attacks on church teachings about women. Emma Goldman declared organized religion one of the most vile oppressors of both men and women. In the 1970s Mary Daly, then a professor of theology at a Roman Catholic college, argued that male religious authorities are guilty of gynocide—murder of women—physically, psychologically, and morally.[1]

American feminists have long criticized organized religion for oppression of women. But American feminist history also includes uncountable figures such as Sarah and Angelina Grimké, Lucretia Mott, and Elizabeth Cady Stanton, who recognized that they derived their political principles, strength and bravery, and their speaking and organizing skills from their religions. Many women have fought from the inside to transform their religions and have demanded the opportunity to become religious leaders and authorities. Others have sought alternative forms of religion more suited to their principles of equality and freedom.

Organized religion is one of the most powerful institutions involved in shaping people's beliefs, attitudes, values, and behavior. Gender is such an important part of the theology, cultural precepts, ceremonies, and rituals of most religions that we could not understand the institutional roots of sex/gender systems without analyzing the role of religion. To do this we look first at teachings about women, gender, and sexuality in the major American religions. We then turn to the role of women in shaping religion and the ways in which women have influenced society through their religious activities. Before examining these issues, however, we must first consider some difficulties involved in any discussion of religion.

"Organized religion" is not a single, homogeneous entity. Even within a single family of religions such as Christianity, we find substantial differences among denominations. Quakers and Roman Catholics are both Christians, both believe in a single deity that sent a son to earth, and both use the Old and New Testaments of the Bible as their chief texts, but beyond this they diverge widely, especially on issues of gender. Nevertheless we cannot consider all American religions in detail here because there are scores of them, ranging from those with millions of members to those with a couple thousand or fewer. Our discussion is limited to considering the denominations that have had the most widespread influence on American society and values because of either their size or their distinctive roles.

Studying religion in American society poses some unique problems and questions. Unlike many other countries the United States does not have an established or national religion. Even more important, the principles of American law call for a "wall of separation" between religion and government. Despite this wall, foreign observers are often amazed by the central role religion plays not only in the personal life of Americans but also in public life.

Surveys in the mid 1970s showed that 58% of all Americans considered their religious beliefs very important compared with 36% each of Italians and Canadians, 23% of Britons, 22% of French, and 17% of Germans (Benson 1981). Moreover, 94% of Americans claimed to believe in God, compared with 89% of Canadians, 88% of Italians, 76% of Britons, and 72% each of French and Germans. And 40% of all Americans claim to go to church regularly. During the 1980s and 1990s religious sentiment rose throughout the country. As Table 7-1 shows, the majority of Americans find religion a very important part of their lives, and almost half derive day-to-day guidance from religion. The table also shows that, at least on some questions, women express greater religiosity than men. They are more likely to find religion important in their lives, pray regularly, and read the Bible. More women than men interpret the Bible as the literal word of God.

Americans do not just find their religions personally important; many believe that religion should play a large role in guiding culture and politics. Indeed, despite the traditional American notion of a wall between religion and government, 34% of Americans say that they favor a constitutional amendment making Christianity the official religion of the United States. This attitude is particularly widespread among Protestants, individuals with less than a high school education, and blacks (Benson 1981). The theoretical wall separating church and state is very porous and flexible in practice. Thus it is especially important to understand how religion shapes gender norms and behavior.

Although the long history of each religion is important for understanding its contemporary ideas and practices, we will look primarily at the American religious experience. We will not ask what Jesus and Paul really said or meant but what American Christians have thought they said and meant, and how these interpretations affect American life. We will not ask about the forms

TABLE 7-1
Religious Orientations, by Gender

	Men	*Women*
Religion is an important part of my life.	70	79*
Religion provides a great deal of guidance in my day-to-day life.	46	48
Pray at least once a day.	38	57*
Never read the Bible.	40	28*
The Bible is the actual word of God and is to be taken literally.	43	52
Attend religious services.	66	64
Go to services almost weekly or weekly.	40	39
Born again (% of Christians).	38	42

Note: Numbers show proportion of people in each religion category who agreed with the statement to the left. Based on N = 467.

*Gender differences are statistically significant $p < .05$.

Source: 1991 American National Election Study Pilot Study, analysis by author.

patriarchal principles took among the ancient Israelites but will explore the norms of American Jews.

Religious Teachings About Women and Gender

Religion offers guidelines for moral behavior and thought. In many cases, religion prescribes considerably more than simple guidelines, of course; some doctrines are rules that must be followed for fear of punishment. Religious institutions are like social institutions in an important way: They provide both explicit rules and more generalized norms that people internalize and enforce on themselves.

The Bible is an important source of moral norms for both Christians and Jews, but different denominations find very different messages in this same text. Mormons, for example, referred to the biblical patriarchs to support the institution of polygamy until polygamy was made illegal by an act of Congress. Other Christians and Jews, revering the same patriarchs in the same Bible, have regarded polygamy as uncivilized and sinful or contrary to God's law. Orthodox and many Conservative Jews still follow the laws on female pollution found in Leviticus, which defines a woman's natural bodily functions as unclean and prescribes purification rituals. Other denominations, including many that claim to accept literal biblical dictates, do not enforce these biblical laws even if they still think menstruating women are unclean. Muslims base their beliefs on a different book, the Koran, but its words are also interpreted in different ways.

Despite these differences, there are some remarkable similarities among various denominations' traditional views on gender. Among these are the beliefs that (1) women and men have different missions and different standards of behavior and (2) although women and men are equal in the eyes of the deity, women are to some degree subordinated to men. Let us look in more detail at religious definitions of gender and some of the changes now taking place. We begin with a discussion of images of God and then turn to religious prescriptions for everyday life and morality for women. This section ends with a look at some new and alternative views of women.

God Talk: Is It Male?

God the Father. God the King and Lord. The Father, the Son, and the Holy Ghost. If we believe the words used in Judaism, Christianity, or Islam to describe God, the deity is male. Some people argue that the use of *He* to refer to God is a generic term, but it is difficult to say the same of *Father*, *Lord*, and *King*. To see the importance of "he" words in religion, try taking a religious text or prayer and substituting female-gender words. Think about your reactions as you hear yourself refer to God as *She*, *the Queen*, or *my Lady*. Adults are not supposed to make the "childish" error of anthropomorphism, that is, seeing God as a human being. Even theological sophistication, however, is not a sufficiently powerful force to eliminate what we might call "andromorphism." God may not be human like us, but "he" is still male.

The gender images of Jesus in Christian theology and tradition are especially interesting. Whereas the character attributed to God has generally been unambiguously masculine, the character of Jesus is considerably more androgynous. God's compassion is often described as *fatherly*, a term that seems less appropriate to describe the compassion of Jesus. Although Jesus was male, his unfailing gentleness, humility, simplicity, and nonviolence; his healing qualities and immediately forgiving nature; and his suffering for others are usually regarded as feminine. Nevertheless, the fact that Jesus and the disciples were male has often been used to argue that women should not hold the highest positions of religious authority. Many leaders in the Anglican and Episcopal churches used this view to argue against the installation of the first female bishop in the Episcopal church in 1989.

Religious language helps define our conception of God, authority, goodness, and holiness. If God is a Father but not a Mother, that says something not just about our conception of God but also about our conceptions of fathers and mothers and, by extension, men and women. Religious language and thought teaches us not just about our religions but about other aspects of life as well. If we look at American history, we can see the crucial role religion has played in defining the roles of women in American life and culture.

Defining Male and Female

Religion played a crucial role in the formation of American ideology on gender as well as other things during the colonial and early post-Revolution eras. Although the Anglican colonials of the South had a somewhat less stern outlook than the Puritans of the North, a literal reading of the Bible and a patriarchal view of God and society were important bases of thought in either case. When people learned to read, their text was the Bible; even if they could not read, they learned their lessons in church each Sunday or, if they were farther from "civilization," from the traveling preacher.

The Puritans based their views of women on the Old Testament and their interpretation of the patriarchal ancient Hebrew values. Woman's purpose was to be a helpmeet for her husband, to be fruitful and to multiply. Both men and women must fear God and Satan (although in different ways), but women should also be submissive to their husbands, the moral authority of the household. Women's work, especially the pain of childbirth, was viewed by Christians as a punishment for Eve's insubordination: "I will increase your labor and your pain, and in labor you shall bear children. You shall be eager for your husband, and he shall be your master" (Gen. 3:16).[2]

Puritans and others found more warnings for women to submit themselves to their husbands in the New Testament: "For man did not originally spring from woman, but woman was made out of man; and man was not created for woman's sake, but woman for the sake of man" (1 Cor. 11:8–10). Women should be silent in church and learn from their husbands (1 Cor. 14:34–35; 1 Tim. 2:9–15). "Wives, be subject to your husbands as to the Lord; for the man is the head of the woman, just as Christ also is the head of the Church. Christ is, indeed, the Savior of the body; but just as the church is subject to Christ, so must women be to their husbands in everything" (Eph. 5:22–24). Although more egalitarian than other denominations in matters concerning public speaking, even the gentle Friends, or Quakers, accepted the patriarchal view that man is to woman what Christ is to humans (Frost 1973).

Religion and the Bible provided examples of female character to serve as lessons for all, particularly in the persons of Eve and Mary. Religious people found proof in Genesis that woman was created as man's auxiliary and also that woman is likely both to sin and to tempt men to sin if left to her own devices. The main lesson of this story has been that if women are not controlled they will reenact the Fall. Rather than providing a maternal image (as the mother of us all), Eve has come to represent woman's treachery. Although Jews interpret the story of the Garden of Eden somewhat differently from Christians (neither the Fall nor Original Sin are part of Jewish theology), women and men are customarily separated in Orthodox synagogues because of the belief that women would otherwise distract men from their piety. In Islam this separation is achieved through veiling and *purdah.*

Within the Christian tradition (especially among Roman Catholics) the primary contrasting female image to Eve is Mary, the mother of Jesus, who, according to some Catholic traditions, was conceived without sin (that is, without recourse to sexual relations) and who most Christians believe conceived Jesus "without sin." She is the ideal woman and, most important for understanding religious norms of womanhood, an unattainable ideal. Although the cult of the Virgin has perhaps never taken hold in the United States to the same degree that it has elsewhere, Mary is a powerful model in Christian life.[3]

Biblical stories are interpreted differently by different people and traditions. Many Jewish and Christian feminists have reinterpreted the story of Eve; they see her as the person responsible for making humans capable of knowledge of good and evil. Jewish feminists have rehabilitated Vashti in the book of Esther in the Apocrypha. Vashti was rejected as a wife by King Ahasuerus in favor of Esther because Vashti refused to dance before her husband and his drunken friends at a party. The feminist intention is not to diminish Esther's accomplishments, but rather to reject the assumption that women who do not unquestioningly submit to their husband are bad. Other commentators point to additional female religious models such as Deborah, the judge, or Ruth and Naomi.

Despite these alternative stories and interpretations, the predominant message of most religions is that women and men have very different roles and characters; that religious authority speaks mostly in a male voice; and that woman's primary role is to accept that authority and to bear and raise children.

It is important to understand how religions presumably dedicated to holiness and justice support such a system of inequality and submission. Many religious authorities of different denominations have argued that the enforcement of these differences does not create or enforce inequality. They argue that although men and women are different they are equal in value in the eyes of God. For denominations with a concept of heaven, religious teachings claim that by fulfilling their different duties women and men earn equal places in heaven. Some religions simply believe that God designed women as inferior beings. Changes in the texts and practices of many denominations over the past century show that the religious principles of female inferiority are being abandoned.

Religious teachings also have direct effects on gender ideology and attitudes toward women. Historically, theologians have elaborated on the theme of separate spheres and characters for women and men and have equated preservation of women's place with preservation of morality and of a civilized (and American) way of life. A sermon delivered in 1837 by a Presbyterian minister demonstrates the degree to which regulation of women's sphere, Christian morality, and attitudes toward civilization were intricately intertwined. The preservation of the moral order, he argued, depended on the preservation of distinct spheres for men and women. Women were responsible for determining whether civilization would rise or fall. Addressing women, he said,

> Yours it is to decide, under God, whether we shall be a nation of refined and high-minded Christians, or whether, rejecting the civilities of life, and throwing off the restraints of morality and purity, we should become a fierce race of semi-barbarians, before whom neither order, nor honor, nor chastity can stand (Kraditor 1968, 50).

The morality of separate spheres for the sexes, with women's spheres subordinate to men's, has remained an important religious theme; there are numerous examples of God being called on to reinforce limitations placed on women. In 1887 Senator George Vest of Missouri argued against women's suffrage on the floor of the Senate by saying, "I do not believe that the Great Intelligence ever intended [women] to invade the sphere of work given to men, tearing down and destroying all the best influences for which God has intended them" (quoted in Kraditor 1968, 195). Making a similar point at the turn of the century, President Grover Cleveland argued, "I believe that trust in Divine Wisdom, and ungrudging submission to divine purposes, will enable dutiful men and women to know the places assigned to them, and will incite them to act well in their parts in the sight of God " (200). And as we have already seen, Senator Sam Ervin called God into battle against the Equal Rights Amendment. During the national discussion of "family values" surrounding the 1992 election, many representatives of the religious political right emphasized that many of the recent changes in women's roles brought with them the destruction of the moral fiber of the country.

The predominant message of most religious denominations has been that both women and men are to be carefully restricted to their distinct spheres and that women's roles on earth are to be good wives and mothers and to preserve traditional moral values, especially the modesty and domesticity of women. The punishments of religious women who transgressed the boundaries of these spheres have been enormous, including death (during colonial times for witchcraft and homosexuality), damnation to hell, separation from the religious community, and charges of responsibility for the downfall of a religion or of civilization as a whole.

Because of these views religious organizations and clergy have often played active roles in resisting feminism. In the 19th century, for example, many church leaders criticized women for publicly speaking on behalf of reform movements. Citing the biblical injunction "suffer women not to speak," some wrote, "We cannot . . . but regret the mistaken conduct of those who encourage females to bear an obtrusive and ostentatious part in measures of reform, and countenance any of that sex who so forget themselves as to itinerate in the character of public lecturers and teachers" (quoted in Rossi 1988, 305–6).

If public speaking was unfeminine, for many church leaders the idea of women's suffrage was even worse. In 1869 an American Transcendentalist leader said, "The conclusive objection to the political enfranchisement is that it would weaken and finally break up and destroy the Christian family" (quoted in Kraditor 1968, 192). "Let the hand which rocks the cradle teach the coming young men and women of America the Lord's Prayer and the Ten Commandments," said a New York politician in 1894, "and you will do more for your emancipation . . . than you can do with both hands full of white ballots" (198).

Religious organizations have been leading opponents of divorce reform, liberalization of birth control and abortion, educational policies that would reform gender messages in textbooks and make sex education part of the curriculum, legislation supporting civil rights for homosexuals, and the Equal Rights Amendment. In the first decades of the 20th century, some religious organizations opposed the reforms urged by feminist and progressive groups on the grounds that they were socialist and therefore antireligious. Contemporary studies of antifeminist activist groups show that participants in those groups share the characteristics of being particularly attached to religion and particularly antagonistic to communism (Burris 1983; Conover and Gray 1983; Mueller and Dimieri 1982).

Numerous politically and socially active women have been individually punished or reprimanded by their churches such as Anne Hutchinson and Lucy Stone (1818–1893), who was expelled from the Congregational church for her abolitionist activity. In the 1980s the Mormon church excommunicated Sonia Johnson for her support of the Equal Rights Amendment. In 1983 the Catholic church gave Agnes Mary Mansour the choice of resigning her post as director of social services in Michigan or dismissal from her order of nuns for tolerating the use of federal funds for abortions. She left the order (Briggs 1983). In many cases these women were rebuked precisely because they claimed to derive their "deviant" views from their religious values; in these cases they were punished for coming to their own conclusions about spirituality and religiosity.

Research continues to show that religious beliefs help shape people's view of gender and women's roles. Consider the evidence in Table 7-2, which looks at the relationship between fundamentalist beliefs, religiosity, and attitudes toward gender equality in government, the economy, and the family. It shows that fundamentalists, those who see the Bible as the literal word of God, are more likely than other people to think that men should have more power than women in government, the economy, and the family. It also shows that people who claim

TABLE 7-2
Attitudes Toward Gender Equality, by Religious Fundamentalism and Personal Importance of Religion, 1991

	Religion Has Moderate/Little Importance		*Religion Has Great Importance*	
	Not Fundamentalist	*Fundamentalist*	*Not Fundamentalist*	*Fundamentalist*
Men should have more power and influence than women in government and politics.	8	20	21	41
Men should have more power and influence than women in business and industry.	11	22	25	34
Men should have more power and influence than women in the family.	3	16	11	28

Note: People who said that religion provides "a great deal of guidance" in their day-to-day lives are in the Religion Has Great Importance category. Those who agree that "the Bible is God's word and all it says is true" are categorized as fundamentalists. Numbers show proportion of people in each religion category who agreed with the statement to the left. Based on N = 467. All differences between fundamentalists and nonfundamentalists (holding guidance constant) and between those finding moderate/low and high guidance from religion (holding level of fundamentalism constant) are statistically significant $p < .05$.

Source: 1991 American National Election Study Pilot Study, analysis by author.

they find a great deal of guidance from religion in their day-to-day lives are also more likely to believe in male dominance. If we look at the combined effects of these different aspects of religious belief, we see substantial support for male dominance among religious fundamentalists.

Religious organizations have also helped foster women's activism and even, at times, feminism. Many of the 19th-century suffragists were very involved in their religious communities. In recent decades, women have been actively involved in religion-based feminism. But the power of women to define their own terms, goals, and activities in conventional religious institutions has usually been limited; if their message provided too clear an alternative to traditional religious teachings, they found themselves opposed by the higher, male authorities.

Morality, Sexuality, and Gender

Religious authority regulates sexual morality in ways that have profound effects on women and men and that help further define gender and gender difference. Most denominations regard marriage as the cornerstone of the sexual, moral, and, therefore, social order. As we shall see in Chapter 11, marital law is based very heavily on traditional religious views and law. Although their specific views of sexuality and sexual practices vary, most denominations agree that sexual relations may appropriately and rightfully take place only within marriage between a man and a woman. Many—probably most—believe that the primary, if not sole, purpose of sexual relations is reproduction. Two of the Ten Commandments serve as authority here; one forbids adultery, and one forbids a man to covet his neighbor's wife, house, slaves, or other possessions. Notice that the latter not only defines proper sexual relations but also reinforces the idea that women are men's (sexual) property. For some denominations, such as the Roman Catholic church, reproduction is the sole moral reason for sexual activity.

This moral link between sexuality and reproduction has had two important implications. The first is that if only sexual acts that could result in conception are natural and good, sexual acts that could not result in offspring are unnatural and bad. Christians and Jews alike have used religious authority to forbid homosexuality (Lev. 18:22; 1 Cor. 6:9–11), although church authorities were more vigilant in suppressing homosexuality during some historical periods (e.g., the 12th, 13th, and 19th centuries) than in others (Weeks 1977). American laws against sodomy were based directly on religious teaching and sometimes used the language of the Bible. Although sodomy laws are usually discussed in reference to homosexual activities, they also applied to (and were originally enforced against) heterosexual acts that could not result in conception. These laws were serious in their consequences; early in American history some homosexual acts were punishable by death. The Bible also has been used to declare masturbation (Gen. 38:3–10) and transvestism (Deut. 22:5) sinful and wrong.

Among the mainstream Christian denominations, only the United Church of Christ fully accepts homosexual ministers. Events within the Presbyterian church exemplify the kind of debates and conflicts that have taken place in many denominations in recent years. In 1991 a task force report argued that the

Presbyterian church should not condemn sexual acts outside marriage—regardless of whether they involved two people of the same sex or not—if the acts were mutual and caring. Later the same year the Human Sexuality Committee successfully recommended that the Presbyterian General Assembly reject the task force report.[4] In 1992 the highest court of the Presbyterian church nullified the hiring of a lesbian pastor by one church, although it said that if she were celibate she could be hired. At the same time it said an "unrepentent homosexual" could not be ordained.[5] That same year the generally liberal National Council of Churches decided in a divided vote not to give "observer status" to the mostly gay and lesbian Universal Fellowship of Metropolitan Churches, a denomination with about 50,000 members. The most active opposition came from the Eastern Orthodox churches, some of the African American denominations, and the Korean Presbyterian church.[6]

The second implication of basing sexual morality on its reproductive function is that the practice of birth control is considered wrong. Roman Catholic authorities remain adamant that any form of "artificial" birth control is sinful. Most Protestant denominations and Jews, however, officially leave the decision about whether to conceive to individual choice, although many religious authorities informally discourage the use of contraception. Unitarian churches, on the other hand, have often taken very strong stands in favor of birth control.

Abortion is an even more difficult issue than birth control because it involves terminating life that has already begun. Historically, theologians and the common law generally viewed abortion as murder only after quickening of the fetus took place (i.e., when the fetus moves), and abortion was generally tolerated within the first 40 days after conception. In 1869 Pope Pius IX changed the position of the Catholic church, declaring almost all abortions murder and therefore sinful. According to Catholic doctrine it is not acceptable to terminate a life purposely, even to save another life. The Catholic church has remained firm on its stands on both birth control and abortion, although there is widespread controversy within the church, and some Catholics have felt particularly alienated from their religion because of its stands on these matters. Catholics can even be found in the highest ranks of the National Abortion Rights League, an interest group dedicated to reproductive choice for women.

Religions further regulate sexuality and social relations by dictating who may and may not get married. The Bible enumerates forbidden marriages, such as those considered incestuous. Many religious authorities do not allow interfaith marriage within their communities unless the "outsider" agrees to convert or unless they agree to raise the children in their religion. God's law has been used to bar sexual relations and marriage between people of different races (miscegenation), as this quotation from a Virginia court case in the 1960s shows: "Almighty God created the races white, black, yellow, malay, and red, and he placed them on separate continents. And but for the interference with his arrangement there would be no cause for such marriages. The fact that he separated the races shows that he did not intend for the races to mix."[7]

Most denominations have long supported the idea of personal choice with respect to divorce, at least to some degree, although the Eastern Orthodox,

Episcopal, Mormon, and Roman Catholic churches have generally held that marriages are indissoluble. Many denominations do not permit divorce except on strict grounds of adultery or desertion; many religious authorities will not remarry a divorced person unless that person was the "innocent" party in the divorce or the ex-spouse is dead. Some denominations (e.g., Congregationalists, Christian Scientists, Jews, and Unitarians) leave the question of divorce to the conscience of the individuals involved; others (e.g., Baptists and Disciples of Christ) leave it to the conscience of the minister.

We should not overestimate the impact of sexually repressive religious teachings on people's behavior. Historians have found ample evidence of "prematurely conceived" (as opposed to prematurely birthed) babies throughout American history. Indeed, even among the sterner of American clergy, attitudes toward sexuality were not necessarily as repressive as they are sometimes painted. Some Puritan ministers carefully pointed out that they differed from Roman Catholics by not extolling the virtues of virginity to the same degree, even while they condemned sex outside marriage. Historian Edmund Morgan found that "the Puritans were not ascetics; they never wished to prevent the enjoyment of earthly delights. They merely demanded that the pleasures of the flesh be subordinated to the greater glory of God: husband and wife must not become 'so transported with affection, that they look at no higher end than marriage itself' " ([1944] 1978, 364). Morgan even found evidence that a church expelled one of its male members for denying "congiugall fellowship unto his wife for the space of 2 years."

Nevertheless, the conflict between being holy and experiencing sexual feelings is an important theme throughout the history of sexuality and religion. Witness, for example, the sentiments expressed in a love letter the feminist Quaker Angelina Grimké wrote to her husband-to-be in 1838:

> Ought God to be all in all to us on earth? I tho't so, and am frightened to find that He is not, that is, I feel something else is necessary to my happiness. I laid awake thinking why it was that my heart longed and panted and reached after you as it does. Why my Savior and my God is not enough to satisfy me. Am I sinning, am I ungrateful, am I an IDOLATOR? (Rossi 1988, 289)

The Roman Catholic church further emphasizes a conflict between sexuality and holiness by maintaining that those who dedicate their lives to God by becoming priests or nuns must remain celibate. This rule of celibacy has somewhat different connotations for women and men. Nuns wear wedding rings to symbolize their marriage to Christ. Priests, of course, are not married to Christ; such a relationship, even if spiritual, would imply the sin of homosexuality. It is interesting to note the importance of sexuality and marriage in images of women. While nuns are married to Christ, women who were persecuted for witchcraft were said to be married to or to have sexual relations with the Devil. Thus, even in images of profound goodness or profound evil, women are defined by their relations to male authority.[8]

Contemporary sociological studies show that people's religious orientations do shape their sexual views and behavior. In their study of American couples (which included married and unmarried homosexual and heterosexual couples), Philip Blumstein and Pepper Schwartz (1983) found that regular church attenders were more conservative about sexual matters than those who were not as overtly religious. Religious heterosexuals are more opposed to civil rights for homosexuals, for example, than are less religious people. Most research (e.g., Hare-Mustin, Bennett, and Broderick 1983) finds that Catholics have a more conservative reproductive ideology than do other people. James Robbins's (1980) study of black women who had had abortions found that the more involved these women were with religion, the less happy they were with their own decisions to have abortions. Blumstein and Schwartz found that, although there may be differences in attitudes,

> there is very little difference between religious and nonreligious people when it comes to how they act. They have the same amount of sex. They are just as satisfied. They have no more and no less conflict about sex. And they are just as traditional about the woman's right to initiate it. But perhaps the most startling finding is that religious people are as non-monogamous as anyone else. However attached people may be to religious institutions, they do not seem to be insulated from the temptations of the flesh (1983, 285).

It is not entirely clear whether religious messages about morality have more impact in shaping people's attitudes, behavior, or simply feelings of guilt about doing the same things other people do.

Feminist Alternatives and the Women's Spirituality Movement

A few examples show the types of alternatives many feminists have posed to the more orthodox views of their religious bodies.

Two of the best-known feminist religious thinkers of the 19th century were the Quaker sisters Sarah (1792–1873) and Angelina (1805–1876) Grimké. In Angelina Grimké's most famous work, her 1836 "Appeal to the Christian Women of the South,"[9] she urged women to be instrumental in ending slavery, even if their actions brought them suffering, because they had to follow what they knew to be God's will rather than sinful and oppressive laws created by men. Drawing on the New Testament statement that "there is neither male nor female," the Grimké sisters believed that enforcing separate spheres for women and men and withholding religious and political rights for women were un-Christian acts. Their work, like the work of many other feminist religious activists, shows that the same texts and basic ideas can be interpreted in a variety of ways with very different effects.

Certainly many feminist critics of religion offered attacks on what they regarded as misogynist or androcentric theology and practices. Among these are Elizabeth Cady Stanton, Matilda Joslyn Gage, and a committee of other

Sonia Johnson, feminist activist and political candidate, was excommunicated by the Mormon Church for her support of the Equal Rights Amendment.

feminists who wrote *The Woman's Bible* ([1895] 1974), an exegesis and criticism of the Bible, which they regarded as a man-made, error-filled document. A more contemporary example is Mary Daly whose series of critiques and "re-visions" argue that our understanding of God and religion must be "exorcised" to root out the androcentrism of religion, much as the evil influence of Satan was exorcised by traditional Catholic ritual.

But many writers today also stand in the tradition of the Grimkés in working not just to criticize their religions but also to reconstruct them in a more feminist direction. Among the most well-known of these are Rosemary Ruether, Carol Christ, Judith Plaskow, and Elizabeth Schüssler Fiorenza.[10] These and other thinkers and activists focus on both the substance and the practices of their religions to consider possibilities for change. Their work revolves around two different strategies. One is to remove gender-specific content or rituals, the other is to incorporate more woman-centered language and rituals. Let us look at examples of both.

A common strategy to "de-genderize" religion is to focus on removing gender difference from liturgy and ritual. Formerly gender-segregated rituals are integrated. For example, the important Jewish initiation rite of Bar Mitzvah (Son of the Commandments) historically was a male ritual, but for several decades

Reform Jews have celebrated the same ritual for girls, the Bat Mitzvah (Daughter of the Commandments). Traditional Jewish law does not count women among the ten adults whose presence is required to say certain prayers; in more progressive communities women are counted. Traditionally only Jewish men wore prayer shawls and *yarmulkes* (hats); in more progressive communities many women do as well. Women are no longer barred from the rabbinate except among the Orthodox.

One of the most well-known efforts to remove sexist difference within Christianity other than allowing women into the clergy occurred in 1983 when the National Council of Churches began publishing new translations of biblical passages under the title *Inclusive Language Lectionary* amid considerable controversy. The lectionary refers to God as "the Father and Mother" or "Sovereign" rather than as "Father" or "Lord," and it refers to Jesus as the "Child" rather than as the "Son" of God to reduce the emphasis on male religious imagery. Some churches gave the lectionary a warm reception, and others attacked it as "tampering with the word of God."

While many efforts have focused on removing gender difference from religion as a means toward eliminating subordination of women, others revise religious texts and traditions to incorporate more woman-centered aspects to emphasize a specifically female religious and spiritual experience. Here the intention is largely to empower women, often by rediscovering women-created ideas and rituals and female figures that have been forgotten. Many feminist religious activists also work to create new practices and liturgy focused on women's specific experiences, history, and relationship to religion, morality, and spirituality.

Many such feminists, notably those in the women's spirituality movement, emphasize the symbol of the Goddess, a female conceptualization of the deity. Through Goddess symbolism these feminists try to emphasize a changed conception of God that affirms those parts of the universe more traditionally associated with feminine rather than masculine character. Thus, rather than thinking of God primarily as the "King," "Ruler," and "Judge," providing the constancy of the rule of law, the women's spirituality movement emphasizes the life-giving and sustaining power, and the constant fluidity and change in life found in the life course throughout nature and the change of seasons.[11]

Another branch of feminist spiritualism has turned to witchcraft to find a tradition. This witchcraft has nothing to do with the Wicked Witch of the West or even Glenda the Good Witch, but rather the tradition of witchcraft (which comes from the word *wicce*, meaning "wise ones") that has been the general name for female priestesses, healers, and sages throughout the ages, many of whom have been punished only because they knew how to use medicinal herbs to help people. If women have rejected the long tradition of the *wicce*, they argue, it is not because the tradition is itself bad, but because men have feared and therefore punished it, generally by execution. Sometimes, in our eagerness to reject the violence of these men's actions, we have forgotten that many women have practiced witchcraft, although that practice bears little resemblance to the descriptions in the more orthodox religious texts.

These movements for change involve religious authorities, clergy, and members of traditional religious organizations, as well as people outside these organizations who are attempting to create their own. Although all of these people have different points of view, they are linked by the convictions that (1) religious organizations are among the most forceful institutions that shape and define sex/gender systems; (2) women have had very little control over these powers; and (3) religion should free the human spirit rather than keep it in bondage. Although these movements for change have had wide impact, organized religion has also resisted change very strongly.[12]

Women's Religious Activities and Influences

Thus far we have looked at some of the ways that religious teachings help define gender, sexuality, and women's roles. We now look more directly at women's religious activity. What roles have women played in American religious life and religious organizations? How have their activities in religious organizations helped them shape their own and other people's lives? To what degree have women's activities influenced religious and spiritual life in the United States?

Everyday Life as Religious Activity

In "The Cult of True Womanhood, 1830–1860" historian Barbara Welter identifies the central historical role white women were expected to play in American religious life:

> The nineteenth-century American man was a busy builder of bridges and railroads, at work long hours in a materialist society. The religious values of his forbears were neglected in practice if not in intent, and he occasionally felt some guilt that he had turned this new land, this temple of the chosen people, into one vast countinghouse. But he could salve his conscience by reflecting that he had left behind a hostage, not only to fortune, but to all the values which he held so dear and treated so lightly (1966, 21).

That hostage was woman. Although a good woman was supposed to be submissive to her husband and her Lord, she was also supposed to create a religious home. She was responsible for guarding the spiritual life of her family, which sometimes meant acting outside the home and becoming, in effect, the backbone of church organizations and the occasional upsurges in religious activity.

Historians point out that women were central in the second "Great Awakening" of the 1820s in the East, the remarkable growth in evangelical Protestantism with its famous revival meetings that attracted large numbers of women and drew women into a view of everyday life as a moral mission. In her study of women's roles in the frontier West, Julie Roy Jeffrey found that many of the newly gathered congregations of the mid 19th century were composed primarily of women. "Women not only swelled membership rolls but were quickly recognized as recruiters and forcibly reminded of their responsibilities [by ministers]" (1979, 96). Jeffrey also found evidence that women often gave solace and encouragement to the struggling missionary ministers who were depressed and frustrated by their apparent failures to bring God's word to the frontier. What role might religion play in American life today were it not for the women who populated churches and supported their ministers a century ago?

When we look at women's roles historically it is nearly impossible to separate women's specifically *religious* activities and duties from their other activities. Women's family roles often have been understood as expressions of their religious values and the primary means for enforcing women's piety. Consider, for example, the argument made by Catharine Beecher in her manual for the homemaker, *A Treatise on Domestic Economy* ([1841] 1977). She set her advice on topics as diverse as nutrition, clothing, charity, exercise, and flower cultivation in a deeper philosophical and religious context. She began by arguing that "the democratic institutions of this country are in reality no other than the principles of Christianity carried into operation" (10). She then argued that "the success of democratic institutions (and therefore, by logical extension, Christian institutions) . . . depends upon the intellectual and moral character of the mass of the people" (13). According to Beecher the responsibility for securing this character depends on the woman. "The mother writes the character of the future man; the sister beds the fibers that after are the forest tree; the wife sways the heart, whose energies may turn for good or for evil the destinies of a nation" (13). Because every detail of a household must be arranged according to important basic principles, "These general principles are to be based on Christianity" (145). Thus, the activities of household management are expressions of religious duty and participation.

Similar beliefs are held in other religions. A central tenet of Jewish life is that the wife and mother is responsible for creating a Jewish home; she thereby is responsible for maintaining Jewish life and Judaism itself. Every meal eaten in the home of an Orthodox Jewish family is a reminder of religion and woman's role in it; the woman must carefully follow the laws of *kashrut* in buying, preparing, and serving food, thereby enforcing Jewish law and custom within her family. The conflation of women's religious activity and domestic obligation is especially apparent in Judaism because many important rituals and celebrations take place in the home rather than in the synagogue. The Sabbath meal is itself a religious service and includes traditional foods and the lighting of the Sabbath candles by the woman. Passover, one of the most important Jewish festivals, is celebrated entirely in the home. Much of the woman's work during Passover week is regulated by the fact that it is Passover; her very domestic labor is a ritual act.

For women who are the wives of clergy and missionaries, wifehood is itself a religious occupation. The ministry is one of the many male-dominated jobs in which the wife has special tasks that are unpaid extensions of the husband's job; in fact the husband's job creates nearly a full-time job for his untrained, unsalaried wife. The job of a minister's wife varies from denomination to denomination and from congregation to congregation. Generally, however, she is expected to attend most religious functions (or at least those that allow women), regardless of her own interests. She is expected to serve on committees, especially those that revolve around "women's concerns" such as education and entertainment. When the minister entertains congregants, visiting ministers, and others in his line of duty, she does the work. Above all, the minister's wife is the highly visible representative of her husband and his religious values. Ministers' wives, like the wives of other highly visible authorities, are subject to constant criticism and gossip if their homes, children, clothes, and smiles aren't perfect or appropriate for the values of the congregation. The importance of this job is evidenced by the controversy surrounding ministers' wives who choose to pursue independent careers and therefore do not have the time or the inclination to serve their husbands' congregations full-time.

It is easy to underestimate the religious work and influence of ministers' wives, both historically and today. In the 19th century missionaries sent to the frontier West to "civilize" (meaning to Christianize) the new communities were urged to bring wives for help and support they would need. Julie Jeffrey found that most of the wives thought of themselves as missionaries (as well they might have, given the work they did), even if their husbands and churches regarded them only as helpmates. But, as Jeffrey points out, "Few anticipated the potential conflict between [the roles of wife and missionary]. Nor did their religious enthusiasm and lofty idealism prepare them for the reality of missionary work" (1979, 100).

These women performed the hard duties of frontier women, plus many of the difficult duties of missionary work. They recruited women, taught, organized social events, and were responsible for fund-raising—often through their own labor rather than through collections—so that their husbands could tend to more spiritual needs. They were shuffled from one place to another as their husbands were called to new missions. The toll on these women and their families was often great. It is unfortunate that these hard-working women are often forgotten or remembered only as the wives of the men who tamed the West.

Making a home is regarded as a religious activity of central importance; for many people this is proof enough that women are highly regarded by their religions and are free to pursue a full life within their religious communities and to be influential in them. For many other women—including, of course, those who are not wives and mothers as well as those who simply see wider horizons—this is not enough.

Women's Service Outside the Home

Women have always constituted a substantial portion of the people who have practiced their religious values through public or community service, volunteer work, charity, or philanthropy. For many women bound even by the most traditional domestic values, these service activities and the religious organizations that undertake them have often provided the primary or even sole channel for extrafamilial public action and personal development. Religious organizations have provided ways for women to have an impact on their communities and society that they could not achieve in the male-dominated worlds of politics and the professions.

The 19th century witnessed the development of a religiously based gender ideology that regarded charity and service work a necessary part of a homemaker's life, especially but not exclusively among middle-class women (Scott 1984; Ginzberg 1990; Shaw 1991). As Catharine Beecher observed, "It is also one of the plainest requirements of Christianity, that we devote some of our time and efforts to the comfort and improvement of others" ([1841] 1977, 145–46). Such activities were especially appropriate because the focus of women's lives within their families was the comfort and improvement of others. Beecher included service work in her advice to women on how to schedule their time wisely: "The leisure of two afternoons and evenings could be devoted to religious and benevolent objects, such as religious meetings, charitable associations, Sunday school visiting, and attention to the sick and poor" (147).

The impact of women who express the social implications of their religious concerns through organized activities is immeasurable. The number of people who have been fed, clothed, housed, educated, and otherwise comforted by religious organizations of women is uncountable. Through these organizations women have pressed social and political concerns at all ends of the political spectrum and all levels of politics. Indeed, this work became part of the basis on which public welfare policies were constructed. Throughout the 20th century representatives of women's religious organizations have testified frequently before local and state legislatures, as well as before congressional committees. The social issues and concerns of churches are often manifest largely in the work of women.

Women's religiously based service work is important to understand not only because it has had a great impact on American women and U.S. society more broadly, but also because it offers us a good example of the complexities of developing a feminist analysis of the gender basis of social institutions. As Lori Ginzberg writes in her study of 19th-century women's benevolent work, "Ideologies about gender serve broader purposes than either describing or enforcing supposed differences between women and men. It is necessary . . . to understand the uses to which those ideologies are put" (Ginzberg 1990, 216). Women's influence and power in service work stems from a gender ideology of difference. Women were supposed to have moral influence because of their natural moral difference from and superiority over men.

> Women or, more accurately, the belief in women's moral superiority perfectly fit the requirement that charitable endeavors appear unmotivated by self- or class interest. As members of a group that seemed to be defined exclusively by gender, women could have no interest other than to fulfill their benevolent destiny; they could be applauded and recognized without calling into question the purity of their motives (Ginzberg 1990, 216).

Charity *did* serve class interests for the middle-class and business-owning–class women who were so active in late 19th-century charity work. As Ginzberg points out, charity played an important role in economic development by mediating "the most blatant harshness and dislocation of nineteenth-century capitalism and urbanization" and helping to foster a moral culture that supported that form of industrial capitalism. Thus the structure of gender relations impacted the structure of class relations.

Another important complexity in understanding the significance of the gender ideology of difference underpinning the ideal of female benevolence is its dual effect on the charitable women themselves. On the one hand it provided an outlet for public and communal activity, and indeed a base for women to exert a considerable degree of influence over their communities and even over government. Ann Douglas (1977) claims that women thus were powerful agents in the creation of 19th-century American culture, especially in helping it forsake the harsh Calvinist character of the earlier century in favor of Victorian sentimentalism. Historian Sara Evans (1989) argues that women's activities helped forge a new meaning of public and domestic life, in which the moral mission of homemakers reached outward to public works, and public life, they argued, should function to care for people and sustain them morally. Moreover, this notion of the unique spiritual character of women gave them grounds for collective identity, viewing themselves as sisters, and creating the potential for collective action, including the creation of a feminist movement. On the other hand, this gender ideology reinforced the idea of separate spheres, in which women and men had different and, in fact, unequal places. It was an ideology with both a radical and a deeply conservative potential.

Religious organizations continue to provide a means through which women make contributions to others in their communities. Besides the continuing charitable efforts of churches, synagogues, and other religious organizations, many women have participated in efforts to create new forms of spirituality that emphasize a religious basis for accepting public and even political responsibility for justice and social welfare. These women reject what Judith Plaskow calls the "institutionalized separation of spirituality and politics":

> The assigned guardian of spirituality has been religion, which is itself relegated to the margins of society and expected to limit its interests to Saturday or Sunday mornings. As spirituality minds its otherworldly business, transformation of social structures is left to the often dirty work of politics, which catches us up in a realm of compromise, power seeking, struggle over what have been defined as limited resources, and confrontation with the distortions and disease in our social system (1990, 212–13).

Plaskow and others want to go beyond the traditional bounds of female benevolence and charity to argue for a spiritualism that is itself committed to transformational politics. She underscores the idea of *tikkun olam* —the responsibility to participate in restoring the world to its wholeness, just as others, such as Pamela Couture (1991) emphasize the idea of "shared responsibility" grounded in Christianity. Likewise, in the early 1980s many women became involved in new formulations of the political responsibilities of spirituality in the "sanctuary movement," a religion-based movement to give sanctuary to the victims of government violence in El Salvador. At the time, El Salvador was ruled by a U.S.-backed regime that tortured and killed its opponents, including religious workers (Lorentzen 1991).

These notions of responsibility erase the difference between religion and politics. In these cases, religious activists are attempting to link spirituality, feminism, and a progressive political commitment to communal responsibility in the material as well as spiritual world. These more liberal and progressive thinkers are not alone in their arguments for linking spirituality and political action. Those on the right have also done so, for example, in anti-abortion and "rescue" movements, which they also define as based in social justice and social commitments (Ginsburg 1989).

Women as Religious Authorities and Leaders

We already have seen that with some exceptions, most Judeo-Christian religions explicitly reserve leadership and positions of authority for men. Nevertheless, women have assumed a variety of leadership roles, and they are pressing for more.

Women have been the founders of a number of American Christian denominations. Among the most important and well known are Ellen White, who founded the Seventh-Day Adventist church and led it for 50 years; Aimee Semple McPherson, a charismatic evangelist who founded the Church of the Foursquare Gospel; and Mary Baker Eddy (1821–1910), who founded the Church of Christ, Scientist, best known for the beliefs that the spirit and mind are the central facts of life and that illness, disease, and death are mere illusions that can be overcome by spirituality.

Another church founder was Ann Lee (1736–1884), an immigrant from England who, as a young woman, belonged to a religious group known as the "Shaking Quakers" because of members' behavior while praying. While imprisoned in England for heresy and accusations of witchcraft, she experienced revelations. Once freed she led a small group of followers who believed her to be a messenger of Christ to New York, where she established the first Shaker community. The Shakers believed that only through celibacy could a person achieve the highest spirituality; the growth of the community thus depended on new converts. The Shaker community was based on sharing and hard work, and it is noted for its well-crafted furniture. By the middle of the 20th century only a handful of old women were left in the community. These women decided to let the Shaker community die a natural death and sought no more converts.

Much attention has been focused on the issue of ordination of women. Antoinette Brown Blackwell (1825–1921) was the first American woman to be ordained as a minister and to have her own congregation. At least three Protestant denominations have ordained women for a century or more, including the United Church of Christ, the American Baptist churches, and the Disciples of Christ. Change has come much more recently in most denominations, however. Sally Priesand was the first woman ordained as a (Reform) rabbi in 1972. In 1989 Barbara Harris became the first female Episcopal bishop, an event that caused

Mary Baker Eddy, who founded and for many years directed Christian Science.

great consternation in some sectors of the worldwide Anglican church. Orthodox Jews still do not ordain women, women still may not become Roman Catholic priests, and some conservative Protestant denominations remain opposed to female ordination. Although women are still a small fraction of all ministers, these numbers are likely to change as more women train for the ministry. In 1989 the National Council of Churches found that of 172 denominations for which information was available, 84 ordained women, 82 did not, and 6 did not have ordained clergy. It also reported that women constituted about 8% of the clergy in denominations that ordained women.[13]

A survey of male and female Protestant clergy showed that their experiences and motivations differed to some degree (Carroll, Hargrove, and Lummis 1981). Women were more likely to have upper-middle-class backgrounds, highly educated parents, and mothers who were employed. Men were more likely to have attended denominational colleges, partly reflecting the fact that women made their decisions to enter the ministry later than men. Men were more likely to feel that their families and pastors supported their decisions to enter the ministry in the first place. Women entering the ministry tended to have better academic records

Episcopal Bishop Barbara Harris became the first female bishop in the worldwide Anglican Church in 1989.

than men. More women than men said their motivation in seeking clerical training was personal spiritual growth or service to Christ; more men than women said they pursued religious studies to become parish ministers.

The researchers also uncovered other differences. Men were more likely than women to feel that the ordained ministry carried with it particularly high "prestige and dignity." More women than men felt it was very important to "change the sexist nature of the church." Most of the female ministers revealed strongly feminist attitudes toward women in the church, compared with only 24% of the men. Clerical attitudes toward women's roles in the church vary from denomination to denomination. While 39% of the United Church of Christ ministers expressed strongly feminist attitudes, only 15% of the Episcopal clergy did so.

Women in the ministry face some segregation and discrimination just as women do in other jobs. Men find it easier to become ordained after attending the seminary, although this varies by denomination. Ordained women tend to be placed in smaller churches with older members, and their salaries are lower than men's. As we might expect, the congregants in women's churches tend to be less conservative than those in men's, although surveys show that in most denominations, lay leaders tend to be more conservative on gender issues than are the clergy themselves.

As with other jobs, the fact that some women are now working in this male-dominated profession does not mean that their day-to-day experiences are the same as men's. Women and men feel themselves to be especially competent at different aspects of the job. Carroll, Hargrove, and Lummis (1981) found that women felt more confident about their abilities to preach, lead worship, and teach children, and men felt more confident about their abilities to manage the church budget. Women and men both felt they got on well with different age and gender groups within their congregations. Most of the female ministers thought their gender played a role in conflicts or difficulties they encountered in their jobs; 27% thought their sex was a very important factor.

Studies suggest that women change the ministry and its imagery merely by pursuing their vocations. Women have somewhat different attitudes than their male colleagues; they could not believe that church authority is necessarily masculine and remain in the career they have chosen. Women in the ministry have become increasingly aware of the problems of women partly through their own experiences. Carroll, Hargrove, and Lummis (1981) found that clergywomen are somewhat more likely than clergymen to think that their congregations should get involved in social and political issues, including the rights of women and minorities.

There is growing evidence that women have a different effect on their congregants than men have. Rabbi Laura Geller (1983, 210), for example, reported on the following reaction of two of her congregants:

> Rabbi, I can't tell you how different I felt about services because you are a woman. I found myself feeling that if you can be a rabbi, then maybe I could be a rabbi too. For the first time in my life I felt as though I could learn those prayers, I could study Torah, I could lead this service, I could do anything you could do. Knowing that made me feel much more involved in the service—much more involved with Judaism. Also, it made me think about God in a different way. I'm not sure why. (a middle-aged woman)
>
> Rabbi, I realized that if you could be a rabbi, then certainly I could be a rabbi. Knowing that made the service somehow more accessible to me. I didn't need you to "do it" for me. I could "do it," be involved with Jewish tradition, without depending on you. (a young man)

It seems to be an almost universal religious theme that negative aspects of the world can be lessons for the good. Geller's experience might be an object lesson of exactly this sort.

The relatively low status of the female rabbi, at least in these cases, brought people closer to their own spirituality. These two people were reacting in part to women's lower status, to the jarring image of a female leader in a masculine world, to their stereotypes of women. But as Geller noted, "The lessening of social distance and the reduction of the attribution of power and status leads to the breakdown of hierarchy within a religious institution." In this case the breakdown of gender hierarchies did indeed seem to lead to a breakdown of religious institutional hierarchy because the two are interdependent; they mutually reinforce each other. This is, of course, precisely what conservative leaders fear will be the result of the entrance of women into traditionally male leadership roles. But as these quotations also suggest, many people find a new spirituality and a renewed sense of religious affiliation and purpose when the hierarchy of religious institutions is weakened. Geller noted that a female friend of hers who was an Episcopal minister had a similar experience. "When she offers the Eucharist people take it from her differently from the way they would take it from a male priest, even though she follows the identical ritual. People experience her as less foreign, and so the experience is more natural, less mysterious" (1983, 211).

Women take many other leadership roles in religious organizations. Many denominations have long allowed women to be deaconesses, and the Roman Catholic, Eastern Orthodox, and Episcopal churches have orders of nuns. In some cases these women have been instrumental in changing the status of women. Many Roman Catholic sisters have worked for changes within the Church. Most people are aware that many orders of nuns no longer wear habits. But the size and character of the community of Roman Catholic sisters has been changing over the years. First, it is considerably smaller than it once was; while in 1968 there were over 176,000 nuns in the United States, by 1992 the figure was a little over 99,000. Far fewer women enter as novitiates each year. But the women who enter are different also. Today a substantial portion of women who become nuns are much older than in the past; often they are women who have raised families and had careers, sometimes well-paid professional careers. Indeed, many religious orders now discourage younger women from joining in favor of older women with skills and experiences that can benefit the group and their work.[14] At the same time, this trend is likely to exacerbate the discontent of nuns who are already frustrated with the limits placed on them by the male church hierarchy.

Most denominations also allow women to fulfill other organizational leadership roles, such as committee work and leadership in religious education, some of which are designed only for women and some of which are open to both women and men. We should not underestimate the impact women have had in these various roles; however, many of these roles are limited by very specific boundaries, which also limit women's potential impact on religious life. Women who want to reach further within their religious organizations are still forced, for the most part, to ask permission from male authorities, curb their own spiritual needs, or leave.

Religion and Society

Few subjects stir up as much controversy and passion as the relationship between religion and gender norms. Often those on opposing sides of the debate do agree about one point: Organized religion has been one of the most powerful human institutions for defining and controlling gender, sexuality, and "woman's place."

There is strong disagreement, however, about what can and should be done about this power. The solutions offered are wide ranging.

Religious institutions, like the other institutions discussed in this book, are not isolated enclaves; they are integrally linked to the wider society and its values. They both influence and are influenced by it. They are powerful producers and enforcers of gender norms, but they also are affected by changes in these norms in other social institutions. Many aspects of religious teachings and structures depend on specific conceptions of women and their roles; when these begin to change outside of religious institutions, the institutions are also affected.

Religions have promoted inequality between women and men and have supported great violence against women—and men—who step out of their assigned gender and sexual roles. Because women have been assigned the subordinate position, they have been especially subjected to punishments for gender-specific reasons. For example, the crime of the thousands of women accused of witchcraft was not only that they were heretics but also that they had engaged in activities, such as healing, which were part of the province of men. In modern times many religious organizations have formally and officially resisted changes in the status of women, even outside the institutions themselves.

The story of religious institutions is not a simple history of victimization of women. Denominations differ in their treatment of women, and most have changed to some degree in recent years. Millions of women have found strength and inspiration in their religions, which has sometimes allowed them to battle their own religious institutions and to transform themselves and women's roles in subtle ways. A delicate balancing act is required to recognize both the religious power and influence of women especially when it is often so subtle and the very real gender-specific limits that have been placed on women in almost all of their religious activities.

Many women have sought to create a spiritual bond among women through a feminist approach to religion that values women as a group. While this has been an active and important aspect of feminism, the feminist spirituality movement has also made many women more conscious of divisions among women based in their religious beliefs and practices. This is not just because denominations disagree in their beliefs and differ in their practices. The conflict among women in the women's spirituality movement is related to some of the problems of difference discussed in Chapter 4. Let us consider two brief examples here: relations between African American and white Christians and between Christians and Jews.

Many Christian feminist writers have begun to identify a number of problems in developing a feminist theology or spirituality that does not deal specifically with race (Gilkes 1987; Grant 1989; Thistlethwaite 1989). Just as the sexism inside organized religion both reflects and shapes the sexism in other social institutions, so does its racism. In most communities, African Americans have no more been welcomed by whites into their churches than they have been welcomed into white-dominated neighborhoods and schools. Despite the apparent welcome accorded the Whoopi Goldberg character in the movie *Sister Act,* African American nuns face discrimination.[15]

Ethnic and other aspects of cultural heritage become woven together with religious practices; thus, for example, even within the same denominations the worship styles can differ dramatically in white and black churches.[16] But there are other intellectual and theological differences that can cause race-based conflict in the effort to claim a "women's" Christian spirituality. Among them is the problem of freedom and free will, which looks different depending on which side of slavery and other forms of institutionalized oppression shapes one's history. African American and white views of religious claims of universality and the unity of human beings are also shaped by the realities of relationships of subordination. Another important point of difference is evident in discussing Christology, debates over the nature and place of Jesus in religious thought, including dealing seriously with the significance of Jesus' race and gender. These are each important and emotional issues. These conflicts remind us of the problem of the false sense of universalism that comes from not recognizing difference, discussed in Chapter 4.

Many thinkers have also dealt with issues that divide Christians and Jews within the feminist spirituality movement. Judith Plaskow has written influential works on the problem of feminist anti-Judaism, especially in the context of apparently ecumenical spirituality discussions. Here she is not just referring to cultural anti-Judaism reflecting norms in the wider society, although she includes that as well. Rather, she points to a fundamental source of anti-Judaism in Christian theology, especially the versions favored by feminists that emphasize the "feminism" and "femaleness" of Jesus. Historically, part of the forcefulness of the Jesus story is its backdrop—the figures with whom Jesus is compared and the significance of that comparison. The Jesus story depends heavily on what to Jewish eyes are the anti-Jewish caricatures found in Christian images of rabbis, Pharisees, and Jewish life and religion generally. This leads Plaskow to write about the "psychological reality that Christians need Jews in a way that Jews do not need Christians" (1990, 101). She notes that in ecumenical dialog Christians are always asking Jews what they think of Jesus and why they reject Jesus as the Messiah. As she writes,

> Christians seem to find it almost impossible to hear that Jews *don't* think about Jesus—except when Christian questions and a Christian culture force them to do so—and that they do not reject Jesus, they are simply not interested in him (1990, 101).

Plaskow argues, contrary to the spiritualist urges toward universalism, that Christians should take Judaism seriously as an independent religion on its own terms.

One of the most striking aspects of the study of women and religion is the degree to which given rituals and texts can offer different messages to different people. The same Bible has proven to some people that women and men are equal and that women should take full leadership roles in religions and society and to others that women are inferior, periodically unclean, dangerous, and subordinate to men. Some people take religious prescriptions for women's domestic roles as a sign of the high esteem in which women are held; others find them the primary indications of women's subordination and even enslavement. At the same time, various religions and denominations often take their own unique aspects to be the truth and the potential source for universalism. These variations and similarities are sources both of the stability and resilience of religious institutions and of their potential for change, of their possibilities for oppression and liberation.

NOTES

1. To read some of these women's writings, see Rossi (1988), which includes essays by Murray, Martineau, Stanton, and Goldman; Stanton ([1895] 1974); Gage ([1900] 1972); and Daly (1973, 1975, 1978).
2. All biblical quotations are from the *New English Bible with the Apocrypha* (New York: Oxford University Press, 1970).
3. For a history of Mariology, see Warner (1976).
4. Peter Steinfels, "Presbyterian Panel Rejects Sexuality Report," *New York Times*, June 9, 1991.
5. Ari L. Goldman, "Top Presbyterian Tribunal Bars Homosexual Minister," *New York Times*, November 5, 1992.
6. Dennis Hevesi, "Gay Church Again Rejected by National Council Group," *New York Times*, November 15, 1992.
7. This is a quotation from the 1967 Supreme Court case *Loving* v. *Virginia*, which invalidated the Virginia law against miscegenation.
8. The most important Christian book defining witchcraft is *Malleus Maleficarum*, written in 1486 by two Dominican friars. See Kramer and Sprenger (1928).
9. This is reprinted in Rossi (1988).
10. For some of the most basic works, see Ruether (1974; 1983); Heschel (1983); Christ and Plaskow (1979); Fiorenza (1984; 1992); Plaskow (1990).
11. For some influential writing about Goddess religion, see Starhawk (1979) and Christ (1987).
12. For an example of a blistering attack on the women's spirituality movement and feminism more broadly, especially within Roman Catholicism, see Steichen (1991).
13. "Women in Full Ministry Doubles," *Wisconsin State Journal*, May 27, 1989.
14. Jennifer Steinhauer, "Older and More Skilled, New Nuns Are Assuming Wider Roles," *New York Times*, December 27, 1992.
15. Ibid.
16. Ibid.

8

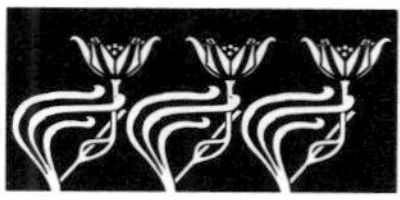

Gender and the Institutional Media of Communication

Females constitute 27.7% of the U.S. population. Half of them are teenagers or in their 20's. They wear revealing outfits, jiggle a lot, but don't do much else. More than a third are unemployed or without any identifiable pursuit or purpose. Most others are students, secretaries, homemakers, household workers, or nurses.

Portrait of American women as presented on television.[1]

MOST OF THE information we receive about the world around us does not come from direct experience. Our knowledge about human life is gained secondhand from the mass media of communication—radio, television, newspapers, and magazines—or from the artistic media of communication such as the performing, graphic, and literary arts. For this reason the collective normative power of the people and organizations who manage these media is enormous.

As the description that opens this chapter suggests, the tremendous normative power of the media has often distorted the image of women in society. This chapter pursues the following questions: What images of women do the institutional media of communication offer us and why? What is the process by which these images appear? What impact do the media have on the construction of gender? To what degree and how do they foster and inhibit social change? What impact do women have on the media?

We begin by looking at the mass media, including radio, television, newspapers, and magazines. We then turn to advertising as a special form of communication that shapes and is shaped by gender. Finally, we consider the arts as an institutionalized medium of communication that plays an important role in sex/gender systems.

The Mass Media

The mass media of communication both reflect and help create and alter social and cultural values. Although the mass media are often blamed for the problems of modern society (ironically, people usually communicate these criticisms through the mass media), they are not monolithic and do not present us with a single message. Indeed, while they are powerful agents in reinforcing dominant cultural norms, they are also among the most important channels for achieving social change. This complexity makes studying the mass media especially important for anyone interested in the social meanings of gender and the position of women. To look at the issues more closely, we turn first to women's roles in the print (newspapers and magazines) and electronic (radio and television) media. We then consider the gender-related content of the media and its impact on the way people think and act.

Women in the Print Media

Although men have clearly dominated institutionalized media of communication, women are by no means newcomers.[2] Women were influential in the print media from its beginning in America; in fact the first printing press was imported and installed by a woman in 1638. There were at least 14 female printers by the Revolution, and 4 women published weekly newspapers. Elizabeth Timothy became the first female editor-publisher in 1738 with the publication of the *South Carolina Gazette*. Political pamphlets, broadsides, and propaganda pieces, perhaps more important than newspapers in the early days of this country, were often written or published by women. It was a woman who first printed the Declaration of Independence complete with the names of all signers (Marzolf 1977; Beasley and Gibbons 1993, 51).

Print shops were often family businesses and, as in many family businesses, women were important contributors. Many early female printers are invisible because history books tend to focus on the male members of printing (and other business) families. Consider the Franklin family, including Deborah, who ran the print shop when her famous husband Benjamin was away; Ann, Benjamin's sister-in-law, the state printer of Rhode Island in 1736 and a newspaper publisher in her own right; and Margaret H. Bache, also a newspaper publisher and the wife of Benjamin's grandson (de Pauw 1975, 35).

As the importance of the public press increased in the 19th century, women continued to exert a clear if restricted influence. By 1831 there were at least 1,297 printers, of whom about 30% were women. Women and boys received about one-third the average wages of men (Marzolf 1977, 9). By 1850 women were about 16% of all newspaper compositors. The tasks they were allowed to do were limited and their pay less than that of similarly occupied men, but women earned more as printers than they could doing most "women's" work (DuBois 1978, 129). Print unions did not accept women as full members until

1873, which helped to restrict the number of women involved in the trade. Some women organized their own union for a time (DuBois 1978).

Even if the number of women in the print media was low, some observers, such as Ann Douglas (1977), argue that women writers helped shape important aspects of 19th-century American culture through their contributions to the periodical press at a time when it was first becoming a *mass* medium. Douglas believes that women were successful in attracting mass readership, and "gain[ed] power through the exploitation of their feminine identity as their society defined it" (7) by influencing the 19th-century culture of moralism. Douglas's argument underscores the complexity of both the mass media and sex/gender systems. The "cult of true womanhood" was oppressive, but some women also found a way to bend it to their needs. By the mid 19th century women's influence in all aspects of periodical production was sufficient to provoke resistance by men, who thought women were feminizing culture too much.

Nineteenth-century women submitted individual stories, poems, and religious pieces to newspapers and magazines, and some became regular contributors. Some were even editors, including Margaret Fuller, who edited the Transcendentalist magazine, *The Dial.* She published some of her own important feminist writing through that journal. Most remarkable, however, was the rise of the women's magazines and other periodicals. Among the most famous was one of the first popular mass-circulation magazines, *Godey's Lady's Book* (1837–97), edited by Sara Josepha Hale (1788–1879). Widely remembered chiefly for its color fashion plates which are now expensive collectors' items, *Godey's* was an arbiter of taste voraciously devoured by women across the country. *Godey's* was only one of many women's magazines, but its circulation outstripped that of most of the others. Most "ladies'" magazines were not explicitly feminist but usually did favor expansion of women's rights and influence.

The mid and late 19th century also witnessed an impressive growth in what we now would call a feminist press, periodicals established by and for women to further the cause of women's rights and change in women's roles. Many were quite radical in their politics (Russo and Kramerae 1991). Among these were the *Free Enquirer*, established in 1828 by Frances Wright as the first reform periodical published solely by women; Amelia Bloomer's *Lily* (1849–59); Pauline Wright Davis's *Una* (1854–56); Elizabeth Cady Stanton and Susan B. Anthony's *The Revolution* (1868–71); Lucy Stone's *Women's Journal* (1870–1917); and *The Woman's Era*, designed for black women. These publications were important links in the 19th-century women's movements.

The popularity of women's magazines did not go unnoticed by the rest of the press, which paid increasing attention to women as an audience. In 1859 Jane Croly (1829–1901) began the first women's page—actually a newspaper column—in a mass-circulation newspaper. After a time most other newspapers followed suit, institutionalizing a segregated portion designed to appeal specifically to women, or at least to a stereotyped view of them. As newspapers and magazines began to use advertising to support themselves, fashion and consumer items related to women's domestic roles were also used to appeal to women.

The last half of the 19th century and the beginning of the 20th century witnessed the rise of the female reporter. Marzolf (1977) found two well-known types of female reporters promoted by the press to its readers: "stunt girls" and "sob sisters." The stunt girls were just that: They performed great, or at least curious, feats and wrote about them. A good example was Elizabeth Cochrane (writing under the pen name "Nellie Bly") who drew on Jules Verne's popular *Around the World in Eighty Days* and beat Phileas Fogg's fictional record by circling the globe in 72 days, 6 hours, and 11 minutes in 1889–90. This rather trivial example masks the fact that many of these stunts were important contributions to the growth of serious investigative journalism. For example, when Cochrane was 22 years old she feigned insanity to investigate conditions in insane asylums and published a book, *Ten Days in a Madhouse*, in 1887. Some investigative journalists did not do stunts but nevertheless performed dangerous acts. Ida B. Wells (1862–1931), the African American editor and part owner of the *Memphis Free Speech* in the early 1890s, published an exposé of lynchings that served as the focal point for agitation against these vicious acts. Ida M. Tarbell (1857–1944), who exposed the monopolistic practices of Standard Oil for *McClure's* magazine, was also part of this tradition of women investigative reporters.

The "sob sisters" focused on crime, often painting the details in lurid colors (Abramson 1990). Many of them later went into other types of journalism. Both sob sisters and stunt girls spurred the sales of newspapers and magazines.

Women's roles in journalism expanded in the late 19th and the 20th centuries. In 1890 women constituted 14% of the people involved in printing and publishing; in 1905 they constituted 20%. They held 24% of the editing and reporting jobs in the early 1920s, 32% in 1950, 37% in 1960, and about 50% by 1990. But they remained restricted in many ways.

Women had to fight for what they gained. We already have discussed the resistance on the part of male printers' unions, and women's relatively low pay. Similar problems were encountered by female journalists. When women became eligible for membership in the Capitol Press Gallery, their numbers in the gallery rose from 4 in 1870 to 20 in 1879, but then women were virtually eliminated from membership by a new rule barring part-time reporters and limiting news organizations to one reporter each. In 1919 only 10 of the 110 reporters accredited to cover Congress were women. During World War II the number of accredited women rose to 98, but it fell to 30 right after the war.

Women in many fields complain that their profession seems like a "men's club"; in journalism it was almost literally true. The National Press Club, founded in the 19th century, did not admit women until 1971. This exclusion prompted women to form their own clubs, such as Sorosis, the Women's National Press Association (1885) and the Women's National Press Club (1919). The prestigious Gridiron Club did not admit women until 1975, when Helen Thomas was admitted. She became its first female president in 1992, 108 years after it was founded. At that time 11 of its 60 members were women. Although women journalists had earned Pulitzer Prizes, no women were admitted as jurors for the prize until 1972. Women often used only their initials or pen names for their articles to avoid the stigma of being identified as females.

Many women became prominent journalists in the years between the two world wars. Anne O'Hare McCormick became a foreign affairs commentator for the *New York Times* and in 1937 won the first Pulitzer Prize awarded to a woman in journalism. Many women covered foreign affairs, including the Spanish Civil War and World War II, including Freda Kirchwey, Martha Gelhorn, and Dorothy Thompson (Wagner 1989). Eleanor Roosevelt helped promote women journalists by allowing only women at her morning press conferences, thus giving good opportunities to such women as Lorena Hickock of the Associated Press and May Craig, who later became a regular interviewer on television's *Meet the Press.* These women differed in their views of women and gender although some were feminist activists and wrote on feminism (Marzolf 1977; Sochen 1973; 1981).

As in other male fields women's influence and involvement rose during World War II and then stalled after the war. Although women's numerical presence in journalism did not decline after the war, their roles became more limited. Many complained that they were relegated to reporting traditional women's issues, and young women seeking entry into journalism were encouraged to stick to these. The difference between men and women's pay and status remained considerable. Despite the impressive activities of women journalists in the mid-century wars, many editors claimed that some stories were just too dangerous for women to handle.

The treatment of women in print journalism has begun to change in the last quarter of the 20th century, largely because of women's political and feminist activism. In the late 1970s women began taking the print media to task, and complaints and lawsuits charging sex discrimination were filed against such major press organizations as the *New York Times*, the *Washington Post*, *Newsweek*, and *Time*. In 1970, for example, female employees charged *Newsweek* with violating Title VII of the 1964 Civil Rights Act by its practice of designating news writing as almost exclusively a male domain and news researching (which was at that time given no byline, or named authorship) as almost exclusively a female domain. In 1974 the Equal Employment Opportunity Commission found that the *Washington Post* engaged in illegal employment practices.

In 1978 women won against the *New York Times* after filing 90 charges of discrimination against that paper. Grace Glueck, an art news reporter, explained how the complaint developed:

> In the beginning, even as a group, we had on our white gloves and party manners. How we got started was that in 1972 Grace Lichtenstein was kvetching about the fact that the *Times* would not permit the use of the title "Ms." in the paper. Several of us, including Grace, got to thinking that this style rigidity was symptomatic of more basic problems. And so we began what you might call a group grope, meeting several times before drawing up a petition to the publisher and his board members. We pointed

out the inequities of male-female salaries, the total absence of women in management jobs, and the stringent patterns of our nonpromotion. The managing editor then took it upon himself to call us troublemakers into his office and complain that our action was divisive.[3]

When the women did not receive satisfaction they filed a lawsuit against the paper. Some things did change at the *New York Times*, including acceptance of the term *Ms.* in 1986.[4]

Efforts to achieve equality in the journalism field continue, aided by women's press organizations and women's own publications, such as the *Media Report to Women*. But although some changes have taken place, much is left to be done. Female bylines in the *New York Times*, for example, rose from 12% in 1974 to 24% in 1992.[5] Another study showed that women had 34% of newspaper bylines.[6] Even with their increasing numbers, women face problems; a survey of journalists showed that many report experiencing sexual harassment on the job.[7]

Women in the Electronic Media

The history of women in radio and television broadcasting parallels their involvement in print media.[8] The electronic media are also managed by gender-segregated, male-dominated organizations in which men hold the visible, high-status positions, and women hold primarily auxiliary and lower-status jobs. Radio and television include a wide variety of programming, especially since the introduction of cable services including channels devoted entirely to a specific genre such as music videos, movies, travel documentaries, news, and even weather reports. Our discussion emphasizes electronic journalism partly to offer a comparison with the print media and partly because unlike most kinds of entertainment, which have clear male and female "parts," broadcast journalism's claim to neutrality offers a good test of how gender structures social institutions. It is a traditionally male-dominated endeavor that allows us to see how much change there has been.

The first female radio news commentator was Kathryn Cravens who in 1934 launched her program "News through a Woman's Eye" in St. Louis. Pauline Frederick joined the American Broadcasting Company (ABC) radio network in 1948 and for 12 years was the only woman hard-news commentator on radio and television (Marzolf 1977). One justification used by mass-media organizations for the small number of women commentators was that people didn't like the sound of women's voices: They were too soft and shrill (that is, high pitched), and they lacked authority. Thus, "Singing and acting and, later, giving cleaning tips and recipes and reading commercials were a woman's place in radio's first decades. Changing that role took a war, an act of Congress [the 1964 Civil Rights Act], and a domestic revolution" (Hoseley and Yamada 1987, 1).

The past 20 years has witnessed a dramatic increase in the number of well-known female broadcast journalists. National Public Radio (NPR) has been a leader with the extraordinary prominence of women among its news staff including, among many others, Susan Stamberg, an early host of "All Things

Considered"; Cokie Roberts, one of the few female congressional reporters; and Nina Totenberg, who became directly embroiled in the Clarence Thomas–Anita Hill hearings.

Women also have become more prominent among television news reporters and anchors including Barbara Walters, who led the way in television anchoring; Jane Pauley, who moved from NBC's "Today" to other news and news magazine shows; Connie Chung, the first Asian-American woman on national network news; and Charlayne Hunter-Gault, who began her career as a newsmaker when she became part of the first group of African American students to attend the University of Mississippi and who eventually became a news reporter on public television's "MacNeil-Lehrer Newshour." Now, fortunately, the number of women involved in broadcast news is too large to list.

By the beginning of the 1980s some improvements were evident, as a 1982 survey by the Radio and Television News Directors Association found.[9] Women in local affiliate and cable news channels did somewhat better than those on the network news, reflecting the usual rule of "the higher the fewer." At that time the top six men were on camera more than all the women put together. A very high proportion of stories reported by women were aired on weekends, a lower-status and less visible slot for reporters (Sanders and Rock 1988, 113). By 1992 women were still only 14% of the network broadcast correspondents, and a study of a month of newscasts that year showed 14% of the news stories were reported by women.[10] Women do not fare any better in other kinds of news and public affairs formats; during 1991 women were 14% of the panelists on the "McLaughlin Group."

Women's experiences as news anchors offers good insight into the status of women in broadcast journalism. Marlene Sanders, involved in television broadcasting since its earliest years, provides this illustrative passage from a *New York Times* article reacting to her appearance in 1964 as a temporary replacement for a news anchor who was ill:

> The masculine evening news line up received a temporary female replacement last night . . . when Marlene Sanders stepped in at 6:45 p.m. . . . People who should know report that never before has a distaff reporter conducted on her very own a news broadcast in prime time. For the record, then, the courageous young woman with a Vassar smile was crisp and businesslike and obviously the sort who wouldn't put up with any nonsense, from anyone. Her 15 minute show was not spellbinding, but that could have been because her delivery was terribly straightforward and her copy somewhat dull (Sanders and Rock 1988, 49–50).

Sanders's reaction at the time was to wonder how one could deliver news other than in a straightforward manner. She was surprised at the suggestion that news anchors were usually "spellbinding" (Sanders and Rock 1988, 49–50).

Women news anchors are much more common now, especially since both morning news magazines and evening local news shows have developed a "Ken and Barbie" formula, as some put it: a male and female pair (Paisner 1989, 32).

The fact that anchoring is an area of special progress should be understood partly as a function of the difference between anchoring and other broadcast news positions. Although most news anchors are drawn from the ranks of television journalists, they usually do not research or write the news stories themselves. They are not reporters. They are performers selected largely for their public appeal as personalities. As anchor Jane Pauley put it, "My daughter aspires now to have four children and be a broadcaster with NBC when she grows up. While I'm flattered . . . I hope she does something more productive with her life." She continued,

> It gives me the creeps when I hear . . . young women aspire to be an anchorwoman. You don't aspire to be an anchorwoman. I mean, that's like aspiring to be a Vanna White, a letter turner or something. You aspire to be a journalist (Paisner 1989, 74).

Other journalists agree.

This distinction between reporter and performer was highlighted in 1983 when Christine Craft, a former reporter serving as local anchorwoman, sued her station because she was demoted on the grounds that she was "unattractive, too

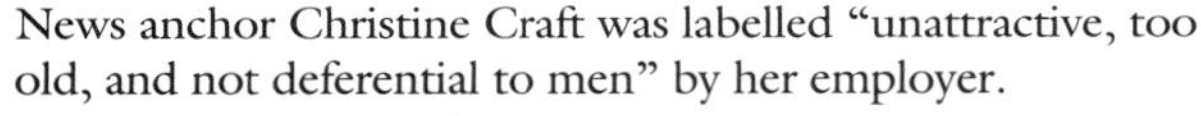
News anchor Christine Craft was labelled "unattractive, too old, and not deferential to men" by her employer.

old, and not deferential to men."[11] The station rebutted, saying that news anchors must be attractive to their audiences if the station is going to keep its audience, and market research showed that audiences regarded Craft as lacking warmth, too casual in her dress, and too opinionated. Craft's lawyers later claimed that the methods used to solicit audience reaction to Craft were discriminatory because they encouraged people to respond in a stereotypic way. Two juries found in favor of Craft, but she lost her case on appeal. Only Justice Sandra Day O'Connor voted to hear the case when Craft appealed to the Supreme Court.

Many female news anchors and journalists contend that higher standards for appearance are set for women on camera than for men and that women are judged on how well they conform to gender stereotypes. Many also believe there is a double standard with respect to aging. As men get older they are viewed as authoritative and perhaps avuncular, whereas women are simply judged less attractive (Paisner 1989, 205–13). Is the problem sexist audiences or sexist media organizations? It is hard to tell, but as early as 1976 one study (Whittaker and Whittaker 1976) found that audiences judged male and female news broadcasters equally acceptable, believable, and effective.

Even the most successful and prominent women in broadcast journalism have experienced some form of discrimination or sexual harassment. Mary Alice Williams recalls a job interview in 1971 when, following an interview focusing mostly on her looks, the executive said, "We don't have anything right now, but we could probably arrange something. Do you fuck?" (Paisner 1989, 179–80). Jane Pauley found that during her time on "Today" all the interviews were given to her on-camera partner, Tom Brokaw (Paisner 1989, 176). When Lesley Stahl visited a set being designed for a prime-time broadcast in 1974, she found the participating journalists' positions labeled, respectively, "CRONKITE," "RATHER," "MUDD," "WALLACE," and "FEMALE" (Paisner 1989, 17–18). Many women journalists find that they are not rid of this aspect of their lives once they become famous.

Many women have been important on camera in other types of television shows, but some have also been influential in shaping the medium. Women like Lucille Ball, Mary Tyler Moore, and others made their mark not just as performers but as shapers of situation comedy as a genre. Because the appearance of women on the air in shows other than news is more directly related to the content, we shall look at these women shortly.

It has been more difficult for women to establish themselves behind the scenes in the production and business aspects of the electronic media. In the early 1970s women were a tiny fraction of the executive and production staff. CBS, for example, had no female directors and one female crew member (U.S. Commission on Civil Rights 1979). Like women in the print media, those in the electronic media began to turn to the courts for help. As a result women's situation has improved, as Table 8-1 shows. Women overall constitute about 34% of the television news staff members and 30% of radio news staff members. They fare much worse as television directors. The organizations that bring us broadcast news remain disproportionately male and white.

TABLE 8-1
Broadcast News Work Force, by Gender and Race, 1992

		TV News		*Radio News*	
		Staff	*Directors*	*Staff*	*Directors*
Total % Women		34	17	30	29
White	Women	27	14	23	24
	Men	56	77	65	67
Black	Women	4	<.5	4	2
	Men	6	2	3	1
Hispanic	Women	2	1	1	2
	Men	3	3	1	1
Asian	Women	1	1	1	2
	Men	1	<.5	<.5	<.5
Native American	Women	<.5	<.5	<.5	1
	Men	<.5	1	1	2
Number		23,100	745	16,900	5,800

Note: Numbers are percentages; columns do not sum to 100% due to rounding error.
Source: *Media Report to Women* 20 (Fall 1992), pp. 4–5.

The Message of the Media

What image of women and norms about gender do the mass media offer people? Very influential analysis in the 1970s argued that media portrayal of women amounts to symbolic annihilation of women by systematically ignoring, trivializing, and distorting them (Tuchman, Daniels, and Benet 1978). George Gerbner (1978) argues that the media are major instruments of cultural resistance to changes in the roles and status of women. He says this happens in three ways.

1. Women and the women's movement are discredited by the media, which focus on the bizarre and the threatening.
2. Women are isolated or segregated and ghettoized. They are shown in special places (for example, the kitchen).
3. Exploitation and victimization of women is shown on television shows as common, routine, and entertaining.

Mass media research suggests that while there have been some improvements, these charges remain true.

Empirical studies of the image of women on television agree: Women appear considerably less than men on most kinds of television programs. Indeed, in all types of programming except soap operas men outnumber women in proportions that would spell demographic disaster in real life. Research also shows that the image of women who do appear on television is highly stereotypic (Vest 1992). Programming for children and adults underestimates the proportion of women in the labor force and shows women mostly in stereotypic roles (Butsch 1992; Signorielli and Lears 1992; Vande Berg and Streckfuss 1992; Vest 1992). This is also true in the newer genres such as the music videos on MTV, which perpetuate gender stereotypes among both black and white characters (Seidman 1992).

Television representations are also class biased. A review of more than 40 years of situation comedies showed that portrayals of middle-class families usually imply that "father knows best," whereas in portrayals of the working class *men* are characterized by "ineptitude, immaturity, stupidity, lack of good sense, or emotional outburst, traits that have been culturally defined as feminine or childlike" (Butsch 1992, 390). Age stereotypes also play an important role. Old women rarely appear in television programs, and when they do they are usually either comic characters lacking both brains and beauty or nasty and bothersome mothers-in-law. Not until the late 1980s did a television show ("Golden Girls") begin to ask us to laugh with rather than at older women.

Representations of African American women are constructed of both gender and race stereotypes, as Jane Rhodes's history shows (Rhodes 1991). In the 1950s the few African American women who appeared played maids, mostly in the character of the friendly Mammy. From 1968 to 1971 actress Diahann Carroll starred as a nurse in "Julia," the first show that avoided this stereotype entirely. Nevertheless, throughout the 1960s and 1970s, although the number of shows with African American characters rose, most were situation comedies in which many of the men played some variety of the Stepin' Fetchitt character and women portrayed a "cocky but nurturing mammy." The late 1980s and early 1990s changes in black women's television roles seemed to follow those of black men almost literally; an increasing proportion of black female characters on television served little dramatic purpose other than appearing as romantic interests for African American male characters.

Despite the overall pattern there has been some change in the kinds of characters portrayed by women on television. Where once we saw only homemakers and the occasional teacher ("Our Miss Brooks"), secretary ("The Lucy Show," "Perry Mason"), saloonkeeper ("Gunsmoke"), or supernatural ("I Dream of Jeannie," "Bewitched"), women in the 1980s and 1990s have played a wider range of roles. Prime-time women's lives are often more complicated and realistic than they were in past decades, even when they have the same occupations. The African American maid in "I'll Fly Away" has thoughts, commitments, and a life of her own outside her job, unlike those of the 1950s and 1960s. She struggles to find her role in the civil rights movement of the early 1960s. The white working-class mother in "Roseanne" faces the painful difficulties of holding her life and family together during hard economic times, and many female characters work hard to balance their public and private lives.

Prime-time television dramas and situation comedies used to avoid dealing with politics. The few exceptions, such as the comedies "Maude" and "All in the Family," were considered daring. Feminism was avoided or treated as funny. By the early 1990s many shows wove political themes into their plots, and although the committed feminist character was rare, more prime-time characters—like those in real life—revealed their anger with violence against women and discrimination, and their frustration with other characters who trivialized women and feminism. Some prime-time shows dealt explicitly with violence against women from the women's point of view instead of the more usual "sexploitation" approach of violent television. Television producer Linda Bloodworth-Thomason, who also applied her production skills to the 1992 Clinton campaign, allowed her characters to react to the news of the day, and she framed a whole show around the negative reactions her characters in "Designing Women" had to the treatment of Anita Hill when she testified against Clarence Thomas's nomination to the Supreme Court in front of the Judiciary Committee. On "Murphy Brown" the protagonist, played by Candace Bergen, testified to the Judiciary Committee in scenes clearly caricaturing the Hill–Thomas hearings.

The most famous incident in the early 1990s involving prime-time women was surely Vice President Quayle's attack on "Murphy Brown" for its immorality and presumed role in undermining "family values" when the main character had a baby out of wedlock. The attack became the subject of national controversy (and international amusement as the world witnessed the vice president appearing to enter a debate with a fictional character), and the show was written to respond to the vice president. The incident led to some constructive discussion about "family values," but mostly it benefited the show: Its ratings and advertising price rose as a result.[12]

Many people have commented on the gender messages aimed at women in newspapers and especially magazines. Many—if not most—magazines are aimed at gender-segregated markets. Among these are the women's service magazines known as the "seven sisters": *Better Homes and Gardens*, *Family Circle*, *Good Housekeeping*, *Ladies' Home Journal*, *McCalls*, *Redbook*, and *Woman's Day*, which target women in general and emphasize women's roles as homemakers. Fashion and style magazines such as *Cosmopolitan*, *Glamour*, *Bazaar*, and *Vogue* also target women as do those with special themes such as home decoration, weddings, parenthood, and weight watching.

Betty Friedan was one of the first to analyze the image of women presented by women's magazines. Friedan, who wrote for women's magazines in the 1950s, documented a postwar change in the portrayal of women in fiction and nonfiction in her book *The Feminine Mystique* (1963). Good fiction, she claimed, left the pages of women's magazines, as did nonfiction that was not concerned with women's stereotypic roles. By the end of the 1950s women were portrayed almost exclusively as mindless but attentive homemakers. "In 1958, and again in 1959, I went through issue after issue of the major women's magazines . . . without finding a single heroine who had a career, a commitment to any work, art, profession, or mission in the world, other than 'Occupation: housewife'" (38). This change in content was paralleled by a change in format: "The very size of [the women's magazines'] print is raised until it looks like a first-grade primer" (58).

In the 1970s the world of women's magazines began to change in two respects. First, new magazines were founded that were aimed at employed women or that assumed women had more interests in, for example, economics and public affairs than the traditional magazines indicated. Since the early 1970s, there has been a significant increase in magazines aimed at employed women such as *Essence*, launched in 1970 for black women, *New Woman* (1971), and *Working Woman* (1976). In 1971 Gloria Steinem founded the major mass-market feminist magazine, *Ms.* In 1988 Frances Lear founded *Lear's*, she claimed, "for women who weren't born yesterday."

One study in the 1970s compared *Ms.* and *Family Circle* finding that besides attention to feminism in *Ms.* there were other differences (Phillips 1978). *Ms.* was much more likely than *Family Circle* to discuss women (by a factor of 20 to 3). Most women spotlighted by *Family Circle* were homemakers, including women who gave up professional careers to be homemakers; none were in politics or public service. *Family Circle* tended to emphasize how employment interferes with women's home lives. Almost half of the women *Ms.* focused on were in politics and public service, and none were presented as homemakers. Women portrayed in *Family Circle* were white; those in *Ms.* were from a variety of racial backgrounds. The two magazines were different in another way as well: *Family Circle* (circulation: about 8 million) was read by many more people than *Ms.* (circulation: about 380,000).

In the 1970s change began to arrive at the traditional women's magazines as well. Beginning in 1970 when feminists entered the offices of the *Ladies' Home Journal* to protest their treatment of women, these magazines became the subject of some controversy. As women entered the work force in ever larger numbers and confronted the issues raised by the feminist movement, these magazines found they had to respond to the times to keep their audience. Some of their editorial policies changed, supplementing articles on domestic and fashion concerns with articles on other aspects of women's lives. Certainly many changes have taken place. *Ladies' Home Journal* is doing a monthly news column in cooperation with CNN. *Family Circle* won a National Magazine Award for public service in 1991 for examination of toxic contamination. *Glamour* won a National Magazine Award in 1992 for public interest for its articles on teen pregnancy and abortion.

But despite changes, the most popular women's magazines continue to be shaped by—and sell—views of women based in gender, race, and class stereotypes as Ellen McCracken's excellent *Decoding Women's Magazines* (1993) shows. Her book focuses on magazines of the 1980s, but consider also the list of cover story topics and "exemplary women" presented by 11 major women's magazines in one month of 1993, summarized in Table 8-2. Although there is some attention to contemporary issues of some consequence, for example, on women's pay and rates of caesarean sections, most of the articles follow the pattern established long ago.

TABLE 8-2
Leading Content: Major Women's Magazines, April 1993

Magazine	*Pictured Cover Stories*	*Other Cover Stories*	*Exemplary Women*
Bazaar ($3.00)	See the Light: Airy Romantic Fashion	Fresh Faced Beauty * Dominick Dunne's Self-Revelatory New Novel	Darcey Bussell (ballerina), Winona LaDuke (Native American activist), Maxine Waters (Congresswoman), Anna Devere Smith (actress)
Cosmopolitan ($2.50)	(Model)	Cosmo's Sex Survey * The Easiest Thing You Can Do to Look 10 Pounds Thinner * No More Nice Girls (A New Generation of Tough, Fighting-Mad Feminists Is on the Warpath)	Sadie Frost (actress), Bridget Fonda (actress)
Glamour ($2.50)	(Model)	Spring Fashion: What Flatters, What Flops * Your Health: The 10 Most Important Questions to Ask * Topless Dancing: Why I Do It, Why I Like It * Ooh La La Lashes! * Cheating: How Couples Recover	Caroline Ellen (jewelry designer), Jenny Silverman (topless dancer)
Good Housekeeping ($1.95)	Marlo Thomas: Phil, Our Marriage, and Me	10 Room Makeovers * 30 All New 30 Minute Menus * Why Doctors Do 500,000 Unecessary Cesareans a Year * My 911 Nightmare	Marlo Thomas (actress, writer)
Ladies' Home Journal ($1.99)	Hillary Clinton: Will She Change Your Life? (What Cindy Knows: Beauty Tips and Tricks * Whitney Houston: Her Private Love Song)	Don't Get Conned! How to Avoid Repairman Rip-Offs * 21 Ways to Handle Stress * Finally Found! The Diet Solution for Women * When What Turns Him On Turns You Off * The Boy Who Divorced His Parents: His Life Today * Help Your Child Do Better in School * Spring Chicken Recipes * Plus Robert Redford, Geena Davis, and Emma Thompson	Hillary Rodham Clinton (First Lady), Whitney Houston (singer/actress), Emma Thompson (actress), Geena Davis (actress), "America's Smartest Women?"

TABLE 8-2

Leading Content: Major Women's Magazines, April 1993 *(continued)*

Magazine	*Pictured Cover Stories*	*Other Cover Stories*	*Exemplary Women*
Mademoiselle ($2.50)	(Model)	Dress Smart * Clothes for Monday to Friday (& Saturdays, Too) * In Love: Bridget Fonda and Eric Stoltz * Arms Control: Pre-Summer Workout * Rape: The Character Issue/Mike vs. Desiree, Round 2	Bridget Fonda (actress), Desiree Washington (beauty queen, boxer Tyson's rape victim)
McCalls ($1.50)	Mariel Hemingway: How She Put Her Troubled Past Behind Her (Kevin Costner: What the Public Never Sees * Mary Emmerling's New Country Look)	6 Common Diseases Doctors Miss * Rape: When and Where You're Most at Risk * The Secrets of Slim Women * How to Look Your Prettiest * 17 Fast Pasta Dishes	
Redbook ($1.95)	Why the Gossips Won't Say a Bad Word about Kathie Lee	Discover the Healing Power of Sex * Drop 10 Pounds: Outsmart Your Fat Cells * The HOT New Haircut for Spring * Urgent! Breast Cancer News for Women Under 40 * America's 177 Best Schools * Why a 36-Year-Old Woman Seduced a 12-Year-Old Boy * Deadly Home Hazards Most Parents Miss	Marilu Henner (television star), Kathie Lee Gifford (talk show host)
Vogue ($3.00)	Fashion's New Deal: 500 Choices from $5 to $500.		Norma Kamali (designer), Anna Devere Smith (actress), Zhang Yimou (film director), Mary Chapin Carpenter and Shawn Colvin (musicians), Dee Dee Myers (president's press secretary), Deborah Berke (architect), Audrey Hepburn (actress), Neneh Cherry (musician)

TABLE 8-2

Leading Content: Major Women's Magazines, April 1993 *(continued)*

Magazine	*Pictured Cover Stories*	*Other Cover Stories*	*Exemplary Women*
Woman's Day ("Only 99¢")	Easy Fresh Lemon Cake (A Killer in the House)	Handywoman's Home-Repair Guide * Free Herb Chart * Is Your Bank Robbing You? * Should You Be Taking More Vitamins? * Decorating with Sheets * 33 Fashion Tips for Size 14 and Up * The 77 Best Family Travel Tips * Consumer Alert: How Not to Be Scammed * Sensational New Orleans Desserts * Fire: Is Your Smoke Detector Enough?	Mariel Hemingway (actress)
Working Woman ($2.50)	The Truth about Women's Pay	Best Hotels for Women * Managing Stress	Sarah Teslik and Nell Minow (shareholders' rights activists), Colleen Barrett (airline executive)

Note: For Picture Cover Stories: If there is more than one cover photograph, the primary one is listed first, others in parentheses. Fashion photographs without explicit tie to headline content are indicated by (Model). Exemplary Women are those (other than models) listed in the contents as subjects of articles.

While women's magazines publish material they think will attract female readers, they do not deal seriously with current issues affecting women. In nearly two decades after the Supreme Court case *Roe* v. *Wade*, the 12 largest women's magazines published only 137 articles on abortion. *Glamour* published 37 of these, meaning that 11 "women's" magazines averaged less than one article every 2 years on one of the most controversial issues affecting women.[13]

Recent decades have also witnessed struggles over the gender content of newspapers. For many years most newspapers had a segregated "women's page." Their content has undergone changes paralleling those in women's magazines. During and just before World War II, women were presented as relatively heterogeneous creatures. In the 1950s, however, they were viewed almost exclusively as homemakers. Most news about women was put on the women's page rather than elsewhere, thus casting stories about women as "soft" (peri-pheral) rather than "hard" (important) news and trivializing significant events:

> In 1965 [the *New York Times* women's page] ran a brief story in which Betty Friedan announced the formation of N.O.W. Placed between a recipe for turkey stuffing and an article announcing that Pierre Henri was returning to Saks Fifth Avenue, the article clearly indicated that Friedan had been interviewed at least several days before. The founding of N.O.W. was treated as soft news (Tuchman 1978, 201–2).

In the 1970s, in an apparent response to the women's movement, newspapers abandoned the "women's page." Careful readers noticed, however, that roughly the same segregated material was simply renamed with titles such as "Style," "Society," or "Living Today."

Even when news about women is not segregated, it is treated differently from news about men. Coverage of women is more likely to mention personal appearance ("the petite blonde lawyer"), marital status, spouses, and children (Foreit et al. 1980). It is also more likely to mention the subject's sex explicitly. Few if any newspapers feel compelled to write about the "male police officer." Judging by the text and pictures of newspapers, women are relatively few in number and of little importance. When they appear they usually either are isolated as though they are a parochial special-interest group or are pictured stereotypically.

It is difficult for women to gain serious recognition for their accomplishments if the press does not cover them properly. Take the case of women's sports. On average, about 8% of the editorial and pictorial coverage in *Sports Illustrated* is about girls and women. An examination of all *Sports Illustrated* issues in 1989 showed a total of 644 photographs of females. Of those only 253—not even 40%—were athletes. The coverage of female athletes was concentrated into a very few sports including especially tennis. Of the nonathletes, 36% were models in the annual swimsuit issue, 27% were male athletes' wives and girlfriends, 8% were male athletes' mothers, and 8% were other family members of male athletes. Models, especially those pictured purely for men to ogle, are more prevalent than athletes among the women who appear in the pages of the highest-circulation sports magazine in the country. And the circulation of that magazine doubles every February for the "swimsuit issue." Research also shows bias in television coverage of women's sports; for example, the camera tends to zoom in on body parts, simulating the eye of the ogling man (Daddario 1992).

One continuing problem has been the trivializing and biased treatment of the women's movement. The mass media were quick to pick up on the image of feminists as "bra-burning libbers" and have often given less than serious, thorough coverage to the women's movement and women's political activities. Consider a study of coverage of the Equal Rights Amendment (ERA) in a prestigious national newspaper. During 1977, an important year in the history of the ERA, the *Los Angeles Times* contained 36 news stories on the ERA. Not one quoted the whole amendment. Only two quoted the first section of it, which consists of only 26 words. None told the status of the amendment in California, and fewer than one-third reported the national status of the amendment.[14] This type of reporting of the women's movement is not unusual.

Research on coverage of abortion politics reveals bias in the mass media in general. A study of the three networks plus three major news magazines for a year beginning in mid-1991 shows that most of the stories were covered by men and that men's and women's coverage differed. Men's stories quote antiabortion sources by a 65-35 margin while women cited pro-choice sources by a 56-44 margin.[15] And as Tiffany Devitt points out, when the *Los Angeles Times* published a lengthy article titled "Can Women Reporters Write Objectively on Abortion?" they never asked whether men can.[16]

The Impact of the Mass Media

Demonstrating that the mass media present an androcentric or distorted view of women is not the same as demonstrating that the mass media have an impact on the way people think about women. Millions of people watch the same television shows, but they do not think alike. What impact do the media have on people's views of women? How is this impact achieved?

Individuals do not receive the images and information transmitted through the media as clay receives thumbprints. People choose to attend to some messages or media and not others; if we are not interested in women's politics, we will not read articles on this topic even if they are in the paper. Psychologists refer to this process as *selective exposure.* Because of the less conscious process of *selective perception* we tend to notice, highlight, or exaggerate certain details out of everything that is presented to us while ignoring or diminishing others. As we saw in Chapter 1, people who are highly gender schematic see gender difference and stereotypes more readily than others. If we expect women to be more emotional than men, we may see emotionality in women more readily than we see it in men. Perception also depends on context. Thus different people can interpret the same picture or text differently. The implications of all of this for identifying the impact of the mass media is that it is not as easy as it might seem. Let us turn first to research looking at media impact on children, then adults.

By the time children enter school they already have spent more hours watching television than they will spend later in college classrooms. Most children spend more hours per week in front of the television than in school (Rickel and Grant 1979). Children prefer to watch programs that contain characters of their own sex, and they watch more carefully and pay more attention when these characters act in gender-typed ways, almost as though they know what they are supposed to be learning (Sprafkin and Liebert 1978). Children who watch a lot of television reflect more stereotypes in their gender views than those who watch little, and stereotyped views, especially those held by males, increase with age among heavy viewers (McGhee and Frueh 1980; Signorielli and Lears 1992).

In one study, some children saw a television show in which women appeared only in gender-typed roles, and others saw one in which a woman was a police officer. The children who saw the latter show were more likely to think later that women really could be police officers. Similar studies yield similar results (Tuchman 1978; Sprafkin and Liebert 1978). In another study, children watched television advertisements portraying various toys as appropriate for one sex or the other. The children were then allowed to choose from a number of toys. Both girls and boys were more likely to pick toys that had been presented as gender appropriate than those that had been presented as gender inappropriate (Cobb, Stevens-Long, and Goldstein 1982). These findings are not unusual.

Gender-based media messages also affect adults. People who watch more television are more stereotyped in their views, and they view themselves in more stereotyped terms (Ross, Anderson, and Wisocki 1982). Sexist language and style in newspapers affects people's perception of female candidates for office. One study showed that sexist language and style in newspaper articles had a negative impact on readers' evaluations of the candidate for stereotypically masculine positions such as sheriff or relatively "neutral" positions but a positive effect on evaluations of female candidates for "feminine" offices such as president of the League of Women Voters (Dayhoff 1983). In other words, linguistic sexism highlights and exaggerates stereotypically feminine details, thus making the woman being described appear less appropriate for "masculine" or even "neutral" positions and more appropriate for "feminine" positions. (We will discuss language and gender more extensively in Chapter 10.)

One of the problems in detecting media effects is the difficulty in gauging the effects of absence. What does it mean to girls' and women's self-image to see not just stereotypes of themselves in the mass media, but not to see themselves at all? If women are rarely highlighted as important figures in world affairs or sports, where can they get the idea that they can excel? Alfred Kidwasser and Michelle Wolf (1992) ask the same question with respect to gay and lesbian adolescents. Very few characters in prime-time television are described as gay. Kidwasser and Wolf ask what that means for gay and lesbian adolescents, who may not feel comfortable talking to anyone and can gain no self-image from television other than invisibility.

The Commercial Media

The mass media are filled with messages aimed at selling us something. Public broadcasting is no exception; sponsors are mentioned not just to thank them for their support but also to show us they are nice companies to buy from. Everywhere we see billboards, bumper stickers, and even T-shirts promoting products. Our mailboxes are stuffed with advertisements and sometimes trial products. Advertisements fill the programs for concerts and plays. The packaging of food and other items in stores is designed to advertise the contents. Newsletters or surveys from our representatives in Congress or our state legislatures are also advertisements.

Women and gender have played important roles in the history of commercial communication, or advertising. Advertising began to develop as serious business with the rise of industrialism in the 19th century and, by the 1920s, was professionalized and later became increasingly technical and scientific in its approach.

In his history of advertising in the United States, Stuart Ewen argues that "the advertising which attempted to create the dependable mass of consumers required by modern industry often did so by playing upon the fears and frustrations evoked by mass society—offering mass-produced visions of individualism by which people could extricate themselves from the mass" (1976, 45). The goal of advertising is to make people feel that they need or want a specific product. An advertisement for a special brand of vaginal douche or cornflakes has to convince people both that they need the product and that they want this brand rather than others. The advertiser therefore transmits the message that without this product potential customers will be less healthy, attractive, happy, secure, or caring than if they purchase the product. Advertisements are aimed at specific audiences; they play on or even create the fears, needs, or desires of specific groups of people. Because of this they can have a powerful influence on creating, or at least maintaining, specific gender norms.

A study of 167 magazine advertisements for menstruation-related products published between 1976 and 1986 provides a good example. Menstruation was consistently presented as a hygienic crisis in which women greatly need the security and peace of mind provided by the product. Women who used the advertised products were always depicted functioning at optimum levels (Havens and Swenson 1988).

Some of the first important efforts at directing advertising at women occurred in the late 19th century as they began to be defined as playing a major role in consumption and therefore the health of American business. Clothing manufacturers had to create markets in the late 19th century for their new products: ready-to-wear clothes. Department stores—sometimes called fashion palaces—were developed at that time. They were designed to convince women that they could be elegant and fashionable, and they sometimes had "experts" available to help women make the "right" choices. We already have seen that women's magazines were filled with fashion plates showing women what they should wear. In such advertisements the function of providing information merges with the sales pitch.

Women still turn to magazine advertising to find out what the fashions are. In many women's magazines almost all the pictures and many of the articles are in fact advertisements even when they do not appear to be. Messages presented as "information" or "advice" are often actually advertisements (McCracken 1993). Ellen McCracken's decoding of magazine advertisements shows that they tend to encourage women into passivity and to see themselves as fragmented, objectified, and, indeed, endangered unless they buy the product.

Observers sometimes exaggerate the power of advertising. For advertising to sell, it must reflect the social values of the time; it cannot create needs out of thin air. At the turn of the century, for example, when science and progress were the catchwords of the day, advertising directed at women began to play on these principles, especially on the new views of scientific home management, or home economics. From then on advertising presented itself as a source of expert information about how women could keep their families healthy, their homes germ-free, and their households efficiently managed. Personal-hygiene product promotion keeps up this tradition today, alerting women to germs and health hazards they never knew existed or that do not exist.

In the 1920s, advertising used feminism and the image of the emancipated woman for its own purposes, just as advertising now uses the image of the liberated woman. The 1970s Virginia Slims campaign, "You've come a long way, baby," hearkens back to a 1929 campaign by the American Tobacco Company that attempted to convince women to smoke.

The 20th century also has been marked by the promotion of "labor-saving devices" to women. These promotion campaigns promise a more healthful and efficient household, as well as release from the drudgery of housework to spend more time in family or social activities or even other occupations. The promise was unfulfilled, as many studies of time use and technology have shown (see, e.g., Vanek 1980; Robinson 1980). Homemakers today spend at least as much time on housework as housewives did in the 1920s. In his study in the mid 1970s John Robinson (1980) found that so-called labor-saving devices make remarkably little difference in the time women spend on housework. Despite the claims of advertisers, a microwave oven reduces the average workday by only 10 minutes, a clothes dryer by only 5 minutes, and a vacuum cleaner by only 1 minute. A freezer adds 6 minutes to the working day, a washing machine adds 4 minutes, and a dishwasher and sewing machine each add 1 minute.

If these figures seem implausible, consider the effects of these goods on a household. A woman with a washer and dryer does not wash the same amount of clothes in less time, she washes clothes more often in about the same time. Special new kitchen appliances such as food processors lead people to do different kinds of cooking from the type they did without them. Although Stuart Ewen is right in suggesting that "rather than viewing the transformations in household work as labor-saving, it is perhaps more useful to view them as labor-changing" (1976, 163), the voice of the expert in advertisements convinces women otherwise.[17]

During the two world wars, business responded by developing the theme that women's efforts could help win the wars. The promotional voice of the expert urged women to participate in programs to save resources needed for the war

Especially these days . . . a man needs a good meal

IN PEACETIME, you owe it to yourself and your family to eat well-balanced, nourishing meals. In critical times like these, it's a patriotic duty.

The food you eat is the fuel which your body turns into *energy* — the energy needed for everything you do, physical and mental.

Your food supplies your body with the materials which *build it* and *keep it in repair*.

From your food, your body also gets the elements which help to *protect it from disease* and *keep it running smoothly*.

Everyone—desk worker, industrial worker, home worker—needs each day a varied selection of the right foods: milk, vegetables, fruits, eggs, meat or fish or poultry, cereals and breads, and fats. From these foods your body can obtain the nourishment it requires. Naturally, the amount of food you require varies with your activity. If your work is hard you can eat more of the foods high in energy value—bread, cereals, potatoes, fats, cheese and dried beans.

Nourishing meals not only help you feel better—they help you do better work and do it more easily. Even your spirits improve and you get more fun from leisure hours. Better eating habits can also build up your resistance to the illnesses which may become more widespread in times of war.

Housewives can do much to see that the members of their families get the nourishing meals they need. Where workers are on night shifts, it is important to arrange meals so that both the workers and the family have nutritious, satisfying meals at the right times. Try to arrange at least one meal so that the whole family may eat together.

To help you select the right amounts of the right foods, Metropolitan will send you on request a free booklet, 92-N, "Your Food—How Does It Rate For Health?"

World War II magazine advertisements showed women how they could contribute to the war effort. This example is from a 1942 *National Geographic*.

efforts. Advertisements showed women how to rearrange their household management to do their part and, incidentally, how this could be accomplished only by using Product X. Particularly during World War II, advertisements promoted the virtues of women working in nontraditional jobs for the sake of the war. They also showed how these good women used the right products; even Rosie the Riveter could keep her hands lovely and feminine. After the war, advertisements showed how happy women were to be back in the household caring for their families.

Commercial images remain gender typed. Television commercials directed at children include many more boys than girls, and girls play passive and gender-typed roles (Feldstein and Feldstein 1982; Macklin and Kolbe 1984). Women in television commercials generally play one of three roles: mother, housekeeper, or "aesthetic" interest (Mamay and Simpson 1981). Women are usually pictured inside the house, especially in the kitchen or bathroom. Women also appear as sex objects in advertisements directed at men; they are draped over cars in revealing outfits, for example, as though for an extra price they could be purchased as optional equipment along with the air conditioning. A content analysis of 1,480 television commercials shows that although by the late 1980s women were shown more frequently outside the home and in a wider range of occupations than they used to be, little else had changed (Ferrante, Haynes, and Kingsley 1988).

The portrayal of expertise and authority in contemporary advertising is also gender based. The "expert" in television commercials (often the unseen "voice-over") is usually a man, even in commercials aimed at women and even when all visuals are of women (Mamay and Simpson 1981). Expertise took an interesting twist with the rise of the women's movement and objections to commercial sexism. Many advertisements emphasized women's expertise, but this expertise was demonstrated in vignettes showing male incompetence at household work. In these portrayals men rather than women were the objects of the jokes, but the underlying message was the same: Housework is for women.

Some changes in advertising were brought about by law. In the late 1960s, for example, it became illegal for "help wanted" columns in newspapers to categorize jobs as "male" or "female." Women's organizations have exerted pressure on companies with sexist advertisements by, for example, writing letters and urging boycotts. The underlying problem, however, is that companies would not use gender-typed techniques if they did not sell products. But they do, so they do.

The Cultural and Artistic Media

The mass and artistic media are not usually analyzed in the same context. But the arts, like other media, are organized in social institutions that are structured in part by gender. Further, it is not always easy to distinguish between the "mass" and "artistic" media. First, the arts are often presented *through* the mass media.

In addition to situation comedies, game and crime shows, news broadcasts, and self-help shows, television and radio also present theater, films, music, poetry readings, and art history. In addition to soap operas, television also may present another kind of opera, such as Wagner's magnum opus, *Der Ring des Nibelungen*.[18] The recent spread of cable television has made this overlap even greater.

There are other similarities between the mass and artistic media. They are, after all, media of communication. They are channels through which some people express themselves and their perceptions of events, people, ideas, and feelings and to which a much larger number of people turn to share, learn about, and possibly evaluate these perceptions. They are part of the cultural traffic of society, their appeal or utility based in part on the relationship of both form and content to surrounding cultural symbols, ideology, and social events.

There are also organizational similarities among the different media. The arts, like the mass media, are often managed by large, bureaucratic organizations with a wide range of goals besides merely "getting the message across." Except under some circumstances their product must sell or gain acceptance in the target audience. Some ideas are too controversial, risky, or unfamiliar to be accepted by the artistic and media organizations for transmission; there is not always complete agreement among the public or coprofessionals on what is most desirable in form and content. Publishing and movie houses, museums, theaters, concert halls are all institutions that can be analyzed in terms of the role they play in the sex/gender system. The arts world has been gender segregated, and women have been valued less than men. The images reflected through the arts, especially the high-status arts, are often gender typed. This link between the arts on the one hand and questions of power, politics, and status on the other has often been ignored. Social scientists have paid less attention to the arts than they have to the mass media.

As with the other media, these messages are not monolithic but reflect the diversity of human nature. But it is impossible to do more here than touch on some art and cultural forms or to take more than a brief look at special issues raised by the arts. We will explore some of the parallels among the cultural and artistic media, the commercial media, and the mass media by looking at examples of some of the issues raised by different forms. We will look first at women's roles in the arts and then at some of the gender messages transmitted through the arts.

Women as Artists

Although anyone can participate in most of the arts on their own or as amateurs, becoming recognized as a great artist requires access to training, the institutions of creation and distribution, and audiences. Historians of women in the arts suggest that access has been the greatest stumbling block for women. As Linda Nochlin (1971) suggests, the often-asked question "Why are there no great women artists?" can be answered in several ways: There have been, but they were not recognized. There have been, but they have been forgotten. There have been some, but not many because women were not allowed to be artists. There have been some, but not many because women are not able enough.

History offers ample evidence that women who might have developed their artistic talents were blocked in their efforts to seek the necessary training. For a long time women were not admitted to the great academies for the graphic arts. They were excluded from one of the most important aspects of art training, life drawing from a nude model. Aspiring female musicians were not allowed into many of the major music academies and courses. Schools of architecture were reluctant to admit women until recently, and from 1915 to 1942 American women who wanted to be architects could train only at the all-female Cambridge School of Architecture and Landscape Architecture (Berlo 1976). Although we know of many great women writers, in the late 18th and early 19th centuries many—such as the Brontë sisters and George Eliot—found it easier to be accepted if they used a male pen name.[19]

It is still relatively difficult for women to gain access to many art fields. Although about 50% of all graphic artists are women, one can find relatively few reviews of women's work in art magazines and newspapers. Women are underrepresented among teachers at professional art schools, among museum administrators, and among exhibiting artists.

The situation in music also shows a long history of discrimination with some recent changes. Until the 20th century, orchestras generally refused to play music composed by women, to admit women instrumentalists, and, until the past couple of decades, to play under female conductors (Jepson 1975–76; Levy 1983). Even by the early 1970s none of the 159 orchestras of the Symphony Orchestra League had a woman music director or conductor. Sarah Caldwell and Margaret Hillis became regularly appointed conductors only by founding their own orchestras (Jepson 1975–76). The New York Philharmonic Orchestra did not include a female instrumentalist until 1966. The lack of orchestra seats for women changed when orchestras introduced blind auditions, in which the judges could not see the player. By 1985 women were 28% of the instrumentalists in major U.S. orchestras and 47% in metropolitan orchestras (Rix 1988, 222). As in other fields, "the higher the fewer" is still the case. In the 1980s about three-quarters of the members of the Music Teachers National Association were female while the same was true of only 22% of full-time college-level music faculty members (Rix 1988, 221).

Women have had a difficult time breaking into film direction. In 1990 women were only 20% of the members of the Directors Guild of America, and they directed only 5% of the feature films that year. Their experience as television directors clearly demonstrates the principle of "the higher the fewer": Women constituted 12% of the directors of half-hour shows, 9% of the directors of hour-long shows, less than 3% of the directors of made-for-television movies, and none of the mini-series. On average, female directors earned a little more than half of what male directors earned.[20] Women directors feel the subtle effects of discrimination against them. Martha Coolidge ("Ramblin' Rose"), for example, says, "You have to look for it to see it, because it's around the corner. It's the people who aren't interested in having a meeting with me or other women. It's the producers who are friends or business associates who don't think of you for something considered a man's piece of material. It's the look of hesitation that comes across their faces when you suggest maybe they should."[21] Even actresses may be implicated in the discrimination against women directors. Actress Dyan Cannon recalls, "I remember once when I was doing a soap opera, I was upset when a woman walked on the set to direct. I wanted a man to direct me, because Daddy ran the house."[22]

Women also have difficulty rising through the ranks of the management of arts industries. Again consider the case of film. Film producer Lynda Obst ("The Fisher King") expressed the view of many women in the film industry when she said, "It is clearly the case for both women executives and producers that, reputation for reputation, experience for experience, we are not on the same levels as our male counterparts."[23] They are not paid the same nor are they given the same opportunities or clout. In 1992, only 2 out of 20 major entertainment companies could claim that 30% or more of their top executives were women. As in many other fields, women sometimes learn to devalue themselves and do not demand as much as men do. As one woman who runs an entertainment law firm said, " I have represented many women executives who find it so difficult to imagine that they deserve what they get paid. Women think they're so lucky. They're afraid someone will get angry if they ask for more." She thinks that "women have a hard time working as little as men do and taking the money as their due."[24]

Women's collective fortunes are better, of course, in fields such as acting and singing that specifically call for women artists. American dance is a field in which women such as Isadora Duncan and Martha Graham had a major impact; in fact only in recent decades have men become as important as women in dance. Although classical music composition has been dominated by men, women have been particularly important in the blues, jazz, and folk genres, where artists such as Bessie Smith, Billie Holliday, Ella Fitzgerald, and Joan Baez are prominent. Even in the traditionally male-dominated fields, women are now achieving recognition; in 1983, for example, Ellen Taafe Zwillich became the first woman composer to win the Pulitzer Prize in music. We can single out names of successful women in most fields of art, but we cannot escape the conclusion that in many of the important fields, women have not been treated as seriously as men.

This leads us to the question of how people judge women as artists. In many fields, opinion leaders have argued that women are incapable of greatness by nature. In music it has been thought that women lack the physical strength to be great pianists, the strength of character to be conductors, and the imagination to be composers (Levy 1983). Could a woman lead a performance of such masculine works as Beethoven's Fifth Symphony (Jepson 1975–76)? Many music professionals have thought that women do not have the mental capacity to teach music theory because it is so technical and mathematical.

Critics of architecture have worried about women's inferior spatial perception, as have critics of painting and sculpture. Literary critics have criticized women's "personalism," lack of strength, and inability to "write like a man." Critics often interpret women's work through gender stereotypes: Regardless of the field they notice its interior dimensions, intuitiveness and sensitivity, and any links with other artists that might mark it as derivative. If the artist is a feminist, critics either notice the "shrillness" of the art or compliment it for not being shrill, as though in the normal course of events it must be.

There is some question whether the works of male and female artists differ. Because men's and women's experiences and training are not the same it would make sense for their artistic expressions to be different. Portions of the art community go beyond this, however, and argue that differences exist and are rooted in the different sexual natures of men and women. Even people in the mainstream of the arts have used this as an argument for women's inferiority. Many radical feminists, especially those who argue for a special "women's aesthetic," also see differences springing from nature, but they place a positive value on "feminine art." Evidence of systematic differences have been elusive, especially where observers do "gender-blind" analysis of different works of art to see whether they can identify male from female (Melosh 1991).

Many feminist artists and art critics have called for the art world to give more serious attention to the art forms that have been the special domain of women including quilting, embroidery, weaving, and certain kinds of pottery. These forms have been virtually excluded from art history courses, books, and museums, not because they have been designed and made by women but because they have been considered crafts rather than fine arts. But crafts—and therefore much of women's artistic work—has lower status in the art world than the "fine" arts. The distinction turns on purpose and function: Crafts spring from the practical purposes of feeding, clothing, and sheltering, for example, and arts are "divorced from use, are 'useless' in any practical sense" (Hedges and Wendt 1980, 2). In music there is also a distinction between "serious," high forms of music, and lower forms such as folk, blues, rock, and pop. Investigating women and the arts thus raises some of the most fundamental questions about the nature and role of the arts in society that we can ask. What is the distinction among arts, crafts, and other forms of expression? What is a "high" form of art? What function do the arts play in society?

Poet Marge Piercy has used her artistry to ask why there is a distinction between arts and crafts: "Who decided what is useful in its beauty/ means less than what has no function beside beauty/ (except its weight in money)?" (1974, 86–87). Anyone who has seen the intricate and beautiful work of quilters or reads about a pieced quilt that contains 30,000 pieces, each one-half inch by three-quarters inch in size[25] wonders why quilts have so often languished in attics and trunks while Mondrian's painted squares hang proudly in the world's great museums. Such skill, taught by ordinary women in their homes rather than by famous people in academies, also makes one wonder how women ever could have been considered technically and cognitively incapable of mastering "higher" forms of art. Women's crafts, like the other arts, have shared symbols, forms, and traditions and are manifest in unique displays of individual creativity and artistry.

Contemporary analysis casts into doubt the appropriateness of making such distinctions between art that is utilitarian and art that is for aesthetic pleasure alone. A review of the history of the arts and the social roles of the arts and

Poet Maya Angelou read a poem she wrote for the inauguration of President Clinton.

artists suggests that these dichotomies are highly suspect. The fine arts are of utilitarian as well as aesthetic value in many senses. Humans need food and shelter, but they also need sensory stimulation. Studies of the effects on people of sensory deprivation show that sense stimulation is almost as necessary to survival as food and water. Is there such a thing as thoroughly useless art?

Consider other links between the "higher" and "lower" arts. Some of the greatest "fine" music in the West originated as church music designed to create a mood and help people praise, glorify, mourn, and celebrate. Do these utilitarian purposes diminish the value of Bach's cantatas, Beethoven's *Mass in B Minor*, or Verdi's *Requiem*? If not, we cannot argue that women's lullabies and native American women's healing songs are necessarily lower forms of music simply because they were composed for specific purposes (Jaskoski 1981).

The history of the sampler provides a fascinating study of utility versus aesthetics, status and art, and gender norms (Fratto 1976–77). Samplers, the small works in which girls and female adolescents demonstrated their skill at embroidery, were made primarily during the 16th through the 19th centuries and reached their greatest popularity in the late 18th century. The skill and beauty of these samplers is amazing to the contemporary eye, particularly considering the age of the artists.

These samplers are important cultural artifacts. Beside the ABCs stitched into them are poems, prayers, and pictorial symbols praising the home and feminine virtues. As Toni Fratto writes, "The sampler was to be the outward sign of a girl-child's willingness and readiness to enter into her place." It "was meant to serve as the sign of gentility, to establish the girl's credentials as 'a lady'" (Fratto 1976–77, 13). Fratto argues that because the samplers became increasingly bound by conventions of status and design, their quality declined in the early 19th century. "What they gained by not being Art they lost by being a symbol of genteel culture" (Fratto 1976–77, 15).

Women play crucial roles in the everyday life of the arts. They decorate their houses, sing lullabies, and tell stories to their children. In some fields, such as singing, dancing, acting, and poetry and novel writing, there have been many great and famous women. In other fields it does not take long to uncover the names of women who should be remembered along with the others. It cannot be argued that the value of all arts and artists is the same; we probably do not want to rank the flower arrangement a woman puts on her dining room table with the sculpture of Barbara Hepworth. But considering the segregation of men and women into different artistic fields and the denigration of women artists and their arts, we can see that the artistic and cultural media of communication are important parts of sex/gender systems.

Gender and Sexuality as Subjects of Art

The treatment of gender in the arts is related to the values, frustrations, and goals of the times. The sexual tensions, role reversals, bawdy jokes, and portrayals of dominant women in Restoration comedies reflect that period of uncertainty and changing roles. In the 19th century these formerly popular plays were considered too lewd and unsuitable for decent people. Cuckolding was a favorite theme of the Restoration, when everything generally worked out well in the end, but by the 19th century the philandering woman became the fallen woman; a fictional female who committed adultery usually died for her sins (often by her own hand), or at least went mad.

Although we could draw examples from any art form, the 20th-century history of film demonstrates powerfully the connections between art and social history with respect to gender. In the earliest days of film, moving pictures were especially popular among urban immigrants. As Elizabeth Ewen (1980) shows, movies were often about common people, and working-class immigrants flocked to neighborhood movie houses to see people acting out their own tensions and problems. Movies presented themes of gender and sexuality from both feminist and antifeminist perspectives. After World War I the growing film industry increasingly reflected middle-class views and perspectives. As the power of film was recognized, there was more pressure to consider its potential effects on audiences. Movies were considered to be potentially powerful tools of assimilation, for example, capable of teaching immigrant women how to be good American housewives.

An important shift in film images of women occurred between the late 1930s and the 1950s. In the late 1930s and early 1940s there were many significant female parts (played by actresses like Katherine Hepburn), often showing women as strong, independent, employed, and even professional. After World War II this began to change as social values stressed the return to the home and domestic values. In the 1950s the strong women went back to being homemakers or became brainless sex objects, or both. In the immediate post–World War II era the remaining strong women were often dangerous temptresses leading men astray in the "film noir."

Parallel historical shifts can also be seen in other art forms, as Kathlyn Fritz and Natalie Hevener (1979) show in their study of 20th-century detective novels. They found that the image of the female detective changed dramatically from the 1920s to the 1970s. Before the 1960s women detectives in these novels often were not really detectives; they were amateurs who solved crimes. They also tended to be unattractive or elderly. In the 1920s and 1930s, 44% of the female detectives did not have a career; the same was true of 40% of the female detectives in novels of the 1940s and 1950s. In recent decades, however, only 10% of the female detectives had no careers, and these characters were often portrayed as attractive women.

Jennifer Waelti-Walters (1979) reminds us of how early in life androcentric norms are taught to us through art forms, in this case, the fairy tale. After reviewing the lives of fairy-tale princesses she concludes, "Nobody in her right mind could possibly want to be a fairy-tale princess" (180). Most fairy-tale princesses are passive victims or merely decorative or must die in order to be loved. If they resist these roles, they are generally portrayed as evil or mad. Although there have been some improvements in children's literature, with publishers making conscious efforts to incorporate into their lists more active, positive representations of women and minority group members, not all is well. A study comparing the original Nancy Drew books of the 1920s and 1930s with those written more recently shows that poor Nancy is not what she was. Whereas in the early days she was described only as "attractive," a more recent edition notes that "the tight jeans looked great on her long, slim legs, and the green sweater complemented her strawberry-blond hair." She is now a much more stereotypic character. Things she surely would have been able to do herself decades ago are now done for her by the boys. She seems to require more help from them than used to be the case.[26]

One of the most interesting sites for investigating the relationship between gendered representations in art and the sociopolitical context in which they were created was the set of publicly funded art projects initiated through the New Deal programs of the 1930s, including especially the Section of Fine Arts, which sponsored sculpture and painting, and the Federal Theater Project (FTP), which sponsored the writing and production of plays across the country, and the Federal Art Project, which was a public relief program for artists. Barbara Melosh's (1991) gender analysis of the productions of the Section and FTP reveals fascinating dimensions to the depiction of gender in light of the political ideology of the New Deal. Farm families were often presented as "comradely" cooperation between strong men and women, whereas depictions of industrial work, projecting an image of "manly" labor, "consistently excluded and hence made invisible women's productive work, privileging the male domains of craft and heavy industry" (Melosh 1991, 83). The antiwar art common in these projects rejected "the sentimental notion of the home as refuge" and "called women to the heroic role of pacifist mothers" (Melosh 1991, 229). The radical aspects of the New Deal political vision often recast women's roles, but at the same time subordinated them in certain settings such as industrial labor and politics.

At times the sexual and gender politics of art has erupted into major battles. One of the best known of these controversies involved a massive work by Judy Chicago called "The Dinner Party," which consists of a large, three-sided dinner table decorated with place settings constructed of various women's arts and crafts representing 39 different well-known women. The names of 999 other women are embedded in the tablecloth and table base. Many viewers and critics have been disturbed by the distinctly vaginal form of much of the design. Whereas critics seem relatively undisturbed by phallic iconography and symbolism, the graphic themes of Chicago's work repulsed and even angered them. Established art critics are less likely to ask, "Is it art?" of androcentric art, because androcentric art is "normal." They ask, "Is it art?" of gynocentric art, because gynocentric art is interpreted as political and therefore not artistic. The role of sexuality and feminism in the arts became extremely contentious in the 1980s and 1990s when the conservative government running the National Endowment for the Arts based some of their funding issues on gender and sexual politics.

One of the most contentious debates in feminist discussion of representations of women revolves around portrayals of sexuality and the erotic and their relationship to violence and pornography. Many feminist critics argue that violence against women is central to dominant male definitions of the erotic and, especially, that pornography usually establishes the dominance or abuse of women as pleasurable, certainly to witness if not to experience. Advertisements for films often present an "erotic" image of a terrified woman. In films, during incidents of terror against women, such as rape, the camera usually takes the assailant's viewpoint rather than the victim's; we watch the victim being terrified rather than the assailant being terrifying. A study of a random sample of "adult" movies available in family video rental stores in southern California found that over half the explicit sexual scenes were predominantly concerned with domination and exploitation (Cowan, Lee, Levy, and Snyder 1988). A considerable amount of pornography involves children. In some films, women are literally mutilated or (in "snuff" films) killed.

What impact do these images of violence have on audiences? Many researchers have investigated the relationship between viewing violent pornography and engaging in violence against women such as rape. Although relatively few find conclusive evidence that such pornographic images cause violence, many argue that it can be a contributing factor. Research on long-term exposure to video violence against women found that as male viewers saw more over time their anxious and other negative reactions to it diminished and they even perceived less violence in the videos than they had at first. The researchers concluded that exposure to violent (but not nonviolent) pornographic images desensitizes men to violence against women over the long haul (Donnerstein, Linz, and Penrod 1987).[27]

The 1980s and 1990s witnessed a heated debate over what to do about artistic and mass-culture representations that devalue and objectify women and eroticize and perhaps encourage violence against them. Feminists share broad agreement that both sexual objectification of women and sexual abuse of women are wrong and that societies need to seek means of eliminating them and helping the victims. Feminists also have tended to agree that these representations and the industries that produce them are part of a larger system of oppression of women.[28] But what should be done about it? Some feminists, most notably Andrea Dworkin and Catherine MacKinnon, have argued that pornography should be made illegal. Activists in many cities worked to create ordinances that would ban pornography. One was passed but vetoed in Minneapolis, one was enacted but overturned by a judge in Indianapolis.[29]

Many feminists have been opposed to this strategy for combating pornography, and some have questioned some claims of the antipornography activists (Vance 1984; Burstyn 1985; Segal and McIntosh 1992). The main question has to do with issues of censorship, civil liberties, and freedom of expression. There is a long history of attempts to regulate representations of sexuality (Kendrick 1987), most of which stem from conservative and moralistic views seeking to regulate people's expression and behavior according to a very limited, usually homophobic and sexist, view. Many people fear that defining the boundaries and limits of censorship of speech and other forms of expression is extremely difficult and dangerous once it has begun. Can we be sure we always know the difference between pornography and other depictions of sexuality? Is there an objective standard for identifying the demeaning? Consider the painting by Monica Sjoo, "God Giving Birth," which pictures, in primitive style, an imposing standing female figure surrounded by the heavens with a head crowning from her vagina.[30] The artist was threatened with an obscenity charge. Indeed, many feminists and others have argued that those most likely to be hurt by censorship of the sort proposed are feminists, gay and lesbian artists and activists, and others who have traditionally fought against censorship.

Analysis of the nude female figure in painting offers important insights into the relationship of art to the surrounding gender culture, including its androcentrism, but also the difficulty—if not impossibility—of straightforward and undebatable interpretation. Feminist and mainstream analysis of the nude painting suggests that it is "a paradigm of Western high culture with its network of contingent values: civilization, edification, and aesthetic pleasure." But it "is also a sign of those other, more hidden properties of patriarchal culture—that is, possession, power, and subordination" (Nead 1992, 283). Different "nudes" will evoke these differing aspects to different degrees, even to the point that some are regarded as high art and some, simply pornographic. The male nude is judged by different standards, especially since the invention of the stone fig leaf. But, as Lynda Nead (1992) points out, these meanings are not found intrinsically in the nude, but in the larger cultural definitions. In discussing New Deal art, Melosh underscores the multiple views of female nudes:

> Insiders viewed female nudes as part of a revered tradition of western art, but the lay public sometimes saw them as pictures of naked women and an affront to public decency. In a few cases, Section administrators defended nude figures even in the face of considerable public outcry; often, they chose to avert possible controversy by censoring nudity (1991, 205).

In the federal art projects, the progressive view generally called for greater openness to representations of sexuality although not, of course, violence and abuse.

The debate has sometimes become bitter. In the course of a dispute among feminists surrounding the contents of an art exhibit displayed as part of a conference on prostitution sponsored by the *Michigan Journal of Gender and Law* in 1992, Catherine MacKinnon summarized her view of the anticensorship argument saying, "My real view . . . is that this is a witchhunt by First Amendment fundamentalists who are persecuting and blacklisting dissidents like Andrea Dworkin and myself as arts censors. I don't see it as a fight within feminism but a fight between those who wish to end male supremacy and those who wish to do better under it."[31] The dispute profoundly concerns the definition of art, sexuality, violence, and feminism.

Media of Change?

We have looked at three overlapping types of media of communication: mass media, commercial media (advertising), and artistic media. In each of these we find evidence of segregation of women, often into lower-status positions. In each we find that the mainstream of the media often project androcentric views of society and a lower status for women. At the same time, we can find women who have had a powerful impact on society through these media. We also find that women working in these fields have organized to look at women's roles in different ways and have worked to provide alternative visions and alternative forms.

Our observations of the relationship between gender and the media leave us with problems and questions that need to be solved. Growing numbers of people work in the media as writers, performers, publishers, market analysts, artists, journalists, and technical personnel. Those of us in these fields have a responsibility to understand how our work reflects or shapes gender roles and ideology. Mere understanding is not enough, however, and individual action is difficult. Individuals are constrained in their ability to bring about change by the organizations in which they work, by the demands and preferences of their audiences, and by the need to earn a living. Few people can afford to sacrifice their incomes for the principle of gender equality in media messages, particularly if lack of compromise means losing the ability to speak through the media. On the other hand, few people aware of the problems of gender messages in the media can ignore these problems entirely in their work. What action can feminists who work in the media take?

Although only some of us work in the media, all of us are consumers. We also face important problems and questions as media consumers. We have a responsibility—to ourselves and, if we have them, our children—to understand how the media reflect and shape gender roles and ideology. It takes effort and expense to identify and use the media that promote less androcentric views of the world, and it certainly takes effort to attempt to influence those who offer us an androcentric view. This, however, is what needs to be done.

NOTES

1. U.S. Commission on Civil Rights, *Window Dressing on the Set: An Update*, 1979, quoted in *Media Report to Women*, February 1, 1979, p. 1.
2. For histories of women in the print media, see Marzolf (1977), Shevelow (1989), Russo and Kramerae (1991).
3. "Grace Glueck Tribute to Attorney Harriet Rabb Recalls Beginning of Suit at 'Times,' " *Media Report to Women*, December 31, 1978, p. 2.
4. For an inside story of women at the *New York Times*, see Robertson (1992).
5. "Women Have Lost Ground in TV and Newspaper Coverage, Cal State Study Finds," *Media Report to Women* 20 (Summer 1992), p. 6.
6. "Front Pages, Network Newscasts Still Overwhelmingly Male Dominated," *Media Report to Women* 20 (Summer 1992), p. 7.
7. "One-Third of Women Journalists Reported Sexual Harassment on the Job," *Media Report to Women* 21 (Winter 1993), pp. 2–3.
8. For some histories see Hoseley and Yamada (1987).
9. *New York Times*, August 6, 1983.
10. "Front Pages, Network Newscasts Still Overwhelmingly Male Dominated," *Media Report to Women* 20 (Summer 1992), p. 6.
11. *New York Times*, August 6, 1983.
12. *Media Report to Women* 20 (Fall 1992), p. 7.
13. Deirdre Carmody, "Grit and Glamour," *Chicago Tribune*, September 6, 1992.
14. "LA Times' News Stories Did Not Give Basic Factual Information on E.R.A," *Media Report to Women*, September 1, 1978.
15. M. P. Taylor, "Abortion Coverage Reveals Bias," *Chicago Tribune*, September 1992.
16. Tiffany Devitt, "Abortion Coverage Leaves Women Out of the Picture," *Extra*, (1992), pp. 18–19.
17. For further discussion of the history and impact of changes in domestic technology, see Cowan (1983).
18. One might argue that Wagner's story of everyday life among the gods is a massive soap opera with music. It has love, hate, incest, illegitimacy, murder, identity and family crises, repetition, and everything else that makes a soap opera work.
19. On the other hand, male writers of romances have often used female pen names.

20. Larry Rohter, "Are Women Directors an Endangered Species?" *New York Times*, March 17, 1991.
21. Ibid.
22. Ibid.
23. Anne Thompson, "Hollywood Is Taken to Task by Its Women," *New York Times*, January 17, 1993.
24. Thompson, "Hollywood Is Taken to Task by Its Women."
25. This quilt is mentioned in Hedges (1980).
26. *Media Report to Women* 21 (Winter 1993), p. 3.
27. For further discussion about sexual violence see Chapter 9 for legal issues and Chapter 11.
28. For some of the most well known arguments on these points see Dworkin (1979), Lederer (1980), Griffin (1981).
29. For a history of these efforts see Downs (1989).
30. See Chadwick (1990, 327).
31. Tamar Lewin, "Furor on Exhibit at Law School Splits Feminists," *New York Times* , November 13, 1992.

9

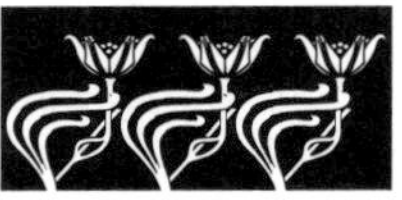

Law and Policy, Government, and the State

OF ALL THE institutions that exert control over people's lives by teaching and enforcing values, those associated with government are the most powerful and authoritative. Government has the power to regulate all other institutions of society at least to some degree. Even the decision that government may not regulate a particular aspect of life is generally made by a governmental institution such as the legislature or courts. Government policy influences most aspects of our lives in one way or another, including even our most intimate relationships and personal choices involving sexuality, family relationships, and reproduction. It necessarily plays a large role in maintaining or changing the sex/gender system.

Many political scientists describe the workings of government as the "authoritative allocation of values." *Values* can refer to tangibles such as goods and services including health care, education, jobs, and wealth, but also less tangible values such as power, legitimacy, and respect. One important difference between the institutions of government and the other social institutions discussed in this book is that when government supports or "teaches" particular values, including those related to gender, it does so with the powers of enforcement and coercion.

The presumption underlying democratic politics is that government is a reflection of the needs, interests, and will of the citizenry as a whole. Examining the role of gender in structuring governmental processes and law and policy leads us to ask fundamental questions about democracy. Are equal values accorded to women and men? Does government work in the equal interests of women and men? Do citizens share equivalent opportunities to shape government policy? Do they play equal roles in government and politics? If not, can we call the political system democratic? In this chapter we seek answers to some of these questions. We begin with a look at government definitions of women as expressed through law and policy. We then turn to the special case of criminal justice. Finally, we consider the role women play in American politics as citizens and leaders.

A key question we asked in an earlier chapter was whether health-care practitioners regard women as normally healthy. When we looked at religion, one of our central questions was whether religious authorities regarded women as normally moral and righteous. In looking at politics, we ask a parallel question: To what degree have women and men been treated as equal members of the political community—as equal citizens?

The law is not a random package of legislation and court decisions. Legal systems differ in their underlying views of rights, obligations, and relations among people and proper procedures for determining how laws should be interpreted and applied. Law and policy are expressions of a political community's underlying set of values or ideology, and they are instruments for enforcing those values. In this section of the chapter we examine the American legal and policy tradition to see its relationship to the ideology of the prevailing sex/gender system.

Protection of Rights

In 1776 a group of people (all men) meeting in Philadelphia wrote a document that read, "We hold these truths to be self-evident; that all men are created equal, that they are endowed by their creator with certain unalienable rights, that among these are life, liberty, and the pursuit of happiness." Their "Declaration of Independence" further argued that the purpose of government is to ensure these rights, and that if government does not do so, the people have a right to "alter or abolish" it.

Seventy-two years later another group of people (mostly women) meeting in Seneca Falls, New York, rebuked the government by rewriting that same document, showing how men withheld from women the rights to which they were entitled. Their "Declaration of Sentiments and Resolutions" included the passage "We hold these truths to be self-evident: that all men and women are created equal. . . ."

In 1868 the 14th Amendment to the U.S. Constitution was ratified. From that day on the Constitution stated that no state shall "make or enforce any law which shall abridge the privileges or immunities of citizens of the United States, nor . . . deprive any person of life, liberty, or property without due process of law, nor deny to any person within its jurisdiction the equal protection of the laws." Unfortunately another part of that same amendment seemed to imply that only men counted as citizens.

Since 1923 thousands, perhaps millions, of people have worked hard to insert words such as the following into the Constitution as well: "Equality of rights under the law shall not be denied or abridged by the United States or by any state on account of sex." This proposed amendment's supporters do not believe that the 14th Amendment has been used rigorously enough to give women and men equal protection of the law. Indeed, until 1971 the Constitution was never used to stop discrimination against women. That was the first time the

Supreme Court declared a law that discriminated against women unconstitutional. For well over a century now, feminists have been arguing that the government has not extended the same protection of the law to women as to men. Most go one step further and argue that law and policy have been based on androcentric and patriarchal norms and therefore maintain and enforce these norms.

The French and American revolutions were fed by the antipatriarchal ideas of Enlightenment political thinkers. Feminist thinkers in this tradition, from Mary Wollstonecraft on, argued that the transformation from a patriarchal to a democratic system took place considerably more quickly for men than for women. Certainly not all men were included equally—racism determined exclusion of African American, Native American, and Asian men, for example—but in effect all women regardless of their race or class retained subject status throughout much of American history, long after most Americans, including most women, thought of themselves as living in a democracy.

What did the Founding Fathers have in mind for women when they began designing the American republic? The evidence of the stray words of Thomas Jefferson, John Adams, Benjamin Franklin, and others is that citizenship was not going to mean the same thing for women and men. Jefferson wrote, "Were the state a pure democracy there would still be excluded from our deliberation women, who, to prevent deprivation of morals and ambiguity of issues, should not mix promiscuously in gatherings of men" (quoted in Kay 1988, 1). From the beginning, government and politics were regarded as a male domain.

In general, free women in the early republic could not vote, hold political office, or serve on juries.[1] Married women especially could not sue or be sued. They could not own property or make contracts and therefore could not seek employment without their husband's permission. Husbands had nearly undisputed rights of control and custody over their children; women had no direct legal control over them. What rationale was used to deny women these rights in a self-proclaimed democratic republic?

The major justification is found in the common law views of women, especially of married women. The common law is an English legal tradition that was the basis for much of the structure of the law in the United States as it affected women.[2] As William Blackstone wrote in 1765 in the *Commentaries on the Law of England*, "By marriage, the husband and wife are one person in law: that is, the very being or legal existence of the woman is suspended during the marriage, or at least is incorporated and consolidated into that of the husband; under whose wing, protection, and cover she performs every thing" (quoted in Kay 1988, 163).

Blackstone pointed out repeatedly that the law cannot treat a woman as having an existence separate from that of her husband. Upon marriage they become one person, and the husband is her "baron, or lord," except he pointed out, "There are some instances in which she is separately considered; as inferior to him, and acting by his compulsion." These instances are primarily in cases of crime. For the most part, however, a married woman was considered "civilly dead"; she had no separate existence apart from her husband.

Women's lack of rights, then, rested largely on the principle that legally women did not exist apart from their husbands. A woman could not represent herself politically by voting because her husband was assumed to vote for the interests of the family; she could not have distinct political interests because she was a part of her husband. Further, women were considered not fully competent, rational, or responsible for themselves, particularly in politics, which was thought to be a man's world.

The 19th century added a new twist to these justifications as democratic reforms spread and it became even more difficult to justify the exclusion of women. The public and private worlds, epitomized by government and economy on the one hand and the family on the other, increasingly came to be seen as separate and even antagonistic arenas of human life. The public domain was a man's world of competition, aggression, and rationality, and the private domain—the family—was a woman's world of compassion, tenderness, and loyalty. While more people acknowledged that it was *possible* for women to be active in the public world of politics, they argued that it would be destructive to human life and values—and femininity—if women actually did so. Women's even more important political role was to raise their sons to be good American citizens, a notion Linda Kerber (1986) calls "republican motherhood." Woman's role, it was argued, was of equal importance to man's, even if women were excluded from public leadership and decision making, because women were responsible for preserving the more human side of life.

The official legal ideology regarding women and women's citizenship can be deciphered from the text of Supreme Court decisions. The courts' job is to interpret the law when the practical meaning of a law is in dispute. The Supreme Court has the additional and critically important power of *judicial review*, meaning that it can nullify a law if it appears to contradict the spirit of the Constitution. This is what is known as "declaring a law unconstitutional." How did the Supreme Court view laws that discriminated between the sexes? Very few cases of sex discrimination reached the Court until the late 20th century, but when they did the message was clear. Granting women fewer rights than men was viewed as consistent both with the Constitution and with the principles of democracy. Following are some examples of this judicial logic.

In the 1873 case *Bradwell* v. *Illinois*, the Court accepted the state's argument that it could prohibit women from admission to the bar because licensing lawyers was a state right with which the federal government could not interfere. One judge offered a different and famous justification for the same decision. He said that women and men have separate spheres and different personalities and that women's naturally disqualify them from many jobs. Further, "Man is, or should be, woman's protector and defender," which presumably means he has the right to protect her from unfeminine jobs. Finally, "The harmony, not to say identity, of interests and views which belong, or should belong, to the family institution is repugnant to the idea of a woman adopting a distinct and independent career from that of her husband." What about unmarried women? "The paramount destiny and mission of women are to fulfil the noble and benign offices of wife and mother. This is the law of the Creator. And the rules

A march for women's suffrage in New York City, 1912.

of society must be adapted to the general constitution of things, and cannot be based upon exceptional cases." In other words, women should be treated as though they are all wives and mothers because that is their natural role. This view was common in American culture.

The next sex-discrimination case was *Minor* v. *Happersett* (1874). Virginia Minor was part of a nationwide protest during the 1872 election in which many women attempted to vote. They claimed that state laws forbidding women to vote were unconstitutional according to the 14th Amendment because they denied women the rights of U.S. citizenship. The Supreme Court dismissed Minor's argument quickly, saying that people (for example, women and children) could be citizens of the United States without being able to vote because states and not the federal government have the power to say who can vote. If the people (meaning men) want women to vote, they will say that through their elected representatives, who will pass appropriate laws.

Another early Supreme Court case shows an important new development in gender-related policies, but one that also had the effect of continuing different treatment of women and men. In *Muller* v. *Oregon* (1908) the question was whether women could be prohibited from jobs requiring more than 10 hours of work per day. The Court agreed that this law had the excellent purpose of protecting women from work that might harm their ability to be mothers. (For further discussion of protective legislation, see Chapter 6.)

The Supreme Court had little else to say about women for the next six decades. Indeed, few courts in the United States did anything about women's roles and status until the 1960s and 1970s other than to protect women in their roles as wives and mothers, usually by restricting their abilities to participate in activities outside the home.

There were some important legislative changes in the 19th century. In the 1840s most states passed "Married Women's Property Acts," which gave (free) married women the right to own and manage property. This change, rarely noted in general history books, was one of the great democratizing reforms of the past few centuries. It probably resulted in more redistribution of wealth than did any other single policy. It also made it possible for women to gain the numerous other rights based on property rights.

In the late 19th century many states began granting women the right to vote and hold public office, which despite the 1874 argument of the Supreme Court already had become a key symbol of full democratic citizenship. The 19th Amendment to the Constitution, ratified in 1920, brought the rest of the states into line.

The history of legislation on women has not been marked by steady progress toward democracy and full citizenship for women, but by struggles that sometimes moved women forward and sometimes backward. Laws on abortion and contraception became more restrictive, and by the turn of the century abortion had become illegal across the country for the first time (Petchesky 1984). The main reasons for this legislation included protection of women from unsafe operations and protection of their morals. (Why would women be engaging in sexual activity if not to procreate?) Only in the 20th century was the "protection of the fetus" argument accepted more widely as the primary justification for banning abortion. (For further discussion of laws on contraception and abortion, see Chapter 12.) The turn of the century also witnessed the beginning of protective labor legislation, which primarily excluded women from certain jobs.

Beginning in the 1880s Congress began to weaken women's tenuous grasp on citizenship by making their citizenship totally dependent on that of their husbands. A succession of laws dictated that a woman's citizenship would now automatically follow that of her husband on the principle that a husband and wife are one and the husband is the pair's representative. Thus, if a foreign woman married an American citizen, she automatically became an American citizen. If an American woman married a foreign man, she automatically lost her citizenship and became an alien even if no other country claimed her as a citizen. Some members of Congress argued that this loss of American citizenship was no great loss to American women, because they couldn't vote anyway.

Some of the more disastrous implications of these laws became clear during World War I, when American women who had previously married Germans found that they were regarded by the American government not just as aliens but as enemy aliens. Once the 19th Amendment was ratified, they found themselves stripped of their right to vote merely because their husbands were not U.S. citizens. Congress began to give women back their citizenship in the 1920s. By the mid 1920s women could keep their citizenship even if they married an alien, but only men could pass their citizenship on to their children. Congress finally equalized the laws of nationality in 1934 (Sapiro 1984).

Each new step forward made it clear that large amounts of legal inequality remained. At every step feminists found that legislators and judges tolerated, approved of, and even reinforced restrictions on women in jobs, education, and other aspects of life, usually because they thought the restrictions protected women, their roles as mothers and wives, and their femininity.

The period of greatest legal progress occurred between the early 1960s and the end of the 1970s. These changes began before the rise of the new women's movement but were certainly spurred on by it once the movement developed. Some of the most important changes in federal law focused on employment, including the 1963 Equal Pay Act, which demanded equal pay for women and men doing the same job; Title VII of the 1964 Civil Rights Act, which barred sex discrimination in hiring, firing, promotions, and working conditions; and the 1978 Pregnancy Discrimination Act, which declared that employers could not discriminate against pregnant women. (Employment discrimination will be discussed thoroughly in Chapter 13.) Other important laws include the 1974 Educational Amendments Act, which barred discrimination in education, and the 1974 Equal Credit Opportunity Act, which increased women's opportunities to get financial credit. In 1972 Congress finally passed the Equal Rights Amendment after 50 years of consideration. The amendment did not become part of the Constitution because it was not ratified by the required number of states.

The force of these laws depends on both the interpretation of courts when there are disputes and the degree to which agencies in the executive branch of government enforce the law. Title VII of the 1964 Civil Rights Act serves as a good example. Dozens of Supreme Court cases have refined the meaning of that statute. What exactly is sex discrimination? Under what circumstances is it illegal? Does discrimination have to be intentional to be illegal? Is the burden of proof on employers to prove they did not discriminate or on employees and job candidates to prove the employer did discriminate? Following 1971, when the Supreme Court first decided a case involving Title VII (*Phillips* v. *Martin Marietta*), it gave increasing force and breadth to the law. As President Ronald Reagan added more conservative judges to the Court in the 1980s, expansion of women's employment and education rights slowed.

The executive branch of the government (the bureaucracy) also became involved, especially through the Equal Employment Opportunity Commission (EEOC), created to enforce the 1964 Civil Rights Act. At first the EEOC was given little real power, and therefore the Act itself had little effect. Only in the 1970s, when the EEOC was given the power to sue on behalf of people who face discrimination, could Title VII be regarded as having any teeth. The executive branch became further involved when Presidents Lyndon Johnson and Richard Nixon issued executive orders outlining the affirmative action employers must pursue to comply with Title VII properly. The force of law changed with the administration in office. Ronald Reagan opposed affirmative action programs and did not vigorously enforce the existing laws.

The Supreme Court has shifted its position on the toleration of sex discrimination. As we have seen, up through the 1960s the Court generally saw no contradiction between democratic and constitutional principles and discrimination against women, even in the face of the 14th Amendment guarantees of equal protection under the law. Not until 1971 (*Reed* v. *Reed*) did the Supreme Court declare unconstitutional a state law that discriminated on the basis of sex. From then through the end of the 1980s the Supreme Court took a dim view of most forms of discrimination against women. The change came late in history, but the change was substantial. For the most part, when a policy is defined in terms of *rights*, the authoritative view now is that it should apply to women and men equally. Indeed, some people oppose some policies aimed at achieving equality, such as special programs to help women enter male-dominated fields, because they claim that these policies violate the idea of equal rights.[3]

Fulfillment of Obligations

Citizenship offers both rights, which governments guarantee, and obligations, which citizens owe to their political communities. Until recently women have not had the same rights as men. Some people have argued that women also have not had the same obligations as men and that if women want equal rights they must accept equal obligations. The three primary obligations citizens owe to the state are taxes, jury service, and military service. Have women had the same obligations as men? If not, why not? Can women share the same rights as men without sharing the same obligations?

Of the three forms of obligation individuals are said to owe the state, taxation is the one that women have historically shared with men. Indeed, if people pay taxes in exchange for guaranteeing that they receive rights, protection, and services from the state, women might be said to have given more than their due. Feminists might well take the revolutionary cry, "Taxation without representation is tyranny!" as an appropriate slogan for their own social movement.

The situation is different when we turn to jury duty. To ensure the constitutional right to a trial by a jury of peers, people are drafted to serve on juries. Moreover, the Supreme Court believes that "the requirement of a jury's being chosen from a fair cross section of the community is fundamental to the American system of justice" (*Taylor* v. *Louisiana*, 1975). Until long into this century, however, women were not well represented on juries. Many states barred women outright. Others said that women could serve if they wanted to, unlike men, who were drafted. Three important Supreme Court cases touched on this question. The first, *Ballard* v. *U.S.* (1946), said that the systematic exclusion of women from *federal* juries "deprives the jury system of the broad base it was designed . . . to have in our democratic society." But this case did not affect state courts, where most of the judicial action occurs.

The 1961 case of *Hoyt* v. *Florida* reflects the historic governmental view of women as jurors. Florida practiced affirmative registration for juries; that is, only women who specifically volunteered for jury duty could serve. Few people ever volunteer for service; thus women virtually never appeared on juries. The Supreme Court found this practice constitutional for the following reason:

> Despite the enlightened emancipation of women from the restrictions and protections of bygone years, and their entry into many parts of community life formerly considered to be reserved to men, woman is still regarded as the center of home and family life. We cannot say that it is constitutionally impermissible for a State, acting in pursuit of the general welfare, to conclude that a woman should be relieved from the civic duty of jury service unless she herself determines that such service is consistent with her own special responsibilities.

In other words, women are exempted from this obligation to the state because they have others—motherhood and homemaking—that come first. Only when those obligations are fulfilled need a woman participate in other acts of citizenship. Only in 1975 (*Taylor* v. *Louisiana*) did the Supreme Court change its opinion, declaring that the motherhood argument was not strong enough to relieve women of their civic responsibilities. Juries should be representative of the community, and the community includes women.

Military service is the third form of obligation citizens are supposed to owe the state on the ground that the defense of citizens cannot be provided unless citizens join in that defense. As in the case of jury duty the government assumes the right to draft people into service. Throughout most of American history, women have been barred from military service except in auxiliary capacities. With the exception of a few famous women, such as the revolutionary fighter "Molly Pitcher," women participated in military action only in the gender-appropriate duties of nursing, cooking, cleaning, and so forth. Although by World War I the military included an auxiliary corps of nurses, women who served in this corps were not at first given formal military status. In World War II a few women served as bomber pilots, but they were not given formal military status and privileges.

In 1948 Congress formalized and integrated women's position into the military more thoroughly, but at the same time it put a ceiling of 2% on women in the military. After the end of the draft in the 1970s, when defense experts were afraid there were not enough people to fill the armed services, the ceiling was raised and women were allowed into the military academies. When Congress reinstituted registration for the draft in 1980, the Carter administration's original intent to include women was dropped in the face of substantial resistance. For the next decade military recruitment remained similar to the process that had been abandoned for jury service: Men were subject to conscription, and women could serve if they wished (up to a limit).

The issue of women and military defense raises a multitude of questions, but discussion here is limited to women's citizenship and obligation to the state and how this compares with men's. Even relatively early in the 20th century it was clear that military service had important implications for how women's citizenship was understood. Consider the 1929 Supreme Court case, *U.S.* v. *Schwimmer*.[4]

Rosika Schwimmer, a lecturer, writer, and pacifist, came to the United States from Hungary in 1921. She petitioned to become a U.S. citizen in 1926. During her citizenship interview, she was asked the usual question, "If necessary, are you willing to take up arms in defense of this country?" She replied that she could not because of her pacifism, adding that she would be ineligible anyway because of her sex and age. "I cannot see that a woman's refusal to take up arms is a contradiction to the oath of allegiance," she said.

Schwimmer's petition for naturalization was turned down because, the Court said, "That it is the duty of citizens by force of arms to defend our Government against all enemies whenever necessity arises, is a fundamental principle of the Constitution." It concluded that "the fact that, by reason of sex, age, or other cause, they may be unfit to serve does not lessen their purposes or power to influence others." A willingness to serve in the armed forces was considered a crucial condition of citizenship, even for people barred from doing so.

That same year another petitioner for citizenship, Martha Jane Graber, said she could go to the front in her profession as a nurse, but she could not bear arms because she was a pacifist. She said, "I could not bear arms; I could not kill; but I am willing to be sacrificed for this country." That was insufficient for the officials; they refused her naturalization. Thus, while claiming that bearing arms in defense of the country was central to U.S. citizenship, the government refused to allow women to do so.

If military service is an important condition of citizenship, why are women not required to serve when men are? This question was asked by a young man who refused his draft call to the Vietnam War and accused the government of sex discrimination because it did not draft women. A U.S. district court ruled against him in 1968, saying:

> Congress made a legislative judgment that men should be subject to involuntary induction but that women, presumably because they are "still regarded as the center of home and family life (*Hoyt* v. *State of Florida* . . .)" should not. In providing for involuntary service for men and voluntary service for women, Congress followed the teaching of history that if a nation is to survive, men must provide the first line of defense while women keep the home fires burning (*U.S.* v. *St. Clair*).

Once again, and depending on the earlier jury duty case, women's role as citizens was held to revolve around their roles as mothers and wives, implying that family care constitutes women's citizen obligations.

By the 1980s many feminists thought that this different treatment of men and women could no longer hold. But even in 1981 the Supreme Court (*Rotsker* v. *Goldberg*) decided that a policy requiring men but not women to register for the draft was constitutional. Congress had been divided over how to draft the law. A congressional subcommittee report states that

> drafting women would place unprecedented strains on family life, whether in peacetime or in time of emergency. If such a draft occurred at a time of

> emergency, unpredictable reactions to the fact of female conscription would result. A decision which would result in a young mother being drafted and a young father remaining home with the family . . . cannot be taken lightly, nor its broader implications ignored (quoted in Kay 1988, 21).

The Supreme Court's acceptance of the inequality turned on a different point. Because women were not allowed to engage in combat and because the purpose of draft registration is to provide a pool of people who can be moved quickly into combat, Congress' decision not to require women to register was acceptable. Two judges dissented, arguing that it is "inconsistent with the Constitution's guarantee of equal protection of the laws."

Although women were not allowed in combat jobs, the proportion of women in the military continued to increase. They were 2.5% of active U.S. military forces in 1973, 9.3% in 1983, and 11.5% in 1993. The various branches of the military differed in their proportions of women, from a low of 4.5% of the Marines to 14.7% of Army personnel on active duty.[5] A turning point in both public and governmental thinking about women in the military occurred during the early 1990s for three reasons: a series of scandals about harassment of women in the military, women's performance during the 1991 Gulf War, and the change of presidential administrations in 1993.

Although there had long been reports about harassment of women in the military, reports increased and became more spectacular by the end of the 1980s and beginning of the 1990s. A report in 1990 identified rampant sexism at the Naval Academy, indicating that "low-level harassment can pass as normal operating procedure" among some people and that "the negative attitudes and inappropriate actions of this minority exert such a disproportionate influence on the Naval Academy climate that most midshipmen readily acknowledge that women are not accepted as equals in the brigade."[6] Even more dramatic was the 1991 annual convention of the Tailhook Association, an organization for top Navy fliers. The Tailhook conventions had long been rowdy stag parties, but in 1991 a scandal broke when four women sued the Tailhook Association and the hotel in which the convention was held because they had been sexually abused. The Inspector General for the Defense Department issued a report in 1993 that described an atmosphere of abuse that included a gauntlet of men who assaulted women trying to walk down corridors and men wearing T-shirts proclaiming, "Women Are Property." An admiral commenting on the report concluded, "Tailhook . . . brought to light the fact that we had an institutional problem in how we treated women. In that regard, it was a watershed event that has brought about institutional change."[7]

The Tailhook scandal probably attracted added attention because of women's participation in the Gulf War earlier in 1991. Five of the 16 participating NATO nations sent women to the Gulf, including the United States, United Kingdom, Canada, Norway, and Denmark. Although none were part of combat units—this was not allowed by the U.S. military at the time—women did come under fire.[8] In all about 35,000 American women served in the Gulf in many roles including as cargo plane pilots. The public was riveted by pictures of uniformed mothers kissing their children goodbye, their honorable service, and the news that women had been taken prisoner of war.

Newspapers covered the story of an Army flight surgeon taken prisoner when her plane was downed. She received no treatment for her broken arms until her third day in captivity, and she suffered sexual abuse during the 8 days she was held. Until that time many people argued that women should not be allowed in combat precisely because they may be sexually abused if taken as prisoners. The flight surgeon reflected that while sexual abuse is serious, "Everything that happens to you as a POW is non-consensual." She continued, "Compared to other things, being shot at, people threatening to shoot you in the back of the head, breaking your bones, it was a terribly insignificant event. Anyone who thinks I'm lying obviously never had those other things happen to them."[9]

These combined images focused public attention on women and the military, leading to intense debates not just about women's capabilities with respect to military activity but also about the nature of the military itself and its relationship to the surrounding society. This debate intensified as arguments over ending the policy banning homosexuals from the military gained prominence.

Much of the top military leadership remained opposed to ending the ban on women in combat, although the Army and the Marine Corps were more opposed than the Navy and the Air Force.[10] A government panel studying the issue recommended in divided opinions that women should continue to be barred from ground combat and flying combat planes, although they might serve on warships. Some of the conservative members argued that it is wrong to allow women to kill, reflecting a continuing influence of a "separate spheres" argument.[11] In contrast, a survey of military women showed a majority favored repealing the ban on women in combat. About three-quarters thought that women should be allowed to *volunteer* for combat, although about half said that they might leave the military if they were *compelled* to serve.[12] Likewise, women who were officers of NATO forces also called for wider roles.[13] The situation changed when Bill Clinton became president. In 1993 the Secretary of Defense ordered the end of the combat exclusion.

This brief review of rights and obligations shows that women's and men's citizenship has not been treated the same way by government and that the exclusion of women from many of the activities, rights, and obligations expected of men has long been held to be consistent with the democratic principles in the Constitution. The reasons offered almost always mention women's unique roles as mothers and wives. Women have not had full citizenship in the "normal" sense—that is, in the male sense. The question that must be resolved is whether citizenship should mean different rights and obligations for men and women.

"Women's Policy Issues": What Are They?

The term *women's issues* is often used to refer to legal and policy issues thought to be of special relevance to women. One argument feminists have often made is that without more women in government "women's issues" will be ignored or will not be resolved "in women's interests." In order to understand the relationship between government and gender, and especially to explore the view of women and gender embedded in public decisions, it is necessary to think more clearly about what these "women's policies" and "women's interests" are. Why are some issues called "women's issues," while others are not?

"Women's issues" usually refers to policies that most obviously affect women's roles and activities, but also those affecting aspects of life stereotypically associated with women and femininity, such as the family and children. The most prominent "women's policy issues" in recent decades are sex discrimination, especially in employment, education, and other financial questions; reproductive rights; family welfare programs; violence against women; and child care and support.

These are obviously women's issues because they have profound implications for the quality of women's lives and the amount of control they have over their lives. There is, nevertheless, a problem with the use of the term *women's issues.* Why are these *only* women's issues? Why is family policy or policy on children a *women's* issue? Don't these policies affect men also? The main reason that family policy is often discussed as a women's issue is that our dominant ideology states that women are more central to families, and families are more central to women than to men.

Many family policies are implemented to affect men as little as possible. Consider the case of child care. In a family headed by a two-career married couple, child care is usually primarily the woman's responsibility, so it is the woman, not the man, whose job is understood to create the need for child care. Child-care centers and baby sitters are thought to change the structure of the woman's time, without any real change in the father's time or responsibility. Moreover, because most child-care workers are still women, even widespread use of day care for children may alter the current structure of gender roles less than we at first think. Women continue to have the main responsibility for child care, although more are paid for their work than in the past.

One aspect of women's issues suggests why male-dominated political systems are so slow to develop policies that would be of specific benefit to women. Many of the conditions that limit or hurt women benefit men in some important way. Men have more access to medical training if medical schools discriminate against women than if they do not. The same is true of access to jobs. If family- and employment-related policies charge women with primary responsibility for child care, men have more freedom to engage in activities outside the home and to make their own independent decisions than if policies support more egalitarian divisions of family labor. If women have more control over marital property, men have less. If the state were more vigorous in its attempts to eradicate wife battery, men would have less power in their personal lives.

Feminist policy experts have concluded that as the term *women's issues* is usually understood it may be much too limiting. Our real question is not simply whether a law or policy affects women, but whether it has gender-specific effects or implications. Many policies that are not stereotypically associated with women do in fact have this kind of gender-based significance. In an androcentric society these gender-based implications may not be noticed, so policy can be constructed to benefit men but not women through unanticipated effects. Thus, some people argue, any public policy problem might be regarded as a "women's issue" if we attend to the gender-specific aspects of it, and not assume gender neutrality where it may not exist. Consider a few examples.

Particular employment policies may cover certain sectors of the economy, such as heavy industry, but not others, such as clerical work. The gender segregation of the labor market can make apparently gender-neutral policies discriminatory in reality. Social welfare policies affect women and men differently because women and men use different social services and benefits. Many benefits are aimed at children, who are usually the primary responsibility of women, or at older people, who are disproportionately female and often cared for by women family members. In fact, social services often involve labor that is otherwise done by women for their families; therefore, there is often a direct trade-off between the availability of social services and the amount of unpaid labor women do.

General fiscal policy (policy on taxes) and monetary policy (policy on the money supply) affect how much money is available to individuals and families and therefore affect consumption patterns. There is a trade-off between certain kinds of consumption and women's labor: Below a certain threshold women will mend clothes rather than buy new ones, do more labor-intensive cooking rather than buy more expensive convenience foods and restaurant meals, or spend more time directly caring for children and other dependents rather than hire other people to do it.

The purpose of law and policy is to put into practice the values and goals of the government. Throughout most of American history one of the government's stated purposes was to protect what was regarded as the traditional family and traditional family values.[14] This resulted in the implementation of government policies that confined women to being wives and mothers or performing other functions consistent with those roles. In the past two decades there has been a growing tendency to see women not just as wives and mothers but also as citizens whose rights need protecting the same as men's do. Although there has been change, the support for traditional and more patriarchal family values is still strong in many parts of the population, so much so that in the 1990s many observers claimed the country has been experiencing a "culture war" and, certainly, a tremendous "backlash" to the change (Faludi 1991; Hunter 1991).

Women, Crime, and Justice

One function of government is to help keep people secure in person and property and, in cases of crime, to dispense justice fairly and equitably. Is the justice system gender-neutral? As the data presented in Chapter 1 show, crime certainly reflects some gender differences. Men commit more crime, especially those involving violence. Women's crimes are concentrated into a few categories, and women are especially likely to be the victims of some categories of injustice, including especially sexual crimes. Our questions, then, are whether and how

Janet Reno, the first woman to serve as U.S. Attorney General, the head of the Department of Justice.

gender shapes the nature of crime and injustice and what is the reaction of the justice system. We begin by looking at the evidence relating first to women as victims of crime and second to women as criminals. To what degree is the disposition of justice determined by gender?

Women as Victims

Two crimes are perpetrated primarily by men primarily against women: domestic violence and rape. Looking at the reaction of the criminal justice system to these forms of violence against women shows some of the special problems women face in gaining justice because of the large degree to which the criminal justice system institutionalized sexist assumptions and perceptions common in the larger sex/gender system. How does the treatment of these crimes compare with the treatment of other kinds of assault? Here discussion is restricted to a focus on the criminal justice system; in Chapter 11 we will focus more on the social dynamics of violence against women and the relationship between this violence and sexuality. (See also Chapter 6 for a discussion of family violence as a health issue.)

Both rape and wife battery are among the most underreported crimes that exist. Perhaps one in four rapes is reported to the police, and one in ten cases of serious wife battery is reported. Only a very tiny proportion of rape and wife battery cases end in conviction and punishment of the offender. In both cases, women fear reprisals if they do anything about these crimes; in both cases, offenders are unlikely to be jailed, thus leaving them free to mete out reprisals. At the same time, convictions have increased dramatically in recent years. The number of sex offenders in prison climbed by almost 47% from 1987 to 1992.[15]

Until recently both rape and wife battery were tolerated by law and public opinion to a shocking degree. The main reasons were (1) men's proprietary rights over their wives and, indeed, over other women and (2) traditional sexual and gender ideology limiting women's autonomy and self-definition, especially within the family. Let us see how these problems apply to criminal justice views of both crimes.

Domestic violence is a gender-based problem. About three-quarters of its victims are women, and over 90% of reported spousal assault cases involve the husband as perpetrator and the wife as victim (Thomas 1991, 313). In 1990 about 40% of female murder victims were killed by their husband or boyfriend; about 20% of women seeking help at hospital emergency rooms were there because of domestic violence.[16] The legal view of domestic violence is also a gender-based problem. Under common law, husbands were allowed to "chastise" their wives physically, as William Blackstone wrote at the end of the 18th century, "In the same moderation that a man is allowed to correct his apprentices or children; for whom the master or parent is also liable in some cases to answer" (quoted in Kay 1988, 192). This law, viewed as enlightened because it stressed moderation, used the "rule of thumb": A man should not hit his wife with a stick any thicker than his thumb. Even relatively recently many lawmakers have been reluctant to facilitate a woman suing her husband for intentional physical attacks because such a suit might destroy the "peace and harmony" of the home. Physical assault between spouses is a crime throughout the country; the problem is enforcement procedures.

The husband's proprietary rights are especially apparent in rape laws. The traditional definition of rape as "unlawful carnal knowledge of a woman without her consent" has been understood throughout the United States until recently to mean that there is no such thing as rape between marital partners. Sexual relations within marriage are not "unlawful,"[17] and the common law tradition (and others) has generally accepted the view that under the marital contract the woman "hath given up herself in this kind to her husband, which she cannot retract" (Thomas 1991, 338). In other words, she gave her irrevocable consent to sexual relations on her marriage day. Since the mid 1980s some states have decided, along with the New Jersey Supreme Court, that this view is "offensive to our valued ideals of personal liberty" (*New Jersey* v. *Smith*, 1981) and limited or eliminated the spousal immunity. Once again, however, neither the law nor the public generally has wanted to interfere in what is viewed as a private matter between husband and wife.

Establishing lack of consent is not just a problem for women married to the men who raped them. It is very difficult for women to prove they did not consent to sexual relations even if it can be established that they said—or screamed—"no." Women's words are not enough as long as they are interpreted through a sexual culture that believes women are supposed to say "no" even when they mean yes and that men are supposed to try to make women's "no" become a "yes." Traditionally, in order to establish lack of consent, women had to make a "fresh complaint" (report quickly) and prove physical resistance even up to an "inch of their lives." In other words, if they show they suffered considerable brutality other than rape, they may be able to get rape convictions. Until recently the victim's past sexual history could be used by the defense to prove she was inclined toward sexual consent. Rape shield laws, first developed in the 1980s, now limit this practice. Nevertheless, women who claim to have been raped often face grueling questions supposedly aimed at identifying consent, such as whether they had an orgasm.

Victims of wife battery also face questions about their consent to victimization. One of the most common questions asked about women is "why don't they leave?" Perhaps on the assumption that women get some sort of neurotic pleasure out of their maltreatment, many cannot believe that women who do not abandon their husband are truly victims of assault. This view shows ignorance about many features of domestic violence, not the least of which is that "leaving" a violent partner is not as simple as walking out the door. It entails abandoning one's own household, often suddenly, with all that is involved if there are children. Moreover, leaving the household does not guarantee the end of "domestic" violence, which needn't take place in one's home. In many cases women need to ensure that their partner cannot find them, which has further implications for women and their children. Shelters for battered women help, but women leaving violent partners face total disruption of their family, personal, and work lives.

Many of the difficulties women face in prosecuting their attackers in battery and rape cases revolve around perceptions of "victim precipitation," the idea that the victim has in some way provoked the attack against herself and that this provocation makes the perpetrator less guilty. Women's clothing or possible drunkenness has been used by police and courts to determine whether the woman "caused" the rape. Victims of battery often find they are interrogated about what they did to "cause" the man's anger. The insensitive treatment of female victims at the hands of the criminal justice system has often been labeled the second or double victimization of women; they are victimized first by the criminal and then by the criminal justice system. One tragic effect of these legal and public views is that many victimized women actually feel guilty for what was done to them.

Prosecutors and police are wary of both rape and domestic violence cases. These and other actors in the criminal justice system often hold stereotypes about women that make them less helpful than they might be to those who have suffered violence and injustice. But other aspects of these crimes affect their behavior. Prosecutors worry about the credibility of rape and battery victims in the eyes of juries. They worry about victims who drop their cases and leave the prosecutors with "wasted time" and records of unsuccessful cases (Stanko 1982). Police often have given low priority to "domestic-disturbance" calls, as they are often termed, partly because they are especially dangerous to the police officers involved. More police are injured or killed when answering these calls than when answering any others.

Until the 1970s and 1980s explicit police policy usually stipulated that police should mediate domestic problems and avoid arresting anyone (Klein 1982). It soon became clear that these policies were pushed to their limits. Police and courts sometimes refused to arrest violent husbands even when their wife requested it, and they refused to enforce restraining orders against violent husbands. Eventually some women responded by suing police officers and court employees on the grounds that they were being denied equal protection in comparison to people assaulted in places other than the home, and second, that the "arrest avoidance policy was based on the broad and archaic sex-based assumptions that a man is privileged to punish his wife" (Woods 1981, 43).

Many changes have occurred recently. Although old attitudes die hard, many police forces have begun to work more closely with shelters for battered women and community-based rape crisis centers, and they employ specially trained police officers, often women, to deal with rape victims. Changes in the law have also helped. Rape shield laws bar courts from referring to women's prior sexual history. Some states have followed the example of Michigan, which in 1974 enacted a rape-reform law that classified sexual offenses by degree in categories ranging from sexual contact to penetration by force with a weapon involved. Some states allow battered women to get protective or temporary restraining orders barring their attackers from contacting them. Some jurisdictions have instituted mandatory arrest policies in cases of domestic violence, which require police to arrest the perpetrator. Women's organizations have worked hard to educate people about the remaining problems and offer assistance to women who need it.

Some new policies are very controversial. By 1992, for example, 22 states had passed laws requiring that convicted sex offenders register with the police at least during their time of parole or probation and, in at least a couple of cases, as long as they live in the state. Some states make the information publicly available, and Louisiana passed a law requiring them to notify their neighbors and giving judges the discretion to require convicted sex offenders to notify others by wearing special clothing, putting signs on their houses, or bumper stickers on their cars. While some experts argue that these are necessary measures because of the high rates of recidivism among sex offenders, others claim this is punishing victims by taking away their rights to privacy.[18] Similar controversies have sprung up on some college campuses, where women who believe there is insufficient attention to violence against women post the names of alleged attackers, thus raising questions about due process.

Change remains slow, and the criminal justice system is still at least partially based on a gender ideology that defines protection differently for women and men. Consider the case of a woman who lost her ability to prosecute her rapist successfully precisely because she was ingenious in finding a way to protect herself. In 1992 in Austin, Texas, a woman found an intruder with a knife demanding sex from her. She escaped to the bathroom and tried unsuccessfully to call 911 before he broke in. Facing the inevitability of rape she tried to convince him to wear a condom. When he told her not to worry because he did not have AIDS, she asked, "How do you know I don't?" When he indicated he didn't have any condoms with him, she gave him one she had in the house. Eventually she fled naked to a neighbor's house. The city did not indict the man because the fact that she had provided a condom indicated consent. As she interpreted it, "The fact that I took extreme measures to protect my life means that I deserve to get raped."[19] It is unfortunate, but perhaps not a surprise that the number of women interested in buying guns doubled in the 1980s. Whereas in 1988 less than 5% of the students in the National Rifle Association's introductory personal protection courses were women, that figure was up to 75% by 1993.[20]

Women as Criminals

Women constitute a very small proportion of the people arrested for crimes and an even smaller proportion of the prison population. They commit a particularly small proportion of the most serious and violent crimes and those involving use of a weapon. Like men, women commit the majority of crimes against others of their own sex except in the case of murder: About 80% of both male and female murderers kill men (Wilbanks 1982, 169). Women are less likely to use weapons, and when they do they often use kitchen knives and other household implements related to female roles (Parisi 1982a, 118–19). Despite the general view that women tend either to be men's accomplices or to get men to commit crimes for them, research shows that, for the most part, they tend to work alone. If they work with someone else, they tend to work with women (Parisi 1982a, 113). So the crime world, like other domains of social life, is segregated by sex.

Women's crime rate, like men's, has increased in recent decades. Women's property crimes and, more recently, drug-related crimes constitute the bulk of the increase; in fact the proportion of women's crimes that are violent has decreased. Why has women's property-crime rate increased faster than men's? Three general answers have been offered. One popular answer in the press is that the women's movement has helped eliminate differences between the sexes in many areas, including criminal activity (see, e.g., Adler 1975). This androcentric view assumes that if men and women become more similar, women will be more like men and men will stay the same. Research that tests the hypothesis does not support it (Parisi 1982a, 123). The androcentric view also assumes women have achieved equality.

A second reason offered for the increase in women's property crimes is that changes in employment give women more opportunity to commit property crimes (see, e.g., Simon and Landis 1991). The evidence for this hypothesis is mixed. Among single women, labor force participation rates are related to property crime (Parisi 1982a, 123). On the other hand, the segregation of the labor force did not decrease much during the years in which the crime rate changed. Moreover, we need evidence not just that more women are employed but also that they are moving into positions which increase opportunities for crime and that the women entering these new positions are the new criminals. Some authors suggest that women's actual crime rate has not changed much but that arrest rates have risen for traditional female crimes such as shoplifting (see, e.g., Steffensmeier 1981; for further review of this theory, see Rafter and Stanko 1982). This hypothesis, of course, is hard to test. Research suggests that it is part but not all of the explanation.

Like other women, female criminals have historically been interpreted through the prism of gender ideology. In their review of research on female criminality, Nicole Hahn Rafter and Elizabeth Anne Stanko note that

> nearly all traditional commentaries on female offenders, whether focused on the serious or the minor criminal, have been overwhelmingly concerned with violations of gender prescriptions. . . . [Theorists] have attributed . . . low arrest rates to the inherently law-abiding nature of women. Accordingly, they have assessed the female criminal by the fit of her crime to men's crime and the extent to which she violated her naturally law-abiding nature. Since crime was assumed to be a masculine phenomenon, women who committed crime were thought to do so either because they were too masculine (the evil women theory) or because they had been led astray (the bad little girl theory) (1982, 6–7).

Such assumptions have clouded research on female criminality, including juvenile delinquency (Chesney-Lind and Shelden 1992).

Some observers worry that women are now even more subject to gender-based regulation under criminal law because a new set of crimes revolving around pregnancy is being recognized (Humphries 1993; Merlo 1993; Reed 1993; Sagatun 1993). Because thousands—perhaps hundreds of thousands—of babies are born each year to mothers who used drugs such as crack and cocaine during pregnancy, efforts to tackle this problem have led to increased use of law enforcement against these women. Another 6,000 to 8,000 babies are born with fetal alcohol syndrome each year (Merlo 1993). More states are now enacting "fetal abuse" statutes that create a new form of female criminal offense.

To what degree is treatment of the female offender shaped by gender? Some states' statutes require indeterminate (and therefore maximum) sentences for women but not for men. Some experts argue that women should have longer sentences because they are more likely than men to benefit from rehabilitation while incarcerated. This idea is connected with the historical practice, stemming back to the establishment of the first separate women's prison in Indiana in 1869, to call women's prisons *reformatories.* Some researchers hypothesize that women receive longer sentences for particularly "unfeminine" crimes—that is, for breaking the law *and* gender norms.

Other observers argue that judges and prosecutors act chivalrously toward women by giving them lighter sentences. Some suggest that people find it difficult to believe that women can be as dangerous as men and therefore don't incarcerate them for as long. Women's responsibility for child care has also led to the notion that judges may be reluctant to create lengthy separation of mothers and children through incarceration.

The evidence seems to suggest that women receive more lenient treatment than men in certain sentencing and parole situations, and "it occasionally appears that negative (punitive) treatment is accorded females for 'manly' crimes" (Parisi

1982a, 215). In any case, it appears that women are now given longer prison sentences than used to be true (Rix 1988, 304).

There are some differences between the prison experiences of men and those of women (Immarigeon and Chesney-Lind 1993; Moyer 1993; Muraskin 1993). Because so few women are incarcerated compared to men, women's prisons and prison programs are much neglected. They are underfunded and poorly equipped, even in comparison to men's prisons. On the other hand, the old reformatory model persists. Nicole Rafter points out that this model is apparent in "its characteristically low security; its tendency to provide living quarters that (to the outsider, at least) resemble college dormitory rooms rather than cells; and in its paternalistic aspects, such as its tendency to treat female inmates as errant children" (1982, 256).

Prisons reinforce gender norms through their rehabilitation programs. Occupational training in women's facilities, for example, typically includes hairdressing and cosmetology, and women's programs traditionally worked to reinforce conventional notions of femininity. In recent years, however, some prisons have developed expanded notions of appropriate occupations and programs for women.

Although prisoners of both sexes may suffer from isolation from their families, mothers—and their children—particularly suffer from separation imposed by imprisonment. As one report indicated, "Male prisoners often have wives or girlfriends to bring children to visit them. Female inmates, more likely to be the child's sole support, often have no one." [21] About three-quarters of women in state and federal prisons are mothers, and roughly half of the children of prison inmates never see their mothers during incarceration.[22] In most prisons even women of infants and those who give birth while in prison are separated from their children. As difficult as the separation may be for the mothers, it may have even more negative impact on their children's development. Many prisons and other organizations have developed programs to maintain contact and relations between mothers and their children.

Thus far we have talked about "crime" in general without focusing on its specific forms. Let us now look briefly at two different types of crime to probe further into the relationship between criminal justice and gender. One is the primarily female crime of prostitution and the other is the apparently gender-neutral crime of murder.

Between 100,000 and 500,000 American women are working prostitutes. Prostitution is a "women's" crime only because most of the people arrested for it are women. The male participants in prostitution, including the pimps and especially the clients, are relatively untouched by the law. The justice system often focuses on prostitutes as though it is only they and not the men who pay for their services who are the wrongdoers.

The state has long had an ambivalent attitude toward prostitution. Officials and other interested parties cannot seem to decide whether prostitution is a crime with victims that must be eradicated, a victimless crime that should be contained and eliminated if possible, an unfortunate aspect of life that should be kept out of sight as much as possible, or an immoral but sometimes useful enterprise.

Does prostitution have victims? Those who are forced to take part in prostitution, as is true for many prostitutes, surely are. Research shows that prostitutes usually have histories of abuse; more than three-quarters were raped before age 14, usually by a relative.[23] Those who become diseased or subject to other crimes because of prostitution are also victims; these include prostitutes, clients, and, in the case of disease, their families. Disease has become an even more vexing problem since the spread of AIDS in the 1980s. A large proportion of prostitutes, including a majority who are intravenous drug users, are HIV-positive. The majority of prostitutes are also mothers, who therefore will leave their children orphaned. Prostitutes do the best they can to protect themselves from violence, but the nature of the job puts them in constant danger.

An influential study of prostitution concludes, "Looking at all the data, one cannot say that prostitution is a victimless crime. On the other hand, the data . . . suggest that prostitution victimizes society only in specific and limited ways" (Milman 1980, 62). Certainly prostitutes themselves are as victimized as anyone else.

It is important to note that the state has accepted and, in some cases, supported prostitution. Police have often turned a blind eye to prostitution, only occasionally hauling in women to increase a lagging arrest rate. Some people claim that the system of charging and fining prostitutes from time to time constitutes a quasi-official license to practice. (This is not to say that prostitutes are not sent to jail. They are.) Police find prostitutes useful informers because they know what is happening on the streets. In the early 1970s, President Nixon allowed prostitutes onto U.S. military bases in Vietnam to "help morale" among the troops. Even though these women were, in a sense, employees of the U.S. government, they were refused free medical treatment for the resulting venereal diseases and pregnancies.[24]

Barbara Milman (1980) argues that if prostitution is more a moral and health problem than a crime problem, criminal sanctions are inappropriate. Many people now recommend alternative treatments of prostitution that do not put the full burden of punishment on the prostitute. Even if rehabilitative programs are more widely used for prostitutes, however, will the public support programs to rehabilitate the men who buy sex? Would most people even think that men who buy sex are in need of rehabilitation?

Whereas prostitution is regarded as a "female" crime, murder seems at first glance to be a gender-neutral crime. However, it also poses some interesting questions for the study of gender and law enforcement.

Most homicides perpetrated by women involve men, especially family members, and tend to take place at home (Wilbanks 1982). Female murderers are more often first offenders than male murderers, and they tend to use as weapons any implements that are handy rather than firearms. These points suggest that a large proportion of the murders committed by women may be done in self-defense, and our earlier discussion of the victimization of women points toward the reasons. The issues surrounding homicide in self-defense committed by women are very revealing of gender-based aspects of criminal justice.

Until 1977 women who killed in self-defense against rape or battery almost always lost their cases in court. The reason is the combined effects of the legal definition of the self-defense plea, the characteristics of murder by females, and stereotyped views of women.

Two criteria must be met to claim justifiable homicide on the grounds of self-defense:

1. The killer must have had a reasonable apprehension of danger and a reasonable perception of the imminence of that danger. In other words, the danger need not have been real as determined by later investigation, but it must have appeared to be real to a reasonable person (traditionally, a "reasonable man"). And killing has to have appeared to be the only viable course of action.
2. Deadly force cannot be used against nondeadly force.

The problem for women who kill in self-defense is whether they can be considered reasonable and what constitutes deadly force. We already have seen how difficult it is for women to convince the criminal justice system they have been victims of rape or battery. It is even more difficult for a woman to convince a court that she had reason to believe she would be killed as well. The courts usually have denied that an "unarmed" man can be interpreted as using deadly force, ignoring the fact that if a relatively small woman is victimized—especially one who has not been trained in the use of physical force against others—an unarmed man may easily exert deadly force with no weapon but his body. Moreover, a self-defense plea must be buttressed by proof that the defendant attempted to flee rather than kill. As one legal analysis put it,

> Only against a wall or at the door of his castle, his home, can the victim take a stand to protect himself with deadly force. A battered woman cannot retreat; she is already home, frequently with her back against a wall. But for her it is no castle. A prejudice persists that she has an obligation to retreat out of her house (Thomas 1991, 365).

As we have seen this is not so simple.

A 1977 state supreme court case (*State* v. *Wanrow*) marked the beginning of change in the treatment of women's self-defense claims. It argued that the courts tend to view women from an androcentric perspective and do not consider the perceptions and physical conditions of women. It also argued that "through the persistent use of the masculine gender" the instructions given to the jury about how to understand self-defense "leave the jury with the impression the objective standard to be applied is that applicable to an altercation between two men." In other words, *he* is not a gender-neutral term. Since that case, courts have moved toward a fairer consideration of women who kill in self-defense. This case represents a dramatic event in the history of criminal justice: a court's recognition that the legal system has been androcentric.

Women face the persistent lack of understanding of rape by the criminal justice system. As one person said during the 1977 trial of Inez Garcia, a rape victim who killed her attacker, "You can't kill someone for trying to give you a good time." Only some states allow deadly force as self-defense in cases of rape against women, which stands in marked contrast to men's situation. The courts have generally acquitted men who use deadly force to protect themselves from rape by another man. These are not the only situations in which men have more rights to violence against what they perceive to be misplaced sexuality. The old "paramour" laws, which permitted murder in reaction to uncovering adultery, were based on similar norms. A man who found his wife in bed with another man could get away with murder; a woman who found her husband in bed with another woman could not.

Women in the Criminal Justice System

There is now considerably more awareness of issues relating to women and criminal justice than was true only a few years ago. Much of the impetus for change has come from the women's movement and from women who have become victims of crime and were politicized by the experiences they had, both during the crime itself and in the course of trying to seek help from the criminal justice system.

Until recently women have had little hand in the formal enforcement and administration of justice. As late as 1987 no major city had a female police chief, although 11 smaller cities did. Women also have been only a small percentage of judges, even in municipal courts. In 1993 President Clinton appointed Janet Reno to be the first woman as Attorney General, the cabinet member who heads the Department of Justice and serves as the "chief cop" of the federal government. Evidence suggests that women have an impact when they become actors in the criminal justice system. The Defense Department investigation of the Tailhook convention offers telling related examples. Donald Mancuso, the Inspector General, said that the female agents were especially valuable in establishing the facts for two reasons. First, the female victims, many of whom were wives, girlfriends, or relatives of the officers, were very reluctant to tell their stories and felt more comfortable talking to women investigators. But also, "Officers were unable to make the impression with the female agents that this was just a guy thing. And the women put many of the men off balance. They weren't used to dealing with professional women who [were] older than they were."[25] Women in professional and official positions do make a difference to women and to men, and this is likely to be encouraged by the formation of women's groups such as the Committee on Women in Federal Law Enforcement and the International Association of Women Police.

Women's Political Participation and Influence

It is commonly argued that women have been kept out of politics and government almost entirely and that for a variety of reasons women do not participate in politics. In fact, women have never been as fully absent from American political life as many people believe. There is no question, however, that women still have considerably less political power than men and that only a small fraction of governmental decision makers are women. To what extent do women participate in politics? How much influence do they have? Does it matter whether more women become active in politics or even obtain positions of political power? (For an introduction to some of these issues, see Chapter 1).

Gender in Electoral Politics

Free elections and the right to vote are supposed to be crucial elements of a democratic polity. People have died for this right. Yet after the long, hard battle for women's suffrage was won, many activists were disappointed to find that women were not as likely to use their right to vote as men were. The gap eventually narrowed, and for many years now there has been little difference between women's and men's voting rates. Indeed, in some elections, among people who are young, highly educated, or black, more women now tend to vote than men. Because male and female turnout rates fluctuate across election, the size of the gender difference depends on the election. Women and men are also about evenly matched in other kinds of campaign activities such as displaying buttons and bumper stickers, going to meetings and rallies, and doing campaign work. Women give less money to political campaigns than men do, but they have less money than men do.

Women's electoral involvement should not be surprising. They have long been known as the backbone of the political parties—making phone calls, ringing doorbells, stuffing envelopes, compiling lists, and watching polls, as well as cooking and cleaning up for party and campaign picnics and other functions. Women were involved in these activities before they had the right to vote.

Research suggests a number of reasons for the early gender differences in political involvement and the more recent achievement of parity. First, voting is a habit that most newly enfranchised groups, including immigrants and young people, take time to develop. Second, education and related socioeconomic factors determine how politically active people are; in general, the greater the gap in education, the greater the gap in electoral participation. Third, gender ideology and gender roles have had an impact. In the 1920s many women didn't vote because they didn't think it was appropriate. Women with an egalitarian gender ideology are still more likely to be active in elections than those who are more androcentric in their views of social and political roles (Sapiro 1983). Women, especially single women, who are responsible for children also are less politically active than women without children.

At higher levels of politics, men's and women's involvement differs more markedly. The more powerful or authoritative, the better paid, or the more visible a political position is, the less likely it is that a woman holds it. Despite women's yeoman work in political parties, until recently they have been a small minority of the delegates selected to participate in decision making at national nominating conventions. Relatively few women are among the major party deci-

Ann Richards, Governor of Texas and a brilliantly witty speaker.

sion makers. Until recently women were not given many top decision-making roles in electoral campaigns, although this is changing. In both 1988 and 1992, for example, women were very prominent among the top levels of presidential campaign management. But women still constitute a relatively small percentage of candidates for local, state, and national offices.

Why is this the case? If women are so active in politics at the mass level, why in a democratic system is there not gender parity in the number of candidates for office? Among the most common reasons cited by political scientists are that (1) women aren't motivated or lack ambitions for office, (2) they aren't as qualified as men for office, and (3) discrimination and sexism have hindered women. Let us look at the evidence for each.

It has often been said that women don't become political leaders because they are not interested in politics or don't want to be leaders. This reason is suspect; differences in interest and mass-level political activity are so marginal that they cannot explain the large gender imbalance in public officials.

Studies of men and women who are already very active in politics—community activists and national nominating convention delegates, for example—show that women are less likely to want to hold a political office, but even by the 1970s the difference was not large enough to explain the substantial gap in the proportion of male and female officeholders (Lee 1977; Sapiro and Farah 1980; Jennings and Farah 1981).

Several reasons have been offered to explain the gender differences in political ambition. Some people argue that women are less competitive and aggressive, which causes them not to seek positions of political power and authority. Research suggests that the problem may be less a lack of competitiveness and more the fact that politically active women have lower expectations of success than men do (Jennings and Farah 1981) and anticipate encountering discouragement and discrimination from male colleagues in politics. Also, the juggling act that politically active women must do among their political activities, jobs, and family life—assuming women remain more responsible at home than men—can lead them to suppress political ambition. Research shows that women and men both feel that family and political roles can conflict but that women tend to resolve these conflicts in favor of the family and men make the opposite choice. This is why comparisons of male and female officeholders show that the women are less likely to be married or to have young children than the men are (Sapiro 1982a).

Do women have the qualifications for office? Certainly they have faced some disadvantages. Political leaders tend to be drawn from the ranks of people in certain occupations, such as the law, which traditionally have been segregated male-dominated fields. One study, however, suggests that occupation does not account for the large differences in the numbers of male and female officeholders, nor are educational differences large enough to explain the power differential (Welch 1978).

A third major reason cited for the low numbers of women in positions of political leadership and authority is discrimination. Women in politics often testify about the discrimination they face in the political parties and other mixed or male-dominated political organizations. There is plenty of evidence of institutionalized gender discrimination. A study of congressional races from 1916 to 1978 shows that women are put forward more often than men as candidates for seats their party is unlikely to win (Gertzog and Simard 1980). Research disagrees over whether women face discrimination in gaining funding for their campaigns. Although studies of male and female candidates show little difference in their ability to attract campaign money, some observers suggest that many women never get to be candidates because of the difficulty of attracting start-up funds. Now many organizations are aimed specifically at raising money for female candidates. The most well known is Emily's List, run by Ellen Malcolm, founded in 1985 under the principle Early Money Is Like Yeast (thus creating the acronym EMILY), which distributed about $6 million to female Democratic candidates in 1992. Other such organizations include the bipartisan National Women's Political Caucus and the Women's Campaign Fund, and the Republican Wish List.[26]

As in other cases, not all political discrimination against women is conscious. One researcher did an experiment in which she gave university students a speech to read that was supposedly given by a candidate for the House of Representatives (Sapiro 1982b). Half the students were told the speech was by Joan Leeds, the other half were told the speech was by John Leeds. Comparing the responses of the two groups showed that John's policy proposals were regarded as better than Joan's and that John was considered more likely to win. Men, but not women, judged John to be more competent than Joan at dealing with military, business, farm, and crime issues.

Attitudes toward women in politics are changing. For example, the Gallup Poll sometimes asks, "If your party nominated a woman for president, would you vote for her if she were qualified for the job?" In 1971, 29% said no; in 1984, 17% said no.[27] In a 1986 national sample of the high school class of 1980, 91% of the men and 96% of the women agreed that "women should be considered as seriously as men for jobs as executives or politicians" (U.S. Department of Education 1988, 334).

Even if the majority of Americans indicate they would seriously consider female candidates, and increasing numbers of women win elections, most people think women and men have different qualifications for public office. Table 9-1 shows women's and men's responses to a public opinion poll asking them to say whether they thought a male or female candidate would be more likely to have certain characteristics. These data reveal a number of interesting patterns. Women and men did not differ very much in their responses. A minority of the people responding to the poll thought a male candidate and a female candidate would be similar in most characteristics. At the same time, they agreed less than one might think about which sex is more marked by which characteristic. They were more likely to give women the edge in honesty, compassion, standing up for their beliefs, and liberalism and more likely to think men would be tougher and back arms control. Women's and men's perceptions differ in only a couple of respects. Men are more likely than women to think men are better at handling crises. Both sexes are more likely to think someone of their own sex works harder and is better able to handle family responsibilities while serving in office.

There is one last explanation for the small numbers of women in public office, one that many scholars are convinced is the major roadblock women now face (Carroll 1985; Darcy, Welch, and Clark 1987). Even if women's ambitions are high, they get the right training, they can manage their public and private roles, and discrimination continues to decrease, the increase in women's numbers in public office depends on certain structural opportunities. Let us take the House of Representatives as an example. Incumbents (current officeholders) are rarely defeated for reelection. A woman's best chance of getting elected to the House and increasing the number of women representatives is to run for an open seat in a district dominated by her party. This fortunate confluence of events rarely occurs. At least one calculation taking into account such structural factors predicts that at best women may constitute about one-third of the House members the decade after the turn of the century. Parity is much further off (Darcy, Welch, and Clark 1987).

The 1992 elections—defined by the press collectively as "The Year of the Woman"—offer a good example. That year an unprecedented number of women ran for seats in the House of Representatives and the U.S. Senate. One hundred fifty women ran for House seats; the highest previous numbers had been 70 in 1990 and 65 in 1984. The 20 female U.S. Senate candidates compared with 10 in 1984 and 8 in 1990. A combination of factors accounted for this dramatic increase. First, there was an unusual opportunity. For a variety of reasons there

TABLE 9-1
Perceived Gender Differences in Candidates for Public Office, 1987

		Candidate Who Would Do a Better Job:		
Characteristic	*Sex*	*Male*	*Female*	*No Difference*
Speaking honestly about issues	Women	10	36	45
	Men	13	28	50
Hard working	Women	16	23	53
	Men	23	17	52
Handling a crisis	Women	27	22	42
	Men	39	10	42
Being compassionate	Women	6	53	34
	Men	7	52	35
Standing up for beliefs regardless of political consequences	Women	12	31	48
	Men	17	26	48
Backing arms control	Women	43	16	22
	Men	37	20	36
Favoring women's rights	Women	5	58	29
	Men	6	54	33
Being tough	Women	31	15	44
	Men	35	12	33
More liberal	Women	19	28	41
	Men	16	31	42
More conservative	Women	26	26	39
	Men	31	20	39
Able to handle family responsibilities while in office	Women	19	34	39
	Men	26	25	40

Note: Based on responses by 1,502 registered voters to a survey conducted by Hickman-Maslin Research.

Source: *New York Times,* August 13, 1987, 8.

were more open seats than there had been for a long time—in other words, more places to run and more possibility of winning. Second, opinion polls and the success of Ross Perot in attracting support indicated that the public wanted some newcomers in office. Women are symbolically the embodiment of newcomers. And finally, many women had become politically energized by the Senate hearings in which law professor Anita Hill accused Supreme Court nominee Clarence Thomas of committing sexual harassment. In many Democratic primaries, women constituted a clear majority of the voters.[28] But also, more than was ever true before, in many races women's votes ensured victory for the winning woman.

One of the most important questions in electoral politics is whether women and men evaluate candidates, parties, and issues differently. Conventional wisdom has been that women are more conservative and moralistic than men in their political thinking and that they tend to oppose the use of force and violence and to support social welfare programs. As usual there has been more stereotype than systematic evidence on the subject. Although it is commonly argued that the supposed differences between women and men are due to their "natures" or women's roles in the family, in fact there have been few differences that are consistent over time or across countries. When gender differences in public opinion show up they are usually relatively small.

Researchers have tracked gender differences in public opinion since the advent of widespread public opinion polling. In the 1950s women were somewhat more likely than men to think of themselves as Republicans and were more supportive of the Republican candidate than men were in 1952 and 1956 (Eisenhower) and 1960 (Nixon). More recently women have identified more with the Democratic party and cast a higher proportion of their votes for the Democrat than men in 1964 (Johnson), 1968 (Humphrey), 1972 (McGovern), 1980 (Carter), 1984 (Mondale), 1988 (Dukakis), and 1992 (Clinton). Rarely were the differences very large, however, and the same candidate usually "won" among both women and men, although by different margins. Only in the 1980s did there seem to be a sizable gender difference in partisanship and preferences, which came to be known as the "gender gap." Many scholars debated the reasons for this gap, concluding that men—especially formerly Democratic men—were more attracted to the hawkishness of the Reagan rhetoric and more favorable to the intended policies of cutting back on social welfare programs (Mueller 1991).

Table 9-2 offers more detail on the voting patterns of women and men during the presidential elections of 1976 through 1992, including gender comparisons within different partisan, racial, age, and education groups. There we can see the gender gap look especially large among Independents but also Democrats in 1980 and 1984, and among both the least and most educated. In 1992 a slightly different pattern emerged. The difference in support for Clinton was larger among African Americans than among whites (although relatively few African Americans supported Republicans throughout this period), and there was a clear gender difference of opinion among the youngest voters and, again, among the least and most educated voters.

An important question is whether there are any notable and stable differences of opinion. There are not as many as people seem to think, and they tend to be small (Shapiro and Mahajan 1986). More women than men oppose policies relying on or encouraging violence and tend to see violence as a last resort. Women are less hawkish on military and defense issues, more opposed to capital punishment, and more supportive of gun control than men are (Sapiro 1983;

TABLE 9-2
Gender Politics in Presidential Elections, 1976–1992

	1976		*1980*			*1984*		*1988*		*1992*		
	Carter	*Ford*	*Reagan*	*Carter*	*Anderson*	*Reagan*	*Mondale*	*Bush*	*Dukakis*	*Clinton*	*Bush*	*Perot*
Women	50	48	47	45	7	56	44	50	49	46	37	17
Men	50	48	55	36	7	62	37	57	41	41	38	21
Democratic												
Women	78	22	23	71	5	22	77	16	84	78	10	12
Men	77	22	29	63	6	28	71	18	80	77	9	14
Independent												
Women	42	55	50	34	13	59	40	52	46	41	32	27
Men	44	53	60	27	10	66	32	58	40	36	33	32
Republican												
Women	10	90	85	10	5	92	8	90	9	10	74	16
Men	9	90	87	8	4	93	7	91	8	10	71	19
White												
Women	46	52	52	39	8	62	38	65	43	41	41	18
Men	47	51	59	32	7	67	32	63	36	37	41	22
Black												
Women	86	14	9	88	3	7	93	9	90	86	9	5
Men	80	19	14	82	3	12	85	15	81	77	15	9

TABLE 9-2
Gender Politics in Presidential Elections, 1976–1992 *(Continued)*

	1976		*1980*			*1984*		*1988*		*1992*		
	Carter	*Ford*	*Reagan*	*Carter*	*Anderson*	*Reagan*	*Mondale*	*Bush*	*Dukakis*	*Clinton*	*Bush*	*Perot*
18–29												
Women	51	47	39	49	10	55	44	49	50	48	33	19
Men	50	47	47	39	11	63	36	55	43	38	36	26
30–44												
Women	49	49	50	41	8	54	45	50	49	44	38	18
Men	49	49	59	31	8	61	38	58	40	39	38	22
45–59												
Women	46	53	50	44	5	57	42	52	48	43	40	17
Men	48	51	60	34	5	62	36	62	36	40	40	20
60+												
Women	49	50	52	43	4	58	42	48	52	51	39	10
Men	44	55	56	40	3	62	37	53	46	49	37	14
< H.S.												
Women	—	—	41	56	2	46	52	38	62	58	27	15
Men	—	—	51	47	2	52	47	49	50	49	30	21
H.S. Grad.												
Women	—	—	50	44	5	58	41	50	50	43	38	19
Men	—	—	53	42	3	62	37	50	49	43	34	23
Some College												
Women	—	—	52	39	8	58	41	54	45	43	38	18
Men	—	—	59	31	8	65	33	60	38	39	37	24
College Grad												
Women	—	—	42	44	12	52	47	49	51	49	35	16
Men	—	—	59	28	11	63	36	63	36	40	41	19

Source: "Portrait of the Electorate," *New York Times*, November 5, 1992.

Conover and Sapiro 1993). A survey of the foreign policy opinions of American leaders shows similar results: Female leaders tend to oppose militarism and the use of the CIA to undermine governments and to support the use of international organizations like the United Nations (Holsti and Rosenau 1981).

Some studies show women are more supportive than men of pro-environmental legislation. Women have voiced more support for government policies to help the poor and guarantee full employment. As a group, women's support of feminism and so-called women's issues is uneven. Women are more moralistic in the traditional sense of many issues, which may account for some of their ambivalence about feminist issues; more women than men support prayer in public schools, for example. Whereas women were once thought to be more trusting of government, polls suggest that women have less confidence than men about the economic future of the United States and are more likely to feel that this country would get into a war. Nevertheless, on most issues gender differences are trivial or nonexistent, and they change over time.

Nonelectoral Citizen Politics

Electoral participation is only one category of political participation. Women have long been noted for engaging in politics and community action through churches, clubs, and numerous other organizations (Scott 1992). Indeed, government figures showing that women constitute a majority of the people involved in volunteer work (U.S. Bureau of the Census 1992, 374) support this view. Women do not provide just the troops for this work but the leaders as well, even while they are not adequately recognized (Daniels 1988).

The importance of community and organization work in politics is underestimated because of the usual emphasis on elections. It is important to remember that a large part of our public problem solving is done by people active in their own communities where issues about education, land use, and the availability of other services are most focused.

The 19th century saw a dramatic growth in women's participation in formal and informal organizations of many sorts involving women of most classes, races, and religions. Some were organized for cultural activities and self-improvement, and others were organized for social philanthropy or volunteer work and community service. Historians point out that even groups not organized explicitly for the purpose of participating in politics nevertheless often engaged women in politics or political discussion. Many women's clubs, for example, served as audiences for suffragists as they traveled across the country lecturing on women and the vote.

In 1890 many of these clubs joined together to form the General Federation of Women's Clubs (GFWC), which had over a million members by 1910. Many GFWC affiliates were instrumental in establishing the early framework for public social welfare programs through their work in health, education, poverty relief, and municipal reform (Skocpol 1992). Club women were among the chief lobbyists for local and state government responsibility for social welfare. Interestingly, although these women thought it was crucial for women to be involved in "social housekeeping" and public affairs, the GFWC did not endorse the women's suffrage amendment to the Constitution until 1914 because many of its members thought that their own successes proved women already had enough power in government, and they did not want women to become involved in "dirty" partisan politics. On the other hand, these same successes may have made it necessary for them to change their minds. As government increasingly took up their concerns with public policy and management, women found their continued involvement limited in those states that barred women from voting or holding office.

There is an unfortunate stereotype that women's organizational and grassroots political activity involved only middle-class white women. This is far from the truth. Although middle-class women historically have had more time to devote to these efforts (at least up until the 1930s when they were unlikely to be employed and likely to have domestic servants), women of different classes and many ethnic and racial groups organized for community action and problem solving. For example, as early as the 1820s to 1840s black women organized literary societies that also helped impoverished black women and gave financial assistance to black newspapers (Giddings 1984, 49). There was a large black women's club movement (Salem 1990). White ethnic immigrant women also formed many organizations around the turn of the century.

Historically women have been active in many social movements and protest actions. In Chapter 14 we will focus on feminist movements. Women's independent labor activity goes back at least to the 1820s (Foner 1982; Kessler-Harris 1982). There are many instances in U.S. history of women organizing boycotts and other consumer-related political actions. A good example is the 1917 boycott that resulted in massive demonstrations among Jewish immigrant women living in New York's Lower East Side (Frank 1985). There have been few major social movements in American history in which women were not involved in large numbers; among the more notable are the movements for abolition, temperance (Bordin 1990), utopian communalism (Chmielewski, Kern, and Klee-Hartzell 1993), health reform, peace (Alonso 1993), progressivism and municipal reform, civil rights (Mills 1993), and welfare rights (Pope 1989). Examples of this activism in different arenas are described in most chapters of this book.

Women are now nearly as active as men in mass-level politics. Thanks in part to education and changing gender-role ideology, more people than ever now think that political activity is appropriate for women. But unfortunately it appears that girls are still socialized to express less interest in politics than boys are (Owen and Dennis 1988). Politics is still stereotypically regarded as a "male domain."

Women's gender-related roles help shape the degree to which women become politically active as well as the ways in which this activism is manifest. Motherhood has a greater impact on political activity than does fatherhood; child-care responsibility can inhibit women's participation in some aspects of politics, especially for single women, but it also can push women, especially homemakers, into political activity in local and school affairs (Jennings 1979; Sapiro 1983). The mere fact that a woman is either employed or a housewife does not have as strong a relationship with political participation as some people think (McDonough 1982; Sapiro 1983). Employment can expand the number of contacts a woman has, and her occupation may help shape the kinds of interests she has. More important, however, may be the way a woman interprets her own roles and how compatible she thinks her roles are with political activism. It is important to remember that for a long time Sojourner Truth's occupation was slavery and Elizabeth Cady Stanton's was homemaking; neither of them shied away from political activity.

The Impact of Women in Politics

What difference does it make whether women participate in politics? One way to answer this is to determine whether women and men act differently or make different decisions when they hold positions of power and influence. Most studies of women legislators, judges, and bureaucrats suggest that most of the time gender doesn't make much difference in how public officials view the issues. Studies of state legislators show women and men voting in similar ways and sponsoring the same number of pieces of legislation. Research on judges shows that, by and large, male and female judges make the same kinds of decisions (Gruhl, Spohn, and Welch 1981). But many women in politics claim that even when males and females say that they support similar policies, it is the women in public office who generally do most of the work to put more egalitarian gender principles into practice.

Nevertheless, recent research sponsored by the Center for the American Woman and Politics at Rutgers points to many instances in which women now seem to be making more of a difference than they did. It is not clear whether this is because only when the numbers of women in office passed a certain critical mass could they be more active or because different kinds of women are now being elected. But consider the findings from a national study of state legislators (Dodson and Carroll 1991). The vast majority of men and women in state legislatures think that women make a difference. More women than men oppose prohibiting abortion, oppose parental consent for abortion, and oppose the death penalty and expansion of nuclear power plants. Women are more likely to think that the private sector can't solve most of our problems. Even within political parties, women legislators tend to be more supportive of liberal and feminist policies than are their male colleagues. More women have worked on women's rights bills. Women and men have somewhat different ideas about qualities that are important for political leaders to have. Women are more likely to think that political leaders should have a sense of mission and a concern for those affected by decisions. Women think that men try to keep them out of leadership positions, but men disagree.

Even though we cannot yet know how many, which, and to what degree policies would be different in a more gender balanced government, some things would surely change. Government would be more representative of society as a whole. Women would have more of a role in governing their own lives as citizens. And, to the degree that government is a model of society's values, that model would show women as leaders and full participants.

The people of the United States have long thought of their government as close to ideal in the principles and practice of democracy. American schoolchildren still learn that theirs is a government "of the people, by the people, and for the people." There is no question that this government is one of the most democratic in the world. But has it been as democratic as Americans have claimed?

Throughout the history of this nation, feminists have argued that we have a long way to go before our democratic claims are truly fulfilled. Our standards for democracy have become tougher over the years; not so long ago we described ourselves as democratic even though at least half the adult population was barred by law from voting. Even now many people find no contradiction between democratic principles and the low degree of governmental power that women share. Most people are unaware of how unequally law and policy affect women and men.

The central theme of democratic theory is the distribution of power in a political community: the degree to which people are free to share in making decisions about the community and, ultimately, themselves. The central theme of feminist theory is the distribution of power between women and men, especially the amount of power women have over themselves. Feminism, therefore, seeks to raise our standard of democracy.

The fall of many authoritarian governments in the late 1980s and early 1990s renewed worldwide attention on the meaning of democracy. Feminists in many of the countries of the former Soviet Union and Eastern Europe are learning the hard way that there are no simple solutions. Following the initial euphoria after the fall of the Berlin Wall and the toppling of dictators, members of those nations are finding that the transition *to* democracy is more difficult than the fall *from* authoritarianism. Women especially are finding that in the shift toward "democracy" they are often left behind, losing the social welfare assistance they had under the old system and being excluded and neglected to a large degree in the new. In response to some of these fears, many feminists in the former Soviet Union adopted as the battle cry of their new movement, "Democracy minus women is not democracy." The United States is one of the many nations that stand to learn from this phrase.

NOTES

1. Unless otherwise stated, the discussion of legal rights refers to the rights of free women (most of whom were white) under the law. Women held in slavery (most of whom were black) did not have legal rights.
2. Because of colonial patterns, the French legal tradition also influences law in Louisiana, and the Spanish legal tradition has influence over much of the Southwest.
3. This does not mean that there are no more problems. There is still the issue of defining exactly what "equal" means. Further, some policies cannot easily be translated into issues of "equal rights," particularly those that concern conditions affecting only one sex or primarily one sex. For readings on feminist views of the law and

especially the notion of "rights," see Rhode (1989), Williams (1991), and Weisberg (1993).

4. The House of Representatives held hearings on this and related cases. The report makes very interesting reading. See U.S. Congress (1930).

5. "Pentagon Plans to Allow Combat Flights by Women; Seeks to Drop Warship Ban," *New York Times*, April 28, 1993.

6. Felicity Barringer, "Four Reports Cite Naval Academy for Rife Sexism," *New York Times*, October 10, 1990.

7. Michael R. Gordon, "Pentagon Report Tells of Aviators' 'Debauchery,' " *New York Times*, April 24, 1993.

8. William Tuohy, "Female NATO Officers Press for Wider Combat Roles," *Los Angeles Times*, May 25, 1992.

9. Mary Daniels, "Prisoner of War," *Chicago Tribune*, September 6, 1992.

10. Eric Schmitt, "Ban on Women in Combat Divides Four Service Chiefs," *New York Times*, June 19, 1991.

11. Michael R. Gordon, "Panel Is Against Letting Women Fly in Combat," *New York Times*, November 4, 1992.

12. Eric Schmitt, "Survey Finds Majority of Army Women Favor Ending Ban on Combat Roles," *New York Times*, September 11, 1992.

13. Tuohy, "Female NATO Officers Press for Wider Combat Roles."

14. For more discussion of women, the family, and the development of U.S. social policy, see Sapiro (1986). In this book, other social policies are further discussed in other chapters, including education policy (Chapter 5), family law and policy (Chapter 11), reproductive policy (Chapter 12), and employment and welfare policy (Chapter 13).

15. "Sex-Offender Registration Laws Pit Victims' Rights Against Civil Rights," *New York Times*, February 20, 1993.

16. Don Terry, "Stabbing Death at Door of Justice Sends Alert on Domestic Violence," *New York Times*, March 17, 1992.

17. This is not strictly true because of the many states with antisodomy laws that technically make such acts as oral or anal intercourse illegal. Thus not all sexual relations within marriage are technically protected.

18. "Sex-Offender Registration Laws Pit Victims' Rights Against Civil Rights," *New York Times*, February 20, 1993.

19. Ross E. Milloy, "Furor Over a Decision Not to Indict in a Rape Case," *New York Times*, October 25, 1992.

20. Mitchell Landsberg, "Women's Fears Lead to Gun Buys," *Wisconsin State Journal*, February 8, 1993.

21. Peter Applebombe, "Holding Fragile Families Together When Mothers Are Inmates," *New York Times*, December 27, 1992.

22. Ibid.

23. Barbara Goldsmith, "A Reporter at Large: Women on the Edge," *The New Yorker*, April 26, 1993, p. 65.

24. For further discussion of the military and prostitution, see Enloe (1983).

25. "Beating Wall of Silence by Navy Pilots."

26. "Evolution, Not Revolution Spurs Women toward Congress," *New York Times*, October 21, 1992.
27. Robin Toner, "Women in Politics: High Goals Mean Higher Bias," *New York Times*, August 13, 1987.
28. R. W. Apple, "Female Candidates Poised for Breakthroughs in 1992," *New York Times*, March 23, 1992.

PART THREE

Choice and Control in Personal Life, the Family, and Work

ONE THEME IN this book is the relationship between gender and power, control, and choice. Throughout Part II we looked at the ways in which values defining individuals and their life choices are shaped by the gender norms embedded in the structures of social institutions. We also looked at some ways in which women have influenced these institutions and attempted to expand their options.

In Part III we look at the areas of life in which people are said to express and act most on their own feelings, abilities, and desires as individuals: the way we talk, walk, and relate to others, our personal and intimate lives, our family and work relationships. The question that unites these chapters is: To what extent does gender limit the control women have over their choices and experiences?

Reflect Before You Read

1. Imagine that tomorrow morning you wake up to find you have become the other sex. Describe in detail what tomorrow will be like. How will you feel? What will you do? How will people treat you? What will you miss about your former sex? What will you like about your new one?
2. You have been restored to your current sex. Describe your adult life as it has been, as you hope it will be, and as you imagine it will be. How much of it—which of your choices, important experiences, major dilemmas, and turning points—is determined by your gender? What would be different if you were of the other sex?
3. Think about the five people who are closest and most important to you. Imagine they all suddenly changed their sex. Can you imagine them being just as they are now in all other respects? If not, what would be different? Would you feel differently about each of these people? Would you act differently? How? Why?

10

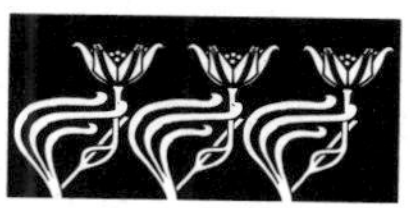

Gender, Communication, and Self-Expression

ONE OF OUR most important tasks in the course of human development is to learn how to communicate with others. Language provides the basis for becoming both social beings able to act and interact with others and independent, autonomous beings, because it is the means by which people know themselves and others.[1]

Studying patterns of communication helps us understand the delicate balance between the individual and social aspects of people's lives. Without communication we are a collection of unconnected individuals, not a society. Communication is, in a sense, the medium of which social structure is built, because it is the medium by which values are transmitted and enforced. Social structure can be maintained relatively "gently" through teaching the young preferred values, or it might be maintained more forcefully by communicating severe threats to a population and using terror against deviants as a symbolic warning to others. Communication, then, is the stuff of power and control. Power is not a lump of something that people possess; it is a characteristic of relationships among people. As such, understanding how sex/gender systems work requires investigating gendered aspects of language and communication.

Marx and Engels called language "practical consciousness"—that is, the means by which we categorize, recognize, or name tangible and intangible objects. When we cannot attach a word to an object we call it "indescribable," something that cannot be identified, defined, or communicated to others. Objects or feelings we consider particularly dangerous or frightening we call "unmentionable" or "unspeakable," as though we could wipe them out of existence by excluding them from social discourse.

Language and *communication* encompass many kinds of nonverbal behavior as well as acts of writing and speaking. Sign language, after all, is a full language based on gesture rather than the spoken word. But almost all of us express ourselves regularly by smiling, shaking our head, raising a hand, walking away, or hitting someone; often these gestures are intertwined with spoken language to create meaning. Both verbal and nonverbal communication have vocabulary and grammar. That is, they are systems of sounds or gestures that symbolize or encode meaning understood by people within a specific language group when they are patterned in a certain way.

Analyzing language is complicated by the fact that there are many variations within any given natural language (such as English, French, or Hindi). Most of us are familiar with regional dialects and similar language variations resulting from cultural factors, such as ethnicity, race, and religion. Language also varies by age, class, occupation, and gender. Sometimes the differences are so great that people from one group unwittingly misinterpret or have difficulty understanding those from another group.

Situation and context also affect people's language use. Most people communicate differently with a stranger and a friend, a parent and a child, a superior and a subordinate, a woman and a man. This is partly due to subcultural variations among these groups and the effects of status and hierarchy rankings on communication behavior.

The remainder of this chapter explores gender and language and communication behavior beginning with the ways in which sex/gender systems are defined, maintained, and changed through the language we use to discuss gender and ourselves as men and women. We then turn to how gender shapes our own communication behavior, including how we speak, carry ourselves, and interact with others. In a hierarchical sex/gender system we should see evidence of these power differences in people's communication behavior. Finally we consider the problem of communication and social change.

Referring to Women, Men, and People

Most of us have had the experience of saying to someone, "Don't put words into my mouth," usually when someone interprets something we said in a way that conflicts with what we were trying to say. This can happen when a word or phrase carries a connotation we do not immediately recognize but which, nevertheless, is understood by the listener as part of the message.

Women's studies scholars in linguistics, psychology, and philosophy have devoted considerable attention to analyzing the connotations of words used to refer to males and females. They find that our gender language reflects the current nature of sex/gender systems and hierarchical social relationships, and often incorporates values we might not recognize or intend. Let us explore our gender vocabulary.

Gender-Specific Terms

Consider some words that obviously refer to gender: *male* and *female*, *man* and *woman*, *girl* and *boy*, *feminine* and *masculine*. Each pair consists of two words usually regarded as antonyms, terms that are "opposites." Indeed, people often talk about "the opposite sex." Here is our first problem: Why are *male* and *female* antonyms? How are they "opposites"?

The answer might seem obvious. Among human beings, those who are not female are male, and those who are not male are female. But to talk about "opposites" implies more than this. *Male* and *female* are antonyms partly because they are culturally linked to other pairs of antonyms generally regarded as traits associated with males and females—the stereotypes we discussed in Chapter 1. The terms *male* and *female* are associated with other pairs of terms, such as *logical/emotional, active/passive, independent/dependent,* and *rough/gentle.* These are not simply words people use to describe men and women; they also reflect the deeper meanings people associate with these terms. Most of the words we use have many possible connotations. These cultural associations raise an important question: Even if we carefully choose the words we use to express ourselves, will other people understand what we mean? What is our power over our own gendered meanings?

We also have different terms to refer to roughly the same things. People use *male* and *female* to refer generally to persons of one or the other sex, but we also use many other words to limit our meaning further to males or females of particular ages, marital status, or other characteristics. Some terms connote respect, some are informal, and some are derogatory. How and when these different words are used depends on what we mean and the situation. Table 10-1 lists some of the words most commonly used to refer to males and females, and their other connotations.

Clearly one important aspect of these terms is that male and female terms are often asymmetrical; that is, there are not always equivalent terms for both sexes. Rather, certain statuses and situations are more important for defining for one sex than the other. Females and males in the same situations are regarded differently. This implies that *male* and *female* are therefore not really antonyms, or opposites, as framed by our language.[2] Some examples follow.

Although most of the words in Table 10-1 imply at least some age characteristic, there are four sets in which age is a very important part of the meaning: *woman/man*, *girl/boy*, *spinster/bachelor*, *matron/?*. Here we find some apparent analogues. We can say that *woman* is to *man* as *girl* is to *boy* because the first pair constitutes the female and male adult analogues of the second pair, the terms for a female child and a male child. Or we could say that *woman* is to *girl* as *man* is to *boy*, because the first pair is composed of the terms for a female adult and a female child, and the second is composed of the terms for a male adult and a male child.

A more careful look casts some doubt on this simplicity. These male and female terms are not precise analogues in common usage because of the extra meaning baggage they carry. *Girl*, for example, is widely used to describe females of all ages, including adults, whereas the use of *boy* for adult males is used under much more limited circumstances. Why is this the case? Some people claim that calling an adult woman a girl is a compliment because it suggests the woman is young. Why not, then, suggest a man is young by calling him a boy? The reason has to do with definitions of both gender and aging. Calling a man a

TABLE 10-1
Gender Referents: Nouns and Titles

Female Referents	*Male Referents*	*Additional Connotations*
Female	Male	Generic.
Woman	Man	Generic. Also implies age. *Man* is also used to mean "human."
Girl, Gal	Guy, Boy	Informal. *Girl* also connotes age. *Boy* is rarely used for adult males.
Dame, Broad, Chick, Skirt	?	Derogatory generic. This is a small selection; some are obscene.
Ms.	Mr.	Generic title. *Ms.* is used less often than *Miss* or *Mrs.* and probably is interpreted as implying feminist attitudes.
Girl	Boy	Age. *Girl* is also used to refer to adult females, especially those in subordinate status. *Boy* also has been used to refer to adult black males by whites.
Lady	Gentleman	Age and class; polite form.
Madam	Sir	Age and class; polite form.
Spinster	Bachelor	Age and marital status.
Wife	Husband	Marital status.
Bride	Groom	Marital status and length of marriage. *Bride* also is used for a young married woman; *groom* is used only on the wedding day. *Bride* is often the object of a possessive noun ("John's bride"); *groom* is not ("Jane's groom").
Housewife, Homemaker	Breadwinner (Househusband)	Marital and occupational status.
Divorcée	? (Divorcé)	Marital status.
Matron	? (Patron)	Marital status, age, social status.
Widow	Widower	Marital status. *Widow* is often the object of a possessive noun ("John's widow"); *widower* is not ("Jane's widower").
Miss, Mrs.	?	Title connoting marital status.
Mistress	? (Master)	Marital status and heterosexual relationship.

TABLE 10-1
Gender Referents: Nouns and Titles *(Continued)*

Female Referents	*Male Referents*	*Additional Connotations*
?	Cuckold	Extramarital relationship of spouse.
Prostitute, Whore, Tramp, Slut, Hooker, Nymphomaniac	Lecher, Stud	Heterosexual behavior outside marriage.
Lesbian, Dyke, Queer, Gay, Homo	Queer, Gay, Fairy, Pansy, Fag, Molly, Homo	Homosexual behavior or personality attributed to homosexuals.
?	Sissy, Pansy, Weak sister, Mamma's boy, Swish, Poof, Wimp	A very "feminine" person.
Tomboy, Amazon, Dyke, Butch	Stud, He-man, Macho man	A very "masculine" person.

Note: Words within parentheses are apparent equivalents that are rarely used or are completely different in meaning.

boy belittles his experience, competence, and manly attributes. This asymmetry coincides with the social view that aging in early and especially middle adulthood detracts more from women's attractiveness than from men's. *Girl* and *boy* do not refer to youth and vigor, but to childhood, a more desirable status for women.

Using childhood terms for some adults but not others reflects status differences. In U.S. society the use of *boy* to refer to an adult male historically was a derogatory means for whites to talk to or about black men. Calling a black man *boy* indicated his subordinate, servile status or "stripped him of his manhood." (Notice, at least in this case, the close ties between the politics of race and gender.) Abolishing the term *boy* was an important symbolic issue during the civil rights movement of the 1960s. Within a generation the usage has virtually disappeared. The connotation of subordinate and servant status is easily detected when people use the word *girl* to refer to their female domestic help ("My girl is wonderful; she's absolutely devoted to the children") or to their female secretaries ("I'll have my girl phone your girl to make the arrangements").

Spinster/bachelor is another word pair with interesting age connotations, this time combined with an indication of marital status. *Spinster* and *bachelor* both refer to unmarried adults, but the words do not have precisely the same meaning. Consider the sentence "They were always careful to have at least one attractive _____ at their parties." One could well imagine *bachelor* but not *spinster* filling in the blank because of the word *attractive*. We talk about a "confirmed bachelor"—a man who chooses to be unmarried—but not a "confirmed spinster." Why is there no positive term to refer to an adult unmarried female?

Consider also the asymmetry in the titles assigned to women and men. The standard title for adult men regardless of marital status is *Mr.* Although the generic female title *Ms.* is now available, most people continue to prefer a title for women that also indicates marital status: *Miss* or *Mrs.*[3] Marital status is a more important determinant of women's status than of men's.

Marital status is so important for defining women that most married women still change not only their title but also their personal identity tag: their name. The law used to force women to give up their surnames of birth and take their husband's on the grounds that a married woman had no legal identity apart from her husband. Most state laws no longer make it difficult for women to retain their birth names, but if a woman gives up her birth name, it can be difficult and expensive to recover it legally. Even if the law does not require women to change their names, social pressure on them to do so can be very strong. Soon after President Clinton's inauguration, considerable public attention focused on the fact that his wife used her birth name as her middle name and (even more shocking) had neglected to use his name at all when they were first married! As Table 10-2 shows, a married woman's name is quite variable.

Some people argue that it is confusing for husband and wife (or, as the traditional marriage service has it, man and wife) to have different surnames. It is confusing only because people *expect* husbands and wives to share a surname. Parents and married daughters usually have different surnames, but they know they are related and so do others who need to know. Sharing a surname does not make life less confusing if the name is very common, such as Smith. The confusion faced by couples with different surnames does not compare with that

TABLE 10-2
What's in a Name?

Lucy Stone Marries Henry Blackwell	
While married, she might be addressed as:	*While married, he might be addressed as:*
Lucy Stone	Henry Blackwell
Ms. Lucy Stone	Mr. Henry Blackwell
Mrs. Lucy Stone	
Lucy Stone Blackwell	
Lucy Blackwell	
Mrs. Lucy Blackwell[1]	
Ms. Lucy Blackwell	
Mrs. Henry Blackwell	
Miss Lucy Stone *and* Mrs. Henry Blackwell[2]	

[1]Many people feel that this is a correct address only for a widow or a divorcée.

[2]Used by women who keep both a professional and a married name.

encountered when we have been trying to find an old friend or business acquaintance who has married and changed her name. Many women add to this potential confusion by giving up both their first and last names, becoming "Mrs. John Smith." This identity tag tells us that it is more important to know her husband's name than to know hers.

Research shows there are many derogatory, or at least disrespectful, generic terms for women, but there are few, if any, for men. What is the male equivalent of *broads* or *chicks*? *Guys* is informal, but it is not belittling or derogatory. What social conditions create the need for so many derogatory terms to describe a particular social group?

It is also interesting to note the difference between the terms used to describe a heterosexually active male or female. *Lecher* or *stud* can be used in an admiring sense, but the female equivalents are clearly derogatory. A woman who likes sexual activity "too much" is a nymphomaniac. What is the name for a man who likes sexual activity "too much"? Is there such a thing? The English language is considerably richer in the number of terms labeling a sexually permissive woman than in terms for a sexually permissive man. One researcher found 220 terms for the former and only 22 for the latter (cited in Eakins and Eakins 1978).

The admiration–derogation distinction vanishes when we look at the terms referring to homosexually active people. In this case, the words used for both men and women are derogatory, and there are more derogatory terms for homosexual men than for lesbians. Likewise, there are more derogatory terms for an "effeminate" male than for a "masculine" female. Our language seems to suggest that if a woman acts "too masculine" (or unfeminine) she is deviant, but at least she is emulating the superior sex; if a man acts "too feminine" (or unmasculine) there is something profoundly wrong with him.

Women notice gender-based modes of address and naming more than men do. For example, a survey of New Jersey attorneys (New Jersey Supreme Court Task Force 1986) showed that although 61% of women claimed to have heard a judge speak to a female lawyer using her first name or a term of endearment while men were addressed by surname and/or title, 76% of men thought they had not heard this happen. While 85% of the women had heard a male attorney use inappropriate forms of address to a woman attorney, only 45% of the men had. Many female attorneys experience courts as gender biased because of their perception of persistent patterns of linguistic discrimination. This is only one example of how language use can become part of an institutionalized system of inequity.

The politics of naming often becomes an important issue in the agenda of social movements. Certainly they often fight for awareness of the impact of using derogatory language against a social group. But social movements sometimes also try to force a reevaluation of names that have been applied to them. The 1960s black power movement declared "Black is beautiful" because up to that time *black* had always had culturally negative connotations. The gay movement used the slogan "Gay and Proud" to combat ideas of the shamefulness of homosexuality, and lesbians used a traditionally derogatory term, *dyke*, as a public symbol of pride. By the early 1990s much of the gay movement had similarly adopted the traditional insult *queer*.

There are many words not initially "about" gender that are often transformed to indicate gender. The most common examples are terms for occupations, especially gender-typed occupations. Nothing in the construction of the words *lawyer*, *poet*, *nurse*, *sculptor*, or *journalist* reveals the gender of the person being described, but many people seem to think it is important to modify with a gender tag if the person being discussed is a woman (lady lawyer, poetess, male nurse, sculptress, lady journalist), even when gender information is irrelevant or even redundant (Mary Jones, a lady lawyer . . .).

Using suffixes *-ess*, *-ette*, or *-ix* to denote female gender in these types of words conveys more than just the female gender. Note that they modify the *standard forms* of the words, suggesting that women are modifications of the standard or normal occupants of these positions. The "male" forms are the ones used to refer to these positions generically. This change is especially significant because most of the standard forms do not linguistically indicate gender in the first place. If *-er* or *-or* indicated male gender, we would have to say not just "waitress" or "sculptress" but also "workress," "professorix," and "stock brokerette." Members of the U.S. Senate might say, "I defer to my colleague from Kansas, Senatrix Nancy Kassenbaum."

The standard form of some occupational names does flag gender, such as *businessman*, *chairman*, *congressman*, and *fireman*. For these terms, the standard practice used to be to use the *-man* form as a generic form or to refer to men, and to use either the *-man* form (as in "Madam Chairman") or the *-woman* form to refer to women. It is now common to omit irrelevant gender connotations by substituting either *person* (as in *businessperson*) or a neutral alternative form, such as *chair* (for *chairman*), *firefighter*, *representative*, or *member* of Congress, for the gender-specific term.

Gender-Neutral Terms

Few controversies over language have aroused as much hostility as that over the use of generic, non-gender-bound terms. The dispute over the use of *man* alone has created considerable debate and innumerable snide jokes about "personhole covers" and the like.

This book began with a consideration of the supposed generic uses of *man* and *he*. At the most practical level, such usage is ambiguous and confusing. Despite the claim that *man* and *he* can be generic terms, research shows people receive a gender-bound meaning from them (Sniezek and Jazwinski 1986). For example, using *man* rather than gender-neutral terms in chapter titles makes students think of males more often (Schneider and Hacker 1973). Another study (Cole, Hill, and Daly 1983) found that *man* is especially likely to bring males to mind when paired with the supposedly generic *he*. These researchers asked students to write a story flowing from the statement: (1) "In a large coeducational institution the average student will feel isolated in his introductory course," or (2) "In a large coeducational institution the average student will feel isolated in his or her introductory course." In the former case, 84% of the men and 52% of the women wrote about a male. In the latter case, 77% of the men and 22% of the women wrote about a male. The change in pronouns had very little effect on the men. It is significant, however, that only with gender-neutral terminology did women focus on their own sex as often as men focused on theirs.

Gender-neutral language is sometimes labeled "inclusive" language, and research like this suggests why. Women may begin to feel the world being described to them actually includes them. Not surprisingly, males both use more gender-biased pronouns and regard sexism as less relevant to language use than females do. In general, people who use gender-biased pronouns hold stronger gender stereotypes about occupations and have less positive attitudes toward nontraditional women than do those who use more inclusive language (Matheson and Kristensen 1987).[4]

The apparent gender neutrality of a word does not necessarily mean it provokes a nonsexist image or has a nonsexist meaning. Claus Mueller argues that the language we use encodes shared understandings of the surrounding social environment and reflects the structure of that environment. He writes,

> Language, . . . or more precisely, the code a group shares, is context specific. The possibility of transcending the content of one's code is contingent upon accepting and learning other codes. Change from one code to another implies, therefore, not only a change of the language spoken but also a change of the social context (1973, 14–15).

If the social context is one in which gender structures roles and hierarchies, can even the most apparently gender-neutral terms still have gender-based meanings for people? There is considerable evidence that they can.

Consider these terms: *engineer*, *kindergarten teacher*, *army officer*, and *telephone operator*. Although all are technically gender-neutral, two of them probably conjure up specifically male images in readers' minds, and two probably conjure up specifically female images. The reason is not that the words are gender-specific but rather that the social reality and cultural expectations to which they refer are structured by gender. Not all engineers and army officers are male, and not all kindergarten teachers and telephone operators are female, but cultural expectations based especially on past social reality structure the mental image provoked by these words. People who do not conform to this image seem out of place. Sociolinguists argue that language can therefore help forestall social change. Under normal circumstances it will change more slowly than social reality.

Research by Erica Wise and Janet Rafferty (1982) demonstrates how hard it is to find genuinely gender-neutral terms in a gender-structured society. Following up on earlier work about mental-health clinicians (Broverman et al. 1970), they asked students to define the characteristics of a healthy man, woman, and adult and a healthy boy, girl, and child. Like the earlier research, they found that males and females were defined differently. They also asked students to write about a healthy adult or child. Most of the students wrote about a male. In other

FIGURE 10-1

Is *Selfish* a Gender-Neutral Word?

The *Oxford English Dictionary* defines *selfish* as "devoted to or concerned with one's own advantage or welfare to the exclusion of regard for others." Imagine a scale like the following on which we might measure the amount of selfishness an individual displays in different situations:

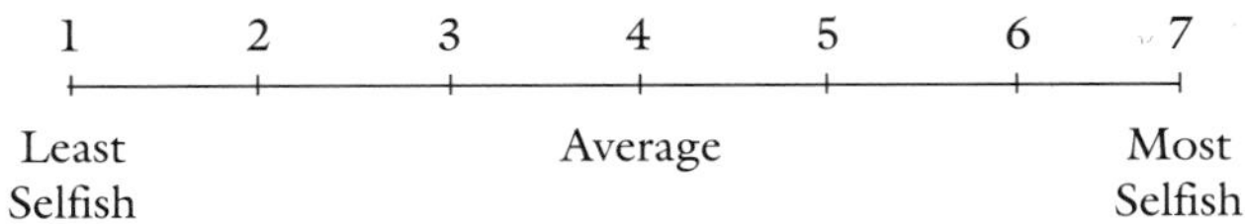

Using this scale we might rate people who always go out of their way to help other people as point 1, least selfish, and people who always expect other people to drop what they are doing so as to serve them as point 7, most selfish.

For each of the following situations, where on the selfishness scale do you think most people would place the individuals involved? Where would you place these individuals?

Most People's Rating	*My Rating*	
______	______	A woman who does not want to entertain her husband's business associates because she finds them boring
______	______	A man who does not want to entertain his wife's business associates because he finds them boring
______	______	A woman who does not want to move to a new town where her husband has found a better job because her own job prospects would be diminished
______	______	A man who does not want to move to a new town where his wife has found a better job because his own job prospects would be diminished
______	______	A woman who refuses to bake cupcakes for her child's school party because she is preparing for an exam
______	______	A man who refuses to bake cupcakes for his child's school party because he is preparing for an exam
______	______	A woman who does most of the cooking and cleaning at home
______	______	A man who does most of the cooking and cleaning at home
______	______	A woman who does not spend much time caring for her children because she is busy with her job
______	______	A man who does not spend much time caring for his children because he is busy with his job

words, the "gender-neutral" terms *healthy adult* and *healthy child* evoked male images on the part of both men and women.

Many apparently gender-neutral words take on different meanings when they are applied to women and men. Consider the words *selfish/generous* and *loving/unloving*. A stereotypic loving wife and mother bends her schedule around her family's needs, is proud to carry her husband's name, and is willing to uproot herself if her husband's job demands it. These things are generally not expected of a loving husband. Is a man considered unloving or selfish if his job usually takes priority in his household or if he refuses to assume his wife's name? Consider your responses to the exercise in Figure 10-1. The definition of many words depends on whether we are talking about a man or a woman. Other examples might include *aggression* and *success*.

Looking at the face values or dictionary meanings of words is not enough to tell us how language maintains or changes the structure of gender. We must also investigate the underlying meanings and associations in the contexts that drive them. Sexism in language is not a trivial matter. Change will not be effected simply by substituting *person* for *man*.

Autonomy and Control in Communication

Research on gender and communication does not focus only on the gender content of words; it also is concerned with the ways women and men speak and interact. Scholars in this field agree that women's and men's communication patterns differ and that the way we communicate depends on the sex of our audience. They also agree that these patterns reflect and help maintain gender differences in status and power. While we display these patterns of behavior every day, we are usually not conscious of what we are doing. This section examines some of these important, but often unconscious, aspects of our lives.

Male and Female Language

Some communications researchers argue that the gender differences in communication are so great we can talk about male and female dialects within the English language (Lakoff 1975). While others do not go that far, there are some important gender differences in our language use and communication behavior.

Women and men use slightly different vocabularies.[5] Because of their different experiences and training they use different specialized vocabularies. Women make finer distinctions in naming colors and, on the average, know and use more technical and precise words connected with clothing (especially words connected with sewing), food and cooking, and so on. Men use numbers more often and more precisely in ordinary conversation than women do. They also swear more and use more language generally regarded as obscene or aggressive. Many people also note differences in women's and men's descriptive vocabularies, especially in adjectives. For example, American men are less likely than American women to describe someone or something as adorable, darling, marvelous, or teeny-weeny.

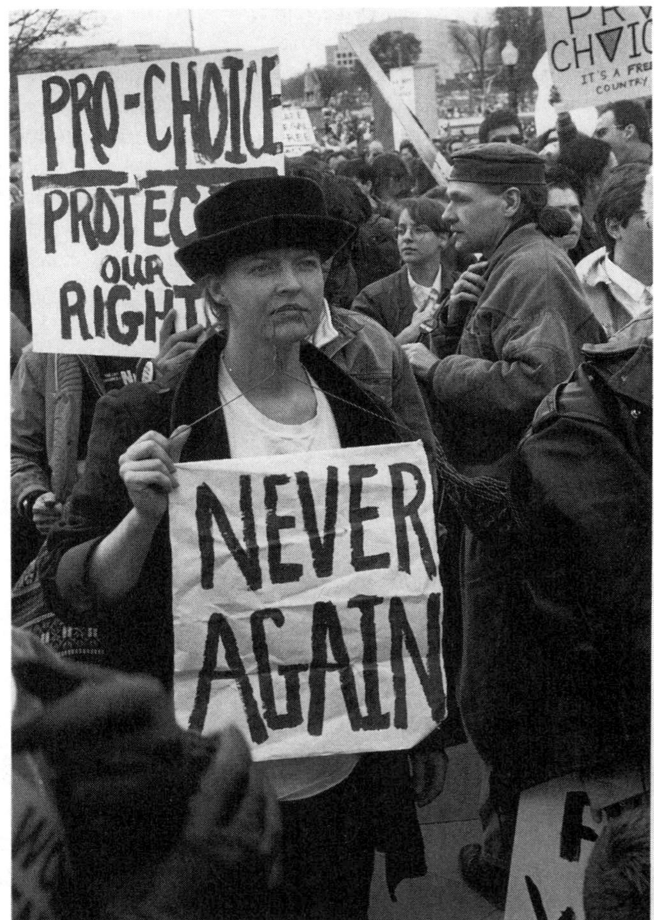

Women have been learning to use forceful language for their own purposes. This woman's coat hanger is a reminder of the results of anti-abortion policies.

Some, but not all, child development experts believe that girls learn verbal language more quickly than boys. Research on adult speech suggests that women are more likely than men to use standard English (the type our English teachers wanted us to learn). Some researchers theorize that this is not because of differences in ability or even knowledge, but because of men's effort to show toughness and independence and women's strategies to obtain higher status or respect (Adams and Ware 1989, 476).[6]

In light of controversies over the use and teaching of black English, it is interesting to note that these gender differences in the use of standard English appear among both African Americans and whites. Patricia C. Nichols, for example, investigated gender differences in the use of a local black dialect in a rural southern area. In one locality, women were more likely than men to use this dialect rather than standard English; in another, the reverse was true. Probing more deeply revealed that use of the more prestigious form was linked to economic differences between the two localities. In the second locality, women had more opportunity to have higher-status jobs requiring standard language skills; in the first, men had greater opportunities. The same underlying principle likely explains gender differences in the use of prestigious language forms regardless of race. For people from working-class or poor families, women's job opportunities (for example, service work involving much social interaction or clerical work) are more likely to depend on language skills, and men's are more likely to depend on physical labor.

Researchers on gender differences in language often argue that women's language tends to be more self-deprecating than men's. In other words, women's speech suggests they are more hesitant and doubt their own credibility more than men do. Some, though not all, research suggests that women are more likely to use the self-qualifying tag question as in "That was a good movie, wasn't it?" Research also indicates that women are more likely to blunt or hedge their statements by adding personalizers ("In my opinion . . . ," or "Personally, I think . . . ") or disclaimers ("I may be wrong, but . . . ") rather than simply stating opinions and observations straight out.

Women are also more likely to hedge their demands by phrasing them as requests or using long, complex sentences that blunt the request. To caricature the difference, the hedging form of the polite demand "Please close the door" might be, "I hope you wouldn't mind terribly, but I would be ever so grateful if you would please close the door—that is, unless you want it open." Women also blunt their communication by using rising intonation as though asking questions or permission when they are making statements. For example, Bob asks his wife, Sally, when dinner will be ready; Sally, who knows exactly when it will be ready, answers, "In ten minutes?" as though asking permission or confirmation.

Men appear to use more words when describing objects (Eakins and Eakins 1978, 25–29). Women often use a higher pitch and more breathy voice than is physiologically required, and they use more variation in intonation than men do (Eakins and Eakins 1978).

It is important not to exaggerate the differences between female and male speech and to remember that there is considerably more similarity than difference. No single speech attribute distinguishes women from men either consistently or dramatically. Nevertheless we can argue that female and male styles differ, as research by Anthony Mulac and Torborg Louisa Lundell (1986) shows. They taped 40 people describing the same photographs. They first asked a group of observers to read the transcripts of the descriptions and guess the sex of the speakers. They were not able to do this very well. They then had the transcripts coded for the presence of the types of characteristics we have been discussing. They found these characteristics did distinguish between female and male speakers in the ways we might expect. "On the basis of the formula determined by [statistical analysis], 85% of the male transcripts could be accurately determined on the basis of the relative presence or absence of the 17 language features" (90). Further analysis showed that the characteristics associated with male speech were viewed as more dynamic and those associated with female speech were viewed as more aesthetic. Even if observers could not name the gender of the speaker, gender made a difference in the impact of the speech.

Communication is an interactive process, depending on social context and the people with whom one is communicating. If I speak hesitantly, it may be because I always do this, because I am unsure of the particular topic I am discussing, or because the person to whom I am speaking makes me feel uncomfortable. Most investigators argue that many of the most important differences between female and male communication behavior are the result of the structure of power and authority relations between them.

The Right-of-Way: Gender and Status

We all follow many rules, usually unconsciously, when we communicate or interact with others. Some of these are the rules of grammar that allow us to put together strings of words in a way that will transmit meaning clearly to others. (Would difficult understand be to if my message not were it correct grammatically through sentences transmitted.) Others are the rules of style that set the tone and indicate, for example, whether we are speaking formally or informally, as intimates or strangers, or as superior and subordinate. (I mean, like, it would be *really* distracting and might screw up your studies really badly—and I wouldn't want to do that!—if I wrote this whole book in the style I'm using in this sentence. Y'know what I mean?) Some of these rules may be regarded as the traffic rules we use to facilitate communication. They include the norms of politeness, which facilitate comfort and ease of communication and have the practical advantage, for example, of requiring people to take turns in conversations.

Communication rules depend on the status rankings of the people involved. Status and hierarchy rankings are reflected through communication behavior. People who break the traffic rules of interpersonal relations, for example, by not taking proper turns in speaking, are not regarded as conversational bad drivers but as impolite or, if the infractions are major enough, crazy. Violations of communication traffic rules by a subordinate in relation to a superior are not just impolite. A subordinate's demand for equality in the traffic rules—for example, by taking even an equal speaking turn without the superior's permission—may be viewed as insubordination. Politeness is the act of granting the socially appropriate amount of respect to others depending on their relative status.

Gender differences in communication and social interaction reflect the existence of a hierarchical sex/gender system. They are governed in part by traffic rules calling for males to have the right-of-way both in the use of social space and in conversation. Other hierarchical gender-related communication patterns also exist.

RIGHT-OF-WAY IN SPACE. Men take up more space than women do. This is not just because men are generally larger than women but also because they occupy, use, and move through space differently from women. Social psychologists and others have noticed that people of relatively high status act as though they have a right to more space or territory than do people of relatively low status. This pattern is reflected by men and women.[7]

Men sit and stand more expansively than women do, much more often spreading their arms and legs outward or sideways or sitting with their head and trunk leaning backward and their legs spread out in front of them. American men

Law professor Anita Hill's testimony before an all-white male Senate Judiciary Committee reminded many women of the effects of communications rights-of-way on their ability to be heard, understood, and believed.

tend to cross their legs in the ankle-over-knee position. Women position themselves as though to shrink themselves, with arms and legs close to the body. No matter how women sit, including when they cross their legs, their knees are close together, and when they sit "properly" their knees touch, a position many find uncomfortable. These leg positions have sometimes been explained on grounds other than status. For example, some people suggest that women keep their legs close together when they wear skirts so that their underwear will not show or that men cannot sit with their legs together (for example, with legs crossed at the knee) because their genitals get in the way. However, women are likely to sit with their legs close together whether they are wearing short or long skirts or slacks; and there are cultural variations in the ways men cross their legs. French men, for example, cross their legs at the knees.

Certainly, gender differences in clothing help maintain some of these differences in demeanor and use of space. It is difficult to walk with long, free strides while wearing high heels. Skirts and some types of women's blouses also inhibit movement if women want to avoid displaying their underwear. Many popular "dress for success" guides of the early 1980s urged businesswomen to wear a female variety of the male business suit precisely because such attire hides the body underneath. But even these outfits, which included a skirt and high-heel shoes, did not eliminate the need to sit and walk in a circumspect, modesty-conscious way.

Men have more personal space than women do, which is another characteristic of people with high status. Like other animals, we need a certain amount of territory. We become uncomfortable or even angry if the wrong people invade that space, for instance, by standing too close when conversing. Two people meeting under these circumstances tend to move in a kind of odd dance, with one person progressively moving backward to create more distance and the other moving forward to diminish that space.

Our personal boundary spaces depend on our relationship to others in our vicinity. The more intimate and friendly a person is, the closer that person is allowed to approach. Status and relationship also determine rights with regard to others' personal space. High-status people assume a right to invade the personal space of lower-status people, whereas lower-status people must respect the personal space of superiors.

The gender-based differences in women's and men's behavior reflect these status-based right-of-way rules. Observers often remark on the relative absence of private places for women as compared with men. It is common in households that can afford it for a man to have his own room or other place that no one else in the family may enter without permission. Even when the household cannot afford such a luxury, it is more common for a man to be allowed to hide behind his newspaper, surrounded by a symbolic "do not disturb" atmosphere that is often enforced by his wife.

Women are less likely to "own" private territory or privacy. "Their" room, the kitchen, is one of the most public in a home. Likewise, secretaries are usually placed out in the open with their tools and desks available to any passerby. Women's work or leisure, therefore, is regarded as less important than men's and more subject to interruption. Indeed, one could argue that a defining characteristic of women's work is that women are supposed to be available, so their space is designed to facilitate interruption.

Women's lack of totally private space does not mean that they lack all control over their surroundings. In the home, for example, women have a relatively large amount of control over the design of the physical environment through their responsibilities for decoration and cleaning. Bedrooms and bathrooms, for example, which are shared spaces, are generally decorated and furnished in what is regarded as conventionally feminine taste. The decoration and furnishing of a man's study or workroom often stands in stark contrast to that of the rest of the house. (For a parallel point, see the discussion in Chapter 6 of women's control of the at-home birthing room.)

There is other evidence of the relatively higher respect for men's personal space. People give men a wider berth on streets and sidewalks than they give women. This type of behavior can easily be observed in any library with narrow stacks. When a man or a woman is sitting or standing in the middle of an aisle that is open at both ends, and another person wants to look at books at the other end of the aisle, women and men respond differently. Women tend to detour through another aisle, especially if the alternative is to brush close to a man, whereas men are more likely to walk straight through, especially if it is a woman blocking the aisle.

As the library example shows, touching behavior is also regulated by status relations. Higher-status people assume a right to touch and sometimes do not even notice what they are doing. Lower-status people, however, arouse a reaction if they touch higher-status people. A male boss may greet a subordinate in the morning by slapping him on the back and saying, "How are you doing there, Sam?" Even if boss and subordinate are on a first-name basis, Sam would not be wise to greet his boss in the same way. Research shows that both men and women respond positively to being touched by someone of higher status than themselves. Research also shows that "when the toucher and the recipient are of equal or ambiguous relative status . . . women generally respond positively to being touched whereas men generally react neutrally or negatively, particularly if the toucher is female" (Major 1981, 28).

In the occupational world, women such as secretaries or nurses are usually subordinate to men and are therefore touched regularly by people they themselves cannot touch, at least not without the contact being misinterpreted. (We will discuss this further shortly.) This touching behavior is not limited to situations in which the male toucher is clearly of higher occupational status than the female being touched. Men in blue-collar jobs touch white-collar female secretaries as freely as do men who are business executives. When receiving change, men of all statuses often prolong touching the hands of female sales clerks.

The differences in touching behavior are also clearly observable in nonoccupational settings. A favorite game for boys of all ages is grazing against women's breasts or bottoms "accidentally." Even when men are not playing this type of sexual game, they are much more likely to touch women than women are to touch men. Women sometimes find strange men holding them by the back or shoulders as they move past in buses and aisles, or they find themselves pushed into small segments of bus seats because the man next to them is using his right-of-way to spread himself out. Men, much more than women, drape their arms across the backs of the chairs of the people sitting next to them.

One of the best-known observers of gender and nonverbal behavior, Nancy Henley, writes of an encounter she had with two high-status administrators at a university where she was working (1977, 95):

> After a large meeting one spring, the Vice Chancellor came over to me and took my upper arms in his two hands, saying he wanted to tell me something; he continued holding me in this restrictive fashion as he proceeded to talk with me. After he finished, and he had finally let go, I grabbed him back, then remarked that I would have to tell him sometime about my thesis which is [about gender and touching behavior]. He expressed interest, so I began telling him about it, and he found it plausible; at this moment the Chancellor approached, the only man on campus with higher authority, laid his hand on the arm of the Vice Chancellor, and urged him to accompany him to the next meeting. The V.C. and I were both struck by the aptness of this action and I think I made my point.

This story also illustrates the point that higher-status people are relatively free to interrupt lower-status people.

Research shows that dominance-deference relations are displayed even in touching behavior between male and female intimates. Among couples it is still expected that sexual contact will be initiated by the male. One study (Borden and Homleid 1978) of heterosexual couples walking together holding hands found that if one member of the couple is left-handed and the other is right-handed, they walk with their dominant hands clasped together. If they are both either left- or right-handed, however, the man tends to hold the woman's weaker hand with his dominant hand.

Gender norms and status also influence eye contact. We sometimes call initiation of contact with another person "catching the person's eye." Initiation of eye contact, especially staring, is the prerogative of higher-status people, and once again both research and common experience suggest that it is also the prerogative of men. When a woman and a man who do not know each other pass on a street and catch each other's eyes, the woman ordinarily drops her gaze first. If the woman holds her gaze, it may be interpreted as an invitation to sexual pursuit.[8] Men are supposed to approach women or initiate relationships, not the reverse (Green and Sanders 1983).

What happens when women violate the traffic rules of space? Think of a woman who sits with her arms and legs spread out, who stares at, touches, and drapes herself on strange men. What message will a man receive from such a woman? Most women are fully aware that if they sit with their arms spread back rather than in front of them, men are likely to become distracted and stare at their chest. (It is difficult to have a serious conversation with someone who is staring at your chest.) Thus, when a woman behaves the same way men do in their use of space, she communicates a very different message.

Some research has examined gender differences in the relationship between the use of public space and status. It seems natural to us, for example, that in groups the leader or the person of highest status should sit at the head of the table or alone in the front of the room. When husband and wife sit at opposite ends of the family dinner table, the man's place is usually called the "head" of the table, and the woman's the "foot." This arrangement helps the higher-status person control the situation and be the focal point of communication.

Natalie Porter and Florence Geis (1981) did some interesting research showing that the differentiated status rankings of women and men are strong enough to overcome the convention that the person of highest status occupies the authoritative position. They showed subjects pictures of a group of people sitting around a table. Some groups were all male or all female, and some were mixed. Each showed one person at the short end of the table and three people down each side. Whenever a man was shown sitting at the head of the table, most observers perceived him to be the leader of the group. In all-female groups, the woman at the head of the table was also perceived to be the leader of the group. In mixed groups, however, when a woman occupied the head of the table, many people chose one of the men at the sides of the table as the leader. Thus space use and positioning is an important indicator of status, but gender may be even more important.

This study is similar in implication to another in which students were given diagrams of a rectangular table and told they were going to meet either Professor Susan Smith or Professor Henry Smith there. When asked where they would seat themselves, most placed the professor at the head of the table. This was not true in all cases, however. The students were more likely to choose the head of the table for themselves when meeting Professor Susan Smith than when meeting Professor Henry Smith (Lott and Sommer 1967).

RIGHT-OF-WAY IN CONVERSATION. Women talk so much that men "can't get a word in edgewise," or so the old stereotype goes. If so, it seems that women must have the right-of-way in conversation. Research shows, however, that in mixed-group discussions not only do men both talk more and take stronger leads in discussions, but also they employ techniques, often unconsciously, that silence women and diminish their abilities to influence the group. Where, then, do people get the idea that women talk too much? Consider this pattern found by linguists: Higher-status people often think that people of lower status talk and interrupt more than they do, even though research shows that it is higher-status people who talk and interrupt more.

Men employ a number of techniques that curb and limit women's speech. The most important is that they interrupt women considerably more often than they interrupt other men or than women interrupt anyone else. One study found that over 90% of all interruptions in conversation were instigated by men (Zimmerman and West 1975; see also Smith-Lovin and Brody 1989). Men are more likely to overlap women's speech or to begin talking after women have begun and continue to talk at the same time. One person may sustain these speech challenges either by forcibly holding his or her ground and continuing to speak or even by saying something such as, "I'm not finished yet." Men are more likely to sustain challenges than women are (Smith-Lovin and Brody 1989).

Despite the assumed right to interrupt and overlap that higher-status people (men) have, there are some variations in the pattern. A study of sex and race differences showed that white males and black females are particularly likely to sustain verbal challenges (Adams 1980), suggesting that white females are especially susceptible to being silenced by men's challenges.

One of the intriguing aspects of studying communication behavior is its complexity and subtlety. A person's speech may be stopped by a verbal challenge, but it may also be stopped by silence. We tend to require some indication that the other person is paying attention in conversation. Listeners demonstrate attentiveness by verbal conventions, such as adding the occasional *mm-hmm*, *uh-huh*, *oh*, *yeah*, or laughing appropriately or, in face-to-face conversations, by nonverbal behavior: nodding or some facial response. If the listener does not use these conventions during a telephone conversation, the speaker is likely to elicit a response purposely or even to ask, "Are you still there?" Showing no response tends to distract the speaker and eventually kill the conversation. Men tend to do this to women more often than women do it to men.

Other patterns emerge in discussions among women and men. Men initiate new topics more than women do, but this is partly because a man is especially likely to introduce a topic other than the one a woman is discussing. A higher proportion of men's sentences are statements, a higher proportion of women's are questions. Some observers even suggest that in a discussion in which a woman has made a valuable point, it is often attributed by others to a male in the group.[9]

These differences in verbal behavior are reinforced in day-to-day life by the different positions males and females who interact are likely to hold. In cases involving a male boss and a female secretary or other subordinate or a male doctor and a female patient, part of the man's right-of-way is derived from the higher status of his position. Males, however, tend to take a right-of-way reflecting higher status regardless of their occupational positions. Even when women hold high-status positions they do not gain, or do not use, the same privileges in communication traffic. Female doctors, for example, are much less likely than male doctors to use their positions to dominate verbal interactions with patients. Patients, moreover, interrupt female doctors more than they interrupt male doctors (West 1984).[10]

THE RIGHT-OF-WAY: CONCLUSION. Thus far we have seen that the traffic rules of communication and interaction are governed in part by a hierarchical relationship between women and men, by patterns of dominance and deference and a male right-of-way. Victor A. Thompson's work (1961) on communication and hierarchy offers an instructive way of looking at this relationship and its impact on communication behavior. Although he was specifically considering the relationship between manager and subordinate in a bureaucratic organization, Thompson's analysis is appropriate for other kinds of hierarchies as well, including the one that exists between women and men.

Thompson argues that status and hierarchy rankings are reflected in the rights and duties individuals have with regard to transmitting and accepting information and directives. Superiors have communication rights, and subordinates have communication duties or obligations. Many of these rights and duties are left unstated, even in formal organizations, because the rules are obvious to everyone.

Thompson (1961, 60–66) listed the communication rights of the superior in a hierarchical relationship:

1. The right to veto or affirm the goals or proposals of subordinates
2. The right to expect obedience and loyalty
3. The right to monopolize communication both within the organizational unit and between the unit and the outside world (especially the latter)
4. The right to expect deference from subordinates
5. The right to be "somewhat insensitive as to subordinates' personal needs"

Thompson further argues that there is a "halo effect of status" that "requires high-status persons to speak out on all sorts of matters from a position of almost complete ignorance" (1961, 67). Subordinates in a hierarchical relationship have a series of obligations that are the inverse of superiors' rights. Subordinates are expected to leave the final word to superiors, to defer to superiors, to be obedient and loyal, and to be aware of and responsive to superiors' needs and desires.

These descriptions aptly characterize the communication behavior between women and men, partly because in most occupations and organizations women remain segregated in the lower-status subordinate positions. Even within the institution of the family women are traditionally supposed to be obedient, loyal, and deferential. The double standard of loyalty is illustrated by the double standard of sexual morality, in which women are expected to be more sexually loyal than men. Family communication is also structured by status relationships. Although women are central to communication within the family (particularly in the absence of the husband/father) and between the family and outsiders, many of the most important communications between the family and other institutions are expected to be carried out by the husband or under his supervision. The trite (and not always true) image of the unequal degree of sensitivity husbands and wives show toward each others' needs and feelings at the end of a hard day of work illustrates the different responses women and men evince toward each others' needs.

Does the interaction between women and men follow hierarchical patterns of communication only because women and men occupy different formal positions in organizations, or do these hierarchical patterns exist between women and men as such? Is gender in and of itself a status marker that leads to hierarchical patterns of interaction? We have much of the answer already: Evidence of the male right-of-way is exhibited in many day-to-day informal interactions. Gender-based communication patterns conform remarkably well to Thompson's analysis of organizations. The male right-of-way allows men to monopolize communication, to veto or affirm subordinates' goals or proposals, to gain deference, and to be insensitive to subordinates' personal needs. When women use patterns of interaction that show hesitation and self-deprecation, they become parties to this dominance–deference system.

Women appear to be better equipped than men to respond to the needs of others. A review of 75 studies shows that women are better able than men to decode other people's nonverbal cues (Hall 1978). The ability to read people's behavior can be interpreted as a defensive skill developed by low-status people; African Americans have also been found to be particularly skillful at behavior decoding. For both women and African Americans these skills are especially strong in detecting negative feelings and reactions. Women also look at people with whom they interact more than men do, which can be interpreted as part of this "reading" behavior. Consider these findings in relation to two characteristics often attributed to women: intuition and "oversensitivity."

The one observation by Thompson that we have not yet discussed is that high status "requires" a person to "speak out on all sorts of matters from a standpoint of almost complete ignorance." We have seen that women speak more hesitantly than men. At least one study suggests that men may indeed be more willing to speak on the basis of little knowledge. Political scientist Ronald Rapoport (1981) studied people who voiced political opinions in public opinion surveys. He divided his sample into three groups: those who seemed, respectively, very, moderately, and unknowledgeable about politics, then compared the first and last groups. Rapoport found that knowledgeable men and women were equally willing or able to offer opinions on political issues to the interviewer. In contrast, unknowledgeable men continued to voice opinions, while unknowledgeable women tended either to acknowledge their ignorance or to offer no opinion. Rapoport's work suggests that, at least in the male-dominated field of politics, men may be more willing to discuss things about which they know very little, perhaps because of gender-role pressure not to appear ignorant.

One of the most important features of the relationship between gender and communication is that people expect women to exhibit the communication and interaction patterns characteristic of subordinates. Consider some of the standard stereotypic traits people define as feminine: yielding, loyal, sympathetic, sensitive to the needs of others, understanding, and soft-spoken (Bem 1975). In contrast, stereotypic male traits include defending one's own beliefs, taking a stand, and acting as a leader (Bem 1975). As we have seen many times, if people expect women and men to conform to gender-stereotyped norms, they will perceive and treat women and men as though they are actually conforming to these norms.

It might seem that the principle "ladies before gentlemen" contradicts the argument about the male right-of-way. Men are supposed to open doors for women and allow them to enter rooms first, to help them put on and remove their coats, to pull out chairs for them, to rise when they enter rooms, and to remove hats in their presence. Men are also supposed to refrain from swearing in women's presence and, in the past, to save their talk about aggressive topics such as sports, business, and politics until the "ladies" left the room. Many a woman has voiced her objection to feminism by saying, "I believe in equal pay for equal work, but I still like a man to open doors for me." What are the implications of these social customs for questions of gender and the right-of-way?

As early as the late 18th century, Mary Wollstonecraft argued that male chivalry was a ruse, albeit an unconscious one. Since that time feminists have continued to ask *which* doors men open for women and why they do so. As with other behaviors and interactions, to understand these acts we must examine the circumstances under which they are done, why they are done, and how they relate to other acts. Most feminists argue that men who take the right-of-way when it really counts but continue to open doors for women or help them put on their coats are showing paternalistic power, symbolically reinforcing the ideas of men as stronger and in control and women as delicate and dependent. Such chivalry sometimes interferes with women's work as when a businesswoman meets chivalrous resistance to picking up the luncheon check for her client. What would be wrong with a system of politeness in which people hold doors for each other? After all, the woman who can manage to carry the laundry or a toddler without male help can surely manage a door.

Strategies of Power and Influence

Thus far we have been discussing research that reconfirms the existence of a hierarchical sex/gender system in both structures of social institutions and in people's everyday behavior. Let us turn directly to questions of power and influence in social interaction. When women and men are trying to influence others or achieve their own goals in a social setting, do they behave differently? There is certainly a widespread view that women and men use different strategies of influence and that they use and react to power differently. But as usual, it is considerably easier to find evidence that people *think* there are gender differences than to find evidence that women and men actually act differently in similar circumstances. Studies of women and men who hold formal positions of power in business, for example, generally find substantial similarity between women's and men's exercise of authority (Colwill, 1982).

Many theorists have argued that men and women do use different styles of influence, although surprisingly few have attempted to provide convincing and systematic empirical evidence. One line of thinking suggests that women's and men's communication goals, and therefore behavior, are different. Sociologist Talcott Parsons (1951) led his field for a long time in arguing that men emphasize instrumental values (getting things done) while women emphasize expressive values (creating group harmony and good feelings).[11] Others have offered variations on this theme, including those who suggest that men emphasize agentic values (concern for the impact of the individual on decisions and activities), and women emphasize communal values (concern for the group, group values, and group activities).

There is some evidence for these theories, but it is not strong and consistent. David Buss (1981) found, for example, that when people were asked about the desirability of 100 different acts of dominance, the ones found less desirable by women than by men were acts of "unmitigated agency" (variations of selfishness). The ones found more desirable by women were more mixed and communal acts. Likewise, the acts Buss's subjects considered less desirable when performed by women than by men were the highly agentic acts. (One of these was "She/he refused to cook or clean the house.") Overall, however, when the subjects were asked which acts they themselves had ever performed, the men claimed to have performed more acts of dominance of almost all sorts.

Other theorists leave aside overall goals and look specifically at strategies of influence. Paula Johnson (1976), for example, argues that the style a person uses to exert influence may fall along three different continua: direct–indirect, personal–concrete, and helplessness–competence. Johnson claims that women's and men's attempts to exert influence can be distinguished along all three lines. Women display a more indirect, and even manipulative, style than men, tend to rely on personal appeals, and use a style that rests on helplessness ("I need your help") rather than on arguments or displays of competence. What causes these differences? For a long time, feminist theorists have argued that women use whatever strategies of influence are open to them. If they are not allowed to be direct and forthright, they will find devious means to obtain their objectives. If this is true, it is easy to see how women might be trapped into fulfilling the stereotype of the sneaky, manipulative woman.

Johnson and others have found evidence that people do consider these different styles particularly masculine or feminine and that they react more positively to someone who uses the "gender-appropriate" style. One study, for example, asked subjects to react to speeches by a man and a woman who used either the "male" power base of expertise or the "female" power base of helplessness. The subjects responded more positively to the male speaker than to the female when both used the power base of expertise, and they responded more positively to the female speaker than to the male when they both used the power base of helplessness. When the investigators compared the subjects' attitudes toward speakers of a single sex according to the style of speech used, they found that the subjects preferred the speakers who used "gender-appropriate" speech, regardless of sex (Falbo, Hazen, and Linimon 1982).

Evidence of actual behavioral differences between men and women are not as easy to find. Certainly, men are more likely than women to employ physical violence to get their way, as crime statistics show, but what of more peaceful means? In one study (Instone, Major, and Bunker 1983), men made more attempts to influence others than women do in similar situations and they used a wider variety of types of influence. At the same time, these small gender differences in the types of influence strategies all but disappeared when the researchers took the subjects' levels of self-confidence into account. In other words, women used different strategies of influence because they had less self-confidence than men. In the same study, both women and men had lower expectations of success when trying to influence the opposite sex than when they were trying to influence members of their own sex.

A number of studies look at use of direct and coercive techniques of influence such as using threats. Not surprisingly, people are more likely to use coercive techniques when they think they have little chance of influencing others otherwise. Interestingly, one study found that men and women trying to influence people of the other sex used more coercive strategies than those trying to influence people of their own sex (Instone, Major, and Bunker 1983). A study of business managers found no overall gender differences in how direct or polite were their efforts to influence others (Hirokawa, Mickey, and Miura 1991). Instead, communication behavior was related to the managers' positions. Those with high "request legitimacy"—that is, whose positions gave them more right to seek compliance of others—tended to use more direct and less polite means of influencing others than did those with less request legitimacy. In real life, of course, men occupy most of the business positions of high request legitimacy. But the same study did find one important gender difference. Among those who had high request legitimacy, men used more direct and less polite means of influence than women. We can interpret this in two different ways. Men might be more likely than women to forget about politeness and consideration of subordinates when they reach high positions. Or, even when women reach high positions, they may still perceive themselves as having less request legitimacy. We cannot tell from this study which is true.

Gender differences in interaction have been detected relatively early in childhood. Patrice Miller, Dorothy Danaher, and David Forbes (1986) observed children's interactions on a playground and found girls and boys both used a range of strategies to deal with conflict, but they also noted some differences. Boys were more likely than girls to start with "heavy-handed" behavior (aggression) whether they were interacting with girls or boys. Girls were also heavy-handed at times, but only with boys and not so quickly. The strategies girls used more often included acknowledging the feelings of others, changing the topic, and displaying anger indirectly.

Overall there is considerable evidence that women and men are expected to use different types of influence and are viewed more favorably when they do. We also have some evidence that there are gender differences in strategies for exerting social influence. As usual in the world of stereotypes, we cannot always trust our eyes. Men are perceived as using more controlling or forceful strategies of influence than women even when they are not actually doing so (Burrell, Donahue, and Allen 1988). The interesting question is why these differences occur. Here are three possible answers:

1. Women and men occupy different positions in social institutions, and they use the forms appropriate to their positions.
2. Strategies for exerting social influence depend in part on self-confidence and expectations of success, and women and men do not experience similar levels of self-confidence or anticipation of success in similar situations.
3. Social pressure is exerted on individuals to make their behavior conform to appropriate gender norms. People are not liked or accepted as much when they deviate from the norm.

Perhaps the most difficult aspect of communication to study is not what people communicate but what they do not communicate. Subordinates have to be careful of how they act in front of those who are more powerful, and there is plenty of evidence that women use their knowledge of gender norms to protect themselves. Women learn to mask their abilities in "masculine" areas in order to avoid the possibility of punishment or rejection. They have variously hidden their sexuality or faked orgasms (as Sally graphically points out in the movie *When Harry Met Sally*) in order to avoid the dangers of offending men's sexual sensibilities. They often expend considerable effort controlling their reactions to sexual harassment. It is more important for women than men to keep smiling no matter how they are feeling (Deutsch, LeBaron, and Fryer 1987).

If gender subordination creates a special need to be strategic about self-presentation, women who face additional problems of social subordination face a multiplied need for care. For example, in a homophobic society lesbian women cannot avoid having to confront issues of whether to mask their sexuality. Darlene Clark Hine has written very powerfully about the culture of dissemblance among black women, or "the behavior and attitudes of Black women that created the appearance of openness and disclosure but actually shielded the truth of their inner lives and selves from their oppressors" (1989, 912).

Hine argues that the effort to appear open while hiding one's persona was an imperative of the conditions of oppression and sexual violence:

> A secret, undisclosed persona allowed the individual Black woman to function, to work effectively as a domestic in white households, to bear and rear children, to endure the frustration-born violence of frequently under- or unemployed mates, to support churches, to found institutions, and to engage in social service activities, all while living within a clearly hostile white, patriarchal, middle-class America (1989, 916).

A study of African American domestics and their employers shows how the relations of dominance and subordination can trick those in a position of power into thinking that they know their subordinates when in fact they do not (Rollins 1985). The exact substance of what one reveals and fears revealing differs from one context of social subordination to another, but close inspection reveals elements of a culture of dissemblance in any group of people with experience of reprisals from a more powerful group. Women are no exception. But Hine recognizes the trap of dissemblance: It serves as an important strategy of self-protection but at the same time buttresses the system that provoked the dissemblance. It is not a trap of the victim's making, but if one plays dumb one looks dumb.

Future Options

The structure of communication has been the subject of heated controversy in recent decades. On one side are feminist activists and scholars who claim that the ways people express themselves and behave in social situations are determined and restricted by a gender ideology that grants men higher status and more power to control their own and others' lives than it grants to women. Moreover, feminists argue, the language we use to refer to men and women captures this androcentric and sexist ideology, thereby limiting the ways women can speak about and express themselves.

These foreclosures on women's options are particularly powerful for three reasons:

1. How to communicate and how to interact with others are among the first skills we learn in infancy. Learning how to express ourselves to other people and how to understand and react to others are in many ways the central tasks of learning to be human. If the structure of communication is determined by gender, the process of learning to be human is at the same time a process of learning how to be male or female, "masculine" or "feminine."
2. Many of the patterns discussed in this chapter become unconscious and automatic once they are learned. Many of the male behaviors described earlier that render women silent or ineffective are done unconsciously; men are unaware of what they are doing. Although we may speak of "choosing our words carefully," anyone who considered all the implications of every word, gesture, facial expression, posture, and reaction would quickly become immobilized.
3. Limiting language and communication patterns is so powerful because it is so ubiquitous, and its effects can be felt in so many ways. This chapter has emphasized everyday communication, but if we return to earlier discussions of the structure and impact of important social institutions it is possible to see numerous practical applications of these patterns. Consider the languages of health, theology, or politics and the gender-based patterns of interaction within health, religious, and political institutions. Any single instance of sexist communication—for example, a married woman's difficulty in getting people to address letters to her under her name rather than her husband's—may seem trivial. But together such instances form a comprehensive and enveloping system with enormous impact.

On the other side of the debate are people who attack any effort to analyze and change the style and structure of communication. Most of these efforts focus on attempts to eliminate sexist language. Let us look at some of the arguments against such efforts.

Some people argue that the movement to use gender-neutral or inclusive language strips our language of its richness and renders it awkward, ungrammatical, and odd sounding. In most cases this is simply because people are unaccustomed to nonsexist forms. Unfamiliar forms often sound awkward, and it feels awkward to have to think about terms that previously were used automatically. Many people worry about the difficulty of pronouncing *Ms.*, for example, when they have done perfectly well with the rhyming words *fizz*, *'tis*, and, certainly, *his*. When used fluently, nonsexist language is no more likely to be ungrammatical than sexist language: People certainly make grammatical mistakes in both forms.[12] But why is language that excludes women more rich and vivid than language that includes them? Some opponents of gender-neutral language claim

FIGURE 10-2

Nonsexist Treatment of Women and Men

1. Avoid typecasting in careers and activities.
   a. Avoid typecasting women in traditional roles.
   b. Avoid showing men as subject to the "masculine mystique" in interests, attitudes, and careers.
   c. Attempt to break job stereotypes for women and men.
   d. Show married women who work outside the home, and emphasize the point that women have choices about their marital status.
   e. Address course materials to students of both sexes.
   f. Portray women and girls as active participants the same as men and boys, and not only in connection with cooking, sewing, shopping.
2. Represent members of both sexes as whole human beings.
   a. Represent women and men with human (not just feminine or masculine) strengths and weaknesses. Characteristics praised in males should also be praised in females.
   b. As in portraying men and boys, show women and girls also as active, logical, accomplishing.
   c. Sometimes show men as quiet and passive, fearful and indecisive, just as women are sometimes portrayed.
3. Accord women and men the same respect, and avoid either trivializing women or describing them by physical attributes when men are described by mental attributes.
   a. Avoid: (1) girl-watching tone and sexual innuendoes; (2) focusing on physical appearance; (3) using female-gender word forms, such as "poetess"; (4) treating women as sex objects or as weak and helpless; (5) making women figures of fun or scorn (not "the weaker sex," but "women"; not "libber," but "feminist").
   b. Avoid references to general ineptness of males in the home or dependence on women for meals.
   c. Treat women as part of the rule, not the exception (not "woman doctor," but "doctor"). Avoid gee-whiz attitude toward women who perform competently.
   d. Represent women as participants in the action, not as possessions of men. (Not "Pioneers moved West, taking their wives and children," but "Pioneer women and men moved West, taking their children.")
   e. Avoid portraying women as needing male permission to act.
4. Recognize women for their own achievements.
5. In references to humanity at large, use inclusive language.
   a. Avoid the generic word *man*, since it is often not interpreted broadly. (Not "mankind," but "humanity"; not "manmade," but "artificial"; not "primitive man," but "primitive peoples.")
   b. Avoid the generic pronouns he, him, his in reference to a hypothetical person or humanity in general.
      (1) Reword sentence. (Not "The average American drinks his coffee black," but "The average American drinks black coffee.")
      (2) Recast into plural. ("Most Americans drink their coffee black.")
      (3) Replace the pronoun with "one," "you," "he or she," and so forth.
      (4) Alternate male and female expressions and examples: "I've often heard supervisors say, 'She's not the right person for the job,' or 'He lacks the qualifications.' "
      (5) If the generic *he* is used, explain in the preface and in the text that the reference is to both females and males.

c. Replace occupational terms ending in -man by inclusive terms. (Not "businessman," but "business manager"; not "fireman," but "firefighter."
d. Avoid language that assumes all readers are male. (Not "you and your wife," but "you and your spouse.")

6. Use language that designates and describes the sexes equally.
a. Use parallel language for women and men. (Not "man and wife," but "husband and wife" or "man and woman." Not "Billie Jean and Riggs," but "King and Riggs" or "Billie Jean and Bobby.")
b. Identify women by their own names, not in terms of their roles as wife, mother, and so forth. (Not "Nehru's daughter," but "Indira Gandhi.") Avoid unnecessary reference to marital status.
c. Use terms that include both sexes; avoid unnecessary references to gender.
d. Use nonsexist job titles. (Not "maid" and "house boy," but "house cleaner" or "office cleaner.")
e. Avoid linking certain pronouns with certain work or occupations. Pluralize or else use "he or she" or "she and he." (Not "the shopper... she," but "shoppers . . . they"; not "the breadwinner . . . his earnings," but "the breadwinner . . . her or his earnings."
f. Do not always mention males first. Alternate the order: "women and men," "gentlemen and ladies," "she or he."

Source: Eakins and Eakins (1978, 186–97).

to find language that includes women less authoritative and weaker than traditional male forms. (See, for example, the discussion of male God language in Chapter 7.) This is precisely the point: Our language reflects and supports the values and power structure of the surrounding society.

Some people object to language change on the grounds that language is a valuable cultural possession with which we must not tamper. They remind us of the horrors of "Newspeak," the language used in the fictional world created by George Orwell in his novel *1984.* In that frightening world the government dictated that language conform to politically correct principles laid down by its Ministry of Truth. In the 1990s many people attacked language reform for exerting a regime of "political correctness." Language is indeed a valuable cultural possession, and Orwell was no doubt correct that language can be used to control the thoughts and lives of individuals and groups in society. This is precisely the point at hand. Who possesses language? Whom shall it serve? Who determines the uses to which it is put? Can a serious argument be made that we should continue to use a language that denigrates the majority of humanity? Can women and men choose to speak in a way that connotes respect for themselves?

Language changes over time as—because—human experience changes. Just as those who view women in ways that are defined by androcentric gender ideology find nonsexist language awkward and irritating, those who view women as complete beings and full members of society find androcentric language awkward and irritating. It is perhaps true that at times feminists and antifeminists do not understand each other; they speak different languages. The difference is that most feminists now alive have been, at least at some point in their lives, bilingual. They grew up with the old androcentric language and have learned the new inclusive language.

Changing the language we speak is not as easy as it might appear. Eliminating the most obvious signs of androcentrism is not difficult with a little thought, and numerous guides offer assistance. Some examples of the types of changes people might make can be found in the list in Figure 10-2, compiled by Barbara Eakins and Gene Eakins. Nonsexist language cannot flow naturally, however, if we do not experience the world in a nonsexist way. As discussed earlier, sexist language is not simply a matter of how one uses the word *man* or whether one retains *man and wife* and the asymmetrical *obey* in a marriage ceremony. If apparently gender-neutral words such as *love*, *selfishness*, *strength*, and *consent* are applied in different ways to men and women, language remains gender laden.[13] Concerning ourselves with language requires considering not only the words we utter but also the way we think.

Changing the patterns of social interaction is even more difficult and requires even more self-consciousness and will. Men and women who try to break free of the gender-based structure of interaction encounter resistance, frustration, and even pain. Some tasks are relatively easy, including extending common courtesies to both sexes rather than maintaining them as acts of male chivalry toward delicate females. But research on communication and interaction behavior suggests that women find acceptance or respect difficult to obtain and may be seen as loud, harsh, demanding, and overly masculine if they do not automatically yield the right-of-way to men or carry and present themselves confidently. Men may be regarded as weak if they choose to share ground with women more equally and treat them as more equal partners. Many feminists claim that the primary reason feminists seem to lack a sense of humor is that they don't find demeaning treatment amusing.

Individuals' choices in self-expression also are limited by the perceptions others have of them. The past two decades have witnessed the organization of numerous seminars, courses, and training groups designed to help people interact with others in a more egalitarian and respectful manner. Assertiveness training is aimed at helping women express themselves clearly and confidently; other groups work on the parallel task of helping men become more aware of what their patterns of behavior have done to women and learn how to change.

Feminist organizations have often experimented with different types of group interaction to try to achieve more open and participatory communication styles and to encourage the shy to assert themselves. Some feminist groups, for example, used to pass out chips or markers at the beginning of meetings. Each time a woman spoke she gave up a marker and could speak no more when she ran out of markers. This seems a very artificial way of managing interpersonal relations, but it can provide a lasting lesson about the nature of power, self-expression, and interaction. Feminist therapists have tied the issue of communication styles to the question of mental health. Feminist therapists not only work on clients' communication skills and abilities but also try to restructure the process of therapy to reflect a less hierarchical structure in the therapeutic relationship itself. Their argument is that therapists cannot meet the needs of clients if therapy takes place within a hierarchical environment.

One issue to which feminists have paid increasing attention in recent years is the degree to which women have used networks of communication. Women and men have always had networks within their separate spheres through which they sought and gave support and information and exerted social control. The system of "old boy" networks has long been recognized as important to men's lives. Unfortunately, although women's networks have been equally important to their lives, the value of these channels of communication has not been recognized until recently and in the past they have been dismissed as "kaffeeklatches," "hen sessions," and "ladies clubs."[14] Women now are taking their communication networks more seriously, partly because they find themselves excluded and isolated as they enter male-dominated occupations. Most recently, the growth of electronic communication has encouraged the growth of feminist electronic mail and bulletin boards. Throughout this book are references to the communication networks that women have established in almost all domains of life. Women are beginning to give voice to their needs and experiences.

NOTES

1. The notion of an "independent, autonomous" self does not imply that an individual is isolated from or unconnected to other people; rather, it refers to the idea that we can see ourselves as morally responsible social agents capable of making at least some choices.
2. Simone de Beauvoir makes a similar argument in *The Second Sex* (1952).
3. Interestingly, some people seem to think that the only people who use *Ms.* are single women, perhaps those who are somewhat embarrassed about being single. Some businesses include only the following options in check-off boxes on application forms: Ms., Mrs., Mr.
4. Recall the discussion of gendered and inclusive language in religion, Chapter 7.
5. Good reviews of this research can be found in Eakins and Eakins (1978).
6. Research also shows, however, that males are more likely than females to have speech impediments and defects (Eakins and Eakins 1978, 92–941).
7. A very good review of the research offering evidence for the points raised in the following discussion can be found in Henley (1977).
8. Try this as an experiment: Next time you are walking in a crowded area, pick a stranger out of the crowd and try to hold that person's eye. Use only your eyes. Observe what happens, how you feel, and how you think the other person feels.
9. This is related to the tendency for people to see women's work in the arts as derivative of men's (see Chapter 8).
10. For an excellent bibliography on women, language, and health care, see Treichler (1984).
11. For more discussion of Talcott Parsons see Chapter 2.
12. Sounding awkward and speaking incorrectly do not always go together. Most Americans seem to feel more comfortable with the split infinitive ("We need to care-

fully explore the gender implications of language") than they do with proper construction ("We need to explore carefully the gender implications of language"). Similarly, many people find it less awkward to say that "many surgeon generals have warned us against smoking" (which is incorrect) than "many surgeons general have warned us against smoking" (which is correct).

13. An excellent discussion of what *consent* means—and doesn't mean—when applied to women can be found in Pateman (1980).

14. For an influential historical view of women's networks, see Smith-Rosenberg (1975).

11

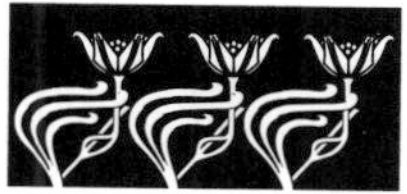

Consenting Adults? Personal and Sexual Relationships

THE MOST ABIDING concern of the centuries-old debate over women's roles and status is the relationship between men and women. Even in this persistence there has been historical change in the specific themes and problems addressed. In the 18th and 19th centuries, the argument focused almost entirely on marital rights and obligations. By the end of the 19th century, attention began to include issues concerning regulation of personal and sexual relations and male violence against women. More critics began to question the institution of marriage and its place in society. Although some theorists and activists in the 19th and especially the early 20th centuries began to rethink dominant assumptions about sexuality and the nature of personal relationships, not until recent decades was there wholesale public discussion of the construction of sexuality and its relationship to social structure and history. Now critiques of sexual and gender relationships focus not just on the way people think about relationships between women and men but also on relationships among women and among men.

This chapter looks at women's personal and, particularly, sexual relationships, focusing especially on the relationships among sexuality, gender, and sex/gender systems. We begin with the role gender plays in defining personal relationships, then turn to sexuality and sexual relationships. Finally we examine the social institution of marriage both to understand its structure and dynamics in relation to gender and to probe its significance as the primary organization through which societies institutionalize sexual and personal relationships. Above all this chapter is concerned with the degree to which women and men have been able to be "consenting adults" in their own lives, that is, to make their own choices about their relationships with other people.

Defining Personal Relationships

Human beings are social animals; few of us can live secluded from human contact. Conventional wisdom and stereotype offer us many statements about gender differences in personal relationships. Some (like Sigmund Freud) say that women cannot get along with each other because of their jealousy. Most people believe that men need sex more than women do. Women are supposedly fickle, although they are also thought to be less promiscuous and to need marriage more than men do. It is said that women are more enmeshed in social relationships than men are, that their lives are more bound by their relationships. Our task here is to look beyond conventional wisdom and even theory, to see what evidence we have about gender and personal relationships.

Gender and Personal Relationships

Because of the different structures of women's and men's lives, it is likely that the role played by personal relationships in their lives has also differed. A large proportion of men in industrialized societies spend much of their time in formal organizations with explicit lines of communication and procedures for dealing with problems. Women, on the other hand, have relied on more informal networks of female relatives, friends, neighbors, and others in their communities. Certainly men face social pressure to avoid showing dependence or weakness, which in turn prevents them from using friendships the way women do.

Contemporary emphasis on gender integration (the increasing tendency for women and men to share interests, activities, and roles) sometimes makes us forget how rich women's social networks can be. Modern ideas of personal networks often scorn the old-fashioned idea of segregated social life, and sometimes dismiss women's traditional relationships and activities as impoverished and limited compared with men's. In contrast, Carroll Smith-Rosenberg's research on relationships among women in the 19th century led her to conclude, "Women . . . did not form an isolated and oppressed subcategory in male society. . . . Women's sphere had an essential integrity and dignity that grew out of women's shared experiences and mutual affection" (1975, 9–10). As Smith-Rosenberg points out, it is no wonder: In a world that is highly sex segregated, to whom would women turn? Women turned to each other for solace and aid. They were each others' teachers; they helped each other give birth; and they helped each other die. Many historians are now investigating the importance of female friendships in women's lives (Freedman 1979; Ryan 1979; Leavitt 1983).

Smith-Rosenberg and others find in women's letters and other available documents evidence that women have long depended throughout their lives on the constancy and intimacy of their female friendships and kin. These historians are now correcting the problems Smith-Rosenberg identified in the early 1970s: "The female friendship of the nineteenth century, the long-lived, intimate, loving friendship between two women, is an excellent example of the type of phenomena which most historians know something about, which few have thought much about, and which virtually no one has written about" (1975, 1).

Research on contemporary women's lives has captured some of the same sense of closeness and interdependence among women including, for example, Carol Stack's (1974) work on black women in urban ghettos. We see hints of it in Mirra Komarovsky's (1967) study of married working-class women. Circumstances make it likely that female friendships have changed over time; for instance, male and female domains are more integrated than they once were and sexual mores have changed. Women can socialize with men more freely today without their relationships being regarded as sexual. Now women too are enmeshed in bureaucratic work places. Ironically the intimacy of some female friendships of the 19th century would today be interpreted as explicitly sexual and therefore might be inhibited.

Social scientists have observed some important gender differences in the types of relationships people have and the way they deal with relationships. Women, for example, are more likely to rate lying as unacceptable within friendship or romantic relationships. For women the act of lying within a relationship is more significant and provokes a more emotional reaction than is true for men (Levine, McCormack, and Avery 1992). If we put this difference together with some of the communication differences discussed in the previous chapter, we see there is considerable scope for misunderstanding between men and women as a normal part of their interaction. This will become even clearer shortly when we discuss sexual cues and perceptions.

It is interesting to compare the claims of anthropologist Lionel Tiger (1969), who argues that men's dominance in society stems in part from their greater "bonding instincts," with theorizing by feminist psychologists such as Carol Gilligan who claim that women define themselves more in terms of the web of social relationships and obligations in which they are enmeshed. In fact there has been more systematic relevant research on women's social relationships than on men's, leaving us with less ability to draw comparative conclusions than many people might think. But men generally report having more same-sex friends than women. At the same time, men seem to define friendship differently. They define as "friends" those with whom they are not as emotionally close or intimate as is true for women's "friends." While men often view their special male friends as people with whom they go in groups to drink or play sports, women are more likely to define their special friends as the people with whom they can share confidences and to whom they can turn when they feel vulnerable.

Robert Lewis (1978) speculates that the relative distance between male friends is the result both of men's fears of appearing vulnerable and of *homophobia* (the fear of homosexuality). He points out that men often discover their most intimate and close male relationships in two special activities: sports and war. Lewis suggests that American men are especially likely to avoid touching each other "unless it is roughly done as in a game of football or other contact sport" (1978, 112). To this we might add ritual greetings such as slaps on the back or handshakes. The link between social and sexual norms is related to people's cultural backgrounds. For example, heterosexual American men generally do not kiss each other or dance with each other, but men in some other countries are more physically expressive; many, for example, have dances that only men do with other men. In recent years, part of the men's movement has focused on developing closer relationships among men.

Defining Sexuality and Sexual Relationships

Studying the social and cultural construction of sexuality is a crucial part of understanding sex/gender systems because women have been defined largely as sexual objects of men within an androcentric society. As work places and other parts of society have become more gender integrated, one problem men have worried over is what to do about the introduction not just of women but of sexuality in places where it doesn't belong. In other words, to introduce women other than those in auxiliary positions such as nurses and secretaries into male-dominated work places is to introduce misplaced sexuality. It is difficult to understand gender relations without understanding sexual relations.

How can we distinguish between a sexual and a nonsexual relationship? This question might seem odd at first. Isn't the answer obvious? The answer is no, as, for example, people trying to develop practical policies to deal with sexual harassment and even rape find out. For that matter, most people have had specific relationships in which they were not at all sure whether there was a sexual or romantic element involved, or to what degree. It is often difficult to distinguish between sexual and other types of intimacy and even between sexuality and violence. These confusions are created partly by the relationship between sexual and gender norms.

Sigmund Freud was the theorist most responsible for alerting us to the difficulties of distinguishing between sexual and other relationships and feelings. Freud's views on the matter were more radical than most people probably accept, but it is worth reviewing them to see some of the most important questions and controversies.[1]

Freud argued that the instincts, or unconscious drives, resemble undifferentiated formless energy. The libido is thus simply a generalized drive for stimulation and pleasure, similar in men and women. For Freud, then, there is no instinctual difference between seeking one or another kind of pleasure, and the libido knows nothing of morality or guilt. Freud, in fact, labeled platonic love and attachment "aim-inhibited eroticism"—in other words, an erotic or pleasure-seeking relationship in which the sexuality is repressed.

Only through socialization, repression (the process of excluding these drives from consciousness), sublimation (transforming basic erotic drives into less threatening or more acceptable forms), and even direct coercion do people channel their pleasure seeking into acceptable forms and make conscious distinctions among feelings and actions they might describe as sexual and nonsexual, aggressive and nonaggressive, good and bad, normal and perverted. Shame, guilt, and morality are alien to the infant and remain alien to the adult unconscious. Unconscious drives threaten our conscious senses of self and morality, so the psyche works to reduce the resulting tension by transforming or reinterpreting the meaning of these drives.

Even if one does not fully accept the psychoanalytic viewpoint, it does illuminate questions that need asking: What is the essential difference between a sexual and a nonsexual caress? What is the fundamental difference between platonic and nonplatonic love and affection? Is the difference merely where and how people touch one another, or whether people consciously initiate genital contact for the purpose of giving or receiving pleasure? Why does there seem to be such a strong link between sexuality and aggression or dominance behavior? As Susan Brownmiller (1975) points out, rape has often been used as an instrument of war and domination. One fast walk through an adult bookstore reveals how much of what people consider erotic involves aggression, violence, and domination. It can, at times, be difficult to distinguish between physical struggle and sexual passion.

Hot flashes. Tingles. Shakes. Dizziness. A need to cling to someone. What are we describing? Fear? A fever? Or sexual arousal? It could be any of these.

The early phases of sexual arousal resemble other states of emotional arousal. How then do we distinguish between sexual and other feelings? Cognitive psychology indicates that people take their cues at least as much from the situation as from their feelings (Rook and Hammer, 1977). Cues offered by the situation make an individual label an instance of emotional arousal as sexual rather than something else. Both cognitive psychology and psychoanalytic theory, then, argue that we have both motive and capability to understand similar feelings in different ways. If our upbringing tells us that we should not be sexually aroused in a given situation or by a particular stimulus, even if we find ourselves aroused in that situation we are likely to label our emotional response in terms other than sexual. People learn what is generally regarded as sexually arousing. Experimental research shows that it is even possible for a person to mislabel an emotional reaction (White, Fishbein, and Rutstein 1981). Most of us probably have heard someone say, for example, "I thought I felt like it—but then I realized I really didn't. It was all a mistake." The implication here is not that the speaker has changed his or her mind, but that the original feeling was misunderstood.

If people have difficulty interpreting their own feelings, they are certainly going to have difficulty interpreting those of others. This is a particularly acute problem for men and women in two additional respects:

1. Males and females communicate differently (see Chapter 10) and therefore can misunderstand each other. This misunderstanding may be especially great on the part of men, who tend to be less able to read nonverbal signals than women.
2. Sexual norms tend to define women as sexual objects and men as sexual pursuers with a right-of-way in sexuality and communication.

What are the practical effects of these problems? As Antonia Abbey notes,

> Available literature on date and acquaintance rape suggests that males are unable to distinguish females' friendly behavior from their seductive behavior because of the differential meaning that the relevant cues have for the two sexes. Men may have been socialized to view any form of friendly behavior from a woman as an indicator of sexual interest (1982, 831).

Abbey's own experimental research provides additional evidence that men read sexual messages into women's behavior that neither the women themselves nor other female observers see. Indeed, men perceive greater sexuality than women in the behavior of both women and men (Shotland and Craig 1988). There are also circumstances in which women read sexual cues into other women's behavior that men claim not to see.

These studies might merely help explain the small dramas of crossed signals between men and women were it not for two points. First, the situations involving conflicting definitions of sexuality are neither random nor merely occasional; they constitute a widespread pattern that reflects a gender-based and androcentric sexual ideology. Women find they have to be on guard constantly to avoid being misinterpreted by men. Second, conflicts in the definition of sexuality play an important role in two serious problems that confront most women at least indirectly: sexual harassment and rape.

Sex, Coercion, and Violence

Male and female sexuality and sexual roles are very different according to the dominant American sexual ideology. Men are still supposed to be more sexually active and interested, playing the role of sexual initiator and leader. In the words of romance novels, men "take" women, while women "give" themselves or, at least, are "swept away." Young men are pressured to conform to this role and to exploit women sexually. The ideology supporting male sexual dominance makes it difficult for men to cope with more independent and self-assured women, and the pressure to conform to the standard of the conquering sexual hero creates strains of its own for men (Komarovsky 1976; Harrison 1978).

Societies differ in their sexual ideologies, and comparative research indicates that the sexual double standard tends to be more apparent in cultures in which women lack power relative to men. As Naomi McCormick and Clinton Jesser write,

> Male-dominated societies seem to permit men to use power to have sex while women are allowed to exercise power only to avoid sex with unsuitable partners. In such a society, a woman who uses power to seduce a man openly is regarded as "bad" and possibly dangerous. A man who uses power to avoid sex with a "turned on" woman is regarded as "religious" at best, and "inept, stupid, and unmanly" at worst (1983, 68–69).

Just as the research provides evidence of a male right-of-way in communication,[2] there is a male right-of-way in sexuality. That right-of-way is an everyday problem for women. It is one of the most important buttresses of male power over women in most domains. Let us look at sexual harassment and rape to see how this sexual right-of-way plays out.

Sexual Harassment

A professor repeatedly suggests that rather than meeting during office hours it might be better to discuss the student's directed reading work in the evening over drinks. During these sessions the professor sits uncomfortably close and keeps turning the conversation to personal issues. A secretary finds herself constantly distracted at work by her boss, who usually gets her attention by putting his hands on her neck or back and often makes comments about her dress. An anatomy instructor mixes pin-ups from *Playboy* among the slides he shows in lecture, making "just us boys" cracks that embarrass the women students and encourage the men to laugh at their female colleagues' discomfort. An employer indicates to an employee that unless they have sexual relations together, the next evaluation will not be a good one.

Sexual harassment involves the use of sexuality as a tool of power or dominance. Most women have been victimized by it at some time or another, although many just thought that "being hassled" was a normal part of life and had no particular name. This became clear in 1991 when a law professor, Anita Hill, testified to a Senate committee that the nominee for Supreme Court judge, Clarence Thomas, had harassed her on the job years before. This case caught the nation's attention and became the subject of tremendous debate in part because of the issues it raised about what constitutes sexual harassment, who the perpetrators are, who the victims are, and what should be done about it. Could a lawyer and high official in charge of equal opportunity policy have engaged in harassment? Could a lawyer actually have been a victim, continued to work for him, and remained silent for 10 years as Hill claimed she had done? Whichever of these two people was telling whatever kind of truth or falsehood, millions of women across the country learned the name of the problem that had afflicted them for years and told journalists, public opinion pollsters, and probably in some cases, their bosses, teachers, doctors, and colleagues that they had had enough.[3]

Sexual harassment of women by strangers in public used to be more common, when most women passing a construction site were bombarded with catcalls, hoots, whistles, and sexual innuendoes. Many women still experience passing groups of men on a street who engage in such public taunting. The purpose of this behavior is, at minimum, to make a woman feel embarrassed and self-conscious—that is, to exert psychological power over her. She is not allowed to be anything but a submissive recipient. If she were to say politely that she didn't like the situation, the laughter and remarks probably would increase. If she were to react angrily, the remarks probably would become more aggressive and abusive, often making the undercurrent of sexual dominance and violence more explicit ("Why don't you go home and make babies," or "What you need is a good fuck"). Women are subject to this kind of psychological assault unless they are accompanied by a male protector, although such assaults appear more subtly in many social settings.

Sexual harassment has taken on a more specific legal meaning because of increasing awareness of how it becomes an instrument of domination in the work place and in educational institutions. Such harassment may take a number of forms, ranging from verbal or physical sexual innuendoes, which women are expected to receive cheerfully or passively, to superiors' expectations of sexual favors in return for career or educational advancement. Harassment can involve making sexual activity or at least toleration of insults a job requirement.

Sexual harassment has serious consequences for women's ability to gain an education and earn a living. Research repeatedly shows that most employed women experience at least some sexual harassment (Backhouse and Cohen 1981).

Women who have been victims of sexual harassment overwhelmingly report that they feel embarrassed, demeaned, intimidated, angry, or upset. Many are frightened or suffer physiological symptoms, such as headaches, tiredness, and nervousness, brought on by stress (Backhouse and Cohen 1981). Thus the pressures of harassment may make it difficult for the woman to work effectively, which has a negative impact on the quality of the woman's work and decreases her employment opportunities. Indeed, a federal government study has estimated that the amount of job turnover, medical insurance claims, absenteeism, and reduced productivity due to sexual harassment may cost the economy $189 million over a 2-year period (Livingston 1982).

At first women who tried to seek legal remedies to harassment through the courts were usually unsuccessful. Most people, including judges, thought sexual harassment was a personal matter based on sexual attraction and that it had little if anything to do with the job. Men, who predominate as judges, are not as convinced as women that harassment is a problem, as shown by large-scale studies of federal employees (U.S. Merit Systems Protection Board 1981) and business executives (Collins and Blodget 1981). The survey of federal employees shows that although less than 25% of the female employees think reports of harassment have been exaggerated, more than 40% of the male employees do (Tangri, Burke, and Johnson 1982).

Catherine Mackinnon, one of the first legal theorists of harassment (1979), argues that there are two types of sexual harassment. The first is the "quid pro quo" type, in which sexual favors are required for a raise, promotion, or good evaluation or simply to retain one's job. Courts have slowly moved toward recognizing this form as illegal. In the 1970s, employers were held responsible for sexual harassment by employees or others at the work place only if the employer had a policy or practice compelling workers to submit to harassment. Employers are now held more responsible: They must show they have policies and procedures to stop harassment, and they must take prompt action when harassment problems are called to their attention.

An important advance was made when courts began to interpret at least some sexual harassment as a form of sex discrimination in employment, thus a violation of Title VII of the 1964 Civil Rights Act. The following passage from a 1977 U.S. Court of Appeals case shows how courts justify claiming that sexual harassment is sex discrimination:

> *But for her womanhood* . . . her participation in sexual activity would never have been solicited. To say, then, that she was victimized in her employment simply because she declined the invitation is to ignore the asserted fact that she was invited only because she was a woman subordinate to the inviter in the hierarchy of agency personnel. Put another way, she became the target of her superior's sexual desires because she was a woman and was asked to bow to his demands as the price for holding her job (*Barnes* v. *Castle*; emphasis added).

This logic raises an interesting problem. Its logic applies when a heterosexual male harasses a woman, when a heterosexual woman harasses a man, or when a homosexual man or woman harasses someone of his or her own sex. In each case the rule applies: But for the victim's sex he or she would not have been victimized. But what about a bisexual perpetrator? They are exempt from the logic of this decision.

The second type of harassment that Mackinnon describes is a constant and negative aspect of the work environment. Consider the secretary who is never asked directly or indirectly to trade sexual services for job benefits but is subjected to a constant flow of sexual remarks and nonverbal innuendoes. Until the early 1980s a woman in this situation had no legal recourse because unless she could show specific harm—mere constant stress wasn't enough—general harassment wasn't covered by the law. Then the law began to change, as the following passage from an important federal court case shows. Here the court made its point by comparing sexual harassment to the situations of workers exposed to constant racial or ethnic slurs at their work places:

> The relevance of these "discriminatory environment" cases to sexual harassment is beyond serious dispute. Racial or ethnic discrimination against a company's minority clients may reflect no intent to discriminate directly against the company's minority employees, but in poisoning the atmosphere of employment it violates Title VII. . . . How . . . can sexual harassment, which injects the most demeaning sexual stereotypes into the general work environment and which always represents an intentional assault on an individual's innermost privacy, not be illegal? (*Bundy* v. *Jackson* 1981)

An atmosphere of sexual harassment is a violation of equal employment law because it poisons the work environment selectively on the basis of sex, which is a violation of the law. Further, according to a 1986 Supreme Court decision, employers can be held responsible if their supervisory personnel engage in harassment (*Meritor Savings Bank* v. *Vinson*).

Although the law on sexual harassment has become stricter, most women still do not complain about harassment either because they don't think anything (or anything serious) would be done to the perpetrator or because they think they would be penalized for complaining. Indeed, men—who are likely to be the supervisors women would need to address—tend to think that harassment is not a serious problem and that women who claim to be harassed are actually misinterpreting men's friendly behaviors. The women, they say, should feel complimented that men pay such attention to them. Many believe that charges of harassment are phony and that what is really occurring is normal sexual interplay between men and women.

Perceptions of victim precipitation are involved in sexual harassment cases much as they are in cases of rape and domestic violence.[4] As in those cases, traditional sexual and gender ideology shapes the view of women as temptresses likely to make irrational charges of harm against men. Consider the evidence provided by a study of over 1,200 people, in which men were more likely than women to blame women for being sexually harassed (Jensen and Gutek 1982). The degree to which women blame themselves and other victims of harassment depends on their gender ideology. The more they believe in traditional divisions of labor and power between men and women, the more they believe it is a woman's own fault if she is the victim of sexual harassment.

It is not always easy to tell the difference between sexual harassment and mutual but difficult relations or mere miscommunication. How can harassment be distinguished from "legitimate" attraction of one person to another that happens to occur in the work place or at school? Most people argue that the test is whether the activity is persistent and continues despite lack of encouragement on the part of the victim. But who is to judge what persistence and lack of encouragement are? Many people argue that any sexual advance by someone in a position of power toward a subordinate is suspect and that superiors have the extra burden of responsibility in making sure their behavior toward subordinates is judicious. But do policies restricting any intimate relations between, for example, employers and employees or students and faculty violate their own freedom of choice? What constitutes insulting or demeaning remarks that might poison the work atmosphere? Who should be the judge? The argument feminists have made is that unequal gender relations in social institutions such as work places and schools interact with the gender basis of sexual relations that give men the sexual right-of-way, leading women to be especially vulnerable.

Rape

The traditional wisdom on rape is that men are at the mercy of their sexual drives and therefore rape when they are overly frustrated or when the opportunity arises.[5] Contemporary sociobiologists often use this argument to show why sex equality will never occur. Social science research, on the other hand, shows that the proclivity to rape and attitudes toward rape depend considerably on culture and ideology. Anthropologist Peggy Sanday's analysis of societies around the world (1981b) indicates that rape is by no means universal. In some societies, rape is virtually unknown: in others it is a normal, ritualized part of men's and women's lives. American society falls somewhere in between (see also Gordon and Riger 1989).

Feminists argue that rape is a logical outcome of an androcentric sex/gender system and its supporting ideology, which grants men a sexual right-of-way. If men are assumed to be sexually demanding by nature and women to be submissive, there is no strong barrier to rape other than men's mutual agreement not to rape because this protects "their own" women from other men. Our sexual ideology says that rape is wrong, but it gives men who do rape an excuse. For this reason at least one author has called the laws about rape a "male protection racket" (Peterson 1977).

The way rape laws have been enforced has provided considerable evidence of such a racket. Penalties assessed against a rapist have been higher when the rape victim was married than when the victim was unmarried, and it was often the husband of the married victim rather than the married victim herself who could sue for damages—of his property. Rape can be a weapon of war because the ability of the men of one nation to rape the women who "belong" to the men of another is an important symbol of domination and humiliation. Conquerors rape for much the same reason that they confiscate or damage other property of the vanquished.

Research by Margaret Riger and Stephanie Gordon (1989) reveals that women and men define rape differently. Almost all the women and men they surveyed thought that "unwanted sexual intercourse with someone when physically forced or overpowered" is rape. About 95% also thought that "sexual intercourse with someone without their consent" was rape. However, the examples of gender differences in definitions of rape are important. About 91% of women and 83% of men defined "a relative having sexual intercourse with a child" as rape. About 80% of women and 64% of men defined "a relative having sexual intercourse with a teenager under age 18" as rape. About 63% of women and 44% of men defined "unwanted sexual intercourse between a husband and wife" as rape. Finally, 23% of women and 10% of men defined "a stranger pinching or grabbing in a sexually suggestive way" as rape (1989, 61).

Martha Burt (1980) did an important empirical study of the role of gender and sexual stereotypes in people's beliefs about rape. She points out that widely accepted cultural rape myths maintain that women are at least in part responsible for their own victimization, that rape is not as common as women believe, and that rapists are in large part not responsible for their own actions. People who accept traditional gender-role stereotypes or who believe that heterosexual relationships are necessarily adversarial are more likely to accept rape myths. And the more people accept interpersonal violence in general, the more they accept rape myths. In other words, acceptance of the predominant rape myths is part of a package of ideas that include belief in men's social and sexual superiority and acceptance of the inevitability of male power and violence. An adaptation of Burt's survey is shown in Table 11-1.

Neil M. Malamuth (1981) has pursued this line of inquiry further by investigating the links between rape and people's beliefs and attitudes. Like most other investigators of rape, he notes that research consistently fails to reveal many psychological differences between men who have raped and men who have not. In other words, rapists are psychologically similar to normal (nonraping) men.

Malamuth discusses several studies asking samples of normal men whether they would rape if they thought they could get away with it. In a typical study, 35% said that there was at least some chance they would and 20% said it was fairly likely they would. In a study of nearly 4,000 college students, 23% of the men said that they had been in a situation in which they had been so aroused that they "couldn't" stop, even though they knew that the woman didn't want to continue. But only 3% of the men in the sample reported that they had actually used physical force. (At the same time, 8% of the women in the study said that a man had used physical force against them.) A proclivity toward rape appears to be widespread.

What psychological differences distinguish rapists from other men? Malamuth (1981) says there are two that show up in the literature on rape: the tendencies "to hold callous attitudes about rape and to believe in rape myths" and "to show relatively high levels of sexual arousal to depictions of rape" (139). Malamuth

TABLE 11-1

Sexual Ideology: Adversarial Sexual Beliefs, Sexual Conservatism, and Rape-Myth Acceptance

Following are three lists of statements that indicate three different but related aspects of sexual ideology. Do you agree or disagree with each of these statements? Do you think most of your friends would agree or disagree? The police? Most people? What difference does it make?

Adversarial Sexual Beliefs

Greater *agreement* with these statements indicated greater belief that heterosexual relationships are adversarial relationships.

A woman will only respect a man who will lay down the law to her.

Many women are so demanding sexually that men just can't satisfy them.

A man's got to show the woman who's boss right from the start or he'll end up henpecked.

A woman is usually sweet until she's caught a man; then she lets her true self show.

A lot of men talk big, but when it comes down to it, they can't perform well sexually.

In dating relationships women take advantage of men.

Men only want one thing.

Most women are sly and manipulative when they want to attract men.

Many women seem to get pleasure in putting men down.

Sexual Conservatism

Greater *agreement* with these statements indicates greater sexual conservatism.

A woman who initiates a sexual encounter will probably have sex with anybody.

A woman shouldn't give in sexually to a man too easily or he'll think she's loose.

Men have a biologically stronger sex drive than women.

A nice woman will be offended or embarrassed by dirty jokes.

Masturbation is not a normal form of sexual activity.

People should not have oral sex.

I have no respect for a woman who engages in sexual relationships without any emotional involvement.

Having sex during the menstrual period is embarrassing.

The primary goal of sexual intercourse should be to have children.

TABLE 11-1
Sexual Ideology: Adversarial Sexual Beliefs, Sexual Conservatism, and Rape-Myth Acceptance *(Continued)*

Rape-Myth Acceptance
Greater *agreement* with *unstarred* statements and greater *disagreement* with *starred* statements indicate greater acceptance of rape myths.

A woman who goes to the home or apartment of a man on their first date implies that she is willing to have sex.

* Any female can get raped.

One reason that women falsely report a rape is that they frequently have a need to call attention to themselves.

Any healthy woman can successfully resist a rapist if she wants to.

Women who go braless or wear short skirts and tight tops are asking for trouble.

In most rapes the victim is promiscuous or has a bad reputation.

If a girl engages in necking or petting and she lets things get out of hand, it is her own fault if her partner forces sex on her.

Women who get raped while hitchhiking get what they deserve.

A woman who is stuck-up and thinks she is too good to talk to men on the street deserves to be taught a lesson.

Many women have an unconscious wish to be raped and may unconsciously set up a situation in which they are likely to be attacked.

If a woman gets drunk at a party and has intercourse with a man she's just met there, she should be considered fair game to other males at the party who want to have sex with her too, whether she wants to or not.

Many women who report rapes are lying because they are angry and want to get back at the man they accuse.

Source: Adapted from Burt, 1980.

further investigated these observations in his own research. He found that compared to other men those who said they were likely to rape if they could get away with it were more accepting of rape myths, more tolerant of interpersonal violence against women, and more readily aroused by depictions of rape.

But are the men's statements about their own proclivity to rape any indication of their real tendency to be violent toward women? Malamuth investigated this question by conducting an experiment in which men were told they could choose to punish another person for incorrect responses in solving a problem. The problem solver was a female confederate. Malamuth arranged for the woman to insult mildly or reject each man before the experiment. In the course of the experiment, the men who had reported that they had a higher likelihood of raping were angrier and more aggressive toward the woman and reported a greater desire to hurt her than did other men.

These results are consistent with studies of men who have been convicted of rape. Rapists often report not on their feelings of sexual arousal or attraction to their victims but on their desire to hurt or dominate them. Even when rapists admit what they have done, they often feel their actions were justified under the circumstances (Wolfe and Baker 1980; Scully 1990). For this reason many people prefer to classify rape as a crime of aggression or violence rather than as a sexual crime. Sexual organs are involved (in part as weapons), and the act of rape resembles other sexual acts in some outward respects. But the main point of the encounter is not fulfillment of sexual or erotic desires unless one accepts violence as an erotic act.

The thesis maintained by feminists is that the tie between sexuality and aggression, and especially the definition of aggression against women as erotic and sexual, is a logical result of an androcentric and even misogynist gender ideology. The research reviewed here shows that (1) an inegalitarian and androcentric gender ideology is associated with an androcentric sexual ideology; (2) these are associated with a belief that aggression against women is justifiable and necessary, at least in some circumstances; and (3) these values help support the existence of actual violence against women.

Men who accept traditional sexual and gender ideologies may find it difficult to understand, at least in the abstract, what is so horrifying about rape. They may wonder why women don't just "lie back and enjoy it." Frances Cherry reports on how she sees this problem and how she tackles it in her teaching:

> When I have introduced the topic of rape in my classes, students often snicker when I raise the possibility that a man can be raped by a woman. Some of the men have sat back in their desks, opened their arms, and sighed, "rape me." When I further suggest we consider that men are raped by men, the men's chortles and sighs abruptly turn to nervous laughter, downward turning of the head and closing of the legs and arms (1983, 247).

It is reasonable to guess this reaction is not just because of the men's fear of homosexuality, although that undoubtedly plays a part. Through this example the men probably are realizing that rape can be violent, aggressive, and truly against one's will and that there may be no recourse if the rapist is at least the victim's physical match in size and strength. It is important to note, however, that whereas men are taught to fight off attackers, women are often counseled to avoid further harm by submitting. These issues became important in the debate over integrating gays into the military. Many feminists suspected that the vehement resistance of many men was based in their fear that they might be treated by other men as men have so often treated women.

Rape myths do not just support men's proclivity to rape; they are also important mechanisms for controlling and limiting women's activities and movements and decreasing their abilities to defend themselves and make appropriate responses to rape. Conventional wisdom is that potential victims, women, can help decrease the incidence of rape by limiting their activities. This is a logical outcome of the view that women are in large part responsible when rape occurs. Such social control over women is made effective by women's fear of rape and their knowledge that there is a very small likelihood that a rapist will be caught, let alone convicted.

Women's lives are indeed limited by a fear of rape; one study of three major cities showed that while 18% of the male residents expressed some fear about being out in their own neighborhoods at night, 40% of the female residents had such fears. Those who felt most vulnerable were the elderly, low-income people, blacks, and Hispanics (Riger and Gordon 1989).

The idea that women are responsible for their own victimization is accepted by many women, so much so that women who have been raped commonly report feeling guilty for their own victimization. This response probably is encouraged by an important difference between the myth and the reality of rape. The myth says that rapes occur on dark, deserted streets between strangers, but in reality a majority of victims and perpetrators know each other (not counting rapes of wives by their husbands) and rapes often occur in the home. One of the most painful issues related to rape concerns "date rape" or "acquaintance rape." Many men on university campuses admit that they use a variety of tactics to try to coerce or trick women into having sexual relations with them; it is a crass game in which affection plays little part.[6]

Women on college campuses are becoming aware of how common it is for women to be raped by a "friend" or a date. In these cases, self-doubt is a particular problem. The fact that women often blame themselves and that they know others will be suspicious of their testimony minimizes the number of victims who report these rapes to the police.

Women who accept the traditional adversarial ideology of sexuality—that normal heterosexual sex involves an active pursuing male and a reluctant female—may not even interpret their own experiences of rape and near rape for what they are. Women who enter shelters for battered wives often report that situations in which their husbands forced them, sometimes violently, to have sexual relations had not occurred to them as incidents of rape for a long time. As in other forms of wife battery, a woman who is dependent on her husband is unlikely to leave home until the situation becomes intolerable.

Women as a group are no longer the passive victims they might once have been. Public awareness is rising, and hundreds of organizations are involved in educating people about the facts of rape and giving psychological and legal assistance to those who have or might become victims. Research by Pauline Bart and Patricia O'Brien (1984) indicates that those who successfully avoid rape attempts have a larger range of preventive actions at their disposal than other women. Among other things, they are able to respond aggressively to their attackers. If nothing else, women who defend themselves successfully know how to kick off their heeled shoes if necessary and run. In many towns, women have organized to establish women's transit systems to help women avoid rape without having to lock themselves away.

Above all, however, the fight against rape involves a struggle against sexual and gender norms, the ideology that increases the likelihood of rape and justifies the crime. Women have given the symbolic message that they intend to do something in "Take Back the Night" demonstrations, in which large numbers of people march through often notoriously dangerous parts of towns at night in a show of strength.

Pornography

Feminists have found some specific targets of action in so-called adult bookstores and movie houses and pornography in general. These specialize not simply in presenting women as sexual objects but also in incorporating a high level of violence against women under the label of erotica. The point feminists make is twofold. First, because sexual values and behavior are in large part learned, pornographic materials that repeatedly associate violence against women with sexual pleasure for men are cultural media that reinforce the idea that violence against women is sexy. The story line of pornography usually depicts at least some of the myths and beliefs listed in Table 11-1.

Demonstrations at the 1968 Miss America contest protested the definition of women as sex objects. This poster of a woman as suitable for meat carving was a well-known restaurant advertisement.

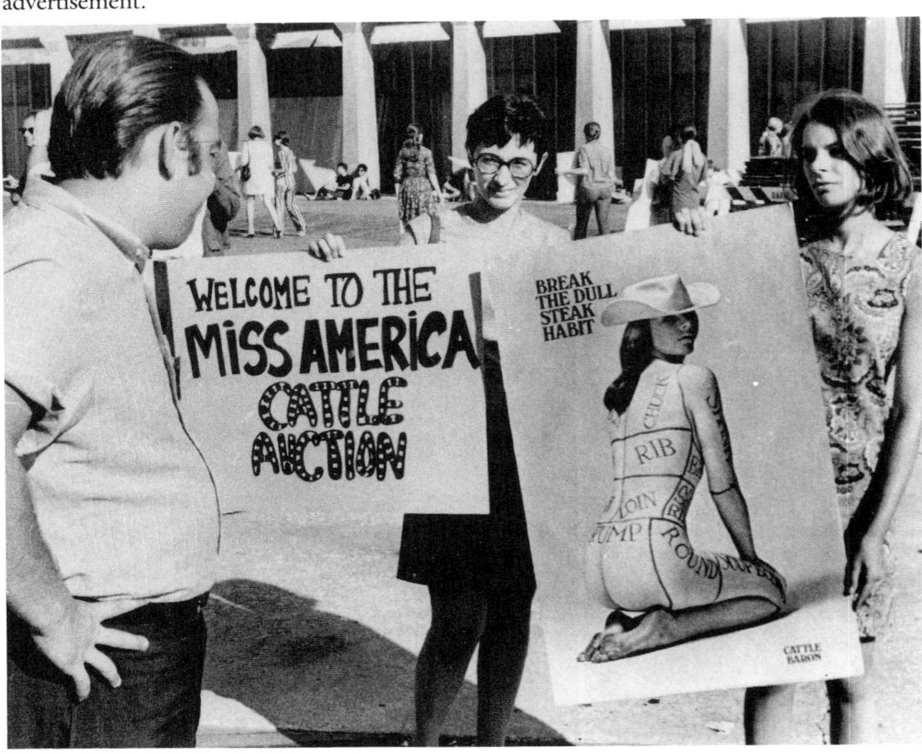

Feminists also point out that although men and women are sexually aroused by similar nonviolent erotica, men also have a tendency to be aroused by depictions of violence against women. Men are certainly more likely to be exposed to these materials; a study in San Francisco found that men constitute 97% of the people who go to adult bookstores and the same proportion of those who frequent adult movie houses.[7] Although researchers are far from agreed on whether pornography encourages rape, research does show that depictions of sexual violence encourage violence against women (Donnerstein, Linz, and Penrod 1987).

Can we distinguish more clearly between acceptable sexuality and eroticism on the one hand and aggression and violence on the other? Who would set the definitions and how? As we saw in Chapter 8, efforts to use the mechanisms of censorship have met with great resistance because of freedom of speech issues. But also, defining "acceptable" sexuality is itself fraught with danger, as will be reemphasized shortly.

Sexual Orientation and Sexual Practices

We already have seen that people's beliefs about sexuality and gender are related and that both are socially constructed. Analysis of sexual orientation—heterosexual, bisexual, or homosexual—shows very clearly that people's ideas about sexuality and gender are not just related but also interdependent; our views of gender depend on our views of sexuality, and our views of sexuality depend on our views of gender. Let us look at the way people think about and act on their sexuality and sexual practices.

Defining Sexual Orientation

Letitia Anne Peplau and Steven Gordon (1983) argue that people often confuse three different components of individuals' identities: (1) gender identity, or a person's understanding of being male or female; (2) gender-role behavior, or a person's repertoire of "masculine" and "feminine" behaviors; and (3) sexual orientation or preference. "Masculinity" and "femininity" are both judged according to how well people conform not just to traditionally prescribed gender divisions of labor but also to traditionally prescribed heterosexual behavior. Indeed, "masculinity" and "femininity" depend not just on appropriate sexual behavior but also on whether a person possesses the characteristics that are sexually attractive to members of the "opposite" sex.

Sociobiologists and much of the public suggest that gender differences in personality and division of labor are actually caused by a particular construction of heterosexual behavior: Men are the pursuers, and women are the pursued and possessed. Many sociobiologists believe that the construction of gender and gender roles inevitably follows from this fact of sexual life. Feminist theorists who analyze sex/gender systems argue that although gender and gender roles have been so constructed as to serve and maintain this sexual system, neither is inevitable.

The logic of the confusion that Peplau and Gordon describe is that to be masculine a person must possess the characteristics "appropriate" to male sexual roles and to be feminine a person must possess the characteristics "appropriate" to female sexual roles. Women who are sexually oriented toward women and men who are sexually oriented toward men are not appropriately feminine or masculine. According to this view, homosexuals must experience confusion in their identities.

The widespread belief that heterosexuality is both the most natural sexual orientation and the primary determinant of people's personalities and behaviors is illustrated by some common myths and stereotypes about homosexuals. Most people think it is easy to distinguish between heterosexuals and homosexuals. Men with stereotypic feminine characteristics and women with stereotypic masculine characteristics generally are suspected of being homosexual. People are surprised when they discover that a very "feminine" woman or a very "masculine" man is lesbian or gay.

Consider some stereotypes of lesbians to see the relationship between sexual and gender ideology. One commonplace idea is that lesbians do not really prefer women as sexual partners; instead, some trauma in their relationships with men made them hate and reject men and turn to women by default. A related stereotype is that gays and lesbians hate people of the other sex. It is often said that if they could just experience a good heterosexual relationship, they would be able to change their sexual orientation. People often have difficulty believing that homosexuals could be as happy with themselves as heterosexuals are.

In fact there is no evidence that homosexuals experience any more confusion about their gender identities than anyone else. It is not even clear how much homosexuals and heterosexuals differ from each other in the degree to which they have "masculine" and "feminine" traits. One study of women from ages 20 to 54, for example, compared lesbians and heterosexual women using the Bem Sex Role Inventory (BSRI). The result was that lesbians scored no less "feminine" than other women did. They were, however, more androgynous, because they scored higher on "masculine" characteristics than did the heterosexual women (Oldham, Farmill, and Bell 1982). No one is exactly sure why people adopt the sexual orientation they do, but homosexuality does not necessarily involve trauma and rejection. In the early 1990s, some influential research suggested that sexual orientation is partly genetically determined. Nor do homosexuals necessarily imitate stereotypic heterosexual roles, with one partner playing the "male" role and the other the "female role."

It is not surprising that people are confused and ignorant about sexual orientation. Until recently, homosexuality was seldom discussed except as a sort of illness. In the 1970s a survey of 3,000 people who had had at least one sex education course revealed that more than 60% had been taught nothing about homosexuality and two-thirds of those who had been taught something were simply taught that homosexuality was wrong (Levitt and Klassen 1974). Before we look more closely at attitudes toward different types of sexual orientation, let us first define *heterosexual*, *bisexual*, and *homosexual* orientations. This is not an easy task, and there are many methods from which to choose.

Some people seem to think that a person who has had any desire for sexual contact with someone of the same sex is a homosexual, despite any behavioral proof to the contrary. Psychologists Philip Blumstein and Pepper Schwartz argue that the reason for this view is ideological: "Our cultural logic holds that it is almost impossible to have only some homosexual feelings. The idea is seldom questioned that a single homosexual act or strong homosexual feelings reveal the 'true person' " (1977, 39). By this definition there can be no such thing as a bisexual; a person is either heterosexual or homosexual. We have no culturally parallel view that if someone who normally prefers homosexual sex has a heterosexual fantasy or encounter, that person is really a heterosexual.

Other people take their cues more specifically from people's sexual behavior rather than their desires or fantasies. It is common, however, for individuals to engage in homosexual relationships, even quite regularly, and still think of themselves as heterosexuals (Blumstein and Schwartz 1977). Likewise, some people are married or live as heterosexuals yet understand their own preferences to be homosexual. How much sexual activity of a given type is required to make one or another label appropriate? In their work on bisexuality, Blumstein and Schwartz write,

> The inescapable—but often escaped—conclusions from Kinsey, et al.'s findings are that a mix of homosexual and heterosexual behaviors in a person's erotic biography is a common occurrence, and that it is entirely possible to engage in anywhere from a little to a great deal of homosexual behavior without adopting a homosexual life-style (1977, 32).

People's sexual orientations often vary considerably over a lifetime. Although many people experience their sexual orientations as stable, many find that at some stages of life they define themselves as heterosexual, whereas at others they see themselves as homosexual or bisexual.

Sexual orientation may also be defined by the way people identify themselves. In a four-city survey, Blumstein and Schwartz found that just as people with extensive homosexual experience may still identify themselves as heterosexuals, many people adopt homosexual or bisexual identities without having had any homosexual experiences. Sexual self-definition does not require any sexual experience at all. People, of course, face tremendous pressure to reject any idea that they might be homosexual. The social sanctions have been so severe that people are often afraid to admit their feelings even to themselves. Research on sexuality and moral reasoning finds that guilt plays an important role in the way people think about sexuality (D'Augelli and D'Augelli 1977). The power of guilt feelings can only be increased when people find themselves with sexual preferences so often described as sick and sinful.

Carmen de Monteflores and Stephen Schultz (1978) have studied the process of "coming out," or acquiring a homosexual social identity, among women and men. They note that coming out is not a single event but a psychological process that takes place over time. They found that the process is generally not the same for women and men. The men they talked to often had their first homosexual experiences before they understood the meaning of homosexuality or thought of themselves as having any sexual preference for men. In explaining their earlier encounters, they tended to emphasize sexual gratification and to deny responsibility for their choices (to say, for example, "I was drunk"). The women tended to act on their sexual preferences only after they had recognized them and to emphasize the emotional bonds they had with their first female partners before having sexual relations with them. The men focused on the special circumstances of their first homosexual encounters, and the women emphasized their special partners. Men also report more difficulty in identifying themselves as homosexual, for reasons we will discuss later (Blumstein and Schwartz 1977).

The process of coming out involves a number of stages. Individuals first grapple with their own sense of identity and personal choice. Next they reveal this new identity to others, generally people in the gay community. Because of the likely negative repercussions, it continues to be difficult for gays and lesbians to express their sexual identity to people in the "straight" world, including family, friends, and employers. Since the issue of sexual orientation has become increasingly politicized, and since gay communities are much more active and cohesive than they once were, for many people coming out also involves becoming a member of an identifiable social and political community.[8]

The process of developing self-identity is not easy for heterosexual people either. Freud, for example, thought the process of becoming heterosexual to be particularly difficult for females, who have to learn to suppress themselves and become relatively passive. Young heterosexual men certainly devote considerable time and effort to proving themselves "healthy," masculine, and heterosexual. But the problems are by no means equivalent to those of people with gay or bisexual orientations. It is precisely the fear of not being heterosexual enough and the fear of homosexuality that motivate some of the struggles of heterosexuals. Parents and others ultimately tend to be understanding of the difficulties of developing heterosexuality; young people developing their homosexuality are more often isolated. Bisexuals face unique problems because they are often not trusted by either the homosexual or the heterosexual communities. Most people do not believe a person can really be bisexual; they believe a person must have one sexual orientation or the other (Blumstein and Schwartz 1977).

These definitional problems suggest that the attempt to label a person heterosexual, bisexual, or homosexual is a misguided effort. Historians note that although people have varied in their sexual orientations since the beginning of recorded history, the designation of a "homosexual role" or of specific individuals as homosexuals is of recent vintage, going back only to the 19th century (Weeks 1977). When we consider both the variability across individuals and within individuals' lifetimes, trying to classify people can seem futile. Shere Hite, for example, argues that "the terms *heterosexual* and *homosexual* should be used not as nouns but as adjectives, and . . . should be used to describe activities, not people. Other than that, these words have no meaning. And even used as adjectives referring to activities, the words are vague" (1981, 809). On the other hand, if these words are used not just as descriptions of sexual relations but also in the more political and sociological senses to refer to communities and life-styles, Hite's suggestion may not be adequate.

One thing is certain. A large number of people are homosexual. Alfred Kinsey and his associates found in the 1940s that 28% of their sample of almost 8,000 women had had some homosexual experience (Kinsey, Pomeroy, and Martin 1948). In Shere Hite's (1981) study of over 7,000 men, 11% said that they preferred to have sex with another man. In her earlier study of women (1976), 8% said that they preferred sex with another woman and 4% said that they were bisexual. Some recent surveys seem to find fewer people who identify themselves as homosexual or admit to having sexual experience with someone of their own sex, sparking a controversy of how adequate any of these social science surveys are for identifying how many people in the population have what kind of sexual orientation.[9]

Much research has been done on attitudes toward homosexuality, especially on homophobia, the fear or hatred of homosexuality. Homophobia is a form of prejudice, like sexism or racism. Table 11-2 shows that although a considerable portion of the American population is now relatively tolerant of homosexuality, a large proportion would place great limits on the lives of homosexuals and, especially, would try to shield their children from them. When research uncovers gender differences in attitudes, the difference is usually that men are more

TABLE 11-2
Attitudes Toward Homosexuality

Homosexuality should be considered an acceptable alternative lifestyle.	36
Homosexual relations between adults are morally wrong.	55
Homosexuals should have equal rights in terms of job opportunities.	78
Would object to having an airline pilot who is homosexual.	11
Would object to having a homosexual as representative in Congress.	38
Would object to having a homosexual as their child's elementary school teacher.	55
Would not permit their child to read a book that contains a story about a homosexual couple.	59
Would not permit their child to watch a prime-time television situation comedy show with homosexual characters.	36
Would not permit their child to play at the home of a friend who lives with a homosexual parent.	58
Would be very upset if their college-age son or daughter revealed that they were homosexual.	49
Think that being homosexual is something people choose to be.	44
Think that being homosexual is something people cannot change.	43

Source: *New York Times*/CBS News Poll, February 9–11, 1993.

hostile to and threatened by homosexuality than are women. A survey of new undergraduates in 1992, for example, found that 49% of the men and only 28% of the women agreed that "it is important to have laws prohibiting homosexual relationships."[10] After looking at a range of possible explanations for male homophobia, including age, education, religion, and various attitudes, one study found that the single best predictor of homophobia was whether a person accepted traditional family ideology. The more strongly men believe that a family should consist of a dominant father, a submissive mother, and obedient children, the more likely they are to show signs of homophobia (Morin and Garfinkle 1978). The second best predictor of homophobia is gender ideology. The more strongly men believe in traditional women's roles and character, the more homophobic they are likely to be.

Several experimental studies show how homophobia and stereotypes affect the way people think. In one study, psychologists provided subjects with a vignette of an individual. Later they gave the subjects information indicating that the individual in the vignette was either a homosexual or a heterosexual, then asked them what they remembered about the individual. As the researchers expected, the subjects mentally reconstructed the facts of the story to fit their stereotypes of the sexual orientation assigned to the individual (Snyder and Uranowitz 1978). It is interesting to compare these findings with those of Carmen de Monteflores and Stephen Schultz (1978), who found the same process of reconstruction in the process of coming out among gays and lesbians. As newly self-identified homosexuals go through the process of labeling themselves, they also tend to reconstruct their past by remembering events and feelings they had forgotten or by reinterpreting the meanings of different events and relationships in their lives.

Most psychologists have long held that homosexuality was a sign of illness. In contrast, Freudian psychoanalysis argues that human beings are essentially bisexual and that only through a process of developmental struggle do people forsake their homosexual tendencies to become exclusively heterosexual. Although Freud did not consider homosexuality an illness in need of a cure, he did consider it a sign of psychosexual immaturity.

Despite the declaration of the American Psychological Association in 1973 that homosexuality is not necessarily a sign of psychological illness, many psychotherapists continue to regard homosexuals as less healthy than other people. In their study of 400 California psychologists, Ellen Garfinkle and Stephen Morin (1978) presented therapists with a profile of a client, whom they described as either male or female and either heterosexual or homosexual. Male therapists were particularly likely to view the "male homosexual" client negatively and see him as less healthy, less masculine, and more feminine than the heterosexual clients.

Homosexuality has always been suppressed in the United States. Leadership in suppression of homosexuality has come especially from organized religion and government. Government, following from religious views, labeled sodomy or "homosexual acts" (especially by men) as criminal activities punishable in certain circumstances in the past by death. As late as 1986 the Supreme Court case *Bowers*

v. *Hardwick* declared that private intimate acts between consenting adults are not protected under the constitutional right to privacy, which means that state laws on sodomy, used primarily against homosexuals, are legal.[11]

Why is sexual orientation, especially homosexuality, a key issue in feminist research and activism? The primary explanation is so obvious that it is often neglected: lesbians are women who defy in an important way the stereotypes of womanhood and femininity. At the same time, the fact that a woman is a lesbian increases the likelihood that she will experience the effects of androcentric values and women's lack of freedom. For example, gender discrimination in employment affects women regardless of their sexual orientation, but lesbians are less likely than others to have a higher-paid male's salary to share. Moreover, lesbians are subject to employment discrimination as both women and homosexuals (Levine and Leonard 1984). Lesbians with children also have the problems of single motherhood, with the additional problem that much of society is antagonistic to the idea that lesbians should raise children. All women are justified in fearing the violence of rape, but lesbians cannot rely on male protectors as they go about their business.

Women in general suffer from constricting stereotypes of femininity. But because they deviate from the stereotypes in an obvious respect, lesbians face the further problem of being defined as unhealthy and as not "real" women. Women are subtly and not so subtly directed to make their lives revolve around a man's. For this reason some feminists, such as Adrienne Rich, argue that one of the most rebellious things a woman can do is to defy the norm of "compulsory heterosexuality" (1980).

Many feminists have argued that homophobia and heterosexism oppress women regardless of their sexual orientations. Feminist theorist Charlotte Bunch (1979; 1981) has made this point very well, arguing that heterosexism (prejudice against homosexuality) and sexism assume that "each woman exists for a man—her body, her children, and her services are his property. If a woman does not accept that definition of heterosexuality and of herself, she is queer—no matter who she sleeps with" (1979, 554). Women are given marginal status in the work force and in education partly because of the assumption that they will ultimately depend on men. Women also gain much of their social status and privileges through their relationship with men. "One of the things that keeps heterosexual domination going is heterosexual privilege; those actual or promised benefits for a woman who stays in line: legitimacy, economic security, social acceptance, legal and physical protection" (Bunch 1979, 554). If a heterosexual woman does not recognize heterosexism and heterosexist privilege, Bunch argues, she cannot see how dependent she is for her rights and privileges on men, and how easily she can lose them if she does not conform to the standards set by men. In at least one respect, radical feminists and right-wing antifeminists are in substantial agreement. Both see increasing equality for women as threatening to traditional sexual mores, and both see the breakdown of traditional sexual mores as threatening to the life of the patriarchal family.

Feminists like Charlotte Bunch and Adrienne Rich also argue that heterosexism is a powerful force limiting the ability of women to respect themselves and organize socially and politically. Homophobia certainly decreases personal intimacy among men (Lewis 1978). Although there appears to be somewhat more intimacy among women, heterosexism defines women as incomplete without a man, and it defines her relationships with men as more important than relationships with women. (For example, a woman often reneges without hesitation on a commitment to go out with another woman if a man later asks her for a date that conflicts with the former engagement.) Turning away from heterosexism implies the ability to imagine limitless love and respect for women as independent and complete people.

The issue here is not necessarily whom one chooses as a sexual partner, but the degree to which one accepts or rejects androcentric sexual and gender ideologies at the most personal level. This is the reason that Adrienne Rich (1979) chooses to define *lesbianism* not by people's habits of sexual behavior but by the way people understand and identify with women. Antifeminists may be right that the women's movement has encouraged more women to choose to be lesbian, but it also can be argued that the women's movement has meant that more women could choose to be heterosexual without having to devalue themselves.

Sexuality, Love, and Power

Thus far we have discussed sexuality, intimacy, and personal relationships in a fairly abstract manner. Much research has been devoted to studying the behavior of males and females in both heterosexual and homosexual relationships. Let us look at some of the conclusions.

As much as it might surprise most people, especially the devotees of conventional wisdom, men seem to fall in love more quickly than women do (Hill, Rubin, and Peplau 1976). But love and the initiation of intimate relationships mean different things to women and men. Sex appears to be more central and important to men in a relationship than it is to women, and men describe their love in slightly more passionate terms than women do (Peplau, Rubin, and Hill 1977; Hatfield 1983). Women are slightly more likely to feel a companionate love for their partners, or a love that emphasizes friendship and sharing. Some research suggests that a woman more carefully considers whether to live with a man because deciding to do so commits her to undertaking domestic labor and responsibility for the two of them. Men still generally expect the women they live with to do most of the cooking and cleaning.

Philip Blumstein and Pepper Schwartz's (1983) study of American couples reveals some interesting characteristics of attachment in relationships. Their study (which will be discussed often here) focused on married couples, heterosexual cohabiting couples, and gay and lesbian cohabiting couples.[12] The researchers found widespread division of emotional labor within the relationships, which generally included one partner who was more oriented toward the relationship than the other was. "The majority of couples, heterosexual and homosexual, have at least one partner who is relationship-centered. Couples without a relationship-centered partner are less satisfied and less committed" (170). The traditional division of labor assigns women this role, although women by no means constitute all of the relationship-centered partners. Of course, among same-sex partners such a division of labor could not be gender based.

Blumstein and Schwartz found some interesting differences in how people managed and felt about their relationships. "Among heterosexual couples, young men have less desire for their partner's companionship than do young women, but the tables are turned as the couple ages" (176). This observation is consistent with earlier studies of marital relationships (see, e.g., Lopata 1971). The early stages of marriage can be difficult for women who expected constant sharing and companionship with their new husbands only to find that the husbands turned much of their attention to their jobs and other interests. With the birth of children wives often withdraw some of their attention from their husband as they devote themselves to care of the children. This is one reason why the early stages of parenthood can be so stressful for husbands. For the relatively few remaining employed husband/homemaker wife couples, the husband's retirement can again pose a problem. The man may now be ready for companionship with his wife, but the woman's well-established life and routines may not fit her husband's new needs.

Same-sex couples appear to share more of their leisure activities and their time than heterosexual couples do (Blumstein and Schwartz 1983, 180). Part of the reason is that just as the economic world is segregated by sex, so are many leisure and social activities. This barrier does not divide homosexual couples.

Private time away from one's partner is also important to a relationship. Of the types of couples that Blumstein and Schwartz studied, "Cohabitors feel most strongly about having time away from their partners" (1983, 186), a characteristic consistent with the generally higher levels of independence that mark these couples. Perhaps a more surprising finding given women's desire for companionship in relationships is that women express a stronger wish than do men for more time to themselves. The need for private time does not necessarily indicate a lack of love for one's partner. As we already have seen, women have less control over their time and space than men do, and women with young children often feel cloistered by their families.

Blumstein and Schwartz also looked at the role of possessiveness in relationships and found women to be slightly more possessive than men. Further analysis revealed the reason: Men tend to have more power and control within their relationships, and women's possessiveness is partly a reaction to insecurity. Only among wives in the study did possessiveness seem to be related to the degree of commitment to a relationship; the more they wanted the relationship to last, the more possessive they were. Men's degree of commitment did not affect how possessive they were of their wives, and perhaps even more important, their level of possessiveness did not indicate how committed they were.

The issue of possessiveness raises a related topic: sexual fidelity and monogamy. Public opinion polls generally show that women are more conservative than men in their attitudes toward extramarital sex and divorce. One possible reason is that women gain protection by safeguarding a traditional sexual morality because they are generally in a weaker position. But also, Blumstein and Schwartz's study suggests that women simply are more likely to define commitment to monogamy as part of a stable relationship. The heterosexual women and lesbians were about equally likely to value monogamy. This finding is consistent with others showing that for women personal commitment and affection more often precede the initiation of sexual relations. Another study of couples in the 1970s also concluded that lesbian and heterosexual women are very similar in their desires for close, permanent, and loving relationships (Peplau et al. 1978; Peplau and Gordon 1983).

Shere Hite's study (1981) of male sexuality provides more insight into men's views of extramarital sex. About two-thirds of the married men in her sample claimed to have had at least one extramarital affair. Most did not view this activity as having anything to do with their marital relationships, and most did not think that it detracted from their love for their wife. What they were searching for in their affairs was sex, often because they thought they didn't have enough with their wife. Most thought that sex within marriage eventually becomes boring. However, most of the men strongly disliked the idea of their wife having an affair.

What do we know about patterns of sexual intimacy within relationships? The frequency of sexual intercourse decreases over the life of a relationship. It is difficult to determine how much of the decrease is the result of habituation and how much the result of aging. Sexual activity does tend to decrease after midlife because of physiological aging, but not nearly to the degree that young people generally suspect. Men's physiological capacities for sex begin decreasing at an earlier age and to a greater extent than women's. But as A. R. Allgeier concludes in his discussion of aging and sexuality, "The North American stereotype of the sexless older person is inaccurate. Sexy young people mature into sexy middle-aged and elderly people. The sexually disinterested elderly person was probably not very enthusiastic about sex in youth" (1983, 144).

Blumstein and Schwartz's couples study also shows that the traditional sexual division of labor is alive and well among heterosexual couples. The majority of people—53% according to female cohabitors and 67% according to husbands—thought that one partner in the couple tended to initiate sex, and in heterosexual couples this partner is more often the man, especially among married as compared with cohabiting couples.

Shere Hite's work is particularly notable for what it reveals about couples' sexual relationships. Above all it shows how little heterosexual couples understand each other's sexuality, especially how little men understand and pay attention to women's sexuality. Such widespread ignorance is hardly surprising: Research on sex education and sexual knowledge shows that American children are retarded in their understanding of sexuality and reproduction compared with those in other countries. By age 9, for example, only 10% of American children know that a woman must have sexual intercourse to have a baby. By the same age, 25% of Australian children, 35% of English children, and 60% of Swedish children know the basic facts of life (Goldman and Goldman 1982).

Hite's male respondents sometimes displayed an amazing ignorance about women's bodies and how they work. Many men could not tell whether their partners had orgasms, and many thought the question not particularly important anyway. Many did not know about the clitoris or its role in women's sexuality. Numerous men equated sexual intimacy with genital penetration and considered that women's orgasms should happen during penetration if they happened at all. Although many men also responded differently to Hite's questions, these responses illuminate why the average man seems more eager for sex in heterosexual relationships than do women. Men have greater control, and sexual encounters are structured more by their desires and needs. This pattern also explains the finding that women in lesbian relationships experience more orgasms than those in heterosexual relationships, even though lesbians have sex less often: Women understand how their own bodies work. Americans, male and female, begin adult life with inadequate knowledge about sexual intimacy and the needs of the other sex, and many are unable to ask for or to give the information needed to make their relationships more fulfilling. The phenomenon is largely attributable to traditional sexual and gender ideology.

Power is an important issue in relationships. One of the major findings in Blumstein and Schwartz's research on couples is that "money established the balance of power in relationships, except among lesbians" (1983, 53). Power is more balanced in households with employed wives than in those of other married women, perhaps because these women earn money of their own.

Feminists have long maintained that married homemakers' lack of financial resources puts them in a dependent situation and gives them little leverage in a marriage. They also argue that such wives do not get the respect they deserve from their husbands because the wives are dependents who can easily (and wrongly) be accused of not earning their keep. The couples study shows that a woman gains additional respect from her husband if she is employed. On the other hand, employment of wives can introduce strains in marriages, especially given the lingering ideology of the patriarchal family with traditional gender roles. Married women continue to do most of the housework regardless of their employment status, which means their days are particularly burdened. Blumstein and Schwartz found that although cohabiting couples are somewhat more egalitarian about the division of domestic labor, even in those couples women do most of the domestic labor.

Both heterosexual and homosexual men feel that a successful partner should not have to do housework, unless that partner is female (Blumstein and Schwartz 1983, 151). Men in general do not demonstrate that they are ready to share domestic labor; the more housework a husband does, the more conflict the couple has (146). We will look more closely at the relationship of work and marriage in Chapter 13.

In addition to financial dependency, it is important to consider the role of psychological dependency, a situation in which an individual's sense of self-esteem, purpose, and ability to get along revolves around another person. Traditional gender ideology encourages psychological dependency in women by defining women's purpose as hinging on others and by defining women as incapable of autonomy and independence. By the same token it is possible to argue that traditional gender ideology also encourages a form of psychological dependency in men. If to feel "masculine" and have a strong sense of self-esteem a man needs to have the woman he cares most about be weak and economically dependent, we can argue that he is psychologically dependent on her weakness relative to him.

Women's dependency in marriage has been empirically demonstrated to have other effects as well. Blumstein and Schwartz discovered that in a heterosexual relationship, the more the power balance tips toward the man, the more the couple's sexual activity will be limited to intercourse with the man in the top position. This means that the balance of sexual satisfaction is also tilted toward the male. Power relations thus can shape almost all aspects of a couple's life together.

Both economic and psychological dependency are related to wife abuse, although in different ways. Women's subjective or psychological dependency seems to be related to relatively minor acts of abuse, whereas economic dependency seems to provide a breeding ground for more major acts of abuse (Kalmuss and Strauss 1982). The role of economic dependency in giving men the power to abuse women is also suggested by a study of women who were subject to wife abuse. It showed that among abused wives, women who were not employed were less likely to leave the relationship than were employed women (Strube and Barbour 1983). Inequality and male dominance in marriage are clearly not healthy for women.

A Sexual Revolution?

In the late 1960s, mass-circulation magazines announced that a new revolution was under way: the sexual revolution. Americans were told that more people were having more different kinds of sexual relations with more people than ever before and that these changes were due in part to the emergence of the new, liberated woman. Public opinion figures and statistics provide evidence that Americans' sexual thinking and behavior have undergone considerable change during the second half of the 20th century. People have become more tolerant of variation in sexual life. They appear to be more knowledgeable about their bodies and sexuality. By the 1970s only a minority of people were virgins on their wedding day, and in some areas of the country the number of babies born to single women now outnumbers those born to married women.

These are significant changes. But have people's views of women's sexuality really changed? Has the balance of sexual power between men and women been altered by this "revolution"? What, after all, is new?

Since the late 1940s, when Alfred Kinsey and his associates announced that women were not engaging in sexual relations solely for the purpose of procreation or even simply to satisfy the needs of men (Kinsey, Pomeroy, and Martin 1948; Kinsey et al. 1953), women's sexuality has been the topic of considerable debate. Once this was realized, the nature of women's sexuality and sexual potential became an open question. We shall look at two such questions in particular: women's orgasms and the double standard.

THE VAGINAL, CLITORAL, NONE, ONE, MANY DEBATE. Considerable attention has been paid to women's orgasms, at least in the scholarly literature on sexuality. This attention has focused on two questions:

1. How many orgasms can and should a woman have?
2. What kinds of orgasms can and should a woman have?

There was once general agreement that women's orgasms were secondary to men's; men had a greater need for relief of sexual tension, and many women were "frigid," or anorgasmic, anyway. As Shere Hite's subjects indicate, many women are not given any alternative by their husbands. Women who know better but are afraid to speak up for themselves find sex a very frustrating experience. Indeed, most women probably always have known better, as research on masturbation shows. But the label "frigid" is applied to women who do not or cannot have an orgasm from the thrusting of a penis inside the vagina. Why should a woman bother getting excited and being responsive when her own sexual tensions will not be relieved?

Public attention then shifted from whether women can have orgasms to how many they can have at a time. Many women felt bad enough that they could not have even one orgasm during sexual intercourse when they were hit with the report that with proper stimulation many women could reach climax many times in succession. The flood of clinical reports has often left women and men unenlightened but more anxious than ever. Women worry about frigidity, while men worry about their performance and whether it was good enough to tap and satisfy women's apparently insatiable sexuality. Some women fake orgasms to protect their own and their partner's self-esteem. These worries are hardly conducive to sexual enjoyment. The facts seem to be that (1) with proper stimulation, which in most cases is not achieved merely by penile penetration, most women can reach a climax, and many can do so more than once; (2) the physiological phases of sexual excitement and resolution are roughly similar in men and women; and (3) sex can be enjoyable to many people even if orgasm is not achieved.

The second issue about orgasms centers on what area people define as the locus of sexual stimulation that can lead to orgasm in women. Following Sigmund Freud's theory of psychosexual development (see Chapter 3), many "experts" argued that there are two kinds of female orgasms: clitoral orgasms, achieved by direct stimulation of the clitoris; and vaginal orgasms, the more "mature" orgasm achieved during penetration. Despite the clinical evidence that most orgasms are physiologically caused by stimulation of the clitoris, many people continue to think that a woman should be able to climax during sexual intercourse, which does not always offer the clitoral stimulation women need to have an orgasm.

The "vaginal imperative" helps preserve the male's place as the dominant and more central character in sexual activity. What people do before a man enters a woman—even if it includes orgasm for the woman—is still usually called foreplay, the overture to the main act. The vaginal imperative helps reinforce the idea that women have less sexual drive than men, because only a minority of women are stimulated enough by sexual intercourse alone to have orgasms. If sexual activity between women and men is to be more responsive to women's needs, men must place more value on sexual activities that cannot directly result in their own orgasms. Both women and men have to stop worrying about their performance and what they are "supposed" to do and feel. *That* would be a revolution.

THE DOUBLE STANDARD, POWER, AND DOMINANCE. Successful revolutions usually result in a redistribution of power or resources. In the past, women had relatively little power over their own sexuality. Has the sexual revolution resulted in a reallocation of power? The answer seems to be yes, within limits.

Women certainly appear to have more opportunity to think, learn, and talk about their sexual needs and experiences than they had in the past, although formal sex education (for both sexes) remains limited. People also seem freer to make choices in their sexual lives. Indeed, controversies rage over the degree to which traditional sexual morality has changed.

The double standard, which essentially validates different rules and degrees of power for men than for women, has been weakened and widely questioned, but it has by no means disappeared. Men are still more likely to initiate sexual relationships. Women retain their power to say "no," although they are pressured to use that power less often than they once were because of misguided interpretations of what constitutes a "liberated woman."

The persistence of the double standard means that women remain more likely to be criticized than men for engaging in "inappropriate" heterosexual relations. The persistence of a gender division of labor means that women are held more responsible if conception occurs. One fact of life will never change: It is the woman who becomes pregnant.

The sexual double standard has become even more dangerous since the spread of AIDS. Are women as free as they should be to make their own responsible choices about sexual relations? Consider the following facts. As we have seen, the belief that men are supposed to coerce or trick women into sex lingers. Men are certainly more accepting of casual sex; a 1992 survey of new college students shows that 59% of men and 32% of women agree, "It is all right for two people who really like each other to have sex even if they've known each other for a very short time," and 17% of men and 6% of women think a man is entitled to have sex with a woman if he thinks she "led him on."[13] Men expect to take the lead during sex, and many women are reluctant to press their own demands. Men are more resistant than women to using condoms (Campbell, Peplau, and DeBro 1992). If the sexual right-of-way means that women are coerced into having more sexual partners than they might otherwise have, and they are prevented from protecting themselves during sexual relations, then the double standard is potentially fatal to them. To see how much, look at Table 11-3, containing a letter to the editor of *The New York Times* written by two psychologists.

Sexual liberation and women's liberation are linked and interdependent. Both involve increasing the power of women to express themselves and make responsible choices about themselves; both raise serious questions about women's power and freedom. Research shows that men with high needs for power tend to hold relatively exploitative views of women and limit their wives' choices (Lips 1981, 28–33). Gender equality and sexual equality must be attained in tandem. It appears that a revolution has begun, but it is not over yet.

TABLE 11-3
This Letter Could Save Your Life

To the Editor:

Magic Johnson, the basketball great, produced unforgettable numbers. Let him, as a spokesman for HIV . . . , continue to talk the numbers and tell every 14-year-old in the world:

Suppose you started having sex when you were 15 and had one new partner each year until you were 23.

Suppose that your partners at 16, 17, 18, had followed the same pattern.

Now suppose also, as the AIDS epidemic makes plain, that when you have sex with one person you also come inevitably into contact with the biochemicals of all that person's previous partners—now your "phantom" partners. At 15, your number of actual and phantom partners was merely 1 plus 0 for a total of 1. At 16, your number of actual partners was 2, and phantom partners, 1, for a total of 3. At 17, 3 actual and 4 phantoms gave you a total of 7: your partner at 17 joined you with 2 actuals and 1 phantom of her or his own; and add the single phantom associated with last year's partner.

Please get out your ballpoint and calculator because at 18, 19, 20, and onward, up you went into the wild blue yonder. Result: at the still tender age of 23, with only 9 actual partners, your still-tender membranes and your still-tender bloodstream were potentially serving as fairgrounds for the entertainment and nourishment of active viruses and other bacterial fellow travelers from no fewer than 502 phantoms!

No one should bet that not one of those hundreds of phantoms had the HIV virus. Play it safe or don't play at all!

Timothy C. Brock
Laura A. Brannon

Source: *New York Times,* November 23, 1991.

Marriage: Family, Property, and State

At the center of our sex/gender system lies a relationship institutionalized by acts of government and religion: marriage. Adult women's status, roles, rights, and obligations historically have been governed by marriage and the norms that underlie it. Female children have been taught to think of marriage as the single most important goal in their lives. Experimental research shows that women who have never married are evaluated more negatively than other women and more negatively than either single or married men (Etaugh and Foresman 1983). Hardly a woman who has reached age 30 without marrying has avoided being barraged with, "So when are you getting married?" or the whispered, "Don't worry, your time will come." After age 30 these comments come less frequently; indeed, a woman who has not married by then is often viewed with pity. In the end most people marry at least once in their lives.

Marriage is an institution that is created and defined by government. In the United States the level of government responsible for regulating marriage is the state; only a representative of the state can marry people. Even if two people are married by a member of the clergy, it is the state that grants the cleric the right to officiate. The only *enforceable* terms of marriage are those established by governmental law and policy. The state decides who may marry, at what age they may marry, and under what circumstances they may marry. Only the state may declare a marriage ended. Sexual relations outside of marriage are illegal in many states. Children born outside of marriage are designated illegitimate, or outside the bounds of law.

The Marriage Contract

When two people marry they agree to live under the terms of a marriage contract. This contract is much like others in one respect: It defines the rights and duties of the contracting parties. Beyond this, the marriage contract is very different from most other contracts in three ways:

1. Most contracts are written, and people are generally advised to "read the fine print" carefully and possibly consult a lawyer before signing on the dotted line. They may even negotiate amendments or alterations to the contract. In contrast, the terms of the marriage contract are not written in any single place, and they are not made available for review. Instead, they are scattered throughout laws and court decisions that have been handed down over time. Most people have very little idea about what is in the marriage contract, and very few consider consulting an attorney to find out what their rights and obligations are before they marry; it just doesn't seem very romantic.
2. The terms of most contracts cannot be changed while they are in force without the knowledge and consent of the signing parties. In contrast, because the terms of the marriage contract are defined by legislators, judges, and other policy makers, the only way to find out what changes have been made is to read newspapers and law reports very carefully. When marriage laws change they affect all married people, but no one sends couples notification that the rules governing their marriages have changed. The most important marriage laws are state laws, and they cover only residents of a particular state. If a couple marries in one state and settles there, they are covered by that state's law. If the same couple moves to another state, they are covered by the laws of the new state as soon as they become residents there. The contractual terms for marriage in that state may be very different from the terms they originally "agreed to."
3. The fact that marriage contracts are defined by state law means that generally no private agreement by husband and wife can contradict the terms set out in those laws. When a man and woman say "I do," they are agreeing to accept these definitions, rights, and obligations, although they may make agreements respecting property rights.

What values do states attempt to support through the regulation of marriage? Most American marital law stems from the common law and as such was structured to maintain the patriarchal gender divisions of roles and power regarded as the moral basis of a stable society.[14] To what degree does the law continue to define a wife's identity as incorporated and consolidated into that of the husband? To answer this question we must look at the legal definition of marriage, or the content of the marriage contract.[15]

Names and Places

The most obvious and immediate results of marriage used to be that a man and woman would begin to live together and that the woman would assume the man's surname. Even though couples now often live together before marriage, only marriage gives them the legal right to do so. The law also grants the husband the right to choose his place of residence, and it imposes on the wife what is almost an obligation to be domiciled in her husband's choice of residence. Even if a couple have different residences, in most states they are assumed to be domiciled at the husband's residence. If a wife refuses to move with her husband to another city, she is assumed by law to have abandoned him; if a husband refuses to move with his wife to another city, she is still assumed to have abandoned him. In many states a woman may now establish a separate domicile for a specific purpose, but the assumption remains that the head of the household—the husband, whenever he is present—determines where a family lives.

The traditional norms about domicile embedded in law are not just remnants of the past but remain part of our cultural values. As Table 11-4 shows, the majority still thinks wives should follow their husbands. It will be some time yet before husbands and wives are considered equal partners.

The surnames that a couple or family use also have been treated as part of the marriage contract. Contrary to what most people believe, the practice of a woman taking her husband's name is derived from custom, and the legal requirement that a woman use her husband's name is of relatively recent vintage. Most states now give women full rights to retain their birth names, although some still require them to use the husband's surname for specific legal purposes such as obtaining a driver's license. Federal courts have declared that such laws do not violate a woman's constitutional rights.[16]

The law also generally has assumed that children take the name of the parent who is the head of the household, usually the husband, unless the child is illegitimate, in which case he or she is given the surname of the mother. This rule has become more flexible since the 1980s, and many states now recognize the right of parents to give their child a name different from the father's. Some unmarried couples are now seeking the right to give their children the father's surname.

Rights and Obligations

If the heart of marital law is the relative rights and obligations of husband and wife, the marriage contract bears a striking resemblance to a (nonnegotiable)

TABLE 11-4
Whither Thou Goest . . .

"Suppose both a husband and a wife work at good and interesting jobs and the husband is offered a very good job in another city. Assuming they have no children, which one of these solutions do you think they should seriously consider?"

	Women	*Men*
Husband should turn down the job	10%	19%
Wife should quit and relocate with husband	72	62
Husband should take new job and move/wife should keep her job and stay	6	5
No opinion/doesn't know	12	14
"If the wife is offered a very good job in another city?"		
Wife should turn down the job	55%	58%
Husband should quit and relocate with wife	20	22
Wife should take new job and move/husband should keep his job and stay	8	6
No opinion/doesn't know	17	14

Note: Data are from a Roper survey of approximately 3,000 women and 1,000 men conducted in 1985.
Source: Simon and Landis (1989, 272).

labor contract. According to law the marital relationship is simply this: The wife owes the husband household, domestic, and companionship services, and the husband, in return, has the duty to support the wife. To what degree and in what ways are these principles enforceable by law?

The husband's right to his wife's services is largely unenforceable by law in any direct sense. There are, however, some extremely important consequences of this aspect of the marriage contract. Because of the notion of "conjugal rights," until recently a wife in most states could not charge her husband with rape, as we have seen. This has begun to change. Also, if a third party injured the wife so that she could not have sex with her husband, the husband could sue the other person for "loss of consortium." Traditionally she could not do the same, although this is changing.

Because the wife is obliged to perform domestic labor and therefore is not entitled to any direct compensation for it, until recently a wife's contribution to the family's economic welfare through her labor was not considered in adjudication of property division, for example, during divorce proceedings. This labor is now sometimes taken into account. Because the wife's obligations are unspecified and can cover any work she does in her home or any assistance she gives her husband as a "helpmeet," if a third party injures her, her husband may sue for the value of the household service he has lost, even though he has no legal obligation to pay his wife, and if he owns a farm or business and the wife performs duties associated with these ventures, she is not entitled to compensation.

The wife's rights to support by her husband are also largely unenforceable. Court cases concerning the husband's duty point to a single conclusion: As long as a husband and wife live together, whatever support he chooses to give her is sufficient. A woman who feels her husband is not providing for her has virtually no legal recourse.

Property

If this book had been written before the middle of the 19th century, this section would be very short. Following the common-law tradition accepted in most states at the time, wives could not own property (with a few exceptions). All property a woman owned when she married, and all income earned by her labor, and all property acquired by other means during the marriage belonged to her husband and could be managed by him without her knowledge or consent. If he wished he could use her income to fulfill his obligation of support and provide her with necessaries.

By 1993, 41 states had marital property systems based in the common law, in which the basic rule for determining who owns what is "property follows title." In common-law property states, as states following this rule are called, the husband and wife are treated as individuals with independent rights to own and manage property. Whoever has proof of title to specific assets owns them. If no one has specific proof of title, however, most courts assume that the husband is the owner, especially if the wife has been a homemaker. Homemakers are assumed to have no income with which to acquire assets. Even joint bank accounts have sometimes been viewed as the husband's property if the wife was a homemaker on the assumption that she had simply been allowed access to her husband's account.

Assuming that most husbands earn more than their wives, and that in a substantial minority of marriages women earn virtually nothing, common-law property states give great leverage to husbands. Even if the husband and wife are both income earners, they have to pay attention to how they divide payment of expenses. If a couple divides its expenses equally, but the husband pays for investment and durable goods and the wife for immediate consumption expenses, the husband ends up with the property and the wife does not.

A second type of marital property regime—community property—is found in nine states, primarily in the Southwest and West plus Louisiana and Wisconsin. In community property states, assets acquired during a marriage, with certain exceptions, are assumed by law to be jointly and equally owned by husband and wife regardless of their employment status. Because the married couple is treated as an economic unit, it does make it difficult for either partner to maintain any separate assets.

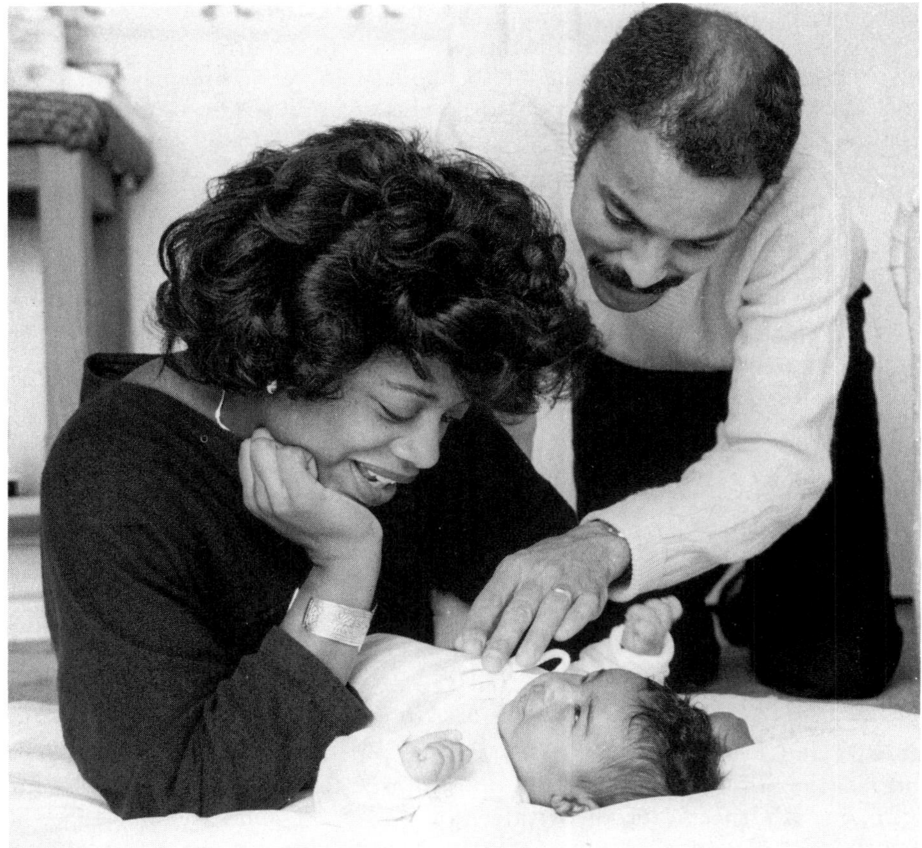

The birth of a child can bring joy, but it also refocuses a couple's relationship.

Property laws affect people most directly when divorce or the death of one partner occurs. Common-law property states compensate widows to some extent for what could be the cruelty of the situation by the principle of the "widow's share," which grants a minimum proportion of the husband's property to the widow. Under common law, property inherited by a widow from her husband is subject to inheritance taxes even if the property is the house in which she lived or the car she drove. These inheritance taxes can prove so burdensome that she must sell the property. In community property states this cannot happen.

In recent years the distinctions between these different kinds of marital property laws have begun to blur, partly in response to claims that women's economic contributions to marriage should be taken into account and partly because of a desire to protect the economic situation of children of divorced and widowed parents. Some of these changes are discussed in Chapter 12.

The State's View of Marriage

What does marital law and policy tell us about the state's definition of marriage? Marriage is viewed in part as a couple's commitment to carry on their lineage by conceiving and raising children. As the Minnesota Supreme Court argued in 1971 (to explain why homosexuals could not be legally married), "The institution of marriage as a union of man and woman, uniquely involving the procreation and rearing of children within a family, is as old as the book of Genesis" (*Baker* v. *Nelson*).

The institution of marriage is also the primary means the state has to regulate the distribution of property within and across generations through the property laws discussed earlier. It also provides labor and services that might otherwise have to be provided by the government. Many conservatives have argued that an important reason why so much public money is spent on social welfare programs is that women are not doing their jobs properly. If women would stay at home and take care of children and elderly people, less money would have to be spent to replace their labor.

The laws that help maintain women in a dependent position do not affect everyone equally. If a husband and a wife continue to love each other and are kind and generous with each other, the law will have little effect on them, especially if they die at the same moment. However, the law continues to define women as subordinates dependent on their husband's good will.

Many people have pointed to a cruel irony in marital law and policy. The women who fulfil their traditional roles most completely are most hurt by these laws and policies. Full-time homemakers have few assets of their own and are most vulnerable during and after marriage. Despite years of labor and service the "displaced homemaker" has few marketable skills that can earn her a living. At the turn of the century, Charlotte Perkins Gilman ([1898] 1966) pointed out the inequity of the familial services-support relationship. The woman from a poor family has the hardest labor as a homemaker and is supported at only the most meager levels by even the most generous husband; the woman from a wealthy family does relatively little strenuous labor but is handsomely supported.

Changes in marital law and related policies have been substantial. There are more choices available to people, and especially women, than ever before. Young women changed their expectations about marriage over recent decades, especially in the 1960s and 1970s (Weeks and Botkin 1987).

Divorce

In 1985 well over 1 million marriages ended in divorce. Ending a marriage was not always so easy. Throughout most of American history the marriage contract had few escape clauses. To sue for divorce one partner had to prove that the other partner had provided the grounds (i.e., violated the marriage contract) by, for example, committing adultery. Only the "innocent" party could file for divorce; the person at fault could not. At the same time, as Glenda Riley (1991) points out in *Divorce: An American Tradition*, there have been debates about divorce throughout American history, and at the end of the 19th century there was much worry about "divorce mills," especially in "godless places" such as Sioux Falls (S. Dak.), Fargo (N. Dak.), and Guthrie (Okla.).

Divorce procedures were not designed to try to achieve amicable agreement; to the contrary, if the partners were amicable there couldn't be much reason for divorce. Indeed, a divorce suit could be turned down if it appeared there was collusion between the divorcing partners in an effort to get a divorce. Property division depended in part on the assignment of fault or innocence. Because the guilty party had committed a crime against state law in violating the marriage contract, he or she could not profit by divorce.

Since the 1970s most states have moved toward no-fault divorce. In a no-fault divorce, one partner does not have to charge the other with a crime; instead, the couple can seek a divorce on grounds of "irretrievable breakdown." Although this has made divorces easier to obtain, these procedures are not without pitfalls. Consider the homemaker who has been the victim of cruelty or finds that her husband has been having affairs. In earlier days she could charge her husband with the fault and seek a divorce. As the innocent party she would likely be rewarded a considerable proportion of the couple's property. Under the current system, if that same woman and her husband divorce on no-fault grounds, there is no reason for the court to award her more than is legally hers anyway. Most states are trying to relieve this problem by giving courts the power to redistribute property, particularly where children are involved.[17]

A major source of contention and controversy in recent years has been the awarding of alimony. Legal scholar Herma Hill Kay (1988) points out that the practice of forcing a husband to pay alimony dates from the time when divorce was not possible except under conditions of fault. Under early laws, following church rules, divorced people could not remarry. In effect a divorce meant that a couple was still husband and wife and could not remarry, but they could no longer live together. Alimony was originally "a judicial order entered during the existence of marriage fixing a husband's duty to support his wife while they were living apart due to his fault." Kay calls this a "functional substitute for the duty of the husband to support his wife" (272).

By the middle of the 20th century, alimony was granted to wives in only a minority of cases, and usually they never received payments. In the 1960s and 1970s, many states declared that either the husband or the wife could be awarded alimony, depending on the circumstances of the case. In 1979 the Supreme Court reinforced this principle by declaring unconstitutional an Alabama law restricting alimony to payments by husbands to wives (*Orr* v. *Orr*). The court argued that alimony is awarded on the basis of need, and "there is no reason . . . to use sex as a proxy for need."

Property settlements have become more difficult than they used to be. Most states now allow courts discretion in apportioning marital property equitably as opposed to equally—in other words, according to the merits of the case. As attorney Martha Davis points out, this change results from changes in the views of gender roles in marriage: "This modification of the common law system reflects changed ideas of economic fairness which dictate that the homemaker's nonmonetary contributions to the marriage be recognized and acknowledges that title is an inaccurate indicator of participation in marriage" (1983, 1092–93). It also allows courts the flexibility to decide what is best for each case individually, especially where children are involved.

The Law on "Living in Sin"

Most states did away with common-law marriage by the 1920s. A common-law marriage was one in which two people were declared married after 7 years of living together, that is, after the statute of limitations had run out on the crime of having fornicated outside of marriage. Such a definition makes it clear that common-law marriages were merely tolerated; they were not favored practice.

Increasing numbers of couples are now choosing to live together and run households without getting married. In some cases this choice reflects a conscious rejection of the problems raised by marital law and policy. But if marriages are not always made in heaven, neither are the relationships of unmarried couples. As we have seen, divisions of labor do not tend to be any more equitable among cohabiting couples than among married couples. If a relationship breaks up, does the woman get adequate compensation for her unpaid domestic labor? What happens to accumulated property?

The law remains in a state of confusion. Unmarried individuals are in a better position than married people to have their private contracts enforced, although there are limitations. If it seems that the couple is exchanging sex for support, the contract is not enforceable because it is in effect a criminal agreement for prostitution. Moreover, when people simply move in together, their agreements are usually oral or even simply implied.

The most famous court case on cohabitation is *Marvin* v. *Marvin*, which was decided in the California Supreme Court in 1976. Actor Lee Marvin and Michelle Triola (who used Marvin's surname) lived together for 7 years. After breaking up, Triola claimed that he had reneged on an agreement that she would provide household services, he would support her, and they would share their property. The court declared that such an agreement had to be honored. At the same time, the court made its view of marriage clear:

> We take this occasion to point out that the structure of society itself largely depends on the institution of marriage; and nothing we have said in this opinion should be taken to derogate that institution. The joining of the man and woman in marriage is at once the most socially productive and individually fulfilling relationship that one can enjoy in the course of a lifetime.

In the end Triola received very little.

Most other states have refused to enforce marriage-like norms in the dissolution of nonmarital arrangements, largely because of fears of weakening the institution of marriage. An influential example occurred in 1979 respecting a couple who lived in an "outwardly appearing conventional family relationship" complete with children. The court argued that treating an unmarried couple as though they were married would contravene the state "policy strengthening and preserving the integrity of marriage." To do otherwise would be to recreate the common-law marriage, which the court did not want to do (*Hewitt* v. *Hewitt*).

Some people argue that enlightened law would respect people's choices and treat the unmarried as though they are married. But would this eliminate the problems we have discussed? Or would it just allow more people to share the same old problems, plus create some new ones? Consider the problems with marital law itself. What fundamental principles governing people's personal relationships do we want enforced? The question cannot be dismissed by saying simply that people should make their own choices. These personal choices affect the community as a whole and are sometimes mere reflections of the larger, androcentric sex/gender system.

The Politics of Personal Life

One of the reasons feminism is so threatening to many people and creates so much contention is that it questions our personal lives—our friendships, intimacies, and sexual relationships—in unaccustomed ways. The structure of sex/gender systems affects the most private aspects of our lives, not just because our private relationships are in part governed by law but also because the gender ideologies we have learned affect the way we interact with others. Social institutions are based to some degree on expectations about the nature of relationships among people. Most of us don't want to think about intimacy in political terms as matters involving struggles over power, but research supports feminist arguments that our personal lives, particularly our sexual lives, constitute a key arena for both oppression and liberation.

This analysis suggests why change in sex/gender systems is both difficult and frightening. Sexuality is central to our sense of identity, and at least in American culture, it is also a source of tremendous anxiety. To question our sexuality and the patterns it takes is to question our sense of self. Men who have learned that masculinity requires them to be the successful pursuer and to dominate women in sexual and other intimate relations are threatened by women who either demand equality in their personal relationships or do not see their relationships with men as sexual.

Increasing numbers of women and men are thinking carefully about the significance of their intimate behavior and the choices they make in their private lives. Awareness is not sufficient, however. Making these choices in the face of ingrained ideology and personal feelings and even state enforcement means that making choices can hurt. But feminists argue that the reward for facing these challenges is great: a chance for friendship, love, and intimacy not based on domination and coercion.

Over a century ago the feminist Margaret Fuller summed up her ideal of a personal relationship between a husband and a wife, not as a couple in which two were merged into one and thus lost individual autonomy or equality, but as the progress of "two pilgrims toward a common shrine" (Fuller [1845] 1971,

80–81). As Fuller's words show, the application of feminist theory and the pursuit of autonomy for women does not mean we must abandon all sense of mystery and romance in our lives.

NOTES

1. See the earlier discussion of Freud in Chapters 2 and 3.
2. See Chapter 10.
3. There are many fascinating readings on this event. See, for example, Morrison (1992). For one of the few major accounts that is completely unsympathetic to Anita Hill, see Brock (1993).
4. See the discussion of victim precipitation in Chapter 9.
5. See, for example, the discussion of sex-war theories in Chapter 2.
6. Michele N-K Collson, " 'A Sure-Fire Winner Is to Tell Her You Love Her; Women Fall for It All the Time': Men Talk Frankly with Counselor to Assess Harassment and Acquaintance Rape," *Chronicle of Higher Education*, November 13, 1991.
7. Why are the institutions in which men obtain vicarious pleasure from watching other people having sex and men hurting women labeled "adult"?
8. See also Penelope and Wolfe (1989) and Phelan (1989).
9. Felicity Barringer, "Measuring Sexuality through Polls Can Be Shaky," *New York Times*, April 25, 1993.
10. "Fact File: This Year's Freshmen: A Statistical Profile," *Chronicle of Higher Education*, January 13, 1993.
11. For a discussion of privacy and gay rights, see Samar (1991).
12. This study surveyed over 12,000 people, including 4,314 heterosexual couples, 969 gay male couples, and 788 lesbian couples. More recent research suggests that the findings of this study probably remain valid, with the exception of certain changes in sexual behavior that resulted from the AIDS epidemic, which occurred after Blumstein and Schwartz did their research.
13. "Fact File: This Year's Freshmen: A Statistical Profile," *Chronicle of Higher Education*, January 13, 1993. See also Oliver and Hyde (1993).
14. This was discussed in Chapter 9.
15. Remember during this discussion that because marriage is generally governed by state law its legal definition varies to some degree.
16. For further discussion see Chapter 10.
17. For an influential discussion of the faults of no-fault divorce, see Weitzman (1985).

12

Reproduction, Parenthood, and Child Care

MOTHERHOOD HAS GENERALLY been seen as the destiny and the special mission of women. Through the ages in any discussion of women's roles, status, and activities, one of the first questions anybody is likely to ask concerns the possible effects of changes in women's lives on their roles as mothers. Law, theology, and medicine each have their special perspectives on the matter, but for the most part when authorities in these areas think about women, they are thinking about women as mothers and potential mothers.

In the past century, motherhood and reproduction have become questions for analysis and debate for at least three reasons:

1. Childhood was a historical "invention." In his influential book, *Centuries of Childhood*, the historian Philippe Ariès (1962) showed that the idea of childhood as a special time of life when people are supposed to be nurtured and protected from adult concerns historically evolved in Western culture only in recent centuries. A walk through an art museum shows how people's perception of children has changed. Up to the 18th century children in paintings look like miniature adults; only later do they begin to look like children as we know them today.

   Although Ariès had little to say about mothers, it is reasonable to expect that only when the child became a special category of person did the mother also become a special category of person. In colonial America even the suckling of infants was not necessarily the biological mother's work (Matthaei 1982); indeed, 18th-century philosophers like Rousseau and Wollstonecraft tried to convince more mothers to breast-feed their babes. Those who could afford it hired wet nurses. Child raising meant introducing children to their adult work as soon as possible. Because women and men had different work to do, child raising was done by mothers, fathers, and other family and nonfamily members who were gender-appropriate for the job. Thus, fathers played an important role in child raising.

2. The growth of industrialization separated production from the home. As a distinct sphere of "family life" emerged, so did distinct roles within that sphere. As Julie Matthaei writes, "Family relationships—between husband and wife, between parents and children—began to gain a content of their own" (1982, 110). Homemaking, including motherhood, became a vocation.
3. Motherhood was transformed into an activity regarded as having great social importance. Part of the reason for this change was the growing realization that people could actually control and make choices about whether and when to reproduce and the ways to raise children. As more people realized that choices could be made, they began to evaluate and weigh alternatives. One of the questions they considered was which choices would be beneficial and which detrimental to society as a whole.

In the 19th century, numerous debates began to flow from this new consciousness. Should control be exerted over the number of people born? What was the best way to raise children? How much control should individual men and women have over reproduction? What type of mother would produce the best children? What responsibilities did society as a whole (especially through the force of government and law) have for the production and care of children? The debate over these questions continues today. Let us look more closely at these issues.

To Be or Not to Be a Parent

"If the right of privacy means anything, it is the right of the individual, married or single, to be free of unwarranted governmental intrusion into matters so fundamentally affecting a person as the decision whether to bear or beget a child." This was the view taken by the U.S. Supreme Court in 1972, when it declared unconstitutional laws barring single people from purchasing contraceptives (*Eisenstadt* v. *Baird*). The major breakthrough in giving individuals more control over their own decisions had come in 1965, when in *Griswold* v. *Connecticut*, the Supreme Court first declared that there is a constitutional right to privacy, and indicated that this right meant that married people could not be barred from purchasing contraceptives. The Court restated and further developed its point in 1977 in *Carey* v. *Population Services International* when it declared that an unmarried minor should be able to obtain contraceptives: "The Constitution protects individual decisions in matters of childbearing from unjustified intrusion by the State." How well protected is this constitutional right? How free are people, and especially women, to make their own decisions over whether and when to become a parent?

Reproduction and Choice

Women are about as likely to have children as they ever were, but their reproductive behavior with respect to how many children they have is influenced

The right and ability to choose how many children to have has been the privilege of very few women until recently.

by historical conditions. During the Depression women had fewer children than they do now, and right after World War II they had more.

Socialization and social pressure play important roles in people's thinking about reproduction and parenthood. Not having children is generally viewed negatively, especially for women. Women without children are often viewed and treated as not quite adult themselves. Consider how we describe adults who have no children: There are mothers, fathers, parents, and childless people. Lucia Valeska (1975) asks what would be people's reaction if more women without children described themselves as "child free." The term sounds jarring because it suggests that one might be happy about being without children—that not having children might be a good choice for some people.

Joanna Ross and James Kahan (1983) did an interesting study to investigate reactions to married couples' decisions about having children. They read to college students one of three versions of a story about a married couple. One version said the couple did not want children, another that the couple already had two children, and the third said nothing at all about children. The students were then asked to imagine what the couple's life would be like in 1 year and in 25 years. Of those who heard the story about the couple who did not want children, 50% thought the couple would have children anyway. Only 37% thought the couple would remain child free. Among the 38 people who received no information about the couple's parental status and wishes, 26 specifically mentioned that the couple were parents in their projections. In the 25-year projections, the child-free couples were much more likely than the other couples to be described as divorced. An interesting gender difference emerged in the reactions of the students. Women regarded the couple with children as most satisfied, and men regarded the couple without children as most satisfied.

Children are somewhat more central to a woman's sense of self than they are to a man's. In a Canadian survey, nearly 800 people were asked to list up to 20 items in response to the question "Who am I?" Women were more likely than men to mention their parental status (94% versus 85%), and they put parental status higher up on their lists of self-descriptions. Note that although motherhood seems more central to women than fatherhood is to men, the vast majority of both sexes included parenthood in their lists (Mackie 1983). Even by adolescence, however, females feel more pressure than males to have children (Thompson 1980).

About 10% of all women who are married at some point in their lives never have children, about half of these by choice (Macklin 1980). Child-free women are more likely to have college educations and high-status jobs than are other women, they tend on average to be older when they first marry, and they are more likely than average to believe that having children has some negative effects on parents' lives (Macklin 1980). Psychological studies show that they are more likely to be androgynous, and they appear to have above-average mental health. A 1981 study found married couples with and without children were not different in family background or marital happiness, but the child-free couples had less traditional attitudes toward women and tended to interact with each other more than couples with children did (Feldman 1981).

There are many reasons why people choose not to have children. Those who are single face particular burdens if they want children or find themselves confronted with an unwanted or unplanned pregnancy. People who are married may reject parenthood because child raising does not fit their goals and interests, they do not have the financial resources to care for children adequately, they feel they would not be good parents, or they worry about overpopulation.

Why do people have children? Again, there are reasons, although few parents ever have to think of their reasons. Many people, of course, do not regard reproduction as a choice; it is simply what adults do.

In certain kinds of economies such as preindustrial and nonwelfare state industrial societies (as existed in the United States in earlier years), having children is an important economic resource. Children are needed to work in the family, and parents hope that children will provide old-age insurance. Those who make a conscious choice to have children now may do so because they like the idea of having children, they think they would be good parents, they view having children as fulfilling in their marital relationship, they believe having children will provide personal fulfillment, or they believe having children is a way to leave a mark on the world. Some minority and religious groups urge their members to have children to preserve or expand the group itself.

One decision that increasing numbers of people seem to be considering more carefully is the timing of births. In the late 1960s and early 1970s, the press began to worry that women were giving up having babies. After a while it became clear that the primary change was not in whether women were having children, but in when they did so. In 1970 the majority of mothers had had their first child by the time they were 25 years old: about 36% before they were 20 and 46% between 20 and 24 years old. In 1987 about 23% had had their first child before age 20 and 33% between 20 and 24. The trend toward older first births is also marked in the increased proportion of women who have their first birth at age 30 and older. In 1970 this included 4% of births while in 1987 the figure was 16%.[1]

There are at least three reasons for the trend toward later births. First, the availability of contraception and abortion makes choice possible. Second, because of changing health-care technology and medical views pregnancy at older ages is not considered as dangerous as it used to be. Doctors are changing the advice they give women. Third, women's increased education and work force participation make childbearing at a later age more desirable. Whereas women once believed that motherhood necessarily came first and perhaps could be followed by a career, now more women, especially those entering professional careers, are establishing themselves in their careers first and then having children.

Another change that has been greeted with alarm is that a higher proportion of single women than ever before are having children. In 1950, 4% of all births involved single women, in 1970 the figure was almost 11%, in 1980 it was 18%, and in 1989 it was 27%. There are very large race differences; about 19% of all births to white women, 12% of births to Asian American women, 36% of births to Hispanic women, 46% of births to native Americans, and 65% of births to African American women involved single women (U.S. Bureau of the Census 1992, 68). A large proportion of these births involve very young women, many in their teens. Thirteen percent of births involve teenage mothers, ranging from a low of 6% among Asian Americans to 23% among African Americans.

It is clear that many, perhaps most, of these births are not the result of considered decisions, especially among those who have barely passed childhood themselves. For the young and poor, lack of adequate knowledge about contraception and access to medical care hurts an increasingly sexually active population. People of lower socioeconomic status tend to begin their sexual activity younger than other people, which means they begin with less information (Weinberg and Williams 1980). A 1990 study of pregnant teens, for example, found that many thought abortion causes sterility or that it is illegal (Stone and Waszak 1992). Governmental decisions allowing states to refuse public funding for abortions also mean that poor women do not have the options wealthier women have. Young motherhood is especially prevalent in communities in which young women do not stay in school much longer than they have to and have no careers for which they are likely to be making long-term plans.

On the other hand, many single women are having children by choice. Between 16% and 25% of teenagers say that they intended to become pregnant (Resnick 1984; Stone and Waszak 1992). For many of these young women, however, the "choice" is based on misunderstanding. Large numbers of teens who have children by choice believe that having children will make them more adult, make others treat them more like adults, or at least give them a way to leave home and their family. Tragically, childhood abuse is often a contributing factor to adolescents' pregnancies. One study of pregnant and parenting teens found that at least half had experienced rape, and many had been abused by their own caretaker, including 31% who had been hit with an object like a stick and 18% who had been hit with a closed fist (Boyer and Fine 1992).

Even if there has not been abuse in the home, adolescents often do not feel they can seek help from their parents if they become pregnant. A study of pregnant African American teens found that those who were more likely to tell a parent about their pregnancy were younger, lived further from the clinic, did not attend religious services very often, and had generally good communication with their mothers and anticipated a supportive reaction (Zabin, Hirsch, Emerson, and Raymond 1992).

Many relatively wealthy professional women who have the financial means to provide a home for a child are choosing to have children regardless of their marriage prospects. For some of these women the reason for their choice is age. As they move into and through their thirties they worry that their biological aging will take away the choice to have a child they may want. These women face important moral dilemmas: Is it right to marry a man just because one wants a child? Is this fair to the man? Because having a husband tends to increase the amount of work women have to do at home, is it fair to the woman? Some people argue that it is fairer to children to provide them with two parents, but if the marriage was really only an expedient, how long will it last? For many women, especially African American women, the question of whether to avoid childbearing without marriage is also contingent on the available pool of potential husbands and the likelihood of settling into a stable marital household.

The theme of choice in reproduction has been persistent in the past century of feminism. Choice, however, means more than simply the availability of birth control and abortion. Many 19th-century feminists who fought for voluntary motherhood were not arguing for birth control but for ways to manage reproduction to bolster the dignity of mothers and their abilities to carry out their important social functions (Gordon 1982). Anarchist Emma Goldman argued forcefully for wider availability of contraception, but she, like Margaret Sanger, saw this as only one of the ways to give women the chance to be the best mothers they could be. Some feminists, including some of the best-known suffragists, even supported the idea of eugenics, the "science" of determining which people should be allowed to reproduce. The goal of eugenics is to produce a better race of people, and its proponents generally support racist, conservative points of view.

In her utopian novel *Herland* ([1915] 1979), progressive feminist Charlotte Perkins Gilman envisioned a society of women who had decided that only women with the right temperament and skills for motherhood would conceive. Only babies who were wanted would be conceived; in Herland the idea of abortion was considered utterly appalling. In the real world, however, if we are to consider control over reproduction, we must investigate the questions of both contraception and abortion.

Margaret Sanger, birth control activist.

Contraception

There have been many changes in the technology of contraception over the past century and a half. Changes in the process of manufacturing rubber in the 19th century produced more effective and comfortable condoms and led in the latter part of the century to the development of the diaphragm as we know it. The design of intrauterine devices (IUDs) has changed radically in recent years. Spermicidal agents and douches differ in content from those that were used for centuries. In the late 1980s a contraceptive implanted under the skin, marketed as "Norplant," was developed, and in the early 1990s the new vaginal condom was approved for public use. Methods of sterilization have changed since the

1960s. Even the rhythm method has changed in technique with the use of basal temperature charting, although the principle and the results are the same. Of course abstinence is now, as it always has been, the safest and most effective method of preventing conception.

Despite the changes that have occurred, there is only one form of contraception used now that was completely unknown in any form before the 19th century: the Pill. The approval of the birth control pill by the Food and Drug Administration (FDA) in 1960 was regarded as the harbinger of a new revolution. As we shall see, there are now questions about how successful that revolution was.[2]

Various means of contraception were widely used in the 19th century (Gordon 1977; Degler 1980; Petchesky 1984). The fact that there was a massive political and governmental onslaught against contraception in the 1870s demonstrates how widespread the growing use of birth control techniques was. The governmental response came in the form of the Comstock laws, inspired and promoted by a self-proclaimed emissary of God, Anthony Comstock. These laws were intended to control pornography. The following quotation from one such law reveals the definition of pornography:

> Whoever (within the United States) shall sell . . . or shall offer to sell, or to lend, or to give away, or in any manner to exhibit, or shall otherwise publish or offer to publish in any manner, or shall have in his possession, for any such purpose or purposes, any obscene book, pamphlet, paper, writing, advertisement, circular, print, picture, drawing or other representation, figure, or image on or of paper or other material, or any cast, instrument, or other article or any drug or medicine, or any article whatever, for the *prevention of conception*, or for causing unlawful *abortion*, or shall advertise the same for sale, or shall write or print, or cause to be written or printed, any card, circular, book, pamphlet, advertisement, or notice of any kind, stating when, where, how, or of whom, or by what means any of the articles . . . can be purchased or obtained, or shall manufacture, draw, or print, or in any wise make any of such articles, shall be deemed guilty of a misdemeanor (quoted in Kerber and Mathews 1982, 438).

In other words, the means to control reproduction was defined as pornography. The punishment was between 6 months and 5 years imprisonment at hard labor, or a fine of between $100 and $2,000.

Women's first birth control battle was for access to information about their reproductive systems and birth control techniques. Poor and uneducated women—those most affected by the repression of such information—were especially vulnerable to anticontraception or pronatalist policies suppressing information. Margaret Sanger and Emma Goldman were among those who understood this and worked to help poor, working-class, and immigrant women find the solution they needed and wanted. They were arrested under the Comstock laws for their efforts.

A cruel irony of history is that although in effect poor women have sometimes been denied access to contraception, at other times contraception has been forced on these women. In the 1960s and 1970s, a new issue arose when it became known that many poor women, especially poor black women, were being forced to undergo sterilization without their consent or under considerable pressure to consent. Coerced sterilization has been performed most often on women on the welfare rolls by doctors or hospitals who argue that women who have too many children and cannot afford the medical treatment should be stopped from having more children. Earlier in the century, sterilization of prisoners and the "feeble-minded" was a respected practice. Although the government now has issued guidelines to eliminate abuse of this kind, it has apparently not been stopped completely. As recently as 1977, a U.S. Court of Appeals decided in favor of a doctor who refused to treat pregnant patients who already had two children if they could not pay their own medical bills (for example, if they were on Medicaid) unless they underwent sterilization (*Walker* v. *Pierce*).

Coerced or involuntary sterilization is an important issue. In 1942 the Supreme Court, declaring a right to parenthood, showed a realization of what sterilization could mean if it was guided by the wrong rules and practices:

> We are dealing here with legislation which involves one of the basic civil rights of man. Marriage and procreation are fundamental to the very existence and survival of the race. The power to sterilize . . . may have subtle, far-reaching and devastating effects. In evil or reckless hands it can cause races or types which are inimical to the dominant group to wither and disappear. There is no redemption for the individual whom the law touches (*Skinner* v. *Oklahoma*).

It is no wonder that many black feminists do not define the right to contraception or abortion as a central issue for them. Control over reproduction is a question not simply of whether the means to avoid pregnancy or childbirth is available but also of whether the means to choose parenthood is available.

Comstock-style contraception policy was not attacked effectively until 1965. Many different groups had been fighting for legalization of birth control, but it was a Supreme Court decision that made the difference. In *Griswold* v. *Connecticut*, one of the most historically important Supreme Court cases, the court declared a state law prohibiting contraceptive use by married people unconstitutional. The significance of this decision was far-reaching because in it the court argued for the first time in American history that the Bill of Rights grants Americans a constitutional right to privacy. In this case it concluded that the law could not invade the privacy of the marriage bed. Later applications of the same principle covered contraception more comprehensively and, eventually, abortion.

The Supreme Court expanded its application of the right to privacy in the 1972 case, *Eisenstadt* v. *Baird*, in which it concluded that the decision whether to have a child was a private decision protected by the Constitution regardless of the marital status of the individuals involved even though it also did not favor single people engaging in sexual relations. The Court noted that barring single people from obtaining contraceptives does not keep them from fornicating, and in any case it would be unreasonable to make "the birth of an unwanted child

[a] punishment for fornication." The Court again reinforced this view when it protected the right of minors to obtain contraceptives (*Carey* v. *Population Services International*, 1977).

Legalization of contraception does not mean that people have the knowledge and information necessary to make decisions about birth control. Adolescents in particular often lack a clear understanding of reproduction and of the likelihood that they will become pregnant (Zellman and Goodchilds 1983; Resnick 1984). Young men are certainly under no greater pressure to understand reproduction.

Traditional sexual ideology and guilt also play their roles in guiding people's behavior. Even people who know about contraception may not use it. Women who have learned to feel guilty about having sexual relations are less likely to understand and use contraception than people who do not feel guilty (Rohrbaugh 1980). This is true in part because women who use birth control must admit to themselves that they are preparing to have sexual relations. Alternatively they could think, "I couldn't have *meant* to do this because after all I wasn't prepared." Traditional ideology, which holds men to be the pursuers, may also lead women to assume that men will take care of contraception (an assumption showing more trust than wisdom) and makes men believe it is women's business to avoid getting pregnant.

Traditional sexual ideology and guilt about sex may keep partners from discussing contraception and may make the actual process of donning a condom or inserting a diaphragm more distasteful and sexually inhibiting than it is for people who are more comfortable with themselves and each other. Thus traditional sexual ideology and guilt allow people only two choices: abstinence or unwanted pregnancy.

One study of women aged 18 to 34 found that regular contraception users differed from women who took more risks when they had sex. They were more likely to initiate sex and reported having more orgasms, more likely to be living with their partners and for a longer time, and more likely to be from non-Catholic backgrounds (Harvey and Scrimshaw 1988).

Even for people who seek contraception, good means and complete knowledge are difficult to obtain. Each available method has drawbacks, some of them serious. The rhythm method, douches, withdrawal, and spermicides used with no other contraceptive device have high failure rates. Douches and spermicides can cause irritation, and some intrauterine devices and the birth control pill can cause major medical problems. Many forms of birth control are psychologically difficult for people to use, either because they require considerable attention or distraction from the sexual activity or because they are messy or uncomfortable. Scientists and doctors are unsure about the risks of some methods, such as birth control pills. For women who would like to use Norplant many, including especially the poor who seem most inclined toward the method, can't afford it because even at the cheapest clinics it costs more than $500 to insert.[3]

After it became widely available in the 1960s, the birth control pill quickly became the most popular means of contraception used in the United States, particularly among young people. Doubts about the safety of the Pill, especially for cigarette smokers and women over 35, led to greater caution on the part of many women. Many doctors had special worries about young women's reactions to information about side effects, because for them going off the Pill often meant not using any birth control method. The Pill is the easiest method of birth control to use next to Norplant, and a young woman is especially likely to neglect more interventionist alternatives because she might still be more concerned with not "putting off" her boyfriend than she is with protecting herself.

Nevertheless, the popularity of the Pill increased until the late 1980s, when 76% of women had positive attitudes toward it. The condom had not been a very popular form of birth control among women until the 1980s, when women's attitudes became increasingly positive, partly because of the fear of AIDS. On the other hand, intrauterine devices (IUDs) became less popular because of safety issues and failure rates (Forrest and Fordyce 1988). Of women between menarche and menopause, about 35% rely on their own or their partner's sterilization, 28% take the Pill, 13% use condoms, 10% use no contraceptive method, 5% use diaphragms, 4% use withdrawal, abstinence, or rhythm, and less than 2% use an IUD.[4]

One point is clear: In the sexual division of labor, contraception is still women's responsibility. There are only two relatively effective means of contraception available to heterosexually active men: condoms and vasectomies. Condoms are not as reliable as some other methods (although more reliable than some), and many men object to them on aesthetic grounds. As discussed in the previous chapter, it is tragic for reasons of preventing AIDS that more men will not use them. Vasectomies, or male sterilization, are reversible in most cases, although doctors are reluctant to perform this operation on very young men or men who have not yet had children. Many men find the idea of sterilization distasteful because of mistaken notions that their masculinity or sex drive will be decreased; however, many opt for sterilization, especially if they have had children.

Work on effective male forms of contraception has progressed very slowly. Scientists argue that because the male reproductive system is more complex intervention is more difficult. Moreover, the safety standards now observed in developing a male birth control pill appear to be higher than those used in the development of the female birth control pill, partly because safety standards in general have become more stringent over the past quarter of a century. In any case, contraception probably will remain primarily women's responsibility for the foreseeable future. Even if most people agreed that greater sharing of responsibility is desirable, many women wonder whether they want to entrust contraception to men, who cannot get pregnant.

Abortion

When the United States adopted the English common law, it accepted the view that abortion could not be considered a crime until quickening, that is, the time at which the fetus's movements can be felt. The first law in the United

States that explicitly discussed abortion was an 1821 Connecticut statute that reinforced the common law. The first statute dealing with an unquickened fetus was New York's 1828 statute that made abortion of an unquickened fetus a misdemeanor and abortion of a quickened fetus second-degree manslaughter unless the abortion was necessary to preserve the life of the mother.

The number of abortions rose considerably in the 1840s. Soon more states began to pass restrictive legislation that abolished distinctions among abortions and increased penalties. In the late 1860s, the Roman Catholic Church condemned most abortions. By the beginning of the 20th century, abortion was illegal throughout the United States. The option of a legal abortion was all but foreclosed until the 1960s unless a woman could afford to go to a country that allowed them, such as Sweden.

Why did abortion law become more restrictive? The Supreme Court asked itself precisely this question in 1973 when it was trying to decide what to do about the question in the case of *Roe* v. *Wade*. Justice Harry Blackmun, who wrote the court's opinion, found three reasons:

1. The new abortion laws helped to support the morality of the time, which, as we have seen, defined control over reproduction, including abortion, as pornographic and obscene.
2. Abortion was hazardous when not performed properly, and the medical field was filled with quacks. The restrictive laws, therefore, were sometimes forwarded in an effort to protect women.
3. These laws were viewed (relatively rarely) as ways to protect the life of the unborn from the time of conception. This became much more important to the prevailing public view in the 20th century than it had been previously.

The 1960s saw a rise in the agitation for abortion, and some states began to reform their laws. Once again, however, the real change was instigated by the Supreme Court, which in January 1973 tore down much of the edifice of antiabortion laws in its decisions on two cases, *Roe* v. *Wade* and *Doe* v. *Bolton*. The court again used the right to privacy enunciated in *Griswold* v. *Connecticut* in 1965. The justices argued that abortion must be included in the right of individuals to decide whether to have a child. But they also said, "a State may properly assert important interests in safeguarding health, in maintaining medical standards, and in protecting potential life. At some point in pregnancy, these respective interests become sufficiently compelling to sustain regulation of the factors that govern the abortion decision." At what point? The court decided that it was in no position to argue that theological or philosophical question of when life begins, although it did agree that under the law a fetus is not treated as a legal person with civil rights. It therefore divided pregnancy into three stages, distinguished by the relative claims a state could make in intervening in a woman's decision.

In the first stage, covering roughly the first trimester, the claims of the woman are strongest when weighed against other factors, and therefore the state may not interfere with her right to choose abortion by making restrictive policies. At this stage, the court reasoned, the state does not have sufficiently strong grounds to restrict a woman's constitutional right to privacy.

Whereas in the first trimester, "mortality in abortion may be less than mortality in normal childbirth," during the second trimester abortion becomes riskier for women. In the second trimester, therefore, "the state, in promoting its interest in the health of the mother, may, if it chooses, regulate the abortion procedure in ways that are reasonably related to maternal health."

Finally, "For the stage subsequent to viability, the state in promoting its interest in the potentiality of human life may, if it chooses, regulate, and even proscribe, abortion except where it is necessary, in appropriate medical judgment, for the preservation of the life or health of the mother." In the final stages of pregnancy, states have almost full latitude to ban abortion.

This decision effected a compromise between those who speak unilaterally about the rights of the fetus and those who speak unilaterally about the rights of the woman. Many people regard this case as having attained a delicate balance among conflicting and essentially irresolvable claims. Instead of settling the question, however, the decision increased public debate over abortion.

Many court battles have been fought over abortion since 1973 for two reasons. First, as is generally true when a court makes a major new decision, *Roe* v. *Wade* left many finer points of interpretation unarticulated. Second, the foes of abortion strengthened their political forces considerably and began to do everything in their power to use the law to chip away at and confine the 1973 decision.

One example of a later Supreme Court case that, for the most part, reinforced the expansion of abortion rights is *Planned Parenthood* v. *Danforth* (1976). This case dealt with the constitutionality of several provisions of a Missouri law limiting abortion. The results of this case point to some of the ways states have attempted to narrow the impact of earlier abortion decisions, and the case raises some interesting questions about the nature of choice and justice in abortion decisions. Among the Court's conclusions were the following:

1. States may use a flexible definition of *viability* in deciding when abortion should be forbidden; they do not have to adhere to a strict trimester rule. Given advances in medicine, this enables states to expand the time during which they may ban abortion.
2. A woman may be required to give consent in writing before undergoing first-trimester abortion. Some states have used this provision to require that women review graphic descriptions of even minutely possible risks before having an abortion, as well as pictures of aborted fetuses and fetal development. The purpose of this kind of "informed consent" is to deter women from having abortions.
3. It is unconstitutional to require a spouse's consent for a first-trimester abortion because this would constitute granting the spouse a veto over the woman's decision. In effect she would have the right to choose an abortion only if her husband wanted her to have one. As the Court said,

> Ideally, the decision to [abort] should be one concurred in by both the wife and her husband. . . . But it is difficult to believe that the goal of fostering mutuality and trust in a marriage and of strengthening the marital relationship and the marriage institution will be achieved by giving the husband [an unlimited] veto power.

4. It is unconstitutional to require parents' consent for a first-trimester abortion for an unmarried minor. "Minors, as well as adults, are protected by the Constitution." The Court further argued, "It is difficult . . . to conclude that providing a parent with absolute [veto power] will serve to strengthen the family unit. Neither is it likely that such veto power will enhance parental authority or control." In 1990 the Court allowed states to require that parents be notified of a minor's intention to have an abortion as long as the child can alternatively notify a judge (*Hodgson* v. *Minnesota*, *Ohio* v. *Akron Center for Reproductive Health*).
5. It is unconstitutional to make amniocentesis illegal. Some states attempted to do this on the grounds that the primary purpose of amniocentesis was to screen the fetus for certain defects which, if found, might end in the woman's choosing to abort.
6. States may require that hospitals keep records of every abortion performed in a state.
7. It is unconstitutional to require doctors to make every effort to save the life of the fetus without specifying the stage of fetal development at which this must take place. In an effort to dissuade doctors and hospitals from performing abortions, Missouri's law had made a blanket statement that doctors were required to try to save the aborted fetus.

The Supreme Court reached a legal turning point in *Webster* v. *Missouri* (1989). For the first time since *Roe* and *Doe*, a majority of the judges signaled their intention to restrict the legal right to have abortions, although they did not make clear how far they would go. *Webster* reemphasized the court's identification of viability rather than trimesters as the key to whether abortion is a protected constitutional right of a woman. The decision made it clear that if women have a constitutionally protected right to abortion as *Roe* and *Doe* stated, this right exists only while there is no chance the fetus could be viable. Four of the judges indicated that they disagreed with the earlier decision that abortion is part of a constitutional right to privacy. They believed instead that it is a political issue that should be decided by legislatures. In the end, Justice Sandra Day O'Connor refused to cast the vote that would overturn the original decision. The *Webster* decision signaled states to formulate new, more restrictive policies if they wished, and gave strong hints that it would reconsider the issue of constitutionality in a future case. Later cases, however, continued to preserve the original logic.

There have been a number of unanticipated consequences of the Supreme Court decision that first legalized abortion. The method of analysis the court used was to say that at the early stages of pregnancy states could not interfere with the private abortion choice in part because the mother had the deciding claim against any notion of fetal rights. At the same time, the decision opened the way not just for closing off the possibility for abortion later in the pregnancy, but also for asserting other rights of the fetus in the later stages. In fact, *Roe* paved the way for court-ordered caesarean sections and other interventions on behalf of the child in the womb (see, e.g., Gallagher 1985).

Federal Funding

One of the most successful strategies used by those opposed to individual choice in abortion falls particularly heavily on the poor: the curtailing of federal and other public funds for abortions.

As part of the "Great Society" legislation of the 1960s, Congress added an amendment to the Social Security Act (Title XIX) establishing the Medicaid program. Medicaid provides federal funding to states for medical services rendered to the poor. Participation in the program by any given state is voluntary, but all states that choose to participate must accept certain federal regulations. One of these is that Medicaid cannot be denied to anyone if the services rendered are medically necessary. All states have chosen to participate in the Medicaid program.

The Supreme Court decided that states could refuse to use Medicaid funds to pay for abortions (*Beal* v. *Doe*, 1977), that Congress could pass a law forbidding the use of federal funds (including Medicaid) to pay for abortions of certain types including even abortions caused by rape (*Harris* v. *McRae*, 1980) and that Congress could pass a law allowing states to refuse to use public funds even for medically necessary abortions (*Harris* v. *McRae*, 1980). The Court also decided that cities may refuse to allow nontherapeutic abortions to be performed in public hospitals.

The rationale used in these cases is important to understand. In the case of *Harris* v. *McRae*, the Court discussed the Hyde Amendment, which had called for restricting public funding of abortion. It argued that the amendment does not violate the statutory intent of the Medicaid program to provide financial assistance to the poor who require medically necessary services. The "Hyde Amendment . . . is rationally related to the legitimate governmental objective of protecting potential life." Although Medicaid funds are used to fund medical costs incurred during pregnancy and childbirth, the court also ruled that it is not discriminatory to treat the medical needs of one class of pregnant women (those who need to have abortions) differently from those of another (those who carry the fetus to term). The court argued that the government had a right to offer incentives to make childbirth more attractive than abortion, ignoring the plight of women whose health is threatened by pregnancy and childbirth. This pattern continued. *Webster* v. *Missouri* (1989) upheld a state's right to bar medical personnel from performing abortions in public hospitals.

These court cases, of course, do not affect all women equally; all decrease the likelihood that a poor woman can obtain a safe abortion. As dissenting Justice Thurgood Marshall pointed out in the *Harris* case, the sponsors of these pieces of legislation specifically and openly wished to interfere with women's choices to have abortions, and such intention was specifically declared unconstitutional in the *Roe* and *Doe* cases. Moreover, the legislation places special burdens on the poor, an act which, Marshall argued, is unconstitutional discrimination. The majority of the Court, however, claimed that they were not creating discriminatory burdens, but were simply not going out of their way to remove barriers that were not of the government's making.

One argument in favor of Hyde-type legislation is that the public cannot afford and should not be required to pay for abortions. However, those who need public funds for abortions also need them for prenatal, delivery, and postnatal care; and additional children pose financial burdens on poor women, a burden that will fall on the public treasury and make it more difficult for women to seek employment or additional training to improve their financial situations. One study calculates that the cost to the public of an unwanted birth averages 100 times the cost to the public of the abortion it turned down (Sommers and Thomas 1983). It is also the sad case that the availability of abortion decreases the rate of infanticide in the first hour of human life dramatically ("*Roe* and Neonatal Homicide" 1992). Of course these arguments carry no weight with people who define abortion as murder.

Current Abortion Politics

Public attitudes toward abortion have fluctuated over the years. Although the majority have consistently favored allowing abortions in cases where a woman's health was endangered by pregnancy and childbirth, in cases of rape, and in cases in which the baby would be born with severe defects, a smaller proportion has tended to support it in other cases, such as when a married or unmarried woman feels she cannot afford or does not want another child (Ebaugh, Fuchs, and Haney 1980).

A public opinion poll from early 1989 shows that a majority of Americans believed abortion should be legal under at least some circumstances, and very few believe abortion should be illegal under all circumstances. In that poll, 87% said that they thought a woman should be able to get a legal abortion if her health was seriously endangered by the pregnancy and 69% believed in abortion if there was a strong chance of a serious defect in the baby. A minority agreed that abortion should be legal if a family had a very low income and could not afford any more children (43%) or if the pregnancy interfered with her work or education (26%).[5] Table 12-1 shows that different groups in society react differently to questions about abortion. These data agree with most earlier studies: Women and men do not differ much in their attitudes toward the legal standing of abortion, although women may be slightly more favorable toward some restriction.

The lack of gender differences in public opinion polls does not mean that men and women think about abortion in precisely the same way. The question of abortion can touch men very deeply, and many feel hurt when their partner makes a unilateral decision to have an abortion. But even when stated abstractly

TABLE 12-1
How Groups Differ on Abortion Attitudes, 1989

	Percent saying abortion should be . . .			
	Legal as it is now	*Legal only in certain cases*	*Not permitted at all*	*Know someone who had abortion*
Total Adults	49	39	9	51
Sex and Marital Status				
All women	47	40	11	54
Unmarried	54	37	7	60
Married	42	42	14	50
All men	51	38	8	48
Unmarried	60	31	7	55
Married	46	41	8	45
Age				
18–29 years	56	35	8	66
30–34 years	49	40	9	64
45–65 years	45	39	12	36
65 and over	39	45	9	26
Education				
Less than high school	37	41	16	39
High school graduate	47	41	9	47
Some college	56	35	7	60
College graduate	58	35	5	67
Race				
White	49	39	9	51
Black	45	42	13	54
Religion				
All Protestants	44	44	9	51
Religion very important	34	49	13	46
Not so important	61	36	1	59
All Catholics	48	36	13	45
Religion very important	28	49	22	41
Not so important	72	22	4	50
Political Philosophy				
Liberal	65	28	5	61
Moderate	54	38	6	54
Conservative	38	46	13	46

TABLE 12-1
How Groups Differ on Abortion Attitudes, 1989 *(Continued)*

	Percent saying abortion should be . . .			
	Legal as it is now	*Legal only in certain cases*	*Not permitted at all*	*Know someone who had abortion*
Exposure				
Women saying they had an abortion	79	12	9	95
People who know:				
Someone who had an abortion	58	34	7	100
No one who had an abortion	39	44	12	0

Note: Data are from a *New York Times*/CBS News Poll of 1,412 adults conducted April 13–16, 1989.
Source: *New York Times,* April 26, 1989, p. 13.

the question of abortion has a personal significance and complexity for a woman that it cannot have for a man. Barbara Finlay's (1981) study of college students shows that although overall attitudes toward abortion are not very different between women and men, men's attitudes are structured more simply than women's. Whereas men's attitudes toward abortion are related to their degree of conventionality in sexuality and social matters, women's are also tied to questions of the value of children in their own life plans and to their views of life and the right to life.

Table 12-1 also reveals more liberal abortion attitudes among the unmarried, the young, the more educated, the less religious, and the more politically liberal. Race makes little difference in abortion attitudes. The importance of religion is not surprising and is consistent with previous research. Religious Catholics were more opposed to abortion than religious Protestants. Perhaps more surprising is that not very religious Catholics were more prochoice than Protestants.

Earlier research shows other attitudes that distinguish these two groups. Those opposing abortion have more traditional gender ideology and tend to believe in larger families. Those who favor choice are more committed to protecting a range of civil liberties (Baker, Epstein, and Forth 1981; Granberg and Granberg 1981). Overall, however, antiabortion advocates are not very different from prochoice advocates on other "life" issues such as capital punishment, gun control, government spending and programs on health, or military spending, although antiabortionists do tend to oppose right-to-die practices and condemn suicide more strongly than do prochoice advocates.

These differences of opinion do not capture the depth of the political divisions over abortion. These became more evident in the late 1980s and 1990s as parts of the antiabortion movement became more militant and violent. Demonstrations outside clinics providing abortions became more common, and activists also began to hold demonstrations outside the homes of medical personnel who provided abortions. Abortion providers report that most of them receive harassing and threatening phone calls and mail. One group, the Lambs of Christ, is a nomadic group of Roman Catholic activists who devote their lives to engaging in passive resistance against abortion, primarily by trying to block doctors' and patients' access to clinics.[6]

More active and violent is Operation Rescue, founded by Randall Terry in 1986. His work included vandalism against clinics, and using forceful means to stop women from seeking abortions, including using violence against them. The violence of Operation Rescue and other militant antiabortion activists escalated; as Susan Faludi reports, "Between 1977 and 1989, seventy-seven family-planning clinics were torched or bombed (in at least seven instances, during working hours, with employees and patients inside), 117 were targets of arson, 250 received bomb threats, 231 were invaded, and 224 vandalized" (1991, 412). During 1992 there were at least 43 chemical attacks on abortion clinics, in which foul-smelling chemicals such as butyric acid were sprayed into them, making it impossible for the buildings to be occupied.[7] A survey of facilities performing at least 400 abortions a year reported in 1988 that 81% had experienced picketing, including 46% that experienced picketing with physical contact or blocking patients, 36% had bomb threats, 34% had vandalism, and in 17% of the cases homes of the staff were picketed (Henshaw 1991). In early 1993 a doctor was murdered by a member of Operation Rescue on his way to the abortion clinic where he worked.

Defenders of abortion rights sued under the 1871 Civil Rights Act that bars conspiracies to deprive "any person or class of persons" the equal protection of the laws. First used to defend African Americans against the Ku Klux Klan, many hoped that people who deny women access to abortion clinics could be charged under the law with violation of civil rights, a federal offense. In 1993 the majority of the Supreme Court, including the new appointee Clarence Thomas but not Sandra Day O'Connor, said that women seeking abortions do not constitute a "class" of persons. The dissent argued that the original law was designed to protect citizens "from what amounts to the theft of their constitutional rights by organized and violent mobs" and that people violently blocking access to clinics "is designed to deny every woman the opportunity to exercise a constitutional right that only women possess."[8]

The violent wing of the antiabortion movement is motivated by its desire to end what it sees as the murder of babies, but research also shows that many of these activists—in this wing of the movement, the majority and certainly the leaders are men—also see abortion as part of the evils of feminism (Faludi 1991). The grounds on which this battle is waged were altered to some degree by the change of government administrations from the Republicans, who took a strong stand against abortion (although many Republican women leaders strongly objected to this stand[9]), to the Clinton administration, which began to undo some of the antiabortion regulations of the preceding administrations.[10]

But regardless of these changes, the effects of increasing regulation and harassment must have long-term effects. By the early 1990s a substantial proportion of women who wanted abortions couldn't get them. The year of the *Roe* and *Doe* cases, 52% of abortions took place in hospitals and 46% in clinics. By 1988, 86% took place in clinics and 10% in hospitals partly because of the limits on public funding.[11] Doctors are not being trained to do abortions; whereas in 1985, 23% of residency programs in obstetrics and gynecology included abortion training, in 1992 only 12% included routine abortion training and 31% included none.

Parenthood

Most people become parents at some point in their lives. What choices and decisions do people have to make as parents, and how are these shaped by gender? What are the differences between mothering and fathering? What are some of the questions about parenting raised by changes in gender roles and sexuality?

Motherhood and Fatherhood

When young people contemplate growing up, getting married, and having babies, few understand just how much having children will affect their lives and marriages. Couples know to prepare the baby's space at home and that their time and movements will not be as free as they were. But the new baby will bring additional shocks to family life, some of which are related to gender roles and ideology. Let us begin with a discussion of the impact of children in two-parent families.

Conventional wisdom says that having a child brings couples together and fulfills and cements marriages. This can be true, and the joy of new parents who wanted children can be immense, but the birth of a first child changes the marriage relationship. Partners have less time and energy for themselves as a couple and as individuals. Women especially experience a comparatively large reduction in their free time because of the persistence of traditional divisions of labor. Men often feel that they are being cared for less than they were before their wife became a mother. If women leave employment to become full-time mothers, husbands and wives may find that their lives become increasingly dissimilar. Even the most egalitarian marriage may quickly begin to conform to traditional norms once children arrive.

Studies of the effects of parenthood on marital satisfaction and happiness show that the effects are generally negative, partly because people are not prepared for what will happen to them when children arrive, thus creating stress (Glenn and McLanahan 1982). Although most people are aware of the need to find ways of coping with the shock of losing a family member, few realize they may need to learn how to cope with the addition of one (Ventura and Boss 1983). As one study showed, women overall seem to use a wider range of strategies than men to cope with these changes including seeking outside social support, turning inward to the family itself, and working on their attitudes toward life as a parent. In contrast, fathers seem to find only one strategy more useful than mothers: engaging in outside social activities; in other words, leaving family problems behind (Ventura and Boss 1983).

The degree and type of change a woman experiences seem to depend on whether motherhood is structured as an exclusive and isolating relationship, that is, whether it becomes her sole occupation.[12] The effects of motherhood on women are most negative when it cuts them off from the outside world. Studies of child abuse show that solitary confinement of mother and child is not healthy for the child either.

Being a full-time mother is more difficult in some ways than it once was when women were more likely to be able to count on their mothers, grandmothers, and other female family members as well as the women with whom they had grown up to share their experiences, provide a support group, and ease the transition to and through motherhood. Americans' geographic mobility has changed this. Young people move to seek education and job opportunities, and their parents move to seek pleasant locales for retirement. Most women have at least part-time outside employment, even when children are small, which leaves few companions in the neighborhood for full-time mothers.

The post–World War II development of suburbs also increased the homemakers' isolation. Suburbs are designed to provide space and privacy and to make clearer distinctions than ever between private and public space, residence and commerce. On the whole they are also designed with the private automobile in mind. As more women seek employment, the remaining suburban housewives face more loneliness than ever, certainly more than their mothers or grandmothers faced.

The last generation in which full-time mothering was the predominant style was also the first generation to enter motherhood in the post–World War II era. In 1950 about 28% of married women with school-aged children were in the labor force. A decade later the figure was 39%, in 1970 it was 49%, and in 1980 it was 62%; and in 1990, 74% of married mothers of school-aged children and 59% of married mothers of children under 6 years old were in the work force (U.S. Bureau of the Census 1992, 388). More than 38% were employed full-time.[13] Women are continuing to choose motherhood, but that choice no longer forecloses other choices.

The trend toward greater sharing of familial roles has moved much more slowly than the increase in women's employment. In other words, women have changed their behavior more than men have changed theirs, so women's energies are more divided and their lives more frantic than they were. Men often have claimed that they would take on greater responsibilities at home but cannot because of their job commitments and exhaustion at the end of the day. Women who are employed, however, manage both.

Stress is particularly intense for women competing in traditionally male jobs in which employers feel that they are the most important claimants of their employee's time and command it at will. However, many women and men are beginning to reject this assumption. To discuss this possibility we need to explore what people do when they "mother" or "father" a child.

As though the issues raised by parenthood were not already complicated enough, the very definition of motherhood was thrown open in the late 1980s as more people chose to enter parenthood through "surrogate" arrangements, in which a woman is impregnated by a man whose wife cannot conceive or carry a child. The woman then gives the baby up for adoption by the wife of the father. In these arrangements, the biological mother contracts out the use of her womb, not to mention her genes, and is called a "surrogate mother."

Public discussion became heated during the trial about "Baby M," in which the biological/surrogate mother sued for custody of her child and lost. The contract she had made to have a baby and then give it up was viewed as unbreakable. Up through the middle of 1992 about 4,000 babies were born in the United States through surrogate arrangements. Typically the hopeful parents would pay about $16,000 to a broker in advance, then $10,000 to $20,000 to the birth mother ("surrogate") after the birth and they would pay for all expenses incurred.[14] These cases raise many crucial questions: Should women be allowed to make unbreakable contracts to conceive, carry, and give birth to a child and then relinquish the child to the father and his partner? If it is illegal for women to rent their bodies for sex, why is it legal to rent them for baby making? Above all, what is a mother? More states are regulating surrogacy more strictly in order to avoid the appearance or practice of baby selling. (For more discussion, see Field 1988.)

Mothering and Fathering

He fathered that child. She mothered that child. The connotations of these two sentences are different. *Fathering* generally refers to the act of conception, whereas *mothering* refers not only to conception but also to birthing and caring for a child and to the style of care given. The commonsense differences between mothering and fathering are also illustrated in these two sentences: Don't mother me! Don't father me! The first means don't treat me as though I can't stand up for myself; the second doesn't make any sense at all.

The mother is at the same time one of the most revered and one of the most denigrated of our cultural figures. One could hardly begin to describe the feelings of love, tenderness, and reverence that people have for their own mothers and that are expressed through the cultural media. The relationship is a deeply ambivalent one, however. The child, young or otherwise, wants to be nurtured but also wants to be autonomous. The mother who wants to nurture and care for her children also needs that care herself; a mother is also a daughter. The tremendous responsibility accorded to motherhood is double edged. The ties that bind can be interpreted as both supportive and restrictive.

This unequal responsibility for parenting also means that mothers rather than fathers receive the blame for their children's problems. Numerous popular books and studies explore the ill effects of mothers on society. Philip Wylie's book,

A Generation of Vipers (1942), for example, told people how stultifying to young people, especially young men, mothers and "momism" are. Wylie blamed many of society's problems on the selfish overprotectiveness of women.

In a controversial and provocative article, Nancy Chodorow and Susan Contratto (1982) discuss the problem of blame and idealization of mothers as a central theme in our cultural ideology. They argue that good scholarly analysis of motherhood is especially difficult because of our emotional ties to a particular version of reality: the child's-eye view of our own mothers.

> [The ideology of blame and idealization of mothers] gains meaning from and is partially produced by infantile fantasies that are themselves the outcome of being mothered exclusively by one woman. If mothers have exclusive responsibility for infants who are totally dependent then to the infant they are the sources of all good and evil. Times of closeness, oneness and joy are the quintessence of perfect understanding; times of distress, frustration, discomfort, and too great separation are entirely the mother's fault. For the infant, the mother is not someone with her own life, wants, needs, history, other social relationships, work. She is known only in her capacity as mother (651).

In the process of growing up, we are likely to discover that our mothers are indeed human; thus the rage of disillusionment—and blame.

Chodorow and Contratto argue that some feminist writers have also been subject to these "infantile fantasies." They point out that some feminist writing seems to suggest that the only problem with women's mothering is the oppression of women. If liberated, these writers suggest, like the mothers in Charlotte Perkins Gilman's *Herland*, all mothers would be eternally rich, warm, loving, and not only all-giving to their children but also active and fulfilled by their rewarding outside lives. Indeed, many women (and men) may be trying to live up to this ideal in their own lives, with the frequent result of guilt over their own human limitations and emotional and physical stress. This view also helps keep men out of the picture by deemphasizing their potential impact as fathers.

Like motherhood, fatherhood has changed over time. When parenting meant introducing children to their adult roles as soon as possible, men with sons had very important parental roles to perform. Men also used to be regarded as the moral heads of the family, responsible for safeguarding the morals of wife and children. With the separation of production from the home and the extension of schooling and childhood, however, men became more separate from their children than ever before.

Men also lost some of their parental authority through the course of the 19th century. Until that time all legal rights over children rested with the father. Under the common law (although to a lesser degree in the United States than in England) a man had an unquestioned right to the custody of his children in cases of separation or divorce, and he could even turn custody over to someone other than the mother after his own death. Today some vestiges of patriarchal authority over children remain even though the power of mothers over their children has become greater. "Wait until your father gets home" is a token of this authority.

Fatherhood lost some of its clear definition. Fathers often became absentee landlords who crammed their fathering into weekends and holidays. This image is probably as distorted a portrait as the one of the mother. In a sense it is a complement to the image of the mother as the all-powerful parent who deserves all praise and all blame. In contrast, psychological research continues to show that fathers play a central role in child development for girls and boys.

The tasks of child rearing are divided very unevenly. The dominant gender ideology still assumes that those who are naturally fitted to bear children are also naturally fitted to raise them, even if both mother and father are also employed outside the home. Women are responsible for more child care, and women and men continue to believe that most child-care activities are better or more appropriately done by women. One study of 31 middle-class parents showed that of 81 different child-oriented tasks, a large proportion were described by the majority as tasks that mothers should do, a somewhat smaller number were seen as tasks that should be shared, and a very small number were seen as tasks that fathers should do. Fathers' jobs included developing children's skill at sports, self-defense, and mechanical tasks (Kellerman and Katz 1978).

Couples face many difficulties when they attempt to share parenthood. Just as people have been taught that women are naturally better at child care and other domestic tasks, so they have been taught that men do not have the appropriate natural talents for child rearing. Men may lack the confidence to assume roles that have previously been women's, and many women may be reluctant to give up control or trust fathers to be competent. Sharing would require that men and women reorganize their time and commitments. Employed women have learned to manage both work and family life because they have had to do so, but fathers are not under the same kind of pressure.

The norm of self-sacrifice is so central to cultural definitions of motherhood that women have to fight strong guilt feelings to change themselves. Even when women know their children are being well cared for by someone else, even when the caretaker is the father, many still have the nagging feeling they have forsaken a responsibility. In the end the traditional division of roles is often followed simply because it is the path of least resistance. Sharing requires discussion and negotiation, which can take more effort and energy than simply doing what needs to be done. Such discussions would often take place within earshot of the child. How might children react to hearing negotiations over who should take care of their needs? Role sharing may be healthier and more just, but it isn't necessarily easier.

One of the abiding issues in discussions of mothering and fathering is the way gender structures parent–child relations. Although most people accept the idea that children need the nurturance of a female parent, people also tend to believe that proper child development, especially for sons, requires a male parent. The reason most often given for this need is the preservation of gender roles and the suspicion that a boy will not be able to develop into an appropriately masculine man if he does not have the guidance of a father. Child development theories emphasizing imitation or modeling assume that a child must have a same-sex model to follow. Discussion of the need for father figures has tended to arise in the context of two specific areas: child custody following divorce, which we shall examine shortly, and the "black matriarchy."

Debates over the structure of black families highlight two related issues important in understanding mothering and fathering more generally: the existence and effects of the nuclear family consisting of mother, father, and children; and the existence and effects of the patriarchal family, a more specific form consisting of a dominant father, subordinate mother, and children. African American families are defined as "matriarchal" by people who argue that black families tend to be either single-parent maternal families or families in which a father may be present but is not the dominant adult. This matriarchal structure is said to cause many of the problems that blacks, especially black males, face.

The historical forces shaping the family life of black Americans have been very different from those exerted on whites. Slaves were owned as individuals; slaveowners were under no pressure to respect the integrity of the family relationships of the people they owned, and even when the members of a black family were owned by the same person, their first duties were to their master. Despite their anguish when husbands, wives, or children were sold to other masters, black Americans learned to survive outside the nuclear family unit that whites took for granted.

The development of a black patriarchal family unit was further inhibited by an ideology at odds with the predominant beliefs of patriarchal societies that women are the weaker sex and men are the primary breadwinners. Although African cultures are very diverse and defy generalization at least as much as European cultures do, the gender norms regarding sexuality and divisions of labor of the societies from which blacks came were different from those that sent whites to America. In many of the African societies, women were more economically active and men were less sexually dominant than was true in European cultures. To the degree that African Americans preserved any of the values of their ancestors, their cultures were not necessarily consistent with Euro-American patriarchal values.

Moreover, the experience of black women in the United States was inconsistent with the ideology that women were weak. Indeed, whites applied this ideology of frail womanhood to white women only; black women were viewed as workhorses. As slaves black women were expected to do hard labor. After emancipation black women continued to do hard physical labor, and they found employment primarily in the hardest of the jobs classified as women's work, including domestic service, unskilled service work, and farm work. Black women had little opportunity to learn to see themselves as the weaker sex.

In this century, poverty, migration, and continued job discrimination against black women and men continue to militate against the existence of stable two-parent homes, let alone the patriarchal family. In addition, black men tend to die young, partly because of the likelihood that they will be the object of violence, so there is a large demographic imbalance between black women and men. As a result, public attention in the 1960s was drawn increasingly to the black "matriarchal family." Elizabeth Almquist (1984) points out that the usual description of black families contains some gross inaccuracies, but the image that became seared into public perception was of families dominated by women who, because of their strength, "emasculated" and therefore further weakened the family. The strength of women in the family was often blamed for juvenile delinquency, failure in school, and lack of achievement motivation, especially among sons. In 1965 a government report entitled "The Negro Family: The Case for National Attention" (the "Moynihan Report") based its assessment of the situation of American blacks on exactly this kind of analysis.

The discussion and critique of the black matriarchy is of theoretical and political importance in a discussion of motherhood and fatherhood regardless of race. Aside from the important fact that the black matriarchy theories tend to undervalue discrimination as a source of the problems of African Americans, they reveal some important and continuing assumptions about gender and parenting. The analysis does not simply point to broken or single-parent families as the reasons for difficulty in the black community; it underscores female dominance and strength. We are led to believe that black families (and, it follows, white families as well) would be better off if the male would take "his place" as the dominant authority figure in the family. Women again are the scapegoats, this time for being strong and showing a remarkable ability to cope with oppressive circumstances. Male dominance is posed as the center of gravity for a stable society. (For more discussion see Collins 1989b and Zinn 1989).

Fathers tend to reinforce traditional gender ideology in children more than mothers do, and they are more rigid in expecting their children to conform to traditional gender norms (Johnson 1982). Children recognize at a fairly young age that men have more social power than women, and if boys especially see that part of that power means being able to expect the wife-mother to do most of the work around the house, they would be odd indeed not to try to take on that role themselves. On the other hand, child development experts suspect that one of the important aspects of a successful woman's upbringing is a close and encouraging relationship with her father.

There is a double standard in parenting. Most people are not concerned about the effects of unequal power and authority of parents when the dominant parent is the father. There is much greater concern about mother dominance, however, just as a marriage in which a wife is particularly strong tends to be ridiculed (the poor "henpecked" husband). Despite these worries it appears that more people are choosing, or finding themselves in, alternative family arrangements.

Parenting the Other 14 Million Children

Some of the discussion so far in this chapter makes an assumption that leaves out about 23% of America's children: the assumption that minor children live with their mothers and fathers. As the figures in Chapter 1 pointed out, a large proportion of children live with only one parent (usually the mother) or with neither parent. We now look at some of the special issues single parenthood and divorce raise for children and parents. Both sets of problems highlight once again how closely related are questions of gender, sexuality, and economics.[15]

WHEN A MARRIAGE BREAKS UP. Over a century ago, when John Stuart Mill was advocating liberalization of England's very strict divorce laws, he remarked on an idea we hear very commonly today: Married couples should stay together "for the sake of the children." He believed that people should think more before getting married or becoming parents. We cannot tell whether people are now giving more thought to what they are doing when they marry than they were in Mill's time. What we do know is that the divorce rate has climbed dramatically and that it affects the lives of millions of children.

Child development experts are not agreed that staying together for the sake of children is always the best rule to follow. The case in favor of divorce is most obvious when divorce removes children from scenes of physical violence. Many psychologists also support divorce to insulate children from psychological violence and discord. In her review of the effects of marital disruption on children, Mary Jo Bane (1976) concludes that concern for the welfare of children is no reason to restrict divorce reform per se but that such factors as the arrangements made for children's welfare during marriage and during and after divorce must be considered.

Treatment of children during divorce has changed considerably over the years. When the patriarchal family was more strongly enforced by law, the father had as total control over his children after divorce as he did during marriage. In a sense the mother was related to her children only by marriage; when the marriage ended so did her motherhood if that was what the head of the family wanted. Patriarchal authority was weakened in the 19th and early 20th centuries as the "maternal" or "tender-years presumption" in law took hold. This presumption, until recently held by most psychologists and jurists, assumes that a mother's care is needed during the tender years of childhood; all else being equal, child custody should be awarded to mothers following divorce. As a typical court decision (*Muller* v. *Muller*) stated in 1948, "The mother is the natural custodian of her child in tender years, and . . . if she is a fit and proper person, other things being equal, she should be given custody."

Mothers are judged unfit if they abuse their children or are alcoholics or if they are accused of moral faults that create what is deemed an unhealthy environment for children. Sexual activity outside of marriage has often been used as grounds on which to deny women custody of their children. In 1979, for example, the Illinois Supreme Court threatened to deny custody to a mother for immoral conduct (*Jarrett* v. *Jarrett*). The mother, who divorced her husband because of his cruelty to her, originally had been awarded custody of the child, but when she announced that her boyfriend was going to move in with her, the father then sought custody. The court concluded that it was the policy of the state to "safeguard the moral well-being of children" and that the mother's "conduct offends prevailing public policy." Although a moral indiscretion was not sufficient grounds for denial of custody, the court feared that if the boyfriend moved in and lived with the mother, the children "may learn to disregard existing standards" of morality. Therefore, the boyfriend could not reside in the house if the woman wanted to keep her children.

Lesbian activity has also been used as grounds to deny a woman custody of her children, although mere proof of lesbian inclinations is not treated as negatively by courts as it once was, and lesbian activity is coming to be treated similarly to heterosexual activity. One reason is that courts are becoming aware of research that shows that the upbringing children receive from lesbian and gay parents is not very different from the upbringing they receive from heterosexual parents. It appears that children of lesbian mothers even learn conventional gender norms about as well as other children do (Patterson 1992).

Consider a state supreme court decision that illustrates the conflicting views about homosexuality and child custody found in current law (*Schuster* v. *Schuster*, 1978). Two women separated from their husbands to live together. The fathers filed for divorce in a lower court, and the mothers were given custody of their children but were ordered to live apart, which they refused to do. The fathers then sued to obtain custody of the children. The court not only refused to change the custodial arrangements but also lifted the ban on the women's living together. The court was not unanimous, however. One dissenting opinion included a quotation from a law article that illustrates the objections made to allowing lesbians custody of their children:

> In seeking to regulate homosexuality, the state takes as a basic premise that social and legal attitudes play an important and interdependent role in the individual's formation of his or her sexual destiny. A shift on the part of the law from opposition to neutrality arguably makes homosexuality appear a more acceptable lifestyle, particularly to younger persons whose sexual preferences are as yet unformed. . . . If homosexual behavior is legalized, and thus partly legitimized, an adolescent may question whether he or she should "choose" heterosexuality. . . . If society accorded more legitimacy to expressions of homosexual attraction, attachment to the opposite sex might be postponed or diverted for some time, perhaps until after the establishment of sexual patterns that would hamper development of traditional heterosexual family relationships. For those persons who eventually choose the heterosexual model, the existence of conflicting models might provide further sexual tension destructive to the traditional marital unit.

In this view, allowing lesbians custody of their children may not hurt the children themselves, but it could perpetuate marital instability from one generation to the next.

These cases raise a number of important issues. From the point of view of the parents involved, they highlight some of the difficulties that adults who are now single face in their personal lives because they have responsibility for children. Even if a court decision is not involved, divorced parents face particularly difficult problems in deciding how to handle their parental responsibilities.

A further question concerns the values pursued by public policy through legislation and court decisions. Few people would object to judges' attempts to act in the interests of children, especially to protect them where the parents have conflicting interests. But exactly how should the courts protect children? How far should public bodies go in deciding what is morally and socially good for a child? As the cases cited here show, safeguarding the child can mean quite profound regulation of the parents' lives and the parents' understanding of what is good for the child, including on the basis of gender and sexual ideology.

States are moving toward abolishing the maternal presumption, especially in light of the passage of equal rights amendments to state constitutions and the activism of "fathers' rights" groups. Many people prefer to emphasize financial and other resources available in the home in determining the best outcome of custody fights. This move is not without problems, however, including those specifically relevant to the question of gender. If courts awarded judgments on the basis of parents' financial resources and abilities to provide for children, the facts of economic life would point to the father in most cases as the best care provider. One court, for example, awarded custody to the father on the grounds that the mother was intending to go to law school. The court argued that the mother would not have the appropriate amount of time to devote to her child. This decision (*Marriage* v. *Tresnak*) was reversed on appeal in 1980. It now appears that women usually gain custody of children because men do not seek custody. When men do seek custody, they are increasingly likely to win.

In recent years there have been many new developments in the way custody is handled by divorcing couples and courts. Courts take the children's views and preferences into consideration more than they once did, and they often assign an official the special task of representing the child. The standard practice used to be to award custody to one parent and grant visiting rights to the other. Now, more decisions award joint custody, in which children live part-time with one parent and part-time with the other. This arrangement requires that the parents be able to coordinate schedules and that they live in close proximity to each other.

A more common issue than custody is what, if any, child-support payments the father will be ordered to make and whether the court order will be enforced. In most cases, divorced mothers are in a weak financial position. They are likely to have considerably less earning power than the father, particularly if they have been full-time mothers and homemakers. If they gain custody, they have the added financial burden of children, including child-care costs when they must be absent from home.

In the late 1960s, public policymakers became aware of a problem affecting the majority of women who were supposed to be receiving child-support payments: Fathers were not paying. Within a very short time after divorce many mothers assume full responsibility for the financial support of their children. This is almost a reversal of the old patriarchal principle whereby the mother had only an indirect relationship with her child through the father. Now the father has a connection to the child only through the mother, and if his relationship with her ceases, so does his responsibility to his children. Children are regarded as the mothers' property.

For a while only sporadic attempts were made to enforce child-support payments. A man could be fairly sure to escape if he left the state in which the payments were ordered, and many did. As a result, some people charged, the only men who were caught were those who were poor and had financial difficulties making payments. By the late 1970s, states were computerizing their records and coordinating efforts to catch delinquent fathers, partly because the fathers' refusal to take responsibility for their children was causing the states to suffer financially. A large proportion of women seeking public assistance for their children were those who were not receiving the support payments their former husbands had been ordered to pay. This spurred the government to make greater efforts to track down delinquent fathers.

Child support is not the only financial aspect of divorce that affects children. They are also affected by the way in which property is divided. In Chapter 11 we saw the problems of the widespread common-law property system in which ownership follows title, leaving many women, especially homemakers, very poor. In a relatively small number of states, courts are obliged to divide property equally between divorcing partners. As fair as this system may seem in the abstract, it contains what is generally regarded as a major flaw with regard to the welfare of children. If the marital home constitutes the bulk of the marital property, it has to be sold and divided. This means not only that the children must be physically uprooted, another disruption in their lives, but also that their standard of living will almost inevitably be substantially reduced. Even if the home is awarded in full to the custodial parent, lack of additional resources may still mean that the home must be sold and the standard of living must decline for the custodial parent to be able to afford more than the shelter itself.

Most states now allow courts discretion in apportioning marital property equitably. Equitable and flexible systems of property division increase the opportunity for courts to divide property, including the home, in ways that cause minimal disruption in the lives of children. The home in which children live is less likely to be sold out from under them in these states (Davis 1983).

SINGLE PARENTHOOD. Nearly one-quarter of the births in America now involve single women. Regardless of whether a father lives with the mother and child or whether he assists in the support and care of the child, unless he marries the mother or follows the formal legal procedure to acknowledge paternity, the child is regarded by law as having only one parent, the mother, and is designated illegitimate. At one time this meant that although mother and child had full legal claims on each other, as far as the law was concerned father and child were strangers to each other. No claims could be made by or on behalf of the child for support, inheritance, or any other rights of the parent–child relationship.

Lawsuits involving illegitimate children and their parents raise questions about gender and sexual ideology and the influence these have on the choices people make. Part of the reason the law distinguishes between children born in and out of wedlock is that these distinctions help governments enforce certain sexual morals. However, these distinctions punish the children, who obviously cannot choose the circumstances of their birth, for their parents' violation of social norms. Although the United States has not abandoned the classification of illegitimacy as some other countries have, American law is increasingly regarding discrimination between legitimate and illegitimate children as illegal and even unconstitutional under the equal protection clause of the 14th Amendment. As the Supreme Court said, "It is unjust and ineffective for society to express its condemnation of procreation outside the marital relationship by punishing the illegitimate child who is in no way responsible for his situation and is unable to change it" (*Parnham* v. *Hughes*, 1979).

Legitimacy laws do not discriminate among children as much as they once did, but they still discriminate against men. A Supreme Court case, for example, decided that an unwed father had no right to sue for the wrongful death of his child after the child and mother were killed in an automobile accident. The majority decided that because the father had never bothered to make the child legitimate, he could not benefit by the child's death (*Parnham* v. *Hughes*). Another involved a child's natural mother, the mother's new husband, who did not father the child, and the child's natural father. The new husband wished to adopt the child, which by law would give the child a father. The natural father objected to the adoption. The Supreme Court ruled in favor of the husband and wife and against the natural father (*Caban* v. *Mohammed*, 1979).

Herma Hill Kay points out that illegitimacy cases show that "a severe tension exists between the desire that all children be supported and the disinclination to encourage sexual promiscuity at the public expense" (1988, 381). Public policy continues to discourage what is seen as immoral sexual behavior, and the burden of this policy falls differently on men and women. Ultimately, of course, it falls on the child. The father can be inhibited from taking responsibility for his child unless he marries the mother. The child may be discouraged from having a relationship with the father, a relationship that might contribute to his or her well-being. Legitimacy laws also mean that a single woman who finds herself pregnant and cannot or does not want to have an abortion generally has to face taking full responsibility for her child.

People who become single parents by any means share many of the same problems. They must raise their children alone and find the financial means to support them. They have to balance their moral obligations to their children with their own personal needs for adult companionship. The financial problems of single mothers are particularly awesome. Single-parent households headed by women constitute a large percentage of the households that fall below the poverty line, partly because the sex/gender system continues to discriminate against women and discourages them from developing the resources to be financially independent.

Parents without Children

Sooner or later most mothers find themselves with children who no longer need or want their daily care and no longer help them fulfill the child-centered role for which they were trained. These mothers' children have grown up and may have children of their own. On the problem of mothers with grown children Pauline Bart has written:

> Nowhere is [the inadequacy of traditional female roles] more apparent than when studying the super mothers suffering from Portnoy's Mother's Complaint, middle-aged depression, coming not from the hormonal changes of the menopause, but from the life cycle changes, when the children from whom the woman drew her identity depart and she has nothing to replace them with (1975, 12).

Many writers have looked at the "empty nest syndrome," or role loss, in middle-aged women. Bart argues, "It is true that we all lose roles throughout our lives; but when we are young there are new roles to replace the old ones, and rites of passage to ease the transition. But as we age, there are usually not such new roles . . . and there are few rites of passage. There is no Bar Mitzvah for menopause" (1975, 12). We shall discuss shortly whether there are new roles for the "long-distance mother" to adopt, but the problem of loneliness and depression among some women at this stage in life is a serious one.

Bart studied over 500 women between the ages of 40 and 59 who had been diagnosed as depressed at mental hospitals and had had no previous hospitalization for mental illness. In looking at the relationship between marital, maternal, and occupational role loss and depression, she found that maternal role loss was the most important predictor of these women's depression. The relationship between depression and maternal role loss was even stronger among middle-class homemakers, or women who had had "an overprotective or overinvolved relationship" with their children. Her findings seem consistent with common sense: The more a woman's life revolves exclusively around her children, the more she will suffer when they are no longer children. Gender-role norms that prescribe full-time motherhood for women throughout their younger years may lay a treacherous path for them as they age.

The problems of maternal role loss are magnified by other changes in women's situation as they age. There are different standards of beauty and attractiveness in women and men, and in our society aging is viewed as less attractive in women than in men. Many women also find that their marriages indeed endured only "for the sake of the children" when their husbands leave them for younger women around the time the children become independent. In addition, many women take on the new role of mother-in-law when their children leave home, a role that is itself the subject of painful stereotypes. In this role, women become one of the most ridiculed and resented of our cultural figures.

One of the factors that causes problems for women with older children is the view that a woman loses her meaning when her children grow up. Critics of society's treatment of older women should not focus too long on the emptiness of life without young children. As Bart's study shows, maternal role loss depression afflicts a very special group of women, and the majority of women are now protected from it to some degree by employment, especially after their last child has entered school. In poor and working-class families, grandmothers are still relatively likely to be part of the day-to-day lives of families, at least to a greater extent than tends to be true of wealthier, more mobile families.

Changing attitudes toward aging also mitigate the effects of maternal role loss, and preventive medicine and improved health care mean that women are even more likely to be able to begin new lives and activities when children leave home. The popularity of new towns designed mainly for the "postparental" stage of life testifies to the increased tendency for parents to launch new lives. Parents do not want to be cast off by their children, but increasing numbers also do not want to give up their new—or renewed—independence to adult children in need of baby sitters.

Beyond the Family

American society, especially through the instruments of law and public policy, has made great claims about its intention to protect the family and children. Yet, by the end of the 1970s, critics from left to right charged that in many senses America is antichild, antimother, and antifamily.

Feminists and others on the left have argued that public policy regarding the family is based on and reinforces traditional gender and sexual values that place the primary burden for child care and domestic labor on women without giving them much help in performing these important tasks. They charge that public policy has not fully recognized the facts of life in modern society. Men are not the sole breadwinners in families; most women now do and will continue to seek employment to support themselves and their dependents. A growing proportion of women are the sole heads of families.

The androcentric structure of education and the job market means that women do not have the financial resources to provide for their children, and in too many cases the promise that fathers will provide these resources is empty. Social-welfare assistance to provide for children is inadequate and is dispensed so reluctantly as to make recipients feel degraded for turning to the government for help in raising what is claimed to be our "most valuable resource." Restrictions on abortion mean that those who are least in the position to have more children may be forced to do so.

Women who take traditional gender norms at face value and become full-time mothers and homemakers are rewarded by being the most economically and psychologically vulnerable of all women. Carolyn Adams and Kathryn Winston's comparative research led them to conclude, "The United States has the distinction of being the only major industrialized country in the world that lacks a national insurance plan covering medical expenses for childbirth and is one of few governments in industrialized nations that does not provide any cash benefits to working women to compensate for lost benefits" (1980, 33).

The United States was one of the last democratic nations to develop a maternity or parental leave law, and it offers much less than almost all the others.[16] As of 1993, companies with 50 or more employees must allow employees to take up to 12 weeks' unpaid leave for birth or adoption or to care for seriously ill family members.[17] In fact, many companies offered at least that level already.[18] Many other nations provide grants or stipends to families with new children, which is not done in the United States.

There has been inadequate effort to provide care for the children of working mothers. Mothers once relied on other women, such as their mothers, to help them, but this is less possible now.[19] Relatively few people take seriously the idea that fathers and mothers should share the responsibility for child rearing equally. Jobs, particularly men's jobs, are so structured as to make sharing difficult.

Day care is not a new idea in American history.[20] Early in the 19th century, some private nurseries were set up for poor and working-class women. These were merely custodial compared with the kindergartens developed later in the century, which were intended to foster child development. Limited numbers of publicly funded day-care centers were established during the Depression. There were also publicly funded day-care centers during World War II, when the nation had a specific interest in enabling women to enter the work force while men were at war. When the men came home, the funding for this relatively small program stopped. Repeated proposals to start a new program have been defeated. In 1971 a bill that would have instituted a network of federally funded and locally run child-care centers that would be available to all children who needed them passed in Congress, but President Nixon vetoed it on the grounds that it would weaken the family.

Over the past quarter century, a series of new and increasingly popular efforts have been aimed at trying to make the provision of healthy and high-quality day care a part of public policy. Although there have been efforts to expand public programs, most of what has been available is private. Both businesses and local communities are beginning to sponsor day care for children, although the available spaces make only a small dent in the need. Many companies have found that by providing child-care benefits—in some cases, by establishing child-care centers at the work site—the company itself benefits in many ways. As one partner in the investment firm of Goldman, Sachs & Company said, "If people have trouble finding child care, they will be absent, late, or worrying about their arrangements. If we can alleviate that pressure, people will be more effective."[21]

What arrangements do parents make for their children while they are at work? A study of child-care provisions for children less than 5 years old with mothers who are employed full-time shows that only a minority, 28%, attend a day-care center, nursery school, or preschool. Another 24% are cared for in the child's own home, by the father (11%), a grandparent, another relative, or a nonrelative. The largest proportion, 42%, are cared for in someone else's home, by a nonrelative (28%), a grandparent (11%), or another relative (U.S. Bureau of the Census, 1989). This means that one of the most common ways of obtaining child care is to send the child to the home of a nonrelative, who is often running the equivalent of a small, unregulated, and uninspected day-care center. Child care is also expensive, especially for the less well off. Families of preschoolers with incomes under $15,000 spend about 23% of their income on child care, whereas people earning $50,000 or more spend 6% of their income on child care.

The public is becoming increasingly discontented with the current situation. By the mid 1980s, about 55% of Americans agreed that companies should share responsibility for providing day care rather than leaving it up to individual employees to work out, and 63% thought that companies should make day care available to employees as part of benefits packages. There was also growing support for public provision of day care. By 1985, 43% of the public thought that child care should be made available to all preschool children as part of the public school system and supported through taxes. It is no wonder that child care is now a popular issue among politicians and legislators in the late 1980s. The question is, what will be done about it?

There are other problems with public support of the family from the progressive point of view. In many cities, families have difficulty finding a place to live because landlords refuse to rent to families with children and city governments refuse to interfere. Assistance to women and children who have been victims of abuse in the family is minimal, because the public is reluctant to interfere in the private life of the family. Government and business often have very limited understanding of the definition of "the family," sometimes restricting it to married couples with children. In summary, feminists argue that American policy seems most supportive of motherhood and children when the husband–wife family unit is intact, the woman gets pregnant only when she wants to be pregnant, the woman is a full-time homemaker, and the husband can and does provide for the family. In other words, the American system is not supportive of the family or motherhood per se, but of a particular type of family and motherhood.

Conservatives and antifeminists see the world differently. They focus on how much the patriarchal family has been weakened and worry about the eventual collapse of the family order. Sexuality and morality have become unconstrained by traditional morality and family values. Adults have become individualistic and self-serving, putting themselves before the interests of their families. Women are giving up devoting themselves to caring for home and children, which leaves men without incentives to be good husbands and fathers and leaves children without primary caregivers who are personally motivated.

Conservatives further argue that the incentive to provide for the family is being stripped away by the availability of tax-supported programs. Government is intruding in the family by telling parents how to care for and discipline children and how husbands and wives should treat each other. Government is also making it easier for families to break apart. The law is moving in the direction of treating heterosexuals and homosexuals, married couples and cohabiting couples, all the same. Power over children is being taken away from parents, especially in education policies. In some places a fetus is as likely to be killed as to be nurtured to birth, and more marriages end than begin.

Despite the vast differences between these perspectives, both groups claim to be profamily, and these different positions should be taken seriously as reflecting different conceptions of the family. Feminists emphasize the degree to which patriarchal principles still underlie family policy, and antifeminists emphasize how much that order has broken down. The red herring in the debate is the question of whether there should be government interference in the family. Both sides want the government to do something about the family to support the values they are pursuing. Both sides understand that the values that shape and define the family in its various forms have profound effects on all aspects of our lives. That is why the debate is so rancorous.

The public, through the government, has great power to regulate family and personal life, not only through direct regulation but also through the incentives and disincentives. We have seen many examples in the justifications offered for different court decisions. Family lives and structures have changed over time. Perhaps one of the greatest changes is that we now understand that there are both individual and community decisions to be made about our familial values and policies.

One of the core issues in the continuing debate is whether or to what extent child care and the raising of children should be the work of an isolated family unit. More specifically, because of the persistence of gender divisions of labor, the issue is whether and to what degree child care and the raising of children should be the work of *women* in isolated family units. The rise of public education means that some of that duty has long since become a shared societal task. But the history of child-care provisions reveals the continuing assumption that whatever else they do, when their children are not in school women should be with them.

Reproduction and the care of children are among the most important tasks we have as individuals and as a society. Are children, our future generation, indeed a national resource, or are they private property? Given the current structure of society, behind this question is another: What are the relative roles, responsibilities, and options of women and men in creating and caring for those future generations?

NOTES

1. Jane Brody, "Personal Health," *New York Times*, July 13, 1989, p. 17.
2. For discussion about techniques of birth control, see Hyde (1986).
3. Fawn Vrazo, "Many Can't Afford Cost of New Contraceptive," *Wisconsin State Journal*, March 9, 1992.
4. Philip Hilts, "Birth Control Safer than Unprotected Sex," *New York Times*, April 23, 1991.
5. These figures are from a *New York Times*/CBS News poll taken in April, 1989, and reported in the *New York Times*, April 26, 1989.
6. Gina Kolata, "Nomadic Group of Anti-Abortionists Uses New Tactics to Make Its Mark," *New York Times*, March 24, 1992.
7. Tamar Lewin, "Abortion-Rights Groups See a Rise in Attacks on Clinics," *New York Times*, January 4, 1993.

8. "High Court Says U.S. Judges Can't Halt Abortion Clinic Blockades," *New York Times*, January 14, 1993.

9. "Two G.O.P Groups Ask Party to Drop Anti-Abortion Plank," *New York Times*, July 28, 1992.

10. Steven Greenhouse, "Family-Planning Officials Laud Clinton Move on Bans," *New York Times*, January 24, 1993. See also Alan Cowell, "Vatican Attacks Clinton on New Abortion Policy," *New York Times*, January 24, 1993.

11. Tamar Lewin, "Hurdles Increasing for Women Seeking Abortion," *New York Times*, March 15, 1992.

12. Recall the discussion of health issues in Chapter 6.

13. Susan Chira, "New Realities Fight Old Images of Mothers," *New York Times*, October 4, 1992.

14. Lisa Belkin, "Childless Couples Hang on to Last Hope, Despite Law," *New York Times*, July 28, 1992.

15. For discussion of divorce, see Chapter 11.

16. For a review of European countries' policies, see Snyder (1992).

17. Vivian Marino, "Impact of Leave Law? Experts Say Little Need for Businesses to Worry," *Wisconsin State Journal*, February 6, 1993.

18. Ibid.

19. At the same time, it should be remembered that the vast majority of paid child-care workers are women.

20. Much of the following is from Norgren (1989).

21. Carol Lawson, "On-the-Job Child Care Comes to the Rescue," *New York Times*, April 22, 1993.

13

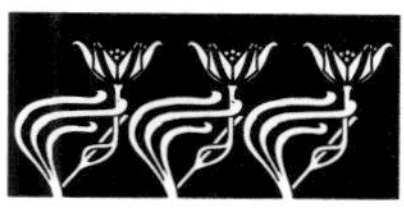

Work, Employment, and the Economics of Gender

WORK IS ONE of the most misunderstood and underestimated facets of women's lives. Until recently the dominant gender ideology led people to believe not only that women do not work as much as men but also that they are too delicate to work as much as men. Many women have tried to open people's eyes to women's labor over the years. Among the most famous was Sojourner Truth, whose 1851 speech, reported by Frances Gage, stands as one of the most powerful in the history of women's oratory:

> Look at me! Look at my arm! I have ploughed, and planted, and gathered into barns, and no man could head me! And ar'n't I a woman? I could work as much and eat as much as a man (when I could get it) and bear de lash as well! And ar'n't I a woman? I have borne thirteen children, and seen' em mos' all sold off to slavery, and when I cried out with my mother's grief, none but Jesus heard—and ar'n't I a woman? (quoted in White 1985, 14)

Sojourner Truth's experience is often quoted as extraordinary and, in many ways, it was. But her speech is not just about her own life. It is also about the lives of the thousands of other women whose "occupation" was slavery. Much of the actual labor she did, including both fieldwork and mother work, has been shared to some extent by millions of women of many colors both before and after her time. Her speech was about the specific experience of African American women who were held in slavery, but it was also about women more generally.

Many feminist scholars have launched critiques of traditional scholarship on economics and economic history, claiming that it has not adequately incorporated women and women's work into its models and explanations (Ferber and Nelson 1993). Indeed, scholarly research on women in society traditionally directly integrated economics questions into understanding men's but not women's lives. Let us look at these claims more closely.

Sojourner Truth, an abolitionist, suffragist, and ex-slave.

Roslyn Feldberg and Evelyn Glenn (1979) argue that sociologists tend to use two entirely different models or sets of assumptions and questions depending on whether they are focusing on men or women. For men there is the "job" model, for women the "gender" model. Social scientists assume that men's social relations and identity are determined by their jobs, their sociopolitical attitudes and behavior are derived from their occupational roles and status, and their central interests and motivations in life are their employment and earnings.[1] Men's primary connection with their families is in their role as economic providers. The job model leads us to assume that the most important thing we can know about a man is his occupation. The job model is not only used by social scientists but also reflected in everyday thought and language. People often use the phrase "the ordinary working man" to refer to the average male. "The ordinary working woman" is not as common a phrase, and it does not have the same connotation as it has when applied to men.

In contrast, Feldberg and Glenn argue, women are analyzed according to a gender or (probably more appropriately named) a family model.[2] Social scientists assume that women's basic social relations are determined by their relationship to the family; their sociopolitical attitudes and behavior are derived from their family roles, status, and gender-role socialization. Women's central interests and motivations in life revolve around the internal dynamics of family life. Women's place is the family, which is not where "work" happens. Women have only a tentative and marginal relationship with the outside occupational world. Women's class is generally defined not in terms of their relationship to production, even if they are employed, but in terms of their husbands' or fathers' occupations. Domestic labor is not regarded as "real work" and is often viewed as only distantly related to the economic world, particularly the world of production, so it does not provide women a class status. The average woman is often referred to as the "average housewife."

The world of work and the world of the family are seen as two places that are parallel and complementary but often in conflict. In the work world, people are (supposed to be) ambitious, competitive, and aggressive and are valued in the currency of money. In the family world, people are (supposed to be) nurturant and more peaceful and are valued in the currency of love and loyalty. Women are assigned to one and men to the other, and their characters are defined by the worlds they are supposed to occupy.

Evelyn Nakano Glenn (1992) has further developed this changed understanding of gender-based models of understanding the structure of economic relations to incorporate race/ethnicity into the model. As she and others have discussed, when feminist scholars develop gendered models of social institutions, very often gender is seen in isolation from race and ethnicity. The mutual isolation of these two aspects of social structure has resulted, by and large, in understanding white women through a primarily gender-based model as though race and gender do not interact in creating their experience, and in understanding women of other races through a race and gender-based model, but in an additive rather than complex and interactive way.[3]

Glenn asks that we use a more complex model to analyze social reproduction, or the "array of activities and relationships involved in maintaining people both on a daily basis and intergenerationally" (Glenn 1992, 1). The term *social reproduction* is useful because it incorporates what is usually narrowly defined as economic activities such as production and consumption, but also activities often excluded from the "economic," including the remainder of domestic and family labor. By using a complex model of gender and race it is more possible to understand the dynamics of who does what social reproduction labor under what circumstances, and it is more possible to see change over time. Glenn's own work on domestic service offers good examples (Glenn 1986; 1992).

Although the majority of women are now employed for pay, there has been less change in the conception of work and family, men and women, than might be expected. As many social scientists have pointed out, one of the reasons that women's work is so little understood is that our definition of work is androcentric, or primarily based on the experience of men. Work is what people are paid to do. For most people, *work* and *employment* are synonymous. Domestic labor, except when performed by a paid servant, is not work. Volunteer work is not work. In other words, much of women's work is defined as something else.

This chapter examines women's work lives, gender divisions of labor, and the resulting economic situation of women. We focus especially on the opportunities women have for making choices in their work and economic lives, and the effects of these choices, or the lack of them, on other aspects of their lives.

Making a Living Versus Making a Home: Defining Differences

If we stopped people on the street and asked them whether their mothers worked when they were children, a large proportion would say "no." What they would mean, of course, is that their mothers were not employed for pay. Their mothers probably spent long hours shopping, cleaning, cooking, and performing the numerous other tasks involved in managing family life, but that is not seen as real work. They might have contributed many hours of labor to voluntary organizations, but that, too, is not considered real work. Only if a woman has done any of these activities for pay, is she likely to be viewed as having worked. Otherwise, she is "just a housewife."

The distinctions between work and family, breadwinning and homemaking, seem so obvious today that many people are surprised to learn that these apparently meaningful distinctions are relatively new and can be applied only to certain kinds of economies. In a subsistence economy, in which all members of a household labor most of their waking hours to provide themselves with the necessities of life, there is little difference between making a home and making a living. In small-farm agricultural societies and urban societies of crafts people, the work place or market is not entirely distinct from the home. In these societies there are gender divisions of labor, but describing one person as a "worker" and one as "just a housewife" does not make sense, especially when many of the goods required in the home are produced there by women. It is true that before this century relatively few women worked outside the home. It is also true that before this century relatively few men worked outside the home.

The Rise and Fall of Homemaking

When did people begin to make a distinction between making a living and making a home? How and when did the distinct role of homemaker arise? Historians point to the rise of industrial capitalism, which increasingly moved production outside the home and provided opportunities for men to seek wage labor there. This does not mean that capitalism *created* gender divisions of labor; it certainly did not create gender inequality. Women in preindustrial American society were already governed by feudal laws denying married women the opportunity to own property and make contracts. If the new jobs available outside the home provided opportunities primarily to men, it was partly because these jobs, as they were created, already were regarded as masculine.

What did happen was that gender divisions of labor were solidified, and men's and women's spheres became more distinct. The value of labor came to be assessed more exclusively in the currency of money, and productivity began to be defined as the amount of monetary profit one's labor returned to one's employer. Women's domestic sphere of labor did not involve wage labor, it could not be assigned a monetary value, and it was no longer seen as productive. It is important to emphasize that the issue is not just whether women and men do different work, but how this different work is valued. As industrial development occurred, women continued to engage in many of the same or similar tasks, but either it became excluded from the wage and profit sector of the economy, as was true for much of domestic labor, or it became routinized, deskilled, and devalued as in the case of mass-market textile production. An interesting example of this process is the shift in Navajo women's production of rugs and blankets over the late 19th and early 20th centuries. Whereas before the development of a cash economy women wove for both personal use and trade, with the United States policy of incorporation of Navajo society and the development of a capitalist economy (but a peripheral one), women lost control over their weaving and became wage-labor weavers with reduced status (Harris 1990).

The nature of households and families also underwent considerable change. As Chapter 12 discussed, in the early stages of American history the structure of the family and the roles of its members were very different from what they later came to be. Children were expected to contribute their labor as soon as they could, and they were often apprenticed to other families to learn their work. If even breast-feeding could be done by a wet nurse, motherhood did not provide a central core to the meaning of homemaking (Matthaei 1982). Although there was a division of labor, roles often overlapped. At harvest time, people did not preserve gender roles and risk letting crops rot. The harvest season signaled not only the work of getting the crops out of the ground but also the work of preserving the food for later use. Women married to men such as sailors, whose work took them away from home for long periods of time, had to carry on all the tasks necessary to keep a household running.

The development of production and wage labor outside the household led to changes in women's and men's lives, especially in the ways people thought about work. Men's lives became fragmented into specific segments known as work, family, and leisure, each with its own particular associations of times, places, and activities. The new structure of work literally and figuratively distanced men from their families. It also provided more of them with at least some opportunity to enter the labor market as individuals to "make something of themselves," and American culture began to promote the idea of the "self-made man." As Matthaei writes, "Under capitalism, men's striving in the economy became, literally, a seeking of their selves, a struggle to establish their own identities by economically competing with other men" (Matthaei 1982, 105).

The measure of men's success was the wealth they were able to accumulate, and one of the important measures of masculinity became the ability to do all the financial providing for the family. The need for a wife to seek employment began to represent the husband's failure as a man. Because of the tie between man's work and earnings and his masculinity, men came under great pressure to deny that their wives worked and, indeed, to deny them employment.

The movement of men and production out of the home did not strip either the home or women of meaning and significance; rather, it transformed them.

> When the development of industrial capitalism separated commodity production from the household, the family was freed from the function of organizing this production, and it was freed from the presence of strangers in the family. The household became a home, a private family place. Family relationships . . . began to gain a content of their own (Matthaei 1982, 110).

Running the private family place became a distinct role with distinct content. That role, homemaking, belonged to women.

The change in women's homemaking roles was not so much a matter of what specific tasks women did, although those did change. The most important change was in the significance and social meaning of homemaking. Homemaking was raised to the status of a vocation embedded in an ideology historians call the "cult of domesticity." Even if the homemaker was not valued in wages, her role slowly came to be seen as the one that held together the very fabric of society. Matthaei writes, "Women's work, as homemaking, was still the process of subordinating oneself to the needs of the family, of emptying oneself of one's own needs and of taking on instead the task of filling the needs of others, of one's family members."

Contrary to what many feminists seem to argue, taking on this new role of homemaker was not a passive process. "It demanded the active self-seeking of women as homemakers, their creative and individual responses to the needs of their families" (Matthaei 1982, 112). Women's success at home became the measure of their femininity. "Femininity began to involve as much self-expression and choice as masculinity—but whereas a man's self-seeking meant striving

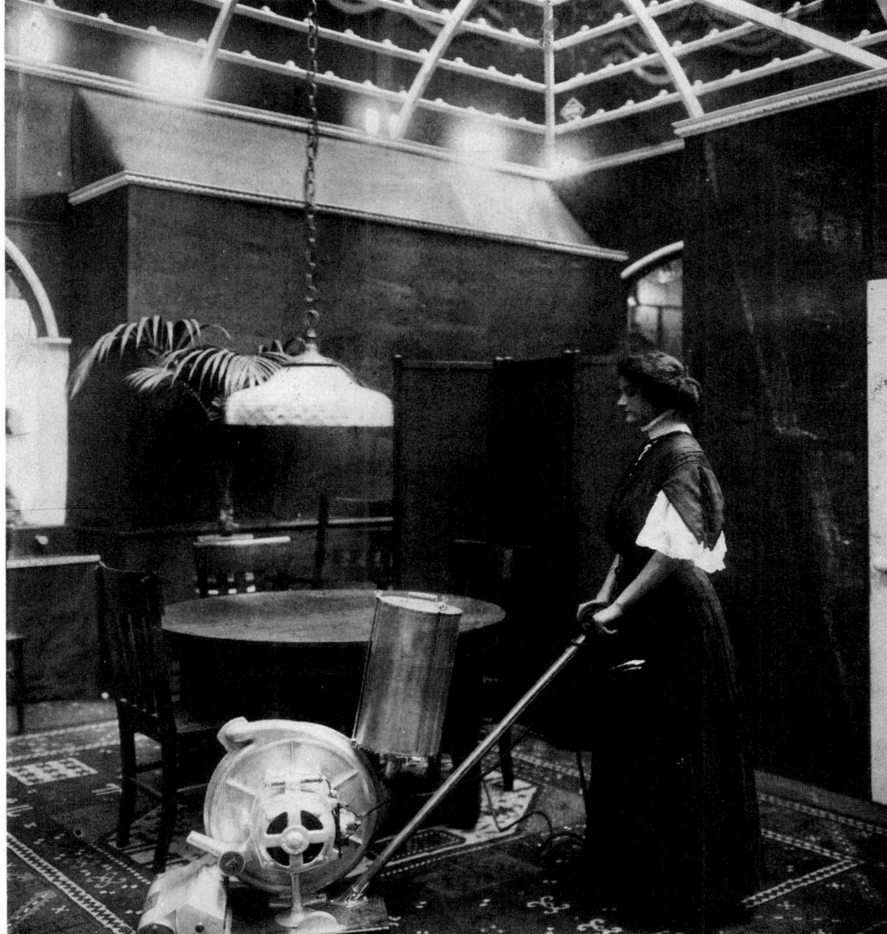

An early "labor-saving" vacuum cleaner.

to subordinate other selves, a woman's self-seeking meant striving to subordinate herself to the self-advancement of her husband and children" (Matthaei 1982, 113). Thus the economy became an important site in which the sex/gender system was developed and maintained, where domestic labor demanded and produced "femininity," and paid employment demanded and produced "masculinity." Women who worked outside their own homes, including especially immigrant women from around the world, African Americans, and Native Americans, could not be considered fully feminine by the dominant society.

By the second half of the 19th century, people had begun to think about homemaking as a vocation and an occupation that could and should be professionalized. It was therefore introduced as a subject of study at school, eventually even at universities. At the turn of the century, experts urged homemakers to apply in their homes management techniques that had been developed in business and industry. Homemaking, many argued, should become more scientific and efficient. Scientific homemaking would help women enter the 20th century, as a 1912 article from the *Ladies' Home Journal* demonstrates:

> I know that any woman who has once felt the comfort, satisfaction, and pride that come from the use of a systematic filing method will never return to the slipshod ways of the past. She will feel that it is just as commendable to have her home run in such a manner that a stranger can run it in the same grooves as herself as it is desirable to have the cogs in the wheels of a great railway system go right on moving, even though the fingers of the president of the road cease to write his dictates (quoted in Matthaei 1982, 161).

The image of homemaking had risen to new heights, but lurking behind this image was the hint of its fall. If homemaking could be done so scientifically and with such a set routine that a homemaker became a replaceable part, what did the homemaker gain from her task? If homemaking really did use the same principles as business and industry, why couldn't women go into business and industry?[4] This question became even more pressing as education, including college education, came to be seen more widely as an appropriate and even necessary part of the training of homemakers who could afford it.

At first the new ideology led married women to pursue their homemaking activities in the larger community while single women increasingly took on paid jobs, such as nursing, teaching, and social work, that were regarded as consistent with domestic roles. Certainly the feminine values of homemaking could be pursued in the outside world. Women who had the resources to do so began to engage in "social homemaking," which meant applying their concerns and skills as homemakers to the community at large. Women's clubs and organizations worked to offset the "masculine" hardness of the outside world by protecting mothers, children, consumers, and others who fell through the cracks of an industrialized society and by working to contain alcoholism and other largely male excesses that hurt the family. As Matthaei argues,

> Their feminine morality—a concern that the needs of particular individuals be filled—was a perfect complement to capitalism's masculinity. Capitalism gave all men a chance to compete; the existence of low-wage and unemployed workers was simply a part of the game. Social homemakers, progressives, and eventually the welfare state charitably "mothered" the losers; they did not try to change the game (1982, 177).

The movement called social homemaking has also been called "social feminism," and it included many of the best-known suffragists.

Homemaking remained a mandatory occupation for adult women, including those who are also employed for pay, through most of the 20th century and it remains a specifically women's role. Despite their protests to the contrary, most men still do very little work in the home. At the same time, many full-time homemakers now view themselves as "just housewives," devaluing the role that society regards as especially theirs. Homemaking is, in many respects, invisible. Those who don't do it don't know what women do with their days.

Homemaking and housework remain central to the identities of a majority of women. When Marlene Mackie (1983) asked nearly 800 people in Calgary to provide up to 20 answers to the question "Who am I?" 75% of the women and 37% of the men put housework somewhere on their lists. Full-time homemakers were more likely than employed women to list housework, and they put it higher on their lists. As we might expect, employed women's lists indicated that their work outside the home was more important to their senses of self than housework. Homemaking is more central not just to women who are homemakers compared with employed women, but to their families as well: Men married to full-time homemakers were more likely to list housework than those married to employed women. Although the family, the marital relationship, and children remain central to men's and especially women's senses of self, the importance of housework is diminishing for people who are or are married to employed women.

The Political Economy of Homemaking

Few people other than homemakers themselves have a clear idea of how the occupation of homemaking works as a whole, and few people have investigated the relationship of homemaking to the larger economy. Given the substantial amount of labor performed in the economy through homemaking, anyone who does not understand the economic functions of homemaking has only a partial understanding of the economy as a whole.

PROBLEMS OF DEFINITION: HOUSEWORK AS WORK. Homemaking does not easily fit into our common definitions of work or, certainly, of occupations. Let us look at three reasons for this difficulty.

1. If work is something people do to earn a living—in other words, for pay—homemaking does not seem to be work. Few have argued that homemakers should be paid for their work, although divorce settlements are beginning to recognize the economic value of homemaking. Indeed, until recently the law stated clearly that women's household labor was required as part of the marriage contract, and therefore women could not expect direct compensation in property or salary for it.

   The issue of wages for housework, or the recognition of its economic value, raises some tricky questions. Do we really want to argue that women perform the role of homemaker for financial support? This view reduces marriage to a purely economic relationship and, as Emma Goldman pointed out at the turn of the 20th century, makes it resemble an insurance pact or prostitution (Shulman 1983). Women are supposed to do their homemaking for the love of their families and because of their nurturant, altruistic, and self-sacrificing natures, not out of economic interests. But if we accept this argument we are back at square one, saying that women's work in the home (if work is a paid occupation) is not really work.

2. Homemaking takes place not in the impersonal world of strangers and acquaintances in the marketplace, but in the intimate, personal, and closely bonded structure of the family. Much of the motivation for homemaking is based on the personal relations of the members of the family and not on economic interests per se; the work and the personal relationships are inseparable. Raising a child is indeed work, but it is difficult to imagine a parent who, having just helped a child walk for the first time, turns to someone else, shrugs, and says, "Well, it's a job." In arguing that household labor is an economic function and therefore is work, we would not want to argue that it is only that. There is something horrifying and inhuman about reducing one's most personal relationships to an economic equation. On the other hand, it is wrong to describe homemakers as people who are not filling an economic role.
3. The home is defined as a place for leisure rather than as a place for work. This view is in part androcentric and stems from the 19th-century definition of the home as a "haven in a heartless world" (Lasch 1977). The home is the place a person goes to rest, relax, and be "rehumanized" after leaving work. This understanding assumes that someone else has cleaned the house and made it comfortable, done the grocery shopping, and cooked the meals; in other words, it is based on men's experiences. It requires that women's work either be invisible or be defined as something other than work. It is also consistent with the idea that the household and the work done in it are distinct and distant from the economic system.

The aspects of homemaking that make it difficult to analyze as work can, in some respects, be applied to other occupations as well. There is not as great a difference between women's domestic labor and other kinds of work as it might seem. People work not solely to make a living; they have many motivations for doing what they do. Many people claim they would continue to work even if they did not need money. People choose their specific work for many reasons other than financial questions. People do develop personal relationships with and loyalties to their coworkers and occupational organizations, and these relationships can provide some of the motivation for doing a task particularly well. For many, if not most, of us a job is not just a job. Some people are more fortunate than others, of course, in being able to get paid for doing something they truly enjoy. The fact that there may be motivations for doing housework other than financial reward, or that housework is regarded as part of a personal relationship, does not mean it is not work.

ECONOMIC FUNCTIONS OF HOMEMAKING. Homemakers provide necessary goods and services that would otherwise have to be supplied by someone else's labor. The homemaker's job responds to changes in the wealth of a family. The wealthier a family, the more a homemaker can replace some of her labor by paying someone else. This process of replacement does not necessarily mean that there is a proportionate decrease in the overall amount of work she does. A wealthier homemaker can decrease the amount of certain kinds of work she does, including physical labor, but to do this she probably will increase her management and purchasing tasks.

Homemakers have at least three important economic roles: They manage household resources, create and maintain the labor force, and serve as an auxiliary labor force. Let us look at each a little more closely.

Women manage household resources and are in charge of day-to-day household consumption. They respond to the financial situation of a family, but they also help create wealth and raise the standard of living. Because homemakers are responsible for managing the day-to-day consumption habits of the family, their skills and choices determine what proportion of family income is depleted by day-to-day needs and what proportion can be saved or put to other uses. In a sense, a full-time homemaker determines the real value of her husband's income. "Labor-saving devices" help in this endeavor. They transform labor by increasing productivity, where productivity is defined as the amount of return for a given amount of time or effort. Labor-saving devices in the home serve the same function as new technology in industry that increases the productivity of workers, who experience no change in the length of their work.

Over the past century, consumption has become an increasingly important aspect of homemaking. Because of their roles as chief consumers, women link the family to the rest of the economy. This is especially true in an unplanned economy, such as that of the United States, which depends to a large extent on market forces and the creation of markets. Producers depend on consumers, and women are the primary consumers. Many women have recognized their potential power in this relationship. At the turn of the 20th century, the consumer movement, composed largely of women, "attempted to constitute consumption as a productive vocation through which woman as homemaker could realize her individuality and social importance. It therefore demanded that women's work of consumption be professionalized and valued" (Matthaei 1982, 165). Among the groups women organized to pursue their interests as consumers were the National Housewives League, the National Consumers' League, and the Pure Food Association. Women continue to use their economic and political power as consumers to organize or threaten boycotts of specific products and producers.

Homemakers also create and maintain the labor force. Women have the primary responsibility for raising children and thereby contribute to the character of the future labor force. They also maintain the labor force on a day-to-day basis by providing essential life services to the members of the current labor force in their families (including themselves).

Homemakers are an auxiliary labor force. Because the homemaker has been defined through law and custom as a helper to her husband, her job is often partly to make direct contributions to his work depending, of course, on the nature of his job and the family's economic situation. Homemakers in the auxiliary labor force include wives whose husbands work as farmers, clergymen, politicians, and owners of small businesses; wives of businessmen for whom home entertaining is a business affair; and even writers' wives ("I'd like to thank my wife" for typing, editorial comments, etc.).

Homemakers serve as an auxiliary labor force in other ways. Many businesses and industries have relied on a flexible work force of homemakers who are willing and able to do paid labor in their own homes without destroying their sense—or their husband's—that they are still full-time homemakers. In the 1980s the spread of home computers and other developments in information processing technology gave the "putting out" system new life as a means of satisfying businesses' clerical needs with home workers. Other businesses that use this system extensively are textile and electronics manufacturers because it allows employers to avoid more expensive union or salaried labor, overhead costs involved in providing workers with a place to work, the payment of benefits to regular staff employees, and the necessity of using proper procedures for hiring and firing employees. Companies such as Tupperware and Avon, depending on telephone canvassing and sales or at-home and door-to-door sales, also rely on homemakers for their work forces.

The auxiliary labor force of homemakers can be called into action and discarded as it suits the needs of companies. Women participate in these types of jobs because of their familial roles as auxiliary earners. These jobs have been particularly important in families that need the woman's income but either cannot spare her for a regular outside job or consider it improper to do so. In many cases, women's paid work at home helps the family preserve the impression that the husband is the breadwinner and does not depend on his wife's labor. Women have long found ways to earn incomes without appearing to abandon their feminine, home-based roles. In the 19th century, many women rented spare rooms to boarders. Farm women still earn their "chicken and egg" money. Other women take in sewing or do baby sitting in their homes.

Homemakers also serve as an auxiliary labor force that can substitute for men, especially their husbands, when necessary. Since colonial times widowhood has allowed women to perform work generally considered unfit for women in the abstract. Julie Matthaei correctly notes that

> such women were not destroying the sexual division of labor, or even challenging it; as widows, daughters, or sisters, they were fulfilling their womanly obligation of replacing an absent or deceased male family member at the helm of a family business. In such cases it was within their duties as women to enter into men's work, and their actions were understood as such (1982, 191–92).

This same framework may be used to understand women's war work. Sometimes the view that women were substituting for their absent husbands was made explicit. During World War II, automobile companies that had turned to war production sometimes deliberately hired the wives of men who had worked in the same plant before going off to war. It then seemed natural to the companies to fire these women at the end of the war in favor of the returning GIs (Milkman 1982).

It is very important to understand the subjective meanings of work, or people's own understanding of what they are doing. Women and men can both engage in activities that seem, at first glance, to be contradictory to gender-based expectations and stereotypes without making a great psychological break from traditional views. Here, for example, we see women doing "men's work" but being defined—and defining themselves—as "helping out" under certain appropriate circumstances. Likewise, it is possible to see men doing "women's work," but defining themselves as "helping" women rather than sharing their roles.

Homemakers' role as an auxiliary labor force has limits, however. In the traditional view of gender roles, a homemaker may assist her husband, bring in some extra money by doing "women's tasks" at home or part-time, or substitute for her husband while he is absent or upon widowhood until an appropriate male member of the family comes of age. The same traditional gender ideology, especially among whites, resists a woman replacing an involuntarily unemployed husband in the labor force or entering the labor force because the husband's income is insufficient to meet basic needs. In other words, a woman can work as an auxiliary but not as a breadwinner because that would threaten both her sense of femininity and her husband's sense of masculinity. For most men, however, an employed wife was still a sign of failure, and before the advent of child-labor laws, children in a poor family were often sent to work instead of the adult woman. Black families were less likely to do this than white families because female employment was less stigmatized, and they were especially eager to gain more education for their children to give them more life chances.

Attitudes toward the employment of wives have changed dramatically, especially since the majority of women entered the labor force. Nevertheless, people continue to regard the wife's income as supplementary to the husband's. Certainly the idea of a woman making more money than her husband is viewed by many as odd and particularly uncomfortable for the husband. Men's sense of masculinity is still tied in part to their roles as breadwinners.

Making a Living Versus Making a Home: Choices

Women have long had more choice about whether to seek employment than they have about whether to do household labor; most married women are still responsible for housework regardless of their employment status. Moreover, women of some classes and races have had little choice of paid employment other than domestic service—that is, to do housework, but for pay. Even as late as 1985, although 57% of women and 50% of men thought they would find a marriage in which the husband and wife share responsibilities such as housekeeping and child care the most satisfying and interesting, 37% of women and 43% of men thought the most interesting and satisfying marriage would be a traditional one in which the husband assumes responsibility for providing for the family and the wife runs the house and takes care of children (Simon and Landis 1989).

TABLE 13-1

Attitudes toward Employment of Married Women, 1938–1986

Proportion approving of a married woman earning money in business or industry if she has a husband capable of supporting her:

Year	*Women*	*Men*	*% of Married Women in Labor Force*
1938	25	19	15[a]
1972	66	62	42
1975	71	69	45
1982	75	73	52
1986	76	78	55

[a]This figure is from 1940.

Source: Simon and Landis (1989, 270); Hesse (1979, 53); and U.S. Bureau of the Census (1989, 385).

Even if there has been less change than we might think in attitudes toward the division of domestic labor, the majority of Americans believe that married women should be able to work for wages. Yet as Table 13-1 shows, a sizable minority still disapprove. A 1992 survey of entering college students found that 21% of women and 31% of men thought that "married women's activities are best confined to home and family."[5]

Why have women sought employment? We can answer the question (1) by taking a historical perspective to see when women as a group move in and out of the labor force and (2) by viewing women's life cycles and personal situations to see patterns of employment in women's individual life histories.

Women's Employment: Historical and Aggregate Views

The proportion of women who are employed has risen dramatically over the course of this century. At the same time, because of changes in education and retirement patterns, the proportion of men who are employed has declined. As a result, women now constitute over 40% of the civilian labor force. Why have patterns of women's labor-force participation changed over time?

Economist Claudia Goldin points out that while we tend to pay attention to the rising female employment rate of the 20th century, it is also important to note the falling rate in the 19th century, when work outside of unpaid family domestic labor became discouraged and ignored (Goldin 1990). By the turn of the century, relatively few women entered the labor market. Even when they were employed, they tended to work within familial and gender norms. This helped create the race difference in women's employment which later decreased as employment became less stigmatized among whites. At the beginning of the 20th century, the average female in the United States was young, unmarried, and from a working-class family. Most ended their employment careers by their early twenties when they married.

The trade-off between employment and marriage is well illustrated by the lives of the growing population of college-educated women who entered professions at the turn of the century. Relatively few of them married at all because marriage would have meant the end of their careers. This trade-off was enforced by employers. Many would not hire married women or would fire female employees who married. A study of female college graduates done in 1900 showed that by age 50 only about half had married (Matthaei 1982, 181).

The ideology that barred married women, especially middle-class women, from employment began to fray with the development of jobs that seemed compatible with women's roles as social homemakers. As the nation needed more nurses, teachers, and social workers, women filled these jobs, partly because these occupations were regarded as incompatible with masculinity. The invention of the typewriter and the telephone created other suitably feminine jobs. The position of secretary, once an entry-level male job in business, was transformed into the dead-end female job more familiar to us today. Many factory owners favored using a labor force of compliant, unorganized females who, their stereotypes told them, would be good at light, repetitive work requiring dexterity.

The major boosts to female employment came in the middle of the 20th century. By 1940 the majority of households had electricity, refrigerators, stoves, washing machines, and automobiles, and women could make time for employment. During World War II employers, the government, and the mass media urged women to join the labor force. Female employment rose dramatically; in the auto industry, for example, it rose by 600% (Milkman 1982).

Although women were later pushed out of their war work, the expansion of the female labor force picked up steam again in the 1950s and 1960s for various reasons:

1. Many women never lost their taste for the independence of employment, even if they left the work force temporarily to have children.
2. After the war both males and females began to stay in school longer, providing women with greater motivation and qualification for employment.
3. The economy grew tremendously for the three decades following World War II and could accommodate—indeed, it demanded—massive growth in the labor force. Some of this expansion was very specifically in the female sectors of the job market. The need for clerical and sales workers ballooned. As baby-boom babies reached school age in the 1950s and early 1960s, there was an even greater need for teachers. The increased wealth of the time sparked the growth of service industries such as restaurants, which call for female labor. The expansion of the welfare state and the growth of the public sector created other jobs, such as clerical work, nursing, and teaching, which also called for women. Millions of women thus entered the labor market without ever competing directly with men.

Labor-force participation by women was also pushed by both the rising divorce rate, leading more women to find themselves in need of jobs, and women's increased control over reproduction through birth control affording women more choice and ability to plan for the future. Finally the new enforcement of antidiscrimination legislation in the 1970s gave women greater employment opportunities.

The ideology barring wives and mothers from seeking employment has been weakened tremendously in recent years. The evidence is not simply in public opinion polls but also in people's behavior. In 1970 half the mothers of 12-year-olds were in the work force, and by 1975 half the mothers of 7-year-olds had joined them. In 1980 half the mothers of 3-year-olds were in the labor force, and by 1983 half the mothers of 2-year-olds were there, too (Waldman 1983). In 1988 half the mothers of 1-year-olds were in the labor force (U.S. Bureau of the Census 1989). The "tipping point," as Jessie Bernard (1975) put it, has now been reached: Regardless of marital or maternal status, more women enter the labor force than stay out of it.

These patterns also point to another change in women's work habits. Until recently most employed women stayed in the labor force for a relatively short period of their lives. This was one of the excuses employers used for excluding women from job categories for which they desired a stable, permanent work force. This excuse is no longer valid. Women now have fewer children; they drop out of the labor force for only short periods, if at all (and many men now demand the right to take leave from the labor force to care for children); and they seek to remain employed for most of their adult lives.

Will these trends persist in the future? To answer this question we must make some educated guesses about the future of the forces that affect women's employment. Surely women's levels of education will not decrease relative to men's. Likewise, although fertility rates fluctuate over time, unless abortion becomes illegal—still a possibility—women probably will not lose their current control over reproduction. Barring a major war that humanity manages to survive, there is little reason to expect a dramatic rise in birthrates. It is unlikely that we will return to a time when women expect to marry at a young age and be supported by their husbands for the rest of their lives. Moreover, we might guess that men's senses of masculinity will decreasingly be tied to their abilities to be the sole supporters of their families. Women increasingly seem to feel they need excuses to stay *out* of the labor force rather than to stay *in*.

Labor-force participation of women may be most affected by the gender division of labor in the family and the kind of assistance parents receive for child care. Will women continue to accept a double burden? Will men come to accept not just women's integration into the work force but also their own responsibilities in the family? As Chapter 12 pointed out, the United States lags behind many other nations in the availability of day care and maternity leave and benefits. Women's employment decisions are likely to depend in part on whether they can keep their jobs and seniority through the maternity period. But above all women have become aware that even if they want to withdraw from the work force for a time to have babies, their entire work life cannot be shaped by those periods. Given the current average birthrate of two closely spaced children per woman, and the view that women do not need to be home past their children's infancy, women may leave the work force to fulfill their maternal roles for only a very small fraction of the approximately 50 years between the time they leave school and the time they retire.

A final influence on the future of women's employment rates is the structure of the job market and the gender division of labor in the work force. Although we may see economic growth again, massive economic expansion like that experienced from about the end of World War II to 1973 seems unlikely. It is unlikely that the job market can tolerate another massive influx of new people, especially with the end of mandatory retirement ages. But as long as the job market remains relatively segregated, we must consider *which* sectors are likely to expand or contract. Women and men do not generally compete for the same jobs. At one point in the 1970s, men's jobs were particularly hard hit by layoffs in the construction and automobile industries. Later on, cutbacks in social services and new developments in information technology caused women's jobs to suffer.

Consider the example of the American Telephone and Telegraph Company (AT&T). In 1971 the Equal Employment Opportunity Commission (EEOC) launched an investigation of sex discrimination at AT&T and filed suit against the company after concluding that it was "the largest discriminator against women in the United States." When AT&T was ordered to draw up affirmative action goals for future hiring and promotion of women, the document it drew up targeted a decline in the number of women to be hired in the future. The reason: Expected technological changes would eliminate the jobs of thousands of women. Because the company could not reasonably expect to hire a compensating number of women in other job categories, there was nothing the government could do (Hacker 1979).

Like men, many women who seek work do not find it. Unemployment rates generally have been higher for women than for men, and economists suspect that unemployment figures are underestimated even more for women than for men. After a period of unemployment, people of either sex often become "discouraged workers"; that is, people are so pessimistic about their job prospects that they no longer try to find work. It is likely that at this point many women may begin to call themselves "homemakers" and are therefore classified as such in government figures even though they would rather be employed. This label, therefore, hides their real employment status because being a homemaker and being unemployed are two different things.

Women's Employment Experiences Through Life

Paid work experience generally begins for both males and females before they finish their schooling. Although there is little available research on patterns of work among children, it appears that boys tend to begin paid work earlier and work longer hours than girls (Greenberger and Steinberg 1983). Young unmarried men and women enter the labor force at roughly similar rates.

Despite changes over recent decades, and although the majority of young women now assume they will spend much of their adult life employed, young women and men still reflect expectations born of a society structured by gender. In her study of a race-diverse group of 1980s college seniors, aptly titled "Talking Careers, Thinking Job," Anne Machung (1989) found that these young adults still saw the woman's employment as secondary to their husband's, more flexible, and more contingent on household and child-rearing demands. The men expected to help out at home, but by "help out" they still meant something far short of full sharing and equality, and when probed further, the men define the equality they are looking forward to as one in which the partners respect each other and the women take more responsibility for domestic tasks. The women defined equality differently. As one African American woman put it, "I'll be damned if I do double shift" (Machung 1989, 45). They didn't seem to expect equality, but they defined it as equal sharing of the various responsibilities.

Marriage depresses women's employment rates somewhat, especially among less educated people, although not nearly as much as was once true. In fact some women are now pushed into the labor market by marriage. These women, who might otherwise have continued their education or training, take low-paid, low-status jobs while their husbands increase their earning potential. Relatively few husbands do the same for their wives. But when a woman's husband disapproves of female employment, she is likely to do volunteer work instead of paid work, thus not violating her husband's gender ideology (Schram and Dunsing 1981). It is important to note, however, that this occurs in fewer and fewer families. In 1990, 58% of married women were in the labor force.

Although many women leave the labor force temporarily when they have children, they do so for a shorter period than used to be the case. Of those who do leave, about 23% return before their child is 3 years old, and another 19% return when their child is between 3 and 5.[6] This change has important effects on women's employment choices and opportunities. A young woman who plans to be employed throughout her adulthood is likely to make very different choices about how much she is willing to invest in training and what kind of a career she will undertake. She may be more likely to look for a career instead of just trying to find a job. As unpredictable as life may sometimes seem, planning one's work life makes a difference. Research shows that women who maintain consistent plans to be employed from their adolescence on tend to have higher wages by their mid thirties than women who had had at least some plans to be homemakers (Shaw and Shapiro 1987).

Women who delay entry into the labor force until after they have children face some special problems. Educators and employers expect good job candidates to follow the male pattern of beginning careers relatively young and are often reluctant to take on people who are over 30, much less over 40. Some employers argue that it is not worthwhile to invest in "late starters" who will have what these employers consider relatively short careers. Therefore, women have often been ruled out of male occupations not because they are women but because they are viewed as too old. The Age Discrimination Act of 1967, which bars discrimination against people between 40 and 70 years old, provides some relief, but it is not sufficient to cover the problems of women who have been housewives.

Women themselves often find it daunting to be surrounded by people who are much younger and have the momentum that going straight from school to career brings. When older women search for their first jobs, they often find the experience even more frustrating than younger people do. One common problem women face is that they have little or nothing to put down under the heading "prior relevant experience" on employment applications that will be considered seriously. Most employers expect to see a listing of the applicant's prior work experience, and as we have seen, work is usually defined as something one is paid to do. The skills and experiences a woman has gained through homemaking or volunteer work usually do not count, even if a woman's volunteer work has amounted to a nearly full-time job with considerable responsibility. Employers are now being urged to look at these experiences more seriously and carefully.

Another problem many women who have been married homemakers face is that they find themselves in need of a job suddenly and unexpectedly because of divorce or widowhood. They must find a job quickly, and they have little opportunity for learning what might be available or for undertaking necessary training. Many communities have now developed programs designed to help such "displaced homemakers." A substantial portion of the female unemployment rate consists of older women trying to reenter the labor market. Partly because of this, many young women are now reversing the traditional pattern and establishing themselves in careers before having children.

As more women enter and stay in the labor force, more also face the experience of retirement. It is incorrect to assume that women fit right back into the home after retirement without any difficulty. A woman who has been employed for much of her adult life has lived a very different life from that of a full-time homemaker. The retiree may have done most of the housework as she went along, but becoming a homemaker means taking on a new role. Like retired men, women change their daily lives dramatically when they no longer spend their days on the job. Because of differences in male and female life expectancy, as well as in divorce and remarriage rates, a woman who retires is considerably more likely than a man to go home to an empty house. In 1990, 34% of women 65 to 74 years old lived alone compared with 13% of similarly aged men; for people over 75 years old, the figures rise to 53% of women and 21% of men (U.S. Bureau of the Census 1992, 51). It is clear that a retired woman is not the same as an older homemaker.

Women's retirement experiences are somewhat different from men's. They are less prepared for retirement than men are. Men are more likely than women to have engaged in financial planning, which eases their way economically (Kroeger 1982). On the other hand, retiring women tend to draw on larger support networks of people who are close to them. Retired women also tend to belong to a relatively large number of organizations through which they can remain active and socialize with people. In this respect they are also more active than homemakers of their own age (Depner and Ingersoll 1982; Keith 1982).

No matter what aspect of women's work life we are considering, it is necessary to remember why women seek employment in the first place. Like men women seek employment to support themselves and, if they have them, their families. They work because they must. They cannot always arrange their work and family roles as they wish; they often find roadblocks in their private lives and in the world around them. The process of making choices is difficult, and unfortunately in the process of coming to grips with the choices they have made, women sometimes denigrate the choices of other women. Those who seek employment belittle those who choose the domestic route; those who base themselves in the family decry the selfishness of women in the work force. These conflicts are encouraged in part by a social and economic structure that militates against combined roles (Gerson 1985).

Gender Divisions of Labor in Employment

So far in this chapter we have discussed whether and under what circumstances women work for pay. Now let us turn to the substance of their work. Are women now working more but doing the same thing? Or have there been substantial changes in the work women do? What are the similarities and differences between women's and men's work and experiences?

We begin with a theoretical and historical look at the definitions of women's and men's work. Although there has been tremendous change in women's employment rates over the past century, there has not been equivalent change in the kinds of work women and men do. We then consider major developments in antidiscrimination law and policy over the past quarter century designed to break down discrimination based on these cultural understandings of "women's" and "men's" work. Finally we look at the social and social-psychological dynamics of gender-based discrimination in the work place to see how it occurs and, especially, why it persists despite the development of powerful antidiscrimination law.

What Is the Difference Between Women's and Men's Work?

There is still substantial occupational segregation by gender in the United States. Women are concentrated into many fewer occupations than men, and the jobs in which there is a high proportion of female workers are those in which the vast majority of workers are women. Women and men in the same general job classifications or sectors are segregated into different types of work, and women's work tends to have lower status and pay. Where women are found in the same sectors, men are more concentrated in the positions of higher status and authority than women. This is true in "women's" jobs as well as in "men's." People are well aware of gender segregation in employment. In fact, people tend to exaggerate the amount of segregation there is by overestimating the number of women in "women's" jobs, underestimating the proportion of women in integrated jobs, and underestimating even more strikingly the number of women in "men's" jobs (Cooper, Doverspike, and Barrett 1985). Table 1-4 shows some of the most and least gender-segregated jobs in the current United States labor market.

How much change has there been in women's work over time? There has been remarkable continuity in the types of jobs women have held over the past century. Table 13-2 lists the 10 jobs employing the largest number of women for each decade from 1880 to 1990. Jobs shift position on the list from decade to decade, but overall the lists contain the same types of jobs year after year. Women clean, cook and serve food, sew, teach, and do clerical and sales work; in other words, much of the work women do for pay is the same kind of work they are expected to do as wives and mothers at home. If we move further down the list past the top 10 jobs in 1990, we find many of the same occupations (or related work) that appeared on earlier lists. The jobs that held 11th through 15th place in 1990 were sewing-machine operators, assemblers, cooks, typists, and child-care workers.

Thus, women and men work in very segregated worlds, although the amount of segregation has decreased over time. In 1980, 53% of all men worked in jobs that had 20% or fewer women. In 1980, about 46% of women had jobs that had 20% or fewer men in them. If a thoroughly integrated occupation is one in which the ratio of one sex to the other is no more than 60 to 40, we find that in 1970 only about 5% of men and 8% of women worked in integrated jobs; in 1980, 11% of men and 15% of women did (Rytina and Bianchi 1984). There is little reason to believe these figures have changed substantially since then. Few people hold jobs in which gender does not seem to make a difference in who does the work.

When women first began to move into the labor market, they had few skills to take with them other than the homemaking skills they had been taught since childhood. What was called "women's work" therefore had the dual advantage of being at least somewhat familiar and seeming gender-appropriate; it allowed women to work for pay without violating norms of femininity too radically. Of course, employers would usually hire women only for work that required what they saw as women's natural skills. In recent years much of this "women's work" has been labeled "pink-collar" work: work that is an obvious extension of women's roles at home, particularly work involving service to other people (Howe 1978).

Clerical work is a particularly good example of pink-collar work and a good illustration of how the gender composition of jobs changes over time and how the content and structure of jobs are related to their gender composition. The history of clerical work also shows how changes in the structure of the economy affect women's work and work opportunities.

Clerical work began to be feminized at the end of the 19th century; until then it was the bottom rung of the male business ladder. As businesses began to grow in size and complexity, employers saw a need for maintaining larger, more specialized staffs. One way to achieve this was to separate the increasingly important but routine tasks of clerical work from those of lower-level managers. After some initial resistance, employers began to see women as well suited to these now dead-end clerical jobs for various reasons:

TABLE 13-2
The 10 Jobs Employing the Largest Number of Women, 1890–1990

1890	*1900*	*1910*	*1920*	*1930*	*1940*	*1950*	*1960*	*1970*	*1980*	*1990*
Servants	Servants	Other servants	Other servants	Other servants	Servants (private family)	Stenographers; typists, and secretaries	Stenographers; typists, and secretaries	Secretaries	Secretaries	Secretaries
Agricultural laborers	Farm laborers (family members)	Farm laborers (home farm)	Teachers (school)	Teachers (school)	Stenographers, typists, and secretaries	Other clerical workers	Other clerical workers	Sales clerks (retail trade)	Teachers (elementary school)	Cashiers
Dressmakers	Dressmakers	Laundresses (not in laundry)	Farm laborers (home farm)	Stenographers and typists	Teachers (n.e.c.)	Saleswomen	Private household workers	Bookkeepers	Bookkeepers	Bookkeepers
Teachers	Teachers	Teachers (school)	Stenographers and typists	Other clerks (except in stores)	Clerical and kindred workers (n.e.c.)	Private household workers	Saleswomen	Teachers (elementary school)	Cashiers	Registered nurses
Farmers, planters, and overseers	Laundry work (hand)	Dressmakers and seam-stresses (not in factory)	Other clerks (except in stores)	Saleswomen	Saleswomen (n.e.c.)	Teachers (elementary school)	Teachers (elementary school)	Typists	Office clerks	Information clerks
Laundresses	Farmers and planters	Farm laborers (working out)	Laundresses (not in laundry)	Farm laborers (unpaid family workers	Operators and kindred workers, apparel and accessories	Waitresses	Bookkeepers	Waitresses	Managers (n.e.c.)	Nursing aides, orderlies, attendants

TABLE 13-2

The 10 Jobs Employing the Largest Number of Women, 1890–1990 *(Continued)*

1890	*1900*	*1910*	*1920*	*1930*	*1940*	*1950*	*1960*	*1970*	*1980*	*1990*
Seamstresses	Farm and plantation laborers	Cooks	Saleswomen (stores)	Bookkeepers and cashiers	Bookkeepers, accountants, and cashiers	Bookkeepers	Waitresses	Sewers and stitchers	Waitresses	Teachers (elementary school)
Cotton mill operators	Saleswomen	Stenographers and typists	Bookkeepers and cashiers	Laundresses (not in laundry)	Waitresses (except private family	Sewers and stitchers, manufacturing	Misc. and not specified operators	Nurses, registered	Sales workers	Sales supervisors and proprietors
House-keepers and stewards	House-keepers and stewards	Farmers	Cooks	Trained nurses	Housekeepers (private family)	Nurses, registered	Nurses, registered	Cashiers	Nurses, registered	Health technologists, technicians
Clerks and copyists	Seam-stresses	Saleswomen (stores)	Farmers (general farms)	Other cooks	Trained nurses and student nurses	Telephone operators	Other service workers (except private household)	Private household cleaners and servants	Nursing aides	Waitresses

Note: Categories within each year show the 10 jobs that employed the largest number of women in descending order according to the U.S. Census Bureau. "N.e.c.": not elsewhere classified.

Source: For 1890–1970, Berch (1982, 12–13); for 1980, calculated by the author from U.S. Bureau of the Census (1982); for 1990 calculated by the author from U.S. Bureau of the Census (1992, 392–94). Note that census classifications are not exactly comparable from one decade to the next.

1. Women constitute a large pool of high-school-educated workers with few job opportunities who could be hired cheaply.
2. It seemed natural that women would willingly accept jobs that did not lead to higher positions, which were left for men.
3. After a promotion campaign by early manufacturers of typewriters using women to demonstrate their use, typewriting came to be seen as a woman's job.

Evelyn Nakano Glenn and Roslyn L. Feldberg (1989) provide figures that document the feminization of clerical work. In 1870, 3 years before the invention of the typewriter, women constituted about 2% of America's clerical workers. By 1890 they were about 17%, by 1900 they were 27%, and by 1910 they were 36% of U.S. clerical workers. The "tipping point" came in the next two decades; women were 45% of clerical workers in 1920 and 52% in 1930. By 1970 three-quarters of all clerical workers were women, and in 1980 over 80% were women. From 1950 on secretarial work employed more women than any other job; 36% of all female workers were employed as clerical workers in 1987 (Glenn and Feldberg 1989, 288).

Why did women flock to clerical work? The most obvious reason is that the jobs were there and expanding, and they fit very comfortably within the definition of feminine work. Glenn and Feldberg also show that clerical work offered women advantages over blue-collar work. The work and environment is relatively clean, and the work involves little physical exertion and offers women more opportunities to use their education and literacy. Traditionally, at least, clerical workers were more likely than blue-collar workers to be paid a fixed and secure salary rather than hourly and fluctuating wages, their hours were more regular, and they had greater job security and greater opportunities for advancement. Further, clerical jobs involved working with people.

Three important changes have occurred in clerical work over the course of this century:

1. The more feminized the job has become, the greater the gap between women's clerical salaries and men's blue-collar salaries. (This may also be due to the greater unionization of male blue-collar work.)
2. Secretaries have come to be seen as personal assistants to the boss, what some call the "office wife." The secretary's position, as Glenn and Feldberg point out, is defined by her attachment to the boss, and she is generally expected to perform a wide range of personal services for him. These services can reach absurd lengths and in many cases go well beyond making coffee, picking up the boss's laundry, or buying presents for his wife.
3. As the need for clerical labor has increased and having a personal secretary increasingly has become the prerogative only of high-ranking people, secretarial work has become more specialized, routine, and unskilled. (See Davies 1983.)

Many women have broken out of female job classifications throughout women's employment history. One example is the women who have taken over their absent or deceased husband's work. Another well-known example is women's war work. "Rosie the Riveter," the symbolic representation of women who worked in heavy industry during World War II, is often cited, but this image is misleading. Ruth Milkman concluded from her study of women in the automobile industry that "Rosie the Riveter did a 'man's job,' but more often than not she worked in a predominantly female department or job classification" (Milkman 1982, 338). Both the automobile industry and the United Auto Workers (UAW), a generally progressive union, fought against integrating women into the plants. The industry preferred to import male workers from the South until the War Production Board forced them to stop causing migration and start hiring women. In 1943 women were 25% of the automobile industry's workers. Following World War II, automobile companies used every means at their disposal to push women out, and within a year of the end of the war women constituted only 8% of the automobile company work force. The women did not go quietly, but they did go, often to other jobs (Gabin 1982). Women continued to have some amount of choice of employment, as long as they chose women's jobs.

In the last couple of decades, women have entered new kinds of jobs, although the degree of change should not be overestimated. Some of the change, especially in the professions, has been more a regaining of lost ground than new gains. The proportion of professors, doctors, and lawyers who are women, for example, fell after 1930 and returned to the 1930 level only around 1970. Some social scientists and historians look at recent changes with pronounced skepticism. Bettina Berch notes that many of the job classifications in which women have increased their proportions are either industries that have undergone substantial growth and are in need of a new labor force or industries that men are leaving because they are declining (Berch 1982, 82–83). An analysis of professions in which women have most increased their proportions shows that these fields, especially the areas in which we find the most women, include many jobs that have become more routine, are relatively low paying, and are undergoing a loss of power and status (Carter and Carter 1981). In some cases, such as the traditionally male steel industry, women made gains only to see some progress lost during a recession in which layoffs took place in order of seniority, thus hurting women's new jobs especially (Deaux and Ullman 1983).

Many observers are beginning to caution that some of the progress observed in gender integration of the labor force has been an illusion. Women's employment has increased substantially in many traditionally male jobs, but sometimes it is because these have been broken down into new specialties, including new female ghettos. Family law or medicine, residential (as opposed to commercial) real estate, and "women's" fields in university education are some examples (Patterson and Engleberg 1978). Bakers are another example. Although the proportion of women in baking shifted from 25% in 1970 to 48% in 1988, much of that is accounted for by the rise of bakeries inside supermarkets, usually staffed by women who appear to do "home baking," but in fact only heat prepackaged dough. A baker in these establishments is a lower-status, lower-paid worker than other bakers, who remain predominantly male (Reskin 1988). At the same time there are many areas, including business management, in which research shows that there has been considerable progress (Jacobs 1992). And although there are "female ghettos" in professions such as law and medicine, this does not account for the shift toward a more even balance of women and men entering those professions in the past two decades.

These caveats underscore a most important point: The gender division of labor in employment is based on both horizontal and vertical segregation. Thus far we have looked primarily at horizontal segregation. Women are in pink-collar jobs, and men are in blue-collar jobs. Women are in the domestic services, men are in the protective services (Matthaei 1982, 197). But we must also look at the considerable degree of vertical segregation. Blue-collar women are in light industry, blue-collar men are in heavy industry. Women are in auxiliary jobs. Men's jobs generally have more authority and higher status, and they are better paid.

Sometimes jobs are accorded lower status and pay *because* they are women's jobs; in other words, the fact that a job is seen as something women can and should do makes it worth less than something regarded as a man's job. Gender segregation creates what Claudia Goldin calls an "aura of gender," a cultural meaning that goes beyond who happens to do the job (Goldin 1990, 81). The business world provides one of the clearest examples of the principle of "the higher, the fewer" with regard to women's work. In 1990 almost 99% of all secretaries and typists were women, while more than 99% of the highest-paid officers and directors of the 799 largest industrial and service companies (Jacobs 1992, 282) and 97% of the top five jobs at Fortune 500 companies were men.[7] No one expects secretaries to rise to the top, although most secretaries know their bosses would be lost in their own offices without them.

Gender is only one of many factors that structures inequality in the labor market. Race is another, and it is therefore important to understand the relationship between the impact of gender and race on employment experience. Inequality between women and men in the labor market is constant across racial and ethnic groups; that is, regardless of what group we consider, women and men are segregated from each other in the work force and women tend to be concentrated in lower-paying, lower-status jobs. The *degree* of gender inequality is not constant across groups, however. A study of gender effects among the 11 largest non-European racial and ethnic minorities found that there was greater gender inequality in the more affluent groups and among those with lower fertility rates—in other words, among those with more resources (Almquist 1987).

Discrimination and Gender Divisions of Labor

Gender divisions of labor begin at a very young age. Male and female children are given different jobs at home that correspond to adult divisions of labor. The first paid work done by children and adolescents also corresponds to these divisions; boys do more manual labor, and girls do child care and clerical, sales, and service work. Even when their work is similar, girls tend to work with people and boys with things (White and Brinkerhoff 1981; Greenberger and Steinberg 1983). Parents and employers thus help to perpetuate gender-based divisions of labor in childhood. Educational and training institutions help sort workers into gender-appropriate jobs and, indeed, into jobs defined as appropriate for women of one or another race/ethnicity (Glenn 1992).[8]

It often has been said that gender segregation results partly from women choosing jobs that are especially compatible with their family responsibilities. In this view, women's choices cause gender segregation. Research using national employment data calls this assumption into question. In fact, as research shows, "Exactly the opposite was found in professional and blue-collar jobs where female concentration was negatively related to compatibility" (Glass and Camarigg 1992, 148). Women are concentrated into positions with low levels of authority, low flexibility, and high levels of supervision in part so that their employers can make sure they are not distracted from their work. "The very job characteristics that would reduce stress and job–family tension among employed mothers are difficult for them to obtain because these rewards are linked to an authority and reward structure that places women in marginalized 'women's jobs' outside central lines of authority" (Glass and Camarigg 1992, 1148). Gender segregation as it is structured makes women's lives worse, not better.

Women, of course, are not just shoved around the job market like passive game pieces; they make choices all along the way. But as they make their job choices they use what they have learned about themselves and their society to assess their chances in the labor market generally and in specific jobs. If a woman knows that very few women occupy one career, but many are successful in another, she is likely to choose the path of less resistance. People are aware of the gender, racial/ethnic, and class compositions of many jobs, and they are aware of the likelihood that they will be relatively welcome or unwelcome in jobs because of some combination of their own gender, race/ethnicity, or class background.

To see the ways in which discrimination works to keep the job market horizontally and vertically segregated, let us look at hiring and promotion processes. It is no longer legal under most circumstances for employers to refuse to hire or promote anyone, female or male, simply on the grounds of sex. Employers may not advertise jobs in ways that suggest only men or women will be considered, and they must make good-faith efforts to consider men and women equally. Title VII of the Civil Rights Act of 1964 was the first and most important piece of congressional legislation on gender discrimination in employment. It makes it illegal to discriminate on the basis of sex in hiring, firing, "compensation, terms, conditions, or privileges of employment" or "to limit, segregate, or classify employees or applicants . . . in any way which would deprive or tend to deprive any individual of employment opportunities."

Most employers, employment agencies, and labor organizations are covered by this law. Title VII states that sex may be used as a criterion in employment only in "those certain instances where . . . sex . . . is a bona fide occupational qualification reasonably necessary to the normal operation of that particular business or enterprise." This phrase, the "bona fide occupational qualification," or "bfoq," is crucial to lawsuits over gender discrimination. The point is that gender cannot be used as a basis of judgment unless an employer can prove that one's gender is crucial to job performance. The question we encounter repeatedly in sex-discrimination suits is: What, exactly, constitutes a "bfoq"? Under what circumstances can we say that being male or being female is necessary to get the job done? The few cases that stand include (among others) jobs for actors and actresses, sopranos and basses, bathroom attendants, and prison guards under certain circumstances.

Although Title VII of the 1964 Civil Rights Act technically went into effect in 1965, the law had very little real impact until the early 1970s. The first case about the meaning of that law with regard to women was decided by the Supreme Court in 1971. Just as important, in 1972 Congress gave the Equal Employment Opportunity Commission (EEOC), a federal agency, the power to sue employers under Title VII. Before that time the EEOC did not have this power, and victims of discrimination had to assume the burden of suing. Governmental procedures can make a great difference in how thoroughly a law is enforced. The EEOC's first major success came in 1973, when a suit against AT&T resulted in the award of millions of dollars of back pay to women employees who had suffered discrimination.

The courts have extended and refined the meaning of Title VII considerably. In the first (1971) Supreme Court case, *Phillips* v. *Martin Marietta*, the Court concluded that a policy of refusing employment to mothers of preschool children but not to fathers of preschool children violated Title VII. The Martin Marietta Corporation claimed that it was not discriminating against women, but rather against a certain classification of women: mothers. The company thought that because mothers but not fathers of small children are likely to take time off from work because of children's illnesses and holidays, it would be fair to say that mothers (but not fathers) were bad risks as employees. The court rejected this argument, observing that the company had "one hiring policy for women and another for men—each having preschool aged children." The company had not shown that not being a mother of preschool children was a bfoq. Discrimination of the "sex plus" type (in this case, sex plus parenthood) is illegal, a decision reinforced in later cases, including one that condemned a company that discriminated against married women, but not married men (*Sprogis* v. *United Airlines*, 1971).

If an employer discriminates against pregnant women, is this a case of sex discrimination? For a while the answer was no because, as the Supreme Court reasoned, there is no such thing as a pregnant man, and therefore there is no sex discrimination. For pregnancy discrimination to be *sex* discrimination, the Court reasoned, we would have to see different treatment of women and men in a similar condition: pregnant (*General Electric Co.* v. *Gilbert*, 1976). Congress tried to take care of this problem by passing the Pregnancy Discrimination Act, which amended Title VII of the 1964 Civil Rights Act to say that discrimination on the basis of pregnancy is sex discrimination. Nevertheless, especially in the difficult economic times of the early 1990s, some observers thought that discrimination against pregnant women may have been rising as companies tried to save money. Reports from the thousands of complaints to the EEOC indicate that the discrimination is often more direct against women in lower-level jobs and more subtle at the higher ends.[9]

It is important to remember that Title VII applies to men as well as to women. In *Diaz* v. *Pan American Airways*, a 1971 case involving discrimination against a man, a federal court found that Pan Am violated Title VII by refusing to hire men as cabin attendants despite the company's evidence that passengers prefer female attendants, but the court said a company cannot justify discrimination on the grounds that it pleases clients.

In 1967 a new policy mechanism was applied to women in an attempt to enforce the spirit of Title VII. This mechanism, introduced by an executive order of President Johnson and later extended by President Nixon, was called *affirmative action*. In 1961 President Kennedy had issued an executive order stating that certain employers must "take affirmative action to ensure that applicants are employed, and that employees are treated during employment, without regard to race, creed, color, or national origin."

Affirmative action policy has been one of the most widely misunderstood of all policies used to combat discrimination. The purpose and underlying theory of affirmative action as it was designed are quite simple. Antidiscrimination policy had hitherto been couched in negative terms; it concentrated on telling employers what they should not do. Affirmative action policy, in contrast, tells employers what positive steps they must take to eliminate discrimination. It ordered them to make "every good-faith effort" to provide equal employment opportunity by participating in an affirmative action program.

What is an affirmative action program to combat discrimination against women? How does an employer engage in good-faith efforts to combat discrimination? The heart of affirmative action was the development of goals and timetables for employers to use to achieve equal opportunity in employment policies and practices. Employers were required to figure out how many women were being used in what capacities and to compare that with an estimate of the number of women available locally who have appropriate skills or who could be given these skills by the employer in a reasonable time and might, therefore, be employed to do the job. Then they could assess where they should have more women and develop a time frame and strategy for hiring them considering the available work force and the probable future vacancies. The original design of the program makes it very clear that "goals may not be rigid and inflexible quotas which must be met, but must be targets reasonably attainable by means of applying every good faith effort to make all aspects of the entire affirmative action program work." A company that seems earnest in its efforts cannot be punished, even if it has made no real changes at all. In fact most organizations under investigation have passed this test to the satisfaction of the government. The worst punishment available under the policy is withdrawal of all government contracts from that institution. This threat is obviously more serious to some institutions than to others, but it is rarely carried out.

Some courts and employers have attempted to use quotas rather than goals as a specific form of affirmative action. The courts have not been favorable to employers who establish their own private program of preferential treatment of women or minorities, because such programs are held to be in violation of Title VII, which forbids discrimination in employment. They have, on the other hand, accepted the idea of taking gender and race into account as one of the characteristics employers are looking for, if taking gender or race into account is part of a plan to pursue more equality in the work force (*Johnson* v. *Transportation Agency, Santa Clara County*, 1987). They also have tended to allow private companies to develop quota-based affirmative action plans if these plans are part of a contract bargained with a labor union. Even stricter nondiscrimination standards are used with public employers, who usually have been forbidden to use quota-based affirmative action programs.

As one result of the widespread misunderstanding of affirmative action policies, many people believe that it is difficult for white males to get jobs and that the women and minorities who are being hired are unqualified. As we have seen, there is already a tendency for women and men and their levels of success to be evaluated differently. This misperception of affirmative action policies reinforces that tendency and leads people to assume that many women have their jobs not because they deserve them but because of preferential treatment.

It is not easy for women who believe they are victims of discrimination to seek and gain relief. The process of litigation is time-consuming, wearing, and expensive. Although it is illegal for employers to punish employees for litigating discrimination cases, it is unlikely that such employees or job candidates will be viewed favorably by employers. Even when the EEOC takes on the case for the victimized person, it is under its own constraints. For example, as a part of the executive branch of the government, the EEOC's effectiveness is ultimately determined by the person who happens to be president at the time. During the relatively unsympathetic presidencies of Ronald Reagan and George Bush, this and other agencies in charge of civil rights were not as vigorous as they might have been.

As Chapter 12 discussed, interpretation of Title VII of the 1964 Civil Rights Act was also expanded in the 1980s to cover sexual harassment. This was a crucial addition. Without antiharassment policies, sexual harassment remains a normal part of the working conditions of a very large proportion of women workers. Without vigorous antiharassment policy, it is difficult to imagine that the demand of Title VII that there be no gender discrimination in working conditions could ever be fulfilled. At this time, awareness and remedies are still in their early stages.

The Dynamics of Gender Discrimination

Certainly a lot of discrimination takes place consciously, when employers believe members of a particular group of people, defined for example by gender or race/ethnicity, are unsuitable for a job or when an employer simply does not want people from that group around. These are the relatively "easy" cases of discrimination to detect, even if many employers go to great lengths to disguise their prejudice. But employers are not always aware that they are discriminating against women. Personnel assessment is not an exact science, and there is much room for bias in perception and judgment by employers and employees who may act on gender-related cues. This book has cited numerous experimental studies that show evidence of nonconscious gender bias in evaluations of men and women.[10] Some of these apply specifically to employment, and some use business people as subjects.

The most telling studies are those in which people are asked to evaluate men and women who have exactly the same credentials or characteristics. Consider the stereotype that women are not as assertive or do not exert the same leadership characteristics as men. Research suggests employers often see women and men through stereotypes that make them look different even if they are not. One study showed that when managers evaluated reports about a fictitious man or woman, they evaluated men who used power strategies at work more favorably and as more effective than women who used similar strategies. The managers were also more likely to believe that a woman rather than a man was a subordinate (Wiley and Eskilson 1982). Another experimental study of managers in a large corporation investigated hiring for two different kinds of engineering jobs, one of which also involved some managerial duties. For the job involving managerial duties, women were rated lower than men with the same qualifications; they were even rated lower than women applying for the technical engineering job without the management component.

Employers are less likely to help female than male job candidates who have spouses that need employment, and men with families are rewarded with higher pay than are women with families (Osterman 1979). Businessmen view male candidates as more likely to remain with a company (Rosen, Jerdee, and Prestwick 1975), and women are expected to hold their jobs for briefer periods than men (Gerdes and Garber 1983).

Not all discrimination is nonconscious, and some occurs so early in the hiring process that employers avoid even considering women or men for nontraditional jobs. Richard Levinson (1975) did an experiment in which men and women phoned employers to inquire about jobs advertised in local newspapers. They selected advertisements for jobs that were clearly traditionally male or female, and initially only someone of the "wrong" sex made an inquiry. When a person of the "wrong" sex was told on the telephone that the job was already filled, a person of the "right" sex telephoned soon after to find out whether the response was the same. In many cases the experimenters were directly told that they were the wrong sex for the job. When the responses were tallied, Levinson found that in about 35% of the cases there was clear-cut sex discrimination, in 27% of the cases the situation was ambiguous, and in 31% of the cases there was no evidence of discrimination.

Muriel Siebert, who became the first woman member of the New York Stock Exchange in 1967, offers many examples from her own career. When she first sent out her résumé in the late 1950s she received no offers, but received many when she sent her résumé under the name of "M. Siebert." Early on she could not attend many important company meetings because they were held in country clubs that excluded women.[11] This was a common practice, and women have sued for entrance into male-only social clubs on the grounds that this exclusion has ramifications for women's employment opportunity. Many men in these clubs claim that they are only social and cannot see why they do not have a right to "freedom of association"—without women.

No law or policy can cancel out the effects of nonconscious discrimination. It is often difficult, and even impossible, for a person to know when she has been the victim of such discrimination. This is of particularly great significance in light of other research showing that women, in contrast with men, tend to attribute their failure to lack of skill. Nonconscious discrimination can depress the aspirations of women who have no ready explanation for their lack of success other than their own abilities. Those who have acted in a discriminatory manner deny they have engaged in wrongdoing because they are not aware of it, and may even be shocked at the idea that they would do such a thing.

There is evidence that nonconscious discrimination has even been activated by attempts to end sex discrimination. Reminding personnel departments that they are obliged to consider women and men equally for jobs can cause resentment or stimulate the belief by people in authority that women are people with special, and inferior, characteristics. In his experimental study, William Siegfried (1982) found that when men were given standard equal opportunity warnings, they tended to find male candidates more likable than females and to hire them more often. Rosen and Mericle (1979) found that strong warnings had no effect on whether men or women were hired but did result in women being hired at lower starting salaries than men. Such evidence makes it clear that job equity will evolve only when sexist beliefs and attitudes disappear. Many people have come to believe that policy changes now mean that unqualified women are given jobs, so their assumption is that the women they see in nontraditional jobs must be unqualified. After all, if they had been qualified, all of these women would have had jobs earlier, wouldn't they? In order to understand the changes, one has to understand how fundamentally discriminatory the system has been, which is difficult for many people to believe. The implication of accepting the idea that the system has been discriminatory is to accept the idea that many white men did not in the past achieve their jobs solely through merit.

Recent attention to sexual harassment points to the lingering problem of hostility toward women in some work places, especially women in traditionally masculine jobs (e.g., Swerdlow 1989). Many women have experienced harassment based in male hostility toward the female invader. Sometimes the hostility takes apparently sexual forms. Women may be subject to hazing or initiation processes by their male colleagues when they enter very male-dominated jobs, and some of the hazing takes dangerous forms. Female police officers, for example, report cases in which male colleagues have refused to answer their calls for assistance or have cut the wires to their radios. When women object to these actions, they are often accused of being oversensitive and not having a sense of humor.

Studies of women in nontraditional blue-collar jobs reveal that more than 25% feel hostility directed against them by male coworkers. Such disapproval poisons the work environment for women, who then experience less job satisfaction than those who are not exposed to coworker hostility (O'Farrell and Harlan 1982). This problem is not limited to blue-collar workers. Female professionals in traditionally male occupations also find a significant number of male colleagues who, if not openly hostile and harassing, show obvious discomfort in their presence and confusion about how to deal with them. In some cases the problem extends beyond the work place. Female police officers, firefighters, and miners know that quite often the wives of their male colleagues are hostile toward them, partly because of the close physical contact required by these jobs and partly because they do not feel comfortable entrusting their husband's safety to a woman (Hammond and Mahoney 1983). Often the burden is on the "newcomer" to make those around her feel comfortable, a responsibility that cannot ease her integration into a new job. In traditional male fields even a few women can feel like a wholesale invasion.

Income, Worth, and Poverty

Thus far we have looked at the work women and men do. Let us now turn to the financial situation of women and their families, beginning with job-related pay and benefits issues, then other problems of financial support and poverty.

Women's Worth at Work

Women may be increasing the amount of time they spend in employment, but they continue to earn considerably less than men do. As Table 1-6 showed, women in full-time year-round employment earned less than men at every education level. In 1990 women employed full-time year-round earned 72 cents for every dollar earned by men. Women are twice as likely to have salaries at or below the minimum wage (Mellor 1987). Table 13-3 suggests some of the joint effects of race and gender on income. There we see how many cents on the male dollar women earn compared within each educational level among Hispanics, blacks, and whites. We also see how many cents on the white male dollar Hispanic and black women earn. These figures do not take account of the difference between full- and part-time work or work lasting only part of the year compared with all year. But they do show the situation experienced by women across the country: Women earn considerably less than men of their own educational level and race/ethnic group. The gender gap among whites tends to be larger than the gender gap within the two other racial groups for a variety of reasons, including the compression of wages by racism. But race makes remarkably little difference in how far behind white men women's wages are. For all groups except the most educated blacks and whites, women's wages are less than 60% of men's, and among the less educated, they are less than 55%.

The gender gap in pay is not simply due to differences in the positions held by women and men or differences in their levels of experience. There are also differences in the pay received by women and men in similar jobs. A study done in the early 1980s highlighted this disparity. At that time the median salary of female Ph.D.s in science and social science fields, for example, was 77% the median salary of male Ph.D.s in those fields. The median salary of female Ph.D.s in chemistry was 81% of the median salary of male Ph.D.s in chemistry, and the median salary of female Ph.D.s in chemistry with 6 to 10 years' job experience was 82% of the median salary of male Ph.D.s in chemistry with 6 to 10 years' job

TABLE 13-3
Women's Wages as a Proportion of Men's Wages, 1990

	1–3 years of high school	*4 years of high school*	*1–3 years of college*	*4+ years of college*
All Women				
as % of all men	.55	.55	.60	.64
Hispanic				
as % of Hispanic men	.61	.65	.60	.68
as % of white men	.54	.50	.57	.57
Black				
as % of black men	.70	.74	.75	.85
as % of white men	.51	.54	.58	.68
White				
as % of white men	.53	.53	.57	.62

Note: These figures can be read as "cents on the dollar"; e.g., the least educated white women earn 53 cents for every dollar earned by the least educated white men.
Source: Adapted from Census Bureau figures presented in Ms. Foundation for Women (1992, 6).

experience (Berch 1982, 14–15). And the earnings gap in professional fields is relatively small compared to that in other fields.

Sex discrimination in pay is illegal and has been since the Equal Pay Act of 1963. That law says, "No employer . . . shall discriminate . . . between employees on the basis of sex by paying wages to employees . . . at a rate less than the rate at which he pays wages to employees of the opposite sex . . . for equal work on jobs the performance of which requires equal skill, effort, and responsibility, and which are performed under similar working conditions." Labor unions were also covered by the law.

Employers reacted quickly to this law. Realizing that "equal pay for equal work" could be very costly, especially because employers could not reduce anyone's salary to comply with the Equal Pay Act, many of them made sure that men and women in their companies had different job titles so that they could justifiably be paid differently. Some employers also made sure there was something slightly different about the actual work that men and women did so that their work could be proven to be of unequal value. A turning point came in 1970 when a federal court decided that in ordering equal pay for equal work Congress "did not require that the jobs be identical, but only that they must be substantially equal. Any other interpretation would destroy the remedial purposes of the Act" (*Schultz* v. *Wheaton Glass Co.*). Thus women and men are supposed to be paid the same for doing *substantially similar* work.

But women and men continue to be paid somewhat differently for the same work. In most jobs, pay is based partly on subjective evaluations of the worker by a supervisor, and in this area conscious and nonconscious discrimination can take its toll. It is usually assumed that women are paid less because they have less experience or credentials, or they make different job choices, such as refusing transfers or refusing to travel as much as men are willing to do. A study of managers employed by Fortune 500 companies in the late 1980s offers this conclusion:

> The female managers . . . had done "all the right stuff." They had relocated within the previous 2 years for their own career advancement, they were as well educated as the male managers, they were as powerful in their families, and they were employed as often as the men in higher paying industries. Although they reported that they were receiving promotions at the same rate as the men, they were moving less frequently . . . and their salaries had progressed over the past 5 years substantially less rapidly than the men's (Brett and Reilly 1992, 257).

Salary differences between women and men doing the same work are not as great as they were, but equality has not yet been achieved.

The greater problem for salary equity is that, as we have seen, the labor market remains segregated. Women and men do not do the same work or even "substantially similar" work for the most part. As long as women and men occupy different jobs, "equal pay for equal work" is, practically speaking, meaningless, unless *equal* is defined to mean something other than similarity in the substance of the job.

This observation has led many experts in the 1980s to look to the principle of *comparable worth* or *pay equity* as the standard for identifying sex discrimination in pay. A comparable worth policy requires assessment of the relative amounts of skill, training, experience, and other valued characteristics required to do different jobs to determine the relative worth of different jobs in terms of pay. Without this kind of policy the only way to determine whether there is gender bias in pay is to compare women and men holding substantially similar jobs. Under pay equity we would compare the pay of women and men holding jobs that we think should be valued equally.

The logic of comparable worth suggests, among other things, that "women's work" is often paid less than "men's work" not because it is of different intrinsic value, but simply because it is done by women rather than by men or because it is identified as traditionally female as compared with male work. The implementation of policies based on the notion of comparable worth would transform the process of determining pay and would cost business considerable sums of money. Despite resistance from business the 1980s witnessed some movement toward acceptance of the idea of comparable worth (Hartmann 1985; Brenner 1987; Steinberg 1987; Evans and Nelson 1989).

The dominant school of economics has tried to teach us that the wage market, if left to its own devices, will provide us with the appropriate pay for jobs. The "unseen hand" works out the best negotiated compromise among employers seeking employees and workers seeking jobs. This school vehemently opposes pay equity policies as disruptive to the market. It may be, they argue, that women take jobs that pay less than the jobs that men take, but this is only due to the mutual choices of workers and employers.

Feminist scholars point out that the "unseen hand" may help work out a position of economic equilibrium in a market; however, the values accorded to workers are shaped not by any essential value but by many features of the culture, including the values they place on people of one gender or race or another. Historian Alice Kessler-Harris (1990) shows how throughout the past century wages have been shaped by the cultural values defining the sex/gender system in which the wages are developed. Historically there has been tremendous pressure to think of a man's wage (and thus fair wages for the kinds of work men do) as one that will help support a family, whereas a woman's wage (and thus fair wages for the kinds of work women do) is an auxiliary or extra wage. Thus Kessler-Harris concludes,

> The market, as it functions in the daily lives of people, is not independent of the values and customs of those who participate in it. Justice, equity, and fairness have not been its natural outcomes. Rather, market outcomes have been tempered by customary notions of justice or fairness. The specific forms these take have been the object of struggle. And just as ideas of fairness influence our response to the market, so, too, do they influence how the market works (Kessler-Harris 1990, 117–18).

Claudia Goldin documents the rise in wage discrimination over this century that resulted in part from conscious policy designed to provide the right workers for the right jobs—many of them gender defined (Goldin 1990). Thus, if parking attendants (mostly male) are paid more than day-care workers (mostly female), it is not necessarily because taking care of children is essentially—or correctly—less valuable than parking cars.

Certainly gender-role choices can affect potential earnings. Marnie Mueller (1982) discusses women's work and earnings in terms of human capital theory. According to this theory, earnings are a function of the amount of schooling and experience an individual worker has; in other words, the investment of time, effort, and money ("human capital") should pay off in earnings. As Mueller points out, this theory generally has been applied to male workers. Those who have investigated women have found that women get less for their investment. Mueller, therefore, refined the human capital theory on the basis of observing women's behavior. She points out that a large proportion of women spend some time out of the labor market to raise children. During this period their skills, and therefore their human-capital investment, depreciate in value; that is, women's education and experience lose their value if they are not "used."

Mueller cites evidence to show that the depreciation of value is greatest among the most educated women, which means that the gender-based decision to stay out of the labor market to raise children ultimately reduces some of the relative advantages of women of one class over another when they attempt to secure jobs later. We need only consider the experience of middle-aged, college-educated, displaced homemakers to see how this works. Mueller also looked at women's alternative to paid labor, volunteer work, and found that if she calculated what the volunteer worker would be paid if her labor were not being donated, the human-capital theory still applies. Even when women are not being paid, the value of their labor outside the home depends on their education and prior experience. If a highly educated woman stays out of the labor market and takes on volunteer work that could command relatively high wages if it were paid, because she is out of the labor market her market value still declines. Many women, therefore, can find work that is more suitable to their skills if they do not seek paid work. Challenging and interesting volunteer work, however, does not put dinner on the table.

Many women seek part-time work in order to balance family and economic responsibilities or because it is more consistent with conceptions of women's roles. As the economy is currently constructed, this also results in a financial loss for women. Part-time employees are generally paid on a lower scale than full-time employees and often do not receive the fringe benefits of full-time employees including valuable health and other insurance coverage. Part-time employees do not usually have the same opportunities for promotion that full-time employees have. Moreover, part-time work is often less challenging and interesting than the volunteer work that is available.

It is important to remember that most women do a considerable amount of work that is valuable but for which they receive no pay: household labor. It is difficult to assess the financial value of women's domestic labor, although many people have tried. What is this work worth in money? Experts generally agree that there are two methods to estimate a dollar value for women's household labor: opportunity cost and replacement value (Berch 1982).

Using the *opportunity cost* approach, the value of the household labor is calculated according to what a woman could be earning if, instead, she held a paid job. In this case, housework's value is calculated in the lost opportunity to earn income. Estimates are that the average opportunity cost of homemaking in 1991 was about \$17,000.[12] Opportunity cost figures are sometimes used in divorce proceedings. There are two problems with this approach. First, the value of the labor has nothing to do with the labor itself; domestic work remains, in an important sense, valueless labor. Second, unpaid domestic labor is not an alternative to employed labor for married women. There are many women who do unpaid domestic labor and do not have paid jobs, but most employed married women also do most of the domestic labor.

Using the *replacement cost* approach, the cost of paying someone else to do housework is calculated. Insurance companies use this method in calculating how much to compensate a widower who insured his wife's value as a housewife. With this approach, the value of housework is tied to the housework itself. In the early 1990s, the average replacement cost of a housewife was calculated to be more than \$16,000.[13]

Some people have even suggested that women should receive wages for housework (Malos 1980). This proposal has serious theoretical and practical problems. The main question is: Who would pay? Who could pay? Do we want our family and personal lives to be judged by market standards? Alternatively, many policymakers around the world have argued that even if housework is not financially reimbursed, its value should be incorporated into government figures such as the calculation of gross national product (GNP) in order to raise the status of the women who do this work and also to make the value and needs of these workers more apparent to the system as a whole. This proposal was made through the United Nations Women's Decade conference in Nairobi, and a bill calling for this action was endorsed by the Congressional Women's Caucus and proposed to Congress.[14]

Jobs do not just provide money wages but also provide a range of other often extremely valuable benefits such as pensions and health insurance. In a system such as that of the United States, one of the few nations historically lacking comprehensive government-sponsored health care, these benefits can be crucial. As the discussion of child care (Chapter 12) pointed out, companies have increasingly included child-care benefits as part of the package they offer workers, and many have on-site child care. Although the executives of companies that offer family-friendly benefits may be progressive in their orientation, companies benefit financially from these policies; research shows that "companies that make it easier for employees to juggle their work and family responsibilities do reap gains in greater loyalty, increased job satisfaction and lower turnover."[15] Many companies are also offering family leave benefits beyond the minimum required by law.[16] These benefits are essential to women being able to support themselves and their families. As sociologist Arlie Hochschild has said, "We have to acknowledge that the majority of American women will work for the majority of their lives through their childbearing years and we have to adapt the work place. Don't pretend they're men who have wives at home to do this."[17]

Other Means of Support

Salaries are not the only sources of income for men or women. The poor, disabled, unemployed, and retired, for instance, may depend on various types of public benefits. The wealthy may receive income from investments. In analyzing the economic situations of women and men, it is necessary to look at all the different sources of financial support for individuals and families.

Assistance to the poor is a woman's issue because women appear in disproportionately large numbers among the poor. Numerous social scientists point to the "feminization of poverty," or the increasing tendency for poor populations in the United States to be composed of women. As figures presented in Chapter 1 show, the poverty rates for female-headed families are substantial, especially among African Americans and Hispanics, where at least half the female-headed families are below the poverty line.

But poverty became a more widespread problem during the 1970s and 1980s; the Children's Defense Fund concluded that "young families with children have significantly less money than their counterparts did a generation ago and suffer from child poverty rates that are twice as high."[18] Although the rise in single-parent families account for some of that increase, both decreasing wages and government policies in that era that cut welfare and unemployment benefits account for about half the increase in child poverty rates. If we consider only families with parents under 30 years old, between 1972 and 1990 incomes of those with completed college education rose by 3%, among those with some college education income fell by 15%, among those who completed high school incomes fell by 30%, and among those who were high school dropouts income fell by 46%.[19]

Poverty, and specifically the feminization of poverty, stems from a number of sources. In the 1980s and early 1990s, changes in the global economy created greater financial pressure that led to widespread job loss and decrease in wages and benefits for the jobs that remained. Public policies of the conservative presidential administrations eliminated some of the means of support that had existed earlier. As we have seen, women have fewer job options than men and women's work is not paid as well as men's work.

For women these problems are added to their responsibilities in the family. Although fathers are charged by courts with remaining financially responsible for their children following divorce from the mother, the fact is that a large proportion of those without custody do not fulfill their responsibility to their children. A 1987 study showed, for example, that of the divorced women who had custody of their children, 59% had been awarded some child support due them from the father, and of those, 51% received the full amount, 25% received part of it, and 24% received none of it, amounting to billions of dollars that have accumulated over time that should have gone to mothers to support their children. It is very difficult to collect from delinquent fathers who have left the state, and mechanisms have been established recently to try to increase the collection rate.[20] Research shows that women of all classes experience a decline in their economic standing as a result of divorce, although the decline is steepest for those whose marital income had been the highest. In other words, divorce has a leveling effect on women, reducing the financial differences among them (Weiss 1984).

Poverty has many self-perpetuating effects that affect women in particular through their roles as mothers. Low-income women are much less likely to receive health care during the terms of their pregnancy, which is part of the reason that infant and maternal mortality rates are higher in the United States than in many other nations.

What do people live on other than wage income? How much do they depend on other sources of income? Table 13-4 shows the sources of financial support for white and black families in the mid 1980s. The first is job earnings. The second, labeled "transfer," includes government payments such as AFDC, Social Security, unemployment compensation, pension income, and child support. The third category includes primarily "unearned" income, such as dividends and interest. The figures reveal a number of important patterns. In dual-earner families, wives contribute a substantial proportion to family income, particularly among black families. Married-couple families in which the wife is not employed are worse off financially than those in which women are employed, particularly among black families. Clearly, married women are employed in order to support their families. The relative importance of transfer payments rises among

TABLE 13-4
Sources of Financial Support for White and Black Families, mid 1980s

	White		
	Married Couple		
	Employed Wife	*Not Employed Wife*	*Single Mother*
Mean income in 1985 dollars	$36,805	$29,320	$11,644
Percentage of income due to:			
Husband's earnings	62.9	83.3	0.0
Wife's earnings	29.6	0.0	70.6
Transfer	3.2	8.4	25.5
Dividend, interest, other	4.3	8.3	3.8
	Black		
	Married Couple		
	Employed Wife	*Not Employed Wife*	*Single Mother*
Mean income in 1985 dollars	$30,777	$17,315	$8,672
Percentage of income due to:			
Husband's earnings	53.5	78.0	0.0
Wife's earnings	40.3	0.0	73.3
Transfer	5.0	18.0	26.2
Dividend, interest, other	1.2	3.4	0.5

Note: "Transfer" includes government transfers (AFDC, Social Security, unemployment compensation, etc.), pension income, and child support.

Source: Rix (1988, Tables 3.3, 3.5).

married-couple families if the wife is not employed, but particularly among black families, which reflects the higher poverty rates. Almost 25% of those families live in poverty.

The heaviest dependence of all on transfer payments, however, is in female-headed households, in which a little over 25% of the income of the family comes from transfers. It is also important to notice that at least in this regard, the impact of being a single mother appears to eliminate the usual race differences. A study of women's reliance on welfare payments and food stamps found that in the first year after divorce 71% of women who had had lower marital income used these sources of support as did 25% of middle-income and 4% of higher-income divorcées. Even more shocking is the fact that in the first year after divorce welfare and food stamps constituted 60% of the income of lower-income women, 37% of the income of middle-income women, and 26% of the income of higher-income women (Weiss 1984).

Public aid is remarkably ineffective in helping people out of poverty. The federal program, Aid to Families of Dependent Children (AFDC), is a case in point. AFDC began in 1935 as a program to aid impoverished children cared for by one-parent families. It is estimated that about 25% of all American children receive AFDC at some time in their lives, and the vast majority of these children live with their mother. The AFDC program slowly grew until the Reagan administration began cutting it in 1981. Even before these cutbacks, however, only in Alaska was a combination of AFDC and food stamps likely to raise the children these programs serve above the poverty level. In the past, many welfare programs were explicitly oriented toward helping men out of poverty on the grounds that they could then help women out. In fact, in the 1960s more male-headed than female-headed families were brought out of poverty by government programs.[21]

One of the problems poor women face is negative public attitudes toward public assistance programs and those who depend on them. Although surveys reveal that Americans claim sympathy with "the poor," they are highly critical of "people on welfare" (Smith 1987). About 40% of the public believe that most people who receive welfare could get along without it if they tried, and 32% favored decreasing spending on Food Stamps, a program used disproportionately by women and children (Shapiro et al. 1987b).

A persistent charge aimed at poor women is that they have children in order to obtain or stay on welfare. A study of recipients of AFDC, Food Stamps, and Medicaid proves the charge baseless. After controlling for factors such as race, education, and age, analysis showed women on welfare had a substantially lower fertility rate than other women, and the longer they remained on welfare the lower the fertility rate became (Rank 1988).

Organization of Women in the Work Force

Julie Matthaei wrote about the entrance of women into the labor force at the turn of the century, "Men and women entered the labor force differently; a man seeking to establish himself as a successful man and head of household, a woman as a daughter or homemaker seeking money to aid her family" (1982, 214). Matthaei claims that women just wanted to earn a wage; as women with no desire to forsake what was labeled their femininity, they presented employers with what Matthaei calls an "invitation to exploitation."

Women entered the labor force in large numbers at the same time that male labor was organizing and seeking recognition and the power to fight for its growing membership. Although the proportion of the U.S. labor force that is unionized is one of the smallest among Western democracies, unions have been successful in improving working conditions and benefits (including pay) in the work place through collective bargaining and lobbying the government. What has been women's relationship to labor organization? What role have such organizations played in the history of gender segregation and equity in the work place?[22]

Most labor organizations were male dominated and androcentric from their inception. The history of the American Federation of Labor (AFL) shows the degree to which labor tended to hold the woman worker at arm's length. Before its official founding in 1886, the AFL had approved the organization of working women and policies of equal pay. Union members and leaders, however, were skeptical of women as workers. Women who had been barred from some kinds of employment because unions excluded them were sometimes used as strikebreakers. Samuel Gompers, the head of the AFL, was opposed to women workers on the grounds that they took jobs from men, reduced men's wages, and destroyed the family. As a result, soon after the first official woman delegate went to an AFL convention in 1890, the AFL supported protective labor legislation. Part of the rationale was that employers would be loathe to hire women—and in some cases would be prohibited from hiring them—if women were "protected" by the law. Gompers went even further and in 1898 unsuccessfully urged the government to place an outright ban on employment of women in government. The female membership of unions declined from 4.6% in 1895 to 2.9% in 1908 (Berch 1982).

Despite considerable opposition, many women tried to organize workers and force labor unions to consider women's needs and interests. One of the best-known efforts was the founding of the National Women's Trade Union League (NWTUL) in 1903 at an AFL meeting. The NWTUL involved working union members and their allies, wealthy women who were sympathetic to the plight of working women. Unfortunately it was the wealthy women who had the time to contribute to the NWTUL, so the policies of that group did not reflect the interests of the workers as much as they might have. The women of the NWTUL fell in behind the cause of protective labor legislation for women.

Women have remained weak within the union movement throughout the 20th century. Until recently unions have not worked very hard to organize workers in "women's" jobs (with certain important exceptions, such as those in the textile trade) and have not been very supportive of women's special interests. Women have tended to view labor unions as inappropriate to their types of jobs. In 1960 women were 18% of union members; by 1980 they were 30%, and in 1987 they were 35% (U.S. Department of Labor 1989, 225). A higher proportion of African American women (18%) are members than is true of white (12%) or Hispanic (13%) women (1990 figures, Ries and Stone 1993, 369). Women are an even smaller proportion of national union leadership. They have made more gains at the regional, district, and local levels. Some people argue that women would not have made even this much progress were it not for the founding in 1974 of the Coalition of Labor Union Women (CLUW), a women's caucus in the AFL-CIO.[23]

Despite these problems, women have made gains through the unions. There are still tensions over the unions' staunch support of the principle of seniority, or "last hired, first fired," which in most occupations means more job losses for women than for men. On the other hand, some unions work with feminist organizations and support feminist positions on various issues.

Although men earn more than women in all occupational sectors, the gap is generally smaller between unionized men and women than between nonunionized men and women. Regardless of sex, workers earn more if they are unionized than if they are not, and in some sectors the gain for women who join unions is even greater than the gain for men (Berch 1982, 162). There are alternative organizations for women workers. Some of the largest are employee associations such as the American Nurse's Association and the National Educational Association. These associations are female dominated in membership, and some, such as the two just mentioned, also have a preponderance of women leaders.

A more recent trend is toward organizations composed specifically of women workers. Among the best known of these is 9 to 5, an organization of secretaries, and Women Office Workers (WOW). Another is La Mujer Obrera (The Working Woman), an organization of Chicana garment workers. Most occupations now have caucuses or organizations of women who seek to promote their own interests. There are also many organizations, such as those concerned with sexual harassment on the job, oriented to special problems of working women rather than to specific occupations. Women are not waiting for other people to organize them or tell them what is in their best interests.

The Uneasy Balance

People have long been worried about conflicts between work and family in the lives of women. Many of these fears were unfounded. Work as such need not conflict with women's traditional family roles or senses of femininity, because, first, women's family roles constitute much of their work. Moreover, as women expanded their work to locations outside the home and began to receive pay, they did so in ways that stretched rather than disregarded the meaning of femininity. Eventually the main issue was not whether women worked for pay, but how they did so. Now a rich body of research examines the juggling and balancing acts performed by people who are just trying to live their daily lives as employees and as members of families (Gerson 1985; Rosen 1987; Hochschild 1989; Crosby 1991; Moen 1992; White, Cox, and Cooper 1992). Women's employment has not destroyed the family, as some people thought might happen. Nor does employment mark a straight path to liberation.

Women's employment does not leave gender and familial roles and ideology untouched. Research shows that among married-couple families, those in which both husband and wife work for pay are more egalitarian. Husbands and wives are more likely to share power in the home, and husbands respect their wives more (Huber and Spitze 1981; Blumstein and Schwartz 1983). But, as one study suggests, the effects of employment on husbands and wives depends on their attitudes toward women's employment in the first place. Among husbands who are not in favor of working wives, a man's wife's employment increases the likelihood that he will experience psychological depression. Likewise, wives who would prefer to be housewives tend to show more signs of depression if they are employed. Wives who would prefer to be employed show more signs of depression if they are homemakers. A wife's employment status makes no difference to husbands who are in favor of working wives (Ross, Mirowsky, and Huber 1983).

Divisions of domestic labor also affect how husbands and wives view themselves and their relationships. Women show fewer signs of depression when their husbands do some housework. This is true regardless of whether the women themselves are employed (Ross, Mirowsky, and Huber 1983). On the other hand, "When husbands do a lot of homework, married couples have greater conflict" (Blumstein and Schwartz 1983, 146). Men appear to believe a successful partner should not have to do housework (151). When wives are employed, husbands and wives also argue more about how children should be raised (Blumstein and Schwartz 1983, 135). These different studies suggest that life may be more peaceful when there is a traditional division of labor in which the man has his world of work outside the home and the woman has hers inside. The reason that this division of labor may foster harmony is because husbands and wives live basically separate, unshared lives and because there is a clearer division of labor and of power, authority, and respect within the family.

Child-development experts have long debated the effects of maternal employment on children. Few have pointed out that for many women—and, given the structure of the economy, now probably the majority—there is no choice. Women must seek employment to keep themselves and their families financially afloat. Poverty, we know, is not good for children. Debates have focused on issues of "bonding," or the attachment relationship between babies and mothers (few scholars have thought about bonding with fathers), in some cases suggesting that full-time contact is necessary, in other cases rejecting that idea.

For many experts now, the issue is to accept an important fact of life, that women need their jobs, and focus on how to develop high-quality alternatives for caring for children. "Whatever their views of the evidence, child-development experts . . . are virtually unanimous in their calls for generous parental-leave policies, improved availability and quality of day care and greater flexibility in the workplace to allow, for example, more part-time work."[24] Consider the situation in France, where parents are allowed 2 years' parental leave without pay. The cost of child care is determined by a sliding fee ranging from about $195 per year for poorest families to $4,700 for wealthiest. From 3 years old preschool is free, and 98% of French children attend. Compared to the American system in which many preschool teachers have no or little training, minimum-wage payment or less, and no benefits, French preschool teachers must earn a graduate degree in early-childhood and elementary education and they receive free college tuition and a stipend if they pledge to do preschool work for 5 years. To be a director of a child-care center one must be a pediatric nurse.[25]

The amount of time women spend working for pay has greatly increased, but women spend only slightly less time doing free domestic labor now than they did formerly (especially if they are employed). Women have increasing incentives to enter the labor force, but it is less clear what will motivate men to do more domestic labor. Many employed women find it easier to avoid conflicts and continue to do the housework themselves. But is this wise, especially in the long run?

NOTES

1. Although they did not point this out at the time, most feminist scholars now probably would agree that this "jobs model" assumed by scholars applied primarily to white men in the United States; men of other races would have been interpreted largely through a "race model." We will focus on this shortly.
2. Although Feldberg and Glenn talked about the *job model* for men and *gender model* for women, in fact both are gender models because both are shaped by gender. For this reason, I use *job model* to refer to the gender-based model used for men, and *family model* to refer to the gender-based model used for women.
3. This was discussed more thoroughly in Chapter 4.
4. For more on the development of scientific homemaking, see Cowan (1983).
5. "Fact File: This Year's Freshmen: A Statistical Profile," *Chronicle of Higher Education*, January 13, 1993.
6. Lynda Richardson, "Cookie-Cutter Roles for Mothers Are Gone," *New York Times*, September 2, 1992.
7. "Daughters Already at Work, and Succeeding," *New York Times*, April 28, 1993.
8. See more complete discussion in Chapter 5.
9. Barbara Presley Noble, "An Increase in Bias Is Seen Against Pregnant Workers," *New York Times*, January 2, 1993.
10. For a review of experimental research on sexism in personnel decision making, see Cash, Gillen, and Burns (1977). Also see the discussion in Chapter 3.
11. Patrick Harverson, "Women Take Stock of Wall Street," *Financial Times*, January 6, 1993.
12. Maria Odum, "If the G.N.P. Counted Housework, Would Women Count for More?" *New York Times*, April 5, 1992.
13. Ibid.
14. Ibid.
15. Barbara Presley Noble, "Making a Case for Family Programs," *New York Times*, May 2, 1993.
16. Vivian Marino, "Impact of leave law? Experts say little need for businesses to worry," *Wisconsin State Journal*, February 6, 1993.
17. Susan Chira, "New Realities Fight Old Images of Mothers," *New York Times*, October 4, 1992.
18. Jason DeParle, "Incomes in Young Families Drop 32% in 17 Years, Study Finds," *New York Times*, April 15, 1992.
19. Ibid.
20. Tamar Lewin, "New Tools Are Helping the States in Collecting Child-Support Funds," *New York Times*, June 15, 1991.

21. For more reading on women and poverty programs, see Gordon (1990).
22. To read more on the history of women in labor unions, see Foner (1982), Cook, Lorwin, and Daniels (1984), and Cobble (1993).
23. The AFL-CIO, formed by a unification of the American Federation of Labor and the Congress of Industrial Organizations, is the largest federation of labor unions in the United States.
24. Eric Eckholm, "Finding Out What Happens When Mothers Go to Work," *New York Times*, October 6, 1992.
25. Fred M. Hechinger, "Why France Outstrips the United States in Nurturing Its Children," *New York Times*, August 1, 1990.

PART FOUR

Feminism and the Global Context

EACH CHAPTER OF this book thus far has considered some of the ways in which women have acted individually and together to try to improve the life options open to them and the quality of their lives as women. In this final section we turn specifically to the questions of feminism and united action among women.

Reflect Before You Read

1. What changes in the status and roles of women and of men do you think need to be made in the future? How can these best be accomplished? What role will you play? Why?
2. You probably are aware of the many different strategies women use to become involved in questions raised by feminism. Some women actively oppose feminist organizations. Some try to do the best they can individually in their own lives. Some become involved in organizations that work through conventional political means. Some become involved in radical kinds of action. Why do you think people choose each of these different paths? Which path are you following? Why? If you have remained aloof from them all, why?
3. Do you think of yourself as a feminist? Why or why not? How would you describe feminists and feminism? Where did you get your ideas about feminism?

14

Feminism and the Future

A GROUP OF people are standing together in a room. Over there is Abigail Adams, wife of a revolutionary who later will become the second president of the United States. Adams is telling her husband (half jokingly) that the ladies are bound to foment a revolution if they are not remembered in the design of the new government. Standing nearby is Elizabeth Cady Stanton, who spent half a century pushing for expansion of women's rights. She is arguing with Ida B. Wells, who exposed the prevalence of lynching at the turn of the century and also pointed out the special sexual oppression of black women. Wells is angry with Stanton for her racist remarks and belief that it is more important for white women than black men to have the vote. There is a young Jewish immigrant who has spent the past 14 hours at a factory sewing machine working to support her family. She is about to strike in support of higher wages and a 10-hour working day. She is gazing at a wealthy patron of the arts who has helped build a concert hall where women's music can be heard. A curious conversation is taking place between Valerie Solanas of the Society for Cutting Up Men (SCUM) and Phyllis Schlafly, who vigorously opposes the Equal Rights Amendment and supports policies she thinks will maintain the dignity of women's roles in the family. Catharine Beecher, looking on, is partly sympathetic and points out that she devoted considerable effort to the task of improving the status of women, although she saw no need for women to vote. One woman is walking away from one of the few men in the room because she can't imagine what he would have to say to her about women's rights that would be useful. She has argued that the only way to seek freedom for women is by working with other women to figure out what they need. John Stuart Mill shakes his head sadly, thinking about the hours he spent trying to convince his colleagues in Parliament to support giving women the franchise. Three women stand at the edge of the room. One is thinking that she certainly is not a feminist, but she does believe women should have a better chance to earn a living and do the things they want to do.

Another thinks she has no time for these arguments because she is too busy working with her welfare rights organization fighting for higher benefits for single mothers. Another impatiently thinks that she has no time for feminism because she works 15 hours a day as the first female head of a corporation in her industry.[1]

Which of these people are feminists? Nearly 200 years separate their birthdates; they are of different sexes, races, religions, and classes; and they would find few points of agreement. They all, however, worked for what they saw as improvements in the status of women, or did things that might have direct and special benefits for women, or lived in defiance of stereotypes of women. After all is said and done, what is feminism? Who are feminists? When and how do feminist movements happen, and what is their social significance? These are the questions this chapter explores.

Ever since the word *feminism* was coined near the end of the 19th century, those attached to it and those antagonistic toward it have struggled among and between themselves to define it (Cott 1987; Offen 1988). Why would people who are not bookish academics struggle over the meaning of a word? The answer to this question begins to point us toward the nature of feminism. Feminism has an inseparably dual character, involving both theory and practice. Feminism is both a way of thinking about the world and a way of acting in it.

The meaning of feminism is derived not just from footnote-dotted books but also from the decisions and actions of generations of people around the world claiming to act on its behalf. So disagreement over the definition of *feminism* is a disagreement over how people should act and interact. This debate is conditioned in part by the historical eras in which it has taken place. It is also an international and cross-cultural argument, involving women (especially) from around the world and from different social groups, each with a different experience and, therefore, with a different view on the needs of women.

Let us start with a general working definition and then turn briefly to some alternative contemporary feminist theories to see what some of the disagreements are. If we sort through all of these different perspectives, we can find a core of characteristics about which most agree.

Feminism is a perspective that views gender as one of the most important bases of the structure and organization of the social world. Feminists argue that in most known societies this structure gives women lower status and value than men, more limited access to valuable resources, and less autonomy and opportunity to make choices about their lives. Feminists further believe that although this gender-based world may be organized around certain biological facts such as the exclusive capacity of men to create sperm and the exclusive capacity of women to bear children, gender inequality is rooted in the social construction of human experience, which means that it should be possible to eradicate it. Finally, feminists believe that these inequities should be eliminated and that to do this, feminists cannot simply try to do better as individuals in the social world as it exists but must work together to change the structure of the social world. Any other action means making the best of an unjust situation.

This general working definition provides only the common denominator in definitions of feminism. Further refinement requires examining various traditions and types of feminism. To understand the meaning of feminism in more depth it is important to undertake two tasks. The first is to survey the history of feminism to understand how it has developed over time and to allow us to ground our understanding of feminism in the historical conditions in which it has been created. The second is to explore the body of literature loosely known as feminist theory, in which feminist scholars and activists have experimented with frameworks for understanding women's situation and sex/gender systems, and have worked to create new visions of the future and strategies to achieve these visions.

American Feminism

Like most social movements, feminist movements are not spontaneous uprisings that occur randomly. A social movement is a collective effort by a large group of people to solve a set of problems they think they share. Participants in social movements generally do not have the political power to achieve the changes they desire through regular governmental channels and procedures, which is why they turn to collective action. But how do these groups of people come together in the first place? Why do they come together when they do? What makes them decide that they share common problems and that they can solve these problems through collective action? How do they choose the particular strategies they do? How and why do they succeed or fail? Historians and social scientists disagree about details, but their study of past social movements offers broad suggestions.[2]

Social movements do not necessarily begin because a group faces a new problem; they begin when a group arrives at a new perception of its problems and the possibilities for change. The women's movement of the 1960s did not arise because inequality in employment or education or marital law and policy had just developed, but because enough women came to a special awareness of these inequities. In fact some theorists and social scientists argue that social movements often begin just when a group's situation is starting to improve.

A social movement is often incited by a precipitating event that sparks a special awareness or new consciousness on the part of a relatively small group of people, who in turn organize and attempt to mobilize others they think should share this consciousness. The success of organization and mobilization generally seems to depend on two factors:

1. The early leaders must be able to draw on some prior frustration or discontent experienced by their potential followers, even if that discontent has not yet been expressed in the specific form the new social movement will give it. In the 1950s, for example, Betty Friedan witnessed the "problem that had no name," a feeling of personal discontent on the part of middle-class women that no one seemed to understand.
2. Social movements generally do not start from scratch but develop from and build on existing networks and organizations. Jo Freeman (1975) shows how the contemporary women's movement was built from earlier networks, and

many historians of 19th-century feminism show the same pattern in the suffrage movement.

The task of mobilizing recruits is the most crucial and difficult aspect of social movements. Early in any movement's history—when they are most likely to fail—mobilization is even more important than attempting to influence the powerful. Unlike most interest groups, which may rely on money or contacts or special forms of power, social movements rely largely on numbers. It is hard to make a credible case, or credible threats, to power holders if they include only a tiny proportion of the group that claims to have a grievance. Mobilization of potential members of a social movement involves identifying those people who share an interest and convincing them that they have a shared problem with a shared solution. The already converted sometimes underestimate the difficulty of doing this.

A social movement that is successful in growing is susceptible to change and fragmentation as it grows for a number of reasons:

1. The methods and strategies appropriate to a large movement are different from those appropriate to a small, new movement. A large group has different resources, is more diverse, and does not need to devote as much effort to consciousness raising among potential members.
2. As a movement grows its actions must adjust to the changing reactions of outsiders and to changes in historical circumstances. The suffrage movement, for example, used different strategies and approaches at the close of the Civil War than it did on the eve of World War I, just as the contemporary women's movement, born in a time of prosperity and optimism in the 1960s, had to adjust to the economic and political hard times of the 1980s and early 1990s. In both cases, even the technological supports for political activities changed dramatically. The later suffragists had modes of transportation and communication not available to their predecessors, and current feminists can use computers, which were not as widely available earlier.
3. The characteristics of the people involved change. Early participants gain experience, learn, and are sometimes left behind by the changes that take place within their own organizations. Elizabeth Cady Stanton was a young woman of 33 when she organized the Seneca Falls Convention; she was 75 when she served her last term as president of a national suffrage organization. Many of the women who first came together at the beginning of the contemporary women's movement are still active, but they are now decades older and changed by their experiences. New women with new experiences, motivations, and skills enter a movement in its later stages. They bring with them fresh ideas of what is to be done and how, and they sometimes feel considerable frustration with the old guard, who may deal with them skeptically.

The history of American feminism exemplifies these patterns. Even the brief sketch provided here points out how varied and continuous the history of feminism in America has been. We will look at four phases in this history: the period before the Civil War, often characterized as the era of the women's rights movement; the period from the Civil War to the ratification of the 19th Amendment in 1920, most remembered for the suffrage movement; the period from 1920 to the establishment of presidential commissions on women's status in 1961, when there was no unified national women's movement; and the era from the early 1960s to the present, when the contemporary women's movement has grown and gained force.

Before the Civil War

If feminism is a self-conscious, collective effort to improve the condition of women, there was little feminism as such before the Civil War.[3] No mass movement attacked the oppression of women as a group, although many individuals and organizations worked to alleviate certain specific problems that particular groups of women faced. By the middle of the 19th century, however, advocates of women's rights had laid the groundwork for the post–Civil War surge in feminism and had contributed to a change in the consciousness of many women that provided the breeding ground for a more comprehensive feminist ideology and action.

In the first decades of the Republic, discussion of the roles and status of American women was part of the more general attempt by intellectuals and other leaders to define the nature of the new nation and its members (Kerber 1986; Evans 1989). Mary Wollstonecraft's *Vindication* made the rounds in these circles, and an American, Judith Sargent Murray, wrote a series of essays (as "Constantia") that explained the need for better education for women (see Rossi 1988). Newspapers often served as a forum for discussion of needed improvements.

Nevertheless it would be incorrect to say that there was no agitation for women's rights before the rise of 19th-century women's movements. Action oriented toward change became more common in the early 19th century. The predominant focus of attention was female education, and it was often promoted by one person or a small group of people working to establish schools for females. Emma Willard (1787–1870), for example, established the Troy Female Seminary in 1821 and successfully lobbied to get partial public funding for her school. Her success is particularly notable because the idea of *public* schools was still in its infancy. People such as Willard and Mary Lyon (1797–1849), who founded Mt. Holyoke in 1837, pursued the principle of women's rights by spreading their ideas and attempting to fulfill their own dreams in individual ways.

Although they had no notion of founding a mass movement, these women inspired those who later led the feminist movement. Lucy Stone (1818–1893), for example, seems to have awakened to feminist ideas as she sat in a sewing circle working to provide the income for a young man to pursue his studies (as many young women did). While she sewed she listened to Mary Lyon speaking of women's education. Stone apparently left her sewing thinking, "Let these men with broader shoulders and stronger arms earn their own education while we use our scantier opportunities to educate ourselves" (Flexner 1975, 34). Stone went on to become one of the first female graduates from Oberlin College and a moving force in American feminism.

The early 19th century was a time of great social and religious activism. At the same time, women's roles became more restricted in many ways with the development of the American nation, its economy, and the resulting cult of true womanhood.[4] Not surprisingly, many women chafed at the change and resisted. This change is usually discussed with respect to white society, but there is evidence that parallel developments were occurring within some of the native American nations as well. As pressures from both white society and Cherokee men began to introduce the cult of domesticity into Cherokee society in the early 19th century, women tried to protest their loss of rights and reduced status (Perdue 1989). Free African American women began organizing mutual aid societies as early as the 1820s (Shaw 1991).

Women became involved in two widespread social movements that transformed their ideas about the condition of women and thus provided the country with a core of feminist leaders and organizers: moral-reform movement and the abolition movement. Barbara Berg (1978) provides an account of the growth of female moral-reform societies during the first half of the 19th century and of their evolutionary role in transforming many women's views of their own conditions. Like other historians, Berg reminds us that the growth of female social activism and feminine—and ultimately, feminist—consciousness occurred during a time of widespread social change and redefinition. On one hand there was the growth of an urban culture and pressures for democratization; on the other there was a groping for security best exemplified by the pursuit of a romantic, orderly, pastoral ideal. That ideal included the cult of domesticity and the belief that woman's place is in the home. The home came to be seen as a place distinct from the public world of politics and markets, and woman, the guardian and symbol of the home, came to be seen as having a character distinct from that of man.

Berg argues that not just the home but also this emerging perception of woman's character provided a base of security to white urban men in a confusing and dynamic world.

> Woman's nature, then, perceived as the opposite of man's gave clear expression to the elusive male identity. Moreover, the alleged and exaggerated difference between the sexes substituted for the absence of rigid class distinctions in the first part of the nineteenth century. Because masculine security depended so heavily on the distance man set between himself and woman, every effort had to be made to indicate vast differences in the nature of the two sexes (Berg 1978, 73–74).

The result was the creation of a relatively rigid theory of sex distinction, as well as a class of women with very little to do.

Many women turned their attention to social activities that seemed appropriate for ladies. In some cases these were clubs and literary societies; in many cases they were benevolent and moral-reform societies.[5] Because these women had no intention of defying social mores, most of their good works primarily involved helping other women. The result, however, was a growing awareness that there was something especially oppressive about women's lives. As Berg writes:

> Voluntarism exposed many facets of woman's oppression. It brought into sharp focus those abuses that generally had the greatest impact on the lives of poorer women. Whether they distributed firewood to widows, shelter to orphans, medicine to the sick, Bibles to the unconverted or education to young girls, the women in philanthropic organizations visited with and listened to hundreds of thousands of destitute females in cities across the country. Their collective experiences vivified the depth and extent of feminine suffering (1978, 170).

The two aspects of women's lives underscored most clearly by this experience were economic inequality and women's "subjugation to masculine brutality." Berg further argues that as the volunteer women began to work more closely with those less fortunate such as poor women, widows, prostitutes, imprisoned women, and the wives of drunkards, many began to see considerable similarity between themselves and these other women. Because the ideology of the time was that men and women have distinct and opposite natures, it was a small step for these early social workers to feel a certain unity with women in apparently very different circumstances.

Some activists began to speak and act in ways that would seem very familiar to feminists today. In New York, for example, members of the Moral Reform Society kept vigil at brothels and reported their findings in their journal. They identified some patrons of the brothels publicly and threatened to do the same to others (Berg 1978, 185). The writing in moral-reform periodicals could be very biting:

> Women have so long been called "angels" that men seem to have come to the conclusion that they have no persons to protect; and as for property, they say women do not know enough to take care of it, and therefore the laws and customs of society virtually say they shall have none to protect . . . the law in its kind care for women . . . takes away every cent from her. This is not exactly burning a woman on the funeral pile of her husband, but is rather a refinement on the Asiatic cruelty (Berg 1978, 209).

Above all, the reformers came to believe that women had to take responsibility for themselves and, as they said repeatedly, to think for themselves. Their work in women's organizations gave many women a new respect and affection for women and their abilities (Degler 1980, 301).

Women in moral-reform and related organizations focused on several specific issues. Some concentrated on marital property reform, especially in the 1830s and 1840s. Others concentrated on the conditions of working women. A large proportion focused on the poor, widows, and orphans. Many of their efforts were aimed at protecting women from male exploitation and brutality, through, for example, temperance and birth control (women's right to refrain from sex) and helping "fallen women," who had already been prey to such exploitation and brutality. Finally, many women became active in the abolitionist movement.

The abolition movement gave many African American and white women their first real taste of collective social and political action. As in the moral-reform movement, they did not simply talk but also engaged in action, which in this case could be fatally dangerous, especially when they served as conductors or provided stations on the Underground Railway. As white women worked toward emancipation of black slaves, they began to see some aspects of their own condition as women more clearly. For example, Sarah (1792–1873) and Angelina (1805–1879) Grimké argued that women had a special role to perform in emancipation work and began to talk about women's roles as well (Lerner 1971; Rossi 1988). In 1870, more than 30 years after Angelina's "Appeal to Christian Women of the South," both sisters cast symbolic ballots in special ballot boxes in Massachusetts to demonstrate their support for the female vote.

It is often said that 19th-century feminism, especially the suffrage movement, was born of the abolition movement (DuBois 1978). Although more of the white women who became involved in the later feminist movements probably came through moral-reform organizations, abolition provided the original cadre of suffrage leaders, and it gave shape to midcentury feminist organizations. The early link between abolition and feminism is direct and well known. In 1833 the "men only" American Anti-Slavery Society was founded in Philadelphia. Undaunted by the fact that they were not allowed to join, interested women founded the Philadelphia Female Anti-Slavery Society. Their separatism was foisted upon them; unwilling to pick a leader from their midst, they chose a black freedman as the head of their organization. At the first convention of the National Female Anti-Slavery Society in 1837, however, the members made it clear that women were quite capable of managing without male leaders such as Theodore Weld (the man Angelina Grimké later married).

In 1840 the World Anti-Slavery Convention in London excluded women, including abolitionist activists Lucretia Mott (1793–1880), one of the founders of the Female Anti-Slavery Society, and Elizabeth Cady Stanton (1815–1902). The two women walked around London angrily discussing their plight, but they went their separate ways for the next 8 years, although they stayed in contact. Eventually Stanton and her husband settled in the small town of Seneca Falls, New York, where she found herself growing increasingly discontented with her own limited domestic roles and with the roles assigned to women in general.

> The general discontent I felt with woman's portion . . . impressed me with the strong feeling that some active measures should be taken to remedy the wrongs of society in general and of women in particular. My experience at the World Anti-Slavery Convention, all I had read of the legal status of women, and the oppression I saw everywhere, together swept across my soul, intensified now by many personal experiences. It seemed as if all the elements had conspired to impel me to some onward step. I could not see

> what to do, or where to begin—my only thought was a public meeting for protest and discussion (quoted in Flexner 1975, 73–74).

The same pattern occurred repeatedly both at that time and later: A woman or a group of women is struck by a combination of personal experiences and events that demand action. But what action? The first step for Stanton, as for others, was to call a meeting to share observations with other women and figure out what needed to be done.

In the summer of 1848, Stanton met with Mott and four other women and "poured out, that day, the torrent of my long accumulating discontent, with such vehemence and indignation that I stirred myself, as well as the rest of the party, to do and dare anything" (Flexner 1975, 74). The meeting they planned came to be known as the Seneca Falls Convention, and it ended in the signing of the Declaration of Sentiments and Resolutions. Elizabeth Cady Stanton's feelings at that time kept her active for more than a half century more. Only one woman present at the meeting, which issued the first tentative call for women's suffrage, lived to vote as a result of the 19th Amendment to the Constitution.

Activists continued their abolitionist work until the Civil War, and added to it their commitment to the rights of women. In 1850 an important women's rights convention held in Worcester, Massachusetts, gained international fame through the writings of Harriet Taylor in England (see Rossi 1988). Conventions were held nearly every year until 1861. The overlap between the abolitionist and women's rights movement is well illustrated by the names of the key leaders who spoke and acted for both. Although Elizabeth Cady Stanton, Susan B. Anthony (who joined Stanton in 1851), Lucretia Mott, and Lucy Stone are usually associated with women's rights, and Sojourner Truth (1797?–1883), Theodore Weld, Wendell Phillips, and William Lloyd Garrison are generally associated with abolitionism, in fact all of these people devoted their efforts to both. Sojourner Truth's most famous speech was delivered to a women's rights convention in Akron, Ohio, in 1851.

Not yet a very large social movement, the women's movement consisted of various groups of political activists pursuing different, discrete goals, often tied to other concerns such as moral reform or abolition. Small as the movement was, the group was criticized for doing nothing but talk. The historian Eleanor Flexner answers the charge as follows:

> At this stage, there was not much else they could do. Having stated their dissatisfaction with things as they were, they had to agree on what they wanted to achieve, and to develop an ideology which would serve to refute their critics and win them new adherents. What was the proper condition of married women? What should be women's place in the church, the community, the professions, the state? On what basis should divorce be permitted . . . ? From the gatherings where these issues were thrashed out there emerged a body of thought, new and dedicated leadership, wide publicity, and new recruits (1975, 81–82).

Many of the feminists began to write about these issues, and some started their own periodicals. There was some attempt to coordinate feminist activity nationally. A central committee was formed in the 1850s with delegates from any state in which there was women's rights activity. Flexner notes that at that time activists had little desire for greater organization for much the same reasons that later feminists were wary of too much organization: They feared that it would stultify growth and inhibit rather than promote action (1975, 83). The intentional building of a strong movement had to wait until after the Civil War.

Fifty Years and More: From Civil War to Suffrage

The Civil War offered women new avenues for their social concern and activism.[6] Many social activists turned their attention to new organizations such as the Sanitary Commission, which did war relief and nursing work. The more politically minded put their efforts to a new task: fighting in Congress for passage of a constitutional amendment that would forever ban slavery in the United States. Elizabeth Cady Stanton and Susan B. Anthony gained their national political organizing skills through their positions as officers in the National Women's Loyal League, which in 1864 presented to Congress a petition with over 300,000 signatures supporting an amendment to ban slavery.

The text that eventually became the 14th Amendment to the Constitution both sparked the organization of a full-blown women's suffrage movement and deeply divided it as it was forming. That amendment, which was to become critical in defining citizenship, contained the first and only use of the word *male* in the U.S. Constitution; it levied a punishment against states that interfered with the voting rights of "male citizens." Activists such as Stanton and Anthony were infuriated and wanted, at least, that the word *male* be removed. But they went further and added their voices to the discussion of another proposed amendment (eventually the 15th), which would guarantee the right to vote regardless of race. But they wanted it also to guarantee the right to vote regardless of sex.

The rift that ensued broke up the Equal Rights Association, which had been organized at the end of the war to pursue the rights of women and blacks. The rift focused on two related questions: First, should the Association fight to get what it could, which might mean legal guarantees of rights for blacks (or at least black men) and not women, or should it press for rights for women as well? And second, which was the more pressing need: legal guarantees for blacks or for women? This insidious type of question is often faced by different oppressed groups attempting to work in coalition. In fact, the question makes no sense at all with respect to a large group of women: those oppressed by both race and gender. Consider Sojourner Truth's argument:

> I feel that I have a right to have just as much as a man. There is a great stir about colored men getting their rights, but not a word about the colored women; and if colored men get their rights, and not colored women theirs, the colored men will be masters over the women, and it will be just

as bad as it was before. So I am for keeping the thing going while things are stirring; because if we wait till it is still, it will take a great while to get it going again (Sterling 1984, 411–12).

The Equal Rights Association chose race rights as its primary goal. In 1869 Stanton and Anthony broke away to form the National Woman Suffrage Association, open to any interested women but only women, on the belief that the men of the Equal Rights Association were selling out and duping the women of that organization. The National became dedicated to a constitutional amendment for women's suffrage. Later that year Lucy Stone and others formed the American Woman Suffrage Association, including both women and men, but restricting its membership to delegates. It preferred the more conservative strategy of pursuing women's rights on a state-by-state basis. The national organization for the late-19th-century women's movement was in place, but it remained split for the next 20 years.

The breakup of the Equal Rights Association caused unforgettable tension between black and white leaders. Stanton and Anthony embellished their break with many racist remarks, just as many later suffragists pitted blacks against whites and "native women" (native-born Americans of European stock) against immigrants. Although these events are often discussed as if they involved only black men and white women, they also involved white men and black women. The white men of the Equal Rights Association by and large stuck with the argument "This is the Negro's hour," and black women faced a most difficult dilemma. An amendment that barred discrimination on the basis of race alone would not give black women the vote. But if clear incursions into racism were not made, no amount of women's rights legislation would help them.

The ambivalence of black women lasted throughout the century because they were "placed in a double bind; to support women's suffrage would imply that they were allying themselves with white women activists who had publicly revealed their racism, but to support black male suffrage was to endorse a patriarchal social order that would grant them no political voice" (hooks 1981, 3). Despite the number of times white suffragists made racist statements and discriminated against black suffragists, many black women fought for women's rights throughout the end of the 19th century and into the beginning of the 20th, sometimes in their own organizations, and sometimes in integrated organizations. In the split between the NWSA and AWSA, most African American suffrage leaders, including Sojourner Truth and Harriet Tubman (1820?–1913), chose to stay with Stanton and Anthony in the NWSA.

The suffrage movement remained active throughout the rest of the 19th century, but it was by no means the only activist women's movement. It mobilized women by drawing on those involved in other kinds of women's organizations. Women's organizations in the postwar period were even more active than they had been before the war. Social activists, including many of the leading suffragists, increased their efforts to influence the morals and social life of the nation, especially as they affected women and children. These efforts in the last decades of the 19th century are often called the "social purity" movement.

One of the best known of the social purity organizations was the Women's Christian Temperance Union, which was founded in 1874 and became the largest single women's organization in the nation. Under the leadership of Frances Willard (1839–1898), it was also linked to the suffragist cause, although many people worried about whether the two issues should be mixed. Willard herself took care not to be associated with "radicals" such as Stanton and Anthony. To most other temperance suffragists (such as Anthony herself), the reason for mixing temperance and suffrage seemed obvious. If men would stop spending their wages on drink and coming home to be useless fathers and husbands or worse, women would be better able to provide themselves and their children with good and healthful lives. If women had the vote, they would also have the political leverage to provide themselves and their children with good and healthful lives, as well as a means to spread their own moral influence.

By the end of the century the movement was also drawing from other sources: women who were receiving advanced degrees and were becoming professionals, some of the women of the new labor movement, and some of the women of the West who had become involved in the labor movement and in populist uprisings and organizations such as the Grange clubs. Even if the suffragist movement began as an alliance primarily of homemakers who had the time to devote to social housekeeping and reform causes, by the end of the century it included many working women who were drawn in not as individuals but as members of work-related groups.

The late-19th-century suffragists used various strategies to pursue their goals. They lobbied, spoke, organized petitions, and got involved in state referendum campaigns. The National Woman Suffrage Association worked on increasing congressional support for a constitutional amendment. Suffragists also engaged in protest and direct actions such as attempting to cast ballots in elections, as they did across the country in the early 1870s. They tried to use the courts. Two famous cases, those of Susan Anthony in New York and Virginia Minor (1824–1894) in the Supreme Court, made it clear that the judicial system could not be used to gain women the vote. Both women attempted to vote and sued unsuccessfully when they were barred from doing so. Other participants in the protest, such as Sojourner Truth, were turned away before they could obtain ballots.[7] By the end of the century only a handful of states and local areas had given women the right to vote, and Congress did not seem to be moving toward support for an amendment. The differences between the two major suffragist organizations (the National and the American Woman Suffrage Associations) blurred, and in 1890 they merged, forming the National American Woman Suffrage Association (NAWSA).

By the turn of the century the early suffrage activists were very old. The last of the original leaders, Stanton and Anthony, died in the early 1900s. The new leaders and activists differed from their predecessors. Carrie Chapman Catt (1859–1947) did not fear organization as earlier feminists had. Catt, who engineered the final successful stage of the campaign, brought with her a modern sense of political organization. Elizabeth Cady Stanton's daughter, Harriot Stanton Blatch (1856–1940), had spent 20 years in England and imported some of the

Alice Paul, a suffragist and activist.

techniques she had witnessed there. She formed a new organization and tried new strategies such as holding open-air meetings and marches and working with trade unions. She captured for suffrage work some of the brightest and eventually best-known women of that era, including Charlotte Perkins Gilman (1860–1935) and Florence Kelley (1859–1932) (Flexner 1975, 261). The movement drew women of all types and classes, from trade union women of the garment district to wealthy wives of bankers and industrialists. Women of all political parties—Democrats, Republicans, Socialists, and Progressives, a new party that endorsed women's suffrage in 1912—were involved. At the same time, the size and complexity of the movement meant that agreement on a single plan was difficult to achieve, and the movement was often torn by disagreements about tactics.

One woman who both breathed new life into the movement and fostered a schism in it was Alice Paul (1885–1977), who had spent some time in England before coming home to the United States to complete her Ph.D. She was much impressed with the radical activities of the Pankhursts (a woman and her two daughters who led the English suffrage movement) and thought she could use the same techniques to call attention to women's plight in America. When she became head of the Congressional Committee of the NAWSA, one of her first acts was to organize a parade of 5,000 women in Washington the day before Woodrow Wilson's inauguration, sparking a near riot (Flexner 1975, 272–73).

Alice Paul's radicalism led to a separation of her group from the NAWSA. Paul wanted to hold whichever political party happened to be in power responsible for the lack of the federal amendment granting suffrage to women. NAWSA opposed this position because this would mean working against some prosuffragist candidates. Paul's group, the Congressional Union, worked in the 1914 election campaigns to punish the party in power at that time, the Democrats. Their activities succeeded in bringing the amendment to a vote, but it was at first defeated.

Paul and her organization then became more militant. In 1917 the Congressional Union picketed the White House, the first time any political group had done so. It changed its name to the National Women's Party and added antiwar slogans to its rhetoric. These demonstrations provoked violence by onlookers, and the women demonstrators (not the violent onlookers) were arrested. Eventually the women held a new kind of protest inspired by the English feminists. They demanded to be called political prisoners and went on a hunger strike in prison. Prison officials reacted by force-feeding them, which caused a public outcry that eventually led to the release of the women.

Many people argued that these radical actions hurt more than they helped and made people unwilling to join the suffragists. This argument is still used against militancy in social movements. The criticism, however, is often launched by people who have not been drawn into the movement by more conservative strategies either. Analysis of the effects of different wings of the suffrage and other feminist movements suggests that the combined or parallel actions of the moderate and radical wings allows more widespread participation and more varied strategies.

Alice Paul's actions called attention to the resolve of the feminists in a way other strategies did not; they showed that women were willing to risk their lives and careers for suffrage. Many people would have been unaware of the suffrage movement were it not for the headlines that Alice Paul and her group provoked, and the public was appalled by the violence with which the state fought against them. Meanwhile, Carrie Chapman Catt's "Winning Plan," as she labeled her strategy of intense but more conventional political campaigning, achieved passage and ratification of the 19th Amendment. The irony is that it is in large part people like Alice Paul who made Catt's strategies appear conventional, conservative, and reasonable. Until that time the political tactics NAWSA was using may have been conventional for men, but they were very unconventional for women.

An interesting perspective on this question of moderation versus radicalism in strategy is offered by Arvonne Fraser, an activist who became a leader in mainstream feminist groups in the 1960s and 1970s, including the Women's Equity Action League.

> Radical feminists identified and publicized "the system's" oppression of women. They also made it respectable for women to work on women's issues. Eventually, establishment women began to work within the system to change laws and regulations and their task was made easier by these earlier efforts. Our group and others like it would never have been formed if the women's liberation groups had not staked out a more extreme position (Fraser 1983, 122).

It is difficult to ascertain whether success would have come if only one strategy had been used, and it is even more difficult to know when one is in the middle of the battle.

Many casual observers paint the suffrage amendment and the feminist movement that supported it as failures for two reasons: that feminist goals were too narrowly focused on getting the vote, and that the feminist movement disappeared after 1920. Let us look at these two points more carefully.

The vote was no small goal to achieve. It is the symbol of citizenship, and without it women could not be seen as free citizens. Before suffrage, political leaders argued that women's rights did not matter because, after all, women couldn't vote. Some rights are contingent on voting either by law or by custom, including holding certain types of political offices and sitting on juries. The vote is an instrument to be used to pursue other goals, and this is how most suffragists saw it.

Although suffrage is the best-known goal of feminists of this period, it was not the only one. We already have seen that the social purity movement was based on the belief that women should have increased control over their destinies. The specific goals of this movement may seem conservative to today's feminists, but they were nonetheless intended to free women. A new and more radical birth control movement developed after the turn of the century, as women like Margaret Sanger (1883–1966) and Emma Goldman (1869–1940) fought to make contraception more widely available.

The same era witnessed the rise of organizations oriented toward alleviating the plight of working women. The Women's Trade Union League (WTUL) was formed in 1903 because of the failure of male-dominated unions to work for women. A related effort was the National Consumer's League established in 1899, which originally worked to alert consumers about whether the products they were buying were made in shops with proper working conditions. Meanwhile, women who had entered various professions formed organizations to fight for women's rights within their own groups.

It is difficult to identify an area of life that was not in some way touched by feminism in the late 19th and early 20th centuries. There were attempts at dress reform for women and continuing debates over women's health and education. There is a rich feminist literature from that time produced by feminists in the social sciences, journalism, and the literary arts. Women's groups intensified their efforts to help immigrants and the poor. Women's organizations within various racial, religious, and ethnic groups focused on some of the special problems these groups faced, including groups as diverse as the San Francisco–based Korean Women's Patriotic Society, focusing on educating and developing social awareness among the picture brides from Korea (Yang 1984) to the New York women who used the Yiddish language *Jewish Daily Forward*'s women's page to formulate a Jewish socialist view of women and feminism (Seller 1987). Increasingly after the turn of the century the various feminist organizations also threw their support behind suffrage, much as the widely divergent feminist groups in the 1970s added their voices and efforts to support of the Equal Rights Amendment.

Suffrage was not the only goal of turn-of-the century feminism; it was not even the only goal of most suffragists. It was only the most widely accepted one, and the only one that many people now remember.

The Quiet Time: From Suffrage to Presidential Commissions

Did feminism disappear after 1920 as so many people charge?[8] If the question is whether a large, well-coordinated movement of women persisted after the vote was won, feminism indeed disappeared. But if the question is whether all the feminists packed their intellectual and activist bags and went home, feminism did not disappear, at least not immediately.

To explain these answers it is necessary to analyze the 40-year period following 1920 by asking first, what happened to the large suffrage organizations and second, what other forms feminism took during the post-suffrage period. The pre-suffrage feminists certainly did not think their war was over when they won the suffrage battle. To understand what happened to them and their movement, we must look at the events that followed in the context of the sociology of social movements.

As this chapter has emphasized, mass social movements are fragile coalitions of different types of people with different motivations pursuing similar goals. The suffrage movement was a carefully constructed coalition of people who agreed that women should have a basic right of citizens: the vote. They disagreed considerably over what other issues they should pursue. Should they work for temperance? for birth control? for equal pay or for protective legislation? for marital and divorce reform? How should they structure their organizations? Should whites and blacks work together, even if that alienated a large block of legislators and white suffragists? Should they work in as "ladylike" a manner as possible, or should they display their anger and frustration and use threats and coercion to achieve their ends? Should they focus on the national or state and local levels? on politics or culture or personal life? It is often more surprising when the coalitions in social movements hang together than it would be if they fell apart. Feminism is one of the largest and longest-lived movements in American history, and although it had its failures, its longevity is an indication of its relative strength and success compared with other American movements. As the suffrage battle was won, an intense and active rethinking of the terms of feminism and feminist action occurred (Cott 1987).

The suffrage coalition weakened and eventually fell apart after the vote was gained because there was no consensus on the next major goal or primary strategy. The goals of different individuals and organizations overlapped, but that was not enough, and other events of the period put obstacles in the feminists' path.

Leaders of the suffrage movement did not wait for ratification to begin planning for the future. Alice Paul and Carrie Chapman Catt, assuming that they should be prepared for the inevitable time when their constituents would be voters, began transforming their respective organizations before the 19th Amendment was in place. The difference between their new organizations reflects feminism's important disagreements over the definitions of feminist goals and strategies.

Alice Paul's Congressional Union became the National Women's Party (NWP), whose offices still stand two blocks from the national Capitol. As the name implies, Paul had visions of an explicitly feminist political party that would continue its battle for women's rights at the highest levels of government. Still believing in the most direct and vigorous route to equality, Alice Paul proposed in the early 1920s that the Constitution should be amended to make discrimination on the basis of sex unconstitutional. The wording of the amendment has changed only slightly over time. The most recent version states simply: "Equality of rights under the law shall not be denied or abridged by the United States or by any state on account of sex." This proposal has been the main goal of the NWP since 1923 (Rupp 1985; Cott 1987).

For most of its history the NWP has stood relatively isolated in its support of an equal rights amendment, although other important organizations eventually joined in support. In 1935 the National Association of Women Lawyers endorsed the amendment, and 2 years later the 90,000-member National Federation of Business and Professional Women's Clubs added their support. The NWP gained important allies in the 1940s when the amendment was endorsed by the General Federation of Women's Clubs (GFWC), the National Education Association, five national women's service organizations, and the Republican and Democratic Parties (Rawalt 1983).

Although the Equal Rights Amendment was introduced in Congress in 1923 and in every successive Congress, it did not pass until nearly 50 years later, in

1972. Ten years later the necessary number of states had not ratified it, and the proposal died—for the time being.

This was not the only focus of the NWP's attention. The post–World War I period was a time of international conferences on law and human rights, and Alice Paul fought to make equality of the sexes part of international law. The NWP took a leading role in the fight to allow women their own nationality distinct from their husband's and to pass their nationality on to their children. As the NWP pointed out, gaining the right to vote in 1920 did not make women full citizens because if an American woman married a foreigner, she was stripped of her citizenship, and if she had a child by an alien, the child was an alien. Members of the NWP, many of them also members of the feminist Women Lawyers Association, continuously lobbied and testified to Congress until their demands were won in 1934 (Becker 1981, 1983; Sapiro 1984).

The NWP met opposition in the feminist community primarily because its goals were incompatible with protective labor legislation. This opposition reflects a fundamental disagreement within feminist theory at the time. Alice Paul and her group wanted equal opportunity and equal treatment for women and men. Most other feminists thought that equal treatment, especially in the labor market, would maintain a system of laissez-faire economics in which women were a cheap and exploited labor force and in which no extra care was given to mothers and children.

Most feminists also continued to see Paul's goals and strategies as too radical and militant, and most rejected a separate women's party on two grounds. First, they preferred a more integrated system in which women and men worked together as responsible citizens for the betterment of all. Second, if women wanted power in the political system, many argued, they would do better to make inroads into the main political system than to form a party of their own.

As head of NAWSA, Carrie Chapman Catt was the leader of the more widely accepted brand of feminism. She transformed the NAWSA into the League of Women Voters. Catt's idea was that the League would be a nonpartisan training ground for female political activities and citizenship. It would be a place where women could develop their political agenda. They could then fight for their goals through the regular political parties and processes as equals. The League was intended to promote women in politics much as the National Women's Political Caucus (NWPC) is today. In its first few years the League drew up an impressive agenda of policy goals covering democratization in government; improvements in health, education, consumer, and welfare policy; better care for children and mothers; and protective labor legislation for women.

The League was strengthened when it initiated an even wider coalition of feminist groups. In 1920 the League became aware that it might be stepping on the toes of other women's groups, such as the GFWC and the WTUL, because its program and leadership overlapped with theirs. Under the leadership of Maud Wood Park (1871–1955), the League negotiated the formation of the Women's Joint Congressional Committee (WJCC). Any federal bill supported by at least three of the member organizations was backed by the financial and labor resources of the WJCC.

The greatest early victory of the WJCC was passage of the Sheppard Towner Act in 1921, drafted by Julia Lathrop (1858–1932), a League of Women Voters member and director of the Children's Bureau, and introduced into Congress by Senator Jeanette Rankin (1880–1973) in 1917. The Sheppard Towner Act, which provided federal funding for child and maternal health care, was an early breakthrough in the development of federal welfare policies. This early success, however, also contributed to the eventual weakening of the coalition responsible for it. The women's groups were caught in the middle of the first "red scare" of this century and a subsequent wave of anticommunism.

Feminists had long been accused of being socialists or Communists; indeed, some feminist leaders were socialists. Such accusations became very serious matters after the 1917 Russian Revolution when many radicals, including Emma Goldman, were deported. In the 1920s anticommunism and xenophobia in general played important roles in American politics. The Sheppard Towner Act, widely regarded as the first step toward socialism in America, signified to many people that feminists were insidious Bolshevik radicals. Different scare tactics were used against the WJCC, including the drawing of a spider web showing the connections between feminism, socialism, and Moscow (Lemons 1972; Cott 1987). This spider web suggested a dangerous conspiracy that could trap the innocent. The resulting backlash helped weaken the coalition and forced many of the women's groups, including the League, to put their heads down to survive.

Other factors aided the demise of widespread, united feminism. The political parties resented groups such as the League, arguing that they were trying to compete with the parties. Women party activists found their loyalties tested, and the League's hold on many of its members was strained by the greater power of the political parties. Many members were also overstretched and had to reevaluate their commitments.

The feminist activists of the 1920s and 1930s were different from their predecessors in one important respect. They were, for the most part, employed as professionals or as blue- or white-collar workers. Some worked in government. They had limited time for activism, and many devoted this time to the organizations most relevant to their work. The specific political goals that dominated their interests diverged—many goals were compatible but different—and the feminist movement became more fragmented. Unfortunately, the breakdown of a coalition can also weaken its constituent parts.

In the 1920s, feminists had difficulty attracting young women to their cause. The young women, especially those who were college educated, believed that there really was no battle left to fight, or at least not one that was significant enough to join. They could vote, drink, smoke, and, it seemed, dress as they liked. Many believed that women had gained their freedom, and the public press agreed with them. Flappers and movie stars were more glamorous than tiresome, serious feminists. The feminist movement thus lost an important pool of new recruits. Finally the stock market crash of 1929 and the ensuing Depression overshadowed the demands of feminists.

Between the two world wars, some women continued to fight for feminist change through their jobs or through women's organizations or religious and ethnic associations. Many women in government and journalism pushed for reforms. The New Deal programs of President Franklin Roosevelt offered a special opportunity for women to achieve some of the types of programs they supported and to participate in their administration. Eleanor Roosevelt (1884–1962) associated herself with women's interests and organizations and, in her position as the first activist first lady, provided an important support for women. People such as Margaret Sanger continued their work on making birth control available, and trade union women continued to organize women. Women in groups such as the International League for Peace and Freedom, many of whom also had been active in other feminist groups, continued their efforts to avert war. At the same time, women began to take their places in formerly male domains of economic and social life. The early 1930s saw a peak in the proportion of higher degrees and some professional jobs held by women. That record was not matched again until the 1970s.

The story of World War II and its effects on women has been told throughout this book. Women plunged into war work at home and abroad, and many gained a new consciousness of their potential and the social inhibitions placed on it. Surveys showed that most women did not want to "go home" after the war, and in some industries women struggled together to keep their jobs (Gabin 1982). The systematic attempt to demobilize women, or at least to bump them down into lower-paying and more traditionally gender-appropriate jobs, proved too strong for them, however (Tobias and Anderson 1982). By the 1950s, feminism was a word associated with what seemed to be ancient history, and as Betty Friedan suggested, women didn't even have a name for the problems they faced (Friedan 1963).

Events of the early 1960s, however, provide evidence that feminism never entirely disappeared. The NWP and some other women's groups had continued to push for an equal rights amendment, which the Senate had passed in 1950 and 1953, and both major parties had supported the ERA in their platforms since 1944. As a liberal Democrat, President John F. Kennedy could not ignore the issue of women's rights, and he established a presidential commission on the status of women to look into the matter. He also urged the states to establish their own commissions, which all did by 1967. This series of study commissions set the stage for the rise of the new women's movement in the 1960s.

Rebirth of Feminism: Emma Said It in 1910 / Now We're Going to Say It Again[9]

If the birth of social movements generally depends on changing perceptions of a group's situation, an established network among potential leaders, and an event that precipitates action, the women's liberation movement fits the pattern very well. The postwar economic boom drew women into education and jobs at an unprecedented rate in the late 1950s and 1960s. Divorce rates began to rise in the early 1960s following a decline from a postwar peak. Finally, although America was increasingly affluent, and its growth potential seemed unlimited, new social movements were asking people to question whether life was as good as it

Kay Clarenbach and Betty Friedan, two of the founders of the National Organization for Women.

could be. The black civil rights movement, the ban-the-bomb and antiwar movements, and the early 1960s Free Speech Movement, which sparked student activism nationwide, were all part of the new social ferment of the times and provided the training ground for many social activists who went on to lead the women's liberation movement.

The first decisive event in the history of the new movement occurred in 1966 after both the Equal Pay Act and the Civil Rights Act already had been passed and the Equal Employment Opportunity Commission (EEOC) had been established. At the annual meeting of the National Conference of State Commissions, some of the delegates became angry when they found that they would not be allowed to do anything to correct the problems they had been assigned to study. A group of women met in the hotel room of Betty Friedan, one of the delegates, to decide what to do. After this and a series of later meetings, the National Organization for Women (NOW) was founded in October 1966 with 300 members and Betty Friedan as president.

NOW has sometimes been known as the more conservative wing of the feminist movement. Certainly many of its early members had been active in politics, including women's politics, for many years. As Jo Freeman (1975) argues, however, the difference among the various feminist organizations is at least as much one of style as of substance. NOW has a formal organizational structure and paid officers. It has concentrated on legal and policy changes and has become one of the foremost lobbyists for the women's movement. NOW may have been criticized as conservative by more radical feminists, but this is not how the larger society viewed it. Some of the first women to break away from NOW formed their own feminist groups because they thought NOW was too radical. Some trade union women withdrew their support at first because NOW supported the ERA and their own unions did not. The Women's Equity Action League (WEAL) was formed as a separate organization in 1968 because it wanted to concentrate on sex discrimination and feared that NOW's pro-abortion stand would damage its effectiveness. However, NOW was particularly visible as it spearheaded the drive for the ratification of the Equal Rights Amendment through the 1970s, and it remains the largest and best-known feminist organization.

At the same time that NOW and other nationally organized groups were developing, very different types of feminist groups emerged for parallel reasons at the local level from the political organizations of the New Left. In the early 1960s, women in New Left organizations such as the Student Non-Violent Coordinating Committee (SNCC) and the Students for a Democratic Society (SDS) began to discuss among themselves the problems that women faced. As the women became more conscious of the status of women in society, they concluded that altering this status should be part of the agenda of the New Left groups that claimed to be fighting for a more egalitarian and democratic society. The women who presented their demands to SDS meetings in 1965 and 1966 and to a national meeting of New Left groups in 1966 were greeted with jeers and verbal violence. The same happened to women in other New Left and antiwar organizations across the country. Like Elizabeth Cady Stanton over a century earlier and the organizers of NOW, these women reacted with rage, confusion, and the desire to meet separately to plan a course of action. The result was the formation of small feminist groups across the country based on the politics of the New Left.

The contemporary women's movement therefore began not as a single organization but as a complex network of very different groups, much as the women's suffrage movement had developed from parallel and sometimes conflicting organizations. At times the differences have seemed to overshadow the similarities. The more radical groups' antipathy toward formal structure and hierarchy has led them to experiment with leaderless structures in an attempt to create a more thoroughly consensual democracy. In the early days, many small local groups emphasized consciousness-raising sessions to awaken women to their situations and help them translate their discontent into political action. As women in consciousness-raising sessions discussed their own personal problems, they became aware that these same problems were commonly faced by other women, and this helped mobilize many women to action. Other groups assumed the task of providing services, such as child-care centers and counseling and assistance services for victims of rape and wife battery.

Feminists quickly began to organize demonstrations to attract national attention to their demands. One of the most infamous was a protest staged at the 1968 Miss America contest, where a Freedom Trash Can was set up to dispose of "women's garbage," and a sheep was crowned Miss America. Despite the fact that no one seems to recall the burning of any bra, from that date feminists were given the trivializing name "bra burners." Certainly feminists burned no bras after that date, if only to avoid adding more fuel to the fires of antifeminism. The next major demonstration on the 50th anniversary of women's suffrage, August 26, 1970—was the Women's Strike for Equality, which involved feminists of all views.

As the feminist movement grew, it developed the rifts and fragmentation common to most social movements. These rifts were apparent both within and across organizations. Because of the growth in the membership of the movement, feminists could specialize in particular concerns—abortion, day care, employment discrimination, sexuality—which made the movement more comprehensive and effective but also made coordination and consensus more difficult to attain. Some women felt their concerns were being neglected, and some argued that concentration on such issues as professional employment, higher education, and women's studies was elitist and of little relevance to most women. Many argued that it was too conservative and ignored the interests of women who were not white, middle class, and heterosexual. Others argued that the tactics of such radical women as the lesbian separatists would scare off the more conservative women who most needed the movement. Some objected to the emphasis on abortion rights.

It is one thing for a social movement to appear united when it consists of a relatively small group of people with an apparently simple demand such as "equality" or "equal pay for equal work"; it is quite another when the movement is large and increasingly precise in its identification of problems and solutions. Because many people mistakenly think that disagreement within a social movement is necessarily a sign of failure, many assumed that the women's movement was about to fall apart, even as it was growing larger.

The history of NOW is a microcosm of the larger movement. As some of its associates moved away because they feared issues such as abortion, others grew dissatisfied because they thought NOW too conservative. The arguments, which at times threatened the organization's existence, revolved around NOW's hierarchical structure, the distribution of power in the organization, and the low priority given to lesbian issues. In the early 1970s, the battle between lesbian activists and the NOW leadership reached its height and caused what many described as a purge of the lesbian leaders. Although NOW later added support for lesbian women to its platform, scars remained. Despite these disagreements, NOW's membership and the membership of the thousands of other women's groups across the country grew tremendously into the middle of the 1980s, and the number of groups multiplied until it is now impossible to list all that exist. It is probably safe to say that a feminist group exists for every social category or interest.

Despite differences in views and strategies, the feminist movement has been remarkably cohesive. The different branches and organizations have learned much from each other, to the point where some earlier differences have become obscured. The move toward multiculturalism has changed the character of the movement. As forces such as the Moral Majority, the policies of the Reagan administration, and the new conservatism of the Supreme Court threatened to eliminate the gains of the previous decade, the women's movement experienced a renewed surge of motivation and activity.

The new women's movement is about a quarter of a century old now and larger than ever. The number of people involved is incalculably large. Besides the well-known national groups, there are hundreds of smaller ones, and many feminist activists press their demands in other types of organizations. Many of the early and prominent organizations of the new women's movement are still influential. These include NOW, the National Women's Political Caucus (NWPC), which was formed in 1971 to promote women in politics, and the Coalition of Labor Union Women (CLUW), which was formed in 1974. There are feminist groups and caucuses in nearly every occupational group containing women, in every field of study, and in most religious denominations. Most major towns and cities have at least some community services run by and for women. Some older women's organizations, such as the League of Women Voters, that had once lost their feminist base are now part of feminist coalitions. Even groups like the YWCA and the Girl Scouts of America occasionally join in the feminist alliance. Although many feminist periodicals have been short-lived, their overall number has continued to rise. The history of this phase of the feminist movement is not yet complete.

Oppositions

In 1991 a new best-selling book became the focus of great discussion across the United States and, indeed, in many other countries: Susan Faludi's *Backlash: The Undeclared War Against American Women*. This book, written by a Pulitzer Prize–winning journalist, argues that following some of the early successes of the new women's movement, a vehement backlash developed in almost all walks of life during the 1980s that warred against the advances women had made and were further claiming, and that sought to restore women to a more traditional and subordinate place. The power of the book—probably more widely known than any feminist book since Betty Friedan's *The Feminine Mystique* (1963)—was enhanced by the vicious attacks on feminism and prominent women activists launched by the right wing of the Republican party during the 1992 presidential campaign.

As Faludi documented, there was tremendous resistence to feminism. But to understand that resistance it is necessary to look not just at the events of that brief period of time but also at the history of opposition to feminism and women's movements, in which we can see considerable continuity over the course of American history. Some of the attacks made on today's feminism were made against the suffragists. The antifeminist arguments are as varied as those of feminist arguments.

One of the chief arguments against feminism has been that if women are given equal treatment and opportunities in society, they will lose their protection and become more overburdened than they already are. Antisuffragist women and men used this argument in the 19th and early 20th centuries, and antifeminists continue to use it today. They claim that equality will, in fact, result in injustice for women.

Much opposition throughout the history of feminism has come from religious groups and leaders. These groups are distressed by feminist attacks on what they see as the moral order of male and female difference and changes in familial, sexual, and reproductive mores.[10]

Some opposition is based on economic arguments. Various business interests, including railroads and liquor producers, opposed suffrage because they feared what women would do with their votes (Flexner 1975). In the 1970s, insurance companies opposed feminist causes because of the money they would lose if they had to treat women and men equally. The National Association of Manufacturers (NAM), which opposes any governmental restraint on business, opposed feminist demands that they prove they treat employees fairly and equitably.

Some opponents to feminism have worried about the domino effect of social change: If changes are accepted for women, who will want changes next? During the later years of the suffrage movement, many political leaders worried that if women were granted new rights, there would be little justification for denying the same rights to blacks or immigrants.

Sometimes the opposition has framed its argument not in terms of feminism or women's roles per se but in terms of the effects any changes might have on the larger society. Because feminists have tended to look to the federal government for assistance, supporters of state rights have tended to be antagonistic to feminism. Feminist proposals support government interference with husbands' traditional abilities to overpower their wives financially and physically. Many opponents see these proposals as demands for big government to expand still further and thus interfere with private rights of commerce and personal relations. Feminist proposals also have tended to call for the expansion of social services, which stirs up opposition on the part of those who see these proposals as socialist or as too costly.

Opposition also comes from those who think that society has been well structured in the past, works well, and is in no need of tampering. Those who believe that American social institutions have operated in a fair and open way in the past regard any effort to change their gender composition as an attack on "merit" systems. They argue that women are underrepresented or receive less reward because they have not wanted or been good enough to do better. Conservative critics of feminist efforts to alter the emphasis of research and education argue that these efforts will result in research agendas and curricula based on political decisions rather than merit decisions. They believe that an objective market of ideas (not men raised in androcentric cultures, even if well educated) has determined that women and their creations are not worth much attention.

Explicit antifeminist activity tends to emanate from the most conservative sectors of society. Throughout this century, feminists have been accused by their opponents of being socialist and anti-American, particularly because they support social programs to help the needy and governmental regulation of industry to benefit the consumer and worker. Studies in the 1970s showed that antifeminist activists tended to be particularly fearful about the spread of communism in the United States.

The argument between feminists and antifeminists generally has not been a battle of equal and opposing parties appealing to the government for change. The battle usually has been between groups of mostly women (and generally led by women) on the one hand and the mostly male leaders of government, business, and religion on the other. Of course many women are opposed to feminism, including members of such women's organizations as Phyllis Schlafly's Stop-ERA and Women Who Want to Be Women (WWWW). In the 19th century, many of the most active female opponents were wives of men in government or business who had power to maintain the old system of discrimination and oppression. The most effective opposition then and now is from those who are in power.

It is generally easy to see why these institutional leaders want to forestall change: It is costly to those already in power. Although men can derive many benefits from feminism, women who argue that men can "only benefit" by equality for women are naive, and most men know it.

The contemporary women's movement may be the first in American history to face the opposition of an organized antifeminist social movement. From the mid 1970s to the 1990s, a coalition of groups calling themselves profamily and prolife emerged. These groups, which drew from right-wing political organizations and the Moral Majority, were formed in reaction to feminist successes in reproductive, family, and antidiscrimination policies. These antifeminists use all the opposition arguments already mentioned, but they focus on the "protection" of women and the preservation of what they define as traditional Christian moral values.

Antifeminist women are not generally opposed to women's holding jobs or engaging in political activity; many of them do the former and all, by their involvement in the antifeminist movement, are doing the latter. They are willing to use all the political rights won for them by earlier feminists: They organize, demonstrate, petition, lobby, litigate, vote, and hold office. Some even use violence, for example, firebombing abortion clinics or physically harassing women going in and out of these clinics. They use these means to defend what they define as women's interests, just as feminists use most of these tactics (except violence against women) to defend what they define as women's interests. How can antifeminist women reconcile their opposition to demands for equality and liberation with their claims that they are fighting for women?

A clue to the answer lies in what we now define as 19th-century feminism, where women's rights activists and moral and social purity campaigners were often one and the same because these were seen as two sides of the same equation. Moral and social purity, they claimed, could give women the dignity and protection they needed from the brutal masculine world and the men in it. Men, they argued, are not trustworthy. They will exploit, neglect, and hurt their families if left to their own devices. Women need protection from men, and men need protection from themselves. Giving women more strength as women to spread their influence as nurturers and preservers of traditional values was seen as a key to the solution.

Contemporary antifeminists often use much the same argument, except they argue that contemporary feminists have gone too far in the wrong direction. Today's antifeminists say that by emphasizing a social structure of genderless individuals with precisely the same rights, roles, and characters and by destroying the foundations of familial morality, the feminists are taking away men's motivation to remain loyal to their families and women's motivation to be anything but self-seeking, individually competitive people, just like men. If feminist goals are achieved, they argue, women, children, old people, and others will be left unprotected or taken care of by sterile, bureaucratic public institutions.

Just as many conservatives of today resemble 19th-century liberals, many antifeminist activists of today resemble 19th-century feminists. They reject the overwhelming emphasis modern liberal feminists place on individualism, they distrust reliance on public institutions, and although they agree in a sense with the radical feminist view that women and men have different characters, they reject segregation and separation because it necessitates rejecting traditional family and moral values.[11]

Myra Marx Feree's study of attitudes among working-class women (1983) shows that feminists and antifeminists, whether activist or not, not only disagree about specific issues but also look at feminism in different ways. Among the women Feree interviewed, those who favored the feminist movement emphasized its contributions to women's senses of self-worth and entitlement. Those who opposed the movement emphasized its effects on sexual morality and the belief that it fostered social segregation of the sexes. Those who were mildly sympathetic—most of Feree's sample—emphasized the benefits it offered to future generations of women.

Feree's research and that of others indicates that feminists and antifeminists focus on quite different aspects of feminist issues. Those who wish to restrict or prohibit abortion, for example, tend to focus on moral questions concerning the life of the conceived but unborn, and those who want abortion to remain relatively unrestricted focus on the rights of women to determine their own reproductive lives. The two sides do not simply disagree about what should be done about abortion, they disagree about what the key issues are.

It is important to understand not just the social bases of the conflict over women's status, but also how people perceive the conflict itself. If people believe the real battle is between men and women, for example, they might hold different views than if they think it is between older and younger generations of people. One study (Sapiro 1980) investigated these perceptions using a 1976 national survey in which people were asked how they felt about equal social roles for women and men and then how they thought most women, most men, most young people, and most older people felt. There was considerable agreement between men and women on the general question of women's roles: They tended to agree that women and men should have equal roles in society and to reject the idea that woman's place is in the home. Younger people were more egalitarian in their attitudes than were older people.

Regardless of their own age or sex, people believed there was considerable conflict between the sexes and generations over women's rights. They thought that most women were more egalitarian than most men and that most younger people were more egalitarian than most older people. Men saw about equal levels of sex and age conflict, and women tended to see more conflict between the generations than between the sexes. Most people thus viewed conflict between women and men as only half the problem, at most.

How did people see themselves in relation to sex and generational conflict? Most tended to place themselves on what they saw as the more progressive side: in alliance with women and the young. Women identified themselves as agreeing with most women and most younger people and as much more egalitarian than most men and older people. Although most men thought they were slightly less egalitarian than most women, they saw themselves as agreeing with most young people and as much more egalitarian than most men and most older people. They seemed to be saying, "Most men aren't as egalitarian as they might be, but I'm okay."

An important question for contemporary feminism is how women come to define themselves as feminist or as linked to other women in some common set of experiences, problems, or strategies for change (Sapiro 1989; 1991). It is clear that the sources of feminism—and of opposition to it—are as varied as women's experiences themselves and are lodged both in the facts of individuals' lives and in the historical and cultural situation in which women find themselves.

There are many ways of thinking about why people are feminists or antifeminists, why people join one movement or the other or simply remain aloof. Probably the least useful way is to regard the opposition (be it feminist or antifeminist) as evil or ignorant. One of the most important writings along these lines was contributed by Robyn Rowland (1984). Rowland wrote to many different women around the world, feminist and antifeminist, and asked them to write about their understanding of and attitudes toward feminism. These essays, collected under the title *Women Who Do and Women Who Don't Join the Women's Movement*, offers an unparalleled opportunity to hear many different women speak for themselves. The number of different paths they took to reach their conclusions is striking.

Despite the disagreements and the different paths, research shows that a substantial proportion of the American population shares some of the feminist critique of society as it has been structured and sees room for change. In the early 1990s, about 62% of Americans thought that men have more power than they should relative to women in government and politics and 65% thought that men have more power than they should relative to women in business and industry. They were more divided about the balance of power in the family. About 25% thought that men have too much power relative to women, 24% thought that women have too much power relative to men, and 51% thought that the balance of power between women and men is just right as it is. The vast majority of those people (86% of the population) thought that women and men currently have equal power in the family.[12]

A *New York Times*/CBS News Poll in 1989 found widespread support for the women's movement. Most—68% of men and 75% of women—thought the movement had made both work-related and personal relationships between women and men more honest and open than they had been 20 years ago. Many thought that the women's movement had made life somewhat harder for men. About 36% of women and 42% of men thought that things are now harder on men in the work place, and 51% of women and 55% of men thought that it is harder for men at home. Nevertheless, the poll showed that regardless of marital status, race, or family income, a majority of women are supportive of a women's movement, including 85% of African American, 76% of Hispanic, and 64% of white women. Men, not surprisingly, are somewhat less supportive. Only a majority of African American men believe in a need for a women's movement.[13]

Feminism in Theory

In the first few chapters of this book we looked at different theories that have been offered to explain why societies develop particular sex/gender systems and how individuals in any given society come to fit into those societies. That discussion pointed out that both feminist and nonfeminist theorists form a part of each tradition. Although both feminists and nonfeminists have used the basic structure of liberal, Marxist, and other types of theories, they interpret them and use them in different ways and reach different conclusions.[14]

Here we return to a discussion of theory, focusing on how different theories—different frameworks of understanding—are used by feminists to shape their feminism, to try to construct a vision of a more egalitarian or liberated sex/gender system, and to develop a means to create this system in reality. This discussion compares four broad approaches to feminist theory and action that are important parts of current American feminism: liberal, socialist, radical, and multicultural feminism. Although any brief outline is bound to be an oversimplification, there is some sharp divergence among approaches to thinking about feminism. At the same time, it should become clear that when we consider how people really apply these theoretical frameworks when they are not just writing academic treatises, these different strands are often woven together.[15]

Liberal Feminism

Liberal feminism has been the predominant form in the United States or, for that matter, in most of the best-known feminist movements throughout the world.[16] The earliest explication of a liberal feminist theory can be found in Mary Wollstonecraft's *Vindication of the Rights of Woman* ([1792], 1975), although it was left to later liberal feminists to develop the structure of liberal feminist political action.

The underlying emphasis of liberal feminism is best illustrated by the Declaration of Rights and Sentiments drawn up at the 1848 Seneca Falls Convention, which translated the American Declaration of Independence into feminist terms. Although liberal feminism has changed in detail over time and differs in certain respects from one place to another, its vision is based on liberal democratic principles. Its complaint about the world is, as Alison Jaggar observes, "that the treatment of women in contemporary society violates, in one way or another, all of liberalism's political values, the values of equality, liberty, and justice" (1983, 175–76).[17]

Liberal feminists argue that women are not given the same opportunities as men to pursue their individual interests, because women as a group are blocked by informal and formal discrimination and an ideology learned through socialization that views women differently from men. They argue not that men's lives are necessarily free and fulfilled, but that the privileges, rights, and powers that allow individuals to pursue freedom and fulfillment are unequally distributed and give men a disproportionate share of control over themselves and women. Liberal feminists do not want to change liberal democratic principles of individual freedom and autonomy; they want these principles applied to women and men equally.

The history of feminism shows how the liberal feminist interpretation of society has shaped the political action pursued by its proponents. The method of liberal feminism is to survey the quality and quantity of rights and privileges and the extent of choice granted to women and men, pinpoint the areas of inequality, and then set about making adjustments to create equality of opportunity. The liberal feminist agenda is derived in large part from the more general agenda of liberalism and therefore has focused on extending to women the rights that men have gained in education, employment, and civic and political life.

Above all, liberal feminists emphasize the importance of sexist ideology and ignorance as the basis for the inequality and oppression of women. They argue that the real key to liberation is changing people's values and beliefs with respect to gender. If people can be resocialized to believe that women and men are equal, they will treat them that way. If there are institutional structures that stand in the way of according these rights and choices, they should be altered. Although within the United States liberals focus primarily on trying to equalize the system already in existence, it is important to remember that liberal theory has been the basis of a number of revolutions, including some of the most recent ones.

Socialist Feminism

A second major branch of feminism is socialist feminism, which developed within the framework of Marxist thought as a critique of liberal reformist views. It also, however, criticizes some of the traditional Marxist understanding of "the woman question." Because the premises of liberal feminism are probably familiar to most readers, this discussion will define socialist feminism by pointing out some of the ways in which it most clearly diverges from liberal feminism.[18] Given the demise of most of the world's communist systems it is important to note that "socialist feminism" is not feminism as formulated within communist regimes (indeed, in most of them feminism was suppressed), but rather, is a feminism nurtured primarily within liberal democratic systems.

Socialist feminists argue that the liberal framework does not account for the sources and processes of oppression and liberation, and therefore is misguided in its strategies. Socialist feminists focus on the relationship between the material conditions of societies and the social structures and ideologies that flow from them. The socialist framework leads feminists not just to ask whether women have the same opportunities as men within given social institutions but also to look more deeply at the structure and relationship of the institutions themselves. They do not take specific institutions such as the work place or the family as givens but view them as historically changing social relationships created and recreated by people, especially those in power, to meet changing material needs and capacities. Above all, socialists focus on people not just as individuals with abstract rights but as essentially social beings whose meaning depends on historical context and social relations.

Because liberal feminists argue from the perspective of individual abstract rights, they are very much bound to strategies that tear down specific barriers. Socialists argue that this is not enough. Because they believe that the central feature of human life is social relations, socialist feminists must look not just at what is good for given individuals but also at what is good for people as part of a community. Socialist feminism therefore includes in its strategy the distribution of both specific rights and obligations and the alteration of individuals' relationship to others.

The issue of day care for children offers a good example of the difference between liberal and socialist feminists. Both argue that day care should be more readily available and that more public money should be devoted to these arrangements. These proposals are more central to socialist feminist theory and are easier to justify by socialist arguments. The following discussion shows why.

Liberal feminists generally argue for day care in terms of individual rights: Day care should be made available because without it women have less opportunity to seek employment than men have; provision of day care can help break down barriers to equal opportunity. Liberal feminism, however, provides little justification for claiming that those who don't need such services should be required to pay for them, which is necessary if day-care centers are to be publicly funded, and provides a major source of resistance to it. Liberal views also reinforce the idea that children are the private property of individual families and that child care is women's job. There is a trade-off between women's employment and child care, and women will be responsible for child care in their families unless outside help is provided.

Socialist feminists take a different approach. They begin with the premise that reproduction, including the care and nurturing of children, is a social activity and responsibility, not an individual one determined by biological ties. Society can and has cared for its children in many different ways. As Chapter 12 noted, the structure of child care has varied even within American history. For different historical reasons, child care has been done sometimes by women only and sometimes by women and men; sometimes by biological parents and sometimes by others; sometimes by single individuals and sometimes by many different people. What is valued in child care also differs from time to time. Socialists start with this historical view and ask what arrangements most benefit the community as a whole, where community refers to individuals in their different social relations and to the social relations themselves. The answer socialist feminists arrive at is that child rearing should be a communal responsibility shared by women and men, parents and nonparents alike.

Many socialists use the concept of alienation to argue that the current arrangement of responsibility for child care is alienating to men, women, and children. It is alienating to men because they are separated both from the vital human task of child care and from the mothers of their children because of the strict division of domestic labor. It is alienating to women because, although they do most of the work of reproducing human life, they do not "control the conditions of their motherhood." They are thus engaged in "alienated labor" in the Marxist sense (Jaggar 1983, 310). Women's motherhood has been used as an excuse to limit their activities and resources.

These observations suggest to social feminists that current child-raising arrangements are also alienating to children. They breed hostility between child and mother, distance between child and father, and incomplete bonds between child and society. To socialist feminists, then, the argument for the provision of day care is that it is a mechanism for organizing the task of child care into a truly social endeavor.

The perspective of socialism thus focuses primarily on social relations rather than on individual rights, and it suggests that the entire structure of institutional arrangements must be questioned, not just the apparent inequities within these arrangements. It also suggests that although feminists must focus on questions of gender, the problems women face are also rooted in other social structures—primarily class—that alienate people from their own labor and human society.

Radical Feminism

A third branch of feminism is radical feminism.[19] Radical feminists define sexual relations and sexuality as the center of their feminist framework and argue that societies as they are currently arranged are patriarchal; they are run, organized, and defined by men for their own benefit. In men's societies, women serve as a colonized people. They are made dependent on men and not only are forced to serve the interests of men but also are tricked into regarding what amounts to sexual slavery as in their own interest. Men accomplish this trickery by perverting the bond of love through "compulsory heterosexuality," which makes women dependent on men and separates them from other women, and by coercing women into repressive forms of motherhood.

Radical feminists see rape and other forms of sexual violence as mechanisms men use to enforce their rule. The solution radical feminists offer is the rebellion of the colonized against the colonizer—in other words, unity among women against male authority. The task of women is to look among themselves to discover their own feelings and interests and their own culture and to refuse to participate in the male order. The problem they see is not that women's opportunities have differed from men's, but that women have been coerced into thinking in a way that serves male interests, not their own. It is for this reason that many radical feminists use the rallying cry "The personal is the political." They argue that the governing of women by men means that women have sung their own songs, written their own words, and felt their own feelings only at great risk to themselves.

According to radical feminists, women must fight back first by seizing control of their own bodies, both by liberating them from the control of men and by liberating themselves to be able to share intimacy with other women. Most radical feminists do not believe it is possible for women to free themselves if they remain sexually involved with men, because men use sexuality to control women. They also believe it is impossible for women to free themselves and discover a female reality and culture if barriers to intimacy among women remain. For this reason, many radical feminists describe lesbians as the vanguard of feminism.

Some radical feminists advocate a life-style and strategy of separatism, although they disagree about how much separatism is necessary. By separatism, radicals mean not just sexual separation of women from men but also a wider separation from male culture and institutions. If the social institutions and dominant culture are patriarchal, women cannot free themselves by accepting and working within them. Many radicals also believe that women and men have different natures or, at least, that women working together would create a society and culture different from any created by men. Separatism therefore also means working together to create or rediscover a "woman culture" based on what radicals regard as the specifically female virtues of nurturance, sharing, and intuition. Radical feminists seek to rediscover the lost and devalued aspects of women's culture and to create their own alternative organizations and communities.

Radical feminist strategy differs from other forms of feminism in other ways as well. Radical feminists claim it is no coincidence that most social institutions are hierarchically organized. Hierarchy, they claim, is a key ingredient of male culture. Radicals therefore try to organize themselves nonhierarchically, communally, and democratically. They often also reject the values they see as perpetrated by male culture, especially the view that scientific and analytic reasoning (which they sometimes describe as "elitist") is superior to intuition and knowledge gained from personal experience. In many ways, radical feminism is based on a transformation of the old view that equates male with mind and female with body and nature.

Because of the radical feminist view that political institutions as they are generally defined are patriarchal and that "the personal is the political," radical feminists often eschew strategies to influence law and policy and concentrate on what is sometimes called "witness politics." The arena for political action is personal life, so changing one's way of life is political activity.

Multicultural Feminism

One of the most important changes in feminism and feminist theory in the 1980s was a shift toward a *multicultural* feminism. Up to that point the search

Women such as Whoopi Goldberg are finding ways to express pride in themselves as both women and members of their cultural communities.

for, or emphasis on, commonality among women made it difficult for feminist theory and practice to take full account of the differences among women. This is not to say that feminist movements and organizations were homogeneous, as we have seen. There were feminist writers, activists, and organizations of all different types and in most nations around the world. However, there was little sense of coherence or relationship among these different people and groups. More important, even if feminism was heterogeneous it was dominated by white, middle-class, well-educated women, especially those based on campuses, leaving the voices and contributions of other women more marginal.[20]

Two developments effected a shift in the frame and terms of feminist discussion and debate:

1. International contact among women concerned with the condition of women increased. The United Nations International Women's Decade (1975–1985) was the largest and best known of many efforts to bring together women from around the world. Feminism organized most quickly in the United States in the 1960s and 1970s, but by the 1970s and 1980s there were many large

or well-organized feminist movements around the world. Feminism began to have a major impact on theory and scholarship in different countries. The feminist practice and theory that developed around the globe was different in different countries because of their different histories, cultures, social structures, and problems. As the growth of feminist organization and influence within different countries facilitated contact across countries, the debates among feminists, which highlighted differences among women's situations, became important. Increased contact between First World and Third World feminists enriched feminism considerably.

2. Increased feminist activism and involvement of women of color, poor women, and others whose experiences had been marginalized forced feminists to take account of the differences among women's social circumstances. The growing strength of organization among African American and Hispanic women and those in the battered woman movement, for example, became important forces within feminism and demanded greater reckoning with the diversity of women's lives from everyone involved.

Thus, multicultural feminism is a form of feminism that does not just recognize that women live in many different kinds of situations; that recognition forms a core part of multicultural feminism. It not only looks for the obvious similarities in women's lives but also analyzes the varying effects of androcentric sex/gender systems, as Chapter 4 suggested. The idea of difference among women is central to multicultural feminism, not something that is ignored or explained away. We cannot really understand the role of gender in people's lives unless we also understand its relationship to such other aspects of social life as race and class.

Multicultural feminism itself is necessarily various, drawing from arguments of the liberal, socialist, or radical traditions in feminist theory. Because of the importance of highlighting diversity in multicultural feminism, it also recognizes conflict among women, even those who consider themselves feminists. This is unusual in social movements, which usually emphasize a kind of solidarity among their members that attempts to minimize difference and conflict. In multicultural feminism, the recognition of diversity and the acceptance of some conflict are interpreted as part of a healthy political process.[21]

It is important to note that a piece of feminist writing about women of different cultures or social groups is not necessarily multicultural, and a piece of writing about women of one culture or social group is not necessarily *non*-multicultural feminism. Merely adding some focus on women of color to thinking that is otherwise dominated by the experience of whites is not sufficient to make it multicultural just as it is not sufficient simply to add some focus on women to otherwise androcentric thinking to make it feminist. Multiculturalism depends on the framework and method of analysis. Patricia Hill Collins's effort to construct an Afrocentric or black feminist thought incorporates different and conflicting ways of understanding African American women without "trying to synthesize competing worldviews that . . . may defy reconciliation" (Collins 1989a, 773). She does not try to make single what is multiple.

Bell hooks emphasizes the importance of understanding the differing relationships to domination each individual can have.

> I understand that in many places in the world oppressed and oppressor share the same color. I understand that right here in this room, oppressed and oppressor share the same gender. Right now as I speak, a man who is himself victimized, wounded, hurt by racism and class exploitation is actively dominating a woman in his life—that even as I speak, women who are ourselves exploited, victimized, are dominating children (1989, 20–21).

She argues that "to understand domination, we must understand that our capacity as women and men to be either dominated or dominating is a point of connection, of commonality" (1989, 20). Her argument is part of a multicultural feminism because it is her awareness of difference among women that helps her understand gender relations and because she "shifts the center" of her focus and tries to take account of the multiple standpoints and experiences of the people she talks about.

The Feminist Umbrella

Liberal, socialist, radical, and multicultural feminism are only umbrella terms for a wide range of different viewpoints. None of the branches of feminism has a catechism or list of articles of faith; the many different organizations of women have developed certain shared perspectives and certain clear differences of opinion during the course of their thinking, talking, and acting. In fact these perspectives cannot always be distinguished because each has contributed to what constitutes feminism today. Any given feminist might, for example, participate in one of the liberal feminist organizations that have been so effective in achieving legal and policy reforms, yet at the same time accept the need for more fundamental changes in social structure, agree that feminists must learn to be more "woman identified," and have learned the flaws of generalizing from the experience of particular groups of women.

The reality of feminist theory and practice is that it is a constant discussion among many perspectives and continues to change over time. Ideas that seem radical at one time seem downright conservative at another. As long as feminism has stayed alive it has responded to changed historical circumstances.

Outsiders sometimes paint the arguments among feminists as petty bickering typical of females. This characterization is no more appropriate than it would be to say that the arguments between John Adams and Thomas Jefferson, between one branch of the trade union movement and another, or between the NAACP and the Black Muslims were petty bickering typical of males. They are serious arguments among people trying to define as accurately and effectively as possible the problems they see and the best means to solve them.

Feminism is a worldwide movement, and American feminism must therefore be understood in this context. American feminists often have learned from their sisters abroad, and they often have influenced the feminists of other nations. Feminism has long crossed national borders as women from different nations have worked together for their common cause.

American feminists have been influenced by those from other nations since the 18th century. They found their intellectual roots, for example, in the writings of people such as Mary Wollstonecraft, an Englishwoman. Late 19th and early 20th century feminists like Margaret Sanger, Harriot Stanton Blatch, and Alice Paul gained considerable training and inspiration from European activists during travels abroad. American feminists also have been effective in exporting their ideas and strategies to the outside world through their travels, their publications, and the impressions they have made on foreign women who have traveled in the United States.

The turn of the 20th century witnessed the rise of international organizations of feminists, including the International Woman Suffrage Alliance (IWSA) and international meetings of trade unionists. At these meetings, women exchanged ideas about goals and strategies to support each other in their struggles at home. Carrie Chapman Catt was particularly active in these efforts, and through her, the NAWSA agreed to contribute to the IWSA.

The 1930s were a time of heightened feminist international activity. Governments and international lawyers made numerous efforts to construct a more coherent and enlightened system of international law, particularly as it concerned human rights. Women quickly seized the opportunity to advocate women's rights, as they did at an international conference specifically on women's rights held in Montevideo in 1933. The National Women's Party was particularly active in this regard. The United Nations and its agencies have continued to promote international agreements and conventions on women's rights, as have the Organization for Economic Cooperation and Development (OECD), of which the United States is a member, and the European Community, a confederation of western European nations.

Changes in transportation and communications technology have facilitated the coordination of international feminist organizations. International women's conferences are held yearly around the world, women's caucuses meet in the context of larger international meetings and organizations, and thousands of feminists around the world communicate with each other daily through the medium of electronic mail networks. These international efforts are important not just because they offer an opportunity for feminists to compare notes but also because it has become increasingly obvious that women's problems are not local in origin and sometimes arise from countries' foreign policies.

Sometimes the collective action among feminists globally is very specific. For example, some dangerous birth control drugs or devices banned by the U.S. Food and Drug Administration have been channeled to women in countries without

A soldier hugs her son before she leaves for duty during the Gulf War. International politics has profound impacts on women and their families.

such strong consumer protections. American feminists have fought such policies and have also sought less sexist and discriminatory administration of American foreign aid programs (Jaquette and Staudt 1985; Staudt 1985). During 1992, when mass rape and "ethnic cleansing" became an instrument of war used by the Serbians in the former Yugoslavia, the news traveled fast by electronic means among feminists.

International feminism has its own special problems. The three international conferences held in 1975, 1980, and 1985 as part of International Women's Decade made some of these problems painfully clear. In 1975 the United Nations sponsored an International Women's Year Conference in Mexico City. When it became clear that some women delegates were being used to foster their governments' own aims, an alternative meeting, called the Tribune, was convened. Most of the feminist activists went to this other meeting rather than the official meeting. In 1980 a meeting was held in Copenhagen to evaluate progress since 1975. That meeting was also disrupted by official delegates less concerned with feminism than with their countries' nationalistic goals. Some delegates went so far as to try to bar and censure women from other countries simply because of their nationalities. Many feminist delegates left bitter and skeptical about the potential of international efforts, especially those organized through official governmental bodies. Nevertheless, feminists of different nations met again in Nairobi in 1985—more successfully this time—and continue to cooperate where they can (Ashworth and Bonnerjea 1985).[22]

One of the hardest lessons for feminists in the United States to learn is that they are part of a global system in which there are many different societies and cultures, each with their own subjectivities. In the 20th century, Americans have become used to thinking of themselves as the leaders and the central players on the world scene. This parochialism extends to feminism, to the extent that Americans define their situation as "women's" situation and their feminism as "feminism." Even the particular character of American diversity is different from other forms, so a United States–based understanding of social structure—of how race/ethnicity or class works—is a limited one. Feminisms are shaped by the historical and cultural experiences of specific societies. One nation's or one culture's feminism is as partial as any other.

Feminists around the world are beginning to realize how central sex/gender systems are not just to domestic societies but to the international system as well. Defense and foreign policies often depend on gendered assumptions, and they certainly have gendered effects.[23] In a world that is as economically interdependent as ours, feminism must look beyond national borders.

One of the most exciting developments is the fall of many authoritarian governments that took place in the late 1980s and early 1990s. After a first euphoria, women in those and other countries began to realize what women should have known anyway: The fall of an authoritarian system does not necessarily usher in the rise of a democratic one, and in the course of struggling toward democracy women's interests may be left behind. We have seen this story in the older democracies such as the United States, and we are seeing it in the newer ones.

Feminism and the Future

During the past two centuries there seem always to have been at least some people thinking about and working to improve the status of women. At some times there have been large mass movements, and at others there have been only isolated actions by individuals and small groups. In each generation, people have continued the debate over what equality or liberation would mean and how it could best be achieved. In each generation, there have been many women who were frightened by the changes proposed or thought that they had all the choice and freedom they needed. In each generation, there have been masses of people who have remained ignorant both about their own history and about the turmoil of the present.

As feminism has achieved some goals and failed to meet others, its agenda for the future has grown longer rather than shorter. The solutions to problems always seem to reveal many other problems. Each turning point in feminist history has revealed the degree to which gender continues to be used to restrict people's options. Moreover, as human societies change over time and develop new ways of making their lives better and worse, women's situation changes.

Anyone who needs confirmation that there is still much to be done need only consider that many people regard feminism and women's studies as frivolous and of only peripheral importance. Women who take an interest in their own status and roles in society are seen as selfish or divisive, and men who take an interest in women's status and roles in society are seen as odd or even pitiful. Nevertheless, many women and men persevere.

There has been much change in the definition of female gender and male gender in recent centuries. As we have seen, many of the changes have been liberating, and some have not. What is left to be done? This book is filled with suggestions that come from today's feminism and social analysis. Beyond this, future generations will have to decide for themselves.

NOTES

1. My thanks to Sarah Slavin, who suggested this approach to the differences and commonalities among different thinkers (see Schramm 1979).
2. For works on social movements, see Tilly (1978) and Morris and Mueller (1992).
3. For more reading on feminism in this period, see Flexner (1975), Berg (1978), DuBois (1978), and Evans (1989).
4. This was discussed more completely in Chapter 2.
5. For histories of these associations, see Ginzburg (1990), Scott (1990; 1992), and Shaw (1991).
6. The literature on this period of feminism is voluminous. For some different approaches, see Kraditor (1965), Stanton, Anthony, and Gage ([1881], 1969), Sochen (1972), Flexner (1975), and DuBois (1978).
7. For further discussion, see Chapter 9.

8. For further reading on this period, see Lemons (1972), Sochen (1973), Becker (1981), Ware (1981; 1983), Hartmann (1983), Scharf and Jensen (1983), Honey (1984), Kaledin (1984), and Higgonet et al. (1987).
9. For further reading on this period, see Hole and Levine (1971), Freeman (1975), Boles (1979), Evans (1979), Klein (1984), Echols (1989), and Costain (1992).
10. At the same time, many religious organizations have worked as part of the feminist coalition. Among the principal supporters of the ERA were the American Association of Women Ministers, the American Jewish Committee, Disciples of Christ, Lutheran Church in America, National Council of Churches, Union of American Hebrew Congregations, United Church of Christ, United Jewish Congress, United Methodist Church, and the United Presbyterian Church, plus a number of Catholic organizations and many women's organizations in numerous denominations.
11. For works on or by antifeminists, see Decter (1973), Gilder (1973), Andelin (1974), Morgan (1975), Petchesky (1981), Dworkin (1983), Conover and Gray (1983), and Faludi (1991).
12. Analysis by the author of the 1991 American National Election Study Pilot Study.
13. E. J. Dionne, Jr., "Struggle for Work and Family Fuels Movement," *New York Times*, August 22, 1989.
14. The following discussion assumes familiarity with Chapters 2–4.
15. Feminist theorists have offered many different ways of viewing and categorizing feminist theory. As most would admit, there are problems with any attempt at classification. I have not, for example, included discussion of postmodern and psychoanalytic feminism because those are influential primarily as intellectual and scholarly movements and have relatively little impact on the mass politics of the women's movement or on feminist policy development. For discussion of these approaches, see Marks and de Courtivron (1980), Gallop (1982), Eisenstein and Jardine (1985), Moi (1985), Flax (1987), Spivak (1987), Alcoff (1988), and Diamond and Quinby (1988).
16. For further discussion of liberal feminism, see Okin (1979), Eisenstein (1981), Jaggar (1983), and Pateman (1988).
17. Some critics argue that discussion of rights is necessarily liberal (or vice versa) or that liberalism "just wants reforms and not structural changes." Both of these points are wrong. One problem is that it is important to distinguish between the liberal tradition in theory, which we are discussing here, and the people who, in any given society, are given the political label "liberal" regardless of their relation to the liberal tradition of political philosophy.
18. For further discussion of socialist feminism, see Editors of *Quest* (1981), Sargent (1981), Jaggar (1983), Sayers (1987), and Barrett (1988).
19. For further discussion of radical feminism, see Daly (1978), Editors of *Quest* (1981), Morága and Anzaldúa (1981), Jaggar (1983), and Bunch (1987).
20. It would be a mistake to think of even this group as homogeneous. Too often people forget there are sharp and crucial differences even among "middle-class, college-educated, white women." They are diverse in ethnicity and religion, family history and experience, sexual orientation, and exposure to violence against women, to name just a few things that would make a difference in their understanding of women's situation.

21. *Multicultural feminism* is a name I have chosen for this new turn in feminist theory. It is important to note that, contrary to common perceptions, even at the beginning of this century many feminists were struggling with questions of diversity (Cott 1987). For some examples of multicultural feminism, see hooks (1981; 1984; 1989), Collins (1989a), Morága and Anzaldúa (1981), Aptheker (1982), Spivak (1987), Spelman (1988), Hurtado (1989), and Minhha (1989).
22. For reading on international feminism, see Bouchier (1984), Rowland (1984), Bassnett (1986), Chafetz and Dworkin (1986), Dahlerup (1986), Jayawardena (1986), O'Barr et al. (1986), Gelb (1989), Jaquette (1989), Alvarez (1990), Mohanty, Russo, and Torres (1991), and Eisenstein (1992).
23. Works on women and international politics include Enloe (1983; 1989), Jaquette and Staudt (1985), Staudt (1985), Afshar and Dennis (1992), and Peterson (1992).

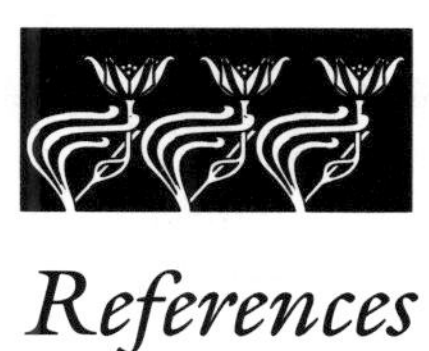

References

Abbey, Antonia. 1982. "Sex Differences in Attributions for Friendly Behavior: Do Males Misperceive Females' Friendliness?" *Journal of Personality and Social Psychology* 42:830–38.

Abbott, Pamela, and Roger Sapsford. 1988. *Women and Social Class.* New York: Routledge.

Abel, Emily. 1981. "Collective Protest and the Meritocracy: Faculty Women and Sex Discrimination Lawsuits." *Feminist Studies* 7:505–38.

Abramowitz, Stephen I., Christine V. Abramowitz, Carolyn Jackson, and Beverly Gomes. 1973. "The Politics of Clinical Judgment: What Non-Liberal Examiners Infer about Women Who Don't Stifle Themselves." *Journal of Consulting and Clinical Psychology* 41:385–91.

Abramson, Phyllis. 1990. *Sob Sister Journalism.* Westport, Conn.: Greenwood.

Adams, Carolyn Teich, and Kathryn T. Winston. 1980. *Mothers at Work.* New York: Longman.

Adams, Karen L., and Norma C. Ware. 1989. "Sexism and the English Language: The Linguistic Implications of Being a Woman." In *Women: A Feminist Perspective,* edited by Jo Freeman, 470–84. Mountain View, Calif.: Mayfield.

Adams, Kathryn A. 1980. "Who Has the Final Word? Sex, Race, and Dominance Behavior." *Journal of Personality and Social Psychology* 38:1–8.

Adler, Freda. 1975. *Sisters in Crime.* Lexington, Mass.: D. C. Heath.

Afshar, Haleh, and Carolyn Dennis, eds. 1992. *Women, Recession and Adjustment in the Third World.* New York: St. Martin's.

Albers, Patricia, and Beatrice Medicine, eds. 1983. *The Hidden Half: Studies of Plains Indian Women.* Lanham, Md.: University Press.

Alcoff, Linda. 1988. "Cultural Feminism versus Post-Structuralism: The Identity Crisis in Feminist Theory." *Signs* 13:405–46.

Allgeier, A. R. 1983. "Sexuality and Gender Roles in the Second Half of Life." In *Changing Boundaries: Gender Roles and Sexual Behavior,* edited by Elizabeth Rice Allgeier and Naomi B. McCormick, 135–57. Palo Alto, Calif.: Mayfield.

Almquist, Elizabeth. 1975. "Untangling the Effects of Race and Sex: The Disadvantaged Status of Black Women." *Social Science Quarterly* 56:129–42.

———. 1984. "Race and Ethnicity in the Lives of Minority Women." In *Women: A Feminist Perspective*, edited by Jo Freeman, 423–53. Palo Alto, Calif.: Mayfield.

———. 1987. "Labor Market Gender Inequality in Minority Groups." *Gender and Society* 1:400–14.

Alonso, Harriet Hyman. 1993. *Peace as a Women's Issue: A History of the U.S. Movement for World Peace and Women's Rights.* Syracuse, N.Y.: Syracuse University Press.

Alvarez, Sonia E. 1990. *Engendering Democracy: Women's Movements in Transition Politics.* Princeton, N.J.: Princeton University Press.

American Association of University Women. 1992. *How Schools Shortchange Girls.* Washington, D.C.: AAUW Educational Foundation.

American Psychiatric Association. 1987. *Diagnostic and Statistical Manual of Mental Disorders-III-R.* Washington, D.C.: American Psychiatric Association.

Andelin, Helen. 1974. *Fascinating Womanhood.* New York: Bantam.

Anderson, Lynn R., Martha Finn, and Sandra Leider. 1981. "Leadership Style and Leader Title." *Psychology of Women Quarterly* 5:661–69.

Andrade, Vibiana M. 1981. "The Toxic Workplace: Title VII Protection for the Potentially Pregnant Woman." *Harvard Women's Law Journal* 4:71–104.

Aneshensel, Carol S., Carolyn M. Rutter, and Peter A. Lachenbruch. 1991. "Social Structure, Stress, and Mental Health: Competing Conceptual and Analytic Models." *American Sociological Review* 56:166–78.

Aptheker, Bettina. 1982. *Woman's Legacy: Essays in Race, Sex, and Class.* Amherst: University of Massachusetts Press.

Aquinas, Saint Thomas. 1945. "Question XCII: The Production of Women." In *Basic Writings of Saint Thomas Aquinas*, edited by Anton C. Pegis, 879–84. New York: Random House.

Ariès, Philippe. 1942. *Centuries of Childhood.* London: Jonathan Cape.

Ashby, Marylee Stoll, and Bruce C. Whittmaier. 1978. "Attitude Changes in Children after Exposure to Stories about Women in Traditional or Nontraditional Occupations." *Journal of Educational Psychology* 70:945–49.

Ashworth, Georgina, and Lucy Bonnerjea, eds. 1985. *The Invisible Decade: UK Women and the UN Decade, 1976–1985.* Hants, U.K.: Gower Publishing.

Aslin, Alice. 1977. "Feminist and Community Mental Health Center Psychotherapists' Expectations of Mental Health for Women." *Sex Roles* 3:537–44.

Backhouse, Constance, and Lea Cohen. 1981. *Sexual Harassment on the Job.* Englewood Cliffs, N.J.: Prentice-Hall.

Baker, Ross K., Laurily K. Epstein, and Rodney D. Forth. 1981. "Matters of Life and Death: Social, Political, and Religious Correlates of Attitudes on Abortion." *American Politics Quarterly* 9:89–102.

Bane, Mary Jo. 1976. "Marital Disruption and the Lives of Children." *Journal of Social Issues* 32:103–17.

Bank, Barbara J., Bruce J. Biddle, and Thomas L. Good. 1980. "Sex Roles, Classroom Instruction, and Reading Achievement." *Journal of Educational Psychology* 72:119–32.

Banton, Michael. 1983. *Racial and Ethnic Competition*. New York: Cambridge University Press.

Barrett, Michelle. 1988. *Women's Oppression Today: Problems in Marxist Feminist Analysis.* London: Verso.

Bart, Pauline B. 1971. "Depression in Middle Aged Women." In *Women in Sexist Society*, edited by Vivian Gornick and Barbara K. Moran, 99–117. New York: Basic Books.

———. 1975. "Emotional and Social Status in the Older Woman." In *No Longer Young: The Older Woman in America*, 3–22. Ann Arbor: Institute for Gerontology, University of Michigan.

Bart, Pauline B., and Patricia H. O'Brien. 1984. "Stopping Rape: Effective Avoidance Strategies." *Signs* 10:83–101.

Barth, Robert J., and Bill N. Kinder. 1988. "A Theoretical Analysis of Sex Differences in Same-Sex Friendships." *Sex Roles* 19:349–63.

Basow, Susan A., and Nancy T. Silberg. 1987. "Student Evaluations of College Professors: Are Female and Male Professors Rated Differently?" *Journal of Education Psychology* 79:308–14.

Bassnett, Susan. 1986. *Feminist Experiences: The Women's Movement in Four Cultures.* New York: Allen & Unwin.

Baxter, Sandra, and Marjorie Lansing. 1980. *Women and Politics: The Invisible Majority.* Ann Arbor: University of Michigan Press.

Beasley, Maurine H., and Sheila J. Gibbons. 1993. *Taking Their Place: A Documentary History of Women and Journalism.* Washington, D.C.: American University Press.

Bebel, August. [1910] 1970. *Women and Socialism.* New York: Schocken.

Becker, Susan D. 1981. *The Origins of the Equal Rights Amendment: American Feminism between the Wars.* Westport, Conn.: Greenwood.

——— . 1983. "International Feminism between the Wars: The National Women's Party versus the League of Women Voters." In *Decades of Discontent*, edited by Lois Scharf and Joan M. Jensen, 223–43. Westport, Conn.: Greenwood.

Beecher, Catharine. [1841] 1977. *A Treatise on Domestic Economy.* New York: Schocken.

Bem, Sandra L. 1974. "The Measurement of Psychological Androgyny. *Journal of Consulting and Clinical Psychology* 42:155–62.

Bem, Sandra Lipsitz. 1975. "Sex Role Adaptability: One Consequence of Psychological Androgyny." *Journal of Personality and Social Psychology* 31:634–43.

———. 1983. "Gender Schema Theory and Its Implications for Child Development: Raising Gender-Aschematic Children in a Gender-Schematic Society." *Signs* 8:596–616.

Benson, John M. 1981. "The Polls: A Rebirth of Religion?" *Public Opinion Quarterly* 45:576–85.

Berch, Bettina. 1982. *The Endless Day: The Political Economy of Women and Work.* New York: Harcourt, Brace, Jovanovich.

Berg, Barbara. 1978. *The Remembered Gate: Origins of American Feminism: The Woman and the City, 1800–60.* New York: Oxford University Press.

Berlo, Janet Catherine. 1976. "The Cambridge School: Women in Architecture." *Feminist Art Journal* 5:27–32.

Bernard, Jessie. 1972. *The Future of Marriage*. New York: Bantam.

———. 1975. *Women, Wives, Mothers: Values and Options*. Chicago: Aldine.

Bernstein, Barbara, and Robert Kane. 1981. "Physicians' Attitudes toward Female Patients." *Medical Care* 19:600–608.

Bethune, Mary McLeod. [1941] 1982. "How the Bethune-Cookman College Campus Started." In *Women's America*, edited by Linda K. Kerber and Jane De Hart Mathews, 260–62. New York: Oxford University Press.

Bigler, Rebecca S., and Lynn S. Libem. 1992. "Cognitive Mechanisms in Children's Gender Stereotyping: Theoretical and Educational Implications of a Cognitive-Based Intervention." *Child Development* 63:1351–63.

Birnbaum, Judith A. 1975. "Life Patterns and Self-Esteem in Gifted Family Oriented and Career Committed Women." In *Women and Achievement: Social and Motivational Analyses*, edited by Martha T. Mednick, Sandra Tangri, and Lois Hoffman, 396–419. New York: Wiley.

Blau, Francine D., and Anne E. Winkler. 1989. "Women in the Labor Force: An Overview." In *Women: A Feminist Perspective*, edited by Jo Freeman, 265–86. Mountain View, Calif.: Mayfield.

Blee, Kathleen M. 1991. *Women of the Klan: Racism and Gender in the 1920s*. Berkeley: University of California Press.

Bleier, Ruth. 1984. *Science and Gender: A Critique of Biology and Its Theories on Women*. New York: Pergamon.

Blumstein, Philip W., and Pepper Schwartz. 1977. "Bisexuality: Some Social Psychological Issues." *Journal of Social Issues* 33:30–45.

———. 1983. *American Couples: Money, Work, Sex*. New York: William Morrow.

Boles, Janet. 1979. *The Politics of the Equal Rights Amendment*. New York: Longman.

Bonafede, Dom. 1982. "Women's Movement Broadens the Scope of Its Role in American Politics." *National Journal*, 11 December, 2108–11.

Bonvillain, Nancy. 1989. "Gender Relations in Native North America." *American Indian Culture and Research Journal* 13:1–28.

Borden, Richard J., and Gorden M. Homleid. 1978. "Handedness and Lateral Positioning in Heterosexual Couples: Are Men Still Strongarming Women?" *Sex Roles* 4:67–73.

Bordin, Ruth. 1990. *Women and Temperance: The Quest for Power and Liberty, 1873–1900*. New Brunswick, N.J.: Rutgers University Press.

Boston Women's Health Book Collective. 1992. *The New Our Bodies, Ourselves: A Book by and for Women*. New York: Simon & Schuster.

Bouchier, David. 1984. *The Feminist Challenge: The Movement for Women's Liberation in Britain and the USA*. New York: Schocken.

Boyer, Debra, and David Fine. 1992. "Sexual Abuse as a Factor in Adolescent Pregnancy and Child Maltreatment." *Family Planning Perspectives* 24:4–11.

Brabeck, M. 1983. "Moral Judgment: Theory and Research on Differences between Males and Females." *Developmental Review* 3:274–91.

Breines, Wini, and Linda Gordon. 1983. "New Scholarship on Family Violence." *Signs* 8:490–531.

Brenner, Johanna. 1987. "Feminist Political Discourse: Radical versus Liberal Approaches to the Feminization of Poverty and Comparable Worth." *Gender and Society* 1:447-65.

Brett, Jeanne M., and Anne H. Reilly. 1992. "All the Right Stuff: A Comparison of Female and Male Managers' Career Progression." *Journal of Applied Psychology* 77:251–60.

Briggs, Kenneth A. 1983. "Women and the Church." *New York Times Magazine*, 6 November.

Brock, David. 1993. *The Real Anita Hill: The Untold Story*. New York: Free Press.

Brooks-Gunn, Jeanne. 1986. "Differentiating Premenstrual Symptoms and Syndromes." *Psychosomatic Medicine* 48:385–87.

Brooks-Gunn, Jeanne, and Diane K. Ruble. 1982. "The Development of Menstrual-Related Beliefs and Behaviors during Early Adolescence." *Child Development* 53:1567–77.

Broverman, Inge K., Donald M. Broverman, Frank E. Clarkson, Paul S. Rosencrantz, and Susan R. Vogel. 1970. "Sex Role Stereotypes and Clinical Judgments of Mental Health." *Journal of Consulting and Clinical Psychology* 34:1–7.

Brown, Diane Robinson, and Lawrence E. Gray. 1988. "Unemployment and Psychological Distress among Black American Women." *Sociological Focus* 21:209–22.

Brownmiller, Susan. 1975. *Against Our Will: Men, Women, and Rape*. New York: Simon & Schuster.

Bruch, Hilde. 1978. *The Golden Cage: The Enigma of Anorexia Nervosa*. Cambridge: Harvard University Press.

Buckley, Thomas, and Alma Gottlieb, eds. 1988. *Blood Magic: The Anthropology of Menstruation*. Berkeley: University of California Press.

Buczek, Teresa A. 1981. "Sex Biases in Counseling: Counselor Retention of the Concerns of a Female and Male Client." *Journal of Counseling Psychology* 28:13–21.

Bunch, Charlotte. 1979. "Learning from Lesbian Separatism." In *Issues in Feminism: A First Course in Women's Studies*, edited by Sheila Ruth, 551–56. Boston: Houghton Mifflin.

———. 1981. "Not for Lesbians Only." In *Building Feminist Theory: Essays from Quest*, 67–73. New York: Longman.

———. 1987. *Passionate Politics: Feminist Theory in Action*. New York: St. Martin's.

Burrell, Nancy A., William A. Donahue, and Mike Allen. 1988. "Gender-Based Perceptual Biases in Mediation." *Communication Research* 15:447–69.

Burris, Val. 1983. "Who Opposed the ERA? An Analysis of the Social Bases of Anti-Feminism." *Social Science Quarterly* 64:305–17.

Burstyn, Varda, ed. 1985. *Women Against Censorship*. Vancouver: Douglas and McIntyre.

Burt, Martha R. 1980. "Cultural Myths and Supports for Rape." *Journal of Personality and Social Psychology* 38:217–30.

Buss, David M. 1981. "Sex Differences in the Evaluation and Performance of Dominant Acts." *Journal of Personality and Social Psychology* 40:147–54.

Bussey, Kay, and Betty Maughan. 1982. "Gender Differences in Moral Reasoning." *Journal of Personality and Social Psychology* 42:701–6.

Butsch, Richard. 1992. "Class and Gender in Four Decades of Television Situation Comedy: Plus ça Change." *Critical Studies in Mass Communication* 9:387–99.

Campbell, Angus, Philip E. Converse, and William L. Rodgers. 1976. *The Quality of American Life: Perceptions, Evaluations, and Satisfaction*. New York: Russell Sage.

Campbell, Susan Miller, Letitia Anne Peplau, and Sherrine Chapman DeBro. 1992. "Women, Men, Condoms: Attitudes and Experiences of Heterosexual College Students." *Psychology of Women Quarterly* 16:273–88.

Caplan, Paula J., Joan McCurdy-Myers, and Maureen Gans. 1992. "Should 'Premenstrual Syndrome' Be Called a Psychiatric Abnormality?" *Feminism and Psychology* 2:27–44.

Caplow, Theodore, and Bruce A. Chadwick. 1979. "Inequality and Life-Styles in Middletown, 1920–78." *Social Science Quarterly* 60:367–86.

Carlsson, Marianne, and Pia Jaderquist. 1983. "Note on Sex Role Opinions as Conceptual Schemata." *British Journal of Social Psychology* 22:65–68.

Carpenter, Eugenia S. 1980. "Children's Health Care and the Changing Role of Women." *Medical Care* 18:1208–18.

Carpenter, Linda Jean, and R. Vivian Acosta. 1991. "Back to the Future: Reform with a Woman's Voice." *Academe: Bulletin of the Association of University Professors*, (January-February): 23–27.

Carroll, Jackson W., Barbara Hargrove, and Adair T. Lummis. 1981. *Women of the Cloth: A New Opportunity for the Churches.* New York: Harper & Row.

Carroll, Susan. 1985. *Women as Candidates in American Politics.* Bloomington: Indiana University Press.

Carter, Michael J., and Susan Boslego Carter. 1981. "Women's Recent Progress in the Professions, or Women Get a Ticket to Ride after the Gravy Train Has Left the Station." *Feminist Studies* 7:477–504.

Cash, Thomas F., Barry Gillen, and D. Steven Burns. 1977. "Sexism and Beautyism in Personnel Consultant Decision Making." *Journal of Applied Psychology* 62:301–10.

Chadwick, Whitney. 1990. *Women, Art, and Society.* London: Thames and Hudson.

Chafetz, Janet Saltzman, and Anthony Gary Dworkin. 1986. *Female Revolt: Women's Movements in World and Historical Perspective.* Totowa, N.J.: Rowman & Allanheld.

Chavkin, Wendy, ed. 1984. *Double Exposure: Women's Health Hazards on the Job and at Home.* New York: Monthly Review Press.

Cherry, Frances. 1983. "Gender Roles and Sexual Violence." In *Changing Boundaries: Gender Roles and Sexual Behavior*, edited by Elizabeth Rice Allgeier and Naomi B. McCormick, 245–60. Palo Alto, Calif.: Mayfield.

Chesler, Phyllis. 1971. "Patient and Patriarch: Women in the Psychotherapeutic Relationship." In *Women in Sexist Society*, edited by Vivian Gornick and Barbara K. Moran, 251–75. New York: Basic Books.

Chesney-Lind, Meda, and Randall G. Shelden. 1992. *Girls, Delinquency, and Juvenile Justice.* Pacific Grove, Calif.: Brooks/Cole.

Chmielewski, Wendy E., Louise J. Kern, and Marilyn Klee-Hartzell, eds. 1993. *Women in Spiritual and Communitarian Societies in the United States.* Syracuse, N.Y.: Syracuse University Press.

Chodorow, Nancy. 1978. *The Reproduction of Mothering: Psychoanalysis and the Sociology of Gender.* Berkeley and Los Angeles: University of California Press.

Chodorow, Nancy, and Susan Contratto. 1982. "The Fantasy of the Perfect Mother." In *Rethinking the Family: Some Feminist Questions*, edited by Barrie Thorne and Marilyn Yalom, 54–72. New York: Longman.

Chow, Esther Ngan-Ling. 1987. "The Development of Feminist Consciousness among Asian-American Women." *Gender and Society* 1:284–99.

Chrisler, Joan C., and Karen B. Levy. 1990. "The Media Construct a Menstrual Monster: A Content Analysis of PMS Articles in the Popular Press." *Women and Health* 16:89–104.

Christ, Carol. 1987. *Laughter of Aphrodite: Reflections on a Journey to the Goddess.* San Francisco: Harper & Row.

Christ, Carol, and Judith Plaskow, eds. 1979. *Womanspirit Rising: A Feminist Reader in Religion.* New York: Harper & Row.

Christensen, Dana, and Robert Rosenthal. 1982. "Gender and Nonverbal Decoding Skill as Determinants of Interpersonal Expectancy Effects." *Journal of Personality and Social Psychology* 42:75–87.

Christoplos, Florence, and JoAnn Borden. 1978. "Sexism in Elementary School Mathematics." *The Elementary School Journal* 78:275–77.

Cixous, Hélène. 1976. "The Laugh of the Medusa." *Signs* 1:875–94.

Clarke, Cheryl. 1981. "Lesbianism: An Act of Resistence." In *This Bridge Called My Back: Writings by Radical Women of Color*, edited by Cherrie Morága and Gloria Anzaldúa, 128–37. Watertown, Mass.: Persephone Press.

Clinton, Catherine. 1985. "Women and Southern History: Images and Reflections." *Perspectives on the American South* 3:45–62.

Cobb, Nancy J., Judith Stevens-Long, and Steven Goldstein. 1982. "The Influence of Televised Models in Toy Preference in Children." *Sex Roles* (October): 1075–80.

Cobble, Dorothy Sue, ed. 1993. *Women and Unions: Forging a Partnership.* Ithaca, N.Y.: ILR Press.

Cohen, Claudia. 1981. "Person Categories and Social Perception: Testing Some Boundaries of the Processing Effects of Prior Knowledge." *Journal of Personality and Social Psychology* (March): 441–52.

Cole, C. Maureen, Frances A. Hill, and Leland J. Daly. 1983. "Do Masculine Pronouns Used Generically Lead to Thoughts of Men?" *Sex Roles* 9:737–50.

Cole, Johnetta B., ed. 1986. *All American Women: Ties That Divide, Ties That Bind.* New York: Free Press.

Collins, Eliza G. C., and Timothy Blodget. 1981. "Sexual Harassment . . . Some See It . . . Some Won't." *Business Review* 59:76–94.

Collins, Patricia Hill. 1989a. "The Social Construction of Black Feminist Thought." *Signs* 14:745–73.

———. 1989b. "A Comparison of Two Works on Black Family Life." *Signs* 14:875–84.

Colwill, Nina. 1982. *The New Partnership: Women and Men in Organizations.* Palo Alto, Calif.: Mayfield.

Commission of the European Community. 1979. *European Men and Women, 1978.* Brussels: European Community.

Conover, Pamela, and Virginia Gray. 1983. *Feminism and the New Right: Conflict over the American Family.* New York: Praeger.

Conover, Pamela Johnston, and Virginia Sapiro. 1993. "Gender, Feminist Consciousness, and War." *American Journal of Political Science* 37.

Cook, Alice H., Val R. Lorwin, and Arlene Kaplan Daniels, eds. 1984. *Women and Trade Unions in Eleven Industrialized Countries.* Philadelphia: Temple University Press.

Cook, Ellen Piel. 1985. *Psychological Androgyny.* New York: Pergamon.

Cooper, Elizabeth A., Dennis Doverspike, and Gerald V. Barrett. 1985. "Comparison of Different Methods of Determining the Sex Type of American Occupations." *Psychological Reports* 57:747–50.

Cooperstock, R. 1971. "Sex Differences in the Use of Mood Modifying Drugs: An Exploratory Model." *Journal of Health and Social Behavior* 12:238–44.

Costain, Anne N. 1992. *Inviting Women's Rebellion: A Political Process Interpretation of the Women's Movement.* Baltimore: Johns Hopkins Press.

Cott, Nancy F. 1987. *The Grounding of American Feminism.* New Haven, Conn.: Yale University Press.

Couture, Pamela D. 1991. *Blessed Are the Poor? Women's Poverty, Family Policy, and Practical Theology.* Nashville, Tenn.: Abingdon.

Cowan, Gloria, Carole Lee, Danielle Levy, and Debra Snyder. 1988. "Dominance and Inequality in X-Rated Videocassettes." *Psychology of Woman Quarterly* 12:299–311.

Cowan, Ruth Schwartz. 1982. "The 'Industrial Revolution' in the Home: Household Technology and Social Change in the Twentieth Century." In *Women's America: Refocusing the Past*, edited by Linda Kerber and Jane de Hart Mathews, 324–38. New York: Oxford University Press.

———. 1983. *More Work for Mother: The Ironies of Household Technology from the Open Hearth to the Microwave.* New York: Basic.

Crosby, Faye J. 1991. *Juggling: The Unexpected Advantages of Balancing Career and Home for Women and their Families.* New York: Free Press.

Daddario, Gia. 1992. "Swimming Against the Tide: *Sports Illustrated*'s Imagery of Female Athletes in a Swimsuit World." *Women's Studies in Communication* 15:49–64.

Dahlerup, Drude, ed. 1986. *The New Woman's Movement: Feminism and Political Power in Europe and the USA.* Newbury Park, Calif.: Sage.

Dalton, Katarina. 1964. *The Premenstrual Syndrome.* Springfield, Ill.: Thomas.

Daly, Mary. 1973. *Beyond God the Father: Toward a Philosophy of Women's Liberation.* Boston: Beacon.

———. 1975. *The Church and the Second Sex.* New York: Harper & Row.

———. 1978. *Gyn/Ecology: The Metaethics of Radical Feminism.* Boston: Beacon.

Daniels, Arlene Kaplan. 1988. *Invisible Careers: Women Civic Leaders from the Volunteer World.* Chicago: University of Chicago Press.

Darcy, R., Susan Welch, and Janet Clark. 1987. *Women's Elections and Representation.* New York: Longman.

D'Augelli, Judith Frankel, and Anthony R. D'Augelli. 1977. "Moral Reasoning and Premarital Sexual Behavior: Toward Reasoning about Relationships." *Journal of Social Issues* 33:46–66.

Davies, Margery. 1983. *Woman's Place Is at the Typewriter: Office Work and Office Workers: 1870–1930.* Philadelphia: Temple University Press.

Davis, Martha F. 1983. "The Marital Home: Equal or Equitable Distribution?" *The University of Chicago Law Review* 50:1089–1115.

Dawson, Debra L. A. 1988. "Ethnic Differences in Female Overweight: Data from the 1985 National Health Interview Study." *American Journal of Public Health* 78:1326–29.

Dayhoff, Signe. 1983. "Sexist Language and Person Perception: Evaluation of Candidates from Newspaper Articles." *Sex Roles* 9:527–40.

Deaux, Kay. 1976. *The Behavior of Women and Men.* Monterey, Calif.: Brooks/Cole.

Deaux, Kay, and Joseph C. Ullman. 1983. *Women of Steel: Female Blue-Collar Workers in the Basic Steel Industry.* New York: Praeger.

de Beauvoir, Simone. 1952. *The Second Sex.* New York: Knopf.

Deckard, Barbara Sinclair. 1979. *The Women's Movement: Political, Socioeconomic, and Psychological Issues.* New York: Harper & Row.

Decter, Midge. 1973. *The New Chastity and Other Arguments against Women's Liberation.* New York: Coward, McCann, and Geoghegan.

Degler, Carl N. 1980. *At Odds: Women and the Family in America from the Revolution to the Present.* New York: Oxford University Press.

Delaney, Janice, Mary Jane Lupton, and Emily Toth, eds. 1988. *The Curse: A Cultural History of Menstruation.* Urbana: University of Illinois.

DeLoache, Judy S., Deborah J. Cassidy, and C. Jan Carpenter. 1987. "The Three Bears Are All Boys: Mothers' Gender Labelling of Neutral Picture Book Characters." *Sex Roles* 17:163–78.

de Monteflores, Carmen, and Stephen J. Schultz. 1978. "Coming Out: Similarities and Differences for Lesbians and Gay Men." *Journal of Social Issues* 34:59–72.

de Pauw, Linda Grant. 1975. *Founding Mothers: Women of America in the Revolutionary Era.* Boston: Houghton Mifflin.

Depner, Charlene, and Berit Ingersoll. 1982. "Employment Status and Social Support: The Experience of Mature Women." In *Women's Retirement: Policy Implications of Recent Research*, edited by Maximiliane Szinovacz, 77–91. Beverly Hills, Calif.: Sage.

Deutsch, Francine M., Dorothy LeBaron, and Maury March Fryer. 1987. "What's in a Smile?" *Psychology of Women Quarterly* 11:341–52.

Deutsch, Sarah. 1987. "Women and Intercultural Relations: The Case of Hispanic New Mexico and Colorado." *Signs* 12:719–39.

Diamond, Irene, and Lee Quinby, eds. 1988. *Feminism and Foucault: Reflections on Resistance.* Boston: Northeastern.

Dibble, Ursula, and Murray Straus. 1980. "Some Social Structure Determinants of Inconsistency Between Attitudes and Behavior: The Case of Family Violence." *Journal of Marriage and the Family* 42:71–82.

Dill, Bonnie Thornton. 1979. "The Dialectics of Black Womanhood." *Signs* 4:543–55.

Dodson, Debra L., and Susan J. Carroll. 1991. *Reshaping the Agenda: Women in State Legislatures.* New Brunswick, N.J.: Center for the American Woman and Politics.

Doering, Charles H., H. K. H. Brodie, H. Kramer, H. Becker, and D. A. Hamburg. 1974. "Plasma Testosterone Levels and Psychologic Measures in Men Over a Two Month Period." *Sex Differences in Behavior*, edited by R. Friedman, R. Richart, and R. Vande Wiele, 413–31. New York: Wiley.

Donnerstein, Edward, Daniel Linz, and Steven Penrod. 1987. *The Question of Pornography: Research Findings and Policy Implications.* New York: Free Press.

Douglas, Ann. 1977. *The Feminization of American Culture.* New York: Knopf.

Downs, Donald Alexander. 1989. *The New Politics of Pornography.* Chicago: University of Chicago Press.

DuBois, Ellen Carol. 1978. *Feminism and Suffrage: The Emergence of an Independent Women's Movement in America, 1848–69.* Ithaca, N.Y.: Cornell University Press.

Durio, Helen F., and Cheryl A. Kildow. 1980. "The Nonretention of Capable Engineering Students." *Research in Higher Education* 13:61–71.

Dweck, Carol S., William Davidson, Sharon Nelson, and Bradley Enna. 1978. "Sex Differences in Learned Helplessness." *Developmental Psychology* 14:268–76.

Dworkin, Andrea. 1979. *Pornography: Men Possessing Women.* New York: G. P. Putnam's Sons.

———. 1983. *Right Wing Women.* New York: G. P. Putnam's Sons.

Dwyer, Carol A. 1974. "Influence of Children's Sex Role Standards on Reading and Arithmetic Achievement." *Journal of Educational Psychology* 66:811–16.

Dwyer, Johanna, and Jean Myer. 1968. "Psychological Effects of Variations in Physical Appearance during Adolescence." *Adolescence* 3:353–80.

Eagly, Alice H., and L. L. Carli. 1981. "Sex of Researchers and Sex-Typed Communications as Determinants of Sex Differences in Influenceability: A Meta-Analysis of Social Influence Studies." *Psychological Bulletin* 90:1–20.

Eagly, Alice H., and Maureen Crowley. 1986. "Gender and Helping Behavior: A Meta-Analytic Review of the Social Psychological Literature." *Psychological Bulletin* 100:283–308.

Eakins, Barbara Westbrook, and R. Gene Eakins. 1978. *Sex Differences in Human Communication.* Boston: Houghton Mifflin.

Eaton, W. O., and L. R. Enns. 1986. "Sex Differences in Human Motor Activity." *Psychological Bulletin* 100:19–28.

Ebaugh, Helen, Rose Fuchs, and C. Allen Haney. 1980. "Shifts in Abortion Attitudes, 1972–78." *Journal of Marriage and the Family* 42:491–500.

Echols, Alice. 1989. *Daring to Be Bad: Radical Feminism in America, 1967–1975.* Minneapolis: University of Minnesota Press.

Editors of *Quest.* 1981. *Building Feminist Theory: Essays from Quest.* New York: Longman.

Ehrenreich, Barbara, and Dierdre English. 1979. *For Her Own Good: One Hundred Fifty Years of the Experts' Advice to Women.* Garden City, N.Y.: Doubleday.

Eichler, Margrit. 1980. *The Double Standard: A Feminist Critique of Feminist Social Science.* New York: St. Martin's.

———. 1988. *Nonsexist Research Methods: A Practical Guide.* Boston: Allen & Unwin.

Eisenberg, N., and R. Lennon. 1983. "Sex Differences in Empathy and Related Capacities." *Psychological Bulletin* 94:100–31.

Eisenstein, Hester. 1992. *Gender Shock: Practicing Feminism on Two Continents.* Boston: Beacon.

Eisenstein, Hester, and Alice Jardine, eds. 1985. *The Future of Difference.* New Brunswick, N.J.: Rutgers University Press.

Eisenstein, Zillah. 1981. *The Radical Future of Liberal Feminism.* New York: Longman.

Elder, Ruth Gale, Winnefred Humphreys, and Cheryl Laskowski. 1988. "Sexism in Gynecology Textbooks: Gender Stereotypes and Paternalism, 1978–1983." *Health Care for Women International* 9:1–17.

Engels, Friedrich. [1884] 1972. *The Origin of the Family, Private Property, and the State.* New York: Pathfinder.

English, Jane. 1982. "Sex Equity in Sports." In *"Femininity," "Masculinity," and "Androgyny": A Modern Philosophical Discussion*, edited by Mary Vetterling-Braggin, 259–67. Totowa, N.J.: Littlefield Adams.

Enloe, Cynthia. 1983. *Does Khaki Become You? The Militarization of Women's Lives.* Boston: South End.

———. 1989. *Bananas, Beaches, and Bases: Making Feminist Sense of International Politics.* London: Pandora.

Estler, Suzanne. 1975. "Women as Leaders in Public Education." *Signs* 1:363–85.

Etaugh, Claire, and Ethel Foresman. 1983. "Evaluations of Competence as a Function of Sex and Marital Status." *Sex Roles* 9:759–65.

Evans, Sara M. 1979. *Personal Politics: The Roots of Women's Liberation in the Civil Rights Movement and the New Left.* New York: Vintage.

———. 1989. *Born for Liberty: A History of Women in America.* New York: Free Press.

Evans, Sara M., and Barbara J. Nelson. 1989. *Wage Justice: Comparable Worth and the Paradox of Technocratic Reform.* Chicago: University of Chicago Press.

Ewen, Elizabeth. 1980. "City Lights: Immigrant Women and the Rise of Movies." *Signs* 5:45–66.

Ewen, Stuart. 1976. *Captains of Consciousness: Advertising and the Social Roots of Consumer Culture.* New York: McGraw-Hill.

Faderman, Lillian. 1991. *Odd Girls and Twilight Lovers: A History of Lesbian Life in Twentieth-Century America.* New York: Penguin.

Fagot, Beverly I., and Mary D. Leinbach. 1989. "The Young Child's Gender Schema: Environmental Input, Internal Organization." *Child Development* 60:663–72.

Fagot, Beverly I., Mary D. Leinbach, and Cherie O'Boyle. 1992. "Gender Labeling, Gender Stereotyping, and Parenting Behaviors." *Developmental Psychology* 28:225–30.

Falbo, Toni, Michael D. Hazen, and Diane Linimon. 1982. "The Costs of Selecting Power Bases or Messages Associated with the Opposite Sex." *Sex Roles* 9:147–57.

Faludi, Susan. 1991. *Backlash: The Undeclared War against American Women.* New York: Crown Publishers.

Faust, Drew Gilpin. 1992. " 'Trying to Do a Man's Business': Slavery, Violence, and Gender in the American Civil War." *Gender and History* 4:197–214.

Feldberg, Roslyn K., and Evelyn Nakano Glenn. 1979. "Male and Female: Job versus Gender Models in the Sociology of Work." *Social Problems* 26:524–38.

Feldman, Harold. 1981. "A Comparison of Intentional Parents and Intentionally Childless Couples." *Journal of Marriage and the Family* 43:593–600.

Feldstein, Jerome H., and Sandra Feldstein. 1982. "Sex Differences in Televised Toy Commercials." *Sex Roles* 8:581–88.

Ferber, Marianne A., and Julie A. Nelson, eds. 1993. *Beyond Economic Man: Feminist Theory and Economics.* Chicago: University of Chicago Press.

Feree, Myra Marx. 1983. "The Women's Movement in the Working Class." *Sex Roles* 9:493–505.

Ferrante, Carol L., Andrew M. Haynes, and Sarah M. Kingsley. 1988. "Images of Women in Television Advertising." *Journal of Broadcasting and Electronic Media* 32:231–37.

Field, Martha A. 1988. *Surrogate Motherhood.* Cambridge, Mass.: Harvard University Press.

Finlay, Barbara Agresti. 1981. "Sex Differences in Correlates of Abortion Attitudes among College Students." *Journal of Marriage and the Family* 43:571–82.

Fiorenza, Elizabeth Schüssler. 1984. *Bread Not Stone: The Challenge of Feminist Biblical Criticism.* Boston: Beacon Press.

———. 1992. *But SHE Said: Feminist Practices of Biblical Interpretation.* Boston: Beacon Press.

Firestone, Shulamith. 1970. *Dialectic of Sex.* New York: Bantam.

Flax, Jane. 1987. "Postmodernism and Gender Relations in Feminist Theory." *Signs* 12:621–43.

Flexner, Eleanor. 1975. *Century of Struggle: The Women's Rights Movement in the United States.* Cambridge: Harvard University Press.

Foner, Philip S. 1982. *Women and the American Labor Movement: From the First Trade Unions to the Present.* New York: Free Press.

Ford, M. R., and C. R. Lowery. 1986. "Gender Differences in Moral Reasoning: A Comparison of the Justice and Care Orientations." *Journal of Personality and Social Psychology* 50:777–83.

Foreit, Karen G., et al. 1980. "Sex Bias in the Newspaper Treatment of Male-Centered and Female-Centered News Stories." *Sex Roles* 6:475–80.

Forrest, Jacqueline Darroch, and Richard R. Fordyce. 1988. "U.S. Women's Contraceptive Attitudes and Practice: How Have They Changed in the 1980s?" *Family Planning Perspectives* 20:112–18.

Foster, D. C., D. S. Guzick, and R. P. Pulliam. 1992. "The Impact of Prenatal Care on Fetal and Neonatal Death Rates for Uninsured Patients: A 'Natural Experiment' in West Virginia." *Obstetrics and Gynecology* 7:40.

Foster, Martha A., Barbara Strudlar Wallston, and Michael Berger. 1980. "Feminist Orientation and Job Seeking Behavior among Dual Career Couples." *Sex Roles* 6:59–65.

Fox, Mary Frank. 1989. "Women and Higher Education: Gender Differentials in the Status of Students and Scholars." In *Women: A Feminist Perspective*, edited by Jo Freeman, 217–35. Mountain View, Calif.: Mayfield.

Fox, Mary Frank, and Sharlene Hesse-Biber. 1984. *Women at Work.* Palo Alto, Calif.: Mayfield.

Frable, Deborah E. S., and Sandra Lipsitz Bem. 1985. "If You Are Gender Schematic, All Members of the Opposite Sex Look Alike." *Journal of Personality and Social Psychology* 49:459–68.

Frank, Dana. 1985. "Housewives, Socialists, and the Politics of Food: The 1917 New York Cost-of-Living Protests." *Feminist Studies* 11:255–86.

Fraser, Arvonne S. 1983. "Insiders and Outsiders." In *Women in Washington: Advocates for Public Policy*, edited by Irene Tinker, 120–39. Beverly Hills, Calif.: Sage.

Fraser, Nancy. 1987. "Women, Welfare, and the Politics of Need." *Thesis Eleven* 17:88–106.

———. Fratto, Toni Flores. 1976-77. "Samplers: One of the Lesser American Arts." *Feminist Art Journal* 5:11–15.

Freedman, Estelle. 1979. "Separatism as Strategy: Female Institution Building and American Feminism, 1870–1930." *Feminist Studies* 5:512–29.

Freeman, Jo. 1975. *The Politics of Women's Liberation*. New York: Longman.

Freud, Sigmund. [1930] 1961. *Civilization and Its Discontents*. New York: Norton.

———. [1933] 1965. "Femininity." In Sigmund Freud, *New Introductory Lectures in Psychoanalysis*, 112–35. New York: Norton.

Friday, Nancy. 1977. *My Mother/Myself*. New York: Delacorte.

Friedan, Betty. 1963. *The Feminine Mystique*. New York: Dell.

Fritz, Kathlyn Ann, and Natalie Kaufman Hevener. 1979. "An Unsuitable Job for a Woman: Female Protagonists in the Detective Novel." *International Journal of Women's Studies* 2:105–29.

Frost, J. William. 1973. *The Quaker Family in Colonial America*. New York: St. Martin's.

Fulenwider, Claire. 1980. *Feminism in American Politics: A Study of Ideological Influence*. New York: Praeger.

Fuller, Margaret. [1845] 1971. *Women in the Nineteenth Century*. New York: Norton. Also excerpted in Rossi (1988).

Gabin, Nancy. 1982. "They Have Placed a Penalty on Womanhood: The Protest Actions of Women Auto Workers in Detroit Area UAW Locals, 1945–47." *Feminist Studies* 8: 373–98.

Gage, Matilda Joslyn. [1900] 1972. *Women, Church, and State: A Historical Account of the Status of Women through the Christian Ages, with Reminiscences of the Matriarchate*. New York: Arno Press.

Gallagher, Janet. 1985. "Fetal Personhood and Women's Policy." In *Women, Biology, and Public Policy*, edited by Virginia Sapiro, 91-116. Beverly Hills, Calif.: Sage.

Gallion, Jane. 1970. *The Woman as Nigger*. Canoga Park, Calif.: Weiss, Day, and Lord.

Gallop, Jane. 1982. *The Daughter's Seduction: Feminism and Psychoanalysis*. Ithaca, N.Y.: Cornell University Press.

Garfinkle, Ellen M., and Stephen F. Morin. 1978. "Psychologists' Attitudes toward Homosexual Psychotherapy Clients." *Journal of Social Issues* 34:101–12.

Gelb, Joyce. 1989. *Feminism and Politics: A Comparative Perspective*. Berkeley: University of California Press.

Gelb, Joyce, and Marian Palley. 1987. *Women and Public Policies*. Princeton: Princeton University Press.

Geller, Laura. 1983. "Reactions to a Woman Rabbi." In *On Being a Jewish Feminist*, edited by Susannah Heschel, 210–13. New York: Schocken.

Gelles, Richard J. 1980. "Violence in the Family: A Review of Research in the 1970's." *Journal of Marriage and the Family* 42:873–76.

Gerbner, George. 1978. "The Dynamics of Cultural Resistance." In *Hearth and Home: Images of Women in the Mass Media*, edited by Gaye Tuchman, Arlene Kaplan Daniels, and James Benet, 46–50. New York: Oxford University Press.

Gerdes, Eugenia Proctor, and Douglas M. Garber. 1983. "Sex Bias in Hiring: Effects of Job Demands and Applicant Competence." *Sex Roles* (March): 307–19.

Gersh, Eileen S., and Isadore Gersh. 1981. *The Biology of Women*. London: University Park Press.

Gerson, Kathleen. 1985. *Hard Choices: How Women Decide about Work, Career, and Motherhood*. Berkeley: University of California Press.

Gertzog, Irwin, and Michele Simard. 1980. "Women and 'Hopeless' Congressional Candidates: Nomination Frequency 1916–78." *American Politics Quarterly* 9:449–66.

Giddings, Paula. 1984. *When and Where I Enter: The Impact of Black Women on Race and Sex in America*. New York: Bantam.

Giele, Janet Zollinger, and Audrey Roberts Smock, eds. 1977. *Women: Roles and Status in Eight Countries*. New York: Wiley.

Gilder, George. 1973. *Sexual Suicide*. New York: Quadrangle.

Gilkes, Cheryl Townsend. 1987. "Some Mother's Son and Some Father's Daughter': Gender and Biblical Language in Afro-Christian Worship Tradition." In *Shaping New Visions: Gender and Values in American Culture*, edited by Clarissa W. Atkinson, Constance H. Buchanan, and Margaret Miles. Ann Arbor, Mich.: UMI Research Press.

Gilligan, Carol. 1982. *In a Different Voice: Psychological Theory and Women's Development*. Cambridge: Harvard University Press.

Gilligan, Carol, Nona P. Lyons, and Trudy J. Hanmer. 1990. *Making Connections: The Relational Worlds of Adolescent Girls at Emma Willard School*. Cambridge: Harvard University Press.

Gilligan, Carol, Janie Victoria Ward, and Jill McLean Taylor, eds. 1988. *Mapping the Moral Domain: A Contribution of Women's Thinking to Psychological Theory and Education*. Cambridge: Harvard University Press.

Gilman, Charlotte Perkins. [1898] 1966. *Women and Economics*. New York: Harper & Row.

———. [1903] 1972. *The Home*. Urbana: University of Illinois Press.

———. [1911] 1970. *The Man-Made World: Our Androcentric Culture*. New York: Charlton.

———. [1915] 1979. *Herland*. New York: Pantheon.

Ginsburg, Faye D. 1989. *Contested Lives: The Abortion Debate in an American Community*. Berkeley: University of California Press.

Ginzberg, Lori D. 1990. *Women and the Work of Benevolence: Morality, Politics, and Class in the Nineteenth-Century United States*. New Haven: Yale University Press.

Glass, Jennifer, and Valerie Camarigg. 1992. "Gender, Parenthood, and Job-Family Compatibility." *American Journal of Sociology* 98:131–51.

Glenn, Evelyn Nakano. 1986. *Issei, Nisei, Warbride: Three Generations of Japanese-American Women in Domestic Service*. Philadelphia: Temple University Press.

———. 1992. "From Servitude to Service Work: Historical Continuities in the Racial Division of Paid Reproductive Labor." *Signs* 18:1–43.

Glenn, Evelyn Nakano, and Roslyn L. Feldberg. 1989. "Clerical Work: The Female Occupation." In *Women: A Feminist Perspective*, edited by Jo Freeman, 287–312. Mountain View, Calif.: Mayfield.

Glenn, Norval D., and Sara McLanahan. 1982. "Children and Marital Happiness: A Further Specification of the Relationship." *Journal of Marriage and the Family* 44:63–72.

Glick, Peter, Cari Zion, and Cynthia Nelson. 1988. "What Mediates Sex Discrimination in Hiring Decisions?" *Journal of Personality and Social Psychology* 55:178–86.

Goldberg, Philip. 1968. "Are Women Prejudiced Against Women?" *Transaction* 4:28–30.

Goldin, Claudia. 1990. *Understanding the Gender Gap: An Economic History of American Women*. New York: Oxford University Press.

Goldman, Ronald, and Juliette Goldman. 1982. *Children's Sexual Thinking*. Boston: Routledge & Kegan Paul.

Goldstein, Leslie Friedman. 1988. *The Constitutional Rights of Women: Cases in Law and Social Change*. Madison: University of Wisconsin Press.

Gordon, Linda. 1977. *Woman's Body, Woman's Right: A Social History of Birth Control in America*. New York: Viking.

———. 1982. "Why Nineteenth Century Feminists Did Not Support 'Birth Control' and Twentieth Century Feminists Do: Feminism, Reproduction, and the Family." In *Rethinking the Family: Some Feminist Questions*, edited by Barrie Thorne and Marilyn Yalom, 40–53. New York: Longman.

———. 1988a. *Heroes of Their Own Lives: The Politics and History of Family Violence, Boston 1880–1960*. New York: Viking Press.

———. 1988b. "What Does Welfare Regulate?" *Social Research* 55:609–30.

———. 1991. "On 'Difference.'" *Genders* 10:91–111.

Gordon, Linda, ed. 1990. *Women, the State, and Welfare*. Madison: University of Wisconsin Press.

Gordon, Margaret T., and Stephanie Riger. 1989. *The Female Fear*. New York: Free Press.

Gove, Walter R. 1972. "The Relationship between Sex Roles, Marital Status, and Mental Illness." *Social Forces* 51:34–44.

Gove, Walter R., Corlynn Briggs Style, and Michael Hughes. 1990. "The Effect of Marriage on the Well-Being of Adults." *Journal of Family Issues* 11:4–35.

Granberg, Donald, and Beth Wellman Granberg. 1981. "Pro-Life versus Pro-Choice: Another Look at the Abortion Controversy in the United States." *Sociology and Social Research* 65:424–33.

Grant, Jacqueline. 1989. *White Women's Christ and Black Women's Jesus: Feminist Christology and Womanist Response*. Atlanta: Scholar's Press.

Green, Susan K., and Philip Sanders. 1983. "Perceptions of Male and Female Initiators of Relationships." *Sex Roles* 9:849–52.

Greenberger, Ellen, and Laurence D. Steinberg. 1983. "Sex Differences in Early Labor Force Experience: Harbinger of Things to Come." *Social Forces* 62:467–86.

Griffin, John Howard. 1961. *Black Like Me*. Boston: Houghton Mifflin.

Griffin, Susan. 1981. *Pornography and Silence: Culture's Revenge Against Nature*. New York: Harper & Row.

Gruhl, John, Cassia Spohn, and Susan Welch. 1981. "Women as Policy Makers: The Case of Trial Judges." *American Journal of Political Science* 25:308–22.

Haavio-Mannila, Elina, et al., eds. 1985. *Unfinished Democracy: Women in Nordic Politics*. New York: Pergamon.

Hacker, Sally L. 1979. "Sex Stratification, Technology, and Organizational Change: A Longitudinal Case Study of AT&T." *Social Problems* 26:539–57.

Hafkin, Nancy J., and Edna G. Bay, eds. 1976. *Women in Africa: Studies in Social and Economic Change*. Stanford, Calif.: Stanford University Press.

Hagler, D. Harland. 1980. "The Ideal Woman in the Antebellum South: Lady or Farmwife?" *Journal of Southern History* 46:405–18.

Hall, Elaine J. 1988. "One Week for Women? The Structure of Inclusion of Gender Issues in Introductory Textbooks." *Teaching Sociology* 16:431–42.

Hall, Jacqueline Dowd. 1989. "Partial Truths." *Signs* 14:902–11.

Hall, Judith A. 1978. "Gender Differences in Decoding Nonverbal Cues in Conversation." *Psychological Bulletin* 85:845–57.

Halperin, Marcia S., and Doris L. Abrams. 1978. "Sex Differences in Predicting Final Examination Grades: The Influence of Past Performance, Attributions, and Achievement Motivation." *Journal of Educational Psychology* 70:763–71.

Hammond, Judith A., and Constance W. Mahoney. 1983. "Reward-Cost Balancing among Women Coalminers." *Sex Roles* 9:17–29.

Hare-Mustin, Rachel T., Sheila Kaiser Bennett, and Patricia C. Broderick. 1983. "Attitudes Toward Motherhood: Gender, Generational and Religious Comparisons." *Sex Roles* 9:643–61.

Harley, Sharon, and Rosalyn Terborg-Penn, eds. 1978. *The Afro-American Woman: Struggles and Images*. Port Washington, N.Y.: Kennikat.

Harris, Betty J. 1990. "Ethnicity and Gender in the Global Periphery: A Comparison of Basotho and Navajo Women." *American Indian Culture and Research Journal* 14:15–38.

Harrison, James. 1978. "Warning: The Male Sex Role May Be Dangerous to Your Health." *Journal of Social Issues* 34:65–86.

Hartmann, Heidi, ed. 1985. *Comparable Worth: New Directions for Research*. Washington, D.C.: National Academy Press.

Hartmann, Susan M. 1983. *The Home Front and Beyond: American Women in the 1940's*. Boston: Twayne.

Hartz, Louis. 1955. *The Liberal Tradition in America*. New York: Harcourt, Brace, and World.

Harvey, S. Marie, and Susan C. M. Scrimshaw. 1988. "Coitus-Dependent Contraceptives: Factors Associated with Effective Use." *Journal of Sex Research* 25:364–78.

Hatfield, Elaine. 1983. "What Do Women and Men Want from Love and Sex?" In *Changing Boundaries: Gender Roles and Sexual Behavior*, edited by Elizabeth Rice Allgeier and Naomi B. McCormick, 106–34. Palo Alto, Calif.: Mayfield.

Havens, Beverly, and Ingrid Swenson. 1988. "Imagery Associated with Menstruation in Advertising Targeted to Adolescent Women." *Adolescence* 23:89–97.

Hayden, Dolores. 1981. *The Grand Domestic Revolution: A History of Feminist Designs for American Homes, Neighborhoods, and Cities.* Cambridge, Mass.: MIT Press.

Hayes, Kathryn E., and Patricia L. Wolleat. 1978. "Effect of Sex in Judgments of a Simulated Counseling Interview." *Journal of Counseling Psychology* 25:164–68.

Hayghe, Howard. 1983. "Married Couples: Work and Income Patterns." *Monthly Labor Review* 106:26–34.

Hedges, Elaine. 1980. "Quilts and Women's Culture." In *In Her Own Image: Women Working in the Arts,* edited by Elaine Hedges and Ingrid Wendt, 13–19. New York: McGraw-Hill.

Hedges, Elaine, and Ingrid Wendt, eds. 1980. *In Her Own Image: Women Working in the Arts.* New York: McGraw-Hill.

Henley, Nancy M. 1977. *Body Politics: Power, Sex, and Nonverbal Communication.* Englewood Cliffs, N.J.: Prentice-Hall.

Henshaw, Stanley K. 1991. "The Accessibility of Abortion Services in the United States." *Family Planning Perspectives* 23: 246–52.

Heschel, Susannah, ed. 1983. *On Being a Jewish Feminist.* New York: Schocken.

Hesse, Sharlene. 1979. "Women Working: Historical Trends." In *Working Women and Families,* edited by Karen Wolk Feinstein, 35–62. Beverly Hills, Calif.: Sage.

Higginbotham, Evelyn Brooks. 1992. "African-American Women's History and the Metalanguage of Race." *Signs* 17:251–74.

Higgonet, Margaret Randolph, et al., eds. 1987. *Behind the Lines: Gender and the Two World Wars.* New Haven, Conn.: Yale University Press.

Hill, Charles T., Zick Rubin, and Letitia Anne Peplau. 1976. "Breakups before Marriage: The End of One Hundred Three Affairs." *Journal of Social Issues* 32:147–68.

Hine, Darlene Clark. 1989. "Rape and the Inner Lives of Black Women in the Middle West: Preliminary Thoughts on the Culture of Dissemblance." *Signs* 14:912–20.

Hirokawa, Randy Y., Jeffrey Mickey, and Steven Miura. 1991. "Effects of Request Legitimacy on the Compliance-Gaining Tactics of Male and Female Managers." *Communication Monographs* 58:421–36.

Hite, Shere. 1976. *The Hite Report: A Nationwide Study of Female Sexuality.* New York: Macmillan.

———. 1981. *The Hite Report on Male Sexuality.* New York: Alfred Knopf.

Hochschild, Arlie. 1989. *The Second Shift.* New York: Avon.

Hoeffer, Beverly. 1981. "Children's Acquisition of Sex-Role Behavior in Lesbian-Mother Families." *American Journal of Orthopsychiatry* 51:536–44.

Hole, Judith, and Ellen Levine. 1971. *Rebirth of Feminism.* New York: Quadrangle.

Holmes, Douglas S., and Bruce Jorgensen. 1971. "Do Personality and Social Psychologists Study Men More Than Women?" *Representative Research in Social Psychology* 2:71–76.

Holsti, Ole, and James N. Rosenau. 1981. "The Foreign Policy Beliefs of Women in Leadership Positions." *Journal of Politics* 43:326–47.

Honey, Maureen. 1984. *Creating Rosie the Riveter: Class, Gender, and Propaganda during World War II.* Boston: Northeastern University Press.

hooks, Bell. 1981. *Ain't I a Woman: Black Women and Feminism.* Boston: South End Press.

———. 1984. *Feminist Theory: From Margin to Center*. Boston: South End Press.

———. 1989. *Talking Back: Thinking Feminist, Thinking Black*. Boston: South End Press.

Horgan, Dianne. 1983. "The Pregnant Woman's Place and Where to Find It." *Sex Roles* 9:333–39.

Hornbrook, Marc C., and Marsha G. Goldfarb. 1981. "Patterns of Obstetrical Care in Hospitals." *Medical Care* 19:55–67.

Horney, Karen. 1967. *Feminine Psychology*. New York: Norton.

Hornung, Carlton A., Claire McCullough, and Taichi Sugimoto. 1981. "Status Relationships in Marriage: Risk Factors in Spouse Abuse." *Journal of Marriage and the Family* 42:71–82.

Hoseley, David H., and Gayle K. Yamada. 1987. *Hard News: Women in Broadcast Journalism*. Westport, Conn.: Greenwood Press.

Hoskin, Fran P. 1980. "Women and Health: Genital and Sexual Mutilation." *International Journal of Women's Studies* 3:300–316.

Howe, Lucy Kapp. 1978. *Pink Collar Workers*. New York: Avon.

Hrdy, Sarah Blaffer. 1981. *The Woman That Never Evolved*. Cambridge, Mass.: Harvard University Press.

Huber, Joan, and Glenna Spitze. 1981. "Wives' Employment, Household Behaviors and Sex-Role Attitudes." *Social Forces* 60:150–69.

Hull, Gloria T., Patricia Bell Scott, and Barbara Smith, eds. 1982. *All the Women Are White, All the Blacks Are Men, But Some of Us Are Brave: Black Women's Studies*. Old Westbury, N.Y.: The Feminist Press.

Humphries, Drew. 1993. "Mothers and Children, Drugs and Crack: Reactions to Maternal Drug Dependency." In *It's a Crime: Women and Justice*, edited by Roslyn Muraskin and Ted Alleman, 130–45. Englewood Cliffs, N.J.: Prentice-Hall.

Hunter, James Davison. 1991. *Culture Wars: The Struggle to Define America*. New York: Basic Books.

Hurtado, Aída. 1989. "Relating to Privilege: Seduction and Rejection in the Subordination of White Women and Women of Color." *Signs* 14:833–55.

Hyde, Janet Shibley. 1984. "How Large Are Gender Differences in Aggression? A Developmental Meta-Analysis." *Developmental Psychology* 20:722–36.

———. 1986. *Understanding Human Sexuality*. New York: McGraw-Hill.

———. 1991. *Half the Human Experience: The Psychology of Women*. Lexington, Mass.: D. C. Heath.

Hyde, Janet Shibley, Elizabeth Fennema, and Susan J. Lamon. 1990. "Gender Differences in Mathematic Performance: A Meta-Analysis." *Psychological Bulletin* 107:139–55.

Hyde, Janet Shibley, and Marcia C. Linn. 1988. "Gender Differences in Verbal Ability: A Meta-Analysis." *Psychological Bulletin* 104:53–69.

Hyde, Janet Shibley, and Marcia C. Linn, eds. 1986. *The Psychology of Gender: Advances Through Meta-Analysis*. Baltimore: Johns Hopkins Press.

Immarigeon, Russ, and Meda Chesney-Lind. 1993. "Women's Prisons: Overcrowded and Overused." In *It's a Crime: Women and Justice*, edited by Roslyn Muraskin and Ted Alleman, 242–59. Englewood Cliffs, N.J.: Prentice-Hall.

Instone, Debra, Brenda Major, and Barbara A. Bunker. 1983. "Gender, Self Confidence, and Social Influence Strategies: An Organizational Simulation." *Journal of Personality and Social Psychology* 44:322–33.

Irvine, Jacqueline Jordan. 1986. "Teacher-Student Interactions: Effects of Student Race, Sex, and Grade Level." *Journal of Educational Psychology* 78:14–21.

Jackson, Linda A. 1992. *Physical Appearance and Gender: Sociobiological and Sociocultural Perspectives.* Albany: State University of New York Press.

Jacobs, Jerry A. 1992. "Women's Entry Into Management: Trends in Earnings, Authority, and Values Among Salaried Managers." *Administrative Science Quarterly* 37:282–301.

Jaggar, Alison M. 1983. *Feminist Politics and Human Nature.* Totowa, N.J.: Littlefield, Adams.

Jaquette, Jane S., ed. 1989. *The Women's Movement in Latin America: Feminism and the Transition to Democracy.* Boston: Unwin Hyman.

Jaquette, Jane S., and Kathleen A. Staudt. 1985. "Women as 'At Risk' Reproducers: Biology, Science, and Population in U.S. Foreign Policy." In *Women, Biology, and Public Policy*, edited by Virginia Sapiro, 235–68. Beverly Hills, Calif.: Sage.

Jaskoski, Helen. 1981. " 'My Heart Will Go Out': Healing Songs of Native American Women." *International Journal of Women's Studies* 4:118–34.

Jayawardena, Kumari. 1986. *Feminism and Nationalism in the Third World.* London: Zed Books.

Jeffrey, Julie Roy. 1979. *Frontier Women: The Trans-Mississippi West, 1840–1880.* New York: Hill & Wang.

Jennings, M. Kent. 1979. "Another Look at the Life Cycle and Political Participation." *American Journal of Political Science* 23:755–71.

Jennings, M. Kent, and Barbara G. Farah. 1981. "Social Roles and Political Resources: An Over-Time Study of Men and Women in Party Elites." *American Journal of Political Science* 25:462–82.

Jennings, Thelma. 1990. "Us Colored Women Had to Go Through a Plenty': Sexual Exploitation of African-American Slave Women." *Journal of Women's History* 1:45–74.

Jensen, Inger W., and Barbara A. Gutek. 1982. "Attributions and Assignment of Responsibility in Sexual Harassment." *Journal of Social Issues* 38:121–36.

Jepson, Barbara. 1975–76. "American Women in Conducting." *Feminist Art Journal* 4:13–18.

Jessell, John C., and Lawrence Beymer. 1992. "The Effects of Job Title vs Job Description on Occupational Sex Typing." *Sex Roles* 27:73–83.

Johnson, Miriam M. 1982. "Fathers and 'Femininity' in Daughters: A Review of the Research." *Sociology and Social Research* 67:1–17.

Johnson, Paula. 1976. "Women and Power: Toward a Theory of Effectiveness." *Journal of Social Issues* 32:99–110.

Jones, Jacqueline. 1980. "Women Who Were More Than Men: Sex and Status in Freedman's Teaching." *History of Education Quarterly* 19:47–60.

———. 1985. *Labor of Love, Labor of Sorrow: Black Women, Work, and the Family from Slavery to the Present.* New York: Basic.

Jones, Warren H., Mary Ellen Chernovetz, and Robert O. Hansson. 1978. "The Enigma of Androgyny: Differential Implications for Males and Females?" *Journal of Consulting and Clinical Psychology* 46:298–313.

Jones, W. T. 1963. *Masters of Political Thought*. Vol. 3. London: George Harrap.

Joseph, Gloria, and Jill Lewis. 1981. *Common Differences: Conflicts in Black and White Feminist Perspectives*. Garden City, N.Y.: Doubleday.

Kaledin, Eugenia. 1984. *Mothers and More: American Women in the 1950's*. Boston: Twayne.

Kalmuss, Debra S., and Murray A Strauss. 1982. "Wife's Marital Dependency and Wife Abuse." *Journal of Marriage and the Family* 44:277–86.

Kandiyoti, Deniz, ed. 1991. *Women, Islam, and the State*. Philadelphia: Temple University Press.

Kay, Herma Hill. 1988. *Sex Based Discrimination*. St. Paul, Minn.: West.

Keith, Pat M. 1982. "Working Women versus Homemakers: Retirement Resources and Correlates of Well Being." In *Women's Retirement: Policy Implications of Recent Research*, edited by Maximiliane Szinovacz, 77–91. Beverly Hills, Calif.: Sage.

Kellerman, Jonathan. 1974. "Sex Role Stereotypes and Attitudes toward Parental Blame for the Psychological Problems of Children." *Journal of Consulting and Clinical Psychology* 42:153–54.

Kellerman, Jonathan, and Ernest R. Katz. 1978. "Attitudes toward the Division of Child-Rearing Responsibility." *Sex Roles* 4:505–12.

Kendrick, Walter. 1987. *The Secret Museum: Pornography in Modern Culture*. New York: Viking.

Kerber, Linda K. 1982. "The Daughters of Columbia: Educating Women for the Republic, 1787–1805." In *Women's America*, edited by Linda K. Kerber and Jane de Hart Mathews, 82–94. New York: Oxford University Press.

———. 1986. *Women of the Republic: Intellect and Ideology in Revolutionary America*. New York: Norton.

Kerber, Linda K., and Jane de Hart Mathews. 1982. *Women's America: Refocusing the Past*. New York: Oxford University Press.

Kerber, Linda K., et al. 1986. "On *In a Different Voice*: An Interdisciplinary Forum." *Signs* 11:304–33.

Kessler-Harris, Alice. 1982. *Out to Work: A History of Wage-Earning Women in the United States*. New York: Oxford University Press.

———. 1990. *A Woman's Wage: Historical Meanings and Social Consequences*. Lexington: University of Kentucky Press.

Kidwasser, Alfred P., and Michelle A. Wolf. 1992. "Mainstream Television, Adolescent Homosexuality, and Significant Silence." *Critical Studies in Mass Communication* 9:350–73.

Kierstead, Diane, Patti D'Agostino, and Heidi Dill. 1988. "Sex Role Stereotyping of College Professors: Bias in Students' Ratings of Instructors." *Journal of Educational Psychology* 80:342–44.

Kinsey, Alfred C., Wardell B. Pomeroy, and Clyde E. Martin. 1948. *Sexual Behavior in the Human Male*. Philadelphia: Saunders.

Kinsey, Alfred C., Wardell B. Pomeroy, Clyde E. Martin, and Paul A. Gebhart. 1953. *Sexual Behavior in the Human Female*. Philadelphia: Saunders.

Kirkpatrick, Martha, Catherine Smith, and Ron Roy. 1981. "Lesbian Mothers and Their Children: A Comparative Study." *American Journal of Orthopsychiatry* 51:545–51.

Kirshenbaum, Gayle. 1992. "U.N. Exposé: Inside the World's Largest Men's Club." *Ms.* (October): 16–18.

Klebanov, Pamela Kato, and John B. Jemmett III. 1992. "Effects of Expectations and Bodily Sensations on Self-Reports of Premenstrual Symptoms." *Psychology of Women Quarterly* 16:289–310.

Klein, Dori. 1982. "The Dark Side of Marriage: Battered Wives and the Domination of Women." In *Judge, Lawyer, Victim, Thief: Women, Gender Roles, and Criminal Justice*, edited by Nicole Hahn Rafter and Elizabeth Anne Stanko, 83–110. Boston: Northeastern University Press.

Klein, Ethel. 1984. *Gender Politics.* Cambridge, Mass.: Harvard University Press.

Koehler, Lyle. 1982. "The Case of the American Jezebels: Anne Hutchinson and Female Agitation During the Years of Antinomian Turmoil, 1636–40." In *Women's America*, edited by Linda K. Kerber and Jane De Hart Mathews, 36–51. New York: Oxford University Press.

Kohlberg, Lawrence. 1966. "A Cognitive-Developmental Analysis of Children's Sex Role Concepts and Attitudes." In *The Development of Sex Differences*, edited by Eleanor Maccoby, 82–173. Stanford, Calif.: Stanford University Press.

Komarovsky, Mirra. 1967. *Blue Collar Marriage.* New York: Vintage.

———. 1976. *Dilemmas of Masculinity: A Study of College Youth.* New York: Norton.

Kraditor, Aileen S. 1965. *The Ideas of the Woman Suffrage Movement, 1890–1920.* New York: Columbia.

Kraditor, Aileen, ed. 1968. *Up from the Pedestal: Selected Writings in the History of Feminism.* New York: Quadrangle.

Kramer, Heinrich, and James Sprenger. 1928. *Malleus Maleficarum.* London: Arrow.

Kramer, Pamela E., and Sheila Lehman. 1990. "Mismeasuring Women: A Critique of Research on Computer Ability and Avoidance." *Signs* 16: 158–72.

Kravetz, Diane, and Linda E. Jones. 1981. "Androgyny as a Standard of Mental Health." *American Journal of Orthopsychiatry* 51:502–509.

Kroeger, Naomi. 1982. "Preretirement Preparation: Sex Differences in Access, Sources, and Use." In *Women's Retirement: Policy Implications of Recent Research*, edited by Maximiliane Szinovacz, 95–112. Beverly Hills, Calif.: Sage.

Lakoff, Robin. 1975. *Language and Women's Place.* New York: Harper & Row.

Lamke, Leanne K. 1982. "The Impact of Sex Role Orientations on Self-Esteem in Early Adolescence." *Child Development* 53:1530–35.

Lander, Louise. 1988. *Images of Bleeding: Menstruation as Ideology.* New York: Orlando Press.

Lasch, Christopher. 1977. *Haven in a Heartless World: The Family Besieged.* New York: Basic.

Leach, William. 1980. *True Love and Perfect Union: The Feminist Reform of Sex and Society.* New York: Basic.

Leavitt, Judith Walzer. 1980. "Birthing and Anesthesia: The Debate Over Twilight Sleep." *Signs* 6:147–64. Also in Leavitt (1984).

———. 1983. " 'Science' Enters the Birthing Room: Obstetrics in America Since the Eighteenth Century." *Journal of American History* 70:281–304.

———. 1986. *Brought to Bed: Childbearing in America, 1750–1950.* New York: Oxford University Press.

Leavitt, Judith Walzer, ed. 1984. *Women and Health in America: Historical Readings.* Madison: University of Wisconsin Press.

Leavitt, Judith Walzer, and Whitney Walton. 1982. "Down to Death's Door: Women's Perceptions of Childbirth in America." In *Proceedings of the Second Motherhood Symposium: Childbirth: The Beginning of Motherhood*, edited by Sophie Colleau, 113–36. Madison, Wis.: Women's Studies Program. Also in Leavitt (1984).

Lederer, Laura, ed. 1980. *Take Back the Night.* New York: William Morrow.

Lee, Marcia Manning. 1977. "Towards Understanding Why Few Women Hold Political Office." In *A Portrait of Marginality*, edited by Marianne Githens and Jewel Prestage, 118–38. New York: Longman.

Leinhardt, Gaea, Andrea Mar Seewald, and Mary Engel. 1979. "Learning What's Taught: Sex Differences in Instruction." *Journal of Educational Psychology* 71:432–39.

Lemons, Stanley. 1972. *The Woman Citizen: Social Feminism in the 1920's.* Urbana: University of Illinois Press.

Lerner, Gerda. 1971. *The Grimké Sisters from South Carolina: Pioneers for Women's Rights and Abolition.* New York: Schocken.

Levine, Martine P., and Robin Leonard. 1984. "Discrimination against Lesbians in the Workforce." *Signs* 9:700–710.

Levine, Timothy R., Steven A. McCormack, and Penny Baldwin Avery. 1992. "Sex Differences in Emotional Reactions to Discovered Deception." *Communication Quarterly* 40:289–96.

Levinson, Richard M. 1975. "Sex Discrimination and Employment Practices: An Experiment with Unconventional Job Inquiries." *Social Problems* 22:533–43.

Levitt, Eugene E., and Albert D. Klassen. 1974. "Public Attitudes toward Homosexuality." *Journal of Homosexuality* 1:29–47.

Levy, A. H. 1983. "Double-Bars and Double Standards: Women Composers in America, 1880–1920." *International Journal of Women's Studies* 6:162–74.

Lewis, Robert A. 1978. "Emotional Intimacy Among Men." *Journal of Social Issues* 34:108–21.

Lifton, P. D. 1985. "Individual Differences in Moral Development: The Relation of Sex, Gender, and Personality to Morality." *Journal of Personality* 53:306–34.

Linn, M. C., and A. C. Peterson. 1985. "Emergence and Characterization of Gender Differences in Spatial Ability: A Meta-Analysis." *Child Development* 56:1479–98.

Lips, Hilary M. 1981. *Women, Men, and the Psychology of Power.* Englewood Cliffs, N.J.: Prentice-Hall.

———. 1993. *Sex and Gender: An Introduction.* Mountain View, Calif.: Mayfield.

Livingston, Joy A. 1982. "Responses to Sexual Harassment on the Job: Legal, Organizational, and Individual Actions." *Journal of Social Issues* 38:5–22.

Locksley, Anne. 1982. "Social Class and Marital Attitudes and Behavior." *Journal of Marriage and the Family* 44:427–40.

Lopata, Helena Z. 1971. *Occupation: Housewife.* New York: Oxford University Press.

Lorde, Audrey. 1984. "Man Child." In Lorde, *Sister Outsider.* Trumansburg, N.Y.: Crossing Press.

Lorentzen, Robin. 1991. *Women in the Sanctuary Movement.* Philadelphia: Temple University Press.

Loring, Marti, and Brian Powell. 1988. "Gender, Race, and DSM-III: A Study of the Objectivity of Psychiatric Diagnostic Behavior." *Journal of Health and Social Behavior* 29:1–22.

Lott, Dale F., and Robert Sommer. 1967. "Seating Arrangements and Status." *Journal of Personality and Social Psychology* 7:90–95.

Lull, James, Catherine A. Hanson, and Michael J. Marx. 1977. "College Students' Recognition of Female Stereotypes in Television Commercials." *Journalism Quarterly* 54:153–57.

Lull, James, Anthony Mulack, and Shelly Lisa Rosen. 1983. "Feminism as a Predictor of Mass Media Use." *Sex Roles* 9:165–78.

Lynch, Robert N. 1986. "Women in Northern Paiute Politics." *Signs* 11:352–66.

Lynd, Robert S., and Helen Merrell Lynd. 1929. *Middletown: A Study of American Culture.* New York: Harcourt & Brace.

———. 1937. *Middletown in Transition: A Study in Cultural Conflict.* New York: Harcourt & Brace.

Lynn, Naomi. 1979. "American Women and the Political Process." In *Women: A Feminist Perspective*, edited by Jo Freeman, 404–29. Mountain View, Calif.: Mayfield.

Lyons, Judith A., and Lisa A. Serbin. 1986. "Observer Bias in Scoring Boys' and Girls' Aggression." *Sex Roles* 14:301–13.

McClintock, Martha K. 1971. "Menstrual Synchrony and Suppression." *Nature* 229: 244–45.

Maccoby, Eleanor, and Carol Jacklin. 1974. *The Psychology of Sex Differences.* Stanford, Calif.: Stanford University Press.

McCormick, Naomi B., and Clinton J. Jesser. 1983. "The Courtship Game: Power in the Sexual Encounter." In *Changing Boundaries: Gender Roles and Sexual Behavior*, edited by Elizabeth Rice Allgeier and Naomi B. McCormick, 64–86. Palo Alto, Calif.: Mayfield.

McCourt, Kathleen. 1977. *Working Class Women and Grassroots Politics.* Bloomington: Indiana University Press.

McCracken, Ellen. 1993. *Decoding Women's Magazines: From Mademoiselle to Ms.* New York: St. Martin's.

McDonough, Eileen. 1982. "To Work or Not to Work: The Differential Aspect of Achieved and Derived Status upon the Political Participation of Women, 1956–76." *American Journal of Political Science* 26:280–97.

McGhee, Paul E., and Terry Frueh. 1980. "Television Viewing and the Learning of Sex Role Stereotypes." *Sex Roles* 6:179–88.

McGuinnes, Kate, and Trish Donahue. 1988. "Women in Law Enforcement." In *The American Woman, 1988–89: A Status Report*, edited by Sara E. Rix, 252–57. New York: Norton.

Machung, Anne. 1989. "Talking Career, Thinking Job: Gender Differences in Career and Family Expectations of Berkeley Seniors." *Feminist Studies* 15:35–58.

Mackie, Marlene. 1983. "The Domestication of Self: Gender Comparisons of Self-Imagery and Self-Esteem." *Social Psychology Quarterly* 45:343–50.

Mackinnon, Catharine. 1979. *The Sexual Harassment of Working Women*. New Haven, Conn.: Yale University Press.

Macklin, Eleanor D. 1980. "Nontraditional Family Forms: A Decade of Research." *Journal of Marriage and the Family* 42:905–22.

Macklin, M. Carole, and Richard G. Kolbe. 1984. "Sex Role Stereotyping in Children's Advertising." *Journal of Advertising* 13:34–42.

McLanahan, Sara, and Julia Adams. 1987. "Parenthood and Psychological Well-Being." *Annual Review of Psychology* 5:237–57.

MacLeod, Arlene Elowe. 1991. *Accommodating Protest: Working Women, the New Veiling, and Change in Cairo*. New York: Columbia University Press.

McManus, Karen A., Yvonne Brackbill, Lynn Woodward, Paul Doering, and David Robinson. 1982. "Consumer Information about Prenatal and Obstetric Drugs." *Women and Health* 7:15–29.

Major, Brenda. 1981. "Gender Patterns in Touching Behavior." In *Gender and Nonverbal Behavior*, edited by Clara Mayo and Nancy Henley, 15–38. New York: Springer-Verlag.

Malamuth, Neil M. 1981. "Rape Proclivity among Males." *Journal of Social Issues* 37:138–57.

Malos, Ellen, ed. 1980. *The Politics of Housework*. New York: Schocken.

Mamay, Patricia D., and Richard L. Simpson. 1981. "Three Female Roles in Television Commercials." *Sex Roles* 7:1223–32.

Mandelbaum, Dorothy Rosenthal. 1978. "Women in Medicine." *Signs* 4:136–45.

Mann, Susan A. 1989. "Slavery, Sharecropping, and Sexual Inequality." *Signs* 14:774–98.

Marks, Elaine, and Isabelle de Courtivron, eds. 1980. *New French Feminisms: An Anthology*. Amherst: University of Massachusetts Press.

Markus, H., M. Crane, S. Bernstein, and M. Siladi. 1982. "Self-Schemas and Gender." *Journal of Personality and Social Psychology* 42:38–50.

Martin, Elaine. 1984. "Power and Authority in the Classroom: Sexist Stereotypes in Teaching Evaluations." *Signs* 9:482–92.

Marx, Karl, and Friedrich Engels. 1947. *The German Ideology*. New York: International.

Marzolf, Marion. 1977. *Up from the Footnote: A History of Women Journalists*. New York: Hastings House.

Matheson, Kimberly, and Connie M. Kristensen. 1987. "The Effect of Sexist Attitudes and Social Structures on the Use of Sex-Biased Pronouns." *Journal of Social Psychology* 127:395–401.

Mathews, Alice E. 1987. "Tall Women and Mountain Belles: Fact and Fiction in Appalachia." In *Perspectives on the American South: An Annual Review of Society,*

Politics, and Culture, edited by James C. Cobb and Charles R. Wilson, 39–54. New York: Gordon and Breach Science Publishers.

Matthaei, Julie A. 1982. *An Economic History of Women in America: Women's Work, The Sexual Division of Labor, and the Development of Capitalism*. New York: Schocken.

Mazey, Mary Ellen, and David R. Lee. 1983. *Her Space, Her Place: A Geography of Women*. Washington, D.C.: Association of American Geographers.

Mechanic, David. 1978. *Medical Sociology*. New York: Free Press.

Mellor, Earl F. 1987. "Workers at the Minimum Wage or Less." *Monthly Labor Review* 110:34–38.

Melosh, Barbara. 1991. *Engendering Culture: Manhood and Womanhood in New Deal Public Art and Theater*. Washington, D.C.: Smithsonian Institution Press.

Merlo, Alida V. 1993. "Pregnant Substance Abusers: The New Female Offender." In *It's a Crime: Women and Justice*, edited by Roslyn Muraskin and Ted Alleman, 146–60. Englewood Cliffs, N.J.: Prentice-Hall.

Milkman, Ruth. 1982. "Redefining 'Women's Work:' The Sexual Division of Labor in the Auto Industry During World War II." *Feminist Studies* 8:337–72.

Miller, Dorothy C. 1983. "AFDC: Mapping a Strategy for Tomorrow." *Social Service Review* 57:599–613.

Miller, Patrice M., Dorothy L. Danaher, and David Forbes. 1986. "Sex-Related Strategies for Coping with Interpersonal Conflict in Children Aged 5 to 7." *Developmental Psychology* 22:543–48.

Millett, Kate. 1970. *Sexual Politics*. Garden City, N.Y.: Doubleday.

Milliren, John W. 1977. "Some Contingencies Affecting the Utilization of Tranquilizers in Long-Term Care of the Elderly." *Journal of Health and Social Behavior* 18:206-11.

Mills, Elizabeth Anne. 1982. "One Hundred Years of Fear: Rape and the Medical Profession." In *Judge, Lawyer, Victim, Thief: Women, Gender Roles, and Criminal Justice*, edited by Nicole Hahn Rafter and Elizabeth Anne Stanko, 29–62. Boston: Northeastern University Press.

Mills, Kay. 1993. *This Little Light of Mine: The Life of Fannie Lou Hamer*. New York: NAL/Dutton.

Milman, Barbara. 1980. "New Rules for the Oldest Profession: Should We Change Our Prostitution Laws?" *Harvard Women's Law Journal* 3:1–82.

Minh-ha, Trinh T. 1989. *Woman, Native, Other: Writing Postcoloniality and Feminism*. Bloomington: Indiana University Press.

Mirandé, Alfredo, and Evangelina Enríquez. 1979. *La Chicana: The Mexican-American Woman*. Chicago: University of Chicago Press.

Mitchell, Juliet. 1974. *Psychoanalysis and Feminism*. New York: Pantheon.

Moen, Phyllis. 1992. *Women's Two Roles: A Contemporary Dilemma*. Westport, Conn.: Greenwood.

Mohanty, Chandra Talpade, Ann Russo, and Lourdes Torres, eds. 1991. *Third World Women and the Politics of Feminism*. Bloomington: Indiana University Press.

Moi, Toril. 1985. *Sexual/Textual Politics: Feminist Literary Theory*. New York: Methuen.

Morága, Cherrie, and Gloria Anzaldúa, eds. 1981. *This Bridge Called My Back: Writings by Radical Women of Color.* Watertown, Mass.: Persephone.

Morgan, Edmund S. [1944] 1978. "The Puritans and Sex." In *The American Family in Historical Perspective*, edited by Michael Gordon, 363–73. New York: St. Martin's.

Morgan, Marabelle. 1975. *The Total Woman.* Old Tappan, N.J.: Revell.

Morin, Stephen F., and Ellen M. Garfinkle. 1978. "Male Homophobia." *Journal of Social Issues* 34:29–47.

Morris, Aldon D., and Carol McClung Mueller, eds. 1992. *Frontiers in Social Movement Theory.* New Haven, Conn.: Yale University Press.

Morrison, Toni, ed. 1992. *Race-ing, Justice, En-gendering Power: Essays on Anita Hill, Clarence Thomas, and the Construction of Social Reality.* New York: Pantheon.

Moyer, Imogene L. 1993. "Women's Prisons: Issues and Controversies." In *It's a Crime: Women and Justice*, edited by Roslyn Muraskin and Ted Alleman, 193–210. Englewood Cliffs, N.J.: Prentice-Hall.

Ms. Foundation for Women. 1992. *A Policy Guide: Women's Choices: A Joint Project.* New York: Ms. Foundation for Women.

Mueller, Carol. 1991. "The Gender Gap and Women's Political Influence." *The Annals: American Feminism: New Issues for a Mature Movement* 515:23–37.

Mueller, Carol, and Thomas Dimieri. 1982. "The Structure of Belief Systems among Contending ERA Activists." *Social Forces* 60:657–75.

Mueller, Claus. 1973. *The Politics of Communication: A Study in the Political Sociology of Language, Socialization, and Legitimation.* New York: Oxford University Press.

Mueller, Marnie W. 1982. "Applying Human Capital Theory to Women's Changing Work Patterns." *Journal of Social Issues* 38:89–96.

Mulac, Anthony, and Torborg Louisa Lundell. 1986. "Linguistic Contributors to the Gender-Linked Language Effect." *Journal of Language and Social Psychology* 5:81–101.

Muller, Charlotte F. 1983. "Income Supports for Older Women." *Social Policy* 14:23–31.

———. 1990. *Health Care and Gender.* New York: Russell Sage Foundation.

Muraskin, Roslyn. 1993. "Disparate Treatment in Correction Facilities." In *It's a Crime: Women and Justice*, edited by Roslyn Muraskin and Ted Alleman, 211–25. Englewood Cliffs, N.J.: Prentice-Hall.

Nead, Lynda. 1992. "The Female Nude: Pornography, Art, and Sexuality." In *Sex Exposed: Sexuality and the Pornography Debate*, edited by Lynne Segal and Mary McIntosh, 280–94. New Brunswick, N.J.: Rutgers University Press.

Nelson, Barbara J. 1984. "Women's Poverty and Women's Citizenship: Some Political Consequences of Economic Marginality." *Signs* 10:209–31.

Newberry, Phyllis, Myrna Weissman, and Jerome K. Myers. 1979. "Working Wives and Housewives: Do They Differ in Mental Status and Social Adjustment?" *American Journal of Orthopsychiatry* 49:282–91.

New Jersey Supreme Court Task Force. 1986. "The First Year Report of the New Jersey Supreme Court Task Force on Women in the Courts—June 1984." *Women's Rights Law Reporter* 9:129–75.

Nichols, Patricia C. 1978. "Black Women in the Rural South: Conservative and Innovative." *International Journal of the Sociology of Language* 17:45–54.

Nochlin, Linda. 1971. "Why Are There No Great Women Artists?" In *Women in Sexist Society*, edited by Vivian Gornick and Barbara K. Moran, 480–510. New York: New American Library.

Norgren, Jill. 1989. "Child Care." In *Women: A Feminist Perspective*, edited by Jo Freeman, 176–96. Mountain View, Calif.: Mayfield.

O'Barr, Jean, et al. 1986. "Reflections on Forum '85 in Nairobi, Kenya: Voices from the International Women's Studies Community." *Signs* 11:584–608.

O'Farrell, Brigid, and Sharon L. Harlan. 1982. "Craft Workers and Clerks: The Effects of Male Co-Worker Hostility on Women's Satisfaction with Non-traditional Jobs." *Social Problems* 23:252–65.

Offen, Karen. 1988. "Defining Feminism, A Comparative Historical Approach." *Signs* 14:119–57.

Office for Economic Cooperation and Development. 1988. *Labor Force Statistics.* Paris: OECD.

Okin, Susan Moller. 1979. *Women in Western Political Thought.* Princeton, N.J.: Princeton University Press.

Oldham, Sue, Doug Farmill, and Ian Bell. 1982. "Sex Role Identity of Female Homosexuals." *Journal of Homosexuality* 8:41–46.

Oliver, Mary Beth, and Janet Shibley Hyde. 1993. "Gender Differences in Sexuality: A Meta-Analysis." *Psychological Bulletin* 110.

O'Malley, K. M., and S. Richardson. 1985. "Sex Bias in Counseling: Have Things Changed?" *Journal of Counseling and Development* 63:294–99.

Orenstein, Gloria Feman. 1975. "Art History." *Signs* 1:505–25.

Osterman, Paul. 1979. "Sex Discrimination in Professional Employment: A Case Study." *Industrial and Labor Relations Review* 32:451–64.

Owen, Diana, and Jack Dennis. 1988. "Gender Differences in the Politicization of American Children." *Women and Politics* 8:23–44.

Paige, Karen E., and Jeffrey M. Paige. 1981. *Politics of the Reproductive Rituals.* Berkeley: University of California Press.

Paisner, Daniel. 1989. *The Imperfect Mirror: Inside Stories of Television Women.* New York: Morrow.

Parisi, Nicolette. 1982a. "Exploring Female Crime Patterns: Problems and Prospects." In *Judge, Lawyer, Victim, Thief: Women, Gender Roles, and Criminal Justice*, edited by Nicole Hahn Rafter and Elizabeth Anne Stanko, 111–30. Boston: Northeastern University Press.

———. 1982b. "Are Females Treated Differently? A Review of the Theories and Evidence on Sentencing and Parole Decisions." In *Judge, Lawyer, Victim, Thief: Women, Gender Roles, and Criminal Justice*, edited by Nicole Hahn Rafter and Elizabeth Anne Stanko, 205–29. Boston: Northeastern University Press.

Parlee, Mary Brown. 1992. "On PMS and Psychiatric Abnormality." *Feminism and Psychology* 2:105–19.

Parsons, Jacqueline Eccles. 1983. "Sexual Socialization and Gender Roles in Childhood." In *Changing Boundaries: Gender Roles and Sexual Behavior*, edited by Elizabeth Rice Allgeier and Naomi B. McCormick, 19–48. Mountain View, Calif.: Mayfield.

Parsons, Talcott. 1951. *The Social System*. New York: Free Press.

———. 1954. "Age and Sex in the Social Structure of the United States." In *Essays in Sociological Theory*, edited by Talcott Parsons, 89-103. New York: Free Press.

Parsons, Talcott, and Robert F. Bales. 1955. *Family, Socialization and Interaction Process*. Glencoe, Ill.: Free Press.

Pateman, Carole. 1980. "Women and Consent." *Political Theory* 8:149–68.

———. 1988. *The Sexual Contract*. Stanford, Calif.: Stanford University Press.

Patterson, Charlotte J. 1992. "Children of Lesbian and Gay Parents." *Child Development* 63:1025–62.

Patterson, Michelle, and Laurie Engleberg. 1978. "Women in Male Dominated Professions." In *Women Working: Theories and Facts in Perspective*, edited by Anne H. Stromberg and Shirley Harkness, 266–92. Mountain View, Calif.: Mayfield.

Pearce, Diana M. 1989. "Farewell to Alms: Women's Fare under Welfare." In *Women: A Feminist Perspective*, edited by Jo Freeman, 493–506. Mountain View, Calif.: Mayfield.

Pedersen, Darhl M., Martin M. Schinedling, and Dee L. Johnson. 1968. "Effects of Sex of Examiner and Subject Taught on Children's Quantitative Test Performance."*Journal of Personality and Social Psychology* 10:251–54.

Penelope, Julia, and Susan J. Wolfe. 1989. *The Original Coming Out Stories*. Freedom, Calif.: Crossing Press.

Penn, Donna. 1991. "The Meanings of Lesbianism in Post-War America." *Gender and History* 3:190–203.

Peplau, Letitia Anne, Susan Cochran, Karen Rook, and Christine Padesky. 1978. "Loving Women: Attachment and Autonomy in Lesbian Relationships." *Journal of Social Issues* 34:7–27.

Peplau, Letitia Anne, and Steven Gordon. 1983. "The Intimate Relationships of Lesbian and Gay Men." In *Changing Boundaries: Gender Roles and Sexual Behavior*, edited by Elizabeth Rice Allgeier and Naomi B. McCormick, 226–44. Mountain View, Calif.: Mayfield.

Peplau, Letitia Anne, Zick Rubin, and Charles Hill. 1977. "Sex Intimacy in Dating Relationships." *Journal of Social Issues* 33:96–109.

Perdue, Theda. 1989. "Cherokee Women and the Trail of Tears." *Journal of Women's History* 1:14–30.

Perkins, Jerry, and Diane L. Fowlkes. 1980. "Opinion Representation versus Social Representation: Or, Why Women Can't Run as Women and Win." *American Political Science Review* 74:92–103.

Perkins, Linda M. 1983. "The Impact of the 'Cult of True Womanhood' on the Education of Black Women." *Journal of Social Issues* 39:17–28.

Petchesky, Roslyn P. 1981. "Antiabortion, Antifeminism, and the Rise of the New Right." *Feminist Studies* 7:206–46.

———. 1984. *Abortion and Women's Choice: The State, Sexuality, and Reproductive Freedom*. New York: Longman.

Peterson, Susan Rae. 1977. "Coercion and Rape: The State as a Male Protection Racket." In *Feminism and Philosophy*, edited by Mary Vetterling-Braggin, Frederick A. Elliston, and Jane English, 313–32. Totowa, N.J.: Littlefield, Adams.

Peterson, V. Spike, ed. 1992. *Gendered States: Feminist (Re)Visions of International Relations Theory.* Boulder, Colo.: Lynne Reinner.

Phelan, Shane. 1989. *Identity Politics: Lesbian Feminism and the Limits of Community.* Philadelphia: Temple University Press.

Phillips, E. Barbara. 1978. "Magazines' Heroines: Is *Ms.* Just Another Member of the *Family Circle*?" In *Hearth and Home: Images of Women in the Mass Media*, edited by Gaye Tuchman, Arlene Kaplan Daniels, and James Benet, 116–29. New York: Oxford University Press.

Piercy, Marge. 1974. "Looking at Quilts." In *Living in the Open*, edited by Marge Piercy, 86–87. New York: Knopf.

Pistrang, Nancy. 1984. "Women's Work Involvement and Experience of New Motherhood." *Journal of Marriage and the Family* 46:433–47.

Piven, Frances Fox, and Richard A. Cloward. 1988. "Welfare Doesn't Shore Up Traditional Family Roles: A Reply to Linda Gordon." *Social Research* 55:631–47.

Plaskow, Judith. 1990. *Standing Again at Sinai.* San Francisco: HarperCollins.

Poole, Debra A., and Anne E. Tapley. 1988. "Sex Roles, Social Roles, and Clinical Judgments of Mental Health." *Sex Roles* 19:265–72.

Pope, Jacqueline. 1989. *Biting the Hand That Feeds Them: Organizing Women on Welfare at the Grass Roots Level.* Westport, Conn.: Greenwood.

Porter, Natalie, and Florence Geis. 1981. "Women and Nonverbal Leadership Cues: When Seeing Is Not Believing." In *Gender and Nonverbal Behavior*, edited by Clara Mayo and Nancy Henley, 39–62. New York: Springer-Verlag.

Prather, J., and Linda S. Fidell. 1975. "Sex Differences in the Control and Style of Medical Ads." *Social Science and Medicine* 9:23–26.

Rafter, Nicole Hahn. 1982. "Hard Times: Custodial Prisons for Women and the Example of the New York State Prison for Women at Auburn, 1893–1933." In *Judge, Lawyer, Victim, Thief: Women, Gender Roles, and Criminal Justice*, edited by Nicole Hahn Rafter and Elizabeth Anne Stanko, 237–60. Boston: Northeastern University Press.

Rafter, Nicole Hahn, and Elizabeth Anne Stanko, eds. 1982. *Judge, Lawyer, Victim, Thief: Women, Gender Roles, and Criminal Justice.* Boston: Northeastern University Press.

Randall, Vicki. 1987. *Women and Politics.* Chicago: University of Chicago Press.

Rank, Mark R. 1988. "Fertility among Women on Welfare: Incidence and Determinants." *American Sociological Review* 54:296–304.

Rapoport, Ronald B. 1981. "The Sex Gap in Political Persuading: Where the 'Structuring Principle' Works." *American Journal of Political Science* 25:32–48.

Rawalt, Marguerite. 1983. "The Equal Rights Amendment." In *Women in Washington: Advocates for Public Policy*, edited by Irene Tinker, 49–78. Beverly Hills, Calif.: Sage.

Reed, Susan O. 1993. "The Criminalization of Pregnancy: Drugs, Alcohol, and AIDS." In *It's a Crime: Women and Justice*, edited by Roslyn Muraskin and Ted Alleman, 93–117. Englewood Cliffs, N.J.: Prentice-Hall.

Reiss, Harry T., and Linda A Jackson. 1981. "Sex Differences in Reward Allocation: Subjects, Partners, and Tasks." *Journal of Personality and Social Psychology* 40:465–78.

Reskin, Barbara F. 1988. "Bringing the Men Back In: Sex Differentiation and the Devaluation of Women's Work." *Gender and Society* 2:58–81.

Resnick, Michael D. 1984. "Studying Adolescent Mothers' Decision Making about Adoption and Parenting." *Social Work* 29:5–10.

Rhode, Deborah L. 1989. *Justice and Gender.* Cambridge, Mass.: Harvard University Press.

Rhodes, Jane. 1991. "Television's Realist Portrayal of African-American Women and the Case of LA Law." *Women and Language* 14:29–34.

Rich, Adrienne. 1976. *Of Woman Born: Motherhood as Experience and Institution.* New York: Norton.

———. 1979. *On Lies, Secrets, and Silence.* New York: Norton.

———. 1980. "Compulsory Heterosexuality and Lesbian Existence." *Signs* 5:631–60.

Richardson, J. T. 1989. "Student Learning and the Menstrual Cycle: Premenstrual Symptoms and Approaches to Studying." *Educational Psychology* 9:215–38.

Rickel, Annette U., and Linda M. Grant. 1979. "Sex Role Stereotypes in the Mass Media and Schools: Five Consistent Themes." *International Journal of Women's Studies* 2:164–79.

Ries, Paula, and Anne J. Stone, ed. 1993. *The American Woman, 1992–93: A Status Report.* New York: Norton.

Riley, Glenda. 1991. *Divorce: An American Tradition.* New York: Oxford University Press.

Rix, Sara E. 1988. *The American Woman, 1988–89: A Status Report.* New York: Norton.

Robbins, James. 1980. "Religious Involvement, Asceticism, and Abortion among Low Income Black Women." *Sociological Analysis* 41:365–74.

Robertson, Nan. 1992. *The Girls in the Balcony: Women, Men and the New York Times.* New York: Random.

Robinson, John P. 1980. "Household Technology and Household Work." In *Women and Household Labor*, edited by Sara F. Berk, 29–52. Beverly Hills, Calif.: Sage.

"*Roe* and Neonatal Homicide." 1992. *Family Planning Perspectives* 24:146.

Rohrbaugh, Joanna Bunker. 1980. *Women: Psychology's Puzzle.* Brighton, U.K.: Harvester Press.

Rollins, Judith. 1983. *Between Women: Domestics and Their Employers.* Philadelphia: Temple University Press.

Rook, Karen S., and Constance Hammer. 1977. "A Cognitive Perspective on the Experience of Sexual Arousal." *Journal of Social Issues* 33:7–29.

Rosen, Bernard, Thomas H. Jerdee, and Thomas L. Prestwick. 1975. "Dual-Career Marital Adjustments: Potential Effects of Discriminatory Managerial Attitudes." *Journal of Marriage and the Family* 37:565–72.

Rosen, Bernard, and M. F. Mericle. 1979. "Influence of Strong versus Weak Fair Employment Policies and Applicant's Sex on Selection Decisions and Salary Recommendations in a Management Simulation." *Journal of Applied Psychology* 64:435–39.

Rosen, Ellen Israel. 1987. *Bitter Choices: Blue-Collar Women In and Out of Work.* Chicago: University of Chicago Press.

Rosenberg, Dorothy J. 1991. "Shock Therapy: GDR Women in Transition from a Socialist Welfare State to a Social Market Economy." *Signs* 17:129–51.

Rosenkrantz, Paul, Susan R. Vogel, Helen Bee, and Donald Broverman. 1968. "Sex Role Stereotypes and Self-Concept in College Students." *Journal of Consulting and Clinical Psychology* 32:287–95.

Ross, Catherine E., and John Mirowsky. 1988. "Child Care and Emotional Adjustment to Wives' Employment." *Journal of Health and Social Behavior* 29:127–38.

Ross, Catherine E., John Mirowsky, and Joan Huber. 1983. "Dividing Work, Sharing Work, and In-Between: Marriage Patterns and Depression." *American Sociological Review* 48:809–23.

Ross, Joanna, and James B. Kahan. 1983. "Children by Choice or by Chance: The Perceived Effects of Parenthood." *Sex Roles* 9:69–77.

Ross, Laurie, Daniel R. Anderson, and Patricia A. Wisocki. 1982. "Television Viewing and Adult Sex-Role Attitudes." *Sex Roles* 8:589–92.

Rossi, Alice. 1965. "Barriers to the Career Choice of Engineering, Medicine, or Science among American Women." In *Women and the Scientific Professions*, edited by J. A. Mattfield and C. G. Van Aken, 51–127. Cambridge: MIT Press.

Rossi, Alice, ed. 1970. *Essays in Sex Equality: John Stuart Mill and Harriet Taylor Mill.* Chicago: University of Chicago Press.

———, ed. 1988. *The Feminist Papers: From Adams to de Beauvoir.* Boston: Northeastern University Press.

Rothblum, Esther D. 1992. "The Stigma of Women's Weight: Social and Economic Realities." *Feminism and Psychology* 2:61–74.

Rothman, Barbara Katz. 1982. *In Labor: Women and Power in the Birthplace.* New York: Norton.

Rowland, Robyn, ed. 1984. *Women Who Do and Women Who Don't Join the Women's Movement.* Boston: Routledge & Kegan Paul.

Rubin, Gayle. 1974. "The Traffic in Women: Notes on the 'Political Economy' of Sex." In *Toward an Anthropology of Women*, edited by Rayna Reiter, 157–210. New York: Monthly Review Press.

Rubin, Lillian B. 1976. *Worlds of Pain: Life in the Working Class Family.* New York: Basic Books.

Rubin, Jeffrey Z., Frank J. Provenzano, and Zella Luria. 1974. "The Eye of the Beholder: Parents' Views on Sex of Newborns." *American Journal of Orthopsychiatry* 44:512–19.

Ruddick, Sara. 1982. "Maternal Thinking." In *Rethinking the Family: Some Feminist Questions*, edited by Barrie Thorne and Marilyn Yalom, 76–94. New York: Longman.

Ruddick, Sara, and Pamela Daniels, ed. 1977. *Working It Out: Twenty-three Women Writers, Artists, Scientists, and Scholars Talk about Their Lives and Work.* New York: Pantheon.

Ruether, Rosemary. 1983. *Sexism and God-Talk: Toward a Feminist Theology.* Boston: Beacon.

Ruether, Rosemary, ed. 1974. *Religion and Sexism: Images of Women in the Jewish and Christian Traditions.* New York: Simon & Schuster.

Rupp, Leila. 1985. "The Woman's Community in the National Woman's Party, 1945 to the 1960's." *Signs* 10:715–40.

Russo, Ann, and Cheris Kramarae, ed. 1991. *The Radical Women's Press of 1850s.* New York: Routledge.

Ruth, Sheila. 1980. *Issues in Feminism: A First Course in Women's Studies.* Boston: Houghton Mifflin.

Ryan, Mary P. 1979. "The Power of Women's Networks: A Case Study of Female Moral Reform in Antebellum America." *Feminist Studies* 5:66–85.

Rytina, Nancy E., and Suzanne M. Bianchi. 1984. "Occupational Reclassification and Distribution by Gender." *Monthly Labor Review* 107:11–17.

Sadker, Myra Pollack, and David Miller Sadker. 1980. "Sexism in Teacher Education Texts." *Harvard Education Review* 50:36–46.

Sagatun, Inger J. 1993. "Babies Born with Drug Addiction: Background and Legal Responses." In *It's a Crime: Women and Justice*, edited by Roslyn Muraskin and Ted Alleman, 118–29. Englewood Cliffs, N.J.: Prentice-Hall.

Salem, Dorothy. 1990. *To Better Our World: Black Women in Organized Reform, 1890–1920.* New York: Carlson Publishing.

Salzinger, Suzanne, Sandra Kaplan, and Connie Artmeyeff. 1983. "Mothers' Personal Social Networks and Child Maltreatment." *Journal of Abnormal Psychology* 92:68–76.

Samar, Vincent. 1991. *The Right to Privacy: Gays, Lesbians, and the Constitution.* Philadelphia: Temple University Press.

Sanday, Peggy Reeves. 1981a. *Female Power and Male Dominance: On the Origins of Sexual Inequality.* New York: Cambridge University Press.

———. 1981b. "The Socio-Cultural Context of Rape: A Cross-Cultural Study." *Journal of Social Issues* 37:5–27.

Sanders, Marlene, and Marcia Rock. 1988. *Waiting for Prime Time: The Women of Television News.* Urbana: University of Illinois Press.

Sapiro, Virginia. 1979. "Women's Studies and Political Conflict." In *The Prism of Sex: Essays in the Sociology of Knowledge*, edited by Julia Sherman and Evelyn Beck, 253-65. Madison: University of Wisconsin Press.

———. 1980. "News from the Front: Inter-Sex and Intergenerational Conflict over the Status of Women." *Western Political Quarterly* 33:260–77.

———. 1982a. "Public Costs of Private Commitments or Private Costs of Public Commitments: Family Roles versus Political Ambition." *American Journal of Political Science* 26:265–79.

———. 1982b. "If U.S. Senator Baker Were a Woman: An Experimental Study of Candidate Images." *Political Psychology* 3:61–83.

———. 1983. *The Political Integration of Women: Roles, Socialization, and Politics.* Urbana: University of Illinois Press.

———. 1984. "Women, Citizenship, and Nationality: Immigration and Nationalization Policies in the United States." *Politics and Society* 13:1–26.

———. 1986. "The Gender Basis of American Social Policy." *Political Science Quarterly* 101:221–38.

———. 1989. "The Women's Movement and the Creation of Gender Consciousness: Social Movements as Socialization Agents." In *Political Socialization for Democracy*, edited by Orit Ichilov, 266–80. New York: Teachers' College Press.

———. 1991. "Feminism: A Generation Later." *The Annals of the American Academy of Political and Social Science* 515:10–22.

———. 1992. *A Vindication of Political Virtue: The Political Theory of Mary Wollstonecraft.* Chicago: University of Chicago Press.

———. 1993a. "Engendering Cultural Differences." In *The Rising Tide of Cultural Pluralism: The Nation State at Bay?*, edited by M. Crawford Young, 36–54. Madison: University of Wisconsin Press.

———. 1993b. " 'Private' Coercion and Democratic Theory." In *Reconsidering the Democratic Public*, edited by George E. Marcus and Russell Hansen. University Park: Pennsylvania State University Press.

Sapiro, Virginia, and Barbara G. Farah. 1980. "New Pride and Old Prejudice: Political Ambitions and Role Orientations among Female Partisan Elites." *Women and Politics* 1:13–36.

Sargent, Lydia, ed. 1981. *Women and Revolution: A Discussion of the Unhappy Marriage of Feminism and Marxism.* Boston: South End Press.

Sayers, Janet. 1982. *Biological Politics: Feminist and Anti-Feminist Perspectives.* New York: Tavistock.

———, ed. 1987. *Engels Revisited: New Feminist Perspectives.* New York: Routledge.

Scharf, Lois, and Joan M. Jensen, eds. 1983. *Decades of Discontent.* Westport, Conn.: Greenwood.

Schneider, Joseph W., and Sally L. Hacker. 1973. "Sex Role Imagery and the Use of Generic 'Man' in Introductory Texts." *American Sociologist* 8:12–18.

Schram, Vicki R., and Marilyn M. Dunsing. 1981. "Influences on Married Women's Volunteer Work Participation." *Journal of Consumer Research* 7:373–79.

Schramm, Sarah Slavin. 1979. *Plow Women Rather than Reapers: An Intellectual History of Feminism in the United States.* Metuchen, N.J.: Scarecrow Press.

Schwendinger, Loren. 1990. "Property-Owning Free African-American Women in the South, 1880–90." *Journal of Women's History* 1:13–44.

Scott, Anne Firor. 1970. *The Southern Lady: From Pedestal to Politics.* Chicago: University of Chicago Press.

———. 1990. "Most Invisible of All: Black Women's Voluntary Associations." *Journal of Southern History* 56:3–22.

———. 1992. *Natural Allies: Women's Associations in American History.* Urbana: University of Illinois Press.

Scott, Ronald L., and Laurie A. Tetrault. 1987. "Attitudes of Rapists and Other Violent Offenders toward Women." *Journal of Social Psychology* (August): 375–80.

Scully, Diana. 1990. *Understanding Sexual Violence: A Study of Convicted Rapists.* Cambridge, Mass.: Unwin Hyman.

Scully, Diana, and Pauline Bart. 1973. "A Funny Thing Happened on the Way to the Orifice: Women in Gynecology Textbooks." *American Journal of Sociology* 78:1045–50.

Segal, Lynne, and Mary McIntosh, eds. 1992. *Sex Exposed: Sexuality and the Pornography Debate.* New Brunswick, N.J.: Rutgers University Press.

Seiden, Ann M. 1976. "Overview: Research on the Psychology of Women: Gender Differences in Sexual and Reproductive Life." *American Journal of Psychiatry* 133:995–1007.

Seidenberg, Robert. 1971. "Advertising and Abuse of Drugs." *New England Journal of Medicine* 284:789–90.

Seidman, Steven A. 1992. "An Investigation of Sex-Role Stereotyping in Music Videos." *Journal of Broadcasting and Electronic Media* 36:209–16.

Seifer, Nancy. 1976. *Nobody Speaks for Me: Self-Portraits of American Working Class Women.* New York: Simon & Schuster.

Seller, Maxine S. 1982. "The Education of Immigrant Women, 1900–35." In *Women's America*, edited by Linda K. Kerber and Jane de Hart Mathews, 242–56. New York: Oxford University Press.

———. 1987. "Defining Socialist Womanhood: The Women's Page of the *Jewish Daily Forward* in 1919." *American Jewish History* 76:416-38.

Serbin, Lisa A., Daniel K. O'Leary, Ronald M. Kent, and Ilene J. Tonick. 1973. "A Comparison of Teacher Response to the Preacademic and Problem Behavior of Boys and Girls." *Child Development* 44:796–84.

Settin, Joan M., and Dana Bramel. 1981. "Interaction of Client Class and Gender Biasing in Clinical Judgment." *American Journal of Orthopsychiatry* 51:510–20.

Shapiro, Robert Y., and Harpreet Mahajan. 1986. "Gender Differences in Policy Preferences: A Summary of Trends from the 1960's to the 1980's. *Public Opinion Quarterly* 50:42–61.

Shapiro, Robert Y., et al. 1987a. "The Polls: Employment and Social Welfare." *Public Opinion Quarterly* 51:268–81.

———. 1987b. "The Polls: Public Assistance." *Public Opinion Quarterly* 51:120–30.

Shaver, Philip, and Jonathan Freedman. 1976. "Your Pursuit of Happiness." *Psychology Today* 10:26–32.

Shaw, Lois B., and David Shapiro. 1987. "Women's Work Expectations and Actual Experience." *Monthly Labor Review* 110:7–13.

Shaw, Nancy Stoller. 1982. "Female Patients and the Medical Profession in Jails and Prisons: A Case of Quadruple Jeopardy." In *Judge, Lawyer, Victim, Thief: Women, Gender Roles, and Criminal Justice*, edited by Nicole Hahn Rafter and Elizabeth Anne Stanko, 261–73. Boston: Northeastern University Press.

Shaw, Stephanie J. 1991. "Black Club Women and the Creation of the National Association of Colored Women." *Journal of Women's History* 3:10–25.

Sherman, Julia. 1980. "Mathematics, Spatial Visualization, and Related Factors: Changes in Boys and Girls, Grades 8–11." *Journal of Educational Psychology* 72:476–82.

Sherman, Julia, Corinne Koufacos, and Joy A. Kenworthy. 1978. "Therapists: Their Attitudes and Information about Women." *Psychology of Women Quarterly* 2:299–313.

Shevelow, Kathryn. 1989. *Women and Print Culture: The Construction of Femininity in the Early Periodical.* New York: Routledge.

Shoemaker, Nancy. 1991. "The Rise or Fall of Iroquois Women." *Journal of Women's History* 2:39–57.

Shorter, Edward. 1982. *A History of Women's Bodies.* New York: Basic.

Shortridge, Kathleen. 1989. "Poverty Is a Woman's Problem." In *Women: A Feminist Perspective*, edited by Jo Freeman, 485–92. Mountain View, Calif.: Mayfield.

Shotland, R. Lance, and Jane M. Craig. 1988. "Can Men and Women Differentiate between Friendly and Sexually Interested Behavior?" *Social Psychology Quarterly* 51:66–73.

Shulman, Alix Kates. 1983. *Red Emma Speaks.* New York: Schocken.

Siegfried, William D. 1982. "The Effects of Specifying Job Requirements and Using Explicit Warnings to Decrease Sex Discrimination in Employment Interviews." *Sex Roles* 8:73–82.

Signorielli, Nancy, and Margaret Lears. 1992. "Children, Television and Conceptions about Chores: Attitudes and Behaviors." *Sex Roles* 27:157–70.

Silber, Nina. 1989. "Intemperate Men, Spiteful Women, and Jefferson Davis: Northern Views of the Defeated South." *American Quarterly* 41: 614–35.

Simon, Rita J., and Jean M. Landis. 1989. "Report: Women's and Men's Attitudes about a Woman's Place and Role." *Public Opinion Quarterly* 53:265–76.

———. 1991. *The Crimes Women Commit, The Punishments They Receive.* Lexington, Mass.: Heath.

Sinkoff, Nancy B. 1988. "Educating for 'Proper' Jewish Womanhood: A Case Study in Domesticity and Vocational Training, 1897-1926." *American Jewish History* 77:572–99.

Sklar, Kathryn Kish. 1982. "Catharine Beecher: Transforming the Teaching Profession." In *Women's America*, edited by Linda K. Kerber and Jane de Hart Mathews, 140–48. New York: Oxford University Press.

Skocpol, Theda. 1992. *Protecting Soldiers and Mothers: The Political Origins of Social Policy in the United States.* Cambridge: Harvard University Press.

Sloane, Ethel. 1993. *Biology of Women*, 3rd ed. New York: Delmer Publishers.

Smith, M. 1980. "Sex Bias in Counseling and Psychotherapy." *Psychological Bulletin* 87:392–407.

Smith, Tom W. 1987. "That Which We Call Welfare by Any Other Name Would Smell Sweeter: An Analysis of the Impact of Question Wording on Response Patterns." *Public Opinion Quarterly* 51:75–83.

Smith-Lovin, Lynn, and Charles Brody. 1989. "Interruptions in Group Discussions: The Effects of Gender and Group Composition." *American Sociological Review* 54:424–35.

Smith-Rosenberg, Carroll. 1975. "The Female World of Love and Ritual: Relations between Women in Nineteenth Century America." *Signs* 1:1–29. Also in Kerber and Mathews (1982) and Leavitt (1984).

Sniezek, Janet A., and Christine H. Jazwinski. 1986. "Gender Bias in English: In Search of Fair Language." *Journal of Applied Social Psychology* 16:642–62.

Snyder, Mark, and Seymour W. Uranowitz. 1978. "Reconstructing the Past: Some Cognitive Consequences of Person Perception." *Journal of Personality and Social Psychology* 36:941–50.

Snyder, Paula. 1992. *The European Women's Almanac.* New York: Columbia University Press.

Sochen, June. 1972. *The New Woman: Feminism in Greenwich Village, 1910–20.* New York: Quadrangle.

———. 1973. *Movers and Shakers: American Women Thinkers and Activists, 1900–70.* New York: Quadrangle.

———. 1981. *Herstory: A Record of the American Woman's Past.* Sherman Oaks, Calif.: Alfred.

Sommers, Paul M., and Laura S. Thomas. 1983. "Restricting Federal Funds for Abortion: Another Look." *Social Science Quarterly* 6:40–46.

Spelman, Elizabeth V. 1988. *Inessential Woman: Problems of Exclusion in Feminist Thought.* Boston: Beacon Press.

Sperling, Susan. 1991. "Baboons with Briefcases: Feminism, Functionalism, and Sociobiology in the Evolution of Primate Gender." *Signs* 17:1–27.

Spiegel, David. 1982. "Mothering, Fathering, and Mental Illness." In *Rethinking the Family: Some Feminist Questions*, edited by Barrie Thorne, 95–110. New York: Longman.

Spivak, Gayatri Chakravorty. 1987. *In Other Worlds: Essays in Cultural Politics.* New York: Routledge.

Sprafkin, Joyce N., and Robert M. Liebert. 1978. "Sex Typing and Children's Television Preferences." In *Hearth and Home*, edited by Gaye Tuchman, Arlene Kaplan Daniels, and James Benet, 228–39. New York: Oxford University Press.

Stake, Jayne, and Charles R. Granger. 1978. "Same Sex and Opposite Sex Teacher Model Influences on Science Career Commitment among High School Students." *Journal of Educational Psychology* 70:180–86.

Stanko, Elizabeth Anne. 1982. "Would You Believe This Woman? Prosecutorial Screening for 'Credible' Witnesses and a Problem of Justice." In *Judge, Lawyer, Victim, Thief: Women, Gender Roles, and Criminal Justice*, edited by Nicole Hahn Rafter and Elizabeth Anne Stanko, 63–82. Boston: Northeastern University Press.

Stanton, Elizabeth Cady. [1895] 1974. *The Woman's Bible.* New York: Arno Press.

Stanton, Elizabeth Cady, Susan B. Anthony, and Mathilda J. Gage. [1881] 1969. *History of Women's Suffrage.* New York: Arno.

Stanworth, Michelle. 1983. *Gender and Schooling.* London: Hutchison.

Starhawk. 1979. *The Spiral Dance: A Rebirth of the Ancient Religion of the Great Goddess.* San Francisco: Harper & Row.

Staudt, Kathleen A. 1985. *Women, Foreign Assistance, and Advocacy Administration.* New York: Praeger.

Steck, Loren, Diane Levitan, David McLane, and Harold H. Kelley. 1982. "Care, Needs, and Conceptions of Love." *Journal of Personality and Social Psychology* 43:481–91.

Steffensmeier, Darrell J. 1981. "Patterns of Female Property Crime, 1960–78: A Postscript." In *Women and Crime in America*, edited by Leo Bowker, 39–64. New York: Macmillan.

Steichen, Donna. 1991. *Ungodly Rage: The Hidden Face of Catholic Feminism.* San Francisco: Ignatius Press.

Steinberg, Ronnie. 1987. "Radical Challenges in a Liberal World: The Mixed Success of Comparable Worth." *Gender and Society* 1:466–75.

Stellman, Jeanne Mager. 1977. *Women's Work, Women's Health.* New York: Pantheon.

Sterling, Dorothy, ed. 1984. *We Are Your Sisters: Black Women in the Nineteenth Century.* New York: Norton.

Stimpson, Catherine R. 1980. "Power, Presentations, and the Presentable." In *Issues in Feminism*, edited by Sheila Ruth, 426–40. Boston: Houghton Mifflin.

Stipek, Deborah J., and J. Heidi Gralinski. 1991. "Gender Differences in Children's Achievement-Related Beliefs and Emotional Responses to Success and Failure in Mathematics." *Journal of Educational Psychology* 83:361–71.

Stone, Rebecca, and Cynthia Waszak. 1992. "Adolescent Knowledge and Attitudes about Abortion." *Family Planning Perspectives* 24:52–57.

Strober, Myra H., and David Tyack. 1980. "Why Do Women Teach and Men Manage? A Report on Research on Schools." *Signs* 5:494–503.

Stroh, Linda K., Jeanne M. Brett, and Anne H. Reilly. 1992. "All the Right Stuff: A Comparison of Female and Male Managers' Career Progression." *Journal of Applied Psychology* 77:251–60.

Strube, Michael J., and Linda S. Barbour. 1983. "The Decision to Leave an Abusive Relationship: Economic Dependence and Psychological Commitment." *Journal of Marriage and the Family* 45:785–93.

Swerdlow, Marian. 1989. "Men's Accommodations to Women Entering a Nontraditional Occupation: A Case of Rapid Transit Operatives." *Gender and Society* 3:373–87.

Swim, Janet, Eugene Borgida, Geoffrey Maruyama, and David G. Myers. 1989. "Joan McKay versus John McKay: Do Gender Stereotypes Bias Evaluations?" *Psychological Bulletin* 105:409–29.

Taffel, Selma M., Paul J. Placek, and Teri Less. 1987. "Trends in the United States Cesarean Section Rate and Reasons for the 1980–85 Rise." *American Journal of Public Health* 77:955–59.

Tangri, Sandra S., Martha R. Burke, and Leanor B. Johnson. 1982. "Sexual Harassment at Work: Three Explanatory Models." *Journal of Social Issues* 38:33–54.

Tanney, Mary Faith, and Janice M. Birk. 1976. "Women Counselors for Women Clients? A Review of the Research." *Counseling Psychologist* 6:28–32.

Thistlethwaite, Susan. 1989. *Sex, Race, and God: Christian Feminism in Black and White.* New York: Crossroad.

Thomas, Claire Sherman. 1991. *Sex Discrimination in a Nutshell.* St. Paul, Minn.: West Publishing.

Thomas, V. G., and M. D. James. 1988. "Body Image, Dieting Tendencies, and Sex Role Traits in Urban Black Women." *Sex Roles* 18:523–529.

Thompson, Becky Wangsgaard, 1992. " 'A Way Outa No Way': Eating Problems among African-American, Latina, and White Women." *Gender and Society* 6:546–61.

Thompson, Kenrick S. 1980. "A Comparison of Black and White Adolescents' Beliefs about Having Children." *Journal of Marriage and the Family* 42:133–39.

Thompson, Victor A. 1961. *Modern Organization.* New York: Knopf.

Thorne, Barrie, Cheris Kramarae, and Nancy Henley, eds. 1983. *Language, Gender, and Society.* Rowley, Mass.: Newbury House.

Tidball, M. Elizabeth. 1980. "Women's Colleges and Women Achievers Revisited." *Signs* 5:504–17.

Tiger, Lionel. 1969. *Men in Groups.* New York: Vintage.

Tilly, Charles. 1978. *From Mobilization to Revolution.* Reading, Mass.: Addison-Wesley.

Tobias, Sheila, and Lisa Anderson. 1982. "What Really Happened to Rosie the Riveter? Demobilization and the Female Labor Force, 1944–47." In *Women's*

America: Refocusing the Past, edited by Linda K. Kerber and Jane de Hart Mathews, 354–73. New York: Oxford University Press.

Tobias, Sheila, and Carol Weissbrod. 1980. "Anxiety and Mathematics: An Update." *Harvard Educational Review* 50:63–70.

Toth, Emily. 1980. "The Fouler Sex: Women's Bodies in Advertising." In *Issues in Feminism: A First Course in Women's Studies*, edited by Sheila Ruth, 107–14. Boston: Houghton Mifflin.

Treichler, Paula A. 1984. "Women, Language, and Health Care: An Annotated Bibliography." *Women and Language News* 7:7–19.

Trennert, Robert A. 1988. "Victorian Morality and the Supervision of Indian Women Working in Phoenix, 1906–30." *Journal of Social History* 22:113–28.

Tsosie, Rebecca. 1988. "Changing Women: The Cross-Currents of American Indian Feminine Identity." *American Indian Culture and Research Journal* 12:1–38.

Tuchman, Gaye. 1978. "Introduction." In *Hearth and Home: Images of Women in the Mass Media*, edited by Gaye Tuchman, Arlene Kaplan Daniels, and James Benet, 3–38. New York: Oxford University Press.

Tuchman, Gaye, Arlene Kaplan Daniels, and James Benet, eds. 1978. *Hearth and Home: Images of Women in the Mass Media*. New York: Oxford University Press.

Tudor, William, Jeanette F. Tudor, and Walter R. Gove. 1977. "The Effects of Sex Role Differences on the Social Control of Mental Illness." *Journal of Health and Social Behavior* 18:98–112.

Turkel, Sherry, and Seymour Papert. 1990. "Epistemological Pluralism: Styles and Voices within the Computer Culture." *Signs* 16:128–57.

Ulbrich, Patricia, and Joan Huber. 1981. "Observing Parental Violence: Distribution Effect." *Journal of Marriage and the Family* 43:623–32.

Unger, Rhoda K. 1979. *Female and Male: Psychological Perspectives*. New York: Harper & Row.

U.S. Bureau of the Census. 1980. *Statistical Abstract of the United States*. Washington, D.C.: Government Printing Office.

———. 1982. *Statistical Abstract of the United States*. Washington, D.C.: Government Printing Office.

———. 1987a. *Statistical Abstract of the United States*. Washington, D.C.: Government Printing Office.

———. 1987b. *Current Population Reports Series P-70, No.10: Male-Female Differences in Work Experience, Occupation, and Earnings, 1984*. Washington, D.C.: Government Printing Office.

———. 1989. *Statistical Abstract of the United States*. Washington, D.C.: Government Printing Office.

———. 1992. *Statistical Abstract of the United States*. Washington, D.C.: Government Printing Office.

U.S. Commission on Civil Rights. 1979. *Window Dressing on the Set: An Update*. Washington, D.C.: Government Printing Office.

U.S. Congress, House of Representatives Committee on Immigration and Naturalization. 1930. "Supreme Court Decision, Citations, Comment, etc. *In re* Rosika Schwimmer and Martha Jane Graber." 71st Congress, 2d Session, 6 March.

U.S. Department of Education. 1987. *Trends in Bachelor's and Higher Degrees, 1975–85.* Washington, D.C.: Government Printing Office.

———. 1988. *Digest of Education Statistics, 1988.* Washington, D.C.: Government Printing Office.

U.S. Department of Education, Office of Educational Research and Improvement. 1992. *Digest of Education Statistics.* Washington, D.C.: Government Printing Office.

U.S. Department of Labor. 1980. *Perspectives on Working Women: A Databook.* Washington, D.C.: Government Printing Office.

———. 1989. *Employment and Earnings (January, 1989).* Washington, D.C.: Government Printing Office.

———. 1992. *Monthly Labor Review* (November 1992). Washington, D.C.: Government Printing Office.

U.S. Merit Systems Protection Board. 1981. *Sexual Harassment in the Federal Workplace: Is It a Problem?* Washington, D.C.: Government Printing Office.

Valeska, Lucia. 1975. "If All Else Fails, I'm Still a Mother." *Quest* 1:52–63.

Vance, Carole S., ed. 1984. *Pleasure and Danger: Exploring Female Sexuality.* New York: Routledge.

Vande Berg, Leah R., and Diane Streckfuss. 1992. "Prime-Time Television's Portrayal of Women and the World of Work: A Demographic Profile." *Journal of Broadcasting and Electronic Media* 36:195–208.

Vanek, Joann. 1980. "Household Work, Wage Work, and Sexual Equality." In *Women and Household Labor*, edited by Sarah Fenstermaker Berk, 275–92. Beverly Hills, Calif.: Sage.

Ventura, Jacqueline N., and Pauline G. Boss. 1983. "The Family Coping Inventory Applied to Parents with New Babies." *Journal of Marriage and the Family* 45:867–75.

Verna, Mary Ellen. 1975. "The Female Image in Children's TV Commercials." *Journal of Broadcasting* 19:301–9.

Vest, David. 1992. "Prime-Time Pilots: A Content Analysis of Changes in Gender Representation." *Journal of Broadcasting and Electronic Media* 36:25–43.

Vladeck, Judith P. 1981. "Sex Discrimination in Higher Education." *Women's Rights Law Reporter* 7:27–38.

Voydanoff, Patricia. 1984. *Work and Family: Changing Roles of Men and Women.* Mountain View, Calif.: Mayfield.

Waelti-Walters, Jennifer. 1979. "On Princesses: Fairy Tales, Sex Roles, and Loss of Self." *International Journal of Women's Studies* 2:180–88.

Wagner, Lilya. 1989. *Women War Correspondents of World War II.* Westport, Conn.: Greenwood.

Waldman, Elizabeth. 1983. "Labor Force Statistics from a Family Perspective." *Monthly Labor Review* 106:16–20.

Walker, Lawrence. 1984. "Sex Differences in the Development of Moral Reasoning: A Critical Review." *Child Development* 55:667–91.

Walsh, Mary Roth. 1979. "The Rediscovery of the Need for a Feminist Medical Education." *Harvard Education Review* 49:447–66.

Waring, Marilyn. 1988. *If Women Counted: A New Feminist Economics.* San Francisco: Harper & Row.

Ware, Susan. 1981. *Beyond Suffrage: Women in the New Deal.* Cambridge, Mass.: Harvard University Press.

———. 1983. *Holding Their Own: American Women in the 1930's.* Boston: Twayne.

Warner, Marina. 1976. *Alone of All Her Sex: The Myth and the Cult of Mary.* New York: Random House.

Weeks, Jeffrey. 1977. *Coming Out: Homosexual Politics in Britain, from the Nineteenth Century to the Present.* London: Quartet.

Weeks, M. O'Neal, and Darla R. Botkin. 1987. "A Longitudinal Study of the Marriage Role Expectations of College Women: 1961–84." *Sex Roles* 17:49–58.

Weinberg, Martin S., and Colin J. Williams. 1980. "Sexual Embourgeoisment? Social Class and Sexual Activity, 1938–48." *American Sociological Review* 45:33–48.

Weinraub, M., L. P. Clements, A. Sockloff, E. Gracely, and B. Myers. 1984. "The Development of Sex Role Stereotypes in the Third Year: Relationship to Gender Labeling, Gender Identity, Sex-Typed Toy Preferences." *Child Development* 55:1493–1503.

Weisberg, D. Kelly, ed. 1993. *Feminist Legal Theory: Foundations.* Philadelphia: Temple University Press.

Weisfeld, Carol C., Glenn E. Weisfeld, and John W. Callaghan. 1982. "Female Inhibition in Mixed Sex Competition among Young Adolescents." *Ethnology and Sociobiology* 3:29–42.

Weiss, Robert S. 1984. "The Impact of Marital Dissolution on Income and Consumption in Single-Parent Households." *Journal of Marriage and the Family* 46:115–28.

Weitzman, Leonore J. 1979. *Sex Role Socialization.* Mountain View, Calif.: Mayfield.

———. 1985. *The Divorce Revolution: The Unexpected Social and Economic Consequences for Women and Children in America.* New York: Free Press.

Welch, Susan. 1978. "Recruitment of Women to Public Office: A Discriminant Analysis." *Western Political Quarterly* 31:372–80.

Welter, Barbara. 1966. "The Cult of True Womanhood, 1830–1860." *American Quarterly* 18:151–74.

Wertheimer, Barbara M., and Anne H. Nelson. 1982. "Education for Social Change: Two Roads." *Economic and Industrial Democracy* 3:483–513.

———. 1989. " 'Union Is Power': Sketches from Women's Labor History." In *Women: A Feminist Perspective*, edited by Jo Freeman, 312–28. Mountain View, Calif.: Mayfield.

West, Candace. 1984. "When the Doctor Is a 'Lady:' Power, Status, and Gender in Physician-Patient Encounters." *Symbolic Interaction* 7:87–106.

West, Candace, and Don H. Zimmerman. 1987. "Doing Gender." *Gender and Society* 1:125–51.

Wheeless, Virginia Eman, and Paul F. Potorti. 1989. "Student Assessment of Teacher Masculinity and Femininity: A Test of the Sex Role Congruency Hypothesis on Student Attitudes toward Learning." *Journal of Educational Psychology* 81:259–62.

White, Barbara, Charles Cox, and Cary Cooper. 1992. *Women's Career Development: A Study of High Flyers.* Cambridge, Mass.: Blackwell.

White, Deborah Gray. 1985. *"Ar'n't I a Woman?" Female Slaves in the Plantation South.* New York: Norton.

White, E. Frances. 1990. "Africa on My Mind: Gender, Counter Discourse and African-American Nationalism." *Journal of Women's History* 2:73–97.

White, Evelyn C. 1990. *The Black Women's Health Book: Speaking for Ourselves.* Seattle, Wash.: Seal Press.

White, Gregory L., Sanford Fishbein, and Jeffrey Rutstein. 1981. "Passionate Love and Misattribution of Arousal." *Journal of Personality and Social Psychology* 41:56–62.

White, Lynn K., and David B. Brinkerhoff. 1981. "The Sexual Division of Labor: Evidence from Childhood." *Social Forces* 60:170–81.

Whittaker, Susan, and Ron Whittaker. 1976. "Relative Effectiveness of Male and Female Newscasters." *Journal of Broadcasting* 20:177–84.

Wilbanks, William. 1982. "Murdered Women and Women Who Murder: A Critique of the Literature." In *Judge, Lawyer, Victim, Thief: Women, Gender Roles, and Criminal Justice*, edited by Nicole Hahn Rafter and Elizabeth Anne Stanko, 151–80. Boston: Northeastern University Press.

Wiley, Mary G., and Arlene Eskilson. 1982. "The Interaction of Sex and Power Based on Perceptions of Managerial Effectiveness." *Academy of Management Journal* 25:671–77.

Williams, Patricia J. 1991. *The Alchemy of Race and Rights: Diary of a Law Professor.* Cambridge, Mass.: Harvard University Press.

Wilson, E. O. 1975. *Sociobiology: A New Synthesis.* Cambridge, Mass.: Harvard University Press.

Wise, Erica, and Janet Rafferty. 1982. "Sex Bias and Language." *Sex Roles* 8:1189–96.

Wolchik, Sharon L., and Alfred G. Meyer, eds. 1985. *Women, State, and Party in Eastern Europe.* Durham, N.C.: Duke University Press.

Wolfe, J., and V. Baker. 1980. "Characteristics of Imprisoned Rapists and Circumstances of Rape." In *Rape and Sexual Assault*, edited by Carmen G. Warner. Germantown, Md.: Aspen Systems.

Wollstonecraft, Mary. [1792] 1975. *A Vindication of the Rights of Woman.* Baltimore, Md.: Penguin. Excerpted in Rossi (1988).

"Women and the American City." 1980. *Signs* 5: entire issue.

Women on Words and Images. 1972. *Dick and Jane as Victims.* Princeton, N.J.: Know, Inc.

Woods, Laurie. 1981. "Litigation on Behalf of Battered Women." *Women's Rights Law Reporter* 7:39–46.

Worcester, Nancy, and Mariamne H. Whatley. 1988. "The Response of the Health Care System to the Women's Health Movement: The Selling of Women's Health Centers." In *Women's Health: Readings on Social, Economic, and Political Issues*, edited by Nancy Worcester and Mariamne H. Whatley, 17–24. Dubuque, Iowa: Kendall/Hunt.

Wylie, Philip. 1942. *A Generation of Vipers.* New York and Toronto: Farrar & Rinehart.

Yang, Eun Sik. 1984. "Korean Women of America: From Subordination to Partnership, 1903–1930." *Amerasia Journal* 11:1–28.

Yee, Doris K., and Jacquelynne S. Eccles. 1988. "Parent Perceptions and Attributions for Children's Math Achievement." *Sex Roles* 19:317–33.

Zabin, Laurie S., Marilyn B. Hirsch, Mark R. Emerson, and Elizabeth Raymond. 1992. "To Whom Do Inner City Minors Talk About Their Pregnancies? Adolescents' Communication with Parents and Parent Surrogates." *Family Planning Perspectives* 24:148–54.

Zeldow, Peter B. 1976. "Effects of Nonpathological Sex Role Stereotypes on Student Evaluations of Psychiatric Patients." *Journal of Consulting and Clinical Psychology* 44:304.

Zellman, Gail L., and Jacqueline D. Goodchilds. 1983. "Becoming Sexual in Adolescence." In *Changing Boundaries: Gender Roles and Sexual Behavior*, edited by Elizabeth Rice Allgeier and Naomi B. McCormick, 49–63. Mountain View, Calif.: Mayfield.

Zimmerman, Don H., and Candace West. 1975. "Sex Roles, Interruptions, and Silences in Conversation." In *Language and Sex*, edited by Barrie Thorne and Nancy Henley, 105–29. Rowley, Mass.: Newbury House.

Zinn, Maxine Baca. 1989. "Family, Race, and Poverty in the Eighties." *Signs* 14:856–74.

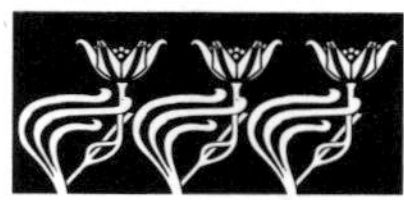

Subject Index

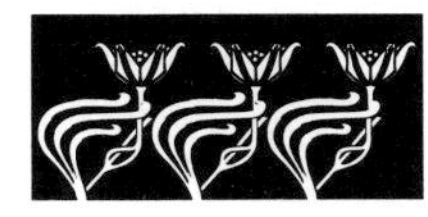

Name Index

ILLUSTRATION CREDITS

Page 12: Elizabeth Crews/The Image Works
Page 16: Reuters/Bettmann
Page 40: Culver Pictures
Page 48: Wyoming State Archives, Museums and Historical Department
Page 60: Wayne Glusker
Page 74: Bob Kalman/Image Works (left)
Page 74: Suzanne Arms/Jeroboam, Inc. (right)
Page 85: Reuters/Bettmann
Page 97: Abigail Heyman
Page 109: Photo Researchers
Page 126: Courtesy of Bethune-Cookman College
Page 142: Sophia Smith Collection, Smith College, photograph by A.J. Schillare
Page 150: Culver Pictures
Page 166: Brown Brothers
Page 176: Museum of the City of New York
Page 194: Kevin Horan/Picture Group
Page 202: The Bettmann Archive
Page 203: UPI/Bettmann Newsphotos
Page 216: AP/Wide World Photos
Page 230: *National Geographic*
Page 236: Reuters/Bettmann
Page 248: Brown Brothers
Page 258: The Bettmann Archive
Page 269: The Bettmann Archive
Page 296: Patsy Davidson/ImageWorks
Page 299: Reuters/Bettmann
Page 332: AP/Wide World Photos
Page 352: Elizabeth Crews/Stock Boston
Page 360: Staten Island Historical Society
Page 364: Brown Brothers
Page 394: Sophia Smith Collection, Smith College
Page 401: Brown Brothers
Page 455: Brown Brothers
Page 463: UPI/Bettmann Newsphotos
Page 476: Laura Luongo/Picture Group
Page 480: AP/Wide World Photos